AUTOCOURSE

The World's Leading Grand Prix Annual

HAZLETON PUBLISHING

CONTENTS

FOREWORD by Michael Schumacher	5
EDITOR'S INTRODUCTION	6
THE TOP TEN DRIVERS OF 1994	15
MICHAEL SCHUMACHER – A MAN APART A profile of the 1994 World Champion by Timothy Collings	30
THE LAW AND ORDER CRISIS by Alan Henry	34
FORMULA 1 REVIEW by Bob Constanduros, Tony Dodgins and Alan Henry	40
BORN TO BE THE FASTEST A tribute to Ayrton Senna	94
1994 GRANDS PRIX by Alan Henry	101
1994 FORMULA 1 STATISTICS compiled by David Hayhoe and Nick Henry	246
FORMULA 3000 REVIEW by Simon Arron	248
FORMULA 3 REVIEW by Andrew Benson	250
SPORTS CAR RACING REVIEW by Adam Cooper	252
BRITISH TOURING CAR CHAMPIONSHIP by Laurence Foster	254
EUROPEAN TOURING CAR RACING REVIEW by Peter Nygaard	266
AMERICAN RACING REVIEW by Gordon Kirby	270
OTHER MAJOR 1994 RESULTS compiled by David Hayhoe	280

Autocourse is published by Hazleton Publishing, 3 Richmond Hill, Richmond, Surrey TW10 6RE.

Colour reproduction by Barrett Berkeley Ltd, London.

Printed in England by Butler and Tanner Ltd, Frome, Somerset.

© Hazleton Securities Ltd 1994. No part of this publication may be reproduced, stored in a retrieval system or transmitted, in any form or by any means, electronic, mechanical, photocopying, recording or otherwise, without prior permission in writing from Hazleton Securities Ltd.

ISBN: 1-874557-95-0

DISTRIBUTORS

UNITED KINGDOM
Bookpoint Ltd
39 Milton Park
Abingdon
Oxfordshire OX14 4TD

NORTH AMERICA
Motorbooks International
PO Box 1
729 Prospect Ave.
Osceola
Wisconsin 54020, USA

AUSTRALIA
Technical Book and Magazine Co. Pty
289-299 Swanston Street
Melbourne
Victoria 3000

NEW ZEALAND
David Bateman Ltd
'Golden Heights'
32-34 View Road
Glenfield
Auckland 10

SOUTH AFRICA
Motorbooks
341 Jan Smuts Avenue
Craighall Park
Johannesburg

PUBLISHER
Richard Poulter

EDITOR
Alan Henry

MANAGING & ART EDITOR
Steve Small

PRODUCTION MANAGER
George Greenfield

HOUSE EDITOR
Peter Lovering

BUSINESS DEVELOPMENT MANAGER
Simon Maurice

SALES PROMOTION
Elizabeth Le Breton

RESULTS AND STATISTICS
David Hayhoe
Nick Henry

F1 ILLUSTRATIONS
Ian Hutchinson
Nicola Fox

CHIEF CONTRIBUTING PHOTOGRAPHERS
Diana Burnett
Paul-Henri Cahier
Lukas Gorys
LAT Photographic
Colin McMaster
John Marsh
Peter Nygaard
Nigel Snowdon
Sutton Photographic
Herke de Vries
Bryn Williams

Dust jacket photographs:
Michael Schumacher
John Marsh/Action Images
Ayrton Senna
Darren Heath, Zooom Photographic
Damon Hill
Paul-Henri Cahier

Title page photograph:
Ayrton Senna memorial
Peter Nygaard/GP Photo

Photograph opposite:
Podium celebration for Mika Häkkinen and Michael Schumacher
John Marsh/Action Images

ACKNOWLEDGEMENTS

The Editor of *Autocourse* wishes to thank the following for their assistance in compiling the 1994-95 edition:
France: ACO, Automobiles Ligier (Frank Dernie, Richard Grundy, Dany Hindenoch and Chris Williams), Fédération Française du Sport Automobile, FIA (Bernie Ecclestone, Robyn Firth, Max Mosley, Francesco Longanesi-Cattani, Sylvie Shanon, Pat Tozer, Martin Whitaker and Charlie Whiting), Peugeot Sport (Jean-Pierre Jabouille), Renault Sport (Jean-Jacques Delaruwière and Bernard Dudot), Larrousse F1 (Robin Herd and Tim Holloway); **Germany:** Mercedes-Benz (Gustav Busing and Wolfgang Schattling), Oberste Nationale Sportkommission; **Great Britain:** Benetton Formula (Maria Bellanca, Ross Brawn, Flavio Briatore, Rory Byrne, Rae Turkington and Tom Walkinshaw), Timothy Collings, Bob Constanduros, Arrows Grand Prix International (Alan Jenkins, Jackie Oliver and John Wickham), Neil Cooper, Ford (Peter Gillitzer, Steve Madinca and Sophie Sicot), Mike Greasley, Peter Hall, Maurice Hamilton, Brian Hart Ltd (Jane Brace and Brian Hart), John Hogan, Ian Hutchinson, Tony Jardine, Denis Jenkinson, Edgar Jessop, Jordan Grand Prix (Gary Anderson, Louise Goodman, Eddie Jordan, Steve Nichols and Ian Phillips), John Judd, Lola Cars, McLaren International (Jocelyne Bia, Justine Blake, Ron Dennis, Norman Howell, Neil Oatley, Jo Ramirez and Peter Stayner), Pacific Grand Prix (Ian Dawson, Mark Gallagher and Keith Wiggins), Stan Piecha, RAC MSA (Derek Tye), Nigel Roebuck, Shell International, Silverstone Circuits (Corinna Phillips), Simtek (Anna Hobbs, Fred Rodgers and Nick Wirth), Team Lotus (Peter Collins, Chris Murphy, Anita Smith and Peter Wright), Tyrrell Racing Organisation (Vincent Franchesini, Rupert Manwaring, Harvey Postlethwaite and Ken Tyrrell), Professor E.S. 'Sid' Watkins, Williams Grand Prix Engineering (Ann Bradshaw, Jane Gorard, Patrick Head, Adrian Newey, Richard West and Frank Williams); **Italy:** Commissione Sportiva Automobilistica Italiana, Scuderia Ferrari (John Barnard, Giancarlo Bacchini and Antonio Ghini), Scuderia Italia Minardi (Leopoldo Canetoli and Giancarlo Minardi); **Japan:** Yamaha ('Herbie' Blash); **Switzerland:** Marlboro Motorsport (Agnes Carlier), Sauber Mercedes (Hans-Peter Brack and Peter Sauber); **USA:** Daytona International Speedway, Goodyear (Barry Griffin, Cal Lint, Leo Mehl, Mike Powell and Tony Shakespeare), IMSA, IndyCar, Indy Lights, NASCAR, SCCA, USAC.

Photographs published in *Autocourse* 1994-95 have been contributed by:
Action Images/John Marsh, *Allsport*/Pascal Rondeau/Mike Cooper/Anton Want, *Bothwell Photographic*/Mark Bothwell/Bill Bothwell, Michael C. Brown, Diana Burnett, Paul-Henri Cahier, David Cundy, Steve Domenjoz, *Empics*/Steve Etherington, *Formula One Pictures*/John Townsend, Lukas Gorys, *GP Photo*/Peter Nygaard, Simon Hildrew, Joseph J. Jiran, Nigel Kinrade, Christine Lalla, *LAT Photographic*/Steve Tee/Peter J. Fox, Pamela Lauesen/*FOSA*, Dominique Leroy, *Steve Mohlenkamp Photography*, Neil Randon, *Royersford International*, Nigel Snowdon, *Sporting Pictures (UK) Ltd*, *Sutton Photographic*/Keith Sutton/Mark Sutton, *Steve Swope Racing Photo*, Denis L. Tanney, Herke de Vries, Kaz Winiemko, *Words & Pictures*/Colin McMaster/Bryn Williams, Tony Di Zinno and *Zooom Photographic*/John Dunbar/Darren Heath.

FOREWORD

by Michael Schumacher

After all the excitement and celebrations, it has finally hit me that I have won my first World Championship title and it is a tremendous feeling. Following a difficult season, the satisfaction and reward for everyone in the Mild Seven Benetton Ford team is great. Despite the trying circumstances during the season, the most notable factor for me was that at all times the team remained united and stronger than ever.

As I said in Australia, I dedicate this championship to the man who should have won it, Ayrton Senna. In my eyes, Ayrton was always the favourite and remained so, even after I had won the two opening races in Brazil and Japan.

It was a terrible tragedy that both Ayrton and Roland lost their lives at Imola and that weekend's memory will always dominate this year, whatever else happened and whatever else has been said or written.

I would finally like to thank everyone at the Benetton Formula headquarters, who have worked so hard all season to make this championship victory possible.

EDITOR'S INTRODUCTION

THE DARKEST

The 1994 Formula 1 World Championship season will always be remembered as one of the most painful in the sport's long history. It wasn't simply that Ayrton Senna, one of the greatest racing drivers of all time, was killed in that black weekend at Imola which also claimed the life of Austrian novice Roland Ratzenberger, nor that the Drivers' World Championship was finally resolved in what might charitably be described as 'unfortunate' circumstances in Adelaide. In reality, these momentous events were simply part of a wider, troubled canvas which saw the F1 business beleaguered and under fire on several different fronts.

The events of the San Marino Grand Prix weekend served abruptly and cruelly to bring the sport face to face with levels of tragedy and despair not known for a generation. It was eight years since Elio de Angelis had been the last driver to be killed at the wheel of a Grand Prix car, testing a Brabham-BMW at Paul Ricard. Yet one had to go back to 1982 to recall the last occasion on which a competitor had been killed at a World Championship race meeting with Gilles Villeneuve's fatal accident at Zolder and Riccardo Paletti's death in a startline collision at the Canadian Grand Prix. Somehow time had moved on and all the safety measures implicit in the F1 business seemed almost to have reduced the risk of such accidents to an infinitesimal outside chance.

Suddenly, all that changed. Without intending any unkindness, had Ratzenberger been the only victim of Imola, it is unlikely that the overall course of the season would have been significantly deflected. But when Senna, arguably the most famous, high-profile sportsman in the world, suffered fatal injuries in a high-speed accident which was shown live, all round the world, on prime-time television, the whole focus of the sport was suddenly and irrevocably changed.

To say that Senna's death left a void at the pinnacle of top-line motor racing is a simplistic understatement. Not since Jimmy Clark's death in the spring of 1968 had a racing accident grabbed the headlines across the globe. Yet Clark's death was largely regarded as simply a legitimate consequence of competing in a hazardous sport. The post-mortems were limited and, to a large extent, shrugged aside.

A generation later, we live in a very different environment where the freedom of the individual to make a personal choice as to how, or indeed whether, he risks his life is very much hemmed in by wider social constraints. Ironically, Senna was not only one of the greatest drivers of his era, but arguably the man with the most finely developed personal assessment of the risks involved in his calling. But to say he knew the risks and willingly stepped forward to embrace them could in no way mitigate the need for a wide-ranging reappraisal of Formula 1 safety in the aftermath of his passing.

The resultant situation presented the sport's governing body with a major dilemma. FIA President Max Mosley's initial reaction was to stand out against pressure for knee-jerk reactions on the safety front. That was commendable, but within a matter of days of the Senna tragedy, it was clear that Mosley was coming under strong governmental pressure from within the EU to be seen to be doing something positive and quantifiable. The result was a controversial package of technical changes, designed to reduce downforce and cornering speeds, rushed through progressively prior to the German Grand Prix.

These changes were met with responses from team chiefs varying from outright hostility to qualified approval. Yet their introduction produced an ironic twist to the way in which the governing body had intended to shape the technical course of the season. For the 1994 season, the FIA had banned virtually all electronic driver aids in an attempt to contain cost inflation within F1 and offer some hope to the smaller teams in their efforts to compete with the large, lavishly funded organisations.

Now Mosley found himself backed into a situation where the well-funded teams were best equipped to deal with short-term rule changes, leaving the smaller teams struggling to make changes as best they could. This had the effect of exaggerating the gap separating the 'haves' from the 'have nots', particularly during the second half of the season.

Another dimension which had to be taken into account was the reintroduction of in-race refuelling, a practice which had been banned at the end of 1983 on the grounds of safety. Nobody explained quite why refuelling was any less dangerous in 1994 than it had been a decade earlier and, indeed, the conflagration involving Jos Verstappen's Benetton in the Hockenheim pit lane during a routine stop in the German Grand Prix far exceeded anything experienced during the previous experiment with this hazardous procedure.

Despite this incontrovertible evidence that the practice was disproportionately dangerous, the FIA did not move to ban it on safety grounds, as they could have. Refuelling may well have brought a renewed tactical dimension to the racing, but such theoretical benefits were negated by the confusion and general muddle it injected into overall race strategy, spoiling more genuinely promising Grands Prix than it ever enhanced. However, the Powers That Be continue to believe it makes good television and F1 seems saddled with it for the next two years at least, although whether by then Ferrari will have been spoon-fed a path to a World Championship title remains rather less certain.

HOUR

Opposite page: Pit stops went largely according to plan (with a couple of notable exceptions). Unfortunately the racing often suffered as different strategies broke up the pattern of races.

Below: The class of '94 line up for the start-of-term team photo. Sadly two of its members would pay the sport's ultimate price in a black weekend at Imola.

It may seem strange to have left the subject of the World Championship battle itself so far down the *Autocourse* Editor's Introduction. Yet somehow that seems strangely appropriate. In some ways, after Senna's death, it was easy to regard the outcome of the title battle as something of a secondary footnote. Indeed, Michael Schumacher remains resolute in his belief that he would not have won the drivers' title had Senna survived to contest the entire season.

Schumacher started the season as the man most likely to challenge Senna, and so it proved. As things transpired, the young German scored eight victories and took the crown by a single point in controversial circumstances at the last race of the season. In terms of pure ability, it is beyond question that Schumacher deserved to be World Champion in 1994. However, the route by which he achieved that objective was so unfortunately overhung by suspicion and controversy, arising from the Benetton team's skirmish with authority over the technical regulations and Michael's own recklessness in ignoring the black flag at Silverstone, that his dazzling talent at the wheel was inevitably eclipsed to a large degree.

Yet he was still the benchmark by which other drivers measured their performances. In that respect, Damon Hill's rise to prominence in the most trying circumstances imaginable proved to be one of the unchallenged high spots of a troubled season. Having been propelled into the Williams team leadership on Senna's death, he had to contend with the destabilising effect of Renault's initial lack of confidence in his ability, which brought Nigel Mansell back onto the scene on a 'guest driver' basis.

Mansell, whose honeymoon with the Indy Car set came to an abrupt end as his Newman-Haas Lola-Ford crashed to defeat after defeat at the hands of the all-conquering Penskes, had four tempestuous races for Williams, culminating in a rather fortuitous victory in the Australian Grand Prix. Many of his fans will undoubtedly react with indignation that such an achievement did not merit his inclusion in the *Autocourse* Top Ten driver ratings, but we did not deem four races out of 16 an adequate basis on which to form a definitive judgement. By contrast, as you will see, David Coulthard's eight consistently impressive performances gain him a desirable rating in the same section.

Hill's emergence as a driver of world class and Coulthard's remarkable confidence as a novice pitchforked into the rarefied atmosphere of a front-line F1 team were two of the season's undoubted highlights. Others included Gerhard Berger's faultless performance to win the German Grand Prix at Hockenheim and the Austrian's dogged chase of Hill's Williams to finish second at Monza after a huge shunt in the race morning warm-up.

In many less obtrusive ways, Berger was the star of the season, his maturity and good judgement after the loss of his close friend Senna marking him out as Grand Prix racing's respected elder statesman at a time when calm objectivity and straightforward commonsense all too often seemed in short supply.

With constructors redesigning their cars and circuits being asked to make massively expensive alterations in the interests of safety, there was an almost unspoken subtext to the whole season which began to make itself felt towards the end of the year. Financially, the costs of F1 seemed to be swirling out of control beyond the reach of all but a handful of top teams.

The financial problems experienced by Team Lotus, which led Britain's once most famous F1 name to seek court-protected administration after the Italian Grand Prix and prompted its subsequent sale to an American consortium, was symptomatic of the challenge involved in keeping one's commercial head above water in difficult economic times. It is to the credit of newcomers Simtek and Pacific that they successfully survived their freshman year and are poised to make more significant progress in 1995.

Elsewhere on the international racing scene, the US Indy Car series continued to thrive, although some might find it ironic that the supremacy of the three-car Penske-Ilmor squad raised memories of the Williams-Renault domination of F1 in 1992. The Indy Car series, of course, benefits from largely taking place in a single, English-speaking continent, which is possibly one fact which explains why its 1995 race calendar was in place last August, whereas at the time of writing the FIA is still wrestling with next season's Grand Prix dates.

The world of touring car racing also continued to thrive, with the British and German championships in particular offering televised excitement on a par with Formula 1, while F3 and F3000, although providing indispensable stepping stones to the upper reaches of F1 stardom, have inevitably been subject to the same chill winds of economic reality as the Grand Prix scene.

Yet, for all this turbulence, international motor racing continued to hold its corner in terms of worldwide televised popularity in 1994. With increased investment in safety developments from the FIA, continuing commitment from major engine manufacturers and renewed competition for the 16 available fixtures on the F1 championship calendar, the future continues to look promising as we head towards the Millennium.

Even so, a certain sense of emptiness pervaded the World Championship contest this year. Time alone will heal the gaping chasm left by Ayrton Senna's death, but for the moment we can only put 1994 behind us in the confident hope of better times ahead.

Alan Henry
Tillingham, Essex
November 1994

WORLD CH

MICHAEL SCHUMACHER - 1994 WORLD DRIVERS' CHAMPION • ROTH

GOODYEAR

AMPIONS
NS WILLIAMS-RENAULT - 1994 WORLD CONSTRUCTORS' CHAMPIONS

#1 in Racing

ADVERTISEMENT FEATURE

GOODYEAR'S LATEST LANDMARK, THE 300TH WIN

GOODYEAR reached another landmark in its historic position as the most successful tyre company ever to be involved in Formula 1 racing when it notched up its 300th Grand Prix victory on the sunny afternoon of Sunday, 29 May, 1994. The place was Barcelona's Circuit de Catalunya, the driver and car to achieve the distinction Damon Hill and the Williams-Renault FW16, the event the 1994 Spanish Grand Prix.

IT WAS A SUCCESS in which history and emotion were firmly entwined. Just as his late father Graham had lifted the Lotus team's spirits by winning the 1968 Spanish Grand Prix at Madrid's Jarama circuit in the wake of his team-mate Jim Clark's death, so Damon's success gave a timely boost to the Williams team only a month after the tragic fatal accident to his team-mate Ayrton Senna.

For Goodyear, of course, this was the latest milestone in a glittering record of Formula 1 achievement in motor racing's most demanding technical gymnasium as well as a further, compelling endorsement of the company's commitment to international Formula 1. It also served as another very public endorsement of Goodyear's unswerving belief that the lessons learned on the race tracks of the world have a powerful and very specific influence in the development of tyres for the everyday motorist.

Goodyear's Grand Prix heritage stretches back to 1960 with a tentative involvement in the unsuccessful F1 foray by the US Scarab F1 team established by the late Lance Reventlow, wealthy only son of Woolworth heiress Barbara Hutton. Unfortunately these front-engined machines were totally outclassed by the revolutionary new generation of central-engined cars being built by the likes of Cooper and Lotus and were withdrawn after a handful of disappointing outings.

After exhaustive testing and evaluation, Goodyear finally made a decisive move into F1 in 1965 with the Brabham and Honda teams for the final season of the 1.5-litre engine regulations. American driver Richie Ginther set the seal on this involvement by scoring Goodyear's first win at the wheel of the Honda in the 1965 Mexican Grand Prix, by which time Goodyear's International Racing Division was established at its UK base in Bushbury, Wolverhampton, where the production of racing tyres began on 10 October 1964 with Fred Gamble as manager and Walt deVinney as Chief Engineer.

In late 1967, Leo Mehl took over as racing manager when Gamble moved on to assume responsibility for Goodyear product sales in New Zealand. By then, Jack Brabham had won the first Goodyear-shod World Championship in 1966 at the wheel of his Repco V8-engined Brabham, thereby becoming the only man in the history of the championship to have won the title at the wheel of a car bearing his own name. Denny Hulme followed this up by winning the title for Brabham in 1967.

Goodyear's next World Championships came with Tyrrell and Jackie Stewart in 1971 and '73, since when Akron has dominated the championship stage. During the halcyon years of the Goodyear/Stewart/Tyrrell alliance, Goodyear not only became the first company to use

Far left: Damon Hill racing to Goodyear's 300th Grand Prix win at Barcelona.
Top: Frantic pitstop action as four new Goodyears go on Gerhard Berger's Ferrari.
Bottom: Bill Sharp, President and General Manager, Goodyear Europe, receives the splendid '300 Wins' Trophy from Bernie Ecclestone, President of the F1 Constructors' Association and F1A Vice-President.
Centre: Jackie Stewart winning the 1971 French Grand Prix on the then-revolutionary Goodyear slicks.
Right: Richie Ginther scores Goodyear's 1st Grand Prix win.

of the F1 service division, and there was a major hiccup in Goodyear's F1 involvement at the end of 1980 when the company withdrew for six months at the height of a political battle within the sport.

By 1983, Akron was ready with its first radial F1 tyre, since when the company has

slick-treaded tyres, but also effectively wrote what amounts to the F1 tyre test and development handbook, setting a trend which has been sustained to this day.

'The rewards of this business are pretty well split 50/50 between advertising benefits and the technical feedback,' explains Leo Mehl. 'Of course, we sometimes encounter an element of opposition within the company which says "why are you still involved when all we're doing is beating ourselves?" but this attitude is only valid if you've stopped developing the product. It might be right if you are no longer contributing, so we've learned that we had better not stop contributing.'

Milestones in Goodyear's Grand Prix history are many and varied. Niki Lauda won the team's 100th victory at the wheel of a Ferrari in the 1977 German GP at Hockenheim. The 200th came up at Adelaide in 1987 when Gerhard Berger emerged victorious, again at the wheel of a Ferrari. In 1979 the manufacture of all racing tyres reverted to Akron, but Bushbury remained the home

consistently met the challenge of adapting its products to suit changes in chassis regulations and the varying requirements of engine power.

'In that respect, there is no doubt that Formula 1 will continue to stretch our engineering expertise and innovation in the forseeable future,' confirms Leo Mehl. 'Which is, of course, what Goodyear's involvement in Grand Prix racing has traditionally been all about.'

Goodyear's unshakeable belief that the technical knowledge derived from participating in Formula 1 produces a sub-

ADVERTISEMENT FEATURE

stantial contribution to the quality and performance levels of the latest generation of high performance road tyres is amply demonstrated by the technology incorporated into the design of the latest Eagle NCT 3 road tyre.

By the end of the 1994 season, Goodyear had surpassed the 300 Grand Prix win barrier, proving that by dint of pushing components to the outer limit of their performance, motor racing continues to supply the company with a consistently demanding and reliable test ground. If a component or material can be seen to function dependably in a highly-stressed racing environment, it can generally be assumed that it will display a significant safety margin when dealing with the normal operating conditions encountered on the road.

Goodyear's unparalleled success in Formula 1 has not only trained engineers and technicians in the disciplines required for long-term success in the racing world, where deadlines are tight and unyielding, but has also resulted in valuable technical transfer onto the road car tyre manufacturing front. This has not only resulted in a range of superior products, but also ensures that the company is pushing the outer edges of the performance envelope when it comes to evaluating and assessing new developments for the future.

It is in the demanding and technically challenging crucible of Grand Prix racing, where the Goodyear Eagle Formula 1 rain tyre has powered a long list of drivers to Grand Prix victories, that the lessons have been absorbed which have contributed to the successful development of Goodyear's high-performance Eagle NCT 3 tyre.

This state-of-the-art product, developed for Europe's most prestigious car manufacturers, decisively advances the cause of safety by significantly reducing the incidence of aquaplaning. This is the situation, so familiar to Formula 1 drivers, where your tyres actually rise up and ride on the surface of the water instead of the road, leading to a possible loss of control.

To prevent this happening, the Eagle NCT 3 has been designed for rapid, more efficient evacuation of surface water. The centreline and circumferential grooves in the tread design, and the tyre's multi-radius shape, all combine to reduce the risk of such aquaplaning.

In addition, the Eagle NCT 3 is constructed using a new compound, a mixture of synthetic and natural rubber, which improves adhesion on wet roads, while running cooler at high speed and thereby prolonging tyre life.

Above: Rubens Barrichello, Formula 1's youngest-ever pole-setter at this year's Belgian Grand Prix.
Below left: An Eagle Aquatred about to be checked for water-dispersion.
Centre, top: The water dispersing action of the tread design is clearly shown.
Centre, bottom: The Eagle NCT 3.
Right: Modern tyre design using computer simulation.

As an added benefit, significant noise reduction is achieved with an optimised block and rib design, while the Eagle NCT 3 actually improves levels of car control as the tyre is so responsive. The car clings to the road with outstanding handling precision and steering response, as a result of the six ribs which progressively widen from the tread centre to the shoulder area.

It is the contribution of such drivers as Michael Schumacher, Damon Hill and Gerhard Berger which continues to prove the key element in achieving Goodyear's unprecedented level of Grand Prix success over the years. They are sustaining a tradition extending back almost 30 years since the first Goodyear Grand Prix victory was scored by the late Richie Ginther at the wheel of a Honda car in Mexico City.

The practical result of their high-speed endeavours on some of the most demanding racing circuits in the world continues to be available to the private motorist through tyres such as the Goodyear NCT 3, again underlining the matchless benefits which accrue from Goodyear's world-wide commitment to this most challenging of sports.

Formula One
Michael Schumacher, winner of the 1994 FIA World Championship of Drivers, Mild Seven Benetton B194-Ford

F3000
Jean-Christophe Boullion
FIA European F3000 Champion
DAMS Reynard 94D-Cosworth AC

Ford-Cosworth Zetec-R Formula One engine

The success of Cosworth engines in international motor racing is legendary.

Continuous research, development and the new manufacturing technology form the centre of our work ethic. Our commitment to excellence ensures that Cosworth will continue to achieve the competitive edge vital for tomorrow's success.

Indy Car
Nigel Mansell, Newman-Haas Racing Kmart/Havoline Lola T94/00-Ford

COSWORTH®

Cosworth Engineering, St James Mill Road, Northampton NN5 5JJ, UK. Telephone: (0) 1604 752444/Fax: (0) 1604 580470
Cosworth Engineering Inc., 3031 Fujita Street, Torrance, CA90505-4004, USA. Telephone: (0) 310 534 1390/Fax: (0) 310 534 2631
A division of Vickers PLC

FIA WORLD CHAMPIONSHIP 1994

TOP TEN DRIVERS

*Chosen by the Editor, taking into account
their racing performances and the equipment
at their disposal*

top ten '94

1

Regarded by many as the star of '93, Damon Hill followed that up by doing a fantastic job throughout the most traumatic season in the Williams team's history. It is no disrespect to Damon to say that he started the year cast in a supporting role to the great Ayrton Senna. Yet within three races the 33-year-old Londoner found himself shouldering the responsibility of leading the team in the most trying circumstances imaginable as a maelstrom of political panic, much of it initiated by Renault, swirled around him like a tropical storm.

Renault got the jitters in the aftermath of Senna's death and had very real reservations about Hill's ability to get the job done. These doubts were only partly assuaged by his victory in the Spanish Grand Prix, but Damon kept his head and his nerve to see off a strong challenge from Nigel Mansell when the former World Champion was invited to make a guest appearance in the French Grand Prix. Hill may be reluctant to concede the point, but his team believe that day at Magny-Cours represented a psychological breakthrough. Chief Designer Adrian Newey recalls that when Damon walked into the team's pit lane garage at Silverstone the Thursday after the French race you could feel the fresh aura of self-confidence surrounding him.

Hill drove some storming races. Schumacher's stop-go penalty at Silverstone certainly dealt him a favourable hand, but many believe he would have won anyway. He also delivered the goods when faced with the challenge of having to win at Monza and Estoril, while Schumacher sat out a two-race suspension, if he was to be in with a realistic chance of the title. It's too glib to dismiss these as 'easy' wins. Stifling psychological pressure and a corresponding sense of expectancy surrounded these two races. But Hill delivered. Then came Suzuka and Adelaide, the best drives of his career to date.

If there was a downside to Damon's season it was the fact that he got embroiled in three first-lap accidents – at Imola (on the restart), Monaco and Hockenheim – which cost him valuable points. He was also less effective than Schumacher in cutting a swathe through heavy traffic, as evidenced by his showings at the Hungaroring and Jerez, although it must be said that the Williams team's continuing adherence to a strategy embracing two refuelling stops at many races, in contrast to Schumacher's three, hardly helped Damon's cause.

Not that Hill would have made a major issue out of it. The calm dignity and rectitude displayed off-track by this very private man was of an order which certainly matched his achievements out on the circuit. Under the circumstances, it would have been hard to ask any more of him.

damon HILL

Damon Hill

Date of birth: 17 September 1960
Residence: Ascot, England
Grand Prix starts in 1994: 16
World Championship placing: 2nd
Wins: 6; Poles: 2; Points: 91

top ten '94

2

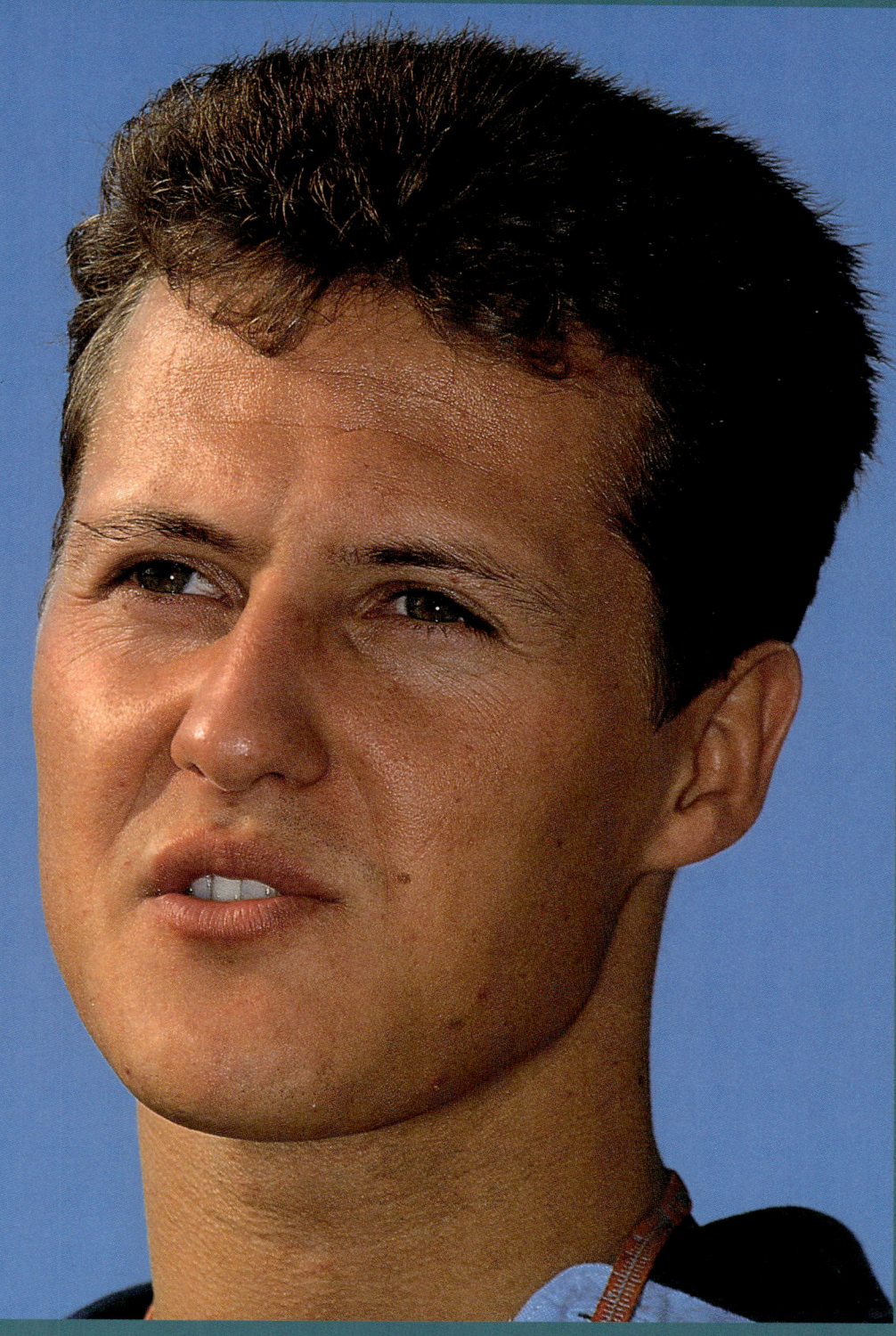

One of the saddest aspects of Michael Schumacher's season is that his outstanding level of achievement has, almost inevitably, been tarnished by Benetton's place at the very epicentre of F1 controversy. It matters not that the team was not proved to be running illegal traction or launch control systems. The whispers continue to hang in the air. Yet, in assessing Schumacher's performances, there is sufficient evidence to back the contention that he was the best driver of the year. The refuelling format could have been tailor-made for his heady blend of speed, stamina, fitness and consistency.

Like the late, lamented Ayrton Senna, he had a magical ability to slice his way through traffic with unerring precision. And, like Senna, he needed no warming-up in the early stages of a race. When the green light came on, it was like flicking a switch; at Monaco, Montreal and Spa he had the opposition on its knees before the race was half a dozen laps old.

Schumacher had successfully marshalled all the qualities necessary to be an outstanding performer behind the wheel. Yet, out of the cockpit, for all his somewhat formal Germanic sense of propriety, he still displayed an innocence which was usually rather attractive, less so perhaps when he chose to flavour it with a dash of arrogance. Was it bad advice or immaturity – or both – which tempted him to ignore the black flag at Silverstone? By the same token, were the same forces at work when he unleashed that unexpectedly vitriolic verbal assault on Damon Hill in the run-up to the European Grand Prix at Jerez?

Either way, Schumacher was guilty of poor judgement on both occasions. Yet his frustration might be seen as understandable. His self-belief was such that he knew he was the best driver in the business once Senna had been plucked from the stage. Only Schumacher knows whether he benefited from any hidden irregularities in the technical specification of his Benetton B194. But the confidence with which he and his advisers demanded a renegotiated contract lasting only until the end of 1995 in the wake of Benetton's problems could be taken as a clear indication that his conscience is clear, although the same perhaps cannot be said when considering his Australian GP collision with Hill which resolved the World Championship in such an unsatisfactory manner.

Michael Schumacher
Date of birth: 3 January 1969
Residence: Monaco
Grand Prix starts in 1994: 14
World Championship placing: 1st
Wins: 8; **Poles:** 6; **Points:** 92

michael SCHUMACHER

top ten '94

3

That we were strongly tempted to place a man who has won but a single Grand Prix as number one in the *Autocourse* Top Ten can be taken as a reflection of just how unusual the 1994 season really was. Berger may not have been the best driver, nor the most successful, but after the Imola disaster he emerged as the best possible advertisement for Grand Prix motor racing at a time when the sport seemed to shake on its very foundations.

Berger produced some of the most remarkable achievements of the entire F1 season. Not only did he put the disappointments of 1993 firmly behind him and establish himself as by far the most convincing of the Ferrari team's drivers, but he also displayed outstanding resilience, maturity and perspective in the aftermath of Senna's death, which probably hit him harder than any other competitor in the pit lane. For a week or so after the Imola tragedy, it seemed possible that Gerhard might quit racing altogether, but the lure of the sport he loved proved irresistible. Once he opted to continue, his resolve never wavered and he waded straight back into the fray to score a hard-won third place at Monaco.

Ferrari's original 65-degree V12 simply wasn't capable of challenging at the front of the pack, but when Gerhard got his hands on the latest 75-degree unit at Silverstone he signalled an upsurge in Maranello form by coming close to taking pole position.

At Hockenheim he proved unbeatable, qualifying on pole and leading every lap, despite having to fend off a strong challenge from Schumacher in the opening stages. In many ways it was absolutely appropriate that the genial Austrian should end Maranello's longest-ever spell without a win. It was a precise re-run of a similar feat in the 1987 Japanese Grand Prix and a success greeted with universal pleasure in the paddock.

However, Gerhard's best race – and perhaps the best race by any driver all year – was unquestionably the Italian Grand Prix at Monza, where he finished second at the wheel of the spare Ferrari, bruised and battered after writing off his race car in a 170 mph accident during the Sunday morning warm-up. This was bravery and commitment of epic proportions, but the Austrian simply shrugged it aside. He was just disappointed that Ferrari had failed to win on its home turf.

Taking a broader perspective, Berger brought just the right blend of persuasive insistence and restraint to the revived Grand Prix Drivers' Association. His enormous experience enabled him to calm the fears of the younger drivers, many of whom had never witnessed disaster remotely on the scale of the Imola tragedy, while at the same time reining in some of the more extreme elements. For that alone, he deserves considerable credit.

John Marsh/Action Images

gerhard BERGER

Gerhard Berger
Date of birth: 27 August 1959
Residences: Wörgl, Austria, and Monaco
Grand Prix starts in 1994: 16
World Championship placing: 3rd
Wins: 1; Poles: 2; Points: 41

top ten '94

4

Remember Estoril, 1993? Having been promoted to the McLaren race team after Michael Andretti's return to America, Mika Häkkinen out-qualified Ayrton Senna at the wheel of the Ford HB-engined MP4/8. Unquestionably, Ayrton was impressed. He climbed from his cockpit and walked over to the blond Finn, patting him approvingly on the shoulder, his face breaking into a sheepish grin.

With that in mind, it should come as no surprise to find many people within F1 firm in the belief that Häkkinen is probably the man best qualified to give Schumacher a genuine run for his money. If only he was afforded comparable equipment. Sadly, McLaren's Peugeot-engined MP4/9 was not the machine for the job. On a good day, it could be adjudged Best of the Rest. More often, it was an extremely disappointing contender. Häkkinen was hard put to conceal his frustration.

An early-season third at Imola boosted his morale and he looked in with a chance of a place on the podium at Barcelona until a cracked water radiator precipitated another major engine failure. Mika's Golden Moment, however, came at Monaco, where he drove brilliantly to qualify second alongside Schumacher's Benetton; then he threw it all away by getting involved in a first-corner collision with Damon Hill's fast-starting Williams.

Going into the second half of the season, Mika's frustration showed signs of getting the better of him. At Hockenheim, he was fingered as the man responsible for the first-corner multiple pile-up, a transgression which earned him a one-race suspension, the Finn missing the Hungarian Grand Prix.

There is much of the late, great Ronnie Peterson in Häkkinen's character. Behind an often impassive façade, he retains an almost impish sense of humour. Walking back across the paddock at Hockenheim after Ron Dennis had offered the stewards an eloquent defence of his first-lap driving tactics, he allegedly turned to his employer and said: 'Bloody hell, Ron, you did such a good job in there that even I began to believe that it wasn't my fault!'

Dennis is an unashamed fan of his lead driver. 'Mika is at an extremely positive, but equally critical stage of his career,' he says. 'He's got the speed, he's maturing well – now he just needs the success to give him the confidence necessary to become World Champion.' Hopefully, in 1995, Mercedes-Benz power will enable him to come closer to realising that ambition.

Mika Häkkinen
Date of birth: 28 September 1968
Residence: Monaco
Grand Prix starts in 1994: 15
World Championship placing: 4th
Wins: 0; Poles: 0; Points: 26

mika HÄKKINEN

top ten '94

5

In the past it has been the *Autocourse* convention not to include in the Top Ten drivers who have failed to start in all the races. However, in the best traditions of F1, rules are there to be broken, and the 1994 season must clearly be something of an exception. Were we to stick to our original terms of reference, six of the drivers cited in this list would automatically be eliminated!

In any event, to omit David Coulthard simply because he has taken part in only half the races would be unreasonable in the extreme, for the 23-year-old Scot was unquestionably one of the most outstanding new stars of the F1 show. When Williams drafted in their latest test driver to fill the gaping void left by Ayrton Senna's death, there were many who thought they were being too ambitious. But when Coulthard made three places on the first lap of his debut race at Barcelona and sat confidently on the tail of Lehto's Benetton and Alesi's Ferrari in the opening stages of the race, it was clear that this newcomer was a cut above the average.

The statistics show that, in his eight outings, he qualified six times in the top half-dozen, set a fastest race lap at Hockenheim, and led three races, with his best result a second place to Hill at Estoril. Yet it was the manner in which he operated which really impressed the Williams team. He was calm, focused and unflustered, capable of switching on an intense level of mental concentration at the drop of a hat. Off-track, he displayed a relaxed and easy manner, perhaps reflecting his apprenticeship under the tutelage of Jackie Stewart in the minor formulae.

It was clearly an enormous disappointment for Coulthard when he was stood down in favour of Nigel Mansell for the last three races, even though he knew it was coming. But he never allowed his frustration to boil over in public. He kept his cool, just as he had done during the Hungarian Grand Prix, when, after throwing away third place under pressure from Brundle, he had come on the radio to explain, in disarmingly matter-of-fact style: 'Sorry about that, chaps. I don't quite know what happened. I'll have a think about it as I walk back to the pits!'

Herke de Vries

David Coulthard

Date of birth: 27 March 1971
Residences: Twynholm, Scotland and London, England
Grand Prix starts in 1994: 8
World Championship placing: 8th
Wins: 0; **Poles:** 0; **Points:** 14

david COULTHARD

top ten '94

6

Jean Alesi had a bitterly disappointing fourth season at Ferrari, during which there were occasions when the whole business of Grand Prix racing seemed to be getting the Frenchman down. Simply scanning the results doesn't tell the full story. The record book may look reasonable enough, but by the end of the season Jean was approaching his 90th Grand Prix start and had still to score his first victory.

The season started off well enough with third place in the Brazilian Grand Prix behind Schumacher and Hill. But then he lost two races recovering from back injuries sustained testing (not his strongest card) at Mugello before returning in time for Monaco, where his over-anxiety saw him tangle with David Brabham's Simtek. Nevertheless, he survived to finish fifth, followed by fourth in Spain, third in Canada and second at Silverstone. After that, his season seemingly ground to a halt and he didn't finish another race until October.

Alesi became weighed down by the frustration of it all, and it told in his driving. Engine failures in the opening moments of the German and Belgian races drove him to the edge of despair, but he took his first pole position at Monza and led the race commandingly in the opening stages, only to scramble his gearbox dogrings as he restarted from his first refuelling stop.

At this point, the accumulated pressure simply became too much to bear. He exploded into a towering rage, stormed out of the circuit and drove his Alfa 164 saloon flat out all the way to the sanctuary of his yacht at Cap d'Antibes. It was a display of the same volatility which saw him screaming at Martin Brundle after an on-track territorial dispute during practice at Spa. Perhaps Jean needs to curb this side of his character if he is ever to score that elusive first Grand Prix victory.

jean ALESI

Jean Alesi
Date of birth: 11 June 1964
Residence: Nyon, Switzerland
Grand Prix starts in 1994: 14
World Championship placing: 5th
Wins: 0; **Poles:** 1; **Points:** 24

top ten '94

7

In 1993, Ken Tyrrell freely admitted that his team ended the season with a chassis that simply hadn't done justice to the fast-improving Yamaha V10 engine. In that respect, the team has done very much better this year but it has come as a surprise to some that Ukyo Katayama has emerged as perhaps the more promising of Tyrrell's two drivers.

Ukyo came close to scoring his first World Championship points for Larrousse in the 1992 Canadian Grand Prix, inadvertently over-revving the engine in the closing stages of the race. He seemed to struggle in 1993, but his talent blossomed dramatically this season at the wheel of the new Harvey Postlethwaite-designed Tyrrell 022. He broke his duck with two points for fifth place in the opening race of the year at Interlagos and duplicated that achievement at Imola.

Yet it was in some of the races he failed to finish that Katayama demonstrated the greatest potential. He qualified a magnificent fifth at Hockenheim, briefly holding second place for a few yards on an opening lap which saw him involved in a collision with Damon Hill which sent the Williams driver heading for the pits to change a bent steering arm. Thereafter he ran an easy third until a stuck throttle deprived him of becoming only the second Japanese driver to take a place on the Grand Prix podium.

At Monza, he started well down the grid, but made the best of a two-stop strategy to soar through the field – as, indeed, did team-mate Mark Blundell – only to lose a chance of more points when a brake disc shattered. Then, at Jerez, he rocketed through to a brilliant seventh place after stalling on the grid and joining in almost half a lap down on the leaders.

Privately, it has been a devastating season for Katayama, who had to contend with the death in childbirth of his sister, who was married to his business manager. But his unyieldingly cheerful, uncomplaining nature has ensured him immense popularity and respect among the Formula 1 fraternity.

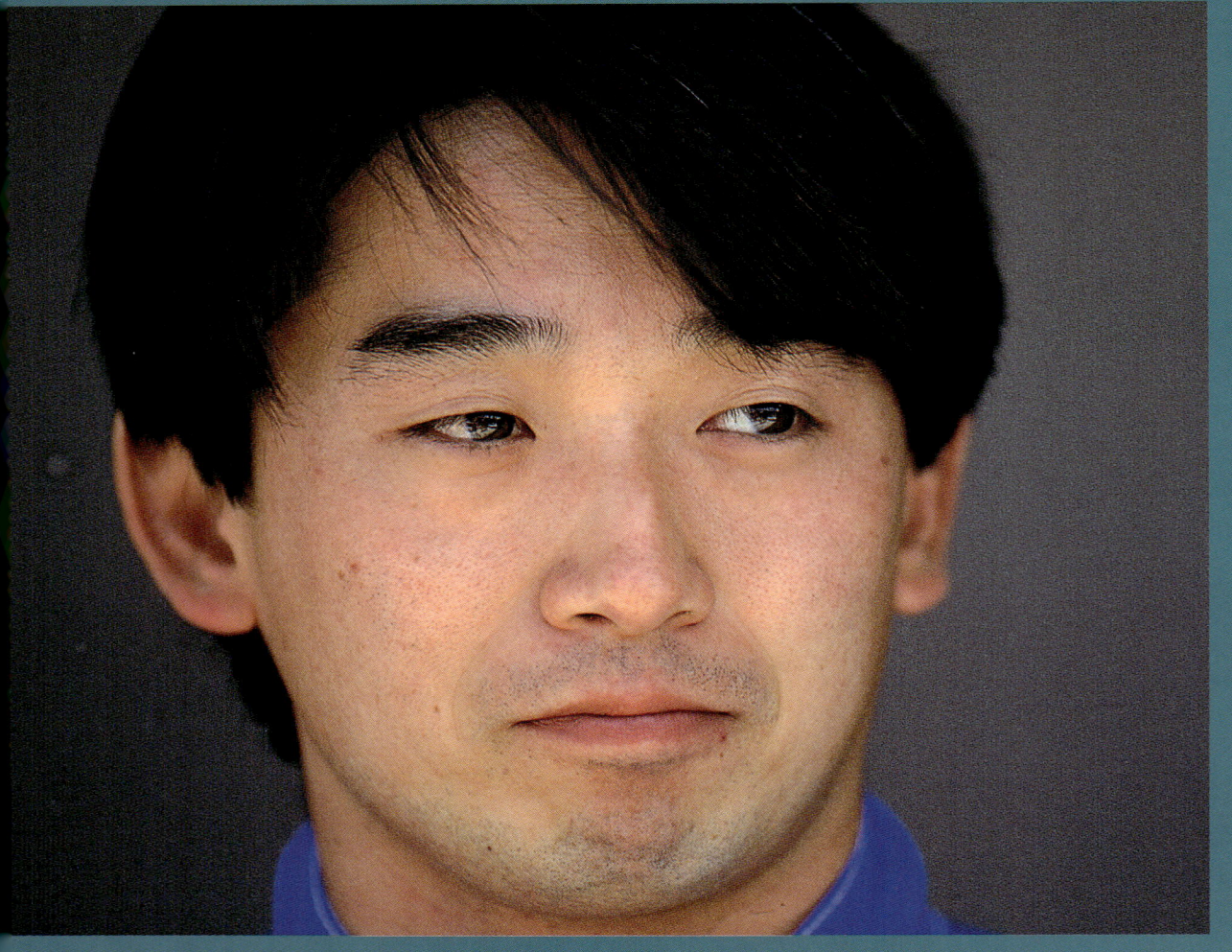

Ukyo Katayama
Date of birth: 29 May 1963
Residences: Tokyo, Japan, Salfords, England, and Monaco
Grand Prix starts in 1994: 16
World Championship placing: 17th
Wins: 0; Poles: 0; Points: 5

ukyo KATAYAMA

top ten '94

8

Eddie Irvine

Date of birth: 10 November 1965
Residence: Dublin, Republic of Ireland
Grand Prix starts in 1994: 13
World Championship placing: equal 14th
Wins: 0; Poles: 0; Points: 6

At the start of the season it seemed as though Eddie Irvine was set to become the Catastrophe Charlie of the Grand Prix community. The Ulsterman first shot to F1 prominence when he matched Ayrton Senna, incivility for incivility, in a post-race verbal brawl at Suzuka where he'd just finished sixth for Jordan on his maiden outing with the team. The storm clouds were just abating when Irvine found himself pitchforked into the centre of another controversy, fingered by the race stewards for triggering a four-car pile-up in the Brazilian Grand Prix at Interlagos.

From a purely personal standpoint, the writer believes it was ridiculous to have blamed anybody for this unfortunate incident – it was simply the almost inevitable result of four cars arriving at the same point on the circuit, at the same moment, each with its driver facing different priorities. He was suspended for a race and very reasonably appealed. Unreasonably, in many people's view, the FIA increased Eddie's suspension to three races in what amounted to a discreet signal to others not to waste the governing body's time with what might all too easily be interpreted as specious objections.

Eddie celebrated his return to the F1 grid with a hard-won sixth place at Barcelona, after which he was bugged by seemingly endless mechanical unreliability, including two rare failures of the generally bullet-proof Hart 1035 engine. It was therefore with some relief that he notched up a fourth place, inches behind Häkkinen's McLaren, to register his best-ever F1 finish at the European GP.

Irvine is rather reminiscent of James Hunt. He projects something of a couldn't-care-less, wild-man image, but Jordan insiders believe this to be a means by which a very intelligent man is disguising a certain lack of confidence. That fourth place at Jerez should have done Irvine the world of good in that particular respect.

eddie IRVINE

top ten '94

9

After the first two races of the season it seemed that Rubens Barrichello was very definitely set for great things. He had delighted his fans at home with a heady drive to fourth place at Interlagos and followed that up with a flawless display to make his first appearance on the podium with third place in the Pacific Grand Prix. He then had a huge accident during practice at Imola which sidelined him from the San Marino GP, followed by an uncomfortable few weeks as he sought to come to terms with the loss of Ayrton Senna, his friend, mentor and inspiration.

Barrichello is a man who seems to have a very clear idea in his own mind of what he wants and where he wants to get to in F1. However, the Jordan team has been aware that he performs best under pressure, and recruiting Eddie Irvine to drive alongside him frequently had the desired effect – although insiders admit it took some time for Rubens to get used to the situation. On his return after Imola, he had a disappointing run at Monaco, but then qualified fifth (Spain), seventh (Canada and France) and sixth (Silverstone) for the next four races in a convincing demonstration of the Jordan-Hart's potential.

The first pole position of his Grand Prix career came at Spa, where he judged things perfectly in patchily damp conditions on the first day, but his race performance was disappointing and he seemed reluctant to acknowledge that it was his own error which eventually sent him off the circuit.

Two more fourth places at Silverstone and Monza were more representative indications of Barrichello's true form. He has all the essential qualities to make a race winner, but he needs to give 100 per cent effort on all 16 outings that make up a World Championship schedule. Sometimes his team formed the impression that he was holding a little in reserve.

Paul-Henri Cahier

Rubens Barrichello

Date of birth: 23 May 1972
Residence: Cambridge, England, and São Paulo, Brazil
Grand Prix starts in 1994: 15
World Championship placing: 6th
Wins: 0; **Poles:** 1; **Points:** 19

rubens BARRICHELLO

top ten '94

10

When Heinz-Harald Frenzten qualified fifth for his first Grand Prix outing in Brazil at the wheel of the Sauber C13-Mercedes, the achievement was greeted with a flurry of excitement. Here, said the pundits, was a man with even greater potential than Michael Schumacher. Moreover, to back up this contention, there were many who stepped forward to point out that he had been as fast, if not faster, than the Benetton team leader when they'd been members of the Mercedes Group C assault back in 1990.

In truth, these are somewhat spurious comparisons. Yet there is no doubt that Frentzen proved himself to be a highly accomplished performer in his maiden Grand Prix season. Even though Sauber was struggling to produce consistent performances from circuit to circuit, the 28-year-old German driver always seemed to be further up the grid than one might have expected of a man with such limited experience. He finished fifth at TI Circuit to score his first points in only his second race, produced an excellent fourth in France and hard-fought seventh places at both Imola and Silverstone.

A regular top-six contender, Frentzen had to assume *de facto* team leadership after Karl Wendlinger's terrible accident at Monaco and he rose to the occasion with impressive confidence. There were moments when his inexperience showed, of course, most notably at Spa, when he spun under pressure at the Eau Rouge chicane and left his Sauber stranded over a high kerb, rear wheels desperately clawing thin air. Equally, he looked strong at Monza before engine failure intervened and might well have finished on the podium at Jerez had his team not taken the strategically inexplicable decision to run through with a single refuelling stop, which simply lost him too much time.

Heinz-Harald Frentzen
Date of birth: 18 May 1967
Residence: Mönchengladbach, Germany
Grand Prix starts in 1994: 15
World Championship placing: 13th
Wins: 0; Poles: 0; Points: 7

heinz-harald FRENTZEN

ADVERTISEMENT FEATURE

FORD IN MOTORSPORT: THE SUCCESS STORY CONTINUES

Ford is the only manufacturer to be involved in what are generally acknowledged to be the world's four major motorsport disciplines: the Formula One World Championship, the World Rally Championship, the PPG Indy Car World Series and the NASCAR Winston Cup. Once again, in 1994, the famous blue and white oval has been to the fore in each of those series.

THE BIGGEST PRIZE of all was secured in November, when Benetton-Ford driver Michael Schumacher won the Formula One World Drivers' Championship in dramatic fashion at the final round of the gruelling 16 race series, in Adelaide, Australia. In clinching the 1994 title, the prodigiously talented young German became the 13th driver in 27 years to win the World Championship with Ford power behind him.

Schumacher also proved that history can repeat itself. In 1967, the legendary Jim Clark took Colin Chapman's brand-new Lotus 49, fitted with the equally new Ford DFV V8 engine, to a debut victory in the Dutch Grand Prix at Zandvoort, announcing the arrival of a new force on the Formula One scene. The Scot followed up this stunning victory with a further three wins before the year was out.

In 1994, armed with Benetton's latest B194 chassis fitted with an all-new Ford Formula One engine, the Zetec-R, Schumacher did even better than his illustrious predecessor. He scored an historic victory for the new combination in the opening round of the World Championship, in Sao Paulo, Brazil, and then went on to notch up a further seven wins on his way to the World Drivers' title.

Schumacher's winning streak also contributed to two other noteworthy statistics in 1994. In Jerez, Spain, at the European Grand Prix, he increased Ford's total of Grand Prix victories to 174, 70 more than nearest rival Ferrari, and in Japan, he recorded Ford's

400th start in Formula One World Championship competition.

For the Ford and Cosworth engineers involved with the new Zetec-R engine, however, one of the most satisfying moments of the year came with a second place finish – in the Spanish Grand Prix at the end of May. With his car stuck in fifth gear for over two-thirds of the race following an hydraulic system failure, Schumacher nonetheless exploited every bit of the new Ford engine's inherent tractability to lap within fractions of a second of the normal race lap times. Such was his pace that his hobbled car even led the race briefly during the second round of pit stops!

When the Ford Electronics telemetry data was analyzed after the race, it revealed that for 44 laps, the Zetec-R in the back of Schumacher's Benetton had pulled from as low as 6200 rpm in the Catalunya circuit's two hairpins up to 14,500 rpm on the start–finish straight – all in the same gear! It was an amazing performance and one which served to demonstrate, in the most graphic way possible, the strength, reliability and performance of Ford's latest Formula One engine. The Zetec-R had definitely arrived.

Unfortunately, the 1994 Formula One season was also one which was afflicted with great sadness. In a mind-numbing double tragedy, three-time World Driving Champion, Ayrton Senna, and Formula One newcomer, Roland Ratzenberger, both lost their lives at the Imola circuit during the weekend of the San Marino Grand Prix. Senna, of course, won the final five Grands Prix of his phenomenally successful driving career at the wheel of the Ford-powered McLaren MP4/8. Early in his career, the Brazilian's driving brilliance was also showcased in the traditional learning category of Formula Ford.

Almost unbelievably, two weeks after the Imola accidents, Karl Wendlinger's Sauber crashed into barriers during qualifying for the Monaco Grand Prix, the Austrian driver suffering serious head injuries which left him in a coma for six weeks. Thankfully, he survived, and has since made a miraculous recovery. He looks set to drive again in 1995.

There was also controversy throughout much of the 1994 Grand Prix season. At various times during the year, the focus of technical officials and the press was on Formula One computer software, the refuelling equipment used at pit stops and the thickness of downforce-reducing 'planks' fitted to the undersides of the cars. Adding to this, Schumacher received a two-race ban for allegedly taking too long to respond to a black flag shown to him during the British Grand Prix at Silverstone in July.

Despite all the side issues, the German and his Benetton Formula team managed to remain focussed on the job in hand – winning the Formula One World Championship. This they eventually did in Australia, and even their rivals would have to admit that over the nine-month haul of the 1994 Formula One season, the combination of Michael Schumacher, Benetton and Ford was the strongest one on the track. Schumacher, in only his third full season of Grand Prix racing, had realised the promise which he so clearly demonstrated on his Formula One debut at the 1991 Belgian Grand Prix. With a mere 52 Grands Prix under his belt, the 25-year-old German had become World Champion.

Next year will see the opening of a new chapter in Ford's Formula One history as the company joins forces with the Swiss-based Sauber team as a highly successful eight-year collaboration with Benetton Formula comes to an end. Also in 1995, Formula One regulations will require that engines are reduced in capacity from 3.5 litres to a maximum of 3.0 litres. Already, the Cosworth engineers who developed this year's winning Zetec-R engine on behalf of Ford have an engine complying with the new regulations running on the test bench and report that it is producing excellent power figures, a point which understandably pleases Peter Sauber. 'No one on the Formula One scene this year can have failed to be impressed by the performance of Ford's Zetec-R engine' he says. 'Quite simply, it has proved itself to be the best engine. I'm overjoyed at the prospect of my team having the exclusive use of this engine next year. I honestly believe that the Sauber-Fords will be able to fight for Grand Prix wins in 1995'.

The Ford Zetec-R will be fitted to a brand-new chassis which will be the work of Team Sauber's Chief Designer, Leo Ress. The Sauber-Ford C14 will be testing early in the new year.

ADVERTISEMENT FEATURE

In addition to the Zetec-R, the Cosworth-developed Ford HB 'customer' engines were the power source of choice for a number of Formula One teams in 1994, including Footwork, Larrousse, Minardi and Simtek. Ford's 'strength-in-depth' through the Formula One field is set to continue again next year.

Ford's 1994 World Rally Championship challenge got off to a fairy-tale start with François Delecour taking an historic win in his Escort Cosworth on the Monte Carlo Rally. The competitiveness of the turbocharged, four-wheel drive Ford was clear for all to see: aside from Delecour's victory, Escort drivers Miki Biasion and Bruno Thiry finished the gruelling event in fourth and sixth places respectively.

Unfortunately, Delecour's Championship challenge was blunted before it had any real chance to get rolling, the Frenchman suffering serious leg injuries in a road accident just before the start of the Corsica Rally in May. During his convalescence, Delecour's place in the Boreham squad alongside Miki Biasion was filled by a number of stand-in drivers, including Ari Vatanen, Malcolm Wilson, Franco Cunico, and Tommi Mäkinen. Thanks to a fine performance from Mäkinen on his 'home' event, Ford scored its second WRC victory of the 1994 season on Finland's 1000 Lakes Rally.

Delecour was firmly back in harness leading the Ford charge into the RAC Rally, the final round of the 1994 World Championship. Despite hobbling about outside his Escort, the Frenchman showed in Sanremo that he was right back on pace once behind the wheel, only a failed head on his Escort's engine preventing him from achieving a strong result in the Italian event.

Carrying the Ford Motorsport colours admirably during Delecour's enforced absence was his team mate, Miki Biasion, the Italian double World Champion and long-time co-driver Tiziano Siviero, both renowned for their consistency. The two have finished fourth in the Driver's Championship four years in succession and, remarkably, they were again lying fourth in the standings going into the final round. They could not catch the leaders at this point, but they were aiming to consolidate their position in the WRC points table with another good result.

Another Ford man to make a strong impression in the 1994 WRC has been Bruno Thiry. The young Belgian and co-driver, Stéphane Prévot, competed for much of 1994 in a 'semi-works' Escort Cosworth tended by the RAS Sport team. Thiry has impressed throughout his first season in a top specification, turbocharged Group A car and has scored points in five rounds of the World Championship. Finishing a commendable third in the final event of the WRC, the RAC Rally, Thiry boosted his World Championship position to fifth place overall, making him the highest placed Ford driver of the 1994 Rally season. Predictably, the RAS Giesse team has confirmed that Thiry will remain in its driver line-up for 1995.

One undisputed star of the rally scene this season has been Malcolm Wilson. Last year, Ford Motorsport's chief test driver finished second in the British Rally Championship and then came home a fine third in the RAC Rally at the wheel of his distinctively liveried Michelin Pilot Team Ford Escort Cosworth.

In the 12 months that have elapsed since achieving that result, Wilson and co-driver, Bryan Thomas, absolutely blitzed the 1994 Mobil 1/Top Gear British Rally Championship, winning four of the five rounds in dominant style. Underlining their ability, the talented duo also ran as high as second on the Sanremo round of the World Rally Championship in October.

Wilson's Escort Cosworth is built by his own preparation company, Malcolm Wilson Motorsport, based in England's Lake District. Wilson's expertise in this area extends far beyond British shores, however, Escorts built in his workshops having claimed both the 1994 Middle East and Portuguese Rally Championships. In fact, that is only part of the Ford success story in rallying this year. At the time of going to press, Escort Cosworths have notched up 48 victories in national and international competition and secured 10 major championship titles. The likelihood is that there will be several more added to that tally before the year is out.

Another motorsport discipline in which Ford vehicles have demonstrated their winning ways in 1994 has been 2-litre Touring Car racing, the Ford Mondeo Ghias of Paul Radisich and Andy Rouse scoring two outright victories in the ultra-competitive Auto Trader RAC British Touring Car Championship. Radisich then went on to score an impressive win in the FIA Touring Car World Cup at Donington Park in October against many of the world's top Touring Car drivers.

This marked the second year in succession that Radisich and Ford have taken the world title. The talented New Zealander then capped a memorable weekend by scything his way through a 15-car field to win the action-packed TOCA Shoot-out and walked away with the £12,000, winner-take-all prize. Aside from being a highly successful road car, the Mondeo has now twice proved that it is also the world's best 2-litre Touring Car.

There is a worldwide upsurge of interest in this form of motor racing and Fords are in

the thick of the action. Andy Rouse Engineering, the Coventry-based company which prepares the BTCC Mondeos, has this year also supplied cars to teams running in the German, French, and Spanish Super Touring Championships.

On the other side of the Atlantic Ocean, the PPG Indy Car World Series was this year almost the exclusive preserve of the Penske team. One

member of Indy Car racing's so-called three-man 'dream team' – Al Unser Jr, Emerson Fittipaldi or Paul Tracy – claimed victory in 12 of the Championship's 16 races and, on five separate occasions, the Penske trio swept the top-three finishing positions.

In spite of this domination, Ford-powered drivers did succeed in carrying the fight to the Penskes, scoring four wins

finishing positions at the Atlanta Motor Speedway.

'It really has been an exceptional year for us,' commented Ford's Director of Motorsport Strategy and Formula One Operations, Peter Gillitzer, after Michael Schumacher secured the World Drivers' Championship in Adelaide. 'When it comes to motorsport, there isn't another motor manufacturer which can touch Ford for its worldwide commitment. Obviously, we're extremely pleased to have helped Michael and the

and 16 podium finishes. Michael Andretti was the most successful at stemming the Penske tide, the American's Ganassi Racing Reynard-Ford taking two victories, in Surfer's Paradise, Australia, and Toronto, while Canadians Scott Goodyear and Jacques Villeneuve, claimed one win apiece for Ford, at Michigan International Speedway and Road America respectively. Robby Gordon and Raul Boesel also made good use of the power of their turbocharged Ford-Cosworth XB IndyCar engines, securing three pole positions and four top-three finishes between them.

The final event of the season, in Laguna Seca, California, also saw two of Indy Car racing's best known Ford drivers taking their leave of the Series. Newman-Haas team mates, Nigel Mansell and Mario Andretti, both departed the scene, Andretti into retirement at the end of an impressive 30-year racing career, and Mansell back to the Formula One arena which he left at the end of 1992. The Andretti name will stay on the side of a Newman-Haas Lola in 1995, Michael moving across to fill the seat vacated by his father, while Mansell's place in the team will be taken by ex-Penske driver, Paul Tracy.

The 1994 season was also an outstanding one for Ford in NASCAR Winston Cup competition, the world's top stock racing championship. The company's Thunderbird coupé won 20 races in the course of a gruelling 31-race schedule, the first time that feat had been accomplished in 10 years. A total of 11 drivers contributed points to Ford's winning NASCAR Manufacturers' Championship tally, the most successful being Rusty Wallace.

The Penske Racing driver won an impressive eight races, four more than the nearest challenger, Dale Earnhardt. It was the Chevrolet driver, Earnhardt, though, the man nicknamed 'The Intimidator' by his rivals for his aggressive driving style, who scooped a record-tying seventh Winston Cup title with his highly consistent finishing record.

Also coming through on consistency was another Ford driver, Mark Martin, who grabbed second spot in the Championship standings from Wallace by winning the final race of the year, the Hooters 500, in Atlanta, Georgia. Thunderbirds occupied six of the top-seven

Benetton team secure their first Formula One World title, but I'm equally gratified by the results that we've achieved in other championships with which we've been involved this year.'

'We may not have won them all, but we've been extremely competitive in all of them. More importantly, we continue to learn valuable engineering lessons from our motorsport involvement which can be applied to current and future road car programmes. This helps us to make better, safer cars for the general public. That is the ultimate reward and one of the key reasons why, as a company, Ford will continue to be involved in motorsport. Whether it's Formula One or Formula Ford, Touring Cars or Ford Fiestas, the technological pay-off makes the cost of involvement worthwhile.'

MICHAEL SCHUMACHER
A MAN APART

by Timothy Collings

In the end, though the means were questionable and the outcome controversial, few could dispute that Michael Schumacher deserved to be the 1994 World Champion. He had displayed an overall supremacy, from the start of the year, that no other driver was able to challenge. He had been outstandingly fast and he had shown a sense of commitment and mental toughness, even when the going became very difficult politically, which earned him respect from everyone. This, more than any analysis of the collision between his Benetton B194-Ford and Damon Hill's Williams FW16B-Renault on the 36th lap of the Australian Grand Prix, explained why Hill declined to criticise, or to lodge a formal protest, after a manoeuvre which most observers regarded as deliberate and dangerous. As Hill himself admitted after his own dream had been shattered, in his heart he knew the title had been won a long time before. That, too, explains why Hill crossed the breakfast room in the Hyatt Hotel in Adelaide to congratulate Michael on the morning after their great contest had been settled.

Schumacher, at 25, became the youngest champion (although it could be argued that Emerson Fittipaldi won the title earlier in the season and therefore at a younger age) and Germany's first. In the process, he fulfilled the predictions of thousands of people who saw him make his Formula 1 debut in a Jordan-Ford at the 1991 Belgian Grand Prix. He had qualified seventh, having previously never seen the circuit, let alone driven on it. His race ended with a burnt-out clutch immediately after the start, but he had done enough to suggest that a rare talent had arrived and Benetton, swooping in the night, had him signed in time to drive for them in the following race, the Italian Grand Prix at Monza. From that day on, Benetton and Schumacher looked set to take the championship together and it was only the timing which remained unresolved.

The death of Ayrton Senna at Imola on 1 May 1994 was the decisive act of fate which made this Schumacher's year. He had won the two season-opening races already, in Brazil and at Aida in Japan, leaving little doubt about his and the B194's potential. When he won the San Marino Grand Prix, he automatically became the new heir apparent to the great Brazilian's position as the fastest and most respected driver of his day. Yet few knew him and even fewer understood him. He was, in short, virtually unknown in global sporting terms compared to the widespread international fame of Senna, Alain Prost or Nigel Mansell.

None of this fazed Schumacher. Indeed, he is rarely fazed by anything at all. His life, from his earlier years as a four-year-old karting prodigy at Kerpen-Mannheim, near Cologne, had been a preparation for Formula 1 and for its unique demands. For him, it was completely natural to race with total mental and physical commitment, as this was what he had been doing since he first began karting as a child. Indeed, his karting years taught him much of the mental toughness he took for granted later when he graduated through Formula Ford, Formula Konig and the German Formula 3 series to the World Sports Car Championship with Mercedes-Benz.

There, under the wise counsel of Jochen Mass, Schumacher learned how to race over a long distance, how to conserve fuel, how to preserve his tyres, how to apply himself most efficiently to his job. He also learned about the importance of diet, fitness, strength, stamina, sponsorship, the media and good communications. In short, by the time he reached Spa-Francorchamps in 1991, he was as near to the finished article as a debutant could be. All this, coupled with his blinding natural talent – Martin Brundle would always say he was 'gifted with speed' – made him a man apart from the rest from the start. He was a dedicated, committed and thoroughly professional racing driver with outstanding talent.

During his youth, Schumacher did little else but race. He entered the German, European and world karting championships as a junior and as a senior, and he grew used to success. He fitness-trained harder than any of his contemporaries, to such a degree that all the weight work he did as a teenager caused chronic knee problems which required surgery on both knees at the end of the 1993 season. He was German junior karting champion in 1984, the European and German senior champion in 1987, Formula Konig champion in 1988, and German Formula 3 Champion in 1990, when he also won the Macau Grand Prix.

All his successes came with ease, his natural speed enabling him to find the limits of his car and the circuit more rapidly than anyone else. This was a rare talent and one he demonstrated frequently. At his first Formula 1 test at Silverstone's South Circuit with Jordan, he was called in three times and told to slow down, and each time he told team manager Trevor Foster that he was in control, he was at the limit. 'We were all just flabbergasted,' said Foster. 'We knew immediately he was something special.' That impression was confirmed in Belgium the following week with his dramatic entrance to Formula 1.

To those who did not know him (and few did), he seemed even in those early days to have an unnatural sense of self-confidence, an arrogance, a Teutonic swagger, but this was only superficial and under the surface was a young man of only 22 who was little more than a hometown boy blessed with speed. Schumacher was not and never has been a playboy, despite the fact that he now lives in sun-tanned splendour in Monte Carlo, but rather a simple fellow with a love of racing. His school friends and those who grew up with him at the karting track all knew this and were impressed as much by his devotion to developing his talent as by his speed. Even in his early teens, he worked out at his local gym on a regular basis, developing the fitness which by 1993 had turned him into the best-equipped athlete ever to have sat in a Formula 1 car. This fitness, which enabled him to finish his races – including the toughest Grands Prix in high temperatures and scorching sunshine – looking cool and relaxed, set him apart from his rivals and gave him an instantaneous advantage.

But he also developed a phenomenal ability to set up his karts and his cars and to understand them during his early years. At first, all this was dedicated to sheer speed, but during his time with Mercedes, under Mass's wise eye, he learned also to consider other things which mattered until he emerged as the complete racer, prepared for Formula 1. On one occasion as a boy, he won a kart race in the German junior series by racing with just one hand on his steering wheel and the other holding a loose screw, on his carburettor mounting, in position. 'It was incredible, it just proved how much he understood about his kart and about engines,' said Jurgen Dilk, who was Schumacher's sponsor and mentor during those early days. 'He just had a tremendous ability and a great will to win. He loved his racing. It was his whole life.'

Dilk had taken over as Schumacher's main benefactor when his father's financial support ran out. For years, as a boy karting star, his father had helped him find secondhand engines, tyres and other parts to keep his kart on the track (his father still works at the same track renting karts to boys to start their careers, and his mother has a fastfood shop there, supplying hot dogs and chips), but when the costs escalated and new and more expensive engines were required Dilk was his saviour. Dilk drove the teenage Schumacher all over Europe in a van to kart races and later, when he moved into single-seater racing, he helped him tackle his first full season, during which he won the German Formula Konig championship.

It was at this time that he was seen, admired and then acquired by Willi Weber, who signed Michael to race for him in his Formula 3 team, WTS Racing, in the process agreeing a ten-year management deal with him. Weber took control of all aspects of Michael's career from then on. In 1990, Schumacher won the Formula 3 championship and the prestigious Macau F3 Grand Prix, after a last-corner collision had removed the threat from Mika Häkkinen, and in the same year he raced for Mercedes-Benz as one of three juniors being groomed for stardom.

The experiences were all vital to his development, but nothing ever changed his fundamental ability to climb into virtually any car and be quick with it immediately. This, as many noted later, was a quality he shared with the late Ayrton Senna, whose mantle he inherited in such tragic circumstances. One man who knew this long before the 1994 season had started and who recognised that Schumacher was the biggest threat to his hopes for further championship successes was Frank Williams. 'There is one man out

WORLD CHAMPION PROFILE

there called Schumacher who is very special,' he said. 'Schumacher is right on the limit. He can just get into the car and go to the limit without having to warm himself up and get his eye in from the day before. It is astonishing.'

This ability came from Schumacher's life-long love of racing (though he readily admits he never gave a thought to Grand Prix racing nor even watched a race until he was 19) and his single-minded pursuit of excellence in all areas which would help him. His humble background and the strict family code imposed by his bricklayer father Rolf and mother Elizabeth had invested him with solid foundations and a strong sense of loyalty. Hence, Dilk and all the friends and supporters from his early days are invited frequently to join him at races, always remembered, never forgotten.

He has never wavered during his Formula 1 career from his attachment to his girlfriend, Corinna Betsch, to whom he is now engaged, and showed similar loyalty under duress when Benetton were besieged by problems at the height of the 1994 season. The black flag at Silverstone, the fuel filter removal at Hockenheim, the fire, the cheating allegations, the skidblock disqualification at Spa-Francorchamps . . . these blows might have flattened a lesser man, but Schumacher, armed with his strong code of life, his almost impenetrable coat of self-confidence and his natural sense of loyalty, rode out the storm. The management factor, in the shape of Willi Weber, steered him towards a new contract, an act of opportunism which matched those Schumacher himself executed so adeptly on the track.

Loyal and courteous, direct and confident, Schumacher can also be ruthless in both racing and business, as was displayed several times in 1994 and not only in Adelaide. His talent is such that he can carve through his rivals on the track, produce lap times that stun everyone and pull together a team which, as Benetton was in September, is struggling for a sense of direction. Coupled with a calculating mind, his supreme confidence in himself and his new status as champion, Schumacher now possesses all the qualities required to retain his title and stay at the top for many years to come.

31

⌞We Are The Ch

"We win by leaving nothing to chance. That is why we use Scanias to get our cars to the circuits. Sca

GRAND PRIX '94 – THE TECHNICAL STORY

THE LAW AND ORDER CRISIS

by Alan Henry

Benetton were quick to adopt a Williams-style rear wing *(left)* in Canada, and Schumacher continued the team's run of success.

Qualifying is about to begin at Spa *(right)*, with many teams still trying to come to terms with the effects of the rule changes that had disrupted the season.

There was certainly turmoil and tragedy from a purely human standpoint in F1 during 1994, but the season's technical challenges proved almost as demanding and unpredictable. During the second half of 1993 the teams and the rule makers had spent much of the time confronting each other over the question of whether or not electronic driver aids would be banned for '94, and when they finally were, the designers were faced with a whole new aerodynamic challenge attempting to make up for the loss of grip which resulted from the ban on traction control systems.

The rules package for 1994 banned not only traction control, but also ABS, power braking systems, fly-by-wire throttle mechanisms and active suspension. In addition, refuelling was imposed on a reluctant F1 fraternity, most teams feeling that they were bounced into agreeing to this dangerous procedure in exchange for the FIA not banning active suspension on the spot midway through the previous summer.

'It was a very deceitful affair achieved by a little manipulation and sleight of hand which I won't go into in any detail,' said one team principal. Understandably, under the circumstances, he did not wish to be identified.

Continuously variable transmission (CVT) was also included on the list of prohibited accessories, a decision which effectively wiped out ten years of behind-the-scenes endeavour on the part of the Williams team.

The reality, of course, was that only Ferrari really wanted refuelling, which was reflected by the fact that the Italian team was the only one which held out against a move by the teams to change their minds and ban it at a meeting of the F1 Constructors' Association held in October 1993. Maranello's standpoint was plain for all to see. Continuing to saddle themselves with an inefficient, thirsty V12 engine configuration, there was clearly little chance of the famous Italian *scuderia* winning a World Championship under the current rules.

Now, with the F1 rule makers demonstrating a long-term commitment to refuelling – which has now been extended to the end of 1996, enabling a proper small-tank car to be built in '95 in order to capitalise on these rules – it seemed as though the FIA was determined to try spoon-feeding Ferrari its first drivers' title in 15 years with all the means at its disposal.

Refuelling was introduced in an effort to jazz up the racing and produce a new dimension in terms of televised entertainment – taking another leaf out of the Indy Car book, if you like. The reality turned out to be slightly different, with otherwise close races sometimes ruined by the mathematical unpredictability which refuelling inevitably introduced to the overall race equation.

Damon Hill was one driver who correctly anticipated this state of affairs. 'Refuelling stops will give people something to get excited about,' he admitted, 'but, by the same token, it takes some of the skill away from the task of setting up a car, because its handling changes very little when you are running a fuel load down from 80 litres to almost zero.

'Last year, when we were running from 200 litres down to zero, we had the active suspension taking care of that transition, but with a passive car it would have been part of the driver's skill to develop a set-up which worked with those varying [fuel] loads throughout a race. That really isn't a factor now, so if they think refuelling is returning some of the advantage to the driver, then they are wrong.'

More immediately, of course, the 1994 season kicked off with the competing teams operating in a distinctly nervous frame of mind. The FIA had made it quite clear that anybody found infringing the rules prohibiting electronic driver aids would be subject to 'draconian penalties'. Exclusion from the championship was clearly a very real threat under these circumstances, to judge by Max Mosley's observations on the subject.

The FIA's position attracted a wide variety of comment. 'Traction control is not impossible to police, but it will be mighty difficult,' observed Frank Williams. 'Charlie Whiting [the FIA Technical Delegate] is obviously operating at Max's behest. Max likes the Bill France, NASCAR approach. He takes his job seriously and likes to control the show.'

McLaren boss Ron Dennis commented: 'The sport should work the way it is structured, but that is not always the case. It is for the governing body to stabilise that lobbying process. It's never been perfect, and it never will be.'

Ken Tyrrell, however, was totally supportive of the FIA's way of handling things. 'I am fully on the side of Max Mosley in bringing in regulations to reduce costs and close up the field. From what we've seen in testing, these rules have achieved their aim.'

There was another crucial aspect to take into account, of course. From the start of 1994, the onus of proving a car's legality was placed firmly on the shoulders of the competing teams. Guilty until proved innocent, if you like.

The first few races of the year showed that the combination of Michael Schumacher and the Ford Zetec R-powered Benetton B194 to be virtually unbeatable. Even Ayrton Senna in the difficult-to-drive Williams FW16 had his work cut out in the face of this dramatic new challenge. But even before the San Marino Grand Prix at Imola, whispers were going round the paddock that all was not as it seemed with Schumacher's new machine.

Senna, for one, was extremely suspicious about its performance out of slow and medium-speed corners. On several occasions, in private, he voiced the view that there was something about the Benetton which worried him. Later, over the weekend of the San Marino GP, he returned to the subject in conversation. It was quite clear from those close to him that he suspected – only suspected, mind you – that the B194 might have some sort of illegal traction control system.

All those suspicions were forgotten in the aftermath of the deaths of Senna and Ratzenberger. At a stroke, F1 suddenly found itself facing its biggest crisis in decades. Calls came for rule changes to slow the cars, but while Max Mosley initially stood up and refused to be bounced into precipitate action, the political pressure quickly became overwhelming. At Monaco two weeks later, the FIA President felt he had no choice but to impose a whole new package of technical

GRAND PRIX '94 – THE TECHNICAL STORY

changes for implementation over the next few races.

As from the Spanish GP, rear diffusers would be dramatically shortened, front wings would be raised by 10 mm and no part of the front wing end plate would be permitted to extend behind the leading edge of the front wheels. As from Canada, increased lateral cockpit protection was demanded (although this was subsequently shelved pending further investigation), strengthened front suspension components were required, the weight limit was raised by 25 kg and the ram effect of the engines eliminated by the cutting of apertures in the rear of the airboxes.

More worryingly for the constructors, the 50 mm stepped undertray rules, originally required from the start of 1995, were brought forward along with further changes to the diffuser panels. The drivers immediately reported that the cars were more difficult to drive in Spain and one leading designer, appalled by the prospect of raising his car's minimum weight by positioning lead ballast beneath the fuel cells, expressed the view that 'anybody who thinks that cars which are heavier are necessarily safer must be quite mad'.

Mosley also revealed that engine fuel-flow restrictors would be introduced to reduce power output from around 750 bhp to 600 for 1995, although this was later changed when the engine makers unanimously submitted the view that a reduction in capacity to 3 litres would have much the same effect. But for the chassis designers, the introduction of a 50 mm stepped undertray was almost impossible in the short term, since it would require a total redesign not only of suspension geometry, but also of gearbox and transmission lines.

Fortunately, the FIA was persuaded to accept a 10 mm stepped undertray as a substitute, interim arrangement from Hockenheim onwards and wood-composite skidblocks were fitted to the cars in time for an intensive programme of testing prior to the German race.

The FIA began the season confident that it had the means by which to police the ban on electronic driver aids, and there was no doubt that the governing body was poised for a wide-ranging check-up on the electronic control boxes of several leading cars after the San Marino GP. But everybody's attention was understandably deflected by Senna's fatal accident and its immediate consequences for the sport.

By the time the question of probing the electronic systems of the Benetton came into the public domain at around the time of the German Grand Prix, the position of the World Championship-leading team looked distinctly beleaguered. Not only had they and Schumacher received severe penalties after the German had ignored the black flag in the British GP – an offence for which Benetton received a $500,000 fine and Schumacher a disqualification plus a two-race suspension – but Flavio Briatore's letter to Mosley at Barcelona, indicating his view that the FIA was not properly qualified to adjudicate on technical matters, had also left the FIA President in a less than sympathetic mood.

It was thus perhaps understandable that the FIA disclosed to the media the report from Charlie Whiting indicating his belief that the Benetton had the facility to run an illegal launch (automatic start) control in the San Marino GP. The FIA finally adjudicated that 'the best evidence' was that the team did not actually use such a system at Imola, but a cloud of doubt had unquestionably been left hanging over Benetton's conformity with the technical rules. And that cloud was not dispelled, even by the end of the season.

The fact that Benetton was also shown to have illegally modified the rig used to refuel Jos Verstappen's car at Hockenheim added another layer to the veneer of doubt concerning the team's conduct. They got away without penalty in the end – but only because the FIA World Council accepted a valid plea in mitigation. As Mosley was quick to remind everybody, Benetton was guilty of the offence.

By any standards, it has been a sad season. Right through to the end of the year there remained sufficient lingering doubt within the ranks of rival F1 engineers to cast doubt over the validity of Benetton's championship challenge. One was also left wondering whether, at the end of the day, the FIA possessed the technical ability to police their own regulations as effectively as they had originally hoped.

One thing is for certain. The governing body is determined to act in 1995 to ensure that none of the technical uncertainty we have seen this year will be repeated. In most people's minds, such a development cannot come a moment too soon. For the F1 fraternity, 1994 was the worst season in living memory.

Right: The distinctive aerodynamics of the Ferrari 412T1 were substantially revised in response to the rule changes introduced at Barcelona. The shapely side pods were cut back and elaborate 'barge boards' added.

Exposed cockpit openings were subject to scrutiny in the aftermath of Karl Wendlinger's accident at Monaco but in the event no changes were introduced. Even small drivers like Ukyo Katayama *(left)* had to squeeze into the tiny apertures.

Below: The celebrated 10 mm wood-composite skidblocks were introduced at Hockenheim.

Nigel Snowdon

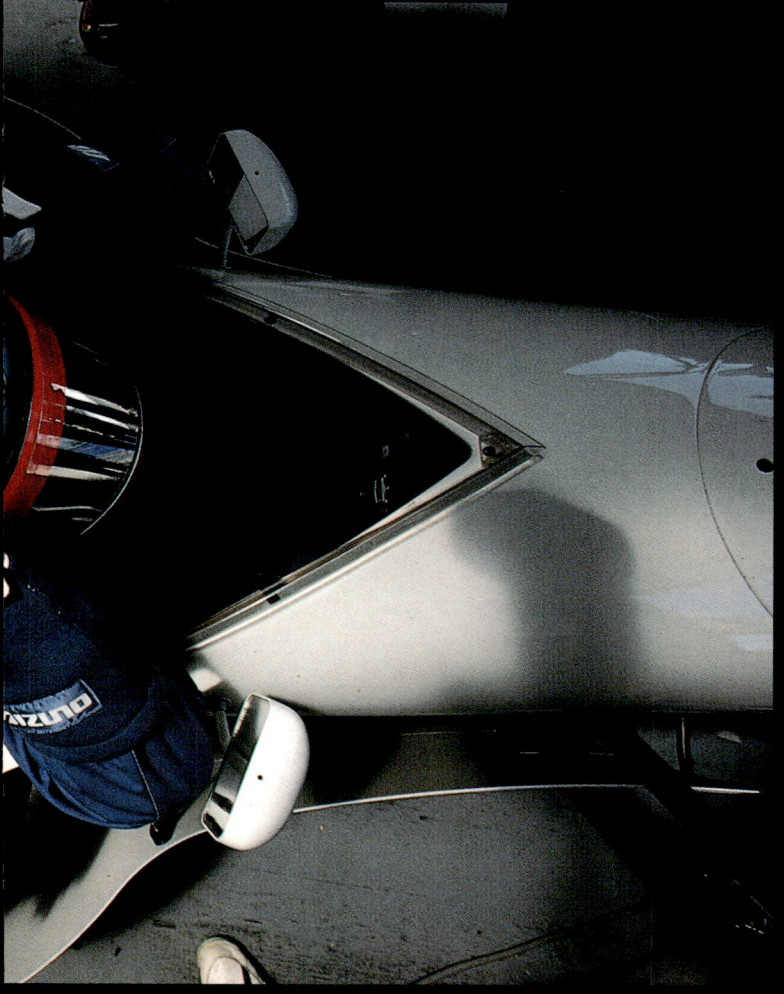

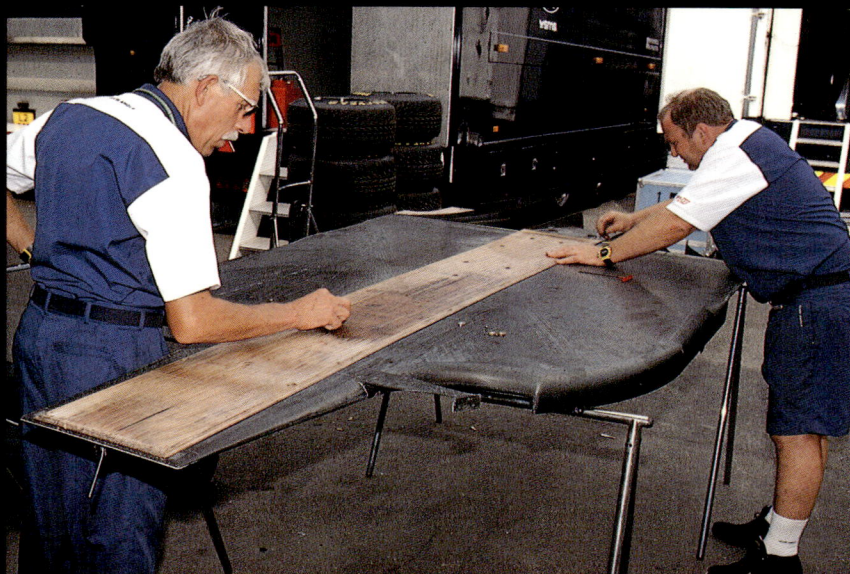

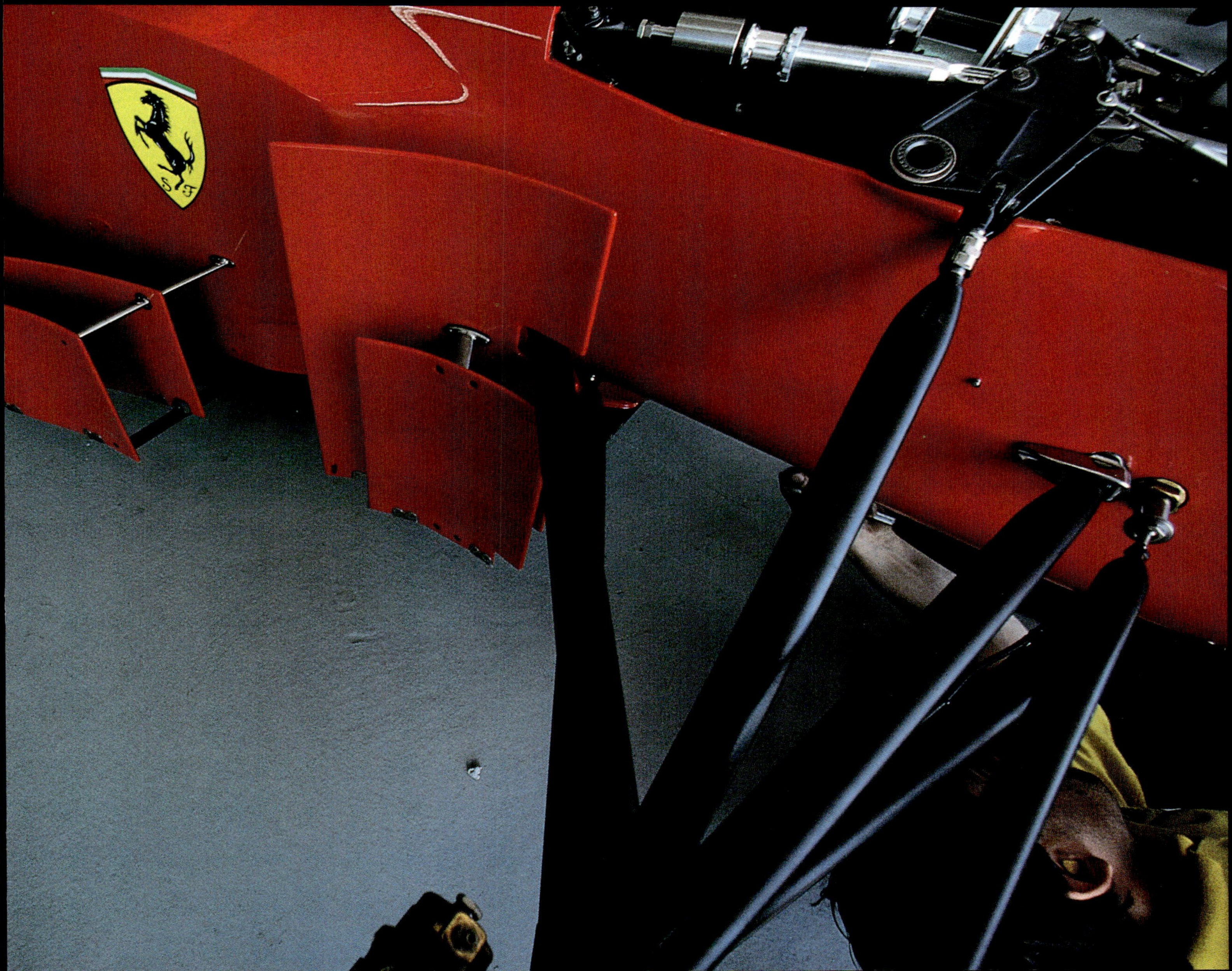

Paul-Henri Cahier

The R1100GS: a motorcycle that doesn't promise anything it can't deliver. Shown in its true light, it is, without a shadow of a doubt, an awesome proposition. Consider its wealth of mid-range torque, its impressive 80bhp at only 6,750rpm, and the security of ABS II braking.

Couple that with BMW's Telelever and Paralever suspension systems and a very imposing motorcycle becomes a pleasure to ride.

RECOMMENDED PRICE: BMW R1100GS £8295. CORRECT AT TIME OF GOING TO PRESS. INCLUDES VAT AND 12 MONTHS BMW ASSISTANCE MEMBERSHIP, BUT NOT DELIVERY, PDI AND NUMBER PLATES, ESTIMA

APPEARANCES CAN BE DECEPTIVE. SOMETIMES.

Suddenly, a journey to the Alps is something to savour, and the R1100GS is just the motorcycle to get you there. With its adjustable windshield and seat height, and a carrying capacity that can take the full complement of BMW luggage, two people can travel in comfort.

So, in the case of the R1100GS, the camera doesn't lie. It really is a motorcycle to overshadow everything else on the road.

THE NEW BMW R1100GS

FORMULA 1 REVIEW

CONTRIBUTORS
Bob Constanduros • Tony Dodgins • Alan Henry

F1 ILLUSTRATIONS
Ian Hutchinson

02 WILLIAMS

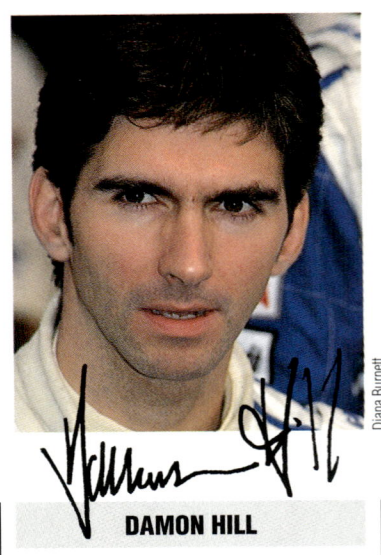
DAMON HILL

21 March 1960 – 1 May 1994
AYRTON SENNA

DAVID COULTHARD

Williams began the year aiming for a hat-trick of World Championships with Ayrton Senna at last joining the team which had originally given him his first F1 test drive a decade earlier at the height of his battle for the 1983 British F3 Championship. The Brazilian star lined up alongside Damon Hill, who had been retained for a second season following an excellent freshman year with the team during which he had scored three Grand Prix wins.

As things transpired, disaster was lurking a short distance down the championship path in the form of Ayrton's tragic fatal accident while leading the seventh lap of the San Marino Grand Prix at Imola. Inevitably, this was not only a catastrophe for the international motor racing community at large, but also a body-blow which sent Williams reeling against the ropes. The resilience, single-mindedness and stoicism subsequently displayed by the team in coming to terms with the loss and fighting back to regain its position as a title contender would rightly earn Williams a great deal of respect.

With no traction control systems, active suspension or other electronic goodies permissible for 1994, Williams Technical Director Patrick Head and Chief Designer Adrian Newey took a completely fresh look at the whole rear-end treatment of the new FW16, which was essentially an evolutionary version of the FW15C which had won the previous year's title in the hands of Alain Prost.

The FW16 was built round a moulded carbon-fibre monocoque, manufactured in-house by Williams. Head and Newey opted for torsion bars at the front – 'a question of packaging, really: a little bit lighter, a little bit neater' – but with coil springs at the rear, where some interesting new thinking had been applied to the business of arranging the suspension components.

In trying to tidy up the airflow over the rear of the car, they came up with a distinctive anhedral rear wing, the effectiveness of which would depend on a low outboard tail section. 'That meant lowering the top wishbone, and once you've lowered it to the point that it is virtually sitting on top of the driveshaft, it made sense to enclose the driveshaft,' explained Newey. The driveshafts on the FW16 were thus contained within wing-section carbon-fibre composite shrouds in a manner approved well in advance by the FIA's Technical Delegate.

The car was powered by Renault's familiar 67-degree V10 engine, which started the season in RS6 specification, and was subsequently uprated to 'B' specification for Hockenheim and 'C' specification for Monza, each offering more revs and enhanced top-end power. It was harnessed to a revised, lightened version of the six-speed transverse gearbox used the previous year, now restricted to semi-automatic control in place of the 'full automatic' system available to the drivers in 1993. The car was also equipped from the outset with a power-assisted steering system, hydraulically driven and reacting to input from electronic sensors, which drew heavily on lessons learned from the team's active suspension technology.

Initially, the FW16 seemed a difficult car to handle, Senna trying so hard on his first outing in Brazil that he spun off during his pursuit of Michael Schumacher's winning Benetton. Both Senna and Hill also experienced rear-end grip problems during practice for the Pacific Grand Prix, having carbon-copy spins at the same corner during the same qualifying session.

'To be honest,' admits Newey, 'we made a bloody awful cock-up. The rear-end grip problem was purely a set-up problem. We were learning about springs and dampers all over again after concentrating on active suspension for two years, whereas most people had been away for only one. We also had a rather silly aerodynamic problem – basically the front wing was too low – but that was raised for Imola by which time I think we were looking in pretty good shape.' Other changes for Imola included a slightly shortened wheel-

WILLIAMS FW16-RENAULT

Sponsors: Rothmans, Renault, Elf, Segafredo, Divella, Goodyear
Designers: Patrick Head, Adrian Newey **Team Principal:** Frank Williams **Team Manager:** Ian Harrison **Chief Mechanic:** Dick Stanford
ENGINE **Type:** Renault RS6/RS6B/RS6C **No. of cylinders/vee angle:** V10 (67°) **Sparking plugs:** Champion **Electronics:** Magneti Marelli **Fuel:** Elf **Oil:** Elf
TRANSMISSION **Gearbox:** Williams six-speed transverse semi-automatic **Driveshafts:** Williams **Clutch:** AP
CHASSIS **Front suspension:** pushrod, bellcrank, torsion spring **Rear suspension:** pushrod, bellcrank, coil spring **Suspension dampers:** Williams/Penske **Wheel diameter:** front: 13 in. rear: 13 in. **Wheel rim widths:** front: 11-11.5 in. rear: 13.7 in. **Tyres:** Goodyear **Brake pads:** Carbone Industrie or Hitco **Brake discs:** Carbone Industrie or Hitco **Brake calipers:** AP **Steering:** Williams **Radiators:** Williams **Fuel tanks:** ATL **Battery:** Williams **Instruments:** Magneti Marelli/Williams
DIMENSIONS **Wheelbase:** 116.1 in./2950 mm **Formula weight:** 1135.3 lb/515 kg **Fuel capacity:** 46.1 gallons/210 litres

FORMULA 1 REVIEW

It was a testimony to the immense courage and resilience of Frank Williams, Technical Director Patrick Head, Chief Designer Adrian Newey, team manager Ian Harrison *(right, top to bottom)* and the rest of the Williams team that they overcame the devastating loss of Ayrton Senna to take the Constructors' Cup at season's end.

Below: Senna studies the timing monitor in the Williams pit garage at Imola. Always magnificent in qualifying, he earned pole position for each of his three races with the team.

NIGEL MANSELL

base and a reshaped cockpit surround to reduce aerodynamic buffeting, which Senna had complained about during the first two races.

It is all too easy to forget that Senna qualified the FW16 on pole for the first three races of the year and was leading Schumacher at Imola when he went off the road. His damaged FW16 was impounded by the Italian authorities, who retain it at the time of writing, and any theorising about the causes of the accident must necessarily remain highly speculative until the magistrate concerned has adjudicated on the matter. However, areas which have been examined include a possible pre-impact failure of the steering column or Senna simply losing control due to the low-set car bottoming out over a bump, a state of affairs which might have been aggravated by low tyre pressures caused by five laps' slow running behind the safety car immediately prior to the accident.

The team opted to run a single car at Monaco, where everybody was in a daze. 'To be perfectly honest, we didn't really know what we were doing,' says Newey. 'It was the most eerie race weekend I've ever experienced.' Hill qualified fourth, then crashed with Häkkinen at the first corner. It was difficult to see how it could all get any worse for Williams.

While Rothmans, the team's prime sponsor, was happy to let Williams sort out its problems without interference, Renault took a distinctly less sanguine view. Put simply, after Senna's death, they panicked and were hard pressed to conceal their initial lack of faith in Hill's ability to lead the team. When Williams nominated test driver David Coulthard as Senna's replacement for Barcelona, they were aghast, suggesting that Olivier Panis might be a better bet, and then embarked on a commercially driven strategy to pressure Williams into signing Nigel Mansell for a guest outing in the French GP, followed by the final three races of the season.

Hill bounced back with a splendid win at Barcelona after Schumacher's Benetton jammed in fifth gear, and this helped restore the team's morale, but Damon was still unhappy with the FW16's handling and it was not until Mansell confirmed its shortcomings at Magny-Cours that the team really began to get behind Hill with the moral support he deserved. By then Coulthard had underlined his potential by running ahead of Hill in the early stages of the Canadian GP before the team asked him to give way to Damon, who finished second to Schumacher.

'Nigel's biggest contribution at Magny-Cours was that he gave the team a morale-boost,' says Newey. 'Damon thought, "I'm blowed if I'm going to be blown off by Nigel," and this had the effect of kick-starting the programme again.'

Patrick Head agrees it was a useful exercise. 'I do think Mansell's presence at Magny-Cours helped in that, while I don't think for one moment he pinpointed any particular problems with the car, his views were similar to Damon's at a time I think Damon was wondering whether it was the car or him, or whatever,' he admits.

The most major specification revision for the FW16 came in time for the German Grand Prix at Hockenheim, where the car sported side pods shortened by 30 cm, enabling longer vertical aerodynamic 'barge boards' to be fitted behind the front wheels, the intention being to regain some of the aerodynamic performance lost through the post-Monaco GP ban on front wing end plate extensions.

'Once the front wing end plates were cut back, there was no way of controlling the front wing vortex, so the only thing possible was to deflect it very crudely with the "barge boards",' explains Newey. 'In turn, we felt this pushed us towards a shorter side pod so we could have a less aggressive plan profile for the boards. That meant cutting back the leading edge of the side pod which, although moulded into the chassis, was not a structural area.'

FORMULA 1 REVIEW

Test driver David Coulthard was given his chance to race the Williams-Renault in the wake of the Imola disaster and the young Scot was soon being talked about as a future World Champion, his remarkable maturity and confidence belying his inexperience.

The distinctive aerodynamics at the rear of the FW16 *(below right)* broke new ground but, initially at least, the car proved difficult to drive.

Bottom: The Williams pit crew at full stretch at the end of the first lap of the German Grand Prix at Hockenheim. While David Coulthard's car receives a new nose section, Damon Hill needs a bent steering arm to be replaced.

This, together with the more powerful Renault RS6B engine, enabled Hill and David Coulthard to close the gap to the Benetton B194 in the second half of the year.

Hill gained in confidence considerably after his Silverstone win and, for Monza, he took a decisive step to maximise his World Championship chances by requesting that the senior F1 engineer, David Brown, move from Coulthard's car to tend his own, replacing John Russell, who switched across to Coulthard's machine.

Hill inherited victory at Spa after Schumacher's disqualification, then went on to score crucial wins at Monza and Estoril while the Benetton driver sat out a two-race suspension. A refuelling glitch at Jerez blunted Damon's challenge to the German driver at a crucial moment when he was only one point behind him in the title chase, compounding the problems caused by his own first-lap accidents at Imola, Monaco and, particularly, Hockenheim, where he tapped Katayama's fast-starting Tyrrell on the opening lap and had to stop for a bent steering arm to be replaced.

Nevertheless, judged as a whole, it was an impressively successful year for Hill, who finished the season with a remarkable victory rate of better than 25 per cent – nine wins from the 34 Grands Prix he has contested during his career thus far.

'Damon is capable of giving absolutely outstanding performances,' says Head approvingly, 'but

as a Grand Prix driver you have to get yourself into a state where you can do that 16 times a year. I sometimes question whether he gets fired up like that on every occasion, but you've only got to watch him out on the circuit to see that those people who say that Damon is like his father – all determination and no skill – are talking rubbish. I don't think we've yet seen the ultimate level he will achieve.'

Right: Frank Williams fulfilled a long-held ambition when he finally secured the services of Ayrton Senna but, by the cruellest of ironies, the brilliant Brazilian's association with the Didcot team was to be tragically brief.

Still a relative novice, Damon Hill found himself carrying the expectations of the Williams team, its sponsors and partners in the most distressing circumstances imaginable. He accepted the burden with characteristic dignity and determination, growing in stature as the season unfolded.

Coulthard's confidence was, if anything, even more impressive and it was somehow appropriate that, after running out of fuel due to a miscalculation at Monza, he finished second to Damon at Estoril. It was the first 1-2 finish for British drivers since Graham Hill's Lotus 49B beat Piers Courage, driving Frank Williams's Brabham-Ford, in the 1969 Monaco Grand Prix.

Mansell's return for the European Grand Prix at Jerez yielded a not particularly distinguished performance, ending with the former F1 and Indy Car champion firmly embedded in a sand trap.

After taking second place behind Schumacher's Benetton at Jerez, Hill finished the season on a high note. His win in the rain at Suzuka was outstanding, as was his spirited pursuit of Schumacher in Adelaide, which unfortunately ended in tears. However, the Australian race at least saw Mansell clinch the constructors' title for Williams with a steady run to the 31st Grand Prix victory of his career.

As usual, the Williams-Renaults displayed fantastic mechanical reliability. In 31 race starts there were only four instances of mechanical failure. Hill suffered a gearbox breakage in the Pacific GP, Coulthard was sidelined by electrical faults at Barcelona and Hockenheim and Mansell suffered a hydraulic pump failure at Magny-Cours, a similar problem causing Coulthard's car to jam in sixth gear in the closing stages at Spa. It was really a terrific effort.

Yet there was still an underlying feeling of 'what might have been' which lingered for a long time after Senna's death. 'He was such a good driver, the way he worked, the way he was able to pull the team along with him' reflects Newey. 'Sadly, we didn't have long enough working with him to develop a rapport, but he had quite incredible powers of recall. He could mention some detail of an individual lap he had done the previous day in immense detail – as if it had happened only two seconds ago.'

Even so, Williams could take comfort from the fact that they had regained their footing on the high wire after suffering such a devastating loss, a tribute indeed to the strength in depth of this remarkable team.

Alan Henry

RENAULT 19 16V

19 FACTS

Leather upholstery

24W Hi-fi with fingertip remote control

Driver's side airbag

Power steering

3 or new 5 door versions

Electric front windows

Electrically adjustable door mirrors

Electric tilt/slide sunroof

Remote control central locking

Height adjustable steering wheel

137 bhp 16 valve engine

0-62 in 8.5 secs

133 mph (where legal)

Alloy wheels

Full sports body kit

Front fog lamps

Engine immobiliser and alarm

Side impact bars

Seat belt pre-tensioners

FROM £13,650*

To Renault UK, FREEPOST, PO Box 21, Thame, Oxon OX9 3BR. For more information about the Renault 19 range, fill in the coupon or call Renault Freephone 0800 52 51 50.   NSVAUC95

Mr/Mrs/Miss (please delete) _____
                                                              BLOCK CAPITALS
Address _____
Town and County _____
Postcode _____ Telephone _____
Present car make and model _____ Registration letter
(eg Renault 19 GTS)   (eg H)
Month/Year you expect to replace /__/__/__/__/ Age (if under 18) ____
                                                M M Y Y
Tick box if your next car may be diesel.☐   ☐ For 'Motability' details.☐

'HAN YOU BARGAINED FOR.

ths Government road fund licence and "Key-in-hand" charge of £465 which covers delivery to the dealer, number plates and security window etching: Other goods or services supplied by agreement between the customer and dealer er. Renault UK Ltd, Western Avenue, London W3 ORZ, and not individual franchise holders. **RENAULT** recommend **elf** lubricants.

3 TYRRELL 4

UKYO KATAYAMA

MARK BLUNDELL

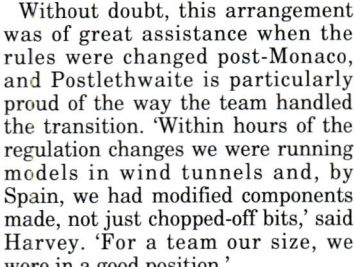

Below left: Ken Tyrrell *(right)* responded positively to his team's dismal showing in 1993 by enticing former Ferrari designer Harvey Postlethwaite back into the fold and was rewarded with a long-overdue return to respectability.

The Tyrrell team had highs and lows in 1993. The high, as far as it went, was that Ken didn't have to pay for his engines. The low, which was much more noticeable, was that the team failed to score a World Championship point for the first time in its history.

With this in mind, any decent results achieved in 1994 would seem like a victory. It might have been hoped that the return of Harvey Postlethwaite, together with aerodynamicist Jean-Claude Migeot, his partner in the design of the successful Tyrrell 019, plus the emergence of the Yamaha V10 as a competitive engine, would see Tyrrell bounce back to the forefront of the F1 scene. However, comebacks sometimes take a little longer than a single season and, in Tyrrell's case, the improvements needed were fairly fundamental. Granted, 1994 was better, but the process of recovery continues.

Harvey Postlethwaite had returned to take over the engineering reins long before the end of the 1993 season and his feet were firmly under the table as the new car began to take shape. Helped by Mike Gascoigne and the design team,

Postlethwaite conceived a good, simple car, what he described as 'the right car for the team at the time'.

The team also enjoyed a special relationship with Gabriele Rumi's Fondmetal Technologies company, which undertook all Tyrrell's research and development work. Migeot defined the aerodynamics of the new 022 in the Ferrara-based organisation's own advanced wind tunnel, although the team still used the Southampton University facility. Fondmetal also supplied free wheels.

Without doubt, this arrangement was of great assistance when the rules were changed post-Monaco, and Postlethwaite is particularly proud of the way the team handled the transition. 'Within hours of the regulation changes we were running models in wind tunnels and, by Spain, we had modified components made, not just chopped-off bits,' said Harvey. 'For a team our size, we were in a good position.'

Although the cars were not exactly adorned with sponsorship identification, to the point that one might have been forgiven for thinking Tyrrell was strapped for cash, the team did enjoy free engines and Fondmetal's assistance. Renowned for managing its funds well, it wasn't badly off, in fact, and tested regularly between races.

While Tyrrell was restoring its credibility, Yamaha's learning process was continuing steadily. After the wilderness years with Zakspeed, Brabham and Jordan, the Japanese company's progress had accelerated in 1993 with Tyrrell, although it had been masked by the unwieldy chassis. Now, with a more competitive car,

TYRRELL 022-YAMAHA

Sponsors: Mild Seven, Calbee

Designer: Harvey Postlethwaite   **Team Principal:** Ken Tyrrell   **Team Manager:** Rupert Manwaring   **Chief Mechanic:** Chris White

ENGINE **Type:** Yamaha OX10A **No. of cylinders/vee angle:** V10 (72°) **Sparking plugs:** NGK **Electronics:** Zytek **Fuel:** BP **Oil:** BP

TRANSMISSION **Gearbox:** Tyrrell/Xtrac six-speed transverse pneumatic semi-automatic **Driveshafts:** Tyrrell **Clutch:** AP

CHASSIS **Front suspension:** double wishbone, pushrod, inboard coil spring/dampers **Rear suspension:** double wishbone, pushrod, inboard coil spring/dampers **Suspension dampers:** Koni **Wheel diameter:** front: 13 in. rear: 13 in. **Wheel rim widths:** front: 11 in. rear: 15 in. **Tyres:** Goodyear **Brake pads:** Hitco/SEP **Brake discs:** Hitco/SEP **Brake calipers:** AP **Steering:** Tyrrell **Radiators:** Secan **Fuel tanks:** ATL **Instruments:** PI Research

DIMENSIONS **Wheelbase:** 114.1 in./2900 mm **Gearbox weight:** 110.2 lb/50 kg **Chassis weight (tub):** 88.1 lb/40 kg **Formula weight:** 1135.3 lb/515 kg **Fuel capacity:** 43.9 gallons/200 litres

KONI SHOCK ABSORBERS THE CHOICE OF TYRRELL

KONI SHOCK ABSORBERS
YOU'LL FIND OUT WHY.

For details of your local stockist:
CAMBERLEY AUTO FACTORS LIMITED, Farnborough, Tel. (0252) 510142, Fax (0252) 371977

FORMULA 1 REVIEW

Although Mark Blundell picked up a couple of points at Spa *(left)*, he was generally outpaced by his diminutive Japanese team-mate Ukyo Katayama *(below far left)*, who looks rather less comfortable with a bat in his hands than he did in the cockpit of the 022. John Judd *(below left)* has been influential in the development of the powerful Yamaha V10 engine *(bottom)*, while chief mechanic Chris White *(below)*, designer Mike Gascoigne *(centre)* and team manager Rupert Manwaring have all contributed to the welcome upturn in Tyrrell's fortunes.

they had a whiff of what might be, what was required, what life was like at the front of the field. They came on in leaps and bounds; but with the occasional fall . . .

The OX10B version of their 72-degree V10, in J1 specification, made its debut at the Pacific Grand Prix, featuring modifications to the intake system and pumps, plus an air compressor to operate the pneumatic valve system. A re-evaluation of all moving parts yielded a reduction of internal friction and an increase in engine speed of more than 1000 rpm to over 14,000 rpm. There was also an increase in power

of eight per cent and a 10 kg reduction in the engine's weight.

An increase in the capacity of the intake system for added power and a further boost in maximum revs was available in time for Monaco and this J2 specification was first raced in the French GP. Specifications K1 and K2 were introduced at Monza, the former featuring more work on the intake valves to improve driveability while the latter further reduced friction losses. Butterfly throttles were introduced for the first time at Jerez and the U – for Ultimate specification – variant was Yamaha's *tour de force* for its home Grand Prix.

The combination of Tyrrell and Yamaha was certainly competitive.

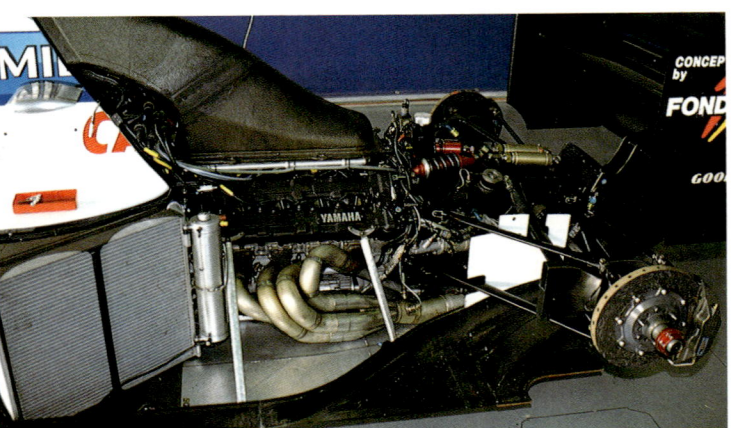

Drivers Ukyo Katayama and Mark Blundell were rarely outside the top half of the field in qualifying and often ran in the top six during the races. But those hoping for an instant return to prominence were disappointed. Mechanical failures or some other incident usually claimed one or other of the cars. However, when they did take the chequered flag, they frequently earned points; Mark Blundell's third in Spain was a deserved high spot of the season.

In fact, the intra-team contest was an interesting one. After his drama-filled 1993 season, Katayama seemed to calm down and progressively improved his qualifying performances, on most occasions lining up ahead of his new team-mate Blundell.

At Monza, Katayama qualified only 14th, yet was in seventh place at the end of the opening lap and was up with the two Williams FW16Bs and Berger's Ferrari within four laps. A slow first pit stop dropped him right back, but he had recovered to fourth place by the time of his second stop. He was running in fifth when he was struck by the brake problem (a shattered disc) which also claimed his team-mate.

Similarly, at Jerez, he charged through the field after stalling on the grid to finish seventh. Admittedly, the fact that there were 19 finishers didn't help! Meanwhile, Blundell showed himself to be a determined fighter and racer. From a decent grid position he would inevitably be in a position to score points, but qualifying wasn't his forte and he will not be retained for 1995.

Although the Tyrrell-Yamaha combination did not seem to be so good on tighter tracks, not liking long, slow corners, the team certainly showed itself to be in the ascendancy in 1994. Yamaha scented success and took the risks that are part of the learning process. With Postlethwaite leading Tyrrell's difficult and comprehensive renaissance, the best is hopefully still to come.

Bob Constanduros

CONGRATULATE MICHAEL SCHUMACHER ON WINNING HIS FIRST FIA FORMULA ONE WORLD DRIVER'S CHAMPIONSHIP TITLE

Kevlar® Pro Series 2000 **M3**

Specific feedback from Bell's European Formula 1 trackside support program led to the M3 design. The Bell M3 is a bold move forward in styling, features and function. Including trip strips to reduce lift, top front and forehead vents for efficient cooling a thick shield and a Kevlar® chin strip, M3 is a feature packed lightweight helmet. Snell SA90 and SFI 31.2 certified.

Kevlar® Pro Series 2000 **XFM-1**

Originally designed with a vision of the future, and still preferred by many top professionals including some Formula 1 drivers. XFM-1 has a long and proven tradition as the choice of top professionals who prefer a non-ventilated helmet with a smaller eyeport. Snell SA90 and SFI 31.2 certified.

S.P.O.R.T.S. Europe
BELL RACING EUROPEAN EXCLUSIVE DISTRIBUTOR
F1 RACING SERVICE
AVENUE DE MESSIDOR 186 B.24
BRUSSELS B1180
TEL: + 32 2 343 3400
FAX: + 32 2 343 8673

5
6
BENETTON

MICHAEL SCHUMACHER

JOS VERSTAPPEN

J.J. LEHTO

When the pundits placed their pre-season World Championship bets, Benetton appeared to have no more than a good outside chance.

The Enstone team and Williams had both retained the same technical partners in Ford and Renault, but at Didcot Ayrton Senna had replaced Alain Prost. Williams, surely, would be stronger still.

The telling difference, Senna's accident apart, was that in 1994 Benetton was ready and Ford had done a superb job with the Zetec-R V8. There are people at Benetton who will tell you that 1993 would have been a different story if the definitive car had appeared at the start of the year, complete with its traction control system.

That is arguable. Williams had significantly greater experience with the electronic technology that had become such an integral part of the Grand Prix car, active suspension in particular.

For 1994, all that was gone. Or, let's say, should have been. It was back to basics. What you needed was a driveable chassis, a strong engine and a top-class man in the cockpit.

There was no doubt that Benetton had all three, although only Schumacher could extract the maximum from the B194. Interestingly, Johnny Herbert found the car critical at the limit when he was drafted in to assist Schumacher and the team's title bids at the end of the season.

As the year began, the biggest worry was whether Ford could wring both power and reliability from the Zetec-R.

'We'd worked on the HB for four years and squeezed everything out of it that we could,' explained Cosworth Engineering's chief development engineer Martin Walters.

'It had limitations that became more obvious the more work we did on it. Mechanically it was very difficult to run it past 13,500 rpm. We had big-end bearing problems which weren't a simple thing to solve. It needed a major redesign.

'What we did was to ask what sort of power we could get out of an eight if we ran it at 14,500 rpm, and what sort of performance that would give us.

'It looked mechanically possible. We had to go for much larger bores, ones that we hadn't been to before, and that made us worry about combustion. We got the work done in time to allow the team to test early, which helped, although we had to limit the engines to around 125 miles before changing them. It was the first time I turned up at the season-opener with Benetton having completed its winter test schedule.'

When Benetton went to Imola pre-season and set times which consistently matched Senna's Williams-Renault on a power track, the fruit of Ford's labour was clear for all to see.

However, a blow, quite literally, was new signing J.J. Lehto's heavy rearward impact in a testing shunt at Silverstone, which left the Finn with cracked vertebrae in his neck. It was a disaster from which J.J. would never properly recover. Sadly, it came at a time when he had been given a car worthy of him for the first time in his Grand Prix career.

A batch of rogue pistons caused minor heart flutters at a Barcelona test but that problem was solved before Schumacher went to Interlagos and threw down the gauntlet to Williams by winning in Senna's back yard. Ayrton led initially but Schumacher eased onto his gearbox after dispensing with Alesi and took the lead at the first refuelling stop. Eddie Irvine was moved to say how stable the Benetton looked when it lapped him, in direct contrast to Senna's Williams. Things were looking good.

Benetton had moved into its 17-acre, 85,000-square foot Enstone technical centre in October 1992, bringing under one roof an operation that had hitherto been fragmented. Engineering Director Tom Walkinshaw and Technical Director Ross Brawn now had the place running like a slick, well-oiled machine and, organisationally, Benetton looked as capable as McLaren or Williams. But controversy was not far away.

Schumacher added Aida, the tragic Imola race, Monte Carlo, Montreal

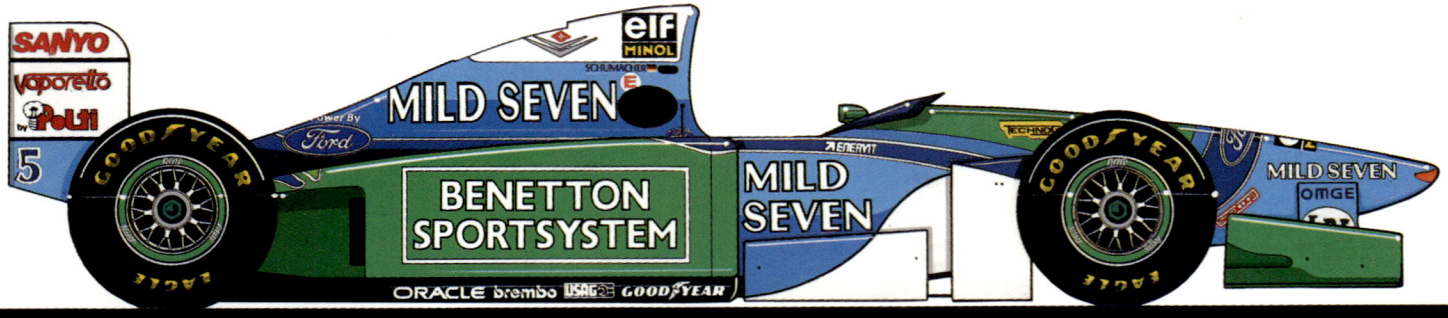

BENETTON B194-FORD

Sponsors: Mild Seven, Benetton Sportsystem, Sanyo, Elf Minol, Technogym

Designers: Ross Brawn, Rory Byrne **Team Principals:** Flavio Briatore, Tom Walkinshaw **Team Manager:** Joan Villadelprat **Chief Mechanic:** Mick Cowlishaw

ENGINE **Type:** Ford Zetec-R **No. of cylinders/vee angle:** V8 (75°) **Sparking plugs:** Champion **Electronics:** Ford **Fuel:** Elf **Oil:** Elf

TRANSMISSION **Gearbox:** Benetton six-speed transverse semi-automatic **Driveshafts:** Benetton **Clutch:** AP

CHASSIS **Front suspension:** double wishbone, pushrod, inboard coil spring/dampers **Rear suspension:** double wishbone, pushrod, inboard coil spring/dampers **Suspension dampers:** WP **Wheel diameter:** front: 13 in. rear: 13 in. **Tyres:** Goodyear **Brake pads:** Carbone Industrie, Hitco or Brembo **Brake discs:** Carbone Industrie, Hitco or Brembo **Brake calipers:** Brembo **Steering:** Benetton **Radiators:** Secan **Fuel tanks:** ATL **Battery:** Benetton **Instruments:** Ford

DIMENSIONS **Formula weight:** 1135.3 lb/515 kg **Fuel capacity:** 43.9 gallons/200 litres-plus

FORMULA 1 REVIEW

JOHNNY HERBERT

Ross Brawn's engineering team is as strong as any in Formula 1, with Rory Byrne *(right)* and Pat Symonds *(far right)* spearheading an intensive research and development programme. The benefits of this concerted effort were apparent in 1994, although the superb Ford Zetec-R V8 *(below)* was a key part of the championship-winning package.

Bottom left: A storm of controversy swirled round Engineering Director Tom Walkinshaw *(left)* and team manager Joan Villadelprat for much of the season, while flamboyant Managing Director Flavio Briatore continued to nurture new driving talent *(bottom right)*, inviting Canadian Indy Car star Paul Tracy *(right)* to test a B194 at Estoril in September.

and Magny-Cours to his winning start in Brazil. Six wins in seven races and it would have been a clean sweep if the gearbox had not given trouble in Barcelona. With just fifth gear for much of the race, a fact confirmed by engineer Pat Symonds from the telemetry, Michael still finished second! But his start at Magny-Cours set the tongues wagging. Out-qualified by both Williams-Renaults, Schumacher was past Mansell and Hill before the first corner and the widely held opinion was that he must have used traction control to do it.

The season had begun under a cloud, with team managers predicting that the FIA did not have the wherewithal to police its ban on driver aids. This was largely fair, during the early part of the season at any rate. By Hockenheim, at midseason, we were only just discovering potential problems with electronic 'black boxes' seized from the first three cars at Imola. And, more to the point, Imola had been the only 'drug test' thus far. By the time they had analysed his urine, the athlete had won another hat full of races.

Max Mosley did prove that the FIA had a far greater level of competence than the teams expected. But the move to have programmes that could activate illegal driver aid devices deleted from the software rather than merely disarmed came too late. Too late for the FIA and too late for Benetton's 1994 achievements to go untainted.

At Hockenheim, the FIA released part of Technical Delegate Charlie Whiting's Imola report which confirmed the presence of 'launch control' – an automatic start system – in Schumacher's Imola black box. But, said the FIA, 'the best evidence is that the team did not use it.'

Rival teams thought that was amusing, preferring to consider the 'best evidence' being that afforded by their eyes at Magny-Cours.

'I know Michael,' said Brawn. 'He would not have used a system that was illegal, with all the consequences it would have brought. I am categoric on that point.'

Brawn had an answer for every anomaly and there was another point to consider. Flavio Briatire had penned a letter to Mosley questioning the governing body's competence in its administration of F1. This had been leaked to the newspapers and it led to a highly stormy round of politicking at Barcelona. Was this Mosley's way of getting even?

Brawn added: 'The risk involved with being caught and eliminated from the championship is tremendous. If we were foolish enough to use such a system willingly and be caught, we would be putting 200 people and their families' future at risk.'

He did not know how ironic those words would become. Not 48 hours later Benetton suffered a fuel spillage with Verstappen's car during the Hockenheim race. Investigation into its causes revealed that a mandatory fuel filter was absent from Benetton's rig, speeding up the fuel flow rate by around one second at the average pit stop. Benetton claimed that it had been removed for the first time in Germany, with the permission of the FIA. The governing body denied it.

FORMULA 1 REVIEW

Although its Ford V8 engine was not as powerful as the Renault used by Williams, the Benetton B194 appeared to enjoy a clear advantage throughout the season – but only when Michael Schumacher was driving it.

Benetton also had the edge where tactics were concerned, although in the wet Friday qualifying session at Spa *(below)* it was the Jordan team which judged the changing conditions best. Schumacher keeps an eye on developments from the cockpit of his car in the pit garage.

This looked serious. Benetton was up before the World Council for a second time. At Silverstone, Schumacher had overtaken Hill on the warm-up lap and, although the stewards had not followed the correct procedure, the No. 5 Benetton was given a stop-go penalty. He did not arrive in the pit lane and so the black flag went out. While remonstrations went on, Schumacher ignored the flag too. If anyone was looking for ammunition, here it was. Schumacher lost the six points for his eventual second place and was banned for a further two races, while Benetton was fined $500,000, with a further $100,000 added for failure to release its computer source codes relative to Imola promptly.

The fuel filter revelations were potentially most serious but, amazingly, the team was let off despite a guilty plea. The mitigating circumstances were a tenuous claim that Larrousse, which coincidentally used a Benetton semi-automatic gearbox, had been told they could remove their filter and had a diagram explaining how this should be done. It may have been an oversight. If the team was intentionally cheating, you had to wonder why, when it knew that its rig was going to be investigated, it did not merely put the filter back. But on the other hand it made you think back to Interlagos and all the other rapid stops Schumacher had made.

The FIA claimed that there were mitigating circumstances because the deed had been carried out by a Benetton junior, which was laughable. Pacific even talked about fitting a turbo and blaming the tea lady...

Whatever, although it was another question mark over Benetton's year, there is no way that Schumacher's superiority was attributable to his pit stops being fractionally quicker than the rest.

To what, then, was it attributable? 'From the telemetry we can see that Michael carries more speed *into* the corner,' explained Brawn, 'especially the high-speed turns.' If 1994 confirmed anything, it was Schumacher's arrival as leader of the New Order. If Senna had lived we would have had a titanic rivalry; in his absence, Schumacher stands head and shoulders above the rest.

With Michael serving his two-race ban at Imola and Estoril, the Benetton performance fell away dramatically. Jos Verstappen, the reigning German F3 Champion, was not up to leading the team and qualified tenth at both races. Lehto was 20th and 14th.

J.J.'s season was a sad catalogue of events. He returned at Imola and was competitive, qualifying fifth, within a second of Schumacher. Then he stalled on the line and was collected by Lamy's Lotus. He had travelled to Imola with poor Ratzenberger. Out of his shattered Benetton, he had a quick check over and then changed, just in time to witness Senna's accident. Both psychologically and physically, J.J. was under the cosh and it was decided to 'rest' him in favour of Verstappen after Montreal, where he finished sixth after qualifying 20th.

Schumacher was back for Jerez and all eyes were on him. How would he fare after the FIA directive that all potentially illegal driver aids had to be removed from computer software rather than disabled? The answer was emphatic: pole position and a dominant eighth win, even if he was helped by refuelling problems at Williams.

The final twist to the Benetton year was the recruitment of Herbert to aid their title aspirations. It was, Brawn said, 'the first time that anyone had remotely approached Michael's times in the car'.

This form was not reproduced in the last two races of the year. Johnny retired from both the Japanese and Australian GPs, while Schumacher, having finished second at Suzuka, claimed the drivers' title by a single point from Hill after a controversial collision in Adelaide which left the possibility of an appearance before the FIA World Council as an uncomfortable footnote to the season.

By then, of course, Benetton and Ford had lost the constructors' title to Williams. Given all the uncertainty, that seemed a just outcome.

Tony Dodgins

DON'T CRACK UNDER PRESSURE

The Sports Elegance chronograph series. 1/10-second accuracy. Intermediate time and fly back hand. Unidirectional turning bezel. Scratch-resistant sapphire crystal. Double protection screw-in crown. Water-resistant to 200 metres (660ft).

TAGHeuer
SWISS MADE SINCE 1860

Available from Harrods, Watches of Switzerland Limited and at selected branches of Leslie Davis, Ernest Jones, Walker & Hall, Goldsmiths, Mappin & Webb, Beaverbrooks and leading jewellers throughout the UK & Ireland. For further information call 0204 862 179.

We're going ahead with this one

A-class study

▶ It's no mere coincidence that our A-class study turned out the way it did. After all, we were out to design a car primarily geared to urban driving. Since road space in city traffic is valuable – and parking space even more so – every centimetre counts. The new car thus had to get by with the dimensions of a hatch. But to provide the right degree of comfort for a longer stay on board we had to fit the generous passenger compartment of a midrange saloon into this limited space. And all without compromising on the traditional safety of a Mercedes.

▶ At first it was far from clear whether we weren't setting out in pursuit of the impossible. But then our engineers came up with a solution as surprising as it is sophisticated: To make room for a top quality Mercedes-Benz safety cell and keep dimensions to a minimum, they hid the engine and transmission safely out of the way – under the floor level of the passenger compartment. This has the additional advantage that in the event of an accident, all the underfloor engineering cannot be pushed into the survival space.

▶ Although some people feel that it is in cars like this that the future lies, this won't be the only car we build in future. Because people's requirements and expectations they place in the car they drive will still be too varied for us to meet them all with only a single model.

We're staying ahead with this one

The S-class

▶ It's no mere coincidence that our S-class turned out the way it did. After all, we build it for people whose above-average professional commitment means they take more passengers than average on longer than average trips. And they all need to arrive in good shape for a hard day's work.

▶ Such people rightly expect their car to go easy on their own personal energy reserves. Which is why, over more than 30 years now. We have constantly returned to thinking of new ways in which the S-class can help them. The result of our efforts to date is a whole spectrum of inventions that make the S-class a paragon of automotive engineering in so many areas. From comfort to safety.

▶ The fact that we're on the right road is constantly reconfirmed when many of the aspects we first introduced in the S-class begin, just a few years later, to appear on a broad front – like the airbag is doing right now. In the meantime, today's S-class has, of course, moved further ahead – and that is where it will stay.

▶ Of course, not everyone needs a car like this. But on the other hand, are many people who need such a car more than ever. And will need one in future, too.

Mercedes-Benz
Engineered like no other car in the world

7 / 8 McLAREN

MIKA HÄKKINEN

MARTIN BRUNDLE

PHILIPPE ALLIOT

It was 28 January 1994 when Ron Dennis and Peugeot Sport boss Jean-Pierre Jabouille took the wraps off the first of the new McLaren-Peugeot MP4/9s at the British team's Woking headquarters. On 25 October – barely ten months later – Dennis was present at a press conference in Paris to explain that McLaren and Peugeot were divorcing by mutual agreement. Much was expected from the new combination, in order to cement which McLaren had turned down a deal to use the Chrysler-Lamborghini V12. More, by far, than it delivered.

The McLaren-Peugeot collaboration had exploded into action with remarkable speed. The partnership hadn't been born until the start of October 1993, while the first of the 72-degree Peugeot V10 engines to be developed by the design team operating under the direction of former Renault engineer Jean-Pierre Boudy was delivered to the team in January.

'Understandably, Jean-Pierre Jabouille and the Peugeot engineers have a cautious approach to what is a very difficult task,' said Dennis at the launch. 'It will take time to equal or surpass the level of Renault performance, but I have a very positive view of the season. Aided by the superior performance we anticipate from Peugeot, I am quite certain we will be competitive and will win races in 1994.'

However, McLaren had unquestionably been weakened by Ayrton Senna's defection to the Williams camp after six years with the team, and although Alain Prost tested the McLaren-Peugeot at Estoril the French triple World Champion eventually elected not to reverse his decision to retire in order to pick up the threads of his previous relationship with the team. As a result, Ron Dennis opted for the services of Martin Brundle as partner to Mika Häkkinen, the reliable English professional sitting on the sidelines until late in the day, correctly judging that McLaren would eventually pick him from the remaining available players. Early-season testing was also shared by Peugeot nominees Yannick Dalmas and Philippe Alliot, the latter standing in for Häkkinen at Budapest after the Finn was given a one-race suspension for triggering the first-corner multiple shunt in the German Grand Prix.

The new MP4/9 chassis was broadly based on the Ford HB-engined MP4/8 with which Ayrton Senna had won on his final outing for McLaren in the 1993 Australian Grand Prix. However, determining the cooling requirements of the five-valves-per-cylinder Peugeot A4 V10 was a problem from the outset as the new engine hadn't run by the time McLaren had to design the cooling package, so much of the work had to be based on McLaren's general experience allied to Peugeot's data from the 905 sports car V10.

McLAREN MP4/9-PEUGEOT

Sponsors: Marlboro, Peugeot, Shell, Courtaulds, Hugo Boss, Goodyear, Camozzi, ABAC

Designers: Neil Oatley, Henri Durand, Tim Goss, Matthew Jeffreys, Dave Neilson, Dave North **Team Principal:** Ron Dennis **Team Manager:** Dave Ryan **Chief Mechanics:** Paul Simpson, Indy Lall

ENGINE **Type:** Peugeot A6 **No. of cylinders/vee angle:** V10 (72°) **Electronics:** TAG Electronics **Fuel:** Shell **Oil:** Shell

TRANSMISSION **Gearbox:** McLaren six-speed transverse semi-automatic **Driveshafts:** McLaren **Clutch:** AP

CHASSIS **Front suspension:** unequal wishbones, pushrod operating inboard spring/damper **Rear suspension:** unequal wishbones, pushrod operating inboard spring/damper **Suspension dampers:** Bilstein **Wheel diameter:** front: 13 in. rear: 13 in. **Wheel rim widths:** front: 11.75 in. rear: 13.7 in. **Tyres:** Goodyear **Brake pads:** Carbone Industrie or Hitco **Brake discs:** Carbone Industrie or Hitco **Brake calipers:** Brembo **Steering:** McLaren **Radiators:** McLaren/Calsonic **Fuel tanks:** ATL **Battery:** GS **Instruments:** TAG Electronics

DIMENSIONS **Wheelbase:** 117.5 in./2985 mm **Track:** front: 66.3 in./1685 mm rear: 63.3 in./1608 mm **Formula weight:** 1135.3 lb/515 kg **Fuel capacity:** 43.9 gallons/200 litres

FORMULA 1 REVIEW

Searching for those elusive fractions of a second: Chief Designer Neil Oatley *(left)* and team manager Dave Ryan confer.

McLaren failed to win a Grand Prix for the first time since 1980 but the team's standards of preparation and presentation remained second to none. However, the mechanics' work on Martin Brundle's MP4/9 at the British Grand Prix at Silverstone *(below)* was in vain when the car suffered a spectacular engine failure as the starting lights turned green.

Ron Dennis *(opposite page)* was inevitably not content to be an also-ran and has forged a formidable alliance with Mercedes-Benz that threatens to dominate Formula 1 in the years ahead.

The MP4/9 aerodynamic package was subtly different from its immediate predecessor, in particular the floor and side pods. The car was fitted with a clutch activated by paddles on the steering column, effectively offering two-pedal control, which number one driver Häkkinen particularly liked, as it enabled him to brake late into the apex of a corner and contributed to the car retaining a more balanced aerodynamic configuration during the cornering process.

'We ran it for the first time on the Ford-powered MP4/8 at a Barcelona test after the end of the '93 season,' explained Chief Designer Neil Oatley. 'It was something which had developed out of general discussions between the engineers and drivers – in particular, Mika, who reckoned if there was no gap between coming off the throttle and going onto the brakes, and vice versa, he would have better control of the car. It was not a problem, but Martin never really used it. He drives more conventionally and, as a consequence, had his pedals positioned slightly differently.'

The team also got into difficulties with the FIA over its interpretation of the technical regulations relating to the transmission. The McLaren's six-speed transverse gearbox had a fully automatic upchange facility which was subsequently declared illegal by the governing body. Its presence was advertised to a wider audience after Philippe Alliot, the team's test driver, commented on the lack of such a facility when he joined the Larrousse team for the Belgian Grand Prix – one race after standing in for Häkkinen in Hungary!

After preliminary tests with the five-valve A4 engine, Peugeot switched straight to the four-valves-per-cylinder A6 engine for the start of the season, these being used exclusively thereafter with the exception of Häkkinen's preference for the A4 installed in the spare car which he used in the Pacific GP. Peugeot made steady progress throughout the season, producing the Version 1 Mk 2 for Imola with an increment of around 20 bhp, then a major revamp with Version 2 for the French GP in July. This unit had revised camshafts, offered 500 rpm more and gained 35 bhp, and was followed by Version 2 Mk 2 for Hungary (plus 15 bhp) and Mk 3 for Jerez (plus a further 10 bhp).

Unfortunately, most of the pre-season McLaren-Peugeot testing was carried out in fairly cool conditions which masked the threshold beyond which the V10's serious overheating problems became terminal – and they turned out to be disastrous in the early-season races.

Alterations were made to the cooling system, in particular the radiator

59

FORMULA 1 REVIEW

The uncompromising lines of the MP4/9 are seen to advantage as Martin Brundle heads for second place at Monaco.

Below, left to right: It was a frustrating season for race engineers Giorgio Ascanelli and Steve Hallam, chief mechanic Paul Simpson, McLaren stalwart Tyler Alexander and the rest of the experienced Woking race team. While the expectations surrounding Peugeot's arrival in Formula 1 were no doubt unrealistic, the performance of its V10 *(bottom)* was a grave disappointment to all concerned – not least Jean-Pierre Jabouille of Peugeot Sport *(centre)*. However, a number of podium finishes, including Mika Häkkinen's third place in Portugal *(opposite)*, offered some comfort.

 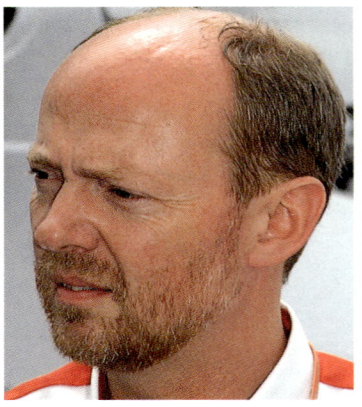  

installations, but the FIA did the team a favour by changing the rules at Barcelona. The shorter diffusers produced resulted in reduced back pressure through the radiators and significantly reduced the engines' operating temperature from that point onwards. Not that the Peugeot V10 had a trouble-free run in other areas, however, for Brundle suffered broken flywheels at Interlagos and Barcelona, and a crankcase pressurisation problem, which caused the Englishman's car to pump out all its oil on the grid at Silverstone, was only solved by a change of piston ring specification.

The MP4/9 was fitted with power steering for the first time at the Monaco Grand Prix, two hydraulic pumps operating the system, the pressure to which was regulated by a Moog electro-valve. The drivers preferred manual steering for the faster circuits like Spa and Monza, but power steering was generally used on the tighter tracks.

The MP4/9's handling was always a little troublesome on slow corners, the problem proving difficult to isolate and identify, although things were definitely improved by the adoption of a revised underbody and different rear wing for the Hungarian GP in mid-August. Häkkinen was undeniably quick, and highly motivated, in both qualifying and the races, but Brundle seemed to have difficulty producing the requisite qualifying speed and invariably lined up too far down the grid to make a worthwhile impact when the green light came on. That said, his race lap times stood close comparison with Häkkinen's and his experience was unquestionably of value to the team as it battled its way through what was a pretty testing year.

In purely relative terms, by the end of the season, the Peugeot V10 hadn't really improved since its debut at Interlagos when one took into account the improvements in form displayed by its key rivals over the 16-race programme.

Ron Dennis managed to keep a smile on the company's corporate face, reiterating his loyalty to Peugeot on many occasions throughout the season. But the bottom line was that 1994 was the first year in which his cars had failed to win a Grand Prix since McLaren International's creation (its first full season was 1981). The McLaren-Peugeot partnership clearly wasn't working in the way both parties had envisaged and, with two races to go, the two companies negotiated a dissolution of the arrangement to go their separate ways.

Peugeot forged a new deal with Jordan, while McLaren announced a new engine-supply partnership for 1995 with Mercedes-Benz only 12 days after the European Grand Prix at Jerez.

Alan Henry

9
ARROWS
10

CHRISTIAN FITTIPALDI

GIANNI MORBIDELLI

In theory, there seemed to have been too many pre-season changes for 1994 to be a real success for Jackie Oliver's Arrows team. In practice, however, it was the post-Monaco regulation changes which eventually cost the team dear. However, if nothing else, they could claim the title of top Cosworth HB customer, even though that engine was no longer a potential race winner.

Last year we predicted that 'the harsh winds of recession in Japan will cause a chill in Milton Keynes'. They did. Not a penny was forthcoming from Footwork, from whom Oliver leased back the team. With the Japanese involvement went Aguri Suzuki and the accompanying finance, plus the Mugen Honda engine, while Derek Warwick was another casualty of the clear-out. So was the name Footwork; Arrows was back, as the team name at least.

The change in identity also signified more independence. Oliver's team was not to be compromised as he searched for drivers, engine and money – preferably interconnected. Marlboro, Lee Cooper, Ford plus new drivers Christian Fittipaldi (from Minardi) and Gianni Morbidelli (after a year's sabbatical) filled the ranks to form the 1994 challenge.

Their equipment was again provided by the engineering and design team led by Alan Jenkins. Experience with TAG's active suspension during the second half of the previous season had helped Jenkins and his colleagues understand more about an F1 car's centre of pressure, and the Footwork FA15's aerodynamics were the fruit of several years' accumulated research.

Early testing, however, was abbreviated – not so much by the gearbox as by the components that controlled its operation. After initial hydraulic pump failures, an interactive vibration problem with Cosworth's ECU took nearly half a season to cure, and vibration from the V8 caused wires that had previously lived happily with Mugen's V10 to break up. This early-season unreliability cost the team test mileage and results at the beginning of the season. Both cars jumped gears at the start in Brazil and retired with gearbox trouble, while Fittipaldi lost an almost certain top six-placing when a wire broke at Monaco.

The promise was considerable; only reliability was needed. Morbidelli qualified sixth for the first race and Fittipaldi was similarly placed on the grid at Monaco. Only once did either driver qualify outside the top half of the field in the first four races and Christian finished fourth in the Pacific GP.

Then came the rule changes. All the team's centre-of-pressure research went out of the window and they felt they were misled as to whether the changes would really take place at all. Consequently they did not put enough effort into the necessary modifications, wind tunnel research and testing. In fact, they were probably the only team not to test prior to Barcelona.

Neither car qualified well for the Spanish GP and neither finished. Canada's circuit configuration tended to favour the FA15s and Fittipaldi finished sixth from 16th on the grid, only to be disqualified when the car was found to be underweight. The next two races, at Magny-Cours and Silverstone, were the worst of the year.

By this point, the team was working towards the ultimate Hockenheim 'stepped undertray' configuration rather than searching for intermediate solutions. Lack of finance meant that they did not test as often as during the previous year, nor as frequently as was necessary. But as they clawed back some of the downforce lost to the regulation changes, they faced the prospect of the faster circuits like Hockenheim, Spa and Monza, where Cosworth's HB – in Series 7 or 8 form – was expected to run out of steam.

Contrary to all expectations, Hockenheim produced the best finish of the year with fourth and fifth places, an admittedly fortuitous result that owed much to the first-lap multiple accident. The Hungarian performance then highlighted another problem, namely that the cars' handling was remarkably susceptible to temperature changes. The loss of

FOOTWORK FA15-FORD

Sponsors: Marlboro, Uliveto, Lee Cooper

Designers: Alan Jenkins, Dave Amey **Team Principals:** Jackie Oliver, Alan Rees **Team Managers:** John Wickham, Alan Harrison **Chief Mechanic:** Ken Sibley

ENGINE **Type:** Ford Cosworth HB **No. of cylinders/vee angle:** V8 (75°) **Sparking plugs:** Champion **Electronics:** Cosworth **Fuel:** Elf **Oil:** Elf

TRANSMISSION **Gearbox:** Arrows/Xtrac six-speed transverse semi-automatic **Driveshafts:** Arrows/Xtrac **Clutch:** AP

CHASSIS **Front suspension:** wishbones, pushrod **Rear suspension:** wishbones, pushrod **Suspension dampers:** Arrows **Wheel diameter:** front: 13 in. rear: 13 in. **Wheel rim widths:** front: 11 in. rear: 13.4 in. **Tyres:** Goodyear **Brake pads:** Carbone Industrie **Brake discs:** Carbone Industrie **Brake calipers:** Brembo **Steering:** Arrows/Xtrac **Radiators:** Secan **Fuel tanks:** ATL **Battery:** FIAMME **Instruments:** PI Research

DIMENSIONS **Wheelbase:** 115 in./2921 mm **Track:** front: 66 in./1676 mm rear: 63 in./1600 mm **Formula weight:** 1135.3 lb/515 kg **Fuel capacity:** 43.9 gallons/200 litres

FORMULA 1 REVIEW

An attractive new livery marked another fresh start for Arrows. Christian Fittipaldi was superb at Monaco (top), qualifying sixth fastest and running in fourth place for many laps. However, by the time of the next race, in Spain, rule changes had been introduced that robbed the cars of their competitiveness.

The withdrawal of Footwork's support allowed Jackie Oliver (above) to regain his independence but the Milton Keynes concern is unlikely to join the Grand Prix élite without major financial backing.

Gianni Morbidelli (right) showed that he had lost none of his sparkle during a year out of Formula 1, repaying Oliver's faith with a number of spirited performances.

grip that accompanied the transition from the cool of the morning to the heat of the afternoon was particularly pronounced.

Belgium produced a good eventual sixth place for Morbidelli, but the first of a couple of engine failures for Fittipaldi. The second was a massive blow-up at peak revs in fifth gear at Monza which blew the bottom out of the car, took out an engine mounting, and left the pumps lying on what was left of the floor and a piston in a radiator. This marked the nadir of Arrows's season in terms of Cosworth engine failures, five of which had been sustained in races and one in testing.

The team also fought to make up lost ground in two key areas, producing a single-spring, twin-shock absorber front suspension set-up which allowed the engineers to regain some control over the FA15's ride height. This finally came into its own at Estoril, coinciding with the introduction of a new diffuser. It also experimented with revised differentials in an attempt to regain some of the traction lost to the reduction in downforce.

These modifications nudged the drivers back into the top half of the field again. As a pair, Oliver's choice of Fittipaldi and Morbidelli had been excellent. Unfortunately Christian's

economy of tyre wear had not been as great an advantage as might have been hoped while Morbidelli proved the perfect team player, although he raced under the threat of losing his seat through lack of finance during the second half of the season.

Fortunately, Oliver showed justifiable confidence in him, with the result that the team was not only one of the handful to end the season with the same drivers as it started, but also finished the year with the same four cars.

Bob Constanduros

11 LOTUS 12

PEDRO LAMY

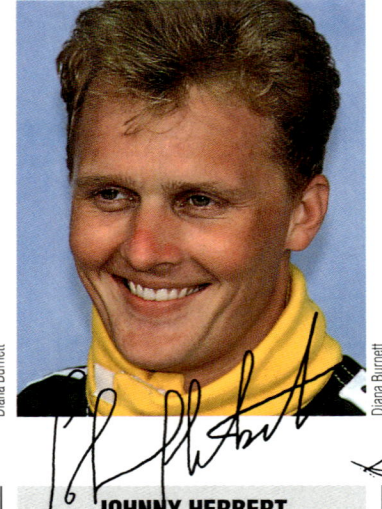
JOHNNY HERBERT

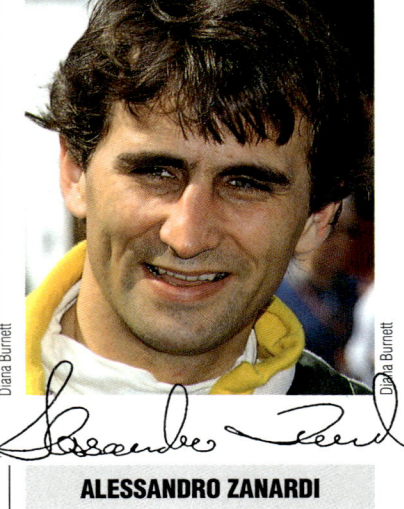
ALESSANDRO ZANARDI

On 12 September Neil Cooper and Nigel Ruddock of chartered accountants Robson Rhodes were appointed joint administrators of Team Lotus. The famous marque seemed to be on its last legs.

At the start of the season Peter Collins had tried to put on a brave face. There was widespread talk of a formidable list of creditors and severe financial problems, but Collins put that down to the destabilising efforts of third parties.

But you did not have to look far to see all was not well. At a pre-season Barcelona test, Herbert already bore the expression of a man who knew he was championing a hopeless cause.

Lotus had agreed terms with Mugen Honda for an exclusive supply of the Japanese V10s. The engines had strong top-end power but they were a little long in the tooth. The unit was a none-too-far-removed derivative of the Honda V10 which had taken Alain Prost to the World Championship in 1989. It had not done kind things to the balance of the Tyrrell 020 when Ken's team secured a supply in 1991 to replace its Hart DFRs.

At Lotus there was a similar problem. An all-new engine was due from Hirotoshi Honda's company, but not before the end of the season. Lotus would start the year with its familiar 107 chassis, itself two years old, revised to take the Mugen. Pre-season testing saw Lotus between four and five seconds from the pace. Herbert was being courted by McLaren and did not disguise his desire to be away from Hethel.

'The car has about as much grip as a Formula Ford,' he said dimissively at a pre-season Barcelona test. Alessandro Zanardi was a little more diplomatic but did admit that the 107 was severely overweight and in need of a trip to Willy Dungl's fitness clinic.

On the engineering side, Nigel Stroud, a man who worked with Nigel Mansell at Lotus in the early Eighties, was back to oversee Jock Clear on Herbert's car and Andy Tilley on Pedro Lamy's.

The season started badly with Herbert qualifing 21st at Interlagos and Lamy 24th. The Lotus-Mugen combination may not have been quick, but it was generally reliable and Herbert got the car home seventh in Brazil and Aida. Lamy was tenth and eighth. The pair both managed to qualify inside the top 20 at Monaco, but that was the last race Lamy did. At Silverstone, testing revisions to the rear aerodynamics in response to the FIA's emergency measures in May, Lamy speared off the road at Abbey and suffered a fearful accident from which he emerged with badly broken legs.

Alessandro Zanardi, who had been relegated to the role of test driver, then made a comeback to the race team for the first time since his own violent accident at Spa the previous season. Anybody who suspected that a demotivated Herbert was giving less than his best was shown otherwise when Alex qualified steadily in 23rd spot for three races in succession.

The Lotus 109 was little more than a mildly reworked 107 and it made no difference when it appeared for the first time in Herbert's hands at Barcelona. Johnny qualified 22nd and spun out of the race.

Morale within the team was at an all-time low and the only glimmer of hope on the horizon was the new engine. Not originally scheduled to race until Suzuka, Lotus got one into the back of Herbert's car for Monza. Johnny qualified in a stunning fourth place.

The lighter weight and lower centre of gravity transformed the car, and Monza was particularly suited to the engine's strong top-end capability. By this time the relationship between Collins and Herbert had deteriorated to the point where they barely spoke, and while Collins thought the performance with the new engine was a vindication of all he had said, Johnny still felt that the car and the team had problems. Collins's view was interesting: 'The old engine was respectable with Footwork last year because with an active system it was possible to con-

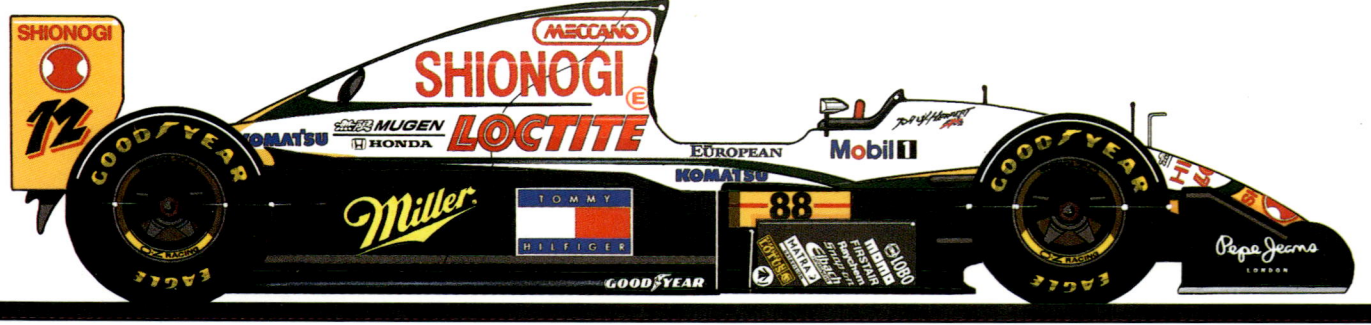

LOTUS 109-MUGEN HONDA

Sponsors: Loctite, Hitachi, Komatsu, Tommy Hilfiger, Shionogi, Miller, Mobil

Designers: Chris Murphy/Lotus design team **Team Principals:** Peter Collins, Peter Wright **Chief Mechanic:** Paul Diggins

ENGINE **Type:** Mugen Honda ZA5C/ZA6C **No. of cylinders/vee angle:** V10 (72°) **Sparking plugs:** NGK **Electronics:** Mugen Honda **Fuel:** BP **Oil:** Mobil

TRANSMISSION **Gearbox:** Lotus/Xtrac six-speed transverse semi-automatic **Driveshafts:** Lotus **Clutch:** AP

CHASSIS **Front suspension:** double wishbones, pushrod, inboard concentric spring/dampers **Rear suspension:** double wishbones, pushrod, inboard concentric spring/dampers **Suspension dampers:** Lotus/Penske **Wheel diameter:** front: 13 in. rear: 13 in. **Wheel rim widths:** front: 11.5 in. rear: 13.7 in. **Tyres:** Goodyear **Brake pads:** Hitco or Carbone Industrie **Brake discs:** Hitco or Carbone Industrie **Brake calipers:** AP or Brembo **Steering:** Lotus/Jack Knight **Radiators:** Lotus/Secan **Fuel tanks:** Lotus/ATL **Battery:** Panasonic **Instruments:** Cranfield/Mugen Honda

DIMENSIONS **Wheelbase:** 117.9 in./2995 mm **Track:** front: 64.9 in./1650 mm rear: 62.9 in./1600 mm **Gearbox weight:** 121.2 lb/55 kg (with rear suspension) **Chassis weight (tub):** 88.1 lb/40 kg **Formula weight:** 1135.3 lb/515 kg **Fuel capacity:** 43.9 gallons/200 litres

FORMULA 1 REVIEW

PHILIPPE ADAMS

ERIC BERNARD

MIKA SALO

Peter Collins *(below left)* refused to concede defeat in his gallant struggle to restore Lotus to its former glories but as the season drew to a close it was beginning to seem that his efforts might have been in vain.

Having been eliminated in the massive startline crash at Imola, Pedro Lamy was back behind the wheel at Monaco *(bottom)*. However, before the next Grand Prix in Spain he suffered unpleasant leg injuries in a frightening testing accident at Silverstone which curtailed his season – and may have ended the talented Portuguese driver's Formula 1 chances.

trol the roll and weight transfer much better. Without active it was difficult. We had to run extremely high rear spring rates to stop the weight transfer, which really hurt us as far as grip was concerned. That meant it was very difficult to balance the car and it wanted to swap ends in a corner every time it was leaned on.

'Alex drove it bloody hard but even he gradually lost motivation because he came up against a brick wall. And until we ran the new engine we actually began to question our own view. We were changing things which we knew should have a dramatic effect on the car but it was making no difference.

'Then, testing the new engine at Silverstone, Johnny found almost three seconds immediately and that was a great boost. At Montreal I'd had a discussion with him, I think that's the polite way to put it, where I accused him of behaving like a spoiled brat. Suddenly here he was doing 1m 28.5s and admitting there was another half-second in him, which would have put him within a second of Schumacher. Which isn't shabby.'

Herbert, meanwhile, was of the opinion that Lotus should have spent less time testing with the old combination and spent what precious little money it did have on new components. Indeed, Johnny claimed, most of the basic aerodynamic moulds went back four seasons.

After Monza, however, the improvement was not maintained. At Estoril Johnny was 20th again and by Jerez the administrators had sold him to Ligier. The hard-working and technically adroit Zanardi was now left to champion the cause and tried manfully as Lotus continued to struggle.

The team was forced to accept rent-a-drivers in its efforts to stay afloat. Philippe Adams turned up at Spa and crashed his chassis within the opening minutes of Friday morning's free session. Although he received quite a widespread panning, the reigning British F2 Champion qualified within two seconds of Herbert using the old engine at Estoril and brought the car home. You could not reasonably have asked for more. Save possibly a cheque . . . Mika Salo arranged to drive alongside Zanardi in Japan and retained the drive in Australia, showing genuine promise.

Lotus was teetering on the brink. Prior to Suzuka it was sold to American businessman Sam Brown, but the long-term future seemed far from secure. Senna and Ratzenberger apart, it was the saddest story of the year.

Tony Dodgins

THE WINNING FORMULA

UNIPART AND JORDAN GRAND PRIX

1994 WAS NOT ONLY the 25th anniversary of the Unipart brand, but it was also the company's most successful year ever, underlining its position as Britain's largest independent automotive parts supplier.

On the other side of the coin, Jordan Grand Prix, one of the leanest organisations in Formula 1, proved theirselves to be truly world class, taking on the established World Championship contenders, and achieving its best results ever.

The link between Unipart and Jordan Grand Prix is, however, more than just a commercial arrangement; there is a meeting of minds in terms of each company's philosophy and their commitment to world class performance.

UNIPART & MOTORSPORT

The involvement of Unipart in the world of motorsport goes back to the beginnings of the company itself.

Since Unipart launched the first truly comprehensive range of automotive prod-

ADVERTISEMENT FEATURE

LEFT: Rubens Barrichello achieves Jordan Grand Prix best ever result - 3rd place in the 1994 Pacific GP.
FAR LEFT: Jordan Grand Prix - one of the smallest but most effective teams in Formula One.
BELOW: Pre-season testing of the Jordan-Hart at Barcelona.

ucts, for all makes of car, in Britain, not only has its portfolio increased to include 41 different product lines, but so has its reputation for quality, reliability, innovation and performance – a reputation which has been continually enhanced by its involvement in the world of motorsport–and particularly the high profile world of Formula 1.

Over the years motorsport fans have seen the Unipart name – and very often Unipart components –up amongst the winners at Le Mans, the most famous international rallies, and almost every Formula category. During 1994 it's the name they have seen on the Jordan Grand Prix cars.

MORE THAN JUST SPONSORSHIP

Whatever the event, one factor remains constant, and that is that the Unipart involvement is wholly comprehensive. Take Jordan Grand Prix for example: in addition to sponsoring the team Unipart has supplied several important components for the Hart V10 which powered the team to its most successful ever season.

The spark plugs Jordan chose are included in the Unipart range (part number GSP 3000, to be precise), though admittedly they are slightly different from the norm, being slimmer, having no exposed electrodes and having the capability to produce over 100 sparks per second at peak revolutions.

Unipart oil and water pump drive belts played an equally important role in the team's pole position performance, cooling and lubricating the 700 plus bhp Hart V10.

Both of these belts running the dry sump lubrication and the water pump, moving the coolant around the sensitive engine hotspots and back through the radiators, were

Some years have a particular significance – for Jordan Grand Prix and Unipart, 1994 was a real milestone.

UNIPART

RIGHT; Unipart sponsored Niki Lauda and John Watson and equipped the McLaren team in the early 1980s.
BELOW: The Unipart range, quality products for all makes of car.

composed of Highly Saturated Nitrile (HSN), a tough, non-stretch material which can cope with the extreme temperatures resulting from the white heat of Formula 1 competition.

You'll find belts made from HSN increasingly available in the Unipart range. In fact, throughout its long association with Formula 1, many Unipart products have found their way into the cars on the track. The innovative, advanced technology of Unipart oil, filters, plugs, and pumps, to name but a few, have all been specified by race engineers and designers for a variety of teams.

Even the products which ensure that the Jordan team cars always look their best – shampoos, polishes, cloths – are the same Unipart products which you can find on the shelf.

TEAMWORK

The comprehensive back up, the high level of involvement and the commitment to teamwork which Unipart demonstrates in its involvement in the world of Formula 1 is equally apparent in its approach to business.

1994 saw Unipart establish even closer links with its network of independent motor traders under the Unipart Car Care Centre banner.

This programme was developed not merely to provide mo-

RIGHT: Nigel Mansell's first international races came in the March F3 team, sponsored by Unipart.
FAR RIGHT: Rubens Barrichello became the youngest ever pole-man in Belgium and finished sixth in the Drivers World Championship.
RIGHT: Eddie Jordan oversees teamwork in preparation for Eddie Irvine's qualifying run in Brazil.

torists with a consistent, high level of customer service, but also to give traders the back-up they need to enable them to provide such service via computerised pricing, product reference and ordering links.

Unipart Car Care Centres offer motorists the security of knowing that skilled mechanics will fit only the highest quality parts, with a unique 'plus', the added security of the Unipart National guarantee. This means that no matter at which Unipart Car Care Centre the part was fitted, in the unlikely event the product should fail, it will be replaced, free, at any other Unipart Car Care Centre anywhere in the UK.

ADVERTISEMENT FEATURE

LEFT: Rubens Barrichello in action in the Canadian GP.
BELOW: The Jordan 194s in tandem at the French GP.

WORKING WITH THE MAJOR MANUFACTURERS

The philosophy of teamwork and the partnership Unipart adopts with its suppliers and trade network also extends to its customers. In fact, over recent years the Unipart Group as a whole has established close links with a number of major motor manufacturers, supplying a range of products for line fit by customers of the magnitude of Rover, Jaguar, Honda, Saab and Toyota.

Major manufacturer involvement was also the big news for Jordan Grand Prix in 1994, when towards the end of October it was announced that next season the Jordans would be running with a new Peugeot engine.

This exclusive three year deal means that Jordan Grand Prix will use Peugeot `works' engines, together with all the technical support, expertise and resource that the Peugeot Sport team brings with it. So, all bodes well for even greater success for the 1995 season.

INVESTING IN TALENT

Eddie Jordan, Jordan Grand Prix founder and Team Owner, would be the first to agree that 1994 was a truly remarkable year for his team. But Eddie himself is no stranger to success during his 24 years in the motorsport business, due in no small part to his eye for spotting talent.

During his career he's given chances to drivers of the calibre of Ayrton Senna, Martin Brundle, Johnny Herbert, Jean Alesi, Michael Schumacher and latterly, Rubens Barrichello and Eddie Irvine (although one big name which Unipart did beat Eddie to was Nigel Mansell, whom the company supported during his Formula 3 career in the late 1970s).

It is more than just spotting talent, however, Eddie Jordan knows that you have to actually invest in this talent to achieve real winning potential, and in this respect his philosophy is very similar to that of Unipart, a company which recognises its future lies in the potential of its staff.

In fact, Unipart has invested in a company 'university', the Unipart U, which offers all employees the chance to acquire the new skills and working techniques which will create the continuous improvement in the levels of service that it can offer to all its customers.

It is this level of investment in its human resource that has not only earned Unipart an excellent reputation in the international business community, but also the prestigious Government sponsored 'Investor in People' award.

Unipart has also become an 'investor in people' itself on the track.

In addition to sponsoring the Jordan Grand Prix team for the 1994 season, Unipart also sponsored both Eddie Irvine and Rubens Barrichello, whose performances during 1994 resulted in Jordan Grand Prix achieving 5th place in the constructors' championship and Rubens achieving 6th position in the drivers' title, including a podium finish – undoubtedly a driver with world championship winning potential.

When it comes to investing in winners with world class potential Eddie Jordan obviously has the knack, and so has Unipart – with its winning range of products, an increasingly successful chain of associated high quality garages, and a multi-million pound investment in its human resources.

When you look at the similar approach and attitudes that Unipart and Jordan Grand Prix have, it comes as no surprise that 1994 was such a successful year.

Here's to an equally successful association next season.

14 JORDAN 15

RUBENS BARRICHELLO

EDDIE IRVINE

AGURI SUZUKI

ANDREA DE CESARIS

In 1994 the Jordan-Hart combination realised the potential which had been masked for most of the previous season but which had become apparent at Suzuka.

Steve Nichols added strength to the design staff, taking some of the pressure off the hitherto overworked Gary Anderson, and the new Jordan 194-Hart was a competitive proposition right from the outset. A personal tragedy for Nichols, however, was the loss of his wife in a car accident.

The team had admirably demonstrated its competence with an impressive maiden F1 season in 1991, but had been hamstrung thereafter by lack of funds. Jordan is not a team on the scale of McLaren, Williams and Benetton, but one in which money is tight and frills non-existent.

A works association with Yamaha in 1992 had been disastrous, but financially necessary, and a switch to Brian Hart's new type 1035 V10 had been made for the following year. Hart is one of the most respected engine builders in racing, but could not really be expected to compete with the full-scale sports divisions at Renault and Peugeot.

A Rover badging deal was rumoured at the beginning of the year, but that came to nought. As things transpired, however, one would have taken a Hart V10 in preference to its Peugeot counterpart for much of 1994, an irony indeed as things turned out. If Brian was ever to come by a generous development budget, there is little doubt that he would inflict serious damage on the opposition.

On the driver front, Eddie Irvine had been a revelation at Suzuka in 1993, even before he squared up to Ayrton Senna! He was confirmed as a full-time member of the team alongside Rubens Barrichello by January as Martin Brundle held out for a McLaren seat. Irvine may not be conventional in his outlook – and more power to him for it – but he was unfortunate to develop a 'wild man' image in the cockpit.

His season opened in dramatic fashion amid his celebrated Interlagos coming-together with Jos Verstappen which resulted in a wrecked Benetton and a cracked helmet and severe headache for Brundle.

Most observers agreed that this was a racing incident, the Jordan bearing down on Eric Bernard's Ligier as Verstappen sought in turn to take advantage of Eddie's slipstream. A three-race ban (after an ill-fated appeal) for Eddie was very

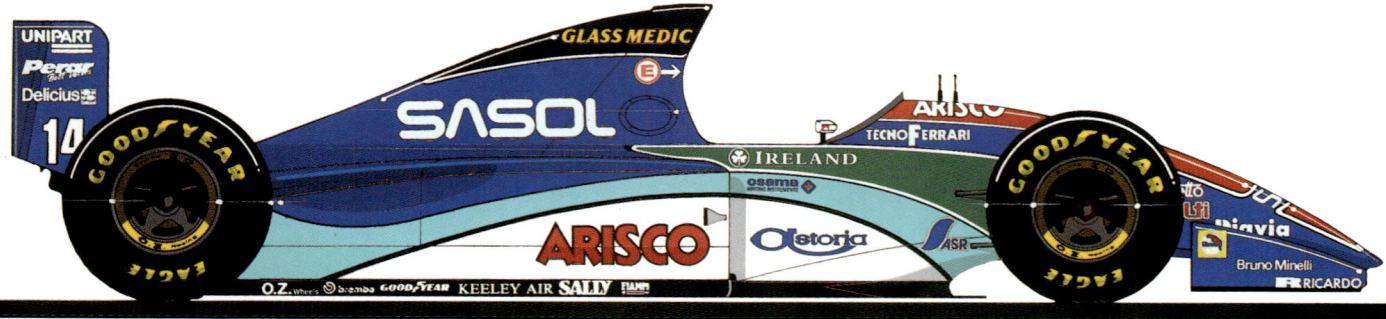

JORDAN 194-HART

Sponsors: Sasol, Arisco, Unipart, Glass Medic, Ireland, Diavia, Osama

Designers: Steve Nichols, Gary Anderson and Jordan design team **Team Principal:** Eddie Jordan **Team Manager:** John Walton **Chief Mechanic:** Jim Vale

ENGINE **Type:** Hart 1035 **No. of cylinders/vee angle:** V10 (72°) **Sparking plugs:** Unipart **Electronics:** Zytek **Fuel:** Sasol **Oil:** Sasol

TRANSMISSION **Gearbox:** Jordan six-speed transverse semi-automatic **Driveshafts:** Jordan/Tripod **Clutch:** AP

CHASSIS **Front suspension:** double wishbone, pushrod, twin damper **Rear suspension:** double wishbone, pushrod, twin damper **Suspension dampers:** Jordan/Penske

Wheel diameter: front: 13 in. rear: 13 in. **Wheel rim widths:** front: 11.5 in. rear: 13.7 in. **Tyres:** Goodyear **Brake pads:** Carbone Industrie **Brake discs:** Carbone Industrie **Brake calipers:** Brembo **Steering:** Jordan/Jack Knight **Radiators:** Secan **Fuel tanks:** ATL **Battery:** FIAMM **Instruments:** PI Research

DIMENSIONS **Wheelbase:** 116.1 in./2950 mm **Track:** front: 65.5 in./1665 mm rear: 62.9 in./1600 mm **Gearbox weight:** 118.6 lb/53.8 kg **Chassis weight (tub):** 83.7 lb/38 kg

Formula weight: 1135.3 lb/515 kg **Fuel capacity:** 48.3 gallons/220 litres

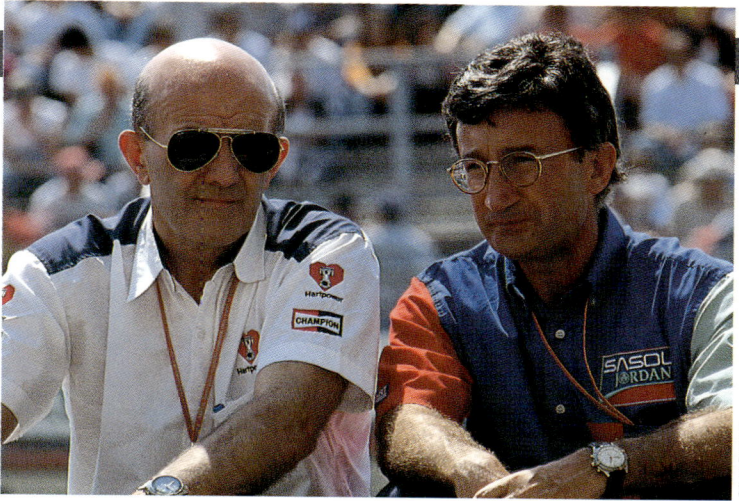

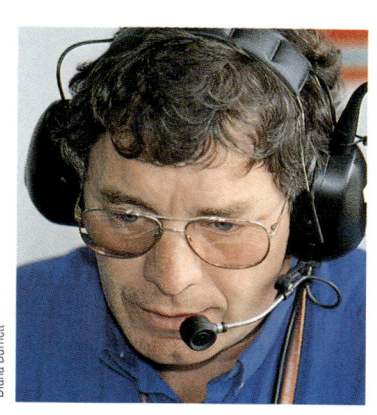

Right: **Although he is quick to acknowledge the contribution made by engine builder Brian Hart *(left)* to his team's emergence as a challenger to Grand Prix racing's Big Four, Eddie Jordan has concluded a deal with Peugeot for the supply of its under-achieving V10 in 1995.**

Developed from the previous year's promising design under the supervision of Chief Engineer Gary Anderson *(far right)*, the colourful Jordan 194-Hart enabled Brazilian prodigy Rubens Barrichello *(below)* to take sixth place in the World Championship of Drivers.

Diana Burnett

Diana Burnett

John Marsh/Action Images

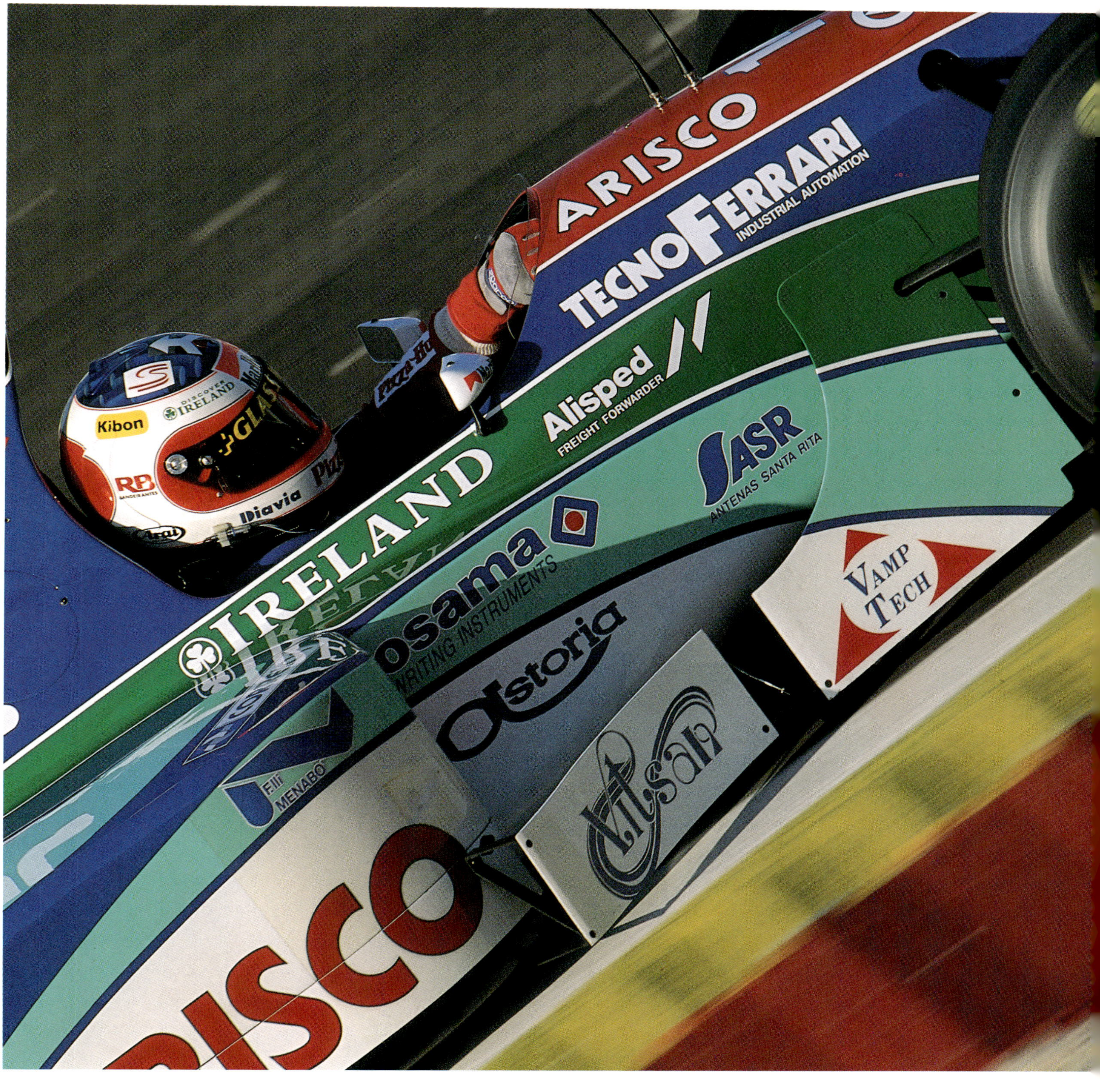

FORMULA 1 REVIEW

It's not how much money you have, but how you use it. The splendid Hart V10 *(right)* humbled engines benefiting from the kind of development budget Brian Hart could only dream of.

Jordan's engineering team was strengthened shortly before the start of the season by the appointment of former McLaren and Ferrari designer Steve Nichols *(below)* as Technical Director.

Despite a number of unfortunate incidents that reinforced his reputation as F1's rebel without a cause, Eddie Irvine *(bottom)* usually proved a match for his highly regarded team-mate, demonstrating growing maturity as the season wore on.

harsh and led to a Jordan return for Andrea de Cesaris (at Imola and Monaco) after a one-off appearance for Aguri Suzuki at Aida. Aguri did nothing special, qualifying 20th and retiring with a broken upright, but in the other car Barrichello delighted the team by recording its first-ever podium finish behind Schumacher and Berger.

There followed a dramatic change of fortune. The disastrous sequence of events at that awful San Marino Grand Prix was started by an enormous accident to Barrichello, from which he was fortunate to escape with a cut nose and mouth. Rubens had simply overdone it. Anderson confirmed that from the telemetry: 'On the previous lap he went through at 208 km/h, whereas on the lap he lost it he was doing 223 km/h. We suggested that he might like to try 215 km/h first . . .'

Senna was Barrichello's idol and, coming on top of his own lucky escape, Ayrton's accident had a sobering effect. Rubens was back fully fit for Monaco after missing the Imola race, but he qualified 15th, his worst showing of the season other than a problematic couple of days at Monza. But then came a points-scoring fifth at Silverstone, despite a last-lap tangle with an aggressive Mika Häkkinen. Irvine, meanwhile, had finished sixth at Barcelona.

On the technical side, Jordan was enjoying strong reliability save for a recurring problem with the gearbox electronics which was prone to leave the car without power.

Within the team there was strong rivalry between Barrichello and Irvine. It was an open secret that McLaren and Ron Dennis were showing a keen interest in the Brazilian, but Irvine was pushing him hard. In fact, there were two successive races where the Jordan duo ended up sharing the same piece of barrier at the first corner – guaranteed to send Eddie Jordan off the clock on the profanity scale. At Hockenheim they were innocent victims, but at Budapest Irvine put the blame squarely at Barrichello's door during some heated exchanges back at the motorhome.

At the next race, Spa, Barrichello played the changing weather conditions superbly to claim the team's first-ever pole, while Irvine qualified fourth. Eddie has a wry sense of humour: 'E.J. seemed surprisingly calm about the whole Budapest thing,' he said. 'So I asked him if Rubens and I were really equal in this team. When he said yes, I fixed him with a serious look and told him I expected the same understanding treatment when I punted Rubens into the boonies at the first corner. He thought I meant it . . .'

If there is any criticism of Barrichello from within the team, it stems from his preoccupation with dashing back home to Brazil after many races and a seeming reluctance to test as often as he might. 'He has the ability, there's no doubt,' mused one of the technical team, 'but could you imagine having to push a young Prost or Senna to test?'

By Japan we knew that Jordan would have works Peugeot engines for 1995 and a three-year deal which should give the team the chance to establish the infrastructure needed to join the big league. After his efforts over the past couple of years, it was tough on Brian Hart, but there is no sentiment in motor racing. Hart understands the situation and Jordan was the first to pay tribute to the part Brian's company has played in his team's rise to prominence.

Tony Dodgins

TO FIND NEW SOLUTIONS WE EXPERIMENT WITH A WELL KNOWN FORMULA

The reason behind Sasol's involvement in Formula One racing may not be all that obvious to the spectator. But it is through our "laboratory on wheels" that we're able to improve our technology. Constantly developing better products such as rubber, paints, resins, filters and engine cleaners used in motoring.

LARROUSSE 19/20

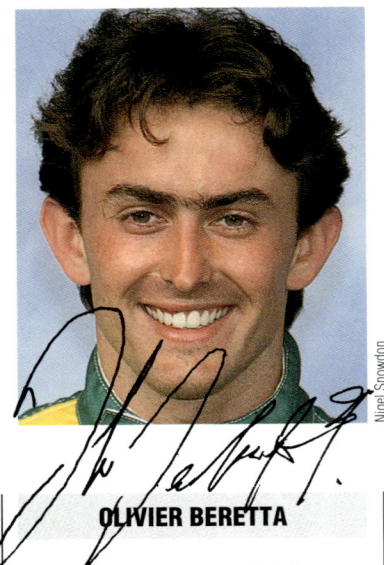
OLIVIER BERETTA

ERIK COMAS

PHILIPPE ALLIOT

Even the appearance of its best sponsor for some years could do little to improve the fortunes of the 35-strong team from the Cote d'Azur. Regulation changes and a rash of engine failures didn't help the cash-strapped Frenchmen and the season ended with the usual quest for additional finance.

It could have been different, of course. At the end of the previous year, McLaren's testing of the Lamborghini engine freed Chrysler finance to further develop the V12 which Larrousse had used during that season. Unfortunately, the programme was halted and Larrousse opted for the Cosworth HB route, the team using Series 7 units throughout 1994.

Larrousse UK, the 15-strong satellite which designs the cars in Bicester, based the new machine on the previous year's monocoque, the back and bottom of which were cut off, with a 200-litre fuel cell being added and modifications carried out to accept the shorter Cosworth engine. The front suspension remained unchanged, as did the suspension uprights. Penske dampers replaced Bilsteins which, in hindsight, was considered a good move.

On the commercial front, Larrousse secured the backing of Tourtel, an alcohol-free beer, but occasionally the team ran in the colours of Kronenbourg, a sister company, in what amounted to an interesting challenge to French alcohol legislation. Their financial input basically replaced that of the French government, which had kept the team going the previous year.

So although the team wasn't much better off financially, Erik Comas would be quick to point out that the LH94s were closer to the pole position times than their predecessors had been the previous season, even if they were lower down the grid. That perhaps reflected the changing calibre of the competition; ninth was the best grid position for Larrousse in 1993, but 13th was the best it could muster this year.

Like so many midfield runners, the team made a promising start to the season, but then came the rule changes. The hacksaws which made the cars conform with the new regulations also chopped off half a dozen places on the grid – and decimated Larrousse's budget, the team having just built up its stock of spares. Now fresh components had to be made and money for testing disappeared.

Traction and power understeer had been a problem from the start of the season and remained so; grip was lacking on low-speed corners and the understeer proved intrusive on medium-speed turns, although the car wasn't bad in fast corners.

The team's development programme went on hold. Wind tunnel testing was abandoned. There was no development after the 'hacksaw job' and, when things remain unchanged in F1, the team goes backwards. This was the case for Larrousse as rival teams developed their cars. These problems were compounded by a rash of mid-season engine failures.

The cars had completed 4000 km of racing and testing at the start of the year without a problem. But in the next 2000 km they had 14 engine breakages. Ten of these were caused by bearing failures, possibly attributable to a shift in Vandervell's manufacturing location. Comas suffered three race engine failures, the second car five.

Yet it wasn't all a hard-luck story. Comas would admit that the gearbox – Benetton's six-speed, semi-automatic, transverse six-speed unit – was really fantastic. 'It makes it fun to drive the car,' said the Frenchman, 'the gearchange is really wonderful.'

Comas would be team leader until the last race of the year, initially showing sometime F3000 winner Olivier Beretta the ropes. Beretta generally kept his nose clean and was beginning to qualify in the top 20 when the rule changes arrived. He suffered most of the engine failures but finished just behind Comas in seventh place at Hockenheim, the team's best race of the year.

By this stage, Comas had proved himself a better racer than qualifier,

LARROUSSE LH94-FORD

Sponsors: Tourtel, Kronenbourg, Zanussi

Designers: Tino Belli, Tim Holloway **Team Principals:** Gérard Larrousse, Robin Herd, Patrick Tambay **Team Manager:** Philippe Leloup **Chief Mechanic:** A. Marguet

ENGINE **Type:** Ford Cosworth HB **No. of cylinders/vee angle:** V8 (75°) **Sparking plugs:** Champion **Electronics:** Cosworth **Fuel:** Elf **Oil:** Elf

TRANSMISSION **Gearbox:** Benetton six-speed transverse semi-automatic **Driveshafts:** Larrousse/Xtrac **Clutch:** AP

CHASSIS **Front suspension:** double wishbone, pushrod, inboard coil spring/damper **Rear suspension:** double wishbone, pushrod, inboard coil spring/damper **Suspension dampers:** Penske/Larrousse **Wheel diameter:** front: 13 in. rear: 13 in. **Wheel rim widths:** front: 11.5 in. rear: 13.7 in. **Tyres:** Goodyear **Brake pads:** Carbone Industrie **Brake discs:** Carbone Industrie **Brake calipers:** Brembo **Radiators:** Secan **Fuel tanks:** ATL **Instruments:** PI Research

DIMENSIONS **Wheelbase:** 115.9 in./2946 mm **Track:** maximum permissible **Chassis weight (tub):** 108.0 lb/49 kg **Formula weight:** 1135.3 lb/515 kg **Fuel capacity:** 43.9 gallons/200 litres

YANNICK DALMAS | **HIDEKI NODA** | **JEAN-DENIS DELETRAZ**

FORMULA 1 REVIEW

Below: Olivier Beretta leads Erik Comas in Canada. The Monégasque failed to make much impact in Formula 1 and when the money ran out, he was shown the door.

The LH94s carried a striking Kronenbourg livery on occasion, but it needed more than a new paint-job to elevate the cars from their lower-middle class status.

Used to better things? Robin Herd *(below left)* was one of the founders of March; Patrick Tambay *(bottom left)* drove for Ferrari; Gérard Larrousse *(bottom right)* ran the Renault F1 effort. Each tasted Grand Prix victory. Now they guide the fortunes of the struggling Larrousse team.

regularly starting in the low twenties in the grid order, but finishing in the top ten when his machinery allowed. He would regularly lap quicker than those with whom he qualified.

By late summer, however, Beretta's finances had dried up. He was initially replaced by Philippe Alliot, fresh from McLaren, and then Larrousse's local driver Yannick Dalmas took over for a couple of races. Finally, the team went back to its traditional route by running its fourth Japanese driver in as many years, Hideki Noda, who had a varied history in F3000, but acquitted himself well on his graduation to Formula 1. In addition, Jean-Denis Deletraz rented the other car for Adelaide, to spectacularly limited effect.

So, on balance, a year on hold for Larrousse. But when will there be light at the end of the tunnel, one wonders?

Bob Constanduros

23 / 24 MINARDI

PIERLUIGI MARTINI

MICHELE ALBORETO

It seemed like just another Minardi year. The odd point here and there, the occasional top-ten qualifying position, the happy-go-lucky Italian team maintaining a foothold in Formula 1 when Osella, Fondmetal, Coloni, Andrea Moda, Life and Scuderia Italia had all failed.

In reality, after a financially marginal 1993, things became slightly better for the team. In fact, they would have been very much better, but for the impact of the regulation changes which hit all the small teams so badly. This was a year of transition. The future looks rosier.

After its disastrous 1993 season with the Lola-Ferraris, the financially stronger Scuderia Italia decided to join forces with Giancarlo Minardi's eponymous team. It wasn't a merger calculated to double the Faenza team in size, or even in finance. What it did do was give the new Scuderia Italia Minardi a guarantee for the future. While the very Latin Minardi has the big family motor and truck business behind him, Scuderia Italia boss Beppe Lucchini is known as the king of Italian steel, and has contacts of similar status within Italian industry.

In fact, it wasn't really a merger at all. The Minardi team effectively increased its number of shareholders and changed its name. But it had acquired renewed credibility; it was now more businesslike, with greater financial stability. Responsibilities were shared between the partners, with Scuderia Italia's Managing Director Paolo Stanzani being appointed Vice-President. There was more expertise across a broader spectrum, encompassing the many areas in which F1 demands total professionalism.

Even the public image of the team was altered. AGIP actually built their PR policy around Minardi, even though they also supplied Ferrari. AGIP's motorhome was parked beside the Minardi bus. The team was also given the use of an aircraft by executive plane manufacturers Rinaldo Piaggio. Minardi was certainly benefiting from its new-found Scuderia Italia-related status!

It was also a numerically larger organisation at the circuits, strengthened by the recruitment of Michele Alboreto's race engineer, Alessandro Maiani, and his chief mechanic from the previous year. But it took time for the two factions to integrate, for them to become accustomed to their different methods of working.

It was wise, perhaps, not to have designed a new car for 1994, but to leave that until 1995. Therefore the team stuck with the M193 monocoque using revised aerodynamics and the same Ford Cosworth HB power units. However, designer Aldo Costa did explore two new routes, designing a semi-automatic gearbox and a new hydraulic suspension system.

The former came on stream during the year and gave little trouble. The latter, however, was a new departure which would require a great deal of testing before it was fully understood. The team was able to test more than it had done the previous year, but perhaps not sufficiently to understand the new suspension, so towards

MINARDI M194-FORD

Sponsors: Beta, Bee Company, Cocif, AGIP, Lucchini, Valleverde, Mercatone Uno

Designers: Aldo Costa, Mauro Gennari, René Hilhorst **Team Principals:** Giancarlo Minardi, Paolo Stanzani **Team Manager:** Giancarlo Minardi **Chief Mechanic:** Gianluca Gradassi

ENGINE **Type:** Ford Cosworth HB **No. of cylinders/vee angle:** V8 (75°) **Sparking plugs:** Magneti Marelli **Electronics:** Magneti Marelli **Fuel:** AGIP **Oil:** AGIP

TRANSMISSION **Gearbox:** Minardi six-speed transverse semi-automatic **Driveshafts:** Minardi **Clutch:** AP

CHASSIS **Front suspension:** wishbone, pushrod, spring/damper **Rear suspension:** wishbone, pushrod, spring/damper **Suspension dampers:** Minardi Idrosystem **Wheel diameter:** front: 13 in. rear: 13 in. **Wheel rim widths:** front: 11 in. rear: 13.7 in. **Tyres:** Goodyear **Brake pads:** Carbone Industrie **Brake discs:** Carbone Industrie **Brake calipers:** Brembo **Steering:** Minardi **Radiators:** Secan **Fuel tanks:** ATL **Battery:** Yuasa **Instruments:** Magneti Marelli

DIMENSIONS **Wheelbase:** 113.3 in./2880 mm **Track:** front: 66.0 in./1678 mm rear: 62.9 in./1600 mm **Formula weight:** 1135.3 lb/515 kg **Fuel capacity:** 43.9 gallons/200 litres

FORMULA 1 REVIEW

Left: Minardi celebrated its 150th Grand Prix start at Spa. The first win seems a long way off. *Left to right:* Paolo Stanzani, Giancarlo Minardi, Beppe Lucchini, Pierluigi Martini and Michele Alboreto.

Piero in action at Imola, the team's home track *(below).* The ban on electronic driver aids was expected to benefit Minardi, which had never embraced the new technology, but after the mid-season rule changes the gap to the front-runners was as big as ever.

Bottom: A hydraulic suspension system developed by designer Aldo Costa (leaning on car) proved to be a blind alley; after a bright start to the year, Michele Alboreto (in cockpit) also ran into a cul-de-sac.

the end of the season it was shelved and the cars returned to the conventional layout. The rule changes did not help the suspension's development and aerodynamic considerations became more of a priority.

Scuderia Italia Minardi's driver pairing was the most experienced in the entire field. As the 1994 entry began to take shape, there was a severe lack of Italians, and while the team comprised French, British and Argentinian staff it also wanted to emphasise its Italian roots. It signed Pierluigi Martini for a seventh year, while Michele Alboreto arrived with Scuderia Italia. Few other teams kept their driver line-up unchanged and none would come close to the combined total of 300 Grands Prix that the pair had accumulated by the year's end.

The season started off well, with Martini climbing up the grid in the first four races to start ninth at Monaco, only to collide with Morbidelli's Footwork at the first corner. But it was there that Alboreto scored the team's first point of the year. In spite of the rule changes, Martini scored another two points in Spain, but that progress up the grid order had been halted. From then on, he would usually qualify in the second half of the grid, among the very competitive midfield bunch, with Alboreto normally a couple of places further back. But points-winning opportunities became progressively rarer.

Alboreto would freely admit that their expectations had been higher, but the rule changes had hit them hard – partly due to the restricted budget, but also because of the lack of a wind tunnel, which meant having to wait until a facility became available to develop aerodynamics to the new rules. The cars did, however, prove quick in a straight line.

Having said that, the team's worst qualifying effort was at Hockenheim, where the Series 7 and 8 Cosworth engines seemed to suffer on the long straights, and the elimination of both cars in startline accidents made it the worst race of the year. Martini retired due to incidents on five occasions, while Alboreto suffered four engine-related retirements as well as three incidents in the first part of the season.

The best, as they say, is yet to come from Scuderia Italia Minardi, if the team is to be believed. Valuable championship points were won and the team certainly gained some stability. Growth and progress had been initiated. Proof of its effectiveness will now be needed in the seasons ahead.

Bob Constanduros

25 LIGIER 26

ERIC BERNARD

OLIVIER PANIS

JOHNNY HERBERT

There is something fundamentally good about Ligier. Any team which can survive three management changes in a year and still finish virtually every race has to have something right, deep down.

There are two strands to this story. One is how Ligier's ownership and management has changed. The other is how, in the face of all this, nothing else has really changed. At the grass roots, the people who actually keep the team racing successfully – the mechanics – did just that, and with great credit.

The year started with everything on hold, including alleged owner Cyril de Rouvre, who was in jail for financial irregularities. All sponsorship monies were frozen, and there was just sufficient to pay the workforce. The situation remained unresolved for the first three Grands Prix; Eric Bernard was signed for the season while F3000 champion Olivier Panis was hired on a race-by-race basis.

However, there had already been destabilising rumours that Benetton boss Flavio Briatore wanted to buy the team and move it to England. The workforce walked out when they heard that story, and Briatore corrected himself. It was rumoured that, in any case, he only wanted the team's Renault engine supply contract for Benetton.

Briatore finally acquired the team just prior to the Monaco Grand Prix, using money borrowed from Bernie Ecclestone. He lost no time in signing Panis on a long-term deal, then sent in a 'rescue package' from Tom Walkinshaw Racing's USA operation. Tony Dowe, who had previously run TWR's IMSA Jaguar sports car programme, and Ian Reed were drafted in in an attempt to prevent Ligier's free-fall down the grid. The test programme was resuscitated and some R&D work carried out.

The French Grand Prix marked the managerial turning point, even if it was Ligier's worst race of the season on the track. Long-serving team manager Dany Hindenoch departed. So too did Gérard Ducarouge, on extended leave.

Frank Dernie returned from Benetton as Technical Director and former Ferrari team manager Cesare Fiorio – a pal of Briatore's – was appointed Sporting Director, prompting the popular Dowe's departure. Reed went too. Commercial and press relations were reopened with the appointment of Richard Grundy. Ligier was back on the road and Briatore made one of his three visits of the summer. He returned after the announcement that Benetton would use Renault power in 1995 to reassure the Ligier team that it would also have competitive power units.

To put it bluntly, that was the unstable side to the year. Thankfully, the equipment with which the team worked was somewhat more consistent. In fact, Dernie returned to find much the same chassis that he had designed back in 1991 and several other familiar features. Admittedly John Davis, who had been with the team almost throughout this period, had worked on some new components, but otherwise Ducarouge's engineering efforts had centred on buying odd bits and pieces from Williams. The car used Williams's gearbox, rear suspension and front wing and Renault's powerful RS6 engine ensured superiority over the Ford HB-powered competition.

Dernie concentrated on running the car in a better, more disciplined manner. A Benetton-style rear wing was developed, while the team scoured the stores for some 1992 low-downforce wings to run at Monza, which worked well. However, the unstable aerodynamics of the JS39B resulted in excessive wear to the stepped-undertray 'plank' and, after a couple of warnings, Panis was disqualified from the Portuguese GP.

'We raised the car 6 mm between qualifying and the race,' said Dernie after one event, 'and it had no effect on wear. The rate was still the same. When lowered, the car will touch the ground more, but if you raise it too far, the aerodynamics become unstable and [the airflow] will attach and detach. We don't really know at the

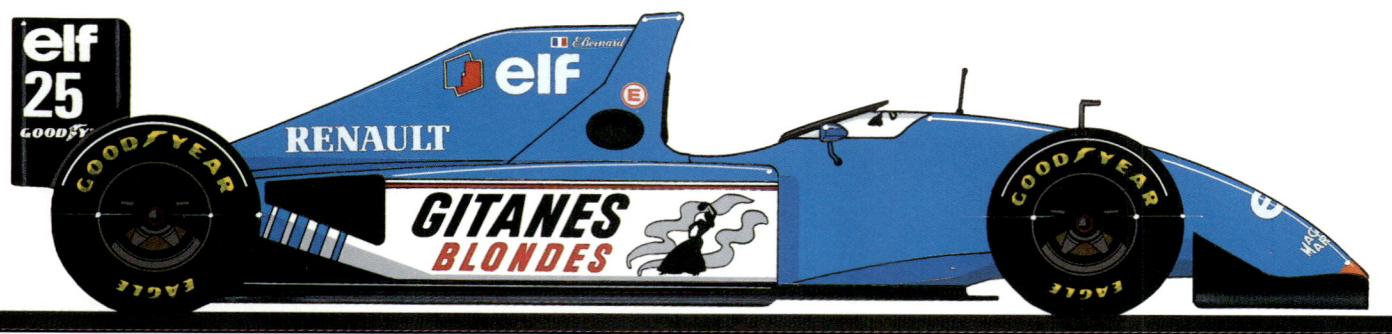

LIGIER JS39B-RENAULT

Sponsors: Gitanes Blondes, Elf, Loto Sportif

Technical Director: Frank Dernie **Sporting Director:** Cesare Fiorio **Chief Mechanic:** Robert Dassaud

ENGINE **Type:** Renault RS6/RS6A/RS6C **No. of cylinders/vee angle:** V10 (67°) **Sparking plugs:** Champion **Electronics:** Magneti Marelli **Fuel:** Elf **Oil:** Elf

TRANSMISSION **Gearbox:** Williams six-speed transverse semi-automatic **Driveshafts:** Ligier **Clutch:** AP

CHASSIS **Front suspension:** double wishbone, pushrod, inboard coil spring/damper **Rear suspension:** double wishbone, pushrod, inboard coil spring/damper **Suspension dampers:** Penske **Wheel diameter:** front: 13 in. rear: 13 in. **Wheel rim widths:** front: 11.5 in. rear: 13.7 in. **Tyres:** Goodyear **Brake pads:** Carbone Industrie **Brake discs:** Carbone Industrie **Brake calipers:** Brembo **Steering:** Ligier **Radiators:** Secan **Fuel tanks:** ATL **Instruments:** Magneti Marelli

DIMENSIONS **Wheelbase:** 115.5 in./2935 mm **Track:** front: 66.6 in./1693 mm rear: 63.3 in./1608 mm **Formula weight:** 1135.3 lb/515 kg **Fuel capacity:** 48.3 gallons/220 litres

FORMULA 1 REVIEW

FRANCK LAGORCE

Au revoir? Hugely experienced engineer Gérard Ducarouge *(right)* and loyal team manager Dany Hindenoch *(far right)* were both casualties of Ligier's mid-season acquisition by Benetton boss Flavio Briatore.

Below: Frank Dernie *(left)* returned to the team as Technical Director in time for the British Grand Prix, while former Ferrari chief Cesare Fiorio was installed as Sporting Director before the Geman GP.

Returning to F1 after a two-year absence, Eric Bernard *(bottom)* was outshone by newcomer Olivier Panis and eventually dropped from the team.

beginning of a race whether it will wear or not, and we don't really have enough time to sort it out in practice.'

Apart from that, the ageing machine was somewhat heavy and tended to suffer from power understeer. Modifications were made to give better downforce at high ride heights – another problem after the rule changes – which improved traction enormously.

In spite of management changes, the Ligier staff remained fairly loyal, its workforce of 140 being slimmed down to 107, but then anyone who has put down roots in the Magny-Cours area has little option but to stay. Sadly, some of the good – but rootless – foreigners did depart.

No doubt familiarity with the machinery helped the mechanics, led by Robert Dassaud, to field perhaps the most reliable cars in the pit lane. A gear selection problem at Magny-Cours caused the team's only retirement due to mechanical trouble in 32 starts, a quite incredible record. Panis retired just once, due to a collision with Morbidelli only a stone's throw from the team's factory, and Bernard had a couple of incidents before he was replaced by Johnny Herbert for Jerez.

Herbert's promotion to Benetton saw newly recruited test driver Franck Lagorce, a Formula 3000 front-runner, join Panis for the last two races of the season. His spin at Suzuka, where he was hit by Martini's Minardi, was only the fifth Ligier retirement of the year!

Panis made a remarkable debut in F1. He qualified ahead of Bernard ten times to three and finished ahead of him nine times to one. It was just reward for the mechanics that the pair should pick up the pieces at the crash-strewn German GP and take second and third places on the rostrum.

While Panis was certainly impressive – except at Monza, where he made several mistakes – Bernard was by no means totally overshadowed. Four times he qualified only one place behind Panis and eight times he finished one place behind the newcomer. His worst race was at Spa, where he spun on the parade lap and stalled during a pit stop, his best at Monza, where he raced from 22nd on the opening lap to seventh at the end.

He perhaps didn't deserve to be replaced by Herbert, but the opportunity was too good to miss. It was another example of Ligier's rather unclear place in the Benetton team management's plans. Were they the reserve team or the dustbin? Either way, it seemed like a potential case of out of the frying pan and into the fire for the men from Magny-Cours.

Bob Constanduros

27 FERRARI 28

JEAN ALESI

GERHARD BERGER

NICOLA LARINI

For the 1994 season, Ferrari Chief Designer John Barnard decided to have a totally fresh look at Grand Prix car design within the tight parameters defined by the current F1 regulations. The result was unquestionably a distinctive, some would say elegant-looking machine. But Barnard was very candid when he discussed its prospects with Luca di Montezemolo and Fiat patriarch Gianni Agnelli. He told them he expected the 412T1 to come on strong in the second half of the 1994 season, leading on to a car which could be a regular winner in 1995, followed by a car which would have a strong chance of winning the World Championship in 1996.

Barnard's design retained the Benetton-style high nose and wing supports, although these were perhaps the most conventional aspects of the 412T1 aerodynamic package. This raised nose meant that the pick-up points for the lower front wishbones were mounted outside the chassis while Barnard adopted a uni-ball type joint where the top wishbones picked up against the outer wall of the monocoque, as an alternative to the original 'flexures' that were used from the start of the season in which the only flexibility at this point was in the joint itself. Inconclusive driver input on this subject tended to blur the benefits of the original concept to the point where one car was running with the uni-ball system and one with the flexures.

The flexures were intended to give added ride stiffness allied to a reduction in operating friction. The side pods began to flare outwards from the side of the monocoque at the point where the under-car aerodynamic 'splitter' started. There was a removable secondary panel on the outside of the pod for added cooling. Suspension at the front was by means of pushrod-activated spring/damper units, with torsion bars the preferred springing medium at the rear.

The tail-end treatment of the car retained Barnard's distinctive 'Coke bottle' flared-in treatment, first pioneered on the flat-bottomed McLaren MP4/1C as long ago as 1983. However, he expended a great deal of time shaping the semi-circular rear underbody diffuser panel, below which were included six vertical 'splitters' which controlled the lateral pressure gradient beneath the rear of the car.

The Ferrari 412T1 began the season equipped with an uprated version of the 65-degree type 041 V12 engine, initially developing around 775 bhp at 15,300 rpm. Towards the end of last year, this unit gained some additional weight when the team equipped it with a seven-bearing crankshaft and it proved consistently frail when revved regularly over the 15,000 rpm mark.

However, this problem seemed to have been largely corrected and the new 75-degree V12 type 043, developing a maximum of around 820 bhp at 15,800 rpm, on which the engine department under the leadership of Claudio Lombardi had been working for more than a year, won on its race debut at Hockenheim. It was hoped that new rules permitting in-race refuelling would tilt the odds in favour of Ferrari's thirsty V12s, but in most cases it only narrowed the engine's performance deficit, never quite eliminating it completely.

Barnard opted for a fabricated chrome-molybdenum casing for the transverse six-speed, semi-automatic gearbox, this enabling him to produce a lighter, stiffer structure than would have been available using a casting. From the French Grand Prix onwards, additional weight was saved by the introduction of a titanium gearbox casing as part of the car's 'B' version revamp in response to the technical rule changes which had been introduced at Barcelona.

Ferrari's season was not without its problems. During free practice for the Pacific Grand Prix at TI Circuit, Larini's 412T1 used a variable rev-limiter which was definitely frowned upon by the FIA. Team Director Jean Todt is absolutely adamant that he discussed the matter with FIA Technical Delegate Charlie Whiting, and although the system

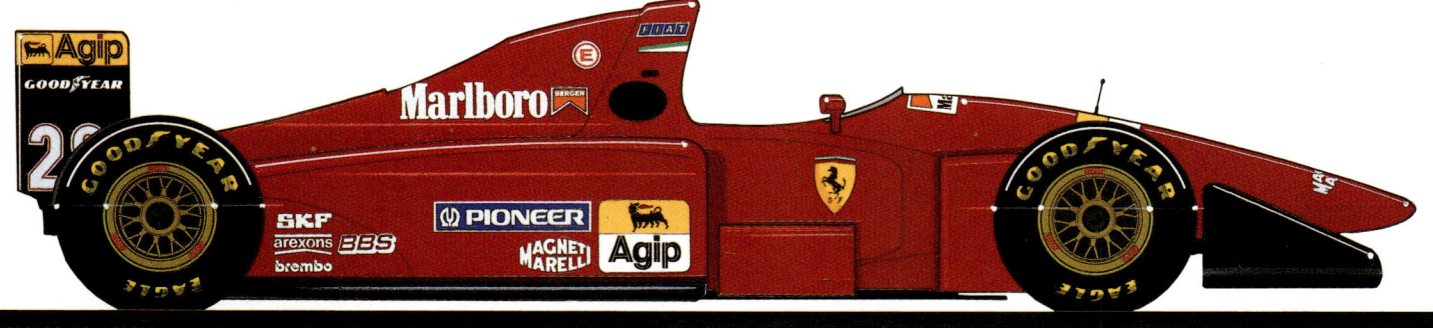

FERRARI 412T1

Sponsors: Marlboro, AGIP, Pioneer

Designer: John Barnard **Team Principal:** Luca di Montezemolo **Team Manager:** Jean Todt **Chief Mechanic:** Nigel Stepney

ENGINE Type: Ferrari 041/043 **No. of cylinders/vee angle:** V12 (65°/75°) **Sparking plugs:** Champion **Electronics:** Magneti Marelli **Fuel:** AGIP **Oil:** AGIP

TRANSMISSION Gearbox: Ferrari six-speed transverse semi-automatic **Driveshafts:** Ferrari **Clutch:** AP

CHASSIS Front suspension: double wishbone, pushrod, separate springs/dampers **Rear suspension:** double wishbone, pushrod, torsion bars, linear dampers **Suspension dampers:** Ferrari **Wheel diameter:** front: 13 in. rear: 13 in. **Wheel rim widths:** front: 11 in. rear: 15 in. **Tyres:** Goodyear **Brake pads:** Hitco or Carbone Industrie **Brake discs:** Hitco or Carbone Industrie **Brake calipers:** Brembo **Steering:** Ferrari **Radiators:** Secan **Fuel tanks:** ATL **Battery:** Magneti Marelli **Instruments:** Magneti Marelli

DIMENSIONS Wheelbase: 116.9 in./2970 mm **Track:** maximum permissible **Formula weight:** 1135.3 lb/515 kg **Fuel capacity:** 46.1 gallons/210 litres

FORMULA 1 REVIEW

Co-ordinating the efforts of team manager Claudio Berri, Chief Designer John Barnard, engine chief Claudio Lombardi *(left to right)* and their departments, Team Director Jean Todt *(below)* has brought a degree of order and purpose to Maranello, which for too long has relied on inspiration and passion alone. In its initial guise, Barnard's 412T1 recorded a number of podium finishes, including Nicola Larini's second place at Imola *(below right)*, but no more. A mid-season aerodynamic revamp undertaken by Gustav Brunner *(bottom)* robbed the car of its distinctive looks but, once united with Lombardi's new 043 V12 engine, the 412T1B was a pacesetter, on fast tracks at least, allowing Jean Alesi to lead the Italian GP at Monza *(bottom right)* in style.

was taken off the cars at Whiting's request, after much consideration it was decided that it did not represent a traction control system – an accessory which was, of course, banned – within the terms of the 1994 technical regulations.

The 412T1 suffered from low-speed understeer in the early races, but this state of affairs was progressively rectified by mid-season. Barnard's original concept was significantly revised in response to the rule changes in time for the French Grand Prix, when heavily modified aerodynamics were incorporated. Shortened side pods and elaborate 'barge boards' were intended to counter major cooling problems experienced since the introduction of new technical rules for the Spanish Grand Prix.

The need to shorten the front wing end plates, and raise the wing itself, had obliged Ferrari to run increased nose wing flap angles, reducing the flow to radiators already marginal on cooling. From the start of the season there had in any case been a problem balancing the pressure drop between the left- and right-hand radiators, which was finally nailed at Magny-Cours with the incorporation of new radiators, but this problem did not fully reveal itself until development work was being carried

FORMULA 1 REVIEW

Gerhard Berger emerged from a testing year with enormous credit, finishing the season on a high note with a battling second place in Adelaide *(left)*.

The Maranello engine department has benefited from the undoubted expertise of former Honda engineer Osamu Goto *(below left)*. The Ferrari V12 *(bottom)* produced plenty of top-end power, but that alone is no longer sufficient to guarantee success.

Right: Jean Alesi drove with his usual unflagging enthusiasm, but by the end of the campaign there were signs that frustration was getting the better of him. After five full seasons in Formula 1, the Frenchman still awaits his first win.

out on the short side pods. Had this imbalance between the radiators been discovered earlier, more performance might possibly have been unlocked from the original 412T1 specification.

In general terms, the Ferrari 412T1B, particularly when fitted with the latest 75-degree V12 from Hockenheim onwards, was a competitive, good-handling proposition on all but the tightest of circuits. But it lacked the mechanical reliability required from a serious World Championship challenger, despite input on the engine side from former Honda engineer Osamu Goto, possibly reminding everybody at Maranello that a V12 with lots of top-end power is perhaps no longer the technical route to pursue.

For Gerhard Berger it was a particularly difficult season, for the Austrian was probably Ayrton Senna's closest personal friend among the ranks of the F1 drivers and the events at Imola hit him especially hard. When the San Marino GP was red-flagged to a halt, he was shaken to find that his car had run over debris from Senna's wrecked Williams and that one of its front suspension members was literally hanging on by a thread.

Even so, he took the restart with gusto to lead Schumacher briefly, but eventually became unnerved by a handling imbalance and came into the pits. Team Director Jean Todt wisely agreed that it was best that he retire, appreciating that his driver had not really got his mind on the job. Later, a faulty rear shock absorber would be diagnosed as the reason behind the handling imbalance.

Berger toyed with retirement for a week or so thereafter, confessing that much of his motivation had been sapped by Senna's death. But he eventually decided to continue and, once set on that choice, displayed an unwavering commitment throughout the balance of the season. He had also developed into an adept and conscientious test driver, much to Barnard's satisfaction, and in this respect was displaying the legacy of three years as Senna's team-mate in the McLaren squad.

By contrast, Alesi seemed more emotional, and distinctly less focused, when it came to development work, and it was Berger who contributed the most to the overall Ferrari equation in this respect. The Frenchman missed two races after injuring his back in a testing accident at Mugello the week immediately following the Brazilian GP, and from his return to the cockpit at Monaco very little went right for him. During his absence, test driver Nicola Larini stepped into the breach and performed with unobtrusive efficiency, finishing a well-judged second to Schumacher in the San Marino GP.

After a succession of patchy performances, Alesi was devastated to suffer engine failure on the opening lap at Hockenheim, but felt his moment had come at Monza, where he qualified on pole position and led through to his first refuelling stop. As he made to rejoin the race, it seems that Alesi pulled the steering wheel 'paddle' to call up first gear a millisecond before fully depressing the foot clutch, with the engine already screaming at 15,000 rpm.

In a split-second, this machined the dogrings off first gear, so he called for second with the same dire mechanical consequences. He then flounced away from the circuit in a fury, leaving Berger to finish second to Damon Hill's Williams after one of the most outstanding drives of the season, the Austrian having taken over the spare car following a big accident during the race morning warm-up.

Taken as a whole, it was only a moderately promising season for Ferrari. But with Barnard's latest 'small tank' challenger poised to take even greater advantage of the refuelling regulations in 1995, the pressure will be on the team to deliver like never before. It is, after all, fifteen years since Jody Scheckter became the last driver to win the World Championship at the wheel of a Ferrari – and eleven since Maranello last took the constructors' title.

Alan Henry

29 SAUBER
30

KARL WENDLINGER — **HEINZ-HARALD FRENTZEN** — **ANDREA DE CESARIS**

Irrespective of the merits of its on-track performance, in retrospect, Sauber's biggest problems in 1994 were financial and commercial. Planned sponsorship from *Broker* magazine failed to materialise, leaving the Hinwil-based team with an estimated operating shortfall of £6.5 million. This sum had to be underwritten by Mercedes-Benz in order to carry the Stuttgart company's nominated F1 team through to the end of the season. It was not a state of affairs which amused the German car maker in the slightest.

The financial safety net was set up through MB's board level connections with SHM, the Swiss corporation which owns Tissot and Omega, through their joint involvement in the Swatch electric car programme. The end result was the Tissot/Watches of Switzerland identification carried by the Saubers throughout the second half of the season.

The year had started with Chief Designer Leo Ress producing an evolutionary version of the 1993 car, the new machine dubbed C13 and built round a monocoque manufactured by the UK-based carbon-fibre specialist company operated by former British F3 entrant Dave Price.

The new car was originally designed to accept a 225-litre fuel cell before refuelling regulations were finally confirmed for 1994. By the time those rules were implemented, there was insufficient time to revise the design, although the actual capacity of the cell was subsequently reduced to 220 litres before the start of the season.

Sauber never made the switch to active suspension in 1993, so most of their winter testing efforts were concentrated on refining the passive set-up used throughout last year, as well as trying out a wide range of geometry variations. Other alterations included a Benetton-style high nose, slightly taller water radiators and an airbox raised by 20 mm to accommodate the very tall Karl Wendlinger in the cockpit.

A large proportion of the wind tunnel development was carried out at the Swiss aerospace facility at Emmen, where a great deal of detailed attention was focused on developing a better rear diffuser. Ress confidently asserted at the start of the season that the C13 profile developed around 10 per cent more downforce than its predecessor, with no additional drag.

The team started the campaign using the Ilmor-built 2175B V10 engine which had first been introduced with Sauber badging at Monza in 1993, but now officially carrying the Mercedes-Benz name. Although not outwardly significantly different from its immediate predecessor, the lower-spec 2175A, which continued to be made available to the Pacific team, the 'B' version was a larger-bore, shorter-stroke version of the engine which laid claim to being the smallest, lightest and most compact of the current breed of F1 powerplant, irrespective of cylinder configuration.

The team started the year with Wendlinger now partnered by the dynamic young German Heinz-Harald Frentzen, whom many rate even more highly than Schumacher. As if to prove his potential, Frentzen qualified fifth for his maiden GP outing in Brazil, but spun off during the race, while Wendlinger managed a strong fourth place in the tragic San Marino GP at Imola.

Two weeks later, the popular Austrian driver sustained serious head injuries in an apparently inconsequential practice accident at Monaco. He would remain in a medically induced coma for almost three weeks, thereafter thankfully making a steady recovery to the point where he was fit enough to visit the Italian Grand Prix at Monza in early September. Peter Sauber remained adamant that Karl's place in the team would remain open, but in the meantime Andrea de Cesaris was recruited to stand in for the Austrian. Remarkably, Wendlinger was sufficiently recovered to test for the team prior to the Japanese Grand Prix, although he elected not to race.

A pneumatic-valve version of the Mercedes V10 first appeared in prac-

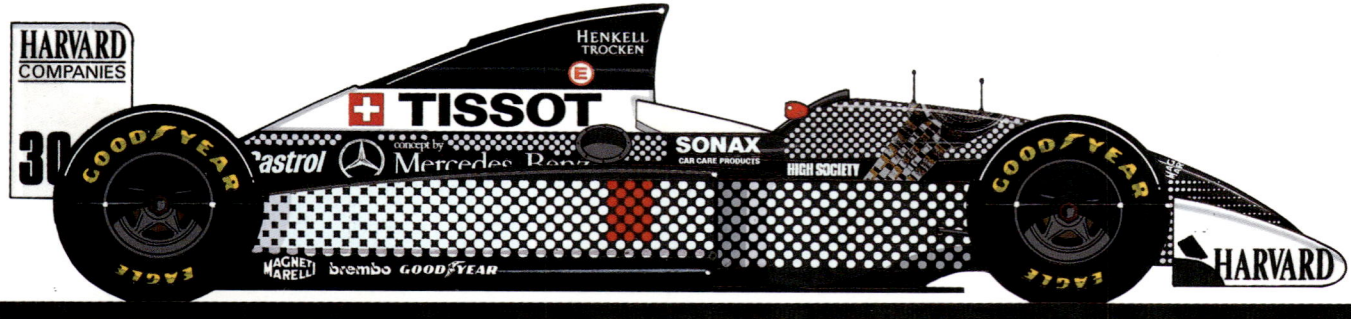

SAUBER C13-MERCEDES-BENZ

Sponsors: Tissot, Harvard, Castrol, Henkell, Sonax

Designer: Leo Ress **Team Principal:** Peter Sauber **Team Manager/Chief Mechanic:** Beat Zehnder

ENGINE **Type:** Mercedes-Benz 2175B **No. of cylinders/vee angle:** V10 (72°) **Sparking plugs:** NGK **Electronics:** Magneti Marelli **Fuel:** Elf **Oil:** Castrol

TRANSMISSION **Gearbox:** Sauber six-speed longitudinal semi-automatic **Driveshafts:** MAT **Clutch:** Sachs

CHASSIS **Front suspension:** double wishbone, pushrod, inboard coil spring/damper **Rear suspension:** double wishbone, pushrod, inboard coil spring/damper **Suspension dampers:** API **Wheel diameter:** front: 13 in. rear: 13 in. **Wheel rim widths:** front: 11.5 in. rear: 13.7 in. **Tyres:** Goodyear **Brake pads:** SEP/Hitco **Brake discs:** SEP/Hitco **Brake calipers:** Brembo **Steering:** Sauber **Radiators:** Behr **Fuel tanks:** ATL **Battery:** Ilmor **Instruments:** Magneti Marelli

DIMENSIONS **Wheelbase:** 115.3 in./2930 mm **Track:** front: 66.9 in./1700 mm rear: 63.3 in./1610 mm **Formula weight:** 1135.3 lb/515 kg **Fuel capacity:** 45.0 gallons/205 litres

J.J. LEHTO

FORMULA 1 REVIEW

tice at Imola, where air pressure leakages resulted in its being shelved for the race. It was first raced in Canada and a more powerful, uprated version made its debut at Spa, where Frentzen ran competitively for 16 laps before spinning over the Eau Rouge kerb. Two major piston failures followed on both cars at Monza, causing the team to revert to the earlier-spec pneumatic-valve engine for the last two European races.

In terms of chassis development, the post-Monaco rule changes hit Sauber particularly hard simply because they lacked the necessary experience to respond quickly enough. Things took a definite step forward at Hockenheim, where revised front suspension geometry was fitted, and at Spa, where new rear suspension and an uprated differential were employed. But by then the writing was on the wall and Sauber's days as MB's prime runners were numbered.

Before the Japanese Grand Prix, the new McLaren-Mercedes partnership was announced, leaving Sauber to negotiate an engine supply deal for 1995 with Ford.

Alan Henry

Now openly bearing allegiance to Mercedes-Benz, the Ilmor-built 2175B V10 *(top)* was impressively compact but had some way to go to match the power and reliability of the standard-setting Renault engine.

Sauber's technical staff, led by long-serving Chief Designer Leo Ress *(above left)* and former Renault and Peugeot engineer André de Cortanze *(above centre)*, have been handicapped by the financial difficulties facing the team, and the succession of rule changes introduced since the Swiss constructor's graduation to Formula 1 have always left it one step behind.

The termination of its special relationship with Mercedes-Benz is a serious blow to the Hinwil team, but Peter Sauber *(above)* lost no time in negotiating a deal with Ford for the supply of works engines in 1995.

Heinz-Harald Frentzen showed great promise in his maiden season of Grand Prix racing, qualifying in fifth place for his first Grand Prix and scoring points in his second, at Aida *(left)*.

85

31 SIMTEK
32

DAVID BRABHAM

4 July 1962 – 30 April 1994
ROLAND RATZENBERGER

ANDREA MONTERMINI

Nick Wirth took on an enormous challenge when he embarked on his Simtek F1 programme at the start of the 1994 season, for although he and his company, Simtek Research, had a great deal of experience in motor racing engineering terms, this was the first time they had actually competed in any category.

With some financial support from former triple World Champion Jack Brabham, which secured one of the seats in the team for his youngest son David, and Konrad Schmidt's SMS Motorsport organisation, the Simtek took shape as a relatively straightforward car using Series 5 'wire valve' versions of the Cosworth HB V8 engine.

The S941 chassis was a distinctively profiled machine distinguished by its high front suspension mounting points, which were intended to provide clean airflow across the side pods. The car was fitted with a six-speed sequential Xtrac gearbox from the start of the season, and although a semi-automatic shift was also developed teething troubles kept it on the back burner.

Popular Austrian driver Roland

SIMTEK S941-FORD

Sponsors: MTV Europe, Barbara MC, Russell Athletic

Designer/Team Principal: Nick Wirth **Team Manager:** Charlie Moody **Chief Mechanic:** Gary North

ENGINE Type: Ford Cosworth HB (Series V) **No. of cylinders/vee angle:** V8 (75°) **Sparking plugs:** Champion **Electronics:** Cosworth **Fuel:** Elf **Oil:** Elf

TRANSMISSION Gearbox: Xtrac six-speed transverse **Driveshafts:** Xtrac **Clutch:** AP

CHASSIS Front suspension: double wishbone, pushrod **Rear suspension:** double wishbone, pushrod **Suspension dampers:** Penske **Wheel diameter:** front: 13 in. rear: 13 in.

Wheel rim widths: front: 11.5 in. rear: 13.7 in. **Tyres:** Goodyear **Brake pads:** Carbone Industrie or Hitco **Brake discs:** Carbone Industrie or Hitco **Brake calipers:** Brembo **Steering:** Jack Knight **Radiators:** Secan **Fuel tanks:** Premier **Battery:** RS **Instruments:** Cranfield/Simtek

DIMENSIONS Wheelbase: 113.3 in./2880 mm **Track:** front: 66.9 in./1700 mm rear: 62.9 in./1600 mm **Formula weight:** 1135.3 lb/515 kg **Fuel capacity:** 46.1 gallons/210 litres

JEAN-MARC GOUNON

MIMMO SCHIATTARELLA

TAKI INOUE

FORMULA 1 REVIEW

Opposite page: The ill-fated Roland Ratzenberger prepares to go out during practice at the San Marino GP. The Austrian's death was a shattering blow to the fledgling Simtek team.

Below: David Brabham leads team-mate Mimmo Schiattarella at Jerez. The Australian's dogged perseverance was a great asset to the F1 novices during a difficult Grand Prix initiation.

In at the deep end. Engineer Nick Wirth *(bottom)* came into Formula 1 without the benefit of any previous competition experience but his team ended the season with its credibility intact.

Ratzenberger, a newcomer to F1, was signed to drive six races for the team. Tragically, he was killed in second qualifying for the San Marino Grand Prix, losing control almost certainly as a result of a slight detour across the grass which damaged his Simtek's nose section on the lap before it flew off at over 170 mph between the Tamburello and Tosa corners at Imola.

This was a frightful loss for the fledgling F1 team, but Brabham's determination proved a welcome tonic as everybody fought to keep up morale. This tragedy was followed by a huge accident that befell Andrea Montermini during practice at Barcelona, but thankfully the Italian driver escaped with superficial injuries. Later in the season Brabham would be fortunate to escape from a violent testing crash at Silverstone, so the structural integrity of the team's cars was certainly not found wanting. Financial considerations meant that the second car was subsequently shared by Jean-Marc Gounon, former Italian F3 exponent Domenico Schiattarella and Japanese novice Taki Inoue. Quite how the last two gentlemen managed to satisfy the FIA that they qualified for F1 superlicences is a question which remains in the realms of speculation.

By the end of the year, it was clear that the Simtek S941 was slightly on the heavy side and, although it handled quite well, Brabham was never able to pull up beyond the edge of the top ten in the races, while qualifying usually saw the cars lining up on the last two rows of the grid. The best result was Gounon's ninth place in the French GP.

For 1995, Simtek is hoping to secure a more competitive engine package in the form of an air-valve Ford HB V8. Overall, Nick Wirth feels the team has learned enough during its maiden season to make a decisive step forward in 1995.

Alan Henry

33 PACIFIC 34

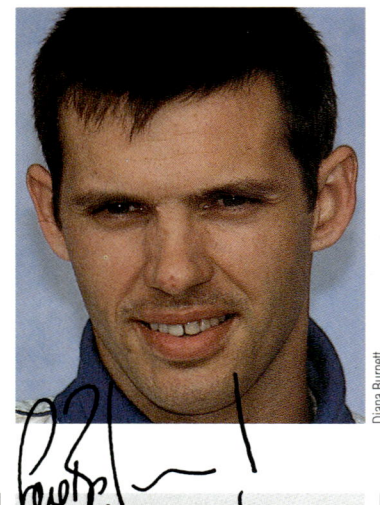

PAUL BELMONDO

BERTRAND GACHOT

During the second half of the season, chief mechanic Jerry Bond *(below far left)* and his men faced the thankless task of preparing the cars in the knowledge that there was little prospect of them qualifying for the race.

Below left: Pacific owner Keith Wiggins has enjoyed success in every other category he has tackled, but appeared to have underestimated the challenge presented by Formula 1.

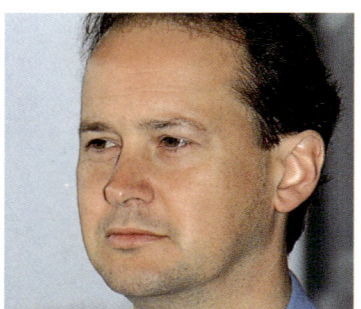

Keith Wiggins's Thetford-based Pacific team had originally intended to enter F1 at the start of 1993, having made a name for itself in both F3 and F3000 over the previous few years. However, the necessary sponsorship could not be raised in time, so Wiggins decided to defer his graduation until this season.

This tiny operation – 18 strong at the start of the year – relied on a Reynard-built chassis which had previously been intended to form the basis of that company's own F1 challenge back in 1991. Designed originally by Rory Byrne and Pat Symonds before their return to Benetton, the design was substantially unchanged when Pacific took over the project for this season, equipping the new PR01 with Ilmor 2175A V10 engines which were maintained under a sub-contractor arrangement by Swiss preparation expert Heini Mader. Ian Dawson, who had joined Pacific from Reynard at the end of 1992 to oversee the F3000 programme and directed the transfer of the F1 project from Reynard, has been team manager throughout.

Bertrand Gachot and Paul Belmondo were signed to drive, but this was very much a learning year and the cars seldom qualified. Even before the season began a whole host of problems surrounding the fitment of minor components had to be addressed, and by Imola the team was beginning to have its suspicions that the stiffness of the chassis left a lot to be desired.

Torsion tests were duly carried out by Reynard, which identified that the back end of the car, behind the rearward cockpit bulkhead, was unacceptably soft. As a result, revised engine mountings were incorporated and a stiffer gearbox casing was also commissioned, both to minimise this problem and alleviate repeated transmission bearing problems.

However, the PR01 was still not performing properly and Wiggins invested in the team's own torsion testing equipment which was installed at the factory by mid-June. This revealed that the additional engine supports which had been incorporated were contributing nothing to the cars' overall rigidity, so more work had to be done before the end of the season. In 32 attempts, Pacific qualified on only seven occasions and scored not a single finish.

As far as engines were concerned, the Pacific struggled for speed with its customer Ilmor V10s, and even when Mader arrived with revised-specification units for Monza, promising an extra 500 rpm, it didn't translate into a measurable performance improvement. In the closing stages of the year new wings, revised side pods, undertray and diffuser were all in the development pipeline, but a totally new car is being prepared for 1995.

The team admits it is lucky to have the finance to continue, but realises that it must perform next year unless its whole future is to be jeopardised. It is unlikely, however, that Pacific will continue to use Ilmor engines.

Alan Henry

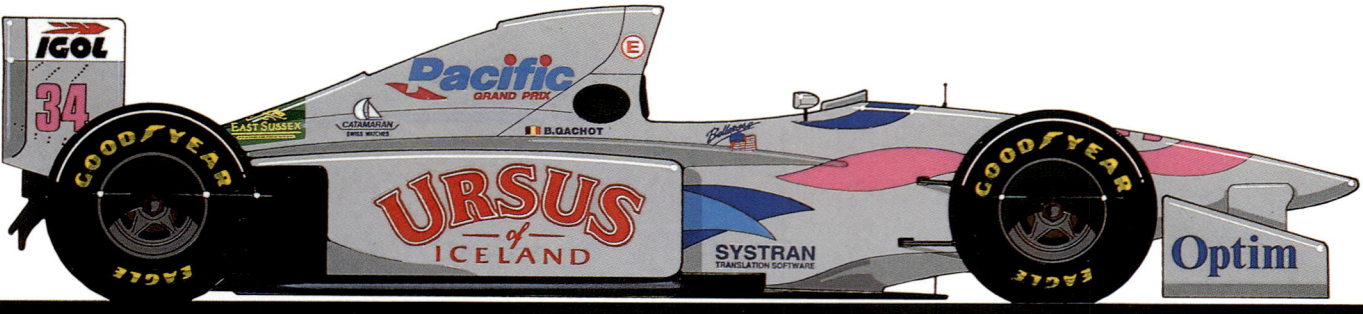

PACIFIC PR01-ILMOR

Sponsors: Ursus, Igol, Catamaran, Belrose, Kenwood, *GQ*

Designer: Reynard Racing Cars **Team Principal:** Keith Wiggins **Team Manager:** Ian Dawson **Chief Mechanic:** Jerry Bond

ENGINE **Type:** Ilmor 2175A **No. of cylinders/vee angle:** V10 (72°) **Sparking plugs:** NGK **Electronics:** PI Research/Zytek **Fuel:** Elf **Oil:** Elf

TRANSMISSION **Gearbox:** Reynard/Hewland six-speed transverse **Driveshafts:** Gemini **Clutch:** AP

CHASSIS **Front suspension:** double wishbone, pullrod, inboard coil spring/damper **Rear suspension:** double wishbone, pullrod, inboard coil spring/damper **Suspension dampers:** Penske **Wheel diameter:** front: 13 in. rear: 13 in. **Wheel rim widths:** front: 11 in. rear: 14 in. **Tyres:** Goodyear **Brake pads:** AP/SEP **Brake discs:** SEP **Brake calipers:** AP **Steering:** Jack Knight **Radiators:** Secan **Fuel tanks:** Premier **Instruments:** PI Research

DIMENSIONS **Wheelbase:** 109 in./2768 mm **Track:** front: 64 in./1625 mm rear: 62 in./1574 mm **Gearbox weight:** 83.7 lb/38 kg **Chassis weight (tub):** 99.2 lb/45 kg **Formula weight:** 1157.4 lb/525 kg **Fuel capacity:** 43.9 gallons/200 litres

AN UNQUALIFIED SUCCESS?

Pacific Grand Prix had something of the 'Dunkirk' spirit throughout the season. There was disappointment immediately following each DNQ, but apart from the initial shock at Aida – the first time in Pacific's ten-year history that its cars had not made a race – the team set about the unenviable task of attempting to qualify the recalcitrant PR01 with remarkable buoyancy.

Never mind the fact that one of the transporters was destroyed by fire on the way back from Imola, that the team frequently had to share a garage, or that the personnel spent 13 hours in a coach driving the 100 km from Suzuka to Osaka, thereby missing their flight to Adelaide. There were the smirks and snide remarks from other teams, and one or two vultures who attempted to prey on the team's sponsors. And there was the Adelaide race organiser who, upon receipt of a telephone call from a sponsor seeking to be put through to the Pacific garage, politely informed the caller that Pacific did not exist and that he would put them through to Simtek . . .

All this contrived to pull staff together and help them become thick skinned.

'Back in January I did an interview in which I said that the car would probably be good for a midfield qualifying position,' admitted team owner Keith Wiggins, 'but as soon as the season started we realised we were in trouble. Goodyear recorded the highest-ever tyre wear on our front tyres in Brazil, while in Aida neither car made the cut and I was totally shocked. We qualified for the next four races but from Magny-Cours to Jerez we weren't in with a chance. I won't say we got used to it, but we learned how to deal with it and decided to get on with finishing '94 and building the programme up for '95.'

With Wiggins and team manager Ian Dawson doubling as race engineers, the team's personnel were nothing if not resourceful. In July former journalist and Jordan press officer Mark Gallagher joined as commercial manager.

'The staggering thing I found was how motivated everyone was,' said Gallagher. 'The only time I ever saw people demoralised was in the half-hour or so after qualifying – particularly in Suzuka and Adelaide, where Bertrand was quick enough to qualify before the rains came – otherwise all the staff, the sponsors and business partners simply regarded the situation as a challenge. On the commercial side the team's biggest asset by far was Bertrand. He worked tirelessly to find the team sponsorship and there is no doubt the team would not have survived were it not for him. As for the sponsors, they recognised the team's longer-term potential based on its track record, and fully understood that with the PR01 we certainly weren't about to take the world by storm.'

Throughout the year the team successfully attracted new backing, pointing out that its string of championship wins in everything from Formula Ford to Formula 3000 shows that Keith Wiggins knows how to win – when the resources are available. As a result both Gachot and team-mate Paul Belmondo remained fiercely loyal to the cause, fully aware of the behind-the-scenes developments.

The team's sense of humour became an important weapon in the fight to survive the potentially devastating impact of not qualifying. Guests were informed that Pacific was the only team operating a policy of asking the drivers to sit alongside the sponsors on a Sunday afternoon to explain what was happening in the race, while the President of Igol, the French oil giant, joked in Magny-Cours that the best thing about Pacific was the fact that the drivers stayed at the Saturday evening party until midnight whereas anyone else he had sponsored had always slunk off to bed at eight.

Making the best of the situation became paramount, but while the black humour was good for the team's collective psyche, beneath lay a mood of quiet determination. Back at base the factory was extended, staff numbers grew to the mid-30s and the 1995 programme began to materialise with Ford customer engines and fresh capital investment coming from a Japanese entrepreneur.

'It wasn't easy, but we came through the season relatively unscathed,' said Wiggins. 'We knew, and our sponsors knew, that we were in the middle of a short-term problem which would just have to be ridden out to the end of the year. Someone has to be first, someone has to be last, and unfortunately it was our turn. Perhaps we were forgiven a little because it was our first year, but then I'd rather have a difficult first year and progress steadily in years two and three than come in with a bang and have nowhere to go but down.'

McLaren International • 1994 FIA Formula 1 World Championship

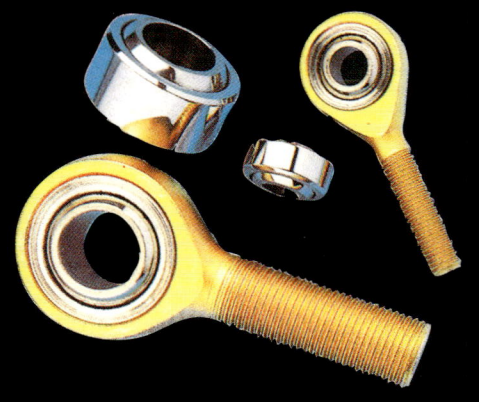

Tomorrow's Technology Winning Today

The suppliers of high quality bearings for high performance cars.

*AMPEP GOLDLINE is a generation of self-lubrication rod end and spherical bearings that have been established to meet the requirements of higher load rate, improved life and maintenance free features demanded by designers and operators of high performance racing cars. To achieve these objectives the bearings have an aerospace pedigree and the designs have been based upon a current state of the art aerospace materials technology applied to configurations and size ranges that have been well established in high performance racing car applications.

*REGISTERED TRADE MARK OF SKF

THE *AMPEP GOLDLINE F1 generation self-lubrication bearing range, has been developed with Goldline bearings Ltd in conjuction with Formula 1 and CART Designers, in order to attain maximum weight savings capabilities. This has been achieved by the use of exotic bearings materials, such as Titanium with very special coatings on the ball and a super finish. This has enabled designers to reduce bearing weight by up to 45% over a conventional joint, with the added benefit of reduced wear rate of the AMPEP X1 liner system and can increase the life by a factor of up to X8 for a .004 inch backlash value over a normal AMPEP Goldline bearing

CONTACT: Mike Jones or Ryan Currier at Stafford Park 17, Telford TF3 3BN England
Tel: 0952 292401 Fax: 0952 292403
24 Hour Delivery Worldwide Export Service

'The best drivers in the world use Shell fuels and lubricants.'

AYRTON SENNA TRIBUTE

BORN TO BE THE

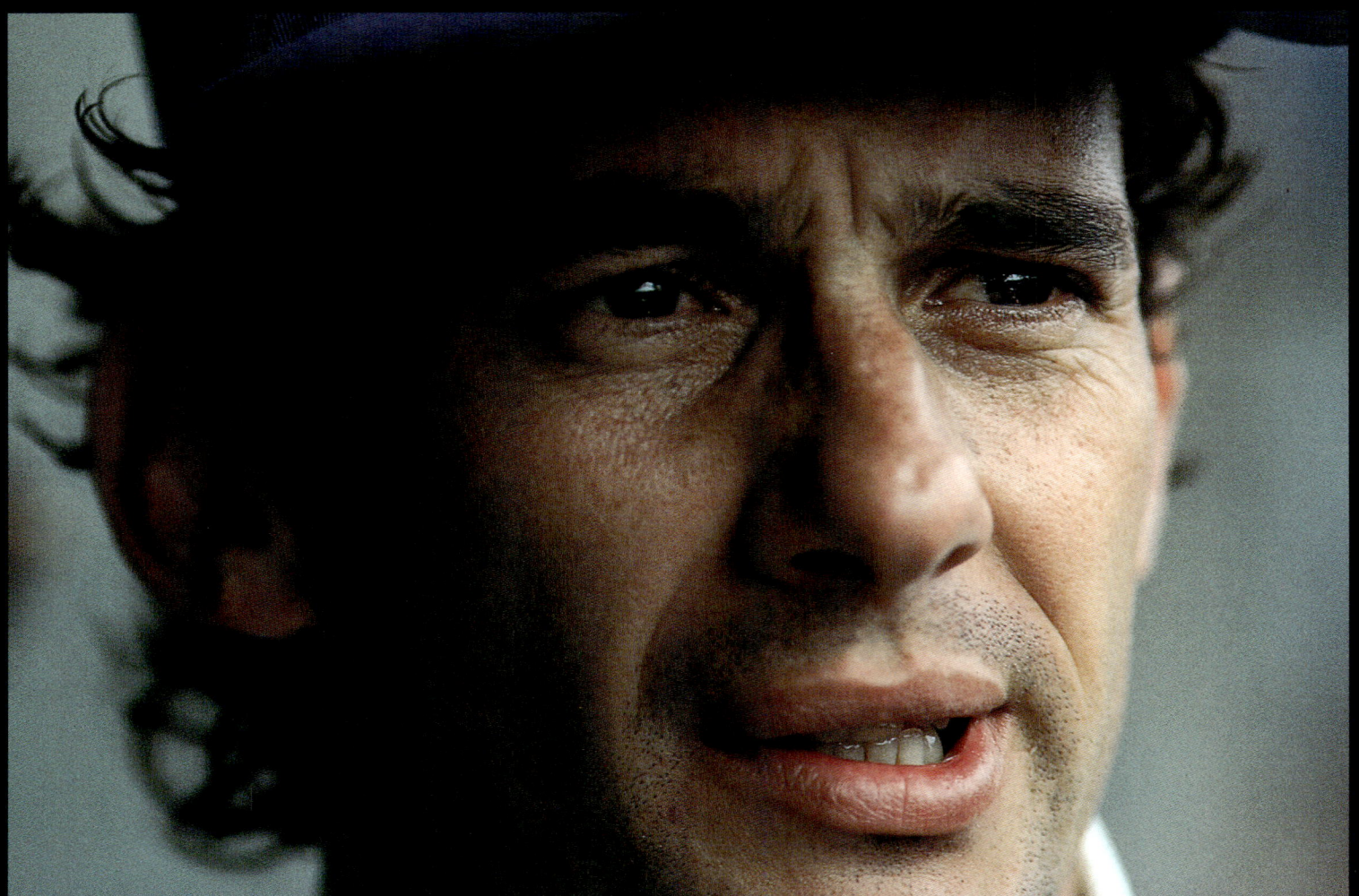

Sunday, 1 May 1994 was the blackest day in motor racing history for a generation. Ayrton Senna's fatal accident while leading the San Marino Grand Prix at Imola not only deprived the sport of one of its greatest-ever exponents, but also left the entire Formula 1 community reeling with shell-shocked disbelief in a manner previously experienced only when the legendary Jim Clark had died in a minor-league F2 race at Hockenheim 26 years before.

Ironically, whereas Clark had always seemed inviolate, a man who appeared to keep something in hand, Senna was a driver who operated on the absolute limit on each and every lap of his career. Winning wasn't enough for this driven, enigmatic genius. He needed to dominate. Not only every race in which he competed, but every qualifying and test session as well. Forty-one race victories – second only to Alain Prost in the all-time winner's list – was a wondrous achievement, but his career tally of 65 pole positions represents a possibly even more compelling indication of what made him tick.

It was Ayrton Senna's absolute refusal to compromise which was probably the single most remarkable facet of his character. When contract negotiation time came round – be it with Lotus, McLaren or Williams – the company's lawyer took a deep breath and braced himself. He knew that he would be required to earn his money like never before as Senna and his advisers went through each individual clause of the proposed agreement in precise and meticulous detail.

He was acutely intelligent, with a calculating mind which could always work out a way of resolving problems to his own best advantage. Yet there was always a defensive quality about his personality – almost as though he expected people to be critical of him before they actually were.

Family values also meant an enormous amount to this complex man – second only, perhaps, to his religious beliefs. Even so, Senna very much kept his emotions to himself. He was not a man who would take you into his confidence and share with you his personal philosophy,

FASTEST

by Alan Henry

either of life or of motor racing. I am also tempted to say that he was not always a model sportsman.

The son of a wealthy Brazilian businessman, Ayrton Senna displayed his single-minded independence almost from the start of his European single-seater racing career. At the end of 1981, he was prepared to abandon his ambitions after a single season of Formula Ford, indignant that commercial reality meant that, despite his successes, he still had to bring sponsorship for 1982. In Ayrton's view, merit should have been enough.

In 1983, McLaren offered to fund Senna's British F3 programme in return for an option on his services. Many youngsters in that position would have jumped at the chance, but Ayrton politely declined. He would raise his own finance, thanks very much, retain his independence – and keep all his options open. It was a disarmingly confident strategy for a 23-year-old to adopt.

Senna graduated to F1 with Toleman in 1984, then switched to Lotus the following year. His first Grand Prix victory came in the pouring rain at Estoril and was followed by five more during his three seasons with the team. But it wasn't until he joined the McLaren-Honda squad at the start of 1988 that Senna began to put an arm-lock on the Grand Prix winner's circle.

Few drivers have ever applied so much mental energy to the business of Formula 1. Ayrton was forever probing, exploring and thinking about every way – any way – in which he could gain an edge. It took him two seasons of psychological warfare to unseat Alain Prost from the team and drive the Frenchman out into the Ferrari camp.

The row which brewed up between Prost and Senna in 1988/89 was, perhaps, inevitable. Prost wanted to protect his position, Senna to undermine it. You could see Alain's point of view, of course. He had been the rock on which most of McLaren's success had been built ever since 1984 and now he could detect the balance of power shifting decisively in Senna's favour.

This undisguised hostility towards Prost, which developed during their second year together at McLaren and was allowed to intensify thereafter, was seen by many people as merely a reflection of Ayrton's burning competitive spirit. I must say I always believed it was irrational and, if anything detracts from Senna's position in the ranks of the all-time great racing drivers, it was this arguably immature attitude towards his greatest rival.

Yet out on the track Ayrton displayed no such insecurities. If anything, his consummate skill prompted an over-confidence which produced as many accidents as Grand Prix victories. This was a rare, if uniquely flawed, talent, by any standards. In particular, the manner in which he rammed Prost's Ferrari off the circuit at Suzuka on the first corner of the 1990 Japanese Grand Prix, after being frustrated in his attempts to have pole position moved to the opposite side of the circuit, suggested that Senna's messianic zeal disregarded even considerations of his own self-preservation.

There was another side to his character, of course, in dramatic contrast to all this. This was revealed in his relationship with a handful of close friends, including McLaren team co-ordinator Jo Ramirez, Gerhard Berger, his McLaren team-mate from 1990 to '92, Professor Sid Watkins, the chief of the FIA Medical Commission, and the first Brazilian driver to win the World Championship, Emerson Fittipaldi. Their comments overleaf offer a valuable insight into Senna's sense of humour, his private generosity and the personal warmth which was not always apparent in his dealings with the outside world.

Ayrton was a difficult man, perhaps, but a master in his chosen sphere. He could be awkward and confrontational, yet perhaps he would not have been such an intensely committed and unremittingly competitive driver without those very qualities.

Race fans – and Senna's rivals – will argue for years over his place in motor racing history. But many of the mechanics and engineers who worked with him have little doubt. They were inspired and motivated by the force of his towering personality, drive and focused energy.

The greatest who ever lived? Possibly so, but it is almost impossible to compare drivers of different generations. Nevertheless, what is beyond question is that Ayrton Senna was one of the all-time Grand Prix legends. Nothing can ever detract from that reality.

AYRTON SENNA TRIBUTE

EMERSON FITTIPALDI became the youngest-ever World Champion when he took the title at the age of 25 in 1972, repeating his triumph two years later. He subsequently embarked on a highly successful career in Indy Car racing, winning the PPG Cup in 1989 and scoring two victories in the Indianapolis 500. Greatly respected by his peers and an immensely popular ambassador for the sport, it was Fittipaldi who blazed the trail that led fellow-Brazilians Nelson Piquet and Ayrton Senna to World Championship glory.

I first saw Ayrton Senna in the late 1970s. I was testing at the Interlagos track, and there was a shy young man there asking questions, watching the test. Ayrton was driving go-karts at that time, doing very well. From time to time I would keep hearing about him – Ayrton is doing really well in go-karts; Ayrton is winning in Formula Ford in England.

The next time I saw Ayrton was when he was racing at the Austrian GP [meeting] in 1981. I took Ayrton to all the top team managers of Formula 1, and I introduced him – 'This is Ayrton Senna, he will be a World Champion.' Some of the team managers looked at me and said, 'How is Emerson sure?' But I knew even then that Ayrton was something special. I think that that was Ayrton's first introduction to the top Formula 1 teams and after that I had a very special relationship with Ayrton.

I felt comfortable with Ayrton, and we shared things about our racing experiences that I never spoke to anyone else about, even my brother Wilson. I had a lot of admiration for Ayrton, but as a friend. From the outside I think he could seem even cold, but it was just a shell; he was very shy with people he did not know. When you were inside the shell he was a very warm person. I have some memories of times we had together, in São Paulo, in Portugal, where we had so much fun. I really enjoyed [those times]. He was fun when he knew people, that was another part of Ayrton that not many people knew. He could look so tense, and almost introverted, but the few times we had were memories I will always keep.

Last year I invited Ayrton to come test my Indy car, and for four days we were there, just the two of us talking about racing, and every second we were enjoying. When he started my Indy car at the Firebird track in Phoenix, I could tell he was very nervous, very tense. He pulled out, not knowing the track or the car, and drove ten laps. He came in, said the seat was uncomfortable and needed to be adjusted. Then he went out and did ten more laps, and he was very quick, and incredibly smooth. I could tell he was enjoying himself, and I could tell he was very comfortable in the cockpit. When he came back into the pits, his eyes were shining, like a little boy who had a new toy. That was how Ayrton was about racing, he enjoyed it, every second. He was dedicated to the sport, never satisfied with his own performance – he always wanted to get better and better. He was the most talented driver I ever met, and a friend.

I was testing in Michigan, the first time, the new Penske-Mercedes car. Chuck Sprague, our team manager, called me into the pits, and told me Teresa, my wife, was on the phone from Florida. I was shocked, and scared that something had happened at home. When I got the news that Ayrton was dead, I could hardly believe it. Just four days before, I had been talking with him. I was devastated, and for nearly four days I could hardly talk to people. I just could not believe that something like that could happen to Ayrton.

He was very special.

Among the Grand Prix drivers, GERHARD BERGER was possibly the closest friend Ayrton Senna had during his F1 career. For three seasons from the start of 1990, Gerhard partnered the Brazilian in the McLaren-Honda squad, during which time he won three Grands Prix.

The Imola weekend, of course, was very bad. Even in my long career I've never experienced a situation where two colleagues died in the same race meeting. I can remember the Elio de Angelis accident, of course, but then I was at the beginning of my career and I wasn't too close to him. But, you know, like everything, after a while, although it still hurts you, it doesn't change your attitude to the sport.

Ayrton was not just a colleague, he was one of my closest friends in Formula 1. Maybe my only real friend among the drivers. We were close, we did a lot of things together, I respected him a lot for the way in which he drove. It might be that he was the best driver ever in Formula 1, I don't know, but during my ten years in the business, nobody could come close to him. This is the picture I remember of him in my mind.

I still miss him. I still see him with his yellow helmet in my mind's eye. Those three years with him at McLaren were great. The team was great and being Ayrton's team-mate was great. I learned a lot from him, and a lot from the way he worked with Honda. He taught me how to work, and I taught him how to laugh!

On one occasion, in a Milan traffic jam, he pulled the keys out of the ignition of the car I was driving and just threw them out into the road. But he'd clearly forgotten that he was Ayrton Senna, I was Gerhard Berger and we were in the middle of Milan! When we climbed out to try and find them, we were recognised and the whole of central Milan seemed to come to a halt. Eventually the police had to rescue us by helicopter. And they were not amused!

PROFESSOR SID WATKINS is the chief of the FIA Medical Commission and came to know Senna first professionally, later on a social basis and in connection with the Brazilian driver's charitable works. He admired Ayrton's single-mindedness and the great generosity of spirit he displayed when outside a Formula 1 cockpit.

I admired his humility, his humour and his kindness, not on the track, perhaps, but off. I found him a very sincere person, always one of the first to ring up if anybody was sick or injured to ask if he could help.

He was a very charitable person and used his money to many good causes. The most recent one, at my instigation, provided sufficient core funding for a medical service to be set up for the children of the Amazon river in the Brazilian Andes, to provide some boats, doctors and medical assistance to work in the villages. With his help it produced £250,000 guaranteed each year for five years, which is a very significant contribution. But Ayrton never wanted any publicity about anything like this.

When he came to my home in the Scottish borders to visit and talk to the pupils at Loretto school, where Jimmy Clark was educated, he asked if he could be taken to the Jim Clark Memorial Room at Duns under the condition that there was no publicity.

At Loretto, he spoke for 45 minutes, and then took questions for another 45 minutes, from boys between eight and sixteen years old. He dealt with them beautifully, and kindly and sincerely. Whenever he was asked a question, he would think a lot before he started to answer. He always engaged his brain before his mouth, which is unusual in a racing driver, indeed in Formula 1 in general.

McLaren team co-ordinator JO RAMIREZ has been involved in Grand Prix racing since the early Sixties, when he tended the cars of his fellow Mexicans, Ricardo and Pedro Rodriguez. He worked with Senna throughout Ayrton's six years at McLaren and they became close friends. Ramirez recalls being at a test session with the Fittipaldi F1 team at Silverstone in 1981 when Emerson introduced him to the young Senna.

Ayrton came to talk to Emerson, and when he left, Emerson said, 'You've just met a guy who will be one of the greatest one day.' After a remark like that, I started to follow Ayrton's career pretty closely.

The difference between him and Prost was that Alain, in a car that he liked, that he was happy to drive, was untouchable, unbeatable. But Ayrton in the end could drive anything, no matter how badly it was handling.

That was the case in his last race at Imola. That Williams FW16 was not a car that should have been in pole position; it was there because Ayrton was driving it. Schumacher said that he could see he was having problems with the car and anybody else might have waited a little.

But Ayrton was born to lead, to be first, to be the fastest. That's just the way he was and it was never going to change.

born to be the fastest

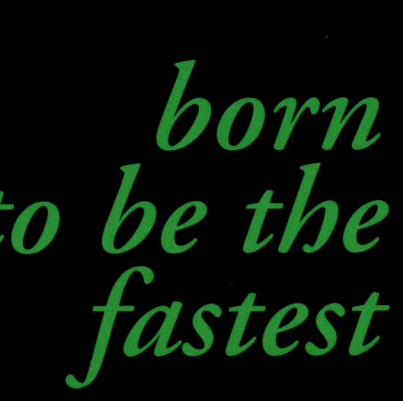

Official Sponsor of the Formula 1 Marlboro McLaren-Team

BOSS
HUGO BOSS

Congratulations Michael Schumacher, 1994 Driver's Championship.
It's a clean sweep for Champion® two years in a row!

Winning is our Formula 1 tradition

CHAMPION®

YOU CAN'T BEAT A CHAMPION

COOPER

1994 GRANDS PRIX

BRAZILIAN GRAND PRIX	102
PACIFIC GRAND PRIX	112
SAN MARINO GRAND PRIX	120
MONACO GRAND PRIX	130
SPANISH GRAND PRIX	140
CANADIAN GRAND PRIX	150
FRENCH GRAND PRIX	158
BRITISH GRAND PRIX	166
GERMAN GRAND PRIX	176
HUNGARIAN GRAND PRIX	188
BELGIAN GRAND PRIX	196
ITALIAN GRAND PRIX	206
PORTUGUESE GRAND PRIX	214

WORLD CHAMPIONSHIP • ROUND 1

BRAZILIAN GRAND PRIX

BRAZILIAN GRAND PRIX

SCHUMACHER
HILL
ALESI
BARRICHELLO
KATAYAMA
WENDLINGER

Michael Schumacher opened what would prove to be a new era of Formula 1 racing with a decisive maiden victory for the Ford Zetec-R-engined Benetton B194, toppling home track hero Ayrton Senna in front of a passionately nationalistic Brazilian Grand Prix crowd at São Paulo's Interlagos circuit. Senna, first time out in the new Williams FW16-Renault, took pole position, but Schumacher ate into his early advantage once the race got under way, slipped ahead at the first refuelling stop and was never headed thereafter. Ayrton fought back gamely in the closing stages, but the prospect of a grandstand finish evaporated when the Brazilian tried too hard, spinning off and stalling his engine on a third-gear left-hander just before the pit straight. That left Schumacher to win by over a lap from Damon Hill's Williams, the Londoner having opted for a less competitive single-stop strategy, with Jean Alesi's Ferrari 412T1 coming home third. The race was punctuated by a four-car accident which eliminated Martin Brundle's McLaren MP4/9, Eddie Irvine's Jordan 194, the Ligier JS39B of Eric Bernard and Jos Verstappen, making his debut in the second Benetton B194 as a stand-in for J.J. Lehto.

Against the backdrop of the São Paulo skyline, the Benetton of Michael Schumacher cuts a swathe through the sea of green. He was out on his own in the opening race of the year, leaving his rivals trailing and with plenty to think about on the long journey home.

Paul-Henri Cahier

1994 TEAM GUIDE

WILLIAMS-RENAULT
World Champion constructors for the past two seasons, going for a hat-trick with the formidable Ayrton Senna signed up as Alain Prost's successor alongside Damon Hill. Reputed £20 million sponsorship package from Rothmans funding challenge from evolutionary FW16 chassis with distinctive rear-end aerodynamic treatment incorporating aerofoil-section upper wishbones encasing driveshafts. Torsion bar front suspension, coil springs at rear, with power from new Renault RS6 V10 engine, 3 kg lighter than its predecessor, transmitted through totally new Williams six-speed semi-automatic gearbox, narrower, smaller and lighter than the unit it replaces.

TYRRELL-YAMAHA
Clean-sheet approach to chassis design with Mark Blundell now partnering Ukyo Katayama in uncomplicated 022 challenger designed under direction of Tyrrell's new Technical Director Harvey Postlethwaite, drawing on aerodynamic input from new partnership with Jean-Claude Migeot at Fondmetal Technologies, with whom the team has a three-year collaborative deal. Retaining further-uprated version of Yamaha OX10A 72-degree V10 engine driving through pneumatically activated semi-automatic gearbox primed by air compressors for the engine's pneumatic valvegear.

BENETTON-FORD
The dynamic Michael Schumacher joined by ex-Sauber man J.J. Lehto in formidable line-up now funded by the Japanese Mild Seven cigarette brand. Challenge based on aerodynamically outstanding Ross Brawn-designed B194 chassis and all-new Ford Zetec-R V8 engine, incorporating titanium connecting rods, magnesium alloy pistons and hollow titanium valves running to 15,000 rpm maximum, driving through further-refined version of transverse semi-automatic six-speed gearbox used on previous year's B193B.

McLAREN-PEUGEOT
Dawn of another Anglo-French F1 partnership with evolutionary two-pedal McLaren MP4/9 chassis powered by all-new Peugeot A6 four-valves-per-cylinder V10 engine designed and built in 26 weeks by Jean-Pierre Boudy's design team at Peugeot Sport's Velizy Viacoublay headquarters. Two-pedal layout offers left-foot braking facility with clutch activation by means of steering column stalk. All-new Dave North-designed gearbox incorporating adjustable hydraulic differentials. Mika Häkkinen confirmed as lead driver with Martin Brundle and Philippe Alliot also signed for the season after Alain Prost tested the car and then declined to reverse his retirement decision, the Englishman lining up to race the second entry while Alliot fulfilled role as test driver.

FOOTWORK-FORD
With Footwork boss Wataru Ohashi forced to scale down his financial involvement due to depressed state of Japan's economy, the team reverted to its original name of Arrows with only the cars continuing to carry the Footwork identification. New Alan Jenkins FA15 design powered by air-valve Ford HB engines with Christian Fittipaldi and Gianni Morbidelli signed to drive.

LOTUS-MUGEN HONDA
Having finalised deal to use Mugen Honda V10 engines with backdoor support from the Japanese car maker, Lotus faced start of season struggling with what amounted to seriously overweight interim Lotus 107C test car while development of new type 109 continued behind the scenes. Johnny Herbert staying on team strength as number one driver, despite approaches from McLaren, with Pedro Lamy as number two and Alessandro Zanardi confirmed in role of test driver.

JORDAN-HART
Logical evolution of 1993 Jordan-Hart package developed under direction of Chief Engineer Gary Anderson with additional input from newly arrived Technical Director Steve Nichols. Chassis aerodynamically improved with revisions to Hart type 1035 V10 engine including redesign of lower crankcase to reduce centre of gravity plus new pistons, revised valvegear and inlet manifolding to slightly increase power output and enhance reliability. Rubens Barrichello joined by Eddie Irvine on full-time basis after two outings at the end of previous season.

LARROUSSE-FORD
Structurally more rigid revised version of the 1993 Larrousse challenger, developed in team's Bicester-based design studio under direction of Robin Herd, Tim Holloway and Tino Belli. Now using Ford HB V8 power driving through 1993 Benetton transverse six-speed semi-automatic gearbox. Erik Comas and Olivier Beretta signed to drive.

MINARDI-FORD
Protracted deal to amalgamate with Beppe Lucchini's Scuderia Italia eventually confirmed early in the New Year. Team relying on uprated versions of M193 chassis, the only competitors to retain manual gearchanges, with Ford HB engine deal continuing and Michele Alboreto paired with Pierluigi Martini behind the wheel.

LIGIER-RENAULT
Long-established French marque starting the season in mood of commercial and financial uncertainty after new owner Cyril de Rouvre encounters legal problems stemming from other business projects. Relying on mildly uprated versions of last year's JS39 chassis driven by former test driver Eric Bernard and 1993 Formula 3000 champion Olivier Panis.

FERRARI
Dramatic new John Barnard-designed 412T1 challenger raising hopes for Maranello revival. Distinctive aerodynamic treatment, particularly around sculptured side radiator intakes, plus direct attachment to chassis of front suspension members, doing away with the need for uni-ball joints. Fabricated chrome molybdenum-cased gearbox transmitting power from familiar 65-degree V12, now reputedly developing 780 bhp at 15,000 rpm. Definitive new 75-degree V12 in the pipeline to offer even more performance for Jean Alesi and Gerhard Berger during the course of the season.

SAUBER-MERCEDES
Totally new Leo Ress-designed C13 chassis, developed from the promising type C12 with which the team had made its F1 debut the previous year. Powered by further-developed bespoke Ilmor-made, Mercedes-badged V10 and driving through the only longitudinal gearbox in the field. Karl Wendlinger joined by highly rated newcomer Heinz-Harald Frentzen on the team's driving strength.

SIMTEK-FORD
All-new team fielded by Nick Wirth's Banbury-based organisation which previously designed abortive Andrea Moda F1 machine and also provided research and consultancy services to the FIA. Simtek Grand Prix established with Wirth retaining controlling interest with Sir Jack Brabham and Schmidt Motorsport (SMS) taking minority shareholdings. All-new S941 chassis built with composite components supplied by SNPE, the major French chemical concern, and powered by basic Series V-spec Ford HB V8 engine, driving through six-speed Xtrac gearbox. David Brabham partnered by Austrian novice Roland Ratzenberger in driver line-up.

PACIFIC-ILMOR
Having geared up for F1 at the start of 1993 only to find that lack of sponsorship obliged him to put the project on hold for a year, Pacific boss Keith Wiggins finally gave the green light to a programme based on what was effectively the stillborn Reynard F1 concept designed by Rory Byrne. The cash-strapped team's PR01s used basic-spec Ilmor V10 engines and were driven by Bertrand Gachot and Paul Belmondo.

Top: Lotus had Mugen Honda power, but started the season with the outdated and overweight 107C chassis.

Ferrari's new car featured beautifully sculptured side radiator intakes.

BRAZILIAN GRAND PRIX

New colours for Martin Brundle, who turned down all other offers in a successful bid to secure a seat in the Marlboro McLaren Peugeot team.

ENTRY AND PRACTICE

The wisdom of Ayrton Senna's switch to the Williams-Renault camp for the 1994 season seemed to be dramatically underlined when the Brazilian displayed a mastery of São Paulo's Interlagos circuit many regarded as totally predictable to set fastest time in both qualifying sessions prior to his home Grand Prix.

Nevertheless, there were definitely signs that, as F1 moved into a new era supposedly free of computer-controlled electronic driver aids, the group of hard-charging pretenders to the Brazilian's throne had received a welcome injection of variety, no fewer than five different cars featuring in the top six placings by the end of the second session.

The ban on such esoteric accessories as active suspension, traction control systems and anti-lock brakes – underpinned by threats of draconian penalties from the sport's governing body should anybody be discovered using such systems – certainly promised to make the cars look more spectacular out on the circuit. In addition, the introduction of in-race refuelling, despite much concern about its obvious inherent dangers, was set to add a fascinating strategic dimension to the way in which the teams ran their races.

From a purely tactical standpoint, the qualifying and practice sessions at Interlagos saw teams doing their utmost to conserve as many tyres as possible. The present rules provided for an allocation of seven sets per car during the course of a Grand Prix weekend, but with some teams planning to make two refuelling stops there was a need for some careful calculations to balance the pressure for a quick lap in qualifying against the need to have sufficient rubber available to maximise the cars' performance on race day.

However, the fact that Senna's Williams FW16 emerged 0.3s ahead of Michael Schumacher's Benetton B194 – after which there was a full second back to Jean Alesi's third-place Ferrari 412T1 – tended to suggest that Ayrton might have things pretty well his own way once the race began. In stark contrast, however, the two days of qualifying proved to be a bruisingly bleak time for Damon Hill, who wound up 1.6 seconds slower than his new team-mate. It was far from the psychological boost the Englishman must have been hoping for at this first race of the season.

Characteristically, Senna applied a meticulous and painstakingly detailed attitude to the setting up of his new machine. On Friday he was definitely not happy with its lively ride over the Interlagos bumps and a lot of work was done on spring and damper settings overnight in preparation for the second timed session.

On Saturday, Ayrton reported that the car felt a little better, although still not perfect by his own high standards. Schumacher was a bit too close for comfort, taking provisional pole position early in the session with a 1m 16.290s.

Senna grabbed it back with a 1m 15.962s just before the session's halfway mark, but then the heavens opened and the São Paulo track was drenched by a torrential shower. That put paid to any prospect of further improvement, although Senna later went out for a few laps – to the delight of his vocal fans in the grandstands – just to find out where the worst puddles were forming.

'Our car, in particular, would perform better on a smooth circuit,' admitted Senna, 'although I am very happy with all aspects of its mechanical reliability on this anti-clockwise circuit which is always very hard work. But I must say that if it rains like this tomorrow during the race, the organisers should put the pace car out immediately – or perhaps even stop the race – because this track just doesn't drain properly when it rains with such intensity.'

Schumacher was similarly satisfied with his own personal performance, despite a tiresome head cold, admitting that he thought there was a little more to come from his Benetton. 'I wasn't really sure how things were going to work out during final qualifying,' he admitted. 'But for the rain, there might have been a chance for a big fight for pole and I'm sure everybody would have enjoyed that!'

Yet while Senna stood poised to make an apparently seamless transition to his new team, sustaining his winning ways into an 11th season of F1 competition, Damon Hill found himself left struggling with a frustrating catalogue of technical problems.

In Friday morning's free practice session the Englishman, battling against flu symptoms, was thwarted by the onboard fire extinguisher discharging into the cockpit of his Williams. In first qualifying, he was then stranded out on the circuit when an electrical fault caused his Renault V10 suddenly to cut out.

'It was obviously very disappointing,' said Damon, 'because by the end of the qualifying session I'd managed only eight flying laps and was two seconds away [from Senna]. I don't think I've sweated so much in a short space of time in all my life. It was a very stressful situation and, although you usually summon up everything for a qualifying lap, I admit I didn't get the best out of this situation.'

On Saturday, Hill's best qualifying lap was thwarted by slower traffic, adding to the difficulty of effectively being a day behind Senna in terms of car set-up. He was fourth fastest overall.

Jean Alesi, meanwhile, raised Ferrari's hopes by taking third place in both sessions with the new John Barnard-designed 412T1, while dynamic newcomer Heinz-Harald Frentzen put in a tremendous performance to qualify the impressive new Sauber C13-Mercedes fifth for his first-ever Grand Prix start.

'Am I really fifth on the grid?' asked Frentzen. 'I still can't believe it. When I saw the clouds getting darker and darker I decided to use the second set of tyres early, which proved to be the right decision.'

His team-mate Karl Wendlinger lined up a slightly disappointed seventh, his progress in the Saturday morning session thwarted by an engine failure which lost him valuable chassis set-up time.

'I wasn't very lucky today,' he admitted. 'On the first set of tyres I had only one clear flying lap and on the second I was delayed when Verstappen spun, then I was stopped by the rain.'

Alesi confessed that there was still some way to go with the development of the new Ferrari, reporting that the transition between its handling on slow and fast corners was insufficiently progressive. By contrast, his team-mate Gerhard Berger experienced nothing but mechanical troubles.

On Friday, he had problems with the gearchange hydraulic pressure system which eventually left him parked on the circuit when it stuck in neutral, then on Saturday he was forced to use the spare car all day after his race chassis developed an electrical problem before the start of the untimed session. The spare then suffered an engine failure, and while a fresh V12 was installed in time for second qualifying, the chassis adjustments were all wrong. 'The way the car is set up today is just not suited to my driving style,' he shrugged.

Diary

December 1993

Ayrton Senna receives suspended three-race licence withdrawal for his involvement in the fracas with Jordan driver Eddie Irvine following the 1993 Japanese Grand Prix.

British F3 Champion Kelvin Burt tests Williams FW15C-Renault at Paul Ricard.

Michael Schumacher renegotiates lucrative new deal with Benetton which is rumoured to be worth $12 million across two seasons.

David Brabham signs for new Simtek F1 team.

Peugeot fires up new F1 V10 engine on the test bed for first time.

January 1994

Former McLaren and Honda engineer Osamu Goto joins Ferrari's F1 engine department.

Larrousse confirms it will use Ford HB V8 engines in 1994 in place of Lamborghini V12s.

British F3 contender Oliver Gavin signs test contract with new Pacific F1 team.

J.J. Lehto suffers serious neck injuries in crash during maiden test outing for Benetton at Silverstone.

Eddie Irvine signs to join Rubens Barrichello in Jordan-Hart squad.

February

Jordan team experiences leak during first refuelling test at Barcelona with new tailor-made equipment.

Footwork team re-adopts original Arrows name.

Gerhard Berger lowers Fiorano record in new Ferrari 412T1.

March

Alain Prost tests new McLaren MP4/9-Peugeot at Estoril.

Michael Andretti scores Indy Car win on maiden outing of new Reynard-Ford.

GP Photo/Peter Nygaard

Nigel Snowdon

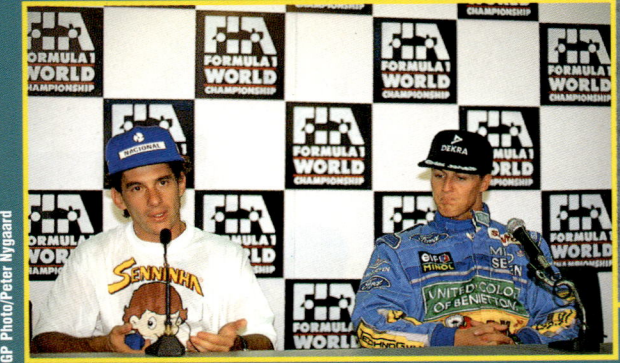

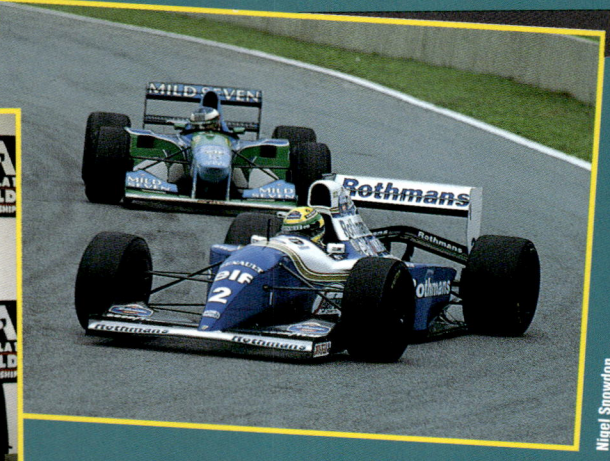

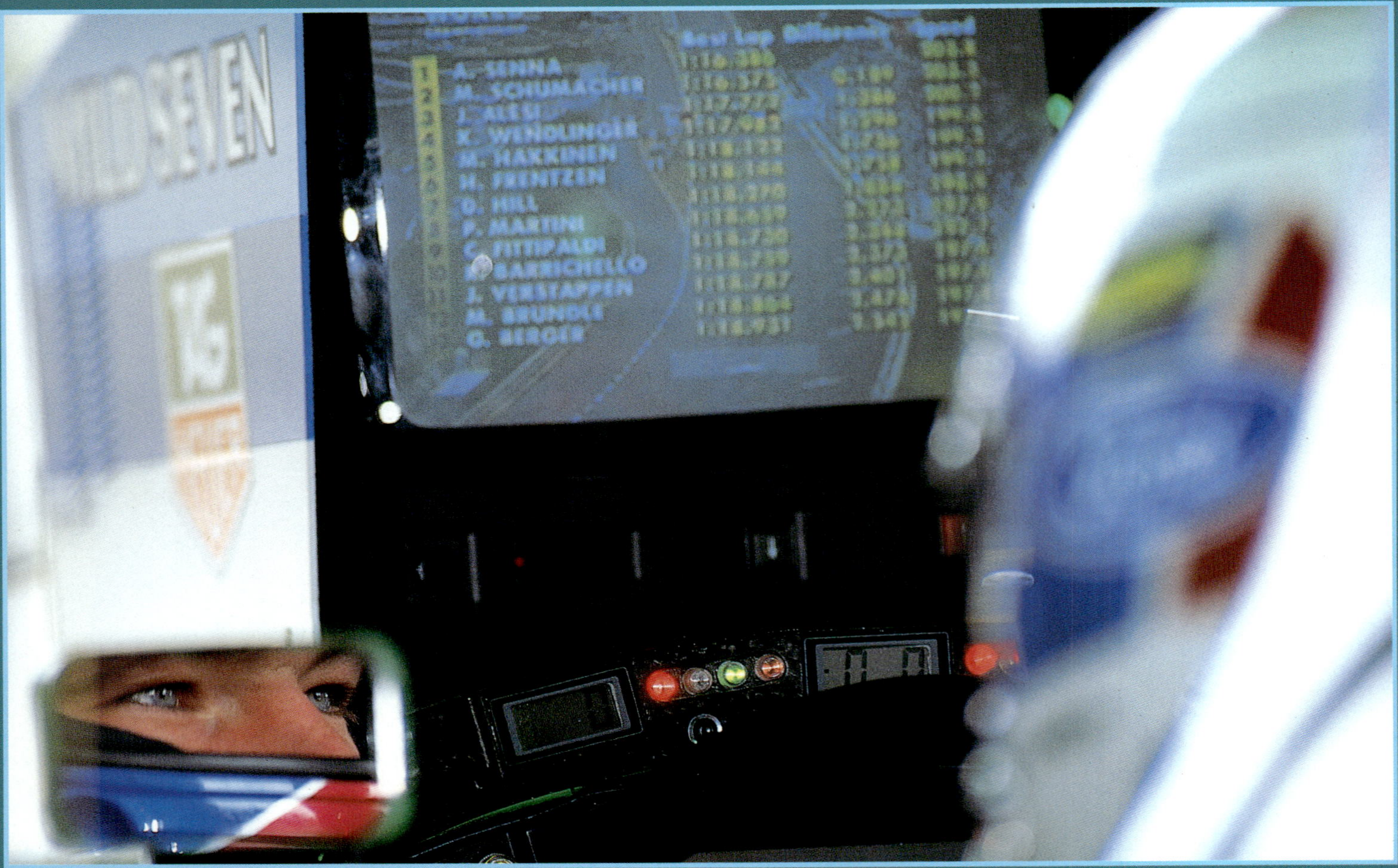

LAT Photographic

Senna's explanations did not impress Schumacher *(top left)*, and although the Brazilian claimed pole position and led in the early part of the race *(top right)*, the Benetton was clearly the superior car in race trim.

Above: **New boy in school. Jos Verstappen stepped into the second Benetton after J.J. Lehto's testing accident and was soon surveying the names at the top of the class.**

Neat and tidy. Powered by the latest Yamaha V10, the new Tyrrell 022 was a huge step forward from last year's machine and Ukyo Katayama *(right)* brought his car home in fifth place to record his first championship points.

Pamela Lauesen/FOSA

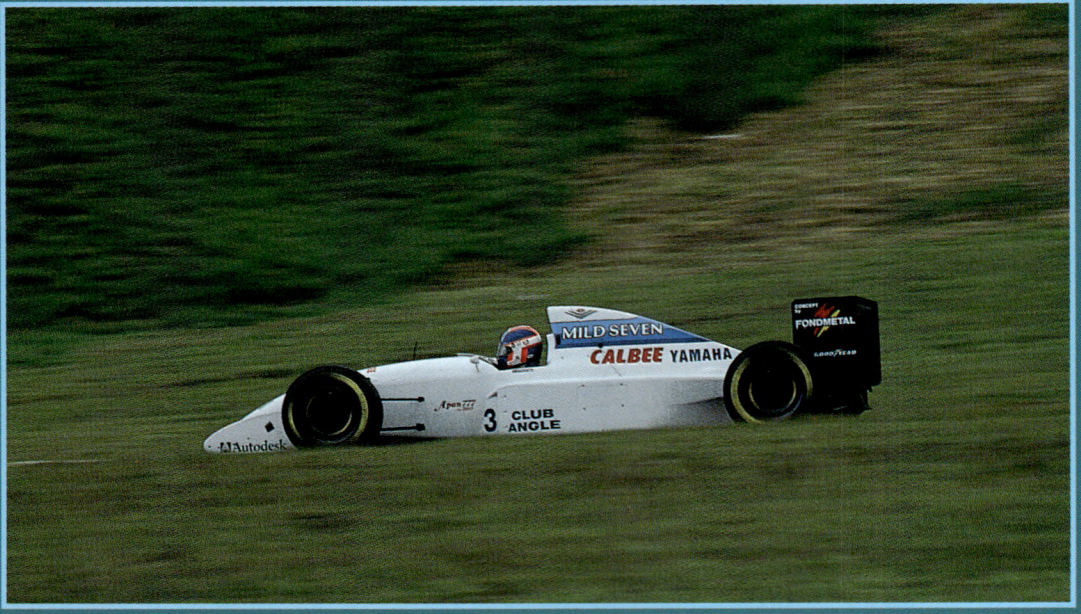

Marked man? After an ill-fated appeal, Eddie Irvine's part in the multiple collision ultimately cost him a three-race ban. *Right:* The Ulsterman leads a midfield train comprising Blundell's Tyrrell, Fittipaldi's Footwork and Brundle's McLaren.

Over in the McLaren camp, both Mika Häkkinen and Martin Brundle also had troubled times with their new Peugeot V10-engined MP4/9s. Both cars were using the four-valves-per-cylinder A6 version of the French engine, but a continuing spate of throttle linkage problems intervened to frustrate their efforts on both days.

On Friday, Häkkinen achieved fifth-fastest time, but Brundle's throttle control problems were more marked. They caused the Englishman to take the first of three unscheduled trips across the bumpy outfield run-off area and cost him valuable familiarisation time with his new machine.

'I was all throttle and brakes for much of the first qualifying session,' Brundle admitted on Friday, 'but then I managed to calm myself down, began to drive smoothly and started to get a feel for the car over the last few laps.'

For Saturday's qualifying session, Häkkinen's MP4/9 was fitted with a new engine, largely rectifying his throttle linkage difficulties. However, the Finn was less than satisfied with the handling and could only manage an eventual eighth place on the grid. Brundle's third trip across the grass, again due to a sticking throttle, capped his efforts in this session. By the time the car's undertray was cleaned out, Martin found himself relegated to a disappointing 18th – with no prospect of bettering his time as the rain arrived.

Ninth and tenth places on the grid were filled by Jos Verstappen's Benetton B194 and Ukyo Katayama's Tyrrell 022. The young Dutch novice took to F1 like the proverbial duck to water and, despite several spins, proved himself an extremely able stand-in for the recuperating J.J. Lehto. Katayama's presence in tenth place lent weight to his team-mate Mark Blundell's prediction that, had he not had some problems, a place in the top six for the new Harvey Postlethwaite-designed machine could have been quite feasible. Mark had been an outstanding fourth in Friday's free practice session before dropping away with a down-on-power engine when it mattered in the afternoon.

'Basically, we showed today that the new car is good and we have the potential to be right up there,' said Blundell. He had to settle for 12th place on the grid behind Christian Fittipaldi's Footwork FA15, finding himself slightly wrong-footed when the rain arrived. Katayama, of course, was delighted to have achieved his best-ever grid position, just as Gianni Morbidelli had with an impressive sixth place in the second Footwork.

In 13th spot, Erik Comas showed that the latest Robin Herd-designed Larrousse LH94 was a respectably promising machine, but new boy Olivier Beretta was disappointing and found himself ten places behind his team-mate.

Neither of the Jordans quite emulated their pre-season form and it was obviously asking too much for the under-developed Ligier JS39Bs to produce much in the hands of Eric Bernard or F3000 champion Olivier Panis. Barrichello qualified 14th, consoled by the fact 'that there is only about half a second between me and the guy in fifth place', but Eddie Irvine was extremely disappointed not to improve on 16th in the final order.

'The car was much better today,' admitted the Ulsterman. 'My first set of tyres were good too, but I didn't do a particularly good lap. On my second set it was a disaster: I had no grip at all.'

By the same token, both Mugen-engined Lotus 107Cs were suffering from excess weight – being effectively little more than test cars intended to finalise the specification of the eagerly awaited 109 – so Johnny Herbert and Pedro Lamy just had to do the best they could and hope for better times ahead.

However, if there had been a prize for the most unlucky man over the two days of practice at Interlagos, it would have had to be awarded to the genial Michele Alboreto. On Saturday morning, he posted a superb fourth-fastest time with his Minardi M193B, then stopped on the circuit when a leak developed in the pneumatic valvegear system of its Ford HB V8. A fresh engine was installed for second qualifying, but he only had time for a single exploratory lap before the rains came. He was thus consigned to an unrepresentative 22nd place, although not before he had impressed sufficiently for some people to wonder why Ron Dennis had not considered this five-times Grand Prix winner to drive the McLaren-Peugeot.

Alboreto's team-mate Pierluigi Martini, eighth fastest on Friday, also failed to post a meaningful time in final qualifying and slipped to 15th place overall.

The Ilmor-engined Pacific PR01s were beset by very severe understeer in the first session, Paul Belmondo in particular being frustrated by the fact that his was a brand-new car which had not turned a wheel prior to arriving in Brazil. On Friday, the wiring loom in the Frenchman's car destroyed itself, and on Saturday morning the chassis cracked at the front, allowing one of the suspension pick-up points to pull out of the monocoque. There was no possibility of repairing the car away from the team's base, so Belmondo had to withdraw and Bertrand Gachot alone took Pacific's first F1 start, in 25th place.

The final position on the grid was taken by the Simtek S941 of David Brabham, overnight changes having improved the new car's handling and given team owner Nick Wirth something to celebrate on his 28th birthday. The team's second car, driven by Austrian novice Roland Ratzenberger, failed to make the cut after suffering from a misfire on Saturday morning followed by a slight damper problem at the start of second qualifying. By the time this had been resolved, the rain had arrived.

Jordan loses out on two counts

Rubens Barrichello's fourth place at Interlagos may have been one of the motivating factors behind the Jordan team's decision to protest the eligibility of Michael Schumacher's winning Benetton B194, for, had the winner been excluded, the young Brazilian would have netted a prestigious top-three finish on his home turf.

As things transpired, the F1 authorities left the Silverstone-based team with a bloodied nose after they had not only rejected the protest but also slapped a one-race ban on Eddie Irvine for triggering a spectacular four-car pile-up at the half-distance mark.

Jordan protested the Benetton over the way in which the front aerodynamic deflectors were attached to the monocoque just inside the B194's front wheels. The rules demanded that the underside of an F1 car lie on one plane from the rear of the front wheels to the front of the rear wheels. 'All these parts must produce a uniform, solid, hard, rigid, impervious surface,' reads Article 3 (3) of the FIA Technical Regulations.

With both the front and rear securing stays on the Benetton falling within that area, as viewed from beneath the monocoque edge, the attachment stays and the deflectors themselves effectively amount to the perimeter of a rectangle. However, Jordan's contention that the rectangle so formed represented an illegal hole in the flat bottom of the car was rejected by FIA Technical Delegate Charlie Whiting.

After examining the facts of the accident, and interviewing the four drivers concerned, the Stewards of the Meeting adjudged Irvine to blame and suspended him from the second race of the season, the Pacific Grand Prix at Japan's TI Circuit. He was also hit with a $10,000 fine.

On Irvine's behalf, the Jordan team appealed against the decision and duly attended an FIA Court of Appeal hearing in Paris eleven days after Interlagos. It was, in retrospect, to prove something of a tactical misjudgement.

The four-man review board, under the chairmanship of Bruce Coles, a British Crown Court Recorder and Deputy Official Referee at London's High Court, multiplied his suspension threefold.

The official conclusion read: 'The board takes the view that Formula 1 is the top of world motor sport and very high standards must be set by drivers participating in these races.

'The board is satisfied that Mr Irvine caused an avoidable collision, forced Mr Verstappen's car off the track and illegitimately prevented Mr Verstappen's legitimate overtaking manoeuvre.

'It is the board's decision that Mr Irvine failed to evaluate the situation in the way that he ought to have done and recklessly pulled out to pass the car driven by Mr Bernard.'

It was small consolation to Irvine that the board cancelled the $10,000 fine. Now he wouldn't be back in action until the Spanish Grand Prix.

RACE

The race morning warm-up saw Senna predictably fastest in front of an adoring home crowd ahead of a mixed bag comprising Karl Wendlinger's Sauber, Michele Alboreto's Minardi, Mark Blundell's Tyrrell, Jean Alesi's Ferrari and Hill in the other Williams.

Berger's Ferrari suffered an engine failure caused by a problem with the O-rings within the pneumatic valve system. The V12 was replaced, only for the team to face a repeat failure the moment the fresh engine was fired up. A second engine change was carried out in record time to get the Austrian out onto the grid, but Maranello's problems didn't end there as Alesi was forced to switch to the spare 412T1 after a problem with the hydraulic system controlling the variable-length inlet trumpets on his race car.

From the touchlines, obviously, few people knew the individual fuel stop strategies which had been adopted by the teams. One stop or two? That was the choice available, the latter clearly the one favoured by Williams

BRAZILIAN GRAND PRIX

Right: With refuelling part of the Grand Prix package for the 1994 season, attention was focused on the pit lane, where races could easily be won and lost. Many pundits were concerned about safety in the crowded environment captured here as Jean Alesi's third-placed Ferrari accelerates away after a scheduled stop.

Heinz-Harald Frentzen's sparkling practice form took the eye, but it was his more experienced team-mate Karl Wendlinger *(below)* who gave Sauber a sixth-place points finish.

for Senna, who seized an immediate advantage at the start to lead the jostling pack into the third chicane.

Alesi elbowed his way through into second place ahead of Schumacher and held up the Benetton to such good effect that Ayrton was able to open out a two-second gap by the end of the opening lap. Schumacher got inside the Ferrari coming into the uphill left-hander leading onto the pits straight, but immediately slid wide, allowing Alesi to repass.

Hill was already dropping away in fourth place, intent on running the race with just a single refuelling stop, ahead of Frentzen's Sauber, Häkkinen's McLaren, Wendlinger's Sauber, Berger and Verstappen's Benetton.

Second time round and Schumacher pulled the same stunt, this time making it stick to take second place, although he was by now four seconds behind Senna. Gachot's Pacific managed to get itself involved in a collision with Beretta's spinning Larrousse, taking both cars out of the race midway round the third lap.

Berger, whose electrifying getaway had carried him from 17th on the grid to eighth on the opening lap, was back in the pits on the fifth lap with his third identical engine failure of the day, just as Morbidelli's Footwork rolled to a halt out on the circuit with gearbox failure.

By lap six, Schumacher had steadied Senna's advantage at 3.9 seconds, then the Benetton began to chip into the Brazilian's lead. From lap eight, the gap was 2.5 seconds, then 2.4s and 1.8s on the next couple of laps. Then Ayrton eased it open to 2.2s, then 2.3s, then 2.1s. Williams FW16 and Benetton B194 seemed closely matched.

Sadly the potential demonstrated by Michele Alboreto's Minardi was to remain unfulfilled, engine gremlins eliminating the Italian after seven laps. Häkkinen, who had been hanging on strongly in fifth place, pulled in at the end of lap 13 to retire with engine problems. 'It suddenly started to cut out on the high-speed corners,' he shrugged. 'It's a great pity, because at the time I had been running quite comfortably behind Hill.'

At the end of lap 15, Martin Brundle made a little bit of Grand Prix history by becoming the first man to make a refuelling stop under the new F1 regulations. His McLaren-Peugeot was stationary for 10.3 seconds before resuming the chase.

On lap 16, Frentzen's F1 debut came to a disappointing end when he spun out of fifth place, promoting Wendlinger, who made his first refuelling stop at the end of the following lap. Alesi made a 9.1-second refuelling stop at the end of lap 18, dropping to sixth between the Tyrrells of Katayama and Blundell.

At the end of lap 21 came the crucial turning point in the Brazilian Grand Prix. Schumacher, who had closed to within a second of Senna, followed the Williams in for their first refuelling stop and got out of the pits ahead of his rival.

Once in front he put the hammer down, opening a 3.9-second advantage over the Williams by lap 24 which expanded to 4.3 seconds on lap 27 and 6.5s on lap 33.

On lap 22, meanwhile, Blundell's fine run came to an end when he slid off the circuit on the climbing left-hander before the pits, half-rolling his Tyrrell in a cloud of mud and debris following a wheel rim breakage. Wreckage was left in the middle of the circuit for his rivals to dodge for a couple more laps, and the Englishman was fortunate to emerge unscathed. Gearbox trouble ended Christian Fittipaldi's race on the same lap.

Hill's one-stop strategy clearly wasn't turning out to be the best choice. By lap 24 the Englishman was 24 seconds behind in third place, fading to 37 seconds behind Schumacher at the end of 30 laps. With 34 laps completed, the order was Schumacher by 6.5 seconds from Senna, then a long gap to Hill, Alesi's understeering Ferrari and Wendlinger's Sauber, which was just

about to be overtaken by Barrichello's Jordan.

As the pack set off on its 35th lap, Brundle's seventh-place McLaren, which had already been hobbled by a malfunctioning rear shock absorber, slowed on the long straight beyond the pits, its transmission suddenly developing a fearful vibration. Martin, who had just lapped Eric Bernard's Ligier, eased back with the intention of heading to the pits at the end of that lap.

As he approached the next left-hander, Bernard moved to unlap himself from the McLaren just as Eddie Irvine's Jordan aimed inside the Ligier – and Jos Verstappen tried to get his Benetton inside the Jordan! Irvine's sudden lurch to the left put Verstappen momentarily on the grass and suddenly all hell let loose: the Benetton snapped sideways, careered back across the track, hitting the Jordan and the innocent Bernard's Ligier, before rolling across the top of Brundle's McLaren with an impact sufficient to crack the Englishman's helmet.

The four cars speared off the road, but everybody emerged unhurt, although Brundle was to suffer the unpleasant effects of whiplash for several days afterwards. By any standards, it was a huge accident and all involved were extremely fortunate to get away with it.

Back at the head of the field, Hill made his sole refuelling stop on lap 38, retaining his third place ahead of Alesi, while Schumacher's ever-more convincing possession of the lead remained secure through the second spate of refuelling stops. Senna made an 8.5-second stop on lap 44 followed by Schumacher in 7.4 seconds next time round. It seemed all over bar the shouting.

Nevertheless, Ayrton remained optimistic. As the race moved into its final 20 laps, the Brazilian began to steady the advantage and it seemed as though he was on the verge of a counter-attack. Then, on lap 56, Ayrton spun off on that final uphill left-hander and stalled the Renault engine. As far as the fans were concerned, that was the end of the Brazilian Grand Prix, and they made for the exits in droves.

'It was a good race,' reflected Ayrton later. 'Fast and very, very quick. Michael was a little bit quicker than us and only at the end was I able to push a little more and go with him. I was driving right on my limit when I got caught out on the exit of that third-gear corner. It was my own mistake as I was pushing a bit too hard.'

That left Schumacher an easy run to victory by over a lap from Hill and Alesi, with Barrichello an excellent fourth ahead of Katayama, Wendlinger and Herbert. Martini's Minardi lasted to take eighth place with Erik Comas's Larrousse leading home Pedro Lamy's Lotus, Olivier Panis's Ligier and David Brabham's Simtek as the sole survivors from the rest of the pack.

In the immediate aftermath of the race came a technical protest against Schumacher's Benetton lodged by the Jordan team and a stewards' post-mortem on the four-car accident. Jordan's protest was rejected (see sidebar), but Irvine got more than he bargained for with a one-race suspension as his negligence was officially blamed for the shunt.

To many people, it seemed as though Jordan's man was being punished for his team's temerity in trying to rock the boat by raising doubts as to the eligibility of the winning Benetton.

109

FIA FORMULA ONE WORLD CHAMPIONSHIP ROUND 1

GRANDE PREMIO DO BRASIL
INTERLAGOS
25-27 MARCH 1994

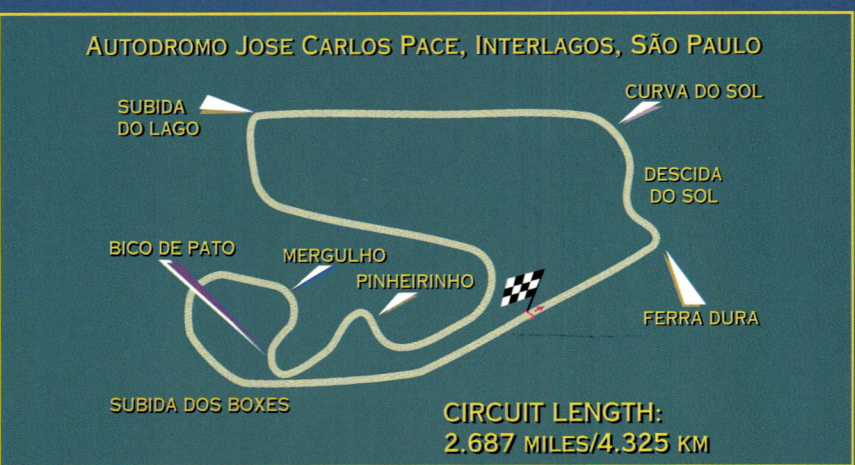

AUTODROMO JOSE CARLOS PACE, INTERLAGOS, SÃO PAULO

CIRCUIT LENGTH: 2.687 MILES/4.325 KM

RACE WEATHER: Warm, cloudy

Place	Driver	Nat.	No.	Entrant	Car/Engine	Laps	Time/Retirement	Speed (mph/km/h)
1	Michael Schumacher	D	5	Mild Seven Benetton Ford	Benetton B194-Ford Zetec-R V8	71	1h 35m 38.759s	119.695/192.632
2	Damon Hill	GB	0	Rothmans Williams Renault	Williams FW16-Renault RS6 V10	70		
3	Jean Alesi	F	27	Scuderia Ferrari	Ferrari 412T1 041 V12	70		
4	Rubens Barrichello	BR	14	Sasol Jordan	Jordan 194-Hart 1035 V10	70		
5	Ukyo Katayama	J	3	Tyrrell	Tyrrell 022-Yamaha 0X10A V10	69		
6	Karl Wendlinger	A	29	Broker Sauber Mercedes	Sauber C13-Mercedes-Benz V10	69		
7	Johnny Herbert	GB	12	Team Lotus	Lotus 107C-Mugen Honda ZA5C V10	69		
8	Pierluigi Martini	I	23	Minardi Scuderia Italia	Minardi M193B-Ford HB V8	69		
9	Erik Comas	F	20	Tourtel Larrousse F1	Larrousse LH94-Ford HB V8	68		
10	Pedro Lamy	P	11	Team Lotus	Lotus 107C-Mugen Honda ZA5C V10	68		
11	Olivier Panis	F	26	Ligier Gitanes Blondes	Ligier JS39B-Renault RS6 V10	68		
12	David Brabham	AUS	31	MTV Simtek Ford	Simtek S941-Ford HB V8	67		
	Ayrton Senna	BR	2	Rothmans Williams Renault	Williams FW16-Renault RS6 V10	55	Spun off	
	Martin Brundle	GB	8	Marlboro McLaren Peugeot	McLaren MP4/9-Peugeot A6 V10	34	Accident	
	Eddie Irvine	GB	15	Sasol Jordan	Jordan 194-Hart 1035 V10	34	Accident	
	Jos Verstappen	NL	6	Mild Seven Benetton Ford	Benetton B194-Ford Zetec-R V8	34	Accident	
	Eric Bernard	F	25	Ligier Gitanes Blondes	Ligier JS39B-Renault RS6 V10	33	Accident	
	Mark Blundell	GB	4	Tyrrell	Tyrrell 022-Yamaha 0X10A V10	21	Accident	
	Christian Fittipaldi	BR	9	Footwork Ford	Footwork FA15-Ford HB V8	21	Gearbox	
	Heinz-Harald Frentzen	D	30	Broker Sauber Mercedes	Sauber C13-Mercedes-Benz V10	15	Spun off	
	Mika Häkkinen	SF	7	Marlboro McLaren Peugeot	McLaren MP4/9-Peugeot A6 V10	13	Electrics	
	Michele Alboreto	I	24	Minardi Scuderia Italia	Minardi M193B-Ford HB V8	7	Electrics	
	Gianni Morbidelli	I	10	Footwork Ford	Footwork FA15-Ford HB V8	5	Gearbox	
	Gerhard Berger	A	28	Scuderia Ferrari	Ferrari 412T1 041 V12	5	Engine	
	Olivier Beretta	F	19	Tourtel Larrousse F1	Larrousse LH94-Ford HB V8	2	Accident	
	Bertrand Gachot		34	Pacific Grand Prix Ltd	Pacific PR01-Ilmor 2175A V10	1	Accident	
DNQ	Roland Ratzenberger	A	32	MTV Simtek Ford	Simtek S941-Ford HB V8			
DNQ	Paul Belmondo	F	33	Pacific Grand Prix Ltd	Pacific PR01-Ilmor 2175A V10			

Fastest lap: Schumacher, on lap 7, 1m 18.455s, 123.315 mph/198.457 km/h.
Lap record: Nigel Mansell (F1 Williams FW14B-Renault V10), 1m 17.578s, 122.865 mph/197.731 km/h (1992).
All cars used Goodyear tyres

All results and data © FIA 1994

QUALIFYING 1

Ayrton Senna	1m 16.386s
Michael Schumacher	1m 16.575s
Jean Alesi	1m 17.772s
Karl Wendlinger	1m 17.982s
Mika Häkkinen	**1m 18.122s**
Heinz-Harald Frentzen	1m 18.144s
Damon Hill	1m 18.270s
Pierluigi Martini	**1m 18.659s**
Christian Fittipaldi	1m 18.730s
Rubens Barrichello	1m 18.759s
Jos Verstappen	1m 18.787s
Martin Brundle	**1m 18.864s**
Gerhard Berger	1m 18.931s
Gianni Morbidelli	1m 18.970s
Erik Comas	1m 18.990s
Mark Blundell	1m 19.045s
Eddie Irvine	1m 19.269s
Olivier Panis	**1m 19.304s**
Eric Bernard	**1m 19.396s**
Michele Alboreto	**1m 19.517s**
Ukyo Katayama	1m 19.519s
Johnny Herbert	1m 19.798s
Olivier Beretta	1m 19.922s
Pedro Lamy	1m 21.029s
David Brabham	1m 22.266s
Bertrand Gachot	1m 22.495s
Roland Ratzenberger	**1m 22.707s**
Paul Belmondo	no time

Friday afternoon
Dry, warm, sunny

QUALIFYING 2

Ayrton Senna	**1m 15.962s**
Michael Schumacher	**1m 16.290s**
Jean Alesi	**1m 17.385s**
Damon Hill	**1m 17.554s**
Heinz-Harald Frentzen	1m 17.806s
Gianni Morbidelli	1m 17.866s
Karl Wendlinger	1m 17.927s
Jos Verstappen	**1m 18.183s**
Ukyo Katayama	1m 18.194s
Christian Fittipaldi	1m 18.204s
Mark Blundell	1m 18.246s
Erik Comas	**1m 18.321s**
Rubens Barrichello	1m 18.414s
Eddie Irvine	1m 18.751s
Gerhard Berger	1m 18.855s
Johnny Herbert	1m 19.483s
Olivier Beretta	1m 19.524s
Olivier Panis	1m 19.533s
Mika Häkkinen	1m 19.576s
Eric Bernard	1m 19.633s
Pedro Lamy	**1m 19.975s**
Bertrand Gachot	**1m 20.729s**
David Brabham	**1m 21.186s**
Roland Ratzenberger	1m 23.109s
Martin Brundle	13m 18.601s
Michele Alboreto	no time
Paul Belmondo	no time
Pierluigi Martini	no time

Saturday afternoon
Overcast, then torrential rain

WARM-UP

Ayrton Senna	1m 18.667s
Karl Wendlinger	1m 18.904s
Michele Alboreto	1m 19.367s
Mark Blundell	1m 19.650s
Jean Alesi	1m 19.872s
Damon Hill	1m 19.884s
Rubens Barrichello	1m 19.892s
Ukyo Katayama	1m 19.903s
Gianni Morbidelli	1m 19.943s
Michael Schumacher	1m 20.035s
Christian Fittipaldi	1m 20.073s
Mika Häkkinen	1m 20.175s
Martin Brundle	1m 20.495s
Heinz-Harald Frentzen	1m 20.533s
Gerhard Berger	1m 21.127s
David Brabham	1m 21.134s
Erik Comas	1m 21.154s
Eddie Irvine	1m 21.237s
Olivier Panis	1m 21.489s
Pedro Lamy	1m 22.162s
Bertrand Gachot	1m 23.543s
Johnny Herbert	1m 23.677s
Jos Verstappen	1m 33.295s
Eric Bernard	1m 34.705s
Pierluigi Martini	1m 36.203s
Olivier Beretta	1m 36.694s

Sunday morning
Damp, warm, sunny

FASTEST LAPS

Driver	Time	Lap
Michael Schumacher	1m 18.455s	7
Ayrton Senna	1m 18.764s	11
Damon Hill	1m 20.386s	21
Jean Alesi	1m 20.452s	12
Martin Brundle	1m 20.717s	17
Rubens Barrichello	1m 20.809s	56
Ukyo Katayama	1m 20.842s	34
Jos Verstappen	1m 20.896s	8
Heinz-Harald Frentzen	1m 20.907s	12
Karl Wendlinger	1m 20.987s	8
Mika Häkkinen	1m 20.989s	6
Mark Blundell	1m 21.039s	19
Gianni Morbidelli	1m 21.570s	3
Christian Fittipaldi	1m 21.582s	8
Eddie Irvine	1m 21.696s	8
Erik Comas	1m 21.756s	30
Pierluigi Martini	1m 21.872s	13
Johnny Herbert	1m 22.007s	40
Gerhard Berger	1m 22.021s	4
Michele Alboreto	1m 22.488s	5
Olivier Panis	1m 22.744s	38
Pedro Lamy	1m 23.234s	11
Eric Bernard	1m 23.459s	13
David Brabham	1m 23.911s	29
Olivier Beretta	1m 38.618s	1
Bertrand Gachot	1m 39.561s	1

STARTING GRID

5 SCHUMACHER Benetton 1m 16.290s		**2** SENNA Williams 1m 15.962s	
0 HILL Williams 1m 17.554s		**27** ALESI Ferrari 1m 17.385s	
10 MORBIDELLI Footwork 1m 17.866s		**30** FRENTZEN Sauber 1m 17.806s	
7 HÄKKINEN McLaren 1m 18.122s		**29** WENDLINGER Sauber 1m 17.927s	
3 KATAYAMA Tyrrell 1m 18.194s		**6** VERSTAPPEN Benetton 1m 18.183s	
4 BLUNDELL Tyrrell 1m 18.246s		**9** FITTIPALDI Footwork 1m 18.204s	
14 BARRICHELLO Jordan 1m 18.414s		**20** COMAS Larrousse 1m 18.321s	
15 IRVINE Jordan 1m 18.751s		**23** MARTINI Minardi 1m 18.659s	
8 BRUNDLE McLaren 1m 18.864s		**28** BERGER Ferrari 1m 18.855s	
25 BERNARD Ligier 1m 19.396s		**26** PANIS Ligier 1m 19.304s	
24 ALBORETO Minardi 1m 19.517s		**12** HERBERT Lotus 1m 19.483s	
11 LAMY Lotus 1m 19.975s		**19** BERETTA Larrousse 1m 19.524s	
31 BRABHAM Simtek 1m 21.186s		**34** GACHOT Pacific 1m 20.729s	

NON-STARTERS

- DNQ **32** RATZENBERGER Simtek 1m 22.707s
- DNQ **33** BELMONDO Pacific no time

LAP CHART

Race distance: 71 laps, 190.807 miles / 307.075 km

1st Lap Order: 2 SENNA, 27 ALESI, 5 SCHUMACHER, 0 HILL, 30 FRENTZEN, 7 HÄKKINEN, 29 WENDLINGER, 28 BERGER, 6 VERSTAPPEN, 10 MORBIDELLI, 14 BARRICHELLO, 3 KATAYAMA, 15 IRVINE, 9 FITTIPALDI, 4 BLUNDELL, 8 BRUNDLE, 23 MARTINI, 12 HERBERT, 20 COMAS, 24 ALBORETO, 26 PANIS, 25 BERNARD, 19 BERETTA, 11 LAMY, 34 GACHOT, 31 BRABHAM

(pink = One lap behind leader)

CHASSIS LOG BOOK

No.	Driver	Chassis
0	Hill	Williams FW16/3
2	Senna	Williams FW16/2
	spare	Williams FW16/1
3	Katayama	Tyrrell 022/2
4	Blundell	Tyrrell 022/1
	spare	Tyrrell 022/3
5	Schumacher	Benetton B194/2
6	Verstappen	Benetton B194/1
	spare	Benetton B194/3
7	Häkkinen	McLaren MP4/9/3
8	Brundle	McLaren MP4/9/2
	spare	McLaren MP4/9/4
9	Fittipaldi	Footwork FA15/1
10	Morbidelli	Footwork FA15/2
	spare	Footwork FA15/3
11	Lamy	Lotus 107C/1
12	Herbert	Lotus 107C/3
	spare	Lotus 107C/2
14	Barrichello	Jordan 194/4
15	Irvine	Jordan 194/3
	spare	Jordan 194/2
19	Beretta	Larrousse LH94/2
20	Comas	Larrousse LH94/1
	spare	Larrousse LH94/3
23	Martini	Minardi M193B/4
24	Alboreto	Minardi M193B/1
	spare	Minardi M193B/3
25	Bernard	Ligier JS39B/6
26	Panis	Ligier JS39B/4
	spare	Ligier JS39B/2
27	Alesi	Ferrari 412T1/150
28	Berger	Ferrari 412T1/151
	spare	Ferrari 412T1/149
29	Wendlinger	Sauber C13/4
30	Frentzen	Sauber C13/3
	spare	Sauber C13/1
31	Brabham	Simtek S194/2
32	Ratzenberger	Simtek S194/1
33	Belmondo	Pacific PR01/1
34	Gachot	Pacific PR01/2

CONSTRUCTORS' CUP

1	BENETTON-FORD	10
2	WILLIAMS-RENAULT	6
3	FERRARI	4
4	JORDAN-HART	3
5	TYRRELL-YAMAHA	2
6	SAUBER-MERCEDES	1

FOR THE RECORD

First Grand Prix start
Jos Verstappen
Olivier Beretta
Olivier Panis
Heinz-Harald Frentzen

First Grand Prix points
Ukyo Katayama

DRIVERS' POINTS

- 1 SCHUMACHER — 10
- 2 HILL — 6
- 3 ALESI — 4
- 4 BARRICHELLO — 3
- 5 KATAYAMA — 2
- 6 WENDLINGER — 1

WORLD CHAMPIONSHIP • ROUND 2

SCHUMACHER
BERGER
BARRICHELLO
FITTIPALDI
FRENTZEN
COMAS

PACIFIC GRAND PRIX

Ayrton Senna may have beaten Michael Schumacher to pole position for the first Pacific Grand Prix to be held at Japan's spanking new TI Circuit, but when the starting light blinked green, Benetton's *Wunderkind* showed a clean pair of heels to the entire field, dominating the second round of the World Championship even more decisively than he had the opening race at Interlagos. Senna's disappointing run continued when he was punted off into the gravel trap at the first corner by Mika Häkkinen's McLaren and then T-boned for good measure by Nicola Larini's Ferrari. Schumacher was thus left to play things as he pleased through to the end of the 83-lap contest, his clear-cut advantage never looking even slightly threatened through his two superbly timed refuelling stops. By the chequered flag, only Gerhard Berger's Ferrari 412T1 was left on the same lap while the remainder of the F1 fraternity could only sit and ponder what was to be done to get on terms with Benetton and Ford across the remainder of the season.

Above: The land of hero-worship offers a seemingly inexhaustible supply of magazines for the country's motor racing fans. They certainly had plenty of time to read them *(left)* while being bussed in and out of the remote circuit.

Ayrton Senna's race was a short one. Having gained pole position, he was pitched off the track at the first corner by Mika Häkkinen. *Below:* Ferrari's Nicola Larini joins the Brazilian in retirement after an 'off' of his own.

PACIFIC GRAND PRIX

Bernie Ecclestone and Hajime Tanaka seem well pleased with the success of the inaugural Pacific Grand Prix held at the Japanese millionaire's lavish new Tanaka International Circuit.

ENTRY AND PRACTICE

Japan's admission to the exclusive group of countries permitted to hold two World Championship Grands Prix in a single year was confirmed with the arrival on the calendar of the so-called Pacific Grand Prix at the lavish new Tanaka International Circuit, modestly named after entrepreneur Hajime Tanaka, the architect of this multi-million-dollar project. The son of a wealthy businessman whose fortune was founded on mining activities in Japan's Yamaguchi prefecture, the area around the city of Aida in which the new circuit was constructed, Tanaka had previously devoted his energies to the operation of highly exclusive golfing resorts, and the TI Speedway owed its origins to a similar concept. Tanaka's plan was to build what amounted to a lavish motor racing country club to which the super-rich could bring their high-performance road and historic racing cars to indulge in some high-price escapism on a certain number of days each year.

The remote but well appointed 2.3-mile facility was completed in 1990, its formal opening celebrated with an historic car meeting graced by distinguished old timers including Stirling Moss and former Le Mans winner Richard Attwood. But once the fanfares had subsided, Tanaka was left facing the challenge of turning his reputed £65 million investment into a workable commercial proposition.

His plans were hampered by the apparent reluctance of the Japanese Automobile Federation to grant the track anything more ambitious than F3 and touring car events. His applications to host a round of the prestigious national F3000 series were consistently turned down on the grounds – somewhat specious, perhaps – that the track was too tight, a verdict allegedly encouraged by lobbying from both Fuji and Suzuka, Japan's best-known and internationally established tracks.

Tanaka admitted that he first discussed the possibility of building the circuit seven years earlier with Bernie Ecclestone, publicly claiming credit for the track layout – 'I did it myself, like I did my golf course, on my own.' This observation produced raised eyebrows from many seasoned F1 hands who had already concluded that the circuit conformed to the slow-corner, television-friendly specifications pioneered by Jerez, the Hungaroring and Barcelona.

Moreover, the fact that the circuit was situated over one hundred miles from Osaka, Japan's second city, seemed strangely at odds with Mr Tanaka's assertion that the apparently isolated location was chosen 'on a 100 per cent commercial basis'.

By the same token, he side-stepped speculation that a provisional five-year deal had been reached with Ecclestone to guarantee the race's future. 'We will try and improve our event for the future,' said Tanaka enigmatically. Bernie added: 'He understands that all he has to do is make this event successful in order to think about the future.'

With no pre-race testing possible at the new circuit, a familiarisation session was held on the Thursday prior to the race, Michael Schumacher providing further evidence of a shift in the balance of F1 power by taking the Benetton B194 round 1.26 seconds faster than Ayrton Senna's Williams FW16 with Damon Hill third fastest.

Hill freely admitted that Williams looked set for a long struggle to get on terms with the Brazilian GP winner. 'We've definitely got our work cut out here,' he said thoughtfully, 'and it could be quite a while before we can make up the difference. We're going to have a tough time in the first half of the season.

'As far as the track is concerned, it has a low-grip surface but it's quite fun, although I think it will be easy to prevent somebody from overtaking you in the race.'

Schumacher echoed those sentiments. 'Even if you are quicker it will be almost impossible to pass,' he admitted. 'Good strategy is going to be the key to this weekend.'

However, by the end of the first day's official qualifying, things didn't look too bad for the Williams duo. Senna tentatively nudged the Williams FW16 back into the limelight by setting fastest time, although he admitted he was still frustrated by the car's handling imbalance on slow corners.

Schumacher remained confident throughout, feeling that he'd only lost Friday's pole after making a chassis set-up change just before the session which didn't pay off. On Saturday, with conditions much hotter, the German driver didn't even bother to do a single flying lap. 'I wanted to save tyres,' he explained. 'Better to be second on the grid and first in the race!

'When we saw that everyone was going slower than yesterday, we had to think about a change that we wanted to do. Jos [Verstappen] went out early, so we made the change on his car. I just waited then until he'd finished his run to get the answer. I waited until 1.45, but David Brabham had just gone off the circuit when we decided to go out.

'So we made the decision to wait until just before the end of the session before trying. But as soon as I went out, I discovered oil on the circuit and I just came straight back in. There was no sense in staying out, doing nothing and wasting tyres.'

Brabham had cracked his Simtek's sump with a wild spin over the high kerbing on the exit of the tight right-hander leading onto the start/finish straight, thus contributing rather more to the overall grid line-up than he could have anticipated before the weekend!

Senna, by contrast, could see problems looming on the horizon. Both he and Hill spun on the same corner. 'We realised that the circuit had some oil [on it] because when the Simtek driver [Brabham] spun, he was losing liquid and fluid and he washed the circuit with it.

'So when I went out the second time, it was just to run the tyres for tomorrow. Then we tried again with another set, but with the circuit so slippery there was no way for anybody to improve. However, when I was on my first run, the car felt fine – engine, everything worked OK.

'But I really don't know what happened when I spun because the car had one of the best positions at that point of the corner throughout the weekend. It was disappointing and frustrating because it looks silly and stupid. I feel very unhappy about it . . . with myself. But better that it happened today and not tomorrow.'

Hill wound up third on the strength of his Friday best, losing most of the Saturday morning session with his FW16 up on stands in the garage while mechanics probed a suspected differential problem. In the afternoon he was anxious to see how close he could get to his Friday best.

'My first run was my first real laps of the day,' said Damon, 'but on my second I thought I would take it a bit easier and I spun, so that was a bit worrying. I hope there is some coincidence why we spun on the same corner as we have got to go round there eighty-odd times tomorrow!'

Fourth place fell to Mika Häkkinen's McLaren MP4/9, although the Finn's energetic performance in the first qualifying session also saw him slide wide coming out of the final right-hander before the pits, wrecking his car's undertray over the high kerb. Like Schumacher, he didn't venture out on the second day, a strategy also adopted by his teammate Martin Brundle, who had managed to qualify sixth on the first day.

Gerhard Berger's Ferrari 412T1 split the McLarens, but the Italian team was at the centre of a major controversy after allegedly running what amounted to an illegal traction control system – in the guise of an adjustable rev-limiter – in Friday morning's free practice session. This whole matter developed a momentum of its own, with thinly veiled allegations about unsporting behaviour from rival teams matched by self-righteously indignant denials from Ferrari sporting chief Jean Todt (see sidebar).

Berger, meanwhile, settled down to produce a strong fifth place in the first qualifying session, despite concern about a potential rear suspension problem and an over-abrupt engine response which caused the car to snap into sudden oversteer, much to the detriment of rear tyre wear.

Test driver Nicola Larini was on hand to deputise for Jean Alesi, the Frenchman having sustained damaged vertebrae in a testing accident at Mugello during the week immediately following the Brazilian GP, and it was around the Italian driver's 412T1 that the speculation of technical non-conformity raged. Larini, meanwhile, did a solid job and took seventh place on the grid, although his Saturday afternoon stint came to a premature end when he clipped Katayama's pirouetting Tyrrell and limped back to the pit lane with broken right-rear suspension and consequent damage to the differential.

Rubens Barrichello produced a storming performance to qualify his Jordan eighth, ahead of the Footwork FA15 of Christian Fittipaldi, the highest-placed competitor to produce his best time in Saturday's hotter conditions. Christian had been handicapped on Friday first by fuel pump trouble, then by a glitch in the Footwork's semi-automatic gearchange system with the result that he was left trailing in an overnight 15th place.

Deputising for the suspended Irvine, Japanese driver Aguri Suzuki took over the second Jordan for this race, but the former Footwork regular was well off the pace, reflecting the fact that he had been

PACIFIC GRAND PRIX

> **Diary**
>
> Mercedes-Benz takes the wraps off totally new engine purpose-made for the Penske team's use in this year's Indianapolis 500.
>
> Eddie Jordan denies rumours that he is to approach Nigel Mansell to stand in for Eddie Irvine at the San Marino GP.
>
> Toyota gears up for a 1995 Indy Car programme in partnership with Dan Gurney's All American Racers organisation.
>
> Doubts are raised over the likelihood of the Argentine Grand Prix taking place on its scheduled date of 16 October. Jerez, Donington Park and the new Nürburgring are named as possible alternative venues.

out of a Grand Prix cockpit since the end of the previous season.

'I had no real problems today,' he shrugged on Friday, 'and it's getting better and better as I have more time in the car. My set-up was quite soft today, though, and maybe tomorrow I will try different settings.' He was able to reduce his time by a tenth of a second in the hotter conditions but remained in 20th place overall.

In tenth place, Jos Verstappen was a touch disappointed with his performance in the second Benetton B194. On Friday morning he had a couple of spins and he then suffered a minor gearchange glitch on the second day and couldn't quite match his Friday best.

'We improved the car a little on Saturday morning,' he explained, 'but when I went out on my first qualifying run, there was a problem with the gearbox and I came back to the pits after only a single lap. When that was sorted out, the car felt better, although it was not behaving particularly well on the slow corners. We tried running more wing, but that affected the straightline speed and I couldn't improve.'

Sauber-Mercedes driver Karl Wendlinger opened proceedings with a spin on Friday morning and was very unhappy with the chassis set-up, complaining of such dire lack of grip that he switched to the spare car for Saturday morning. His efforts were in vain and he slipped to a highly disappointed 19th – eight places behind Heinz-Harald Frentzen, who had been tenth on the first day before plunging into a gravel trap, which brought his session to a premature end.

Mark Blundell lost time with a punctured water radiator on his Tyrrell 022-Yamaha during the first qualifying session and his final run was spoiled by a combination of traffic and marshals removing a car from the track under the cover of a yellow flag. Amazingly, both he and team-mate Ukyo Katayama ended the day with an identical lap in 1m 13.013s, taking overnight 12th and 13th places.

'We made a major revision to the set-up since yesterday's testing, and this has improved the car a great deal,' explained Blundell, 'but we need more chassis work to improve its balance in the slower corners.'

In the second session, that set-up change yielded Mark a 0.3s improvement, enabling him to vault ahead of Gianni Morbidelli's Footwork to retain 12th place in the final line-up despite Fittipaldi's progress. On Saturday Katayama got involved in that brush with Larini's Ferrari and failed to better his time, slipping to 14th place as a result.

Michele Alboreto managed to bag 16th on Friday, despite struggling for chassis balance in his Minardi M193B, and the veteran Italian gained one further place the following day. Pierluigi Martini improved his set-up after Friday morning's free practice session, but then threw his chances away by sliding off early in the crucial first qualifying period, emerging in 17th place. In the second session he somehow contrived to time his quickest run at the wrong moment, going out when the circuit was covered in oil and thus failing to improve.

In the Larrousse camp, Erik Comas had raised team spirits with a strong third-fastest time in Friday morning's free session, but could only manage 14th at the end of the first day. By Saturday morning the team was confident it had pinpointed this apparently abrupt drop-off in form to a fault in its tyre warming blankets. Unfortunately Comas had an unlucky time in second qualifying, being bumped another couple of places by Fittipaldi and Alboreto after another spin.

Olivier Beretta added to the team's workload by going off the track on both Friday morning and Saturday afternoon, on the latter occasion falling foul of Brabham's oil slick. The bottom line was a disappointing 21st grid placing for the French novice.

In 18th place, Eric Bernard performed dependably at the wheel of the under-developed Ligier JS39B while team-mate Olivier Panis found himself down in 22nd, struggling for grip and also taking time off for a spin into a gravel trap on Saturday morning.

For the Lotus drivers, it was just a question of slogging along with the overweight Lotus 107C test car and hoping for the best. Johnny Herbert and Pedro Lamy eventually lined up 23-24, the Englishman bothered more by understeer on Friday than by the acute lack of grip reported by his team-mate. Johnny found the chassis balance slightly improved in second qualifying, but although he shaved 0.1s off his best time it didn't enhance his starting position.

'The balance of my car was a little better, but overall, the level of grip was still very low,' explained a frustrated Herbert. 'Just after I went out for my second run, somebody put some oil down on the track, which, in any case, was around two- or three-tenths of a second slower today due to the higher ambient temperature, so I'm just grateful that I was one of the few able to improve.'

Rounding off the grid were the two Simteks of David Brabham and Roland Ratzenberger, the Australian having turned a praiseworthy 19th-fastest time on Saturday before that sump-cracking excursion. Ratzenberger, meanwhile, was the only man to have raced previously on the TI Circuit, but crashed heavily on Friday morning and had to sit out the first qualifying session while his car was repaired. On Saturday he coped admirably with the pressure to ease out both Pacifics and secure his first F1 start.

Understandably, both Gachot and Belmondo were extremely disappointed not to make the cut. Lack of slow-corner grip plagued both cars and Bertrand suffered an engine failure on Friday morning, a fresh Ilmor V10 being installed for first qualifying. Then on Saturday morning the replacement engine picked up a stone which snapped the oil pump drive belt. Although the engine appeared to have survived intact, this proved not to be the case when he began the second qualifying session, so he switched to Belmondo's car for the final few moments in an unsuccessful attempt to bump Ratzenberger from last place in the line-up.

RACE

The race morning warm-up saw Williams experimenting by slightly raising the ride heights on the FW16s, feeling that their problems in qualifying may have been caused by the cars running a little too low. Senna duly delivered fastest time ahead of Hill, Berger, Wendlinger – whose car now seemed transformed, although nobody appeared to know why – and Schumacher.

Come the start, Senna slightly fluffed his getaway, allowing Schumacher to draw level on the sprint down to the first right-hander. Ayrton seemed to move right slightly in an apparent attempt to squeeze the Benetton ace, but Michael decisively took the line as Senna moved back to the left to make a more suitable approach to the corner.

By this stage, Häkkinen was coming up fast on the right and, as the cars swung into the turn, the McLaren's nose just lightly bumped the rear of the Williams. Senna was suddenly pitched into an elegant spin and came to rest in the sand trap on the left-hand side of the circuit,

---

Ferrari and traction control – a storm in a tea cup?

The Ferrari team found itself embroiled in potential controversy at the Pacific Grand Prix when it was alleged that Nicola Larini's car had run what amounted to a traction control system – banned under the 1994 F1 technical regulations – in the first free practice session on Friday morning.

FIA Technical Delegate Charlie Whiting was alerted to a possible irregularity when he detected a fluttering engine note on Larini's car while watching from the trackside. He subsequently conferred with Ferrari team director Jean Todt and advised the team not to use such a device – understood to be a variable rev-limiter – for the balance of the weekend while the question of its conformity with the regulations was further considered.

Rival teams were extremely sceptical about the way in which the FIA dealt with this apparent problem. 'I rather suspect that if it had been us [Williams] we would have been on our way home by now,' remarked Patrick Head on the morning of the race.

However, Maranello was subsequently cleared of infringing the regulations. A week later the FIA issued an official communiqué which read:

'In essence, these devices [used on the Ferrari] change the characteristics of the engine according to certain predetermined instructions. The "map" of the engine, or the permissible throttle opening, or the rev limit, may be different in each gear. Alternatively, the characteristics of the engine may change according to the whereabouts of the car on the circuit, or be set at will by the driver.

'Devices of this kind are not traction control because they are not influenced in any way by the behaviour of the rear wheels.'

FIA President Max Mosley nevertheless restated his total confidence in the ability of the sport's governing body to detect the use of illegal traction control systems on the current breed of F1 car. 'Nothing that happened in Japan leads me to doubt our ability to police these systems,' he said firmly.

Be that as it may, many rival teams concluded that Ferrari had effectively breached the rules by interfering with the throttle opening and the amount of power given by the engine at a given speed by overriding the driver's throttle input.

'The question that remains is what Ferrari was using this system for,' continued Patrick Head. 'Traction control is not defined specifically in the regulations, so it is my opinion that any means of pre-setting power levels in this way is intended to have a similar effect.'

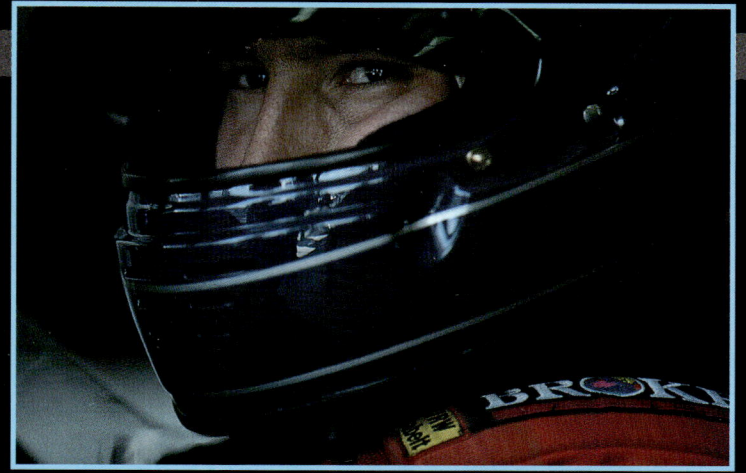

Heinz-Harald Frentzen *(right)* scored his first championship points in only his second Grand Prix.

Rubens Barrichello *(below)* benefited from the late-race retirement of Martin Brundle to take third place. The young Brazilian thus made the podium for the first time in his career.

***Bottom:* Gerhard Berger took second place, and the Ferrari driver was the only runner not to be lapped by the totally dominant Michael Schumacher.**

Paul-Henri Cahier

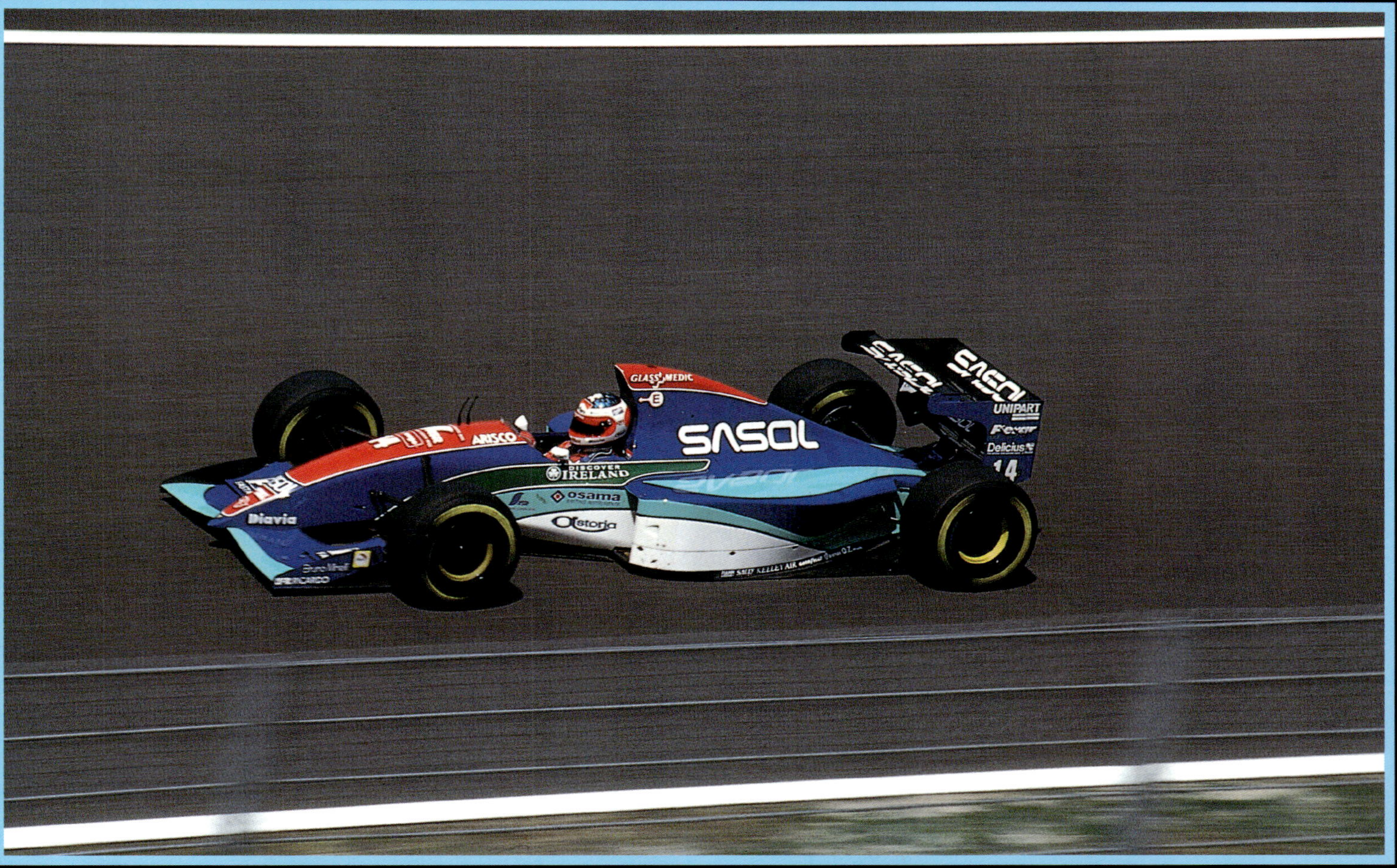

Dominique Leroy

LAT Photographic

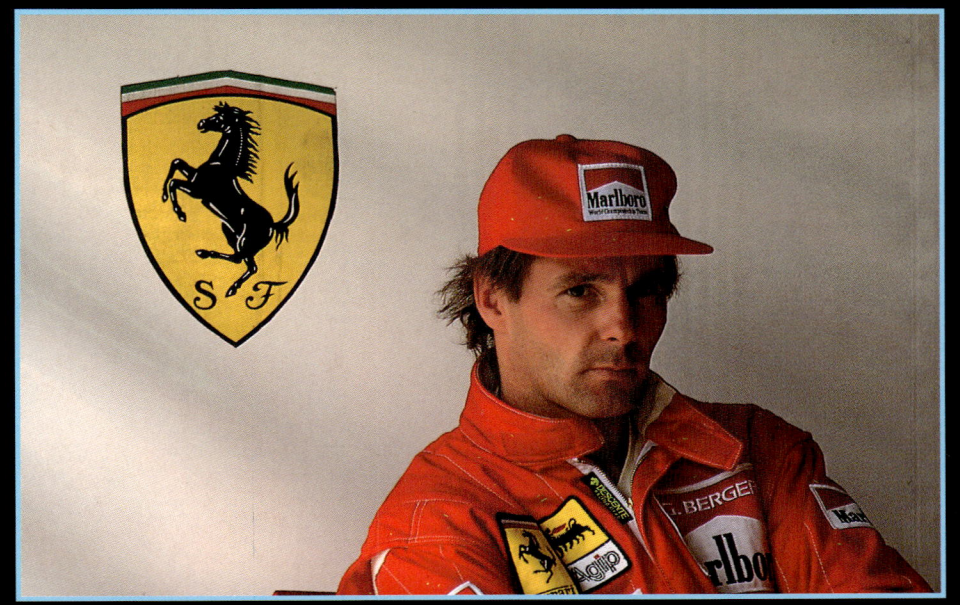

PACIFIC GRAND PRIX

Right: In the enforced absence of Eddie Irvine, Jordan enlisted an able deputy in Aguri Suzuki. The experienced Japanese driver – without any single-seater testing since the end of the previous year – was well off the pace.

Below: A temporary change of livery for the Tourtel Larrousse team was made worthwhile when Erik Comas gained some exposure by taking sixth place.

After crashing out in Friday's first qualifying session, Roland Ratzenberger *(bottom)* did extremely well to make the cut with the Simtek on Saturday. In the race he took things steadily to finish 11th.

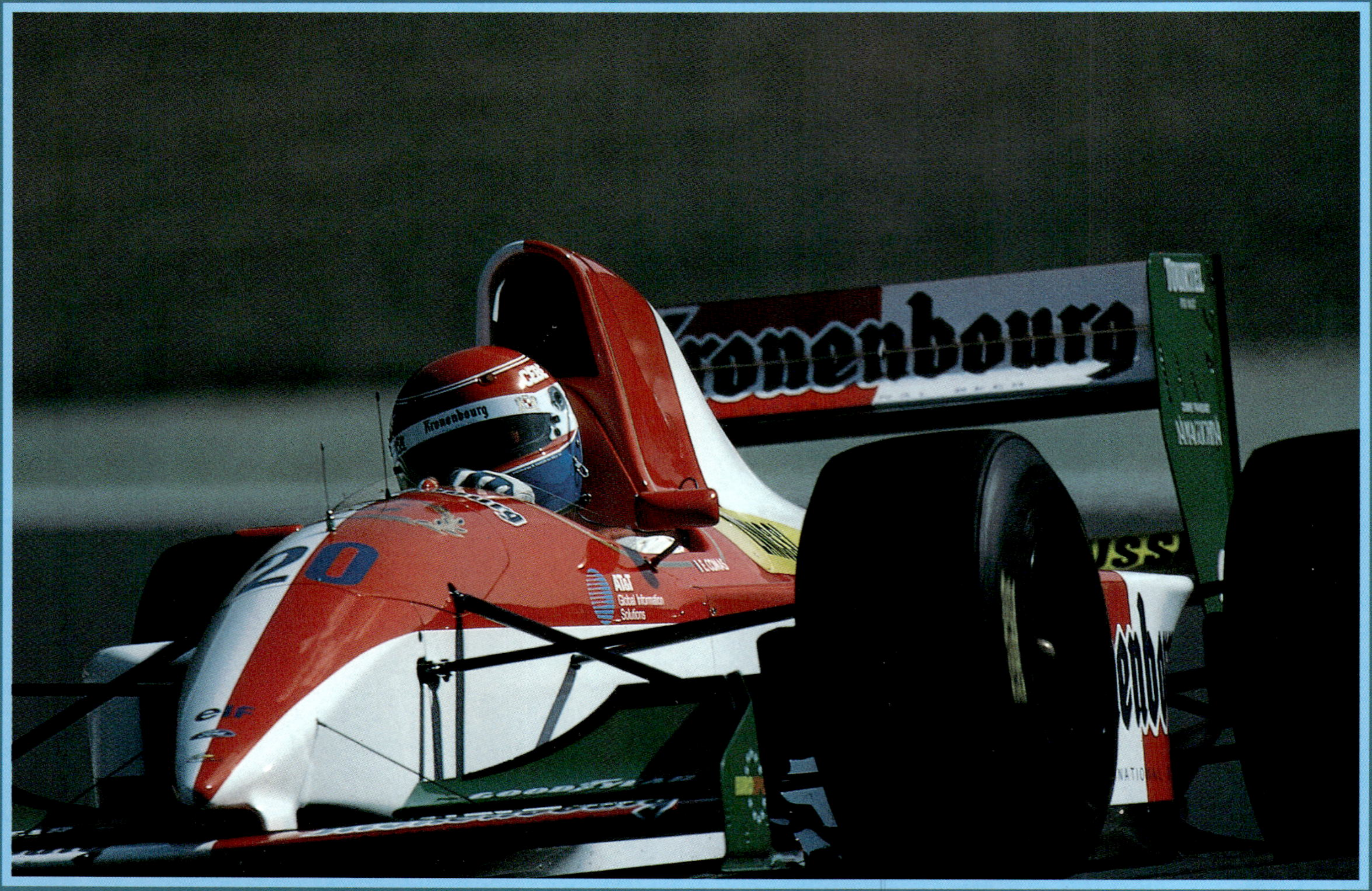

PACIFIC GRAND PRIX

The well-equipped circuit was definitely of the modern, slow-corner variety. Young guns Christian Fittipaldi, Heinz-Harald Frentzen, Jos Verstappen, Gianni Morbidelli, running in line astern, contest the midfield places.

where he was gently T-boned by Larini's Ferrari, the Italian finding himself with nowhere else to go. After his disappointment at Interlagos, this was another bitter blow for the new Williams team leader.

'I made a normal start, but I didn't get a brilliant one,' said Senna for public consumption later in the day. 'I had too much wheelspin, so Michael took the lead. On the first corner we were close together and it was possible to try an overtaking manoeuvre, but that would have been very risky, so I decided to stay second and be safe.

'Then, when I was into the corner, Mika came from behind, hit me and I was out. As a consequence, other cars spun and then Larini came and hit me. I was out of the race.

'He [Häkkinen] should not be allowed to get away with this. His driving was wrong and should not be permitted. Many of these young drivers just don't seem to know the rules.'

One man who had every right to be annoyed with this episode was Blundell. The Tyrrell driver braked hard to avoid the mêlée, but was hit from behind by Comas's Larrousse, spun and stalled his engine.

Häkkinen, by contrast, was matter-of-fact about the whole affair. 'It's a pity I touched Ayrton,' he shrugged, 'but he braked late, as did Michael in front of him. I couldn't avoid him.'

After the race, Häkkinen sought out Senna to apologise, but the incensed Brazilian was not easily placated and hurled a torrent of abuse at the crestfallen Finn. 'I won't tell you what he said,' said Mika, 'but it wasn't complimentary or positive!'

All this early drama meant that it was effectively a cakewalk for Schumacher. Even by the end of the opening lap he was 2.6 seconds ahead, he had opened out 4.03s on Häkkinen by lap three and was 9.3s ahead of the McLaren by lap ten.

Hill, frustrated at being boxed in behind the Peugeot-engined car, attempted to run round the outside of Häkkinen on one of the tight infield hairpins. It was an unsuccessful strategy, the Englishman finding himself edged up the kerb and helped into a spin.

'He closed the door on me,' said Damon, bristling, 'put me on a kerb and I spun off. I should have known it would happen, because he's a bit of a wild boy. He comes up to you on the grid and he shakes your hand, which is jolly sporting and makes him seem like a normal person. But when he gets into the car and puts on his helmet, he turns into some sort of demon.'

That little drama left Damon down in ninth place and had the effect of promoting Berger to third ahead of Barrichello, Brundle and Christian Fittipaldi's Footwork. David Brabham retired with engine failure after two laps, while Häkkinen's McLaren began emitting an ominous haze from around lap ten.

At the end of lap 18, Mika came into the pits for a routine stop. However, the young Finn noticed that the hydraulic pressure had dropped significantly and the engine stalled. He went out for another lap, but the loss of pressure was seriously affecting his ability to select gears, so back in he came for good next time round.

Thus by lap 20 we had Schumacher 41 seconds ahead of Berger, and when Michael made a routine refuelling stop at the end of lap 23 he resumed 25 seconds ahead, which swelled to 33.9 seconds over Barrichello's Jordan when Berger and Brundle both came in to refuel at the end of lap 27.

By now Hill had made his first stop at the end of lap 18 and was poised to capitalise on the flurry of refuelling visits made by his rivals between laps 25 and 30. The net result was that Barrichello's stop at the end of lap 30 promoted Damon to second place, albeit over half a minute behind Schumacher's Benetton.

The sole surviving Williams came in for a second (6.9-second) refuelling stop at the end of lap 42, keeping second place but now almost a full minute behind the leader. Just as it looked as though Damon might be in line for his second consecutive second-place finish, his FW16 abruptly lost drive and he coasted to a halt out on the circuit.

Damon's demise was the cue for Schumacher to make his second refuelling stop (8.3 seconds) at the end of lap 51, the matchless Benetton B194 returning to the fray still over 50 seconds ahead of Berger, who now had Barrichello worryingly close behind.

Verstappen was by now challenging for his first helping of championship points, moving up to sixth place and then fourth by the time of his second stop on lap 54. However, the Dutchman's anxiety to keep ahead of Frentzen's sixth-placed Sauber was his undoing. Benetton's new boy sprinted out of the pit lane and threw the B194 straight into the sand trap at the first corner!

When Berger stopped at the end of lap 56, Rubens surged by into second place, but the young Brazilian's aspirations were almost snuffed out at his third pit stop when he stalled his engine.

'We had decided to go for the harder "B" compound tyres for the first two runs and then leave 20 laps at the finish for softer "Cs",' he explained. 'Then I had a problem with the last pit stop when the engine died. I said to myself, "I can't believe I am not going to the podium today." I wanted to cry!'

Barrichello resumed in fourth place behind Brundle's McLaren, but Martin's Peugeot V10 began to overheat in the closing stages, finally expiring at the end of lap 69. Close examination revealed that one of the McLaren's radiator cooling ducts had been blocked by a plastic rip-off visor from somebody else's helmet. Martin just shrugged it aside stoically and walked away.

This was all merely fine detail compared with Schumacher's utter and complete domination of the race. He surged past the chequered flag well over a minute ahead of Berger's Ferrari, which was the only other car to complete the full 83-lap distance.

Barrichello was promoted back to third place on Brundle's departure from the fray, leaving Fittipaldi, Frentzen and Comas to take the remaining top-six positions, Morbidelli's Footwork having blown its engine and spun out of fifth place on his own oil with an unlucky 13 laps to go.

At the same time, Alboreto got a little too exuberant in his efforts to displace Wendlinger's Sauber from seventh place, trying to pass the Mercedes-engined machine where there was not quite sufficient room going into a tight left-hander. The two cars made smart contact and ended up in the sand trap, a drama which promoted the Lotus duo, Herbert and Lamy, to seventh and eighth places after a couple of unspectacular, if mechanically reliable, runs at the tail of the field.

As Schumacher and the Benetton team revelled in their second win of the season, all that was left for the rest of the field was the long journey back to Europe. The main rump of the season on familiar circuits now beckoned. Surely, it would be different at Imola.

117

FIA FORMULA ONE WORLD CHAMPIONSHIP ROUND 2

PACIFIC GRAND PRIX AIDA
15-17 APRIL 1994

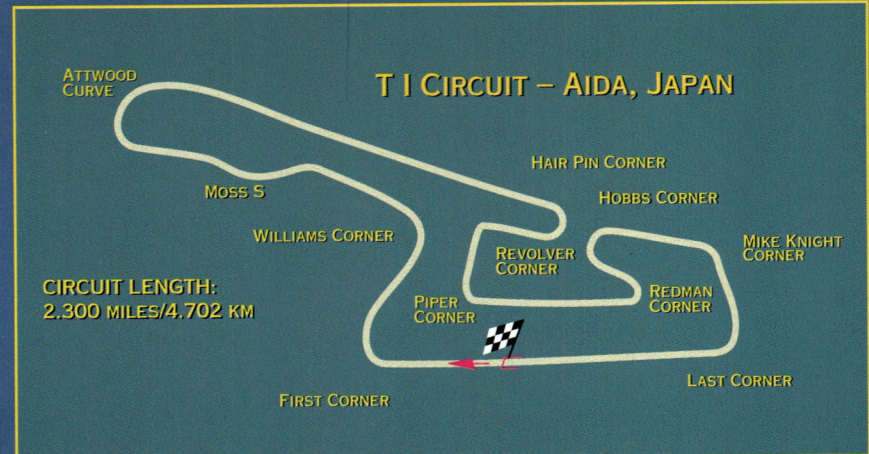

RACE WEATHER: Dry, warm, sunny

Place	Driver	Nat.	No.	Entrant	Car/Engine	Laps	Time/Retirement	Speed (mph/km/h)
1	**Michael Schumacher**	D	5	**Mild Seven Benetton Ford**	Benetton B194-Ford Zetec-R V8	83	1h 46m 01.693s	108.042/173.877
2	**Gerhard Berger**	A	28	**Scuderia Ferrari**	Ferrari 412T1 041 V12	83	1h 47m 16.993s	106.778/171.843
3	**Rubens Barrichello**	BR	14	**Sasol Jordan**	Jordan 194-Hart 1035 V10	82		
4	**Christian Fittipaldi**	BR	9	**Footwork Ford**	Footwork FA15-Ford HB V8	82		
5	**Heinz-Harald Frentzen**	D	30	**Broker Sauber Mercedes**	Sauber C13-Mercedes-Benz V10	82		
6	**Erik Comas**	F	20	**Tourtel Larrousse F1**	Larrousse LH94-Ford HB V8	80		
7	Johnny Herbert	GB	12	Team Lotus	Lotus 107C-Mugen Honda ZA5C V10	80		
8	Pedro Lamy	P	11	Team Lotus	Lotus 107C-Mugen Honda ZA5C V10	79		
9	Olivier Panis	F	26	Ligier Gitanes Blondes	Ligier JS39B-Renault RS6 V10	78		
10	Eric Bernard	F	25	Ligier Gitanes Blondes	Ligier JS39B-Renault RS6 V10	78		
11	Roland Ratzenberger	A	32	MTV Simtek Ford	Simtek S941-Ford HB V8	78		
	Gianni Morbidelli	I	10	Footwork Ford	Footwork FA15-Ford HB V8	69	Engine	
	Karl Wendlinger	A	29	Broker Sauber Mercedes	Sauber C13-Mercedes Benz V10	69	Collision with Alboreto	
	Michele Alboreto	I	24	Minardi Scuderia Italia	Minardi M193B-Ford HB V8	69	Collision with Wendlinger	
	Martin Brundle	GB	8	Marlboro McLaren Peugeot	McLaren MP4/9-Peugeot A6 V10	67	Engine	
	Pierluigi Martini	I	23	Minardi Scuderia Italia	Minardi M193B-Ford HB V8	63	Electrics	
	Jos Verstappen	NL	6	Mild Seven Benetton Ford	Benetton B194-Ford Zetec-R V8	54	Spun off	
	Damon Hill	GB	0	Rothmans Williams Renault	Williams FW16-Renault RS6 V10	49	Transmission	
	Aguri Suzuki	J	15	Sasol Jordan	Jordan 194-Hart 1035 V10	44	Accident	
	Ukyo Katayama	J	3	Tyrrell	Tyrrell 022-Yamaha 0X10A V10	42	Engine	
	Mika Häkkinen	SF	7	Marlboro McLaren Peugeot	McLaren MP4/9-Peugeot A4 V10	19	Hydraulics	
	Olivier Beretta	F	19	Tourtel Larrousse F1	Larrousse LH94-Ford HB V8	14	Electrics	
	David Brabham	AUS	31	MTV Simtek Ford	Simtek S941-Ford HB V8	2	Engine	
	Ayrton Senna	BR	2	Rothmans Williams Renault	Williams FW16-Renault RS6 V10	0	Accident	
	Mark Blundell	GB	4	Tyrrell	Tyrrell 022-Yamaha 0X10A V10	0	Accident	
	Nicola Larini	I	27	Scuderia Ferrari	Ferrari 412T1 041 V12	0	Accident	
DNQ	Bertrand Gachot	F	34	Pacific Grand Prix Ltd	Pacific PR01-Ilmor 2175A V10			
DNQ	Paul Belmondo	F	33	Pacific Grand Prix Ltd	Pacific PR01-Ilmor 2175A V10			

Fastest lap: Schumacher, on lap 10, 1m 14.023s, 111.872 mph/180.041 km/h (record).
Previous lap record: Tom Kristensen (F3 Ralt-Toyota), 1m 27.027s, 95.155 mph/153.138 km/h (1992).

All results and data © FIA 1994

QUALIFYING 1

Ayrton Senna	**1m 10.218s**
Michael Schumacher	**1m 10.440s**
Damon Hill	**1m 10.771s**
Mika Häkkinen	1m 11.683s
Gerhard Berger	**1m 11.744s**
Martin Brundle	1m 12.351s
Nicola Larini	1m 12.372s
Rubens Barrichello	**1m 12.409s**
Jos Verstappen	1m 12.554s
Heinz-Harald Frentzen	**1m 12.686s**
Gianni Morbidelli	1m 12.866s
Mark Blundell	1m 13.013s
Ukyo Katayama	1m 13.013s
Erik Comas	1m 13.111s
Christian Fittipaldi	1m 13.169s
Michele Alboreto	1m 13.342s
Pierluigi Martini	**1m 13.529s**
Eric Bernard	1m 13.613s
Karl Wendlinger	1m 13.855s
Aguri Suzuki	1m 14.036s
Olivier Beretta	**1m 14.101s**
Olivier Panis	**1m 14.106s**
Johnny Herbert	1m 14.538s
Pedro Lamy	**1m 14.657s**
David Brabham	1m 14.946s
Bertrand Gachot	**1m 16.927s**
Paul Belmondo	1m 18.671s
Roland Ratzenberger	no time

Friday afternoon
Dry, warm, sunny

QUALIFYING 2

Damon Hill	1m 12.048s
Gerhard Berger	1m 12.184s
Christian Fittipaldi	**1m 12.444s**
Jos Verstappen	1m 12.681s
Mark Blundell	**1m 12.751s**
Heinz-Harald Frentzen	1m 12.797s
Michele Alboreto	**1m 13.016s**
Gianni Morbidelli	1m 13.090s
Rubens Barrichello	1m 13.172s
Ukyo Katayama	1m 13.411s
Erik Comas	1m 13.550s
Pierluigi Martini	1m 13.758s
Aguri Suzuki	**1m 13.932s**
Karl Wendlinger	1m 14.163s
Eric Bernard	1m 14.204s
Olivier Beretta	1m 14.271s
Johnny Herbert	**1m 14.424s**
Olivier Panis	1m 14.687s
David Brabham	**1m 14.748s**
Pedro Lamy	1m 15.148s
Roland Ratzenberger	**1m 16.356s**
Paul Belmondo	**1m 17.450s**
Bertrand Gachot	1m 18.511s
Ayrton Senna	1m 19.304s
Nicola Larini	5m 32.428s
Michael Schumacher	no time
Mika Häkkinen	no time
Martin Brundle	no time

Saturday afternoon
Dry, hot, sunny

WARM-UP

Ayrton Senna	1m 12.872s
Damon Hill	1m 12.916s
Gerhard Berger	1m 13.653s
Karl Wendlinger	1m 13.665s
Michael Schumacher	1m 13.744s
Mark Blundell	1m 13.825s
Erik Comas	1m 13.834s
Mika Häkkinen	1m 14.096s
Christian Fittipaldi	1m 14.116s
Heinz-Harald Frentzen	1m 14.148s
Martin Brundle	1m 14.197s
Nicola Larini	1m 14.235s
Michele Alboreto	1m 14.607s
Ukyo Katayama	1m 14.637s
Gianni Morbidelli	1m 14.760s
Rubens Barrichello	1m 14.768s
Pierluigi Martini	1m 14.921s
Aguri Suzuki	1m 15.040s
Jos Verstappen	1m 15.512s
David Brabham	1m 15.783s
Olivier Panis	1m 15.876s
Olivier Beretta	1m 16.183s
Eric Bernard	1m 16.635s
Johnny Herbert	1m 16.764s
Pedro Lamy	1m 16.775s
Roland Ratzenberger	1m 17.110s

Sunday morning
Dry, cool, bright

FASTEST LAPS

Driver	Time	Lap
Michael Schumacher	1m 14.023s	10
Damon Hill	1m 14.348s	45
Martin Brundle	1m 14.684s	54
Mika Häkkinen	1m 14.697s	8
Jos Verstappen	1m 15.257s	49
Christian Fittipaldi	1m 15.884s	26
Gerhard Berger	1m 15.931s	24
Michele Alboreto	1m 15.994s	44
Rubens Barrichello	1m 16.061s	64
Erik Comas	1m 16.120s	3
Heinz-Harald Frentzen	1m 16.239s	51
Gianni Morbidelli	1m 16.304s	32
Ukyo Katayama	1m 16.482s	40
Pierluigi Martini	1m 16.639s	56
Karl Wendlinger	1m 16.651s	27
Olivier Panis	1m 16.795s	2
Aguri Suzuki	1m 17.015s	32
Eric Bernard	1m 17.390s	45
Johnny Herbert	1m 17.775s	29
Olivier Beretta	1m 17.880s	9
Pedro Lamy	1m 18.527s	12
Roland Ratzenberger	1m 19.248s	9
David Brabham	1m 19.401s	2

STARTING GRID

Pos	No	Driver	Team	Time
1	2	SENNA	Williams	1m 10.218s
2	5	SCHUMACHER	Benetton	1m 10.440s
3	0	HILL	Williams	1m 10.771s
4	7	HÄKKINEN	McLaren	1m 11.683s
5	28	BERGER	Ferrari	1m 11.744s
6	8	BRUNDLE	McLaren	1m 12.351s
7	27	LARINI	Ferrari	1m 12.372s
8	14	BARRICHELLO	Jordan	1m 12.409s
9	9	FITTIPALDI	Footwork	1m 12.444s
10	6	VERSTAPPEN	Benetton	1m 12.554s
11	30	FRENTZEN	Sauber	1m 12.686s
12	4	BLUNDELL	Tyrrell	1m 12.751s
13	10	MORBIDELLI	Footwork	1m 12.866s
14	3	KATAYAMA	Tyrrell	1m 13.013s
15	24	ALBORETO	Minardi	1m 13.016s
16	20	COMAS	Larrousse	1m 13.111s
17	23	MARTINI	Minardi	1m 13.529s
18	25	BERNARD	Ligier	1m 13.613s
19	29	WENDLINGER	Sauber	1m 13.855s
20	15	SUZUKI	Jordan	1m 13.932s
21	19	BERETTA	Larrousse	1m 14.101s
22	26	PANIS	Ligier	1m 14.106s
23	12	HERBERT	Lotus	1m 14.424s
24	11	LAMY	Lotus	1m 14.657s
25	31	BRABHAM	Simtek	1m 14.748s
26	32	RATZENBERGER	Simtek	1m 16.356s

NON-STARTERS

	No	Driver	Team	Time
DNQ	33	BELMONDO	Pacific	1m 17.450s
DNQ	34	GACHOT	Pacific	1m 16.927s

LAP CHART

1st Lap Order: 5 SCHUMACHER, 7 HÄKKINEN, 0 HILL, 28 BERGER, 14 BARRICHELLO, 8 BRUNDLE, 9 FITTIPALDI, 30 FRENTZEN, 6 VERSTAPPEN, 10 MORBIDELLI, 3 KATAYAMA, 24 ALBORETO, 23 MARTINI, 15 SUZUKI, 29 WENDLINGER, 19 BERETTA, 25 BERNARD, 31 BRABHAM, 11 LAMY, 12 HERBERT, 32 RATZENBERGER, 20 COMAS, 26 PANIS

Lap	Order
1	5 7 0 28 14 8 9 30 6 10 3 24 23 15 29 19 25 31 11 12 32 20 26
2	5 7 0 28 14 8 9 30 6 10 3 24 23 15 29 19 25 31 11 12 32 20 26
3	5 7 28 14 8 9 30 6 0 10 3 24 23 29 15 19 25 11 12 32 20 26
4	5 7 28 14 8 9 30 6 0 10 3 24 23 29 15 19 25 11 12 32 20 26
5	5 7 28 14 8 9 30 6 0 10 3 24 23 29 15 19 25 11 12 32 20 26
6	5 7 28 14 8 9 30 6 0 10 3 24 23 29 15 19 25 11 12 32 20 26
7	5 7 28 14 8 9 30 6 0 10 3 24 23 29 15 19 25 11 12 32 20 26
8	5 7 28 14 8 9 0 30 6 10 3 24 23 29 15 19 25 11 12 32 20 26
9	5 7 28 14 8 9 0 30 6 10 3 24 23 29 15 19 25 11 12 32 20 26
10	5 7 28 14 8 0 9 30 6 10 3 24 23 29 15 19 25 11 12 32 20 26
11	5 7 28 14 8 0 9 30 6 10 3 24 23 29 15 19 25 11 12 32 20 26
12	5 7 28 14 0 8 9 30 6 10 3 24 23 29 15 19 25 11 12 32 20 26
13	5 7 28 0 14 8 9 30 6 10 3 24 23 29 15 19 25 11 12 32 20 26
14	5 7 28 0 14 8 9 30 6 10 3 24 23 29 15 19 25 11 12 32 20 26
15	5 7 28 0 14 8 9 30 6 10 3 24 23 29 15 25 11 12 32 20 26
16	5 7 28 0 14 8 9 30 6 10 24 23 29 15 3 25 11 12 32 20 26
17	5 7 28 0 14 8 9 30 6 10 24 23 29 25 3 11 12 32 20 26
18	5 7 28 0 14 8 9 30 6 10 24 23 15 3 25 11 12 32 20 26
19	5 28 14 8 9 30 6 10 7 0 23 15 29 24 3 25 11 12 32 20 26
20	5 28 14 8 9 30 6 10 23 15 29 3 25 11 12 32 20 26
21	5 28 14 8 9 30 6 0 10 15 29 3 25 11 12 20 32 26
22	5 28 14 8 9 0 10 6 15 29 3 23 25 11 12 20 32 26
23	5 28 14 8 30 0 10 9 6 15 29 24 3 23 25 11 12 20 32 26
24	5 28 14 8 0 10 30 9 6 15 29 24 3 23 25 11 12 20 32 26
25	5 28 14 8 0 10 9 6 15 29 24 3 23 25 11 12 20 32 26
26	5 28 14 8 0 10 9 6 30 29 24 3 23 15 11 12 20 32 26
27	5 14 0 28 10 9 8 6 30 29 24 3 23 15 11 12 20 32 26
28	5 14 28 9 8 6 30 10 29 24 3 23 15 11 12 20 32 26
29	5 14 0 28 9 8 6 30 10 29 24 3 23 15 11 12 25 20 32 26
30	5 14 0 28 9 8 6 30 10 29 24 3 23 15 11 12 20 32 26
31	5 0 28 14 9 8 6 30 10 29 24 3 23 15 11 12 20 32 26
32	5 0 28 14 9 8 6 30 10 29 24 3 23 15 11 12 20 32 26
33	5 0 28 14 9 8 6 30 10 29 24 3 23 15 11 12 20 32 26
34	5 0 28 14 9 8 6 30 10 29 24 3 23 15 11 12 20 32 26
35	5 0 28 14 9 8 6 30 10 29 24 3 23 15 11 12 20 32 26
36	5 0 28 14 9 8 6 30 10 29 24 3 23 15 20 12 11 26
37	5 0 28 14 9 8 6 30 10 29 24 3 23 15 20 12 11 32 26
38	5 0 28 14 8 9 30 10 29 24 23 15 3 12 11 32 26 25
39	5 0 28 14 9 8 6 30 10 29 24 23 15 3 12 11 32 26 25
40	5 0 28 14 9 8 6 30 10 29 24 23 3 15 20 12 11 32 26 25
41	5 0 28 14 8 9 6 30 10 29 24 23 3 15 12 20 11 32 25 26
42	5 0 28 14 9 8 6 30 10 29 23 24 15 3 12 20 11 32 26 25
43	5 0 28 14 8 9 6 30 10 29 23 24 15 12 20 11 32 26 25
44	5 0 28 14 8 9 6 30 10 29 23 24 20 12 11 32 26 25
45	5 0 28 14 8 9 6 30 10 29 23 24 20 12 11 32 26 25
46	5 0 28 14 8 6 30 10 9 29 23 24 20 12 11 32 26 25
47	5 0 28 14 8 6 30 10 9 23 24 20 12 11 32 26 25
48	5 0 28 14 8 6 30 10 9 23 24 20 12 11 32 26 25
49	5 0 28 14 8 6 30 10 9 23 24 29 12 11 32 26 25
50	5 28 14 8 6 30 10 9 23 24 29 12 11 32 26 25
51	5 28 14 8 6 30 10 9 23 24 29 12 11 32 26 25
52	5 28 14 6 8 30 10 9 23 24 20 12 11 26 32 25
53	5 28 14 6 8 30 9 10 24 20 12 11 26 32 25
54	5 28 14 6 8 30 9 10 24 20 12 11 26 32 25
55	5 28 14 8 30 9 10 24 29 23 20 11 12 26 25 32
56	5 14 28 8 9 10 24 29 23 20 11 12 26 25 32
57	5 14 28 8 9 10 30 24 29 23 20 11 12 26 25 32
58	5 14 28 8 9 10 30 29 24 23 20 12 11 26 25 32
59	5 14 28 8 9 10 30 29 24 23 20 12 11 26 25 32
60	5 14 28 8 9 10 30 29 24 23 20 12 11 26 25 32
61	5 14 28 8 9 10 30 29 24 23 20 12 11 26 25 32
62	5 28 8 14 9 10 30 29 24 23 20 12 11 26 25 32
63	5 28 8 14 9 10 30 24 29 23 20 12 11 26 25 32
64	5 28 14 8 9 10 30 24 29 20 12 11 26 25 32
65	5 28 8 14 9 10 30 24 29 20 12 11 26 25 32
66	5 28 8 14 9 10 30 24 20 11 12 26 25
67	5 28 8 14 9 10 30 24 20 11 12 26 25
68	5 28 14 9 10 30 29 24 12 11 26 25 32
69	5 28 14 9 10 30 29 24 12 11 26 25 32
70	5 14 9 30 10 20 12 11 26 25 32
71	5 14 9 30 10 20 12 11 26 25 32
72	5 14 9 30 10 20 12 11 26 25 32
73	5 14 9 30 10 20 12 11 26 25 32
74	5 14 9 30 10 20 12 11 26 25 32
75	5 14 9 30 10 20 12 11 26 25 32
76	5 14 9 30 10 20 12 11 26 25 32
77	5 14 9 30 10 20 12 11 26 25 32
78	5 28 14 9 30 20 11
79	5 28 14 9 30 20 11
80	5 28 14 9 30 20 12
81	5 28 14 9 30
82	5 28 14 9 30
83	5 28

Pink = One lap behind leader

Race distance: 83 laps, 190.925 miles / 307.266 km

CHASSIS LOG BOOK

No	Driver	Chassis
0	Hill	Williams FW16/3
2	Senna	Williams FW16/2
	spare	Williams FW16/1
3	Katayama	Tyrrell 022/2
4	Blundell	Tyrrell 022/1
	spare	Tyrrell 022/3
5	Schumacher	Benetton B194/3
6	Verstappen	Benetton B194/4
	spare	Benetton B194/1
7	Häkkinen	McLaren MP4/9/3
8	Brundle	McLaren MP4/9/4
	spare	McLaren MP4/9/5
9	Fittipaldi	Footwork FA15/1
10	Morbidelli	Footwork FA15/2
	spare	Footwork FA15/3
11	Lamy	Lotus 107C/2
12	Herbert	Lotus 107C/3
	spare	Lotus 107C/1
14	Barrichello	Jordan 194/4
15	Suzuki	Jordan 194/3
	spare	Jordan 194/2
19	Beretta	Larrousse LH94/2
20	Comas	Larrousse LH94/1
	spare	Larrousse LH94/3
23	Martini	Minardi M193B/4
24	Alboreto	Minardi M193B/1
	spare	Minardi M193B/3
25	Bernard	Ligier JS39B/6
26	Panis	Ligier JS39B/4
	spare	Ligier JS39B/2
27	Larini	Ferrari 412T1/150
28	Berger	Ferrari 412T1/151
	spare	Ferrari 412T1/149
29	Wendlinger	Sauber C13/4
30	Frentzen	Sauber C13/3
	spare	Sauber C13/1
31	Brabham	Simtek S941/2
32	Ratzenberger	Simtek S941/1
33	Belmondo	Pacific PR01/1
34	Gachot	Pacific PR01/2

CONSTRUCTORS' CUP

Pos	Team	Points
1	BENETTON-FORD	20
2	FERRARI	10
3	JORDAN-HART	7
4	WILLIAMS-RENAULT	6
5=	FOOTWORK-FORD	3
5=	SAUBER-MERCEDES	3
7	TYRRELL-YAMAHA	2
8	LARROUSSE-FORD	1

FOR THE RECORD

First Grand Prix start
Roland Ratzenberger

First Grand Prix points
Heinz-Harald Frentzen

DRIVERS' POINTS

Pos	Driver	Points
1	SCHUMACHER	20
2	BARRICHELLO	7
3=	HILL	6
3=	BERGER	6
5	ALESI	4
6	FITTIPALDI	3
7=	KATAYAMA	2
7=	FRENTZEN	2
9=	WENDLINGER	1
9=	COMAS	1

WORLD CHAMPIONSHIP • ROUND 3

SAN MARINO GRAND PRIX

The 1994 San Marino Grand Prix will be remembered as 'The Day the Music Died' for those race fans throughout the world who regarded Ayrton Senna as the greatest racing driver of his generation. The 34-year-old Brazilian died as he had lived, setting the pace and running right on the limit, as his Williams FW16 led Michael Schumacher's Benetton B194 into the seventh lap of the race. A startline collision between Pedro Lamy's Lotus and J.J. Lehto's stalled Benetton resulted in the opening phase of the race being run at reduced speed behind the safety car and the restart was barely a lap old when the triple World Champion slammed off the road at Tamburello and into a concrete wall. Just over four hours later he was officially declared dead in Bologna's Maggiore hospital, by which time Schumacher had notched up a commanding, if somewhat inconsequential, victory in the restarted race. Senna's death was the second strike of a double blow that left Grand Prix racing reeling with grief, for Austrian F1 novice Roland Ratzenberger had been killed when his Simtek-Ford crashed during Saturday's second qualifying session.

SCHUMACHER
LARINI
HÄKKINEN
WENDLINGER
KATAYAMA
HILL

SAN MARINO GRAND PRIX

> **Diary**
>
> *FIA President Max Mosley dismisses the controversy over the Ferrari 'traction control' affair at the Pacific Grand Prix as a storm in a tea cup. He vigorously denies any suggestion that the Italian team have been afforded a degree of favouritism by the governing body.*
>
> *Frenchman Franck Lagorce wins Formula 3000 International Trophy race at Silverstone in his Reynard-Cosworth.*
>
> *The Pacific GP team's transporter is burnt out after its brakes overheat following the descent of Mont Blanc on the return from Imola.*
>
> *Bryan Herta, the reigning Indy Lights champion, sets fastest time in Rookie tests in preparation for the Indy 500.*

ENTRY AND PRACTICE

The opening race of the European season at Imola is always one of the most popular events on the Grand Prix calendar. The Autodromo Enzo e Dino Ferrari is a classic venue with a long-established reputation as one of the most challenging tracks in the world, renowned for its convivial atmosphere and the infectious enthusiasm of the Italian fans. Sadly, the events of 30 April/1 May 1994 may have irrevocably altered that perception.

The dreadful sequence of events began on Friday afternoon when Rubens Barrichello was lucky to escape with superficial injuries from a punishingly violent accident which befell his Jordan-Hart.

Seventeen minutes into the session, the 22-year-old Brazilian was on his first flying lap when he lost control coming into the 140 mph Variante Bassa, the tricky right/left flick immediately prior to the pit entrance. The car vaulted the trackside kerb and slammed sideways into the top of the restraining tyre barrier, before bouncing off the debris fencing and somersaulting along the grass verge on the edge of the circuit.

The session was immediately stopped to enable the unconscious driver to be released from the car and transported to the medical centre. Miraculously – for it had been an accident fearful in its sheer ferocity – Barrichello was found to have sustained nothing more than a badly swollen nose and lacerations to his mouth. He underwent X-rays and a brain scan at the track before being transferred as a precaution to Bologna's Maggiore hospital for overnight observation.

The following day, Rubens returned to the circuit with his badly bruised right arm heavily bandaged. 'I feel good now,' he admitted, although he would be on the sidelines for the rest of the weekend. 'I can remember quite a bit of the crash, but I don't know exactly what caused it. It could have been oil, or it could have been my problem. I was certainly going pretty fast!'

Worse was to come. The second qualifying session on Saturday afternoon was overshadowed by another massive accident, this time costing the life of Simtek team novice Roland Ratzenberger, who lost control at over 180 mph on the straight immediately after the flat-out Tamburello left-hander. The car apparently shed parts of its bodywork, causing it to hurtle into the concrete wall on the left-hand side of the circuit at apparently undiminished speed, bouncing back onto the edge of the track and slithering to a halt in the middle of the road at the Tosa hairpin.

Ferrari driver Jean Alesi, still not recovered from his Mugello testing crash injuries, was spectating out on the circuit and reported that the Simtek's front wing flew off seconds before Ratzenberger lost control.

The session was red-flagged to a halt as medical staff rushed to the wrecked car and attempted to revive the Austrian at the trackside. He was briefly removed to the circuit medical centre before being helicoptered on to the Bologna hospital where he succumbed to multiple head injuries.

Ratzenberger was the first driver to be killed at the wheel of a Grand Prix car since Italy's Elio de Angelis crashed his Brabham BT55-BMW at Paul Ricard during a test session in the week immediately following the 1986 Monaco Grand Prix. The last driver to die during a Grand Prix race meeting had been Riccardo Paletti, who crashed his Osella-Ford into the back of Didier Pironi's stalled pole-position Ferrari at the start of the 1982 Canadian GP at Montreal.

Ironically, in the Saturday morning practice session, Ratzenberger had collided with his Simtek team-mate David Brabham under braking for the Tosa corner. The Australian spun off harmlessly into the sand trap on the outside of the turn, but there was no suggestion that any residual damage had been sustained to Ratzenberger's car which might have contributed to the tragedy that lay in wait.

The disaster understandably shocked the current generation of Grand Prix drivers to their very core, many of them having never experienced a fellow driver being killed at any time during their career. When the session resumed following a 47-minute interval to clear the circuit, the Williams, Benetton and Sauber teams all chose not to participate further out of respect for Ratzenberger's memory.

These events totally overshadowed the resumption of the battle between Michael Schumacher and Ayrton Senna for fastest time, a contest joined on this occasion by Gerhard Berger's Ferrari, much to the delight of the ferociously patriotic crowd who lined this circuit deep in the famous Maranello team's heartland.

Despite winning the first two races of the season, Schumacher had come to Imola expecting Senna's more powerful Williams-Renault to seize the initiative. Williams had worked hard to incorporate major front suspension revisions into the FW16 design and Ayrton duly edged out his young German challenger to claim fastest time. The changes included a new nose profile, with the wings positioned slightly higher, revised aerodynamic end plates, altered front wishbones and a reshaped cockpit surround.

Interestingly, during testing at Imola immediately before the start of the season, the Williams FW16 had shown little sign of the unpredictable slow-corner performance which had become so apparent at both Interlagos and TI Circuit, so Senna was optimistic that this initial performance imbalance might have been to a large degree redressed.

Sheer power always tells at Imola. It pays off on the mile-long haul from the tight right-hander by the pits all the way down to the Tosa hairpin. In this environment, despite having two specially developed Ford Zetec-R V8 engines available for qualifying, Schumacher and Benetton returnee J.J. Lehto were having to run as little downforce as they dared in order to wring every ounce of straightline speed from their B194s.

This strategy had a downside, of course, in terms of reduced grip through the two slow chicanes on the return leg, but Schumacher nevertheless managed to round off the first day with a best lap only 0.467s slower than Senna's in the Williams. On Saturday, Michael further trimmed the gap to 0.337s with a quicker lap on his first run, but then Ratzenberger's accident brought this particular contest to a premature end.

Less expected, perhaps, was Ferrari's presence in third place, Berger using a brand-new 75-degree type 043 V12 engine which clearly had sufficient power to compete with the front-runners on this occasion. The Ferrari 412T1s had also been the subject of suspension modifications to improve their handling, including the adoption of Penske shock absorbers in place of the original Konis, and revised trailing-edge flaps on their front wings.

However, it was unfortunate that the Italian team came to this crucially important home race under scrutiny from the sceptical eyes of its rivals following the controversy stirred up over its use of a variable rev-limiter during practice for the Pacific GP. Yet despite lingering doubts expressed by other teams, the Ferrari management steadfastly clung to the assertion that it had 'spontaneously informed' the FIA Technical Delegate that it was using the system at TI Circuit, a standpoint which did not totally convince everybody in the paddock.

Berger was clearly extremely upset by the accident to Ratzenberger, doubtless recalling his own fiery crash in a Ferrari at Tamburello during the 1989 San Marino race. Nevertheless, he boldly went out again once the circuit reopened.

'When I saw the accident on television, I found myself shaking in the car,' he confessed, 'but, of course, in our job we must sometimes be prepared to see these things. Then I got out of the car and went into the motorhome, still shaking, but the question for me was not whether I was going to drive today, but whether I was going to drive tomorrow or at any time in the future.

'When Rubens went off yesterday, I was reminded of how close between life and death we can sometimes be. I eventually asked myself, "Are you going to race or not?" so I went out and tried to concentrate on getting on with it.'

Gerhard failed to improve his Friday time, straight-lining a chicane on his second run, and then running out of fuel at the end of the session, but he still lined up third ahead of Damon Hill, who had vaulted from seventh to fourth on the second day.

Damon had experienced a difficult time on Friday, spinning over a kerb and damaging his Williams's suspension. A front lower wishbone had to be hurriedly replaced in the pits, so the chassis set-up was hardly perfect by the time he rushed back onto the circuit.

'Today was one of those days I would rather put behind me as soon as possible,' he admitted. Fortunately, things were better for him on the morrow.

Lehto wound up an impressive fifth fastest, the Finn returning to F1 for his first race of the season after recovering from a broken neck sustained in a pre-season Silverstone test. He lined up ahead of Nicola Larini's Ferrari and the Sauber C13 of Heinz-Harald Frentzen.

Larini used the earlier-specification 65-degree V12 throughout qualifying, while Sauber initially tried the latest pneumatic-valve Ilmor-built Mercedes V10s on Friday morning, but both cars reverted to regular-spec engines after the new

121

SAN MARINO GRAND PRIX

The blackest weekend in Grand Prix racing for more than three decades witnessed both lurid accidents and double tragedy with the deaths of Roland Ratzenberger and Ayrton Senna.

Below: Rubens Barrichello survived this terrifying crash on Friday. The Jordan driver emerged with no more than superficial injuries, but was forced to sit out the race.

Bottom left: The red sky at night gives no warning of the disaster about to befall poor Roland Ratzenberger the following afternoon as the friendly and popular Austrian chats with compatriots Gerhard Berger and Karl Wendlinger.

Right: A distraught Ayrton Senna and Prof. Sid Watkins confer in the aftermath of Ratzenberger's accident. Little did we know that just over 24 hours later more horror was to follow.

SAN MARINO GRAND PRIX

Left: The start witnessed a massive accident when Pedro Lamy's Lotus tore into the back of J.J. Lehto's stalled Benetton, crashing into the wall to the left of the track before careering back across the circuit. The young Portuguese driver *(above)* emerged unscathed from the cockpit of his wrecked car.

Only luck prevented catastrophe in the pit lane when Michele Alboreto's Minardi shed a wheel that had not been properly secured as he left his pit. *Above left:* The force of the errant wheel can be seen from the Lotus pit as it hurtles on down towards the pit lane exit.

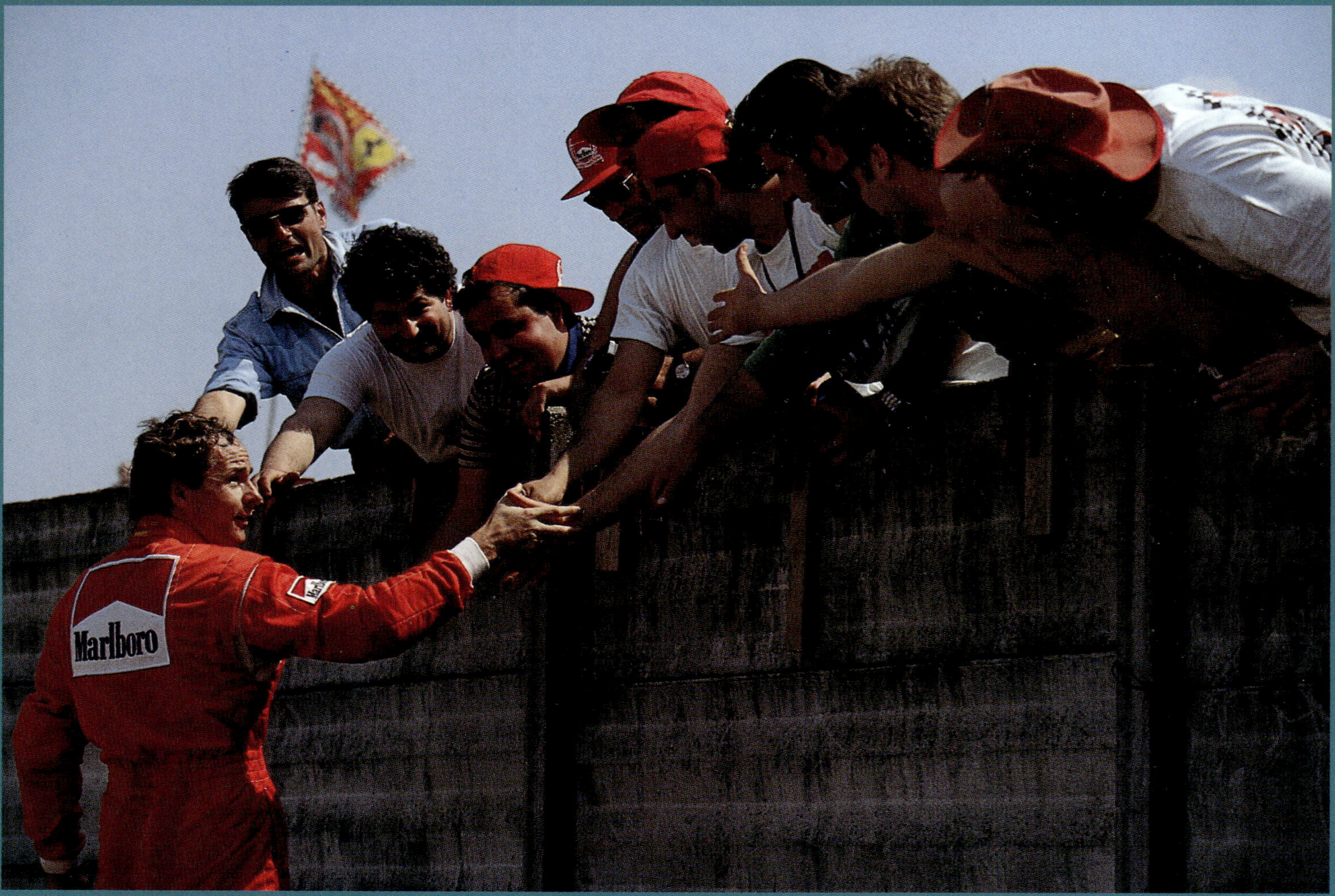

Pascal Rondeau/Allsport

Lukas Gorys

Lukas Gorys

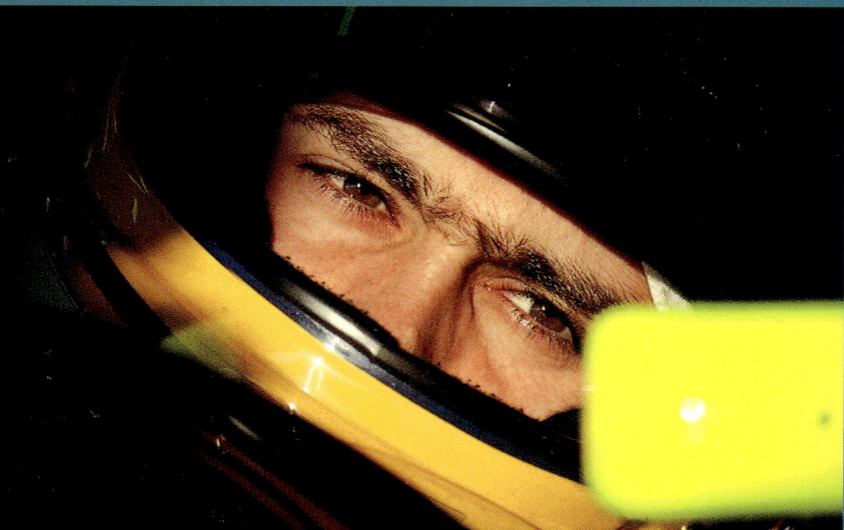

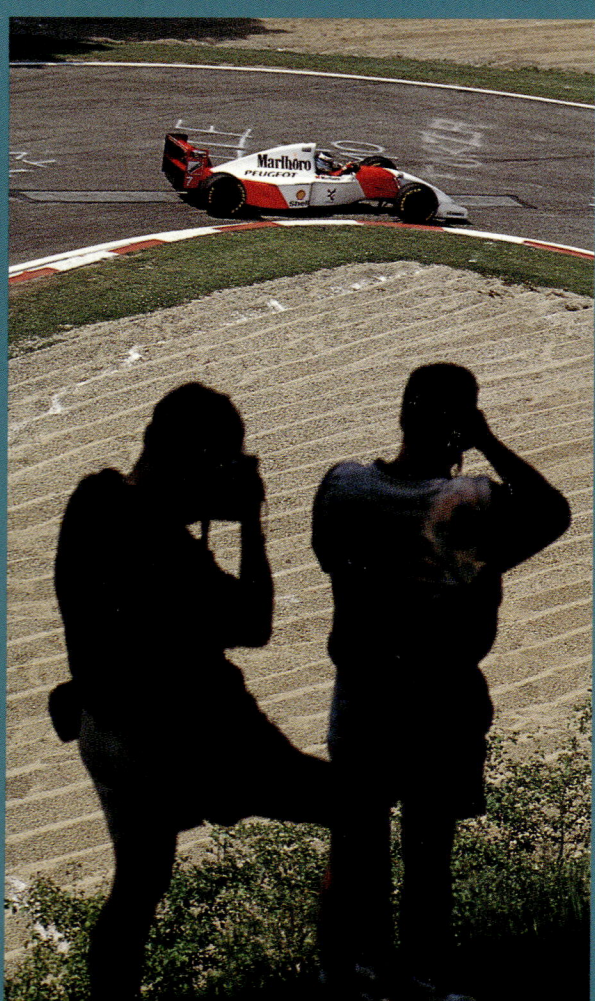

Top: **Gerhard Berger greets a few of the *tifosi* as he makes his way back to the pits after running out of fuel in Saturday's qualifying session.**

The racing was academic, but earned more points for Karl Wendlinger *(above)*, who took fourth place, while Mika Häkkinen *(left)* gained concrete reward for the new McLaren-Peugeot alliance with a third-place finish.

SAN MARINO GRAND PRIX

Nicola Larini proved his talent was not confined to touring cars as, deputising for Jean Alesi once more, he took second place for Ferrari to put his name back in the frame for a possible full-time Grand Prix return in the future.

units suffered a loss of air pressure in the first session.

Mika Häkkinen managed to squeeze eighth place on the grid out of his McLaren MP4/9, but the car's handling balance was by no means perfect and the Peugeot V10, still marginal on cooling despite further recent modifications, simply didn't have the power to compete at the front.

Häkkinen's concerns were echoed by his team-mate Martin Brundle, who slid up a kerb, snapped into a gentle spin and collided lightly with a retaining wall on Friday afternoon. On Saturday morning, Martin's Peugeot V10 suffered from crankcase pressurisation and the replacement seemed badly down on power, preventing him from bettering 13th.

The two McLarens were thus separated by Ukyo Katayama's Tyrrell-Yamaha, Karl Wendlinger's Sauber, Gianni Morbidelli's Footwork and the second Tyrrell of Mark Blundell. Katayama had gearbox problems on Saturday afternoon, while Mark lost a set of tyres running over debris from the Ratzenberger disaster and was disappointed not to have improved his time.

Pierluigi Martini and Michele Alboreto did good solid jobs to line up 14-15 in the Minardi M193Bs, both of which featured modifications destined for eventual incorporation into the definitive new M194 chassis. These included Series VIII Ford V8 engines running on the promising new Agip M26 fuel brew, new rear uprights, revised brakes and a redesigned rear wing.

Christian Fittipaldi was frustrated over his failure to improve on 16th with his stiffly suspended Footwork FA15, the Brazilian just squeezing in ahead of the promising Ligier JS39Bs of Eric Bernard and Olivier Panis, which sandwiched Erik Comas's 18th-placed Larrousse.

Then came Johnny Herbert's Lotus-Mugen in 20th place ahead of F1 guest driver Andrea de Cesaris, deputising for the suspended Eddie Irvine in the second Jordan-Hart. Even before arriving at Imola, the erratic Italian had anticipated his return to the GP scene by writing off a Jordan chassis in testing at Mugello – soon to be followed by another, damaged riding over a kerb during first qualifying. On the face of it, this looked like a problem which the Silverstone-based team could well do without.

Herbert's team-mate Pedro Lamy was next in the final order, with Olivier Beretta, David Brabham and Bertrand Gachot completing the 25-car grid. The second Pacific-Ilmor of Paul Belmondo failed to qualify.

RACE

Senna and Hill both felt quite confident in the half-hour race morning warm-up, setting the fastest and second-fastest times, as well as covering 30 laps – almost half a race distance – between them. Further back, both Benettons seemed off the pace as they finalised their race strategy by experimenting with varying fuel loads, while the Ferrari squad remained guardedly confident about its prospects for the first European race of the season.

Senna duly led the pack round the parade lap, slowing his Williams dramatically as he brought the other 24 cars up to the startline. The field included David Brabham in the remaining Simtek, which the Australian driver had decided to start after seeing the morale-boosting effect his presence in the warm-up had had on the other members of the beleaguered team.

At the green light, however, this seemingly ill-fated weekend witnessed another massive accident. Lehto stalled his Benetton and, while most of the pack managed to avoid the Finn's stationary machine, Pedro Lamy's Lotus plunged straight into the back of it.

Debris from the wrecked cars was hurled into the main grandstand,

SAN MARINO GRAND PRIX

ROLAND RATZENBERGER

It was perhaps inevitable that Ayrton Senna's death the following day should so cruelly overshadow the fatal accident which befell popular F1 novice Roland Ratzenberger in final qualifying at Imola.

The 31-year-old Austrian driver was taking part in only his third Grand Prix meeting, having signed an agreement to drive for the Simtek team in the first six races of the season, but had established a reputation as a briskly professional performer in a number of other categories.

Born on 4 July 1962, Ratzenberger began racing in 1981 at the wheel of a Formula Ford Van Diemen, winning the German, Austrian and European FF titles before coming to prominence in the UK when he triumphed in the 1987 Brands Hatch Formula Ford Festival. That year he also undertook a limited British F3 programme, but he would subsequently achieve most success in touring cars and sports-prototypes, joining the close-knit band of Europeans racing in Japan in 1990.

Immensely popular among his peers, Ratzenberger was just reaping the benefit of a winter's ceaseless sponsorship chasing with the aim of getting his foot firmly on the bottom rung of the Grand Prix ladder when he died.

slightly injuring eight spectators, and while Lehto's car remained on the left-hand side of the circuit Lamy's tattered Lotus pirouetted to a halt in the pit lane exit. Between the two of them, they left wreckage and debris scattered across the entire width of the track. Lehto escaped with a slight arm injury, while Lamy was completely unhurt.

Senna had got away magnificently from pole position, edging out Schumacher to take an immediate lead through the Tamburello left-hander, with Berger slotting into third ahead of Hill and Frentzen's Sauber leading the rest of the pack.

However, the magnitude of the accident on the startline was such that the safety car was despatched to slow the field even before Senna led the pack through to complete the opening lap. Ayrton, already slowing up in response to the 'safety car' signal, eased back the pace of the race and dutifully slotted in behind as the pack went down to Tosa for the second time.

For three laps, Senna steadily circulated in slow formation as the circuit workers did their best to clear up the mess in front of the pits. With the field nearing the end of lap five, Senna calmly acknowledged a radio signal from his engineer David Brown as the safety car pulled into the pits and the race was on once more.

Senna timed the pace of his restart to perfection, deliberately slowing the pack to near-walking pace as he came through the final sequence of slow corners, then accelerating hard out onto the pit straight. Schumacher just managed to see what he was up to and followed hard on his heels, but Berger found himself momentarily wrong-footed and was several lengths adrift even by the time his Ferrari passed the starting line.

At the end of lap six, Senna was 0.6s ahead. Then Schumacher – who had noticed that the FW16 had previously bottomed out badly on a newly resurfaced patch of track midway through Tamburello – watched in horror as Senna's mount again twitched violently over that same bump, failed to negotiate the second part of the long left-hander and speared straight into the concrete wall on the right-hand side of the track.

The Williams bounced back onto the edge of the circuit, with debris being scattered once more all across the track. Out came the red flag and the race was immediately brought to a halt, but not before Berger had run over part of the Williams's nose section and continued full-pelt round to Rivazza before realising that the race was being stopped. When he climbed from the car he saw that the front suspension was virtually broken – 'hanging by a small strand of metal' – which did little to further his appetite for racing.

Meanwhile, the marshals very properly did not go near Senna until authorised to do so by FIA Medical Delegate Professor Watkins, who was soon on the scene. The situation was clearly very bad. Senna was lifted from the car and laid on the ground at the side of the track, where the doctors worked hard to resuscitate him. The medical helicopter landed on the circuit, collected the Brazilian and flew him directly to the Maggiore hospital in Bologna.

In the midst of this nerve-racking tension, Erik Comas's Larrousse mysteriously arrived on the scene, its driver having stopped in the pits for attention and somehow not been prevented from returning to the circuit – despite the fact that the rest of the field was now standing stationary in front of the pits. He was immediately flagged to a flustered halt.

The remainder of the afternoon degenerated into a nightmare. Rumour and counter-rumour as to Senna's condition swirled around the paddock as the teams prepared to restart the race over another 53 laps, giving a total of 58 laps – three fewer than the originally scheduled distance. Although Senna crashed at the start of lap seven, the first part of the race was adjudged to have finished at the completion of the initial five laps.

In the Williams camp, Patrick Head initially heard that Senna had nothing more than a cut on his arm, so there was no compunction about readying Hill's FW16 for the restart. From the telemetry information by then available to the team, Head was also fairly certain in his own mind that there had been no obvious technical failure on Senna's car. Concerned only that there might have been some sort of hydraulic pressure drop-off in the FW16's power steering system, this accessory was switched off on Damon's car for the restart, although the Williams Technical Director had no reason to believe that there was any dangerous shortcoming in this area even though Hill had reported a slight problem in the first part of the race.

However, three months later Head would reflect, 'After the event, reviewing it now, it would have been better if I'd pulled the car out of the race, because, looking back, we didn't have enough information to make the judgement.'

Left: The hollowness of victory this weekend is shown on the faces of Larini, Schumacher and Häkkinen at the post-race press conference.

Eventually the cars lined up for the restart, with Berger taking an immediate lead – on the road, but not on aggregate – as they sprinted down to Tosa and Hill attempting to slice through to take second place from Schumacher. The Williams nosed inside the Benetton only to lose its right-hand nose wing end plate on the B194's left-rear wheel, so Michael accelerated clear on the climb up the hill to Piratella. At the end of the lap, Damon trailed into the pits for a fresh nose section to be fitted, resuming at the tail of the field.

Schumacher quickly hauled up onto Berger's tail, although the German driver was soon to be leading the race on aggregate as the laps ticked away. At the end of lap eight of the restart (lap 13 overall), Schumacher came in to refuel, allowing Berger to move ahead on corrected times for a few laps until he stopped on lap ten. Then it was Häkkinen's turn to lead until lap 13, followed by Larini's Ferrari from laps 14 to 18, with Katayama briefly moving up to second as the leading runners took the opportunity to stop for fuel and tyres.

With 11 laps of the restart completed, Berger pulled in to retire. Emotionally drained by the accident to Ratzenberger, he now found his thoughts focused on Senna and his will to keep going was also compromised by his Ferrari's unnerving rear-end instability. Later it would be discovered that he had had a dud rear shock absorber.

From lap 19 onwards, Schumacher remained totally in control through to the finish to score his third win of the season and retain intact his unbeaten 1994 record. But the German driver was sufficiently frank to admit that winning under such traumatic circumstances gave him no pleasure whatsoever.

Larini's second place was the fully deserved fruit of the Ferrari team's strategy of giving him just a single refuelling stop, on lap 24, and Maranello's test driver was well able to keep ahead of Häkkinen through to the finish, the McLaren-Peugeot making two stops and surviving to the end despite high engine temperatures for much of the distance.

At the chequered flag Mika was only three seconds ahead of Wendlinger's Sauber, relief from the Austrian's challenge coming only in the closing stages of the race when the Mercedes V10 broke an exhaust and lost the fine edge of its performance. Ukyo Katayama drove consistently well throughout, holding off Hill to take fifth place on the last lap by 0.25s, while Heinz-Harald Frentzen came home seventh ahead of Brundle's McLaren, the Norfolk driver hampered by a dire lack of straightline speed and delayed by a slight brush with Martini's Minardi at Tosa.

In the closing stages of the race, even more trouble erupted. At the end of lap 41, Michele Alboreto's 11th-placed Minardi M193B made a final routine pit stop. However, the mechanics did not properly secure his car's right-rear wheel and, as the Italian driver accelerated back onto the circuit, he suddenly found himself only just in control of a three-wheeler.

The wayward wheel flew through a group of three Ferrari mechanics before striking a Lotus mechanic. All four suffered minor injuries and were treated in the local Imola hospital.

This incident was a graphic illustration of what can happen in a crowded pit lane when the action becomes more than usually frenzied, and inevitably gave dramatic added impetus to calls for a pit lane speed limit, a regulation which would be duly implemented prior to the following race at Monaco.

Blundell, his Tyrrell leaking fuel like a sieve, was classified ninth, ahead of Johnny Herbert's reliable but slow Lotus 107C, while Olivier Panis and Eric Bernard plodded round steadily in their Ligiers to complete the list of finishers. Christian Fittipaldi was classified 13th, despite flying into the Tosa sand trap with four laps to go after many miles wrestling with a fading brake pedal.

Meanwhile, back at the Bologna hospital, Senna's condition had slipped beyond hope. Subsequent detailed examination would reveal that his helmet had been punctured by a flying component from the Williams's right-front suspension and he had sustained massive, irreversible brain injuries. He was now in a deep coma and those on the inside already realised there was virtually no chance of his surviving.

Not since Alan Stacey and Chris Bristow were killed in the 1960 Belgian Grand Prix at Spa-Francorchamps had international motor racing known such a desperate day.

Just before 19.00 local time, Dr Maria Teresa Fiandri confirmed the worst: 'Senna's heart stopped beating at 18.40. We did all we could. These are events which upset us too.'

There was simply nothing more to be said.

The mystery behind Senna's accident

Ayrton Senna's Williams FW16 was pulling just over 193 mph when it speared off its prescribed trajectory on the second apex of the Tamburello corner and charged the concrete barrier on the right-hand side of the circuit.

In the ensuing 0.9s before it struck the wall, Senna was hard on the brakes and managed to reduce the impact speed to just in excess of 135 mph. On the face of it, this was a survivable impact. The car dissipated much of its energy by bouncing back onto the edge of the circuit and the FW16 monocoque survived the impact substantially intact.

Senna might well have been expected to jump from the cockpit, ashen-faced, and walk back to the pits. Tragically, the cards did not fall in his favour. At first glance it was assumed that his head had impacted the concrete wall, provoking calls for wider, longer side pods to be incorporated in the 1995 F1 technical regulations. However, detailed analysis of his massive head injuries indicated that he had sustained a fearful, fatal blow from a component torn from his car's right-front suspension.

In truth, whether or not he survived the impact was ultimately a question of pure luck. Pinpointing the reasons behind Senna's loss of control was more complex and has, at the time of writing this report, not been clearly resolved. In the immediate aftermath of the accident there was much speculation that Ayrton had been the victim of a cataclysmic mechanical failure, but others concluded that he had simply been pushing too hard.

Much was made in certain sections of the media of the fact that Ayrton had been in a distant, preoccupied mood prior to the start, totally stunned by Ratzenberger's death the previous afternoon. Certainly, Senna had been very deeply affected by this tragedy – and his frame of mind had not been lightened when he was chastised by race officials for taking it upon himself to go out to the accident scene in the immediate aftermath of the Simtek driver's crash. However, he was probably no more distressed by the episode than most of the other drivers in the field and the atmosphere in the Imola paddock on race morning certainly reflected a sombre overall mood.

It was speculated that perhaps Senna had picked up debris from the Lehto/Lamy accident and that it would, in retrospect, have been wiser if the race had been stopped. This view would subsequently be rejected by FIA President Mosley as being out of step with long-established motor racing traditions, a questionable viewpoint when one considers the number of races that have been prematurely stopped in such dire situations in the recent past.

However, Goodyear was as satisfied as it could be that there was no evidence of pre-impact tyre puncturing and suggestions that Senna might have suffered some sort of physical trauma – possibly a heart attack – were dismissed by the subsequent post-mortem examination.

However, photographs of Senna's wrecked Williams in the immediate aftermath of the accident apparently showed the car's steering wheel lying by the side of the track still attached to a length of shaft. This fuelled speculation that the shaft might have failed, causing the accident, although it could quite obviously also have broken as a result of the massive impact.

Inevitably, many hard words were spoken after the tragedy. Senna's great rival, Alain Prost, for one, expressed the view that the FIA had been deaf to the drivers' concerns about F1 safety. This prompted a very candid, some would say brusque, response from Mosley.

'I would never refuse to take a phone call from a driver,' said the FIA President. 'I would never refuse to see one. But the only driver who's taken the trouble to come and see me in the last three months and talk about safety is Gerhard Berger.

'After his retirement Alain Prost has said we must talk about safety. I said, "Any time." I've even rung him. But he's never rung back.

'The fact is, it's not fun and it doesn't make money. So, most of the time, they don't want to do it. In the past, we've had a drivers' safety commission. When you have the first meeting you have everybody there; second meeting, half; and third or fourth meeting, they just don't bother.

'It's more fun to go and do a promotion, go skiing, or swimming or something. One can understand it. In the end, the drivers' job is to drive. It's our job to see they drive safely. But if it was a question of a driver using a car which was more dangerous, but five seconds a lap faster than a safer one, they would all opt for the quicker one.'

It was a cruel irony that Senna had been poised to spearhead a new drivers' safety committee at the time of his death and, with help and guidance from retired triple World Champion Niki Lauda, the Grand Prix Drivers' Association was duly revived in the days immediately following the Imola tragedy.

Inevitably, there was also concern that Imola was an excessively dangerous circuit – although many of those who voiced such reservations would have earned more credibility if they had advanced similar views before the race. Hindsight represents matchless retrospective wisdom but, as such, is frequently without value.

Needless to say, the wrecked Williams FW16 was impounded by the Italian authorities together with the remains of Ratzenberger's Simtek. Within days notices were served on Imola track boss Federico Bendinelli and representatives of Williams, Simtek and Bell helmets advising them that they might be investigated on suspicion of culpable homicide.

The FIA, meanwhile, prepared to pledge itself to improve the long-term safety of F1. The Williams team faced up to a future without its single most crucial asset. The rest of the paddock was bereft, reduced to a stunned silence and immersed in its own private grief.

Meanwhile, across the world, legions of motor racing fans went into mourning for a man numbered among the exclusive handful of truly pivotal personalities in Grand Prix history.

FIA FORMULA ONE WORLD CHAMPIONSHIP ROUND 3

GRAN PREMIO DI SAN MARINO
IMOLA
29 APRIL–1 MAY 1994

IMOLA – Autodromo Dino e Enzo Ferrari
CIRCUIT LENGTH: 3.132 MILES/5.040 KM

RACE WEATHER: HOT, DRY, SUNNY

Place	Driver	Nat.	No.	Entrant	Car/Engine	Laps	Time/Retirement	Speed (mph/km/h)
1	Michael Schumacher	D	5	Mild Seven Benetton Ford	Benetton B194-Ford Zetec-R V8	58	1h 28m 28.642s	123.176/198.233
2	Nicola Larini	I	27	Scuderia Ferrari	Ferrari 412T1 041 V12	58	1h 29m 23.584s	121.914/196.203
3	Mika Häkkinen	SF	7	Malboro McLaren Peugeot	McLaren MP4/9-Peugeot A6 V10	58	1h 29m 39.321s	121.558/195.629
4	Karl Wendlinger	A	29	Broker Sauber Mercedes	Sauber C13-Mercedes-Benz V10	58	1h 29m 42.300s	121.490/195.520
5	Ukyo Katayama	J	3	Tyrrell	Tyrrell 022-Yamaha 0X10A V10	57		
6	Damon Hill	GB	0	Rothmans Williams Renault	Williams FW16-Renault RS6 V10	57		
7	Heinz-Harald Frentzen	D	30	Broker Sauber Mercedes	Sauber C13-Mercedes-Benz V10	57		
8	Martin Brundle	GB	8	Malboro McLaren Peugeot	McLaren MP4/9-Peugeot A6 V10	57		
9	Mark Blundell	GB	4	Tyrrell	Tyrrell 022-Yamaha 0X10A V10	56		
10	Johnny Herbert	GB	12	Team Lotus	Lotus 107C-Mugen Honda ZA5C V10	56		
11	Olivier Panis	F	26	Ligier Gitanes Blondes	Ligier JS39B-Renault RS6 V10	56		
12	Eric Bernard	F	25	Ligier Gitanes Blondes	Ligier JS39B-Renault RS6 V10	56		
13	Christian Fittipaldi	BR	9	Footwork Ford	Footwork FA15-Ford HB V8	54	Brakes	
	Andrea de Cesaris	I	15	Sasol Jordan	Jordan 194-Hart 1035 V10	49	Accident	
	Michele Alboreto	I	24	Minardi Scuderia Italia	Minardi M193B-Ford HB V8	44	Lost wheel	
	Gianni Morbidelli	I	10	Footwork Ford	Footwork FA15-Ford HB V8	40	Engine	
	Pierluigi Martini	I	23	Minardi Scuderia Italia	Minardi M193B-Ford HB V8	37	Spun off	
	David Brabham	AUS	31	MTV Simtek Ford	Simtek S941-Ford HB V8	27	Accident	
	Bertrand Gachot	F	34	Pacific Grand Prix Ltd	Pacific PR01-Ilmor 2175A V10	23	Engine	
	Olivier Beretta	F	19	Tourtel Larrousse F1	Larrousse LH94-Ford HB V8	17	Engine	
	Gerhard Berger	A	28	Scuderia Ferrari	Ferrari 412T1 041 V12	16	Withdrew	
	Ayrton Senna	BR	2	Rothmans Williams Renault	Williams FW16-Renault RS6 V10	5	Fatal accident	
	Erik Comas	F	20	Tourtel Larrousse F1	Larrousse LH94-Ford HB V8	5	Withdrew	
	J.J. Lehto	SF	6	Mild Seven Benetton Ford	Benetton B194-Ford Zetec-R V8	0	Collision with Lamy	
	Pedro Lamy	P	11	Team Lotus	Lotus 107C-Mugen Honda ZA5C	0	Collision with Lehto	
DNQ	Paul Belmondo	F	33	Pacific Grand Prix Ltd	Pacific PR01-Ilmor 2175A V10			
–	Roland Ratzenberger	A	32	MTV Simtek Ford	Simtek S941-Ford HB V8		Fatal qualifying accident	
–	Rubens Barrichello	BR	14	Sasol Jordan	Jordan 194-Hart 1035 V10		Qualifying accident	

Fastest lap: Hill, on lap 10, 1m 24.335s, 133.682 mph/215.141 km/h (record).
Previous lap record: Riccardo Patrese (F1 Williams FW14B-Renault V10), 1m 26.100s, 130.943 mph/ 210.732 km/h (1992).
All cars used Goodyear tyres

All results and data © FIA 1994

QUALIFYING 1

Ayrton Senna	**1m 21.548s**
Michael Schumacher	1m 22.015s
Gerhard Berger	**1m 22.113s**
J.J. Lehto	1m 22.717s
Nicola Larini	1m 22.841s
Heinz-Harald Frentzen	**1m 23.119s**
Damon Hill	1m 23.199s
Mika Häkkinen	1m 23.611s
Gianni Morbidelli	1m 23.663s
Mark Blundell	1m 23.703s
Karl Wendlinger	1m 23.788s
Ukyo Katayama	1m 24.000s
Pierluigi Martini	**1m 24.078s**
Michele Alboreto	**1m 24.276s**
Martin Brundle	1m 24.443s
Christian Fittipaldi	1m 24.655s
Eric Bernard	**1m 24.678s**
Olivier Panis	**1m 24.996s**
Johnny Herbert	**1m 25.114s**
Andrea de Cesaris	**1m 25.234s**
Erik Comas	1m 26.295s
Pedro Lamy	1m 26.453s
Olivier Beretta	1m 27.179s
David Brabham	1m 27.607s
Roland Ratzenberger	1m 27.657s
Bertrand Gachot	1m 27.732s
Paul Belmondo	1m 28.361s
Rubens Barrichello	**14m 57.323s**

Friday afternoon
Dry, hot, sunny

QUALIFYING 2

Michael Schumacher	**1m 21.885s**
Damon Hill	**1m 22.168s**
Gerhard Berger	1m 22.226s
Nicola Larini	1m 23.006s
Mika Häkkinen	**1m 23.140s**
Ukyo Katayama	1m 23.322s
Karl Wendlinger	**1m 23.347s**
Mark Blundell	1m 23.831s
Martin Brundle	**1m 23.858s**
J.J. Lehto	1m 24.029s
Pierluigi Martini	1m 24.423s
Christian Fittipaldi	**1m 24.472s**
Gianni Morbidelli	1m 24.682s
Michele Alboreto	1m 24.780s
Erik Comas	**1m 24.852s**
Johnny Herbert	1m 25.141s
Olivier Panis	1m 25.160s
Pedro Lamy	**1m 25.295s**
Andrea de Cesaris	1m 25.872s
Olivier Beretta	**1m 25.991s**
David Brabham	**1m 26.817s**
Bertrand Gachot	**1m 27.143s**
Roland Ratzenberger	**1m 27.584s**
Paul Belmondo	**1m 27.881s**
Eric Bernard	1m 40.411s
Ayrton Senna	no time
Heinz-Harald Frentzen	no time
Rubens Barrichello	no time

Saturday afternoon
Dry, hot, sunny

WARM-UP

Ayrton Senna	1m 22.597s
Damon Hill	1m 23.449s
Nicola Larini	1m 23.795s
Karl Wendlinger	1m 23.922s
Gerhard Berger	1m 24.302s
Christian Fittipaldi	1m 24.396s
Gianni Morbidelli	1m 24.468s
J.J. Lehto	1m 24.856s
Mark Blundell	1m 24.891s
Mika Häkkinen	1m 24.924s
Michael Schumacher	1m 24.978s
Pierluigi Martini	1m 25.051s
Heinz-Harald Frentzen	1m 25.133s
Martin Brundle	1m 25.455s
Olivier Panis	1m 26.025s
Michele Alboreto	1m 26.423s
Andrea de Cesaris	1m 26.557s
David Brabham	1m 26.880s
Olivier Beretta	1m 26.906s
Erik Comas	1m 27.080s
Bertrand Gachot	1m 27.623s
Johnny Herbert	1m 28.390s
Eric Bernard	1m 28.774s
Pedro Lamy	1m 42.987s
Ukyo Katayama	no time

Sunday morning
Dry, hot, sunny

FASTEST LAPS

Driver	Time	Lap
Damon Hill	1m 24.335s	10
Michael Schumacher	1m 24.438s	43
Heinz-Harald Frentzen	1m 25.307s	41
Gerhard Berger	1m 25.503s	14
Gianni Morbidelli	1m 25.652s	12
Karl Wendlinger	1m 25.727s	54
Mika Häkkinen	1m 25.737s	18
Martin Brundle	1m 25.774s	54
Nicola Larini	1m 25.825s	18
Christian Fittipaldi	1m 26.067s	12
Mark Blundell	1m 26.259s	25
Ukyo Katayama	1m 26.280s	12
Pierluigi Martini	1m 27.221s	21
Andrea de Cesaris	1m 27.627s	38
Olivier Panis	1m 27.908s	16
Michele Alboreto	1m 27.995s	21
Eric Bernard	1m 28.091s	23
Johnny Herbert	1m 28.407s	11
David Brabham	1m 28.735s	14
Bertrand Gachot	1m 29.094s	12
Olivier Beretta	1m 29.122s	14
Ayrton Senna	1m 44.068s	1
Erik Comas	1m 58.505s	1

STARTING GRID

#	Driver	Team	Time
2	SENNA	Williams	1m 21.548s
5	SCHUMACHER	Benetton	1m 21.885s
28	BERGER	Ferrari	1m 22.113s
0	HILL	Williams	1m 22.168s
6	LEHTO	Benetton	1m 22.717s
27	LARINI	Ferrari	1m 22.841s
30	FRENTZEN	Sauber	1m 23.119s
7	HÄKKINEN	McLaren	1m 23.140s
3	KATAYAMA	Tyrrell	1m 23.322s
29	WENDLINGER	Sauber	1m 23.347s
10	MORBIDELLI	Footwork	1m 23.663s
4	BLUNDELL	Tyrrell	1m 23.703s
8	BRUNDLE	McLaren	1m 23.858s
23	MARTINI	Minardi	1m 24.078s
24	ALBORETO	Minardi	1m 24.276s
9	FITTIPALDI	Footwork	1m 24.472s
25	BERNARD	Ligier	1m 24.678s
20	COMAS	Larrousse	1m 24.852s
26	PANIS	Ligier	1m 24.996s
12	HERBERT	Lotus	1m 25.114s
15	DE CESARIS	Jordan	1m 25.234s
11	LAMY	Lotus	1m 25.295s
19	BERETTA	Larrousse	1m 25.991s
31	BRABHAM	Simtek	1m 26.817s
34	GACHOT	Pacific	1m 27.143s

NON-STARTERS

- DNS — 32 RATZENBERGER Simtek 1m 27.584s
- DNQ — 33 BELMONDO Pacific 1m 27.881s
- DNS — 14 BARRICHELLO Jordan 14m 57.323s

LAP CHART

1st LAP ORDER: 2 SENNA, 5 SCHUMACHER, 28 BERGER, 0 HILL, 30 FRENTZEN, 7 HÄKKINEN, 27 LARINI, 29 WENDLINGER, 3 KATAYAMA, 8 BRUNDLE, 10 MORBIDELLI, 4 BLUNDELL, 23 MARTINI, 9 FITTIPALDI, 12 HERBERT, 26 PANIS, 20 COMAS, 25 BERNARD, 15 DE CESARIS, 19 BERETTA, 31 BRABHAM, 34 GACHOT, 24 ALBORETO

Lap	Order
1	2 5 28 0 30 7 27 29 3 8 10 4 23 9 12 26 20 15 19 31 34 24
2	2 5 28 0 30 7 27 29 3 8 10 4 23 9 12 26 20 15 19 31 34 24
3	2 5 28 0 30 7 27 29 3 8 10 4 23 9 12 26 20 15 19 31 34 24 25
4	2 5 28 0 30 7 27 29 3 8 10 4 23 9 12 26 20 15 19 31 34 24 25
5	2 5 28 0 30 7 27 29 3 8 10 4 23 9 12 26 20 15 19 31 34 25
1	28 5 7 27 29 3 23 9 10 12 4 8 15 26 31 25 19 30 34 24 0
2	28 5 7 27 29 3 23 9 10 12 4 8 15 26 31 25 19 30 34 24 0
3	28 5 7 27 29 3 9 23 10 12 4 8 15 26 31 25 19 30 34 24 0
4	28 5 7 27 29 3 9 23 10 5 4 8 15 26 31 25 19 30 34 24 0
5	28 5 27 29 3 9 10 23 4 8 15 30 26 31 25 19 34 24 0
6	28 5 27 29 3 9 10 23 4 8 15 26 31 25 19 30 34 24 0
7	28 5 27 29 3 9 10 5 4 8 12 30 26 25 31 19 12 34 24 0
8	28 5 27 29 3 9 5 10 4 23 30 12 15 26 31 19 12 34 24 0
9	28 5 27 29 3 9 10 5 4 23 30 12 26 31 19 12 34 24 15 0
10	7 27 29 28 3 9 10 5 4 23 30 4 26 25 31 19 12 34 24 15 0
11	5 27 29 3 5 28 23 4 30 8 26 25 31 19 8 24 12 15 0
12	5 27 3 7 29 5 10 29 23 4 30 26 25 31 19 8 24 34 12 15 0
13	7 3 27 5 9 10 23 4 29 30 26 25 8 24 12 34 15 31 0
14	7 3 5 27 9 10 4 26 8 24 12 15 31 25 34
15	27 3 5 9 7 23 29 30 10 26 8 24 12 15 31 25 34
16	27 5 9 7 23 29 3 10 23 8 24 12 26 15 0 31 25 34
17	5 27 29 3 10 23 4 30 8 24 12 26 15 0 31 25 34
18	5 27 29 3 10 30 4 23 8 24 12 26 15 0 31 25 34
19	5 27 29 3 10 4 30 23 8 24 12 26 15 0 31 25
20	5 27 29 3 10 4 8 23 24 12 26 15 0 31 25
21	5 27 29 9 3 10 4 30 8 23 12 26 0 15 24 31 25
22	5 27 29 9 3 10 4 30 8 23 12 26 15 0 31 25
23	5 27 29 9 3 10 4 30 8 23 0 12 15 26 24 25
24	5 27 29 9 3 10 8 23 0 30 12 26 24 4 25
25	5 27 29 9 3 10 8 23 0 12 30 26 24 4 25
26	5 27 29 9 3 10 8 23 0 30 12 26 4 23 25
27	5 27 29 9 3 10 8 0 30 12 24 4 23 26 4 25
28	5 27 29 9 3 10 8 0 30 15 24 12 23 26 4 25
29	5 27 29 9 3 10 8 0 30 12 15 24 23 26 4 25
30	5 27 29 9 3 10 8 0 30 12 15 24 23 26 4 25
31	5 27 29 9 3 10 8 0 30 15 24 12 23 26 4 25
32	5 27 9 3 10 7 29 8 0 30 15 24 12 23 4 26 25
33	5 27 9 3 10 7 29 8 0 15 24 12 4 26 25
34	5 27 9 3 10 7 29 30 0 15 24 12 4 26 25
35	5 27 9 3 7 29 30 0 15 24 12 4 26 25
36	5 27 9 3 7 29 30 0 8 15 24 12 4 26 25
37	5 27 7 29 3 30 0 8 15 24 12 4 26 25
38	5 27 7 29 9 3 0 30 8 15 24 4 12 26 25
39	5 27 7 29 9 3 0 30 8 15 24 4 12 26 25
40	5 27 7 29 9 3 0 30 8 15 4 12 24 26 25
41	5 27 7 29 9 3 0 30 8 15 4 12 26 25
42	5 27 7 29 9 3 0 30 8 15 4 12 26 25
43	5 27 7 29 9 3 0 30 8 15 4 12 26 25
44	5 27 7 29 9 3 0 30 8 15 4 12 26 25
45	5 27 7 29 9 3 30 0 8 4 12 26 25
46	5 27 7 29 9 3 30 0 8 4 12 26 25
47	5 27 7 29 9 3 0 30 8 4 12 26 25
48	5 27 7 29 9 3 0 30 8 4 12 26 25
49	5 27 7 29 9 3 0 30 8 4 12 26 25
50	5 27 7 29 9 3 0 30 8 4 12 26 25
51	5 27 7 29 3 0 30 8 4 12 26
52	5 27 7 29 3 0 30 8 4
53	5 27 7 29

Race stopped on lap seven. Results taken at end of lap five and combined with those of 53-lap second part to produce aggregate result. Lap chart shows positions on the road. With thanks to FOSA.

One lap behind leader

RACE DISTANCE: 58 LAPS, 181.638 MILES/292.320 KM

CHASSIS LOG BOOK

#	Driver	Chassis
0	Hill	Williams FW16/3
2	Senna	Williams FW16/2
	spare	Williams FW16/4
3	Katayama	Tyrrell 022/2
4	Blundell	Tyrrell 022/1
	spare	Tyrrell 022/3
5	Schumacher	Benetton B194/5
6	Lehto	Benetton B194/4
	spare	Benetton B194/3
7	Häkkinen	McLaren MP4/9/3
8	Brundle	McLaren MP4/9/4
	spare	McLaren MP4/9/5
9	Fittipaldi	Footwork FA15/1
10	Morbidelli	Footwork FA15/2
	spare	Footwork FA15/3
11	Lamy	Lotus 107C/2
12	Herbert	Lotus 107C/3
	spare	Lotus 107C/1
14	Barrichello	Jordan 194/5
15	de Cesaris	Jordan 194/2
	spare	Jordan 194/4
19	Beretta	Larrousse LH94/2
20	Comas	Larrousse LH94/1
	spare	Larrousse LH94/3
23	Martini	Minardi M193B/4
24	Alboreto	Minardi M193B/1
	spare	Minardi M193B/3
25	Bernard	Ligier JS39B/6
26	Panis	Ligier JS39B/4
	spare	Ligier JS39B/2
27	Larini	Ferrari 412T1/150
28	Berger	Ferrari 412T1/151
	spare	Ferrari 412T1/149
29	Wendlinger	Sauber C13/6
30	Frentzen	Sauber C13/3
	spare	Sauber C13/1
31	Brabham	Simtek S941/2
32	Ratzenberger	Simtek S941/1
33	Belmondo	Pacific PR01/1
34	Gachot	Pacific PR01/2

CONSTRUCTORS' CUP

Pos	Team	Points
1	BENETTON-FORD	30
2	FERRARI	16
3=	WILLIAMS-RENAULT	7
3=	JORDAN-HART	7
5	SAUBER-MERCEDES	6
6=	McLAREN-PEUGEOT	4
6=	TYRRELL-YAMAHA	4
8	FOOTWORK-FORD	3
9	LARROUSSE-FORD	1

FOR THE RECORD

First Grand Prix points
Nicola Larini

150th Grand Prix start
Gerhard Berger

50th Grand Prix start
Johnny Herbert

DRIVERS' POINTS

1 SCHUMACHER — 30
2= HILL — 7
2= BARRICHELLO — 7
4= BERGER — 6
4= LARINI — 6
6= ALESI — 4
6= HÄKKINEN — 4
6= KATAYAMA — 4
6= WENDLINGER — 4
10 FITTIPALDI — 3
11 FRENTZEN — 2
12 COMAS — 1

WORLD CHAMPIONSHIP • ROUND 4

MONACO GRAND PRIX

SCHUMACHER
BRUNDLE
BERGER
DE CESARIS
ALESI
ALBORETO

The first race to be held after the tragic deaths of Ayrton Senna and Roland Ratzenberger was obviously going to be a highly charged and intensely emotional affair. Moreover, when Karl Wendlinger sustained serious head injuries after crashing his Sauber-Mercedes during the first qualifying session at Monaco it began to seem as though Formula 1 had become inextricably entrapped in a web of endless disaster. After all that, Michael Schumacher's crushing flag-to-flag victory in the Monaco Grand Prix came as an overwhelming relief. It didn't matter that the race was boring and processional, or that Martin Brundle's McLaren-Peugeot and Gerhard Berger's Ferrari were the only other cars on the same lap as the victorious Benetton at the finish. Granted, it was disappointing that Damon Hill's Williams and Mika Häkkinen's McLaren were both eliminated in a first-corner collision, but the overwhelming feeling to attend the chequered flag was one of unbridled relief that F1 had got through the race free from another serious incident.

MONACO GRAND PRIX

Damon Hill *(below left)* **was left to carry the burden on his own for the Rothmans Williams Renault team at Monte Carlo.**

Bottom left: **Karl Wendlinger's practice accident shook an already nervous F1 hierarchy. One of the marshals at the scene supports the unfortunate Austrian's head as he lies slumped in the cockpit while they wait for expert medical assistance to arrive.**

Diary

Al Unser Jr powers Penske-Mercedes to pole position for Indy 500 on the weekend that his father, four-times Indy winner Al Sr, announces his retirement from racing at the age of 55.

Duncan Hamilton, one of the great Jaguar sports car aces of the 1950s, dies at the age of 73.

Monaco F3 classic won by Italian F3 championship leader Giancarlo Fisichella.

ENTRY AND PRACTICE

Nobody could ever recall the Monaco Grand Prix weekend starting on such a subdued, low-key note. Only ten days had elapsed since the tragedies at Imola when the F1 transporters rolled into the tiny Mediterranean Principality, so sadness and depression were still very much the prevailing emotions in the confined pit lane.

Mechanics worked in near-silence as they prepared the cars, their familiar chatter reduced almost to a subdued whisper. The sense of trauma and loss was still very much to the forefront of their minds. Moreover, those feelings were exaggerated by the fact that Ayrton Senna had been the undisputed King of Monte Carlo.

The meeting took place against a backdrop of anxious expectancy over what steps the FIA would take in the interests of furthering F1 safety. Even before the weekend, a start had been made by the imposition of an 80 km/h pit lane speed limit and barriers positioned to slow cars on both the entry to and exit from the pits.

Undoubtedly the most poignant sight was the single Williams-Renault for Damon Hill in the garage at the entrance to the pit lane. On this historic street circuit Senna had been the dominant force in recent years, winning six times in the last seven outings, and Williams was hoping against hope that Damon might summon up the resilience displayed by his late father Graham, who had helped revive the Lotus team's shattered morale in the aftermath of Jim Clark's death 26 years earlier.

After Clark's fatal crash during a minor-league F2 race at Hockenheim in the spring of 1968, Hill helped Lotus back onto its feet by winning the very next race, the Spanish GP at Madrid's Jarama circuit. Now Damon was trying to do the same at Monaco, a challenge given another historic dimension by the fact that Graham had himself won this challenging street race on five occasions between 1963 and 1969.

Despite this oppressive atmosphere, there was a cautious optimism that F1 might at least get through the weekend without any more misfortune. Tragically, those hopes were dashed in the final seconds of Thursday morning's free practice session when Karl Wendlinger crashed his Sauber C13 at the waterfront chicane.

The 25-year-old Austrian, braking later than ever on what would have been his final lap of the session, lost control over a bump as he left the tunnel and began to slow from around 170 mph. Wendlinger's car spun broadside and slid sideways into the guard rail protecting the chicane escape road.

At first glance it seemed impossible to believe that he had been badly hurt but, despite the relatively low speed of the impact, Wendlinger had sustained serious head injuries. He was taken first to Monaco's Princess Grace clinic, where a scan revealed he had a brain contusion and swelling. Shortly afterwards he was transferred by helicopter to the intensive care unit at the St Roch hospital in Nice, where he would remain in critical condition in a medically induced coma for many days.

Although it came as no surprise that the Sauber team withdrew its second entry for Heinz-Harald Frentzen, the show went on, even though it was not difficult to detect the acute strain lining the faces of many drivers. It also did not take long for rumours to begin circulating to the effect that Prince Rainier was considering cancelling the race should Wendlinger die.

None of these stories was ever confirmed or corroborated, but FIA President Max Mosley gently reminded everybody that the only body which could actually take the decision to cancel the Grand Prix was the AC de Monaco. Thankfully, this acute nervousness eventually passed and everybody settled down to concentrate on the job in hand as best they could.

Martin Brundle led the pursuit of F1's man to beat, Michael Schumacher, with a strong showing in the first qualifying session to set second-fastest time at the wheel of his McLaren-Peugeot. However, Michael had already given a hint of what was to come during the Thursday morning session. After his own race car developed a problem with its revised-spec development Zetec-R V8, he took over team-mate J.J. Lehto's B194 and posted fastest time by more than a second.

Although Schumacher's Benetton wound up fastest by 1.3 seconds, Brundle finished the first day comfortably ahead of his team-mate Mika Häkkinen and the Ferraris of Gerhard Berger and Jean Alesi.

'I drove as smoothly as possible and the time just came,' said a delighted Brundle. 'When you are sliding the car around on opposite lock, it may feel great, but it's not the quick way to do it. We have also benefited from a test at Silverstone which helped me to get to know the car even better.'

Häkkinen's third place was achieved despite a cut tyre and a slight glancing impact against one of the unyielding barriers. Towards the end of qualifying his McLaren also began to trail a smoke haze, but this was traced only to a leaking gearbox oil seal which produced no serious mechanical consequences.

On Saturday afternoon, however, it was Häkkinen who took over as McLaren's most glittering star, jousting closely with Schumacher for the privilege of pole position – more crucial at Monaco than at most places. In fact, the second qualifying session unfolded with Schumacher's Benetton lapping progressively and consistently faster each time it emerged from the pit lane.

Michael had a slight gearchange problem on his first run, but settled down to trim his Thursday best of 1m 20.230s to an amazing 1m 19.974s. Already Nigel Mansell's all-time Monaco circuit record of 1m 19.945s, set in qualifying for the 1992 race, looked set to be toppled.

Berger forced the Ferrari 412T1 into second place with a lap in 1m 20.139s, a superb effort from the Austrian, who had spent the painful days since Imola agonising over whether or not he really wanted to continue racing at all. Then Schumacher breached Mansell's record with a 1m 19.408s, after which Häkkinen pulled out all the stops to draw uncomfortably close to the Benetton star with a 1m 19.488s, relegating Berger to the second row.

With less than five minutes left to run, Schumacher went back out onto the circuit. With barely 40 seconds remaining before the chequered flag came out, he set off on his final flying lap and rocked everybody on their heels with a stunning 1m 18.560s – a full 1.4 seconds faster than Mansell's absolute record.

This was the first pole position of Schumacher's career and only the second ever achieved by a German driver in the 45-season history of the official World Championship. The only previous occasion had been when Wolfgang von Trips took pole for Ferrari at the 1961 Italian Grand Prix at Monza, the race in which he would be killed.

Brundle by now was well out of the picture, having lightly clipped a barrier and damaged a rear suspension link early in the session. The Englishman just couldn't get his McLaren MP4/9 to work properly and faded to eighth in the final order.

'I was really fighting the car, or it was fighting me,' he said. 'To put it mildly, I am seriously disappointed, but I can't really say what might have been wrong with the car until we look at the telemetry results.' Subsequent detailed examination of the car revealed that a friction plate in the differential had seized.

Jean Alesi, now recovered from back injuries sustained in testing and making his return to the cockpit for the first time since Interlagos, complained of poor traction in the slow corners and couldn't quite match Berger's speed.

'I made a big improvement in reducing wheelspin and rear tyre wear,' he explained, 'but my car is still oversteering a lot. I also hit the barrier at Mirabeau with my left-hand wheels.' Fifth place was the result. Both Ferrari drivers tried neck braces in the first free practice session, but discarded them after a couple of laps.

By contrast, Damon Hill had a disappointing time on Thursday, the lone Williams-Renault taking a provisional sixth place on the grid at the end of the first session. Hill's subdued performance mirrored his team's low-key mood, everybody understandably still shell-shocked in the wake of the Senna catastrophe. Midway through Thursday morning's session, Hill's FW16 was switched from Carbone Industrie to Hitco brake discs, the characteristics of which were deemed more suitable for the tight Monaco circuit.

'We have to change quite a few things on the car,' said Damon, 'and hopefully, if it is dry on Saturday, we will improve. I think we are certainly capable of getting the car onto the front row.' This turned out to be a wildly over-optimistic prediction.

Damon's eventual fourth place at the end of Saturday qualifying amounted to a dogged re-run of his qualifying achievement the previous year. But as the Londoner stepped from the cockpit, he nevertheless looked strained and worn out.

'The car is getting better,' he admitted. 'We started off totally out of contention, with no chance. But it is getting better. The biggest problem for me is to shoulder the responsibility for the team. To be honest, I've found that quite hard, but I believe we will be in with a chance when it comes to the race.'

131

Left: Just the first of the losers? Martin Brundle's second place equalled his best-ever Grand Prix result. But for McLaren's Ron Dennis only victory counts.

Bottom left: The vastly experienced Andrea de Cesaris was drafted into the Jordan team and delighted Eddie Jordan by claiming fourth place after a sensibly restrained performance in both practice and the race.

'We can't bring Senna back, but I would have liked ideally to come here with a team-mate, although I realise that could not be organised within the timescale available. The whole thing is awful – a very sorry situation.

'The sooner we get away from Monaco and back to some semblance of normality, the better I think it will be.'

Sixth and seventh places on the grid went to the promising Footwork FA15s of Christian Fittipaldi and Gianni Morbidelli. Christian was particularly happy by the end of second qualifying, but Gianni felt, in retrospect, that he might have managed his tyre strategy in a more efficient manner. Instead of conserving his rubber and trying for three runs, he made only two.

Behind Brundle came Pierluigi Martini, the pint-sized Italian delighted with the feel of his Minardi. With team-mate Michele Alboreto lining up 12th, things looked promising for the compact Faenza-based *équipe*.

Blundell and Katayama were slightly disappointed to have managed only tenth and eleventh places on the grid. Blundell, who admitted that his overriding priority was to score his first points of the season, went straight on at Ste Dévote on his ninth lap during first qualifying, unluckily stalling his Yamaha V10, and was unable to resume.

Katayama, who suffered an engine failure on Thursday morning and was behind on chassis set-up during first qualifying, felt he too could have done better had it not been for a half-spin on his best lap on Saturday afternoon. Even so, the Tyrrell 022s were definitely edging closer to unlocking their undoubted performance potential.

Erik Comas did well to line up 13th for Larrousse, despite his gearbox intermittently selecting neutral during second qualifying, ahead of Jordan duo Andrea de Cesaris and Rubens Barrichello, both of whom had been hoping for a slightly better showing from their Hart-powered cars.

Barrichello, understandably still haunted by the loss of Senna, admitted he was lacking his usual spark while de Cesaris, aware that the team was hoping to capitalise on his proven Monaco expertise, erred on the side of caution as he concentrated on avoiding any silly mistakes.

In a disappointing 17th place was Lehto, the pleasant Finnish driver, clearly dispirited after the events at Imola and generally not in good form, finding the Monaco circuit particularly hard on his neck. In first qualifying he spun under braking for the chicane, sustaining minor front suspension and wing damage, and he finished the day 12th fastest. On Saturday he slipped another five places, seemingly unable to get to grips with the whole business, and he would line up just ahead of Olivier Beretta's Larrousse.

In the Lotus camp, Johnny Herbert was worried by a lack of grip, eventually claiming 16th-fastest time, while Pedro Lamy was three places further back, the Portuguese driver's efforts frustrated when he ran out of fuel on his final lap.

Olivier Panis and Eric Bernard lined up in 20th and 21st places in their Ligier JS39Bs. Both men were plagued by a shortage of grip and suffered from the low priority given to improving their cars in the run-up to Benetton's takeover of the French team, a long-awaited development finally confirmed over the Monaco weekend.

Simtek bravely fielded a single entry for David Brabham, Nick Wirth's car carrying the respectful message 'For Roland' in memory of the popular Austrian driver so cruelly snatched from them at Imola. Brabham's lack of Monaco experience was an obvious handicap and the team was struggling to work out a decent set-up throughout qualifying, eventually lining up 22nd.

Right at the back came the two Pacific PR01s, Bertrand Gachot and Paul Belmondo struggling with a multitude of technical setbacks. Gachot's first qualifying session was punctuated by a major engine problem, while Belmondo spun into a barrier on Thursday afternoon and suffered an Ilmor blow-up on Saturday which prevented him from bettering his first-session efforts.

As the dust cleared after that final qualifying session, there was nothing but admiration for Schumacher. That, and a lingering feeling that something was missing.

If you closed your eyes, just for a moment, you could imagine that bright-yellow helmet in the blue Rothmans Williams slamming out of the tunnel, or wending its fluid path through the ess-bends around the swimming pool. Yes, perhaps Ayrton might have come close to beating Schumacher. But even the Brazilian's most ardent fans could accept that toppling the Benetton driver would have been a tall order. Even for Senna.

Mosley announces dramatic new F1 technical rules

In the immediate aftermath of the Imola tragedies, FIA President Max Mosley seemed determined not to buckle under pressure for precipitate action on safety, rightly fearing that any short-term, knee-jerk action might cause more problems than it solved.

At a meeting held in Paris on the Wednesday following the San Marino Grand Prix, the sport's governing body firmly pledged to improve the long-term safety of F1. But Mosley warned that he would not be bounced into premature action just for the sake of being seen to do something.

'The modern F1 car cannot safely be regulated by snap judgements or panic measures,' he said. 'However, it is right that recent events reinforce the research into increased safety for F1 which continues all the time as part of a wide-ranging programme to improve safety standards in motor sport.'

Little more than a week later, political circumstances found Mosley announcing a dramatic package of new rules to slash aerodynamic downforce, reduce cornering speeds and significantly curtail engine power.

Although it may have been Mosley's initial inclination to take a firm line with Marco Piccinnini, the head of the Italian Automobile Sports Commission, who had demanded immediate action in the Paris meeting, by the time the FIA President arrived at Monaco, the governing body had become the focal point of hysterical pressure from the French and Italian media. The Monaco announcement was seen in some quarters as being intended, at least in part, to defuse threats that both Ferrari and the Italian Grand Prix might withdraw from the World Championship unless something positive was seen to be done.

Mosley's announcement effectively breached the Concorde Agreement, the complex legal protocol governing the implementation and application of F1 racing regulations.

Ironically, this document had originally been drafted by Mosley more than a decade before in his previous incarnation as legal adviser to the F1 Constructors' Association. Its terms require unanimous agreement from the competing teams to effect an immediate rule change, except on the grounds of safety, which were now invoked.

'Unfortunately what we wish to put forward does not meet with everyone's approval,' Mosley explained. 'We did not have the agreement of everyone concerned, so we're going to have to do it despite the Concorde Agreement.

'But I think it is fair to say in the past a number of measures the FIA would have liked to bring in were prevented by the Concorde Agreement.

'The time has come, because of the gravity of the situation and the force of public opinion, to push aside such considerations and simply do what is right in the general interests of the sport.'

Under the new rules, as from the Spanish GP at Barcelona on 29 May, all F1 teams were required to reduce the size of the aerodynamic ramp-like diffuser panels under the rear of the car, raise front wings by 10 mm and remove any part of the front wing end plate extending behind the leading edge of the front wheels. Mosley predicted that this would yield a 15 per cent reduction in aerodynamic downforce which, in turn, would reduce cornering speeds.

From the Canadian GP in Montreal, a fortnight later, increased lateral cockpit protection for the drivers was demanded together with strengthened front suspension components to prevent drivers being struck on the head by flying wheels in the event of an accident.

Added impetus was given to the adoption of this rule after the post-mortem carried out on Ayrton Senna revealed that he had died from a massive blow inflicted by the front-right suspension componentry of his Williams FW16. The minimum weight limit would be raised by 25 kg to accommodate these changes.

In addition, the FIA required that cockpit apertures be lengthened and standard pump fuel become mandatory in addition to the ram effect of the airboxes being eliminated. The fuel companies involved were to be invited to nominate 100 filling stations, any of which could be chosen by the FIA to establish a standard baseline fuel specification.

However, the most dramatic rule change was reserved for the season's midway point, the German Grand Prix at Hockenheim. The FIA proposed the early introduction of the 50 mm 'stepped bottom' regulations originally scheduled for the start of 1995, together with a reduction in rear wing height and a requirement for the reduced diffuser panels to be raised by 50 mm.

Looking further ahead to 1995, the governing body indicated that it intended restricting power from the current average of 750 bhp-plus to below 600 bhp by means of a fuel-flow restrictor. In addition, a special FIA Advisory Expert Group would be established under the chairmanship of Professor Sid Watkins, President of the FIA Medical Commission.

He would be joined by the F1 Technical Delegate, a competing driver, a designer, the F1 Safety Delegate (Circuits) and outside experts chosen by the group. These experts were to be drawn from all the relevent areas (structural design, airbags, absorbent foams, crash testing techniques, etc.) and such funding as necessary would be provided by the FIA.

Most team owners and chief designers remained diplomatically tight-lipped when asked to comment on the rule changes in the immediate aftermath of Mosley's bombshell. More to the point, the team chiefs and designers had met with the FIA only the previous day and the unilateral announcement from the governing body did not seem, in their view, to bear much resemblance to what had been discussed less than 24 hours earlier.

'We're being presented with a *fait accompli*,' said Ferrari designer John Barnard, summing up the prevailing mood in the paddock. 'I doubt the measures would have been announced now were it not for Wendlinger's accident. It's only a week or so since Max Mosley emphasised the need to avoid a knee-jerk reaction to the events at Imola. This has undermined that statement.'

Behind the scenes, most F1 team bosses also believed that Mosley's public stance represented a highly political opening move in a complex chess game which would result in compromise proposals eventually being thrashed out. So it proved.

MONACO GRAND PRIX

Trouble at the start. Michael Schumacher is already well clear of the rest of the field as Mika Häkkinen *(top left)* spins out after colliding with Damon Hill. The Wiliams-Renault was rendered *hors de combat*, as were the Footwork of Morbidelli and the Minardi of Martini, who are seen tangling to the right.

RACE

The race morning warm-up offered an ominous portent for Hill, who spun at Loews due to a throttle response problem and touched the barrier, but he managed to get his race car back to the pits and immediately switched to the spare. Schumacher tried the spare Benetton only to encounter slight electrical problems, but his race car felt just fine.

The prelude to the start served only to tax emotions even further. The drivers all assembled for a minute's silence at the front of the grid, where the first two spaces had been left vacant in memory of Senna and Ratzenberger. After this, there was an understandable degree of nervousness as the cars filed off on the parade lap. Predictably, Schumacher made a clean getaway to take an immediate lead, but Hill tried to catapult down the outside to challenge Häkkinen as the pack jostled into Ste Dévote.

Suddenly all hell broke loose as the Williams's right-front wheel tapped the McLaren's left-rear, spinning Häkkinen, tail out to the right, into the escape road. Mika was out on the spot while Hill, his steering broken, limped as far as the exit to Casino Square before calling it a day.

'I made the best start I've managed all year,' shrugged Damon. 'I was past Berger, closing on Häkkinen and it looked to me as though where he was going to go left me room to get by on the left, but he moved off his line. I had no room, hit the wall, then him. That was it . . .'

Häkkinen saw it differently: 'Coming into the corner, Schumacher braked and so did I. Then I was hit really hard from behind, which pushed me into the barrier.' It was a sad reward for the Finn's first-ever front-row qualifying position. Almost unnoticed, on the opposite side of the circuit, Morbidelli and Martini had somehow tangled, with the result that four of the 24 starters hadn't managed to make it through the first turn!

By the end of the opening lap it was virtually all over. Schumacher had opened out a remarkable 3.7-second advantage over Berger, Alesi, Fittipaldi, Brundle, Blundell and Katayama. By lap three he was 5.7 seconds ahead, by lap five 9.1s and by lap eight a remarkable 13.6s ahead of the Austrian's Ferrari. On lap 15, Katayama's Tyrrell began suffering from gearchange troubles, dropping the Japanese driver from seventh to ninth behind Alboreto and de Cesaris.

Berger ran hard in the opening stages, pulling away from Alesi and Fittipaldi, while Brundle eased back slightly to conserve his rear tyres, mindful that McLaren had a one-stop option in mind as a possible race strategy. By lap 16 the remarkable Schumacher was lining up to lap his team-mate Lehto and four laps later only eight cars remained unlapped by the flying Benetton.

Brundle made the first scheduled refuelling stop at the end of lap 21, dropping back to sixth, while Schumacher made a leisurely 11-second stop three laps later, resuming with his advantage intact. Berger stopped on the same lap, dropping back to fourth and allowing Alesi to hold second until lap 34 when he too came in for what he anticipated would be his sole refuelling stop (10.1 seconds), followed immediately by Fittipaldi's Footwork.

Lap 28 was marked by the first retirement since the fracas on the opening lap. Barrichello, who had been running a frustrated 12th, boxed in amidst a great midfield bunch of cars, opted for an early stop to break the deadlock. Aside from slight problems with his downshift, the Brazilian's Jordan had been running well, so he was surprised when the engine suddenly stopped as he toured into the pits. Despite assiduous efforts, the team was unable to restart the Hart V10 and Rubens was forced to retire.

At the half-distance mark – 39 laps – Schumacher led by 28.2 seconds from Berger, then there was a long gap to Brundle, Alesi, Fittipaldi and Blundell. Going into Ste Dévote to start his 41st lap, Mark could see Schumacher approaching in his mirrors, seconds away from lapping his Tyrrell, when its Yamaha V10 expired spectacularly in a cloud of oil smoke and he skated into the escape road.

Schumacher just managed to keep control as he hit the resultant oil slick. 'The car went sideways and I was lucky to catch it,' he explained. 'I almost hit the barrier.' Berger, next through, was less fortunate. He skated up the escape road and, by the time he resumed the climb to Casino Square, Brundle's McLaren was climbing all over his Ferrari's rear wing. Martin took the long way round, but the outside line at Mirabeau paid off and the Englishman duly moved up into second place.

'When I came out of the escape road, my tyres were covered with oil and dirt, so I just couldn't defend myself against Martin,' shrugged Gerhard. Now he was third ahead of Alesi with Fittipaldi still fifth and de Cesaris, driving with the sort of discipline he seems able to muster only when the conditions are really demanding, a strong sixth.

On lap 46, Brundle made his second stop for tyres and fuel, briefly losing second place to Berger, but the balance of this particular battle was redressed five laps later when it was Gerhard's turn to call at the pits once more. By then Schumacher had also made his second stop, on lap 50, and when Brundle settled back into second place again he was still over half a minute behind the Benetton.

However, on lap 48, Ferrari's one-stop strategy for Alesi had gone out of the window when the Frenchman appeared in the pit lane with a damaged nose cone. 'Brabham blocked me twice when I tried to pass him,' explained Jean, 'first at the Loews, then at the chicane after the tunnel where I could not avoid making contact.' After repairs were effected, he was duly despatched back into the fray behind de Cesaris, cursing 'too many drivers in F1 who do not deserve a superlicence!'

David Brabham, however, had finished the day with a similarly jaded view of Alesi's behaviour. The Simtek was slogging round in 13th place before – in the driver's view – it was dealt a glancing blow as the Frenchman slithered by under braking for the chicane.

'I was aware of Alesi closing behind,' said Brabham. 'I felt I had the racing line and planned to let him by after the corner. To my amazement, he lunged for the inside before the chicane, hitting my offside rear wheel and breaking the suspension in the process. End of story for today.'

On the same lap as Alesi's misfortune, Fittipaldi's great run in fifth came to an end with gearbox failure, promoting de Cesaris to fourth and Alboreto to sixth behind Alesi. With Lehto struggling home seventh, that's how they finished, with the Larrousse duo, Beretta and Comas, sandwiching Panis's ninth-placed Ligier, and Lamy 11th, the final finisher. Gearbox trouble had eliminated the second Lotus of Johnny Herbert with ten laps remaining.

Berger finished the race distinctly less than impressed with Alboreto's behaviour in the closing stages. 'He didn't look in his mirrors for three laps with the result that my engine was overheating madly and losing power,' he complained. 'For the last 15 laps, it was just a question of making it to the finish.' Michele, unceremoniously turfed out of the Maranello ranks at the end of 1988, has a long memory . . .

Several laps before the chequered flag, Schumacher eased off considerably, allowing team-mate Lehto to regain half his two-lap deficit, and Brundle was able to close to within 40 seconds by the finish. For the German ace, it had been another devastating *tour de force*, but it seemed only appropriate that everybody's thoughts should linger on memories of Ayrton Senna.

'I think, for all of us, the two weeks after Imola have been very difficult,' acknowledged Schumacher. 'For myself, I wasn't even sure whether I could continue racing. I did two days of testing at Silverstone before I came here and I knew if I didn't have the right feeling straight away – if I had any feeling of fear – I would not have been able to continue.

'But this was his [Ayrton's] sport and I think he would have wished us to continue with it.'

Brundle echoed those sentiments, recalling with a shudder how he felt when his young daughter asked him if it was really true that Senna was dead. But this second place, equalling his best-ever result, at Monza for Benetton in '92, represented a long-overdue boost for his spirits.

Not that Ron Dennis was about to confirm his tenure of the second McLaren seat for the rest of the season – officially at least. 'He told me, "If you want to drive a McLaren, earn it," ' smiled Brundle. 'I hope I've earned it, but it's not for me to say.'

Back in the paddock, Peugeot were celebrating. Dennis joined in, of course, but with a cautionary reminder to the revellers. 'Remember,' he said, 'second just means you're the first of the losers.'

The McLaren chief's words represented the chill winds of F1 reality. How to bridge the gap to Schumacher, Benetton and Ford remained the challenge facing the rest of the paddock.

Left: Michael Schumacher crushed the opposition in the manner of the late lamented Ayrton Senna, proving himself a worthy successor to the great Brazilian's Monte Carlo crown.

Below: After the disturbing incident at Imola, speed restrictions had been introduced in the pit lane.

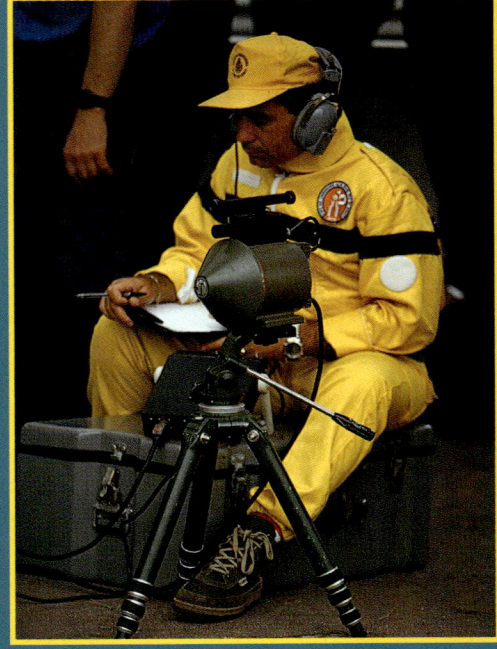

Above: Erik Comas – a study in concentration.

After a moribund year spent with the Scuderia Italia Lola in 1993, Michele Alboreto *(right)* was back in the points for the first time since Estoril in 1992.

Christian Fittipaldi *(above)* drove a superb race in the Footwork, holding fourth place until sidelined by a gearbox failure.

Not in my back yard! Ear defenders help shut out the noise from Gerhard Berger's Ferrari as one resident of the Principality takes the sun during Grand Prix weekend.

Paul-Henri Cahier

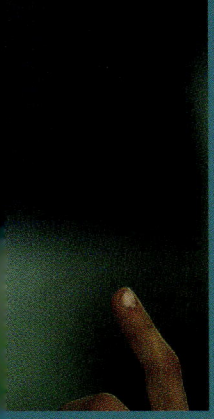

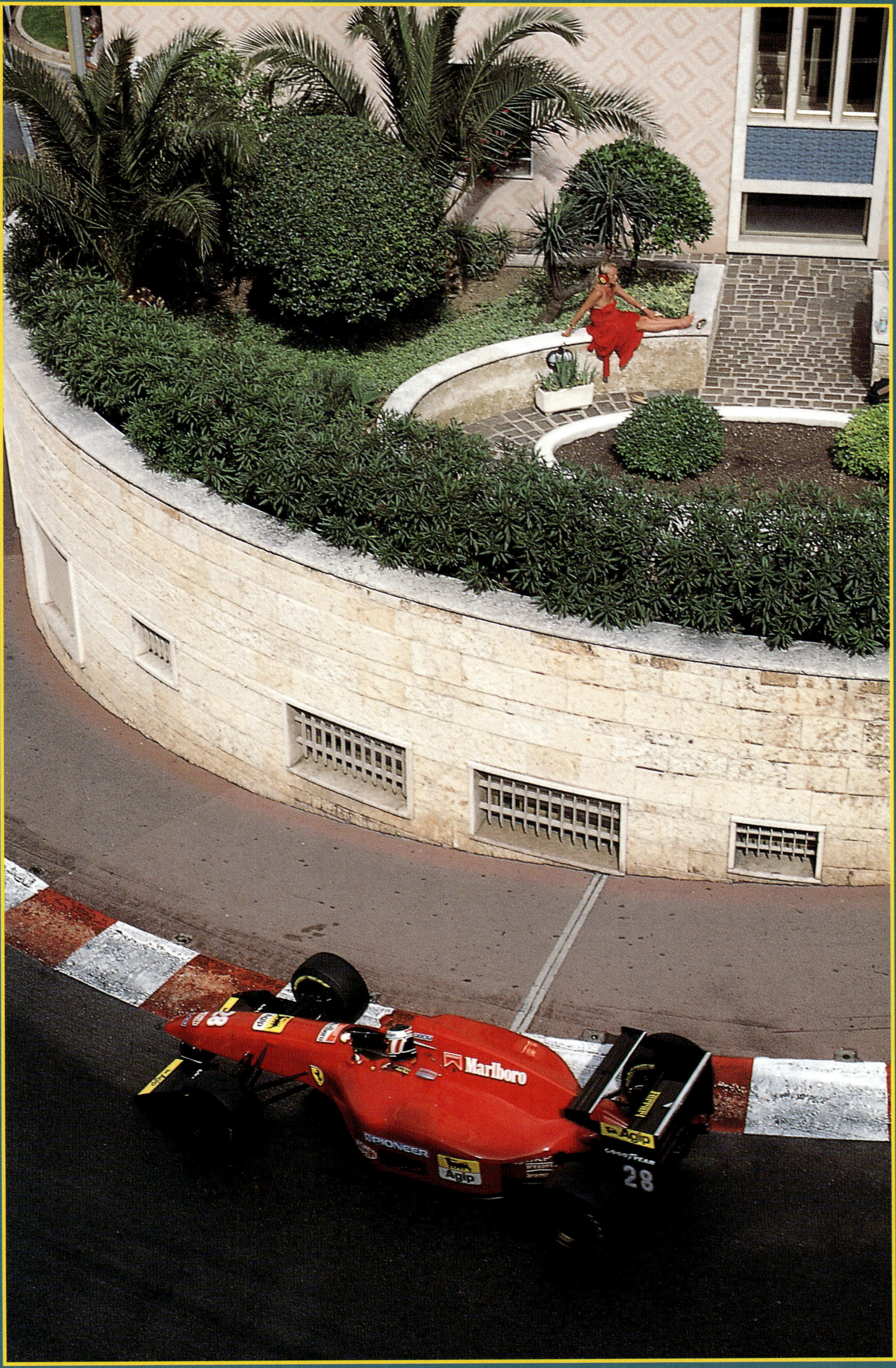

Sporting Pictures (UK) Ltd

FIA FORMULA ONE WORLD CHAMPIONSHIP ROUND 4

GRAND PRIX DE MONACO

MONTE-CARLO
13-15 MAY 1994

Race weather: Dry, warm, bright

Place	Driver	Nat.	No.	Entrant	Car/Engine	Laps	Time/Retirement	Speed (mph/km/h)
1	**Michael Schumacher**	D	5	Mild Seven Benetton Ford	Benetton B194-Ford Zetec-R V8	78	1h 49m 55.372s	88.041/141.690
2	**Martin Brundle**	GB	8	Marlboro McLaren Peugeot	McLaren MP4/9-Peugeot A6 V10	78	1h 50m 32.650s	87.547/140.894
3	**Gerhard Berger**	A	28	Scuderia Ferrari	Ferrari 412T1 041 V12	78	1h 51m 12.196s	87.028/140.059
4	**Andrea de Cesaris**	I	15	Sasol Jordan	Jordan 194-Hart 1035 V10	77		
5	**Jean Alesi**	F	27	Scuderia Ferrari	Ferrari 412T1 041 V12	77		
6	**Michele Alboreto**	I	24	Minardi Scuderia Italia	Minardi M193B-Ford HB V8	77		
7	J.J. Lehto	SF	6	Mild Seven Benetton Ford	Benetton B194-Ford Zetec-R V8	77		
8	Olivier Beretta	F	19	Tourtel Larrousse F1	Larrousse LH94-Ford V8	76		
9	Olivier Panis	F	26	Ligier Gitanes Blondes	Ligier JS39B-Renault RS6 V10	76		
10	Erik Comas	F	20	Tourtel Larrousse F1	Larrousse LH94-Ford HB V8	75		
11	Pedro Lamy	P	11	Team Lotus	Lotus 107C-Mugen Honda ZA5C V10	73		
	Johnny Herbert	GB	12	Team Lotus	Lotus 107C-Mugen Honda ZA5C V10	68	Gearbox	
	Paul Belmondo	F	33	Pacific Grand Prix Ltd	Pacific PR01-Ilmor 2175A V10	53	Driver	
	Bertrand Gachot	F	34	Pacific Grand Prix Ltd	Pacific PR01-Ilmor 2175A V10	49	Gearbox	
	Christian Fittipaldi	BR	9	Footwork Ford	Footwork FA15-Ford HB V8	47	Gearbox	
	David Brabham	AUS	31	MTV Simtek Ford	Simtek S941-Ford HB V8	45	Collision with Alesi	
	Mark Blundell	GB	4	Tyrrell	Tyrrell 022-Yamaha OX10A V10	40	Engine	
	Ukyo Katayama	J	3	Tyrrell	Tyrrell 022-Yamaha OX10A V10	38	Gearbox	
	Eric Bernard	F	25	Ligier Gitanes Blondes	Ligier JS39B-Renault RS6 V10	34	Spun off	
	Rubens Barrichello	BR	14	Sasol Jordan	Jordan 194-Hart 1035 V10	27	Stalled	
	Damon Hill	GB	0	Rothmans Williams Renault	Williams FW16-Renault RS6 V10	0	Collision with Häkkinen	
	Mika Häkkinen	SF	7	Marlboro McLaren Peugeot	McLaren MP4/9-Peugeot A6 V10	0	Collision with Hill	
	Gianni Morbidelli	I	10	Footwork Ford	Footwork FA15-Ford HB V8	0	Collision with Martini	
	Pierluigi Martini	I	23	Minardi Scuderia Italia	Minardi M193B-Ford HB V8	0	Collision with Morbidelli	
–	Karl Wendlinger	A	29	Broker Sauber Mercedes	Sauber C13-Mercedes-Benz V10		Injured in free practice, Thursday	
WDN	Heinz-Harald Frentzen	D	30	Broker Sauber Mercedes	Sauber C13-Mercedes-Benz V10		Withdrawn by team	

Fastest lap: Schumacher, on lap 35, 1m 21.076s, 91.821 mph, 147.772 km/h (record).
Previous lap record: Nigel Mansell (F1 Williams FW14B-Renault V10), 1m 21.598s, 91.234 mph, 146.827 km/h (1992).
All cars used Goodyear tyres

All results and data © FIA 1994

QUALIFYING 1

Michael Schumacher	1m 20.230s
Martin Brundle	1m 21.580s
Mika Häkkinen	1m 21.881s
Gerhard Berger	1m 22.038s
Jean Alesi	1m 22.521s
Damon Hill	1m 22.605s
Pierluigi Martini	1m 23.162s
Erik Comas	1m 23.514s
Mark Blundell	1m 23.522s
Gianni Morbidelli	1m 23.580s
Christian Fittipaldi	1m 23.588s
J.J. Lehto	1m 23.885s
Johnny Herbert	1m 24.103s
Olivier Beretta	1m 24.126s
Ukyo Katayama	1m 24.488s
Andrea de Cesaris	1m 24.519s
Rubens Barrichello	1m 24.731s
Olivier Panis	1m 25.115s
Michele Alboreto	1m 25.421s
Pedro Lamy	1m 25.859s
David Brabham	1m 26.690s
Eric Bernard	1m 27.694s
Paul Belmondo	**1m 29.984s**
Bertrand Gachot	1m 48.173s

Thursday afternoon
Dry, hot, sunny

QUALIFYING 2

Michael Schumacher	**1m 18.560s**
Mika Häkkinen	1m 19.488s
Gerhard Berger	1m 19.958s
Damon Hill	1m 20.079s
Jean Alesi	1m 20.452s
Christian Fittipaldi	1m 21.053s
Gianni Morbidelli	1m 21.189s
Martin Brundle	1m 21.222s
Pierluigi Martini	1m 21.288s
Mark Blundell	1m 21.614s
Ukyo Katayama	1m 21.731s
Michele Alboreto	1m 21.793s
Erik Comas	1m 22.211s
Andrea de Cesaris	1m 22.265s
Rubens Barrichello	1m 22.359s
Johnny Herbert	1m 22.357s
J.J. Lehto	1m 22.679s
Olivier Beretta	1m 23.025s
Pedro Lamy	1m 23.858s
Olivier Panis	1m 24.131s
Eric Bernard	1m 24.377s
David Brabham	1m 24.656s
Bertrand Gachot	1m 26.082s
Paul Belmondo	8m 36.897s

Saturday afternoon
Dry, hot, sunny

WARM-UP

Michael Schumacher	1m 21.294s
Mika Häkkinen	1m 21.560s
Damon Hill	1m 22.038s
Martin Brundle	1m 22.458s
Gerhard Berger	1m 22.943s
Jean Alesi	1m 23.259s
Christian Fittipaldi	1m 23.342s
Andrea de Cesaris	1m 23.925s
Ukyo Katayama	1m 23.972s
Erik Comas	1m 24.024s
Mark Blundell	1m 24.040s
Rubens Barrichello	1m 24.096s
Pierluigi Martini	1m 24.325s
Johnny Herbert	1m 24.363s
Olivier Beretta	1m 24.446s
Olivier Panis	1m 25.113s
Gianni Morbidelli	1m 25.213s
J.J. Lehto	1m 25.643s
Pedro Lamy	1m 26.057s
Eric Bernard	1m 26.279s
David Brabham	1m 26.301s
Michele Alboreto	1m 26.308s
Bertrand Gachot	1m 27.347s
Paul Belmondo	no time

Sunday morning
Dry, warm, sunny

FASTEST LAPS

Driver	Time	Lap
Michael Schumacher	1m 21.076s	35
Martin Brundle	1m 21.998s	29
Gerhard Berger	1m 22.248s	16
Jean Alesi	1m 23.420s	64
J.J. Lehto	1m 23.737s	75
Christian Fittipaldi	1m 23.765s	14
Mark Blundell	1m 23.840s	37
Andrea de Cesaris	1m 23.978s	70
Michele Alboreto	1m 23.996s	26
Erik Comas	1m 24.080s	46
Ukyo Katayama	1m 24.498s	9
Olivier Beretta	1m 25.169s	24
Rubens Barrichello	1m 25.240s	16
Johnny Herbert	1m 25.479s	43
Olivier Panis	1m 25.563s	67
David Brabham	1m 25.844s	18
Eric Bernard	1m 25.904s	14
Pedro Lamy	1m 26.339s	42
Bertrand Gachot	1m 27.711s	21
Paul Belmondo	1m 30.048s	33

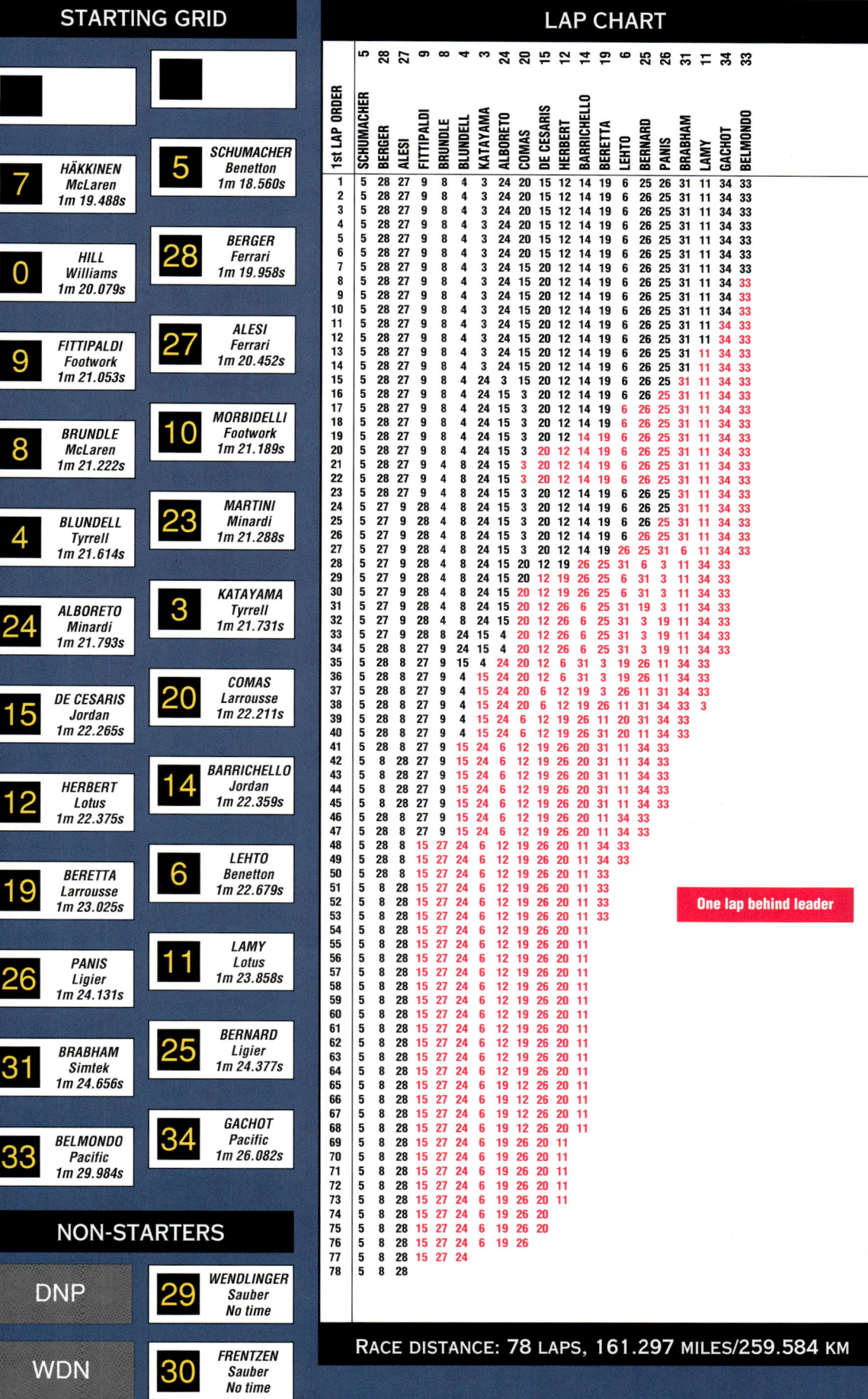

WORLD CHAMPIONSHIP • ROUND 5

SPANISH GRAND PRIX

HILL
SCHUMACHER
BLUNDELL
ALESI
MARTINI
IRVINE

Damon Hill took a decisive step towards rebuilding the Williams-Renault team's shattered morale with a gritty drive to victory in the Spanish Grand Prix at Barcelona. Playing second fiddle to Michael Schumacher's Benetton from the start, Hill was the recipient of a long-overdue slice of good fortune when the World Championship leader's car jammed in fifth gear and he became a sitting duck, the Williams driver surging through to record the team's first victory of the season and a maiden success for its FW16 challenger. Amazingly, Schumacher survived to finish second, lapping with remarkable speed and consistency despite his problems, while Mark Blundell was the fortunate recipient of third place in the Tyrrell-Yamaha, benefiting from the late retirements of J.J. Lehto's Benetton and Martin Brundle's McLaren-Peugeot. Meanwhile, the off-track political scenario remained as volatile as ever with the introduction of revised technical regulations, designed to reduce cornering speeds, accompanied by heated debate behind closed motorhome doors.

Damon's victory put fresh heart into a Rothmans Williams Renault team still coming to terms with the loss of Ayrton Senna.

SPANISH GRAND PRIX

Right: FIA officials and drivers out on the track thrash out a compromise on safety measures at the Nissan curve. The result was a hastily improvised tyre chicane.

Below right: The centre of controversy. Flavio Briatore in discussion with fellow team principals Ron Dennis and Jack Oliver outside the Williams motorhome as the debate on technical regulation changes continued to rage.

ENTRY AND PRACTICE

From the outset this year's Barcelona race looked sure to add yet another turbulent chapter to the chequered history of the Spanish Grand Prix over the past couple of decades.

A trawl through the history books reveals the event to have a remarkable track record. In 1969, at Barcelona's magnificent Montjuich Park circuit, the Lotus 49s of Graham Hill and Jochen Rindt both crashed heavily when the spindly support struts to their absurd high rear wings failed and the aerodynamic appendages collapsed like a pack of cards. Hill emerged unscathed, but Rindt was fortunate to escape with a hairline fracture of the skull. The accidents led to an overnight ban on such wayward aerodynamic devices after the first practice session for the following race at Monaco.

In 1975, at the same venue, the competing teams refused to take part in official qualifying due to concerns over circuit safety. Hasty improvements were made just in time for the race, only for the weekend to be marred by tragedy when Rolf Stommelen's Hill-Cosworth suffered a rear wing failure while leading, vaulted a guard rail and killed four onlookers who were standing in a restricted area.

That marked the end of F1 racing at Montjuich Park, but five years later more controversy erupted when the Spanish event, now held at Madrid's Jarama circuit, became the centre of a political storm over who had the right to sanction its organisation. The underlying problem was a major dispute between the FIA and the predominantly British-based teams who were members of the F1 Constructors' Association.

In the end, the FIA-aligned teams – Renault, Ferrari and Alfa Romeo – declined to take part, leaving Alan Jones's Williams to win an all-FOCA event which subsequently had its championship status removed by the sport's governing body.

Given the existing tensions straining away under the surface of the contemporary F1 landscape, it was with a measure of understandable trepidation that the teams arrived at the Circuit de Catalunya for this year's race. Ever since FIA President Max Mosley had imposed his package of changes to the technical regulations at Monaco, the Grand Prix business had seemed poised on a knife edge with the teams privately simmering with indignation that they had been hustled into accepting the amendments against their better judgement.

These concerns were intensified as testing of the hastily revised cars took place at several circuits across Europe. Lotus blamed Pedro Lamy's Silverstone shunt (see sidebar) on a wing mounting failure directly attributable to the new rules. Ligier suffered two cracked wing mountings while testing their JS39Bs at Lurcy-Levis, near their Magny-Cours base, and Williams also detected a cracked mounting on an FW15D during pre-race testing at Jerez.

There was talk that the race might be cancelled; that it might be run, after all, to the technical rules in place at Monaco. Then Benetton boss Flavio Briatore wrote a highly provocative letter to Max Mosley, exacerbating its effect by simultaneously making copies available to the media.

That provoked a stand-off between Benetton and the race officials, who demanded official assurances that the B194s were in fact safe before allowing them to compete. Briatore countered by saying that the cars had been scrutineered, so that meant that the officials regarded them as safe.

After an exchange of paperwork, the stewards of the meeting had the last say by issuing a communiqué addressed to the Benetton team. It read: 'In the light of the statement contained in your letter of 25th May, addressed to the President of the FIA, that parts of your car may not have been subjected to proper analysis and testing, you are hereby notified under Article 141 of the International Sporting Code, that unless we receive written confirmation from your engineers that all parts of your cars have now been subjected to proper analysis and testing, and that you take full responsibility for them, or such parts have been analysed and tested by the Formula One Technical Delegate, your cars will not be allowed to practise or race at this event.'

Briatore eventually backed down and gave the written assurances required. But Benetton and eight other teams – Williams, McLaren, Lotus, Pacific, Simtek, Jordan, Arrows and Ligier – then declined to contest the Friday morning free practice session, their principals instead convening in the Williams motorhome for a heated debate with Mosley over the question of how future technical regulations would be framed.

None of this was calculated to produce a calm environment in which first qualifying could take place, but eventually a full field of cars settled down to the serious business of the weekend, which seemed in danger of being overlooked amidst the off-track hysteria.

There was also concern about the makeshift chicane – no more than two piles of tyres lashed together to form barriers across the track – which the drivers had demanded be installed on the approach to the 150 mph Nissan curve on Thursday night. There were threats that the drivers would not compete unless the chicane was provided, a position not helped when the FIA reminded the circuit owners that the track needed official approval, for insurance purposes, in the event of such changes being made.

'I know it's not ideal, but it's the best that could be arranged in the time available,' explained Niki Lauda on behalf of the GPDA. 'It's certainly better than hitting a concrete wall at 300 km/h!'

Benetton boss attacks Mosley

Benetton team chief Flavio Briatore weighed into Max Mosley during the run-up to the Spanish Grand Prix, vehemently criticising the FIA President for the manner in which he had introduced the revised F1 technical regulations at Monaco a fortnight earlier.

In a lengthy letter to Mosley, which was also circulated among the media, Briatore accused him of making 'ill-considered, snap decisions' in implementing such rules. He also made it clear that if the teams were obliged to compete at Barcelona under 'these ill-conceived measures' he would be advising Michael Schumacher and J.J. Lehto that they might be racing with components on their cars which had not been subjected to the appropriate analysis and testing.

'It will be theirs and the FIA's responsibility that they race,' he warned. 'Now that the teams have had an opportunity to test and evaluate the Barcelona regulation changes, it has become apparent that there are serious problems. The stability and consistency of the cars has worsened. This can be confirmed by discussions with the majority of teams and their drivers. The cornering speed of the cars may have been reduced, but the likelihood of an accident has been increased.

'Several teams are experiencing structural failures which are attributable to the change in regulations. The loading on key components, such as rear wings, has changed and moved outside the designed range.

'Despite these concerns, you continue to insist on these ill-conceived measures. It is our opinion that the ability of yourself and your advisers to judge technical and safety issues in F1 must be questioned.'

Added weight appeared to be added to Briatore's viewpoint by the accident which had befallen Pedro Lamy at Silverstone the previous week. The 22-year-old Portuguese driver was hospitalised with multiple leg injuries after his Lotus 107C cartwheeled off the circuit at 170 mph on the approach to Bridge Corner, flew through a debris fence and landed in a spectator access tunnel.

Lotus contended that it was most likely the rule changes were responsible for the accident. 'Our wide-ranging investigation is currently concentrating on changes to the dynamic loading conditions (lateral vibration of the wing assembly) caused by changes to the technical regulations mandated by the President of the FIA, Mr Max Mosley, at Monaco and being tested prior to Barcelona,' read the somewhat cool text of the team's official communiqué on the matter.

Mosley, in turn, vigorously rejected such a contention. He explained that all teams had been told they could miss one race without penalty if they felt unable to re-engineer their cars adequately in the time available.

SPANISH GRAND PRIX

Top left: Andrea Montermini's Grand Prix debut ended in a huge crash from which the little Italian was lucky to escape with relatively minor foot injuries.

Bertrand Gachot modified the aforementioned tyre chicane *(top right)* with his Pacific during Friday's eventful qualifying session.

Above: Benetton came armed for every eventuality, as this array of undertrays with different diffusers clearly shows.

Right: Bernie Ecclestone had the happier task of presenting Goodyear's Bill Sharp with a special trophy to commemorate the tyre giant's 300th Grand Prix win.

SPANISH GRAND PRIX

The chicane was duly erected and, despite hopes that the introduction of clipped nose wings and smaller diffusers might serve to erode Michael Schumacher's advantage, the German driver's Benetton B194 remained decisively at the head of the pack throughout the two qualifying sessions.

'Everything went perfectly and the changes we have made to the car have worked well,' he said after clinching the second pole position of his career. 'I'm confident for the race. We've checked the car and tried various things. I don't expect any problems.'

The championship points leader was ably supported on this occasion by his team-mate J.J. Lehto, the Finn having shrugged aside the psychological problems which so seriously compromised his performance at Monaco. Lehto lined up fourth, separated from his colleague by Damon Hill's Williams FW16 and Mika Häkkinen's McLaren MP4/9.

'The big problem with our car is that we're having to run it very close to the track,' explained Patrick Head, 'but we're getting there, I think. It should be better still for the race.'

On Friday, Damon had likened the FW16's feel to 'walking a tightrope' and his mood wasn't improved by having a close view of Andrea Montermini's horrifying accident at the end of Friday morning's free practice session.

The Italian F1 novice lost control of his Simtek coming through the tricky downhill right-hander leading onto the start/finish straight. The car slammed into the outside barrier before spinning back across the track, scattering mechanical debris in all directions.

The front end of the Simtek was ripped off and Montermini did not move once the car skidded to a halt. For a few moments, everybody held their breath, praying that F1 hadn't been visited by yet another disaster. Things looked bad when screens were held up to protect the Italian from the prurient gaze of the television cameras, but, amazingly, Montermini survived with superficial injuries. He was helicoptered to hospital for precautionary X-rays and brain scan, escaping with a broken toe, cracked heel and a deep cut above his right eye.

Even so, this was another body-blow for Nick Wirth's tiny Simtek team so soon after the death of Roland Ratzenberger at Imola, but everybody knuckled down for the second qualifying session, relieved at the new boy's lucky escape.

After the second qualifying session, Hill admitted that his car was getting better. 'I think that the FW16 is a good car, it's got what it takes and I think we are making ground on the Benettons,' he stressed.

Damon's new team-mate David Coulthard had his first taste of the FW16 on Friday afternoon as his scheduled acclimatisation run at Jerez the previous Tuesday had been rained off. He played himself in carefully, then grabbed everybody's attention by popping up in fourth place during Saturday morning's free practice session.

He eventually wound up ninth, a pretty impressive effort for a Grand Prix debutant under such obviously pressured circumstances, although he admitted he was rather disappointed after failing to get the best out of the tyres on his second qualifying run.

'We had a bit of an imbalance from this morning's session, a little too much understeer,' he explained, 'so we made some changes to improve that and the car was better, but I didn't make full use of the second set of tyres.

'On my first lap I was too conservative, on the second I tried to get a tow from Zanardi, but by then the tyres were cold and my run was effectively over. It's a shame because I think that the car was capable of qualifying on the second row, even with me driving it!'

Häkkinen was disappointed to have dropped from second to third, feeling that his McLaren's handling had deteriorated slightly between his two runs on Saturday afternoon. Martin Brundle was similarly annoyed, ending up a frustrated eighth.

'It's the same problem I've had all year,' he admitted. 'I get aggressive and go slower. I am having difficulty getting the right balance between aggression and over-driving. I feel I'm slightly overstepping the line!'

In fifth place, Rubens Barrichello did superbly well to claim the Jordan team's best-ever qualifying position. 'I was a bit cautious on my first set of tyres, but on my second set I went for it and everything came together,' he grinned.

Alesi and Berger were sixth and seventh for Ferrari, neither able to get the best out of their 412T1s running in the lower-downforce trim forced on them by the new regulations. Jean, who opted to use the spare Ferrari on the second day, lost a lot of crucial setting-up time on Saturday morning with an engine problem which the mechanics eventually traced to a faulty spark plug, while Gerhard had a serious leak from the gearbox hydraulic system.

'Today I had to contend with so many problems that I didn't have time to concentrate on the job of setting up the car,' said Gerhard. 'Yesterday we were in a crisis, but today we seem to have fixed at least half of our problems.'

Behind Brundle and Coulthard, Ukyo Katayama and Mark Blundell lined up together in the Tyrrell-Yamahas. 'The car had the potential to qualify much higher on the grid,' shrugged Blundell, 'and I'm very disappointed. Unfortunately, I spun at the first corner on my last flying lap.' Mark's car had been fitted with a fresh H-spec Yamaha V10 for second qualifying after a slight engine problem was detected at the end of the morning session.

Katayama's showing gained particular praise from Tyrrell Technical Director Harvey Postlethwaite. 'I am very satisfied with Ukyo's performance,' he emphasised firmly.

Heinz-Harald Frentzen was expecting much more from the lone Sauber C13, but suffered a transmission problem on Saturday morning, after which a new gearbox was fitted. Unfortunately this had a slightly different differential adjustment which unsettled the car's handling and he could only manage the 12th-fastest time ahead of Eddie Irvine, the Ulsterman admitting that he felt a bit rusty on rejoining the Jordan squad following his three-race suspension.

Michele Alboreto wound up 14th despite his Minardi's cockpit fire extinguisher discharging in the second qualifying session. That left him four places ahead of his team-mate Pierluigi Martini, whose hopes of improvement were thwarted when his engine failed on only his fourth lap of the session.

Gianni Morbidelli's was the quicker of the two Footwork FA15s in 15th slot, six places ahead of a rather dejected Christian Fittipaldi, who went the wrong way on chassis set-up after a spin on Saturday morning. In 16th and 17th places came the two Larrousse LH94s of Erik Comas and Olivier Beretta, the former complaining of excessive understeer in the second session.

Olivier Panis and Eric Bernard completed the top twenty, both Ligier drivers grappling with serious understeer, while Johnny Herbert made a tentative debut with the new Lotus 109, qualifying in 22nd place. However, most of the team's efforts throughout qualifying were understandably focused on trying to ensure that the equipment ran reliably following Pedro Lamy's dreadful accident at Silverstone the previous week. Test driver Alessandro Zanardi was drafted in to handle the second Lotus entry, an old type 107C like the one written off by his unfortunate Portuguese colleague in the Silverstone smash.

Sandro managed to squeeze onto the penultimate row of the grid ahead of David Brabham's Simtek, while the last row was occupied, as usual, by the Pacific PR01s of Bertrand Gachot and Paul Belmondo. Bertrand knocked a wheel askew against the temporary chicane on Friday, bringing out the red flag, then battled excessive understeer on Saturday morning and had a quick spin in the second session. Belmondo complained that his engine felt down on power on Saturday, but the team was guardedly confident that it was at last genuinely closing the gap.

Mosley keeps control

Despite a blistering broadside from Flavio Briatore and several other team chiefs, Max Mosley warned: 'The FIA owns and runs the F1 World Championship. Teams will participate on this basis or not at all.'

However, he did accept a suggestion to extend the F1 Technical Working Group, now to comprise eight engineers and three drivers, who would attempt to formulate a structured programme of new technical rules concerning the passive safety of the cars. Their proposals were scheduled to be communicated to Mosley in advance of the next FIA World Council meeting on 2 June.

'If they [the teams] wish to extend the size of the TWG, under the Concorde Agreement, certainly the FIA would raise no objection,' said the FIA President. 'It would probably be quite useful.'

Nevertheless, he dismissed any notion that he had capitulated to pressure from the team owners. 'We had what might best be described as a full and frank exchange of views,' he said firmly. 'It's business as usual.

'Suggestions that the FIA or any of its officers have made concessions or abandoned any powers are wholly false. At no time did the teams seek concessions or threaten not to run in the qualifying practice session on Friday, 27 May. Had such a threat been made, I would have immediately invited those concerned to carry it out.'

Citing political and governmental pressure, Mosley made it very clear that the governing body would be insisting on reductions in engine power and aerodynamic downforce of the order and to the timetable outlined at Monaco. 'However, delays in implementation can also be proposed provided these are bona fide in the interests of safety,' he explained.

'When you have got serious political journalists writing [about recent events in F1], when there are questions in the Italian, Belgian and European parliaments, you must react. With politicians, who are enemies of motor sport, using the occasion to attack us – possibly very seriously in some countries – it became necessary to do something. Had we been left to our own devices, it might have been easier, but we were faced with a situation and it was necessary to take the initiative.'

Meanwhile, Bernie Ecclestone sought to pour oil on troubled waters by denying any sort of rift between the FIA and the competing teams. 'Max Mosley is the President of the FIA, which runs F1,' he cautioned. 'This situation was not designed to undermine his position.'

However, he did signal his tacit support to those teams which did not take part in Friday morning's practice session at Barcelona. 'The serious people went to the meeting to sort out the future of F1,' he said.

'And the people who weren't serious went practising . . .'

Pierluigi Martini *(left)* took fifth place for Minardi, despite still using an updated 1993 chassis.

Eddie Irvine *(below)* returned to action after his three-race suspension and the controversial Ulsterman gave a good account of himself to take the final point on offer with sixth place.

Overleaf: The midfield pack battle for position on the opening lap with Martin Brundle's McLaren and Mark Blundell's Tyrrell prominent. For Blundell a place on the podium was fitting reward for a splendid afternoon's work.
Photo: Herke de Vries

SPANISH GRAND PRIX

Diary

Silverstone announces major programme of safety upgrading to be completed in time for the 1994 British Grand Prix.

The Argentine Grand Prix, provisionally scheduled for 16 October at Buenos Aires, is dropped from the 1994 calendar. It is replaced by a European Grand Prix at Jerez.

Al Unser Jr wins Indy 500 in Penske-Mercedes.

Jean-Marc Gounon signs to drive for Simtek starting at French GP.

Colin McMaster/Words & Pictures

RACE

The race morning warm-up saw Lehto really flying to set the fastest time ahead of Schumacher, Häkkinen and the impressive Coulthard. It promised to be a busy afternoon, with several teams still pondering whether two or three tyre stops would be necessary and all the drivers mentally reminding themselves that it was single-file through the chicane for the entire race.

Disappointingly, the grandstands were thinly populated as Schumacher led the pack away on the parade lap and, as the Benetton number one eased into the lead on the sprint down to the first corner, everybody settled back to watch what promised to be yet another runaway victory for Germany's brightest. Even before the green light was shown, the field had been reduced by one when Beretta, who had complained of a mysterious vibration during the warm-up, suffered an engine failure on the parade lap and parked his Larrousse amidst a haze of smoke and steam.

Hill slotted into second place ahead of Häkkinen and Alesi, with Lehto completing the first lap in fifth place ahead of a confident-looking Coulthard, the young Scot displaying his proven penchant for excellent starts by making up three places by the first corner.

Schumacher was 2.5 seconds clear on the opening lap, extending his advantage to 4.0s next time round and then 6.5s by the end of lap four. Häkkinen, who was running to a three-stop strategy, easily kept pace with Hill in the opening stages, while Alesi, Lehto and Coulthard ran next in a tight bunch, pulling clear from Barrichello's Jordan, which was momentarily delayed when the Brazilian bumped Berger's Ferrari at the first corner.

Belmondo spun off on the third lap and Alboreto was an early casualty with engine failure fifth time round. Lehto looked really strong and, by lap eight, was all over Alesi's Ferrari trying to find a gap while Coulthard was content to sit behind the Benetton, looking cool and self-assured even though he was grappling with an electronics problem which was affecting the engine at low revs.

On lap 16, Häkkinen made his first refuelling stop, briefly dropping to 12th. The following lap Coulthard came in, keeping his fingers firmly crossed that the engine wouldn't play up. He was to be cruelly disappointed. Twice the engine refused to run at low revs and stalled. By the time David had got everything under control again and accelerated back into the race, he was in 20th place.

Although the new Williams number two settled into a steady rhythm once again and had hauled back to 12th by lap 32, close scrutiny of the telemetry read-outs in the pit lane garage revealed that the electronic glitch was now affecting the semi-auto gearchange system. Erring on the side of prudence, the team brought their new man in and retired the car.

'I had felt relaxed and competitive, and thought I might finish in the points,' shrugged Coulthard philosophically. 'It was comfortable learning how they run in Grands Prix.'

On lap 22, Schumacher made a 9.0-second refuelling stop, resuming in second place behind Häkkinen. Suddenly, on lap 24, Schumacher lost several seconds and dropped back behind Hill. For the first time this season, *das Wunderkind* seemed to be in mechanical trouble.

'The car was running perfectly in the beginning, but then I started to have problems when I wanted to shift into a different gear,' explained Michael. 'Then it stuck in fifth and I asked my pit over the radio whether there was anything they could do, but there was nothing. I never imagined I could finish like this running in one gear!'

Häkkinen led until the end of lap 31 when a 7.4s second refuelling stop dropped him to third behind Hill and the ailing Schumacher. Lehto was a storming fourth with Brundle now fifth and Alesi, who had stopped on lap 20, sixth ahead of Blundell and Fittipaldi.

Berger had dropped to 12th after his first-lap fracas, but had pulled back to tenth by the time he came past, close to the pit wall, slowing and with his arm raised aloft, at the end of lap 27. 'The gearbox went on the blink,' he explained after climbing from the car.

On lap 33 Hill lost over two seconds when he was badly balked by Pierluigi Martini's Minardi, but such a minor delay did not offer Schumacher any hope of launching a counter-attack. By the end of lap 35, Hill was 8.6 seconds ahead and pulling away. On lap 41, Damon made a second refuelling stop which allowed Schumacher and Häkkinen past, but the Benetton and McLaren both came into the pits for fuel and tyres at the end of lap 46, allowing the Williams to re-establish a 5.6-second cushion.

On lap 49 Häkkinen was closing in on Schumacher when his Peugeot V10 suddenly blew up in spectacular fashion. It wasn't a totally unexpected development, for his engineers had detected a water leak from what turned out to be a cracked radiator on the telemetry several laps earlier. Now the order was Hill by 8.1 seconds from Schumacher and Lehto, Brundle, Blundell's Tyrrell and Alesi. Next up were Martini and Irvine, just outside the points-scoring positions.

Hill reeled off the laps to win his fourth Grand Prix — psychologically his most important triumph of all — by just over 24 seconds from Schumacher, who couldn't quite believe that his crippled Benetton had lasted the distance. 'Second place under these conditions is as good as a win,' he enthused.

Lehto stopped with engine failure only 12 laps from the end while Brundle lasted until lap 60 when his McLaren emitted a huge sheet of flame and smoke, the Englishman pulling off at the end of the start/finish straight. Transmission failure was officially given as the reason for this display of pyrotechnics.

That allowed Blundell to take third ahead of Alesi and Martini, with Irvine scoring the final point after losing what he thought might have been a possible fourth place when he clipped the chicane and had to make an unscheduled stop to replace his Jordan's nose section. The Ligier-Renaults of Olivier Panis and Eric Bernard trailed home behind the Jordan-Hart, with Alessandro Zanardi and David Brabham completing the finishers. Brundle was officially classified in 11th place.

'This is better than any of the wins last year, much harder under the circumstances,' said Hill. 'In the opening stages Mika was giving me pressure and I lost a bit of time in traffic when I came into the pits. It was difficult to know what fuel load he was running, and that makes it difficult to know how to drive if you're not on the same footing as the next guy.

'The slowing-down lap was terrific. I took it nice and slowly to take it all in!'

Only a month had passed since Williams's darkest day at Imola. Now Hill's timely win, and Coulthard's heartening debut, had set the team on the road to recovery. They were not yet quite back in the sunlight, but a new dawn was definitely flickering on the horizon.

145

FIA FORMULA ONE WORLD CHAMPIONSHIP ROUND 5

GRAN PREMIO DE ESPAÑA
CATALUNYA 27–29 MAY 1994

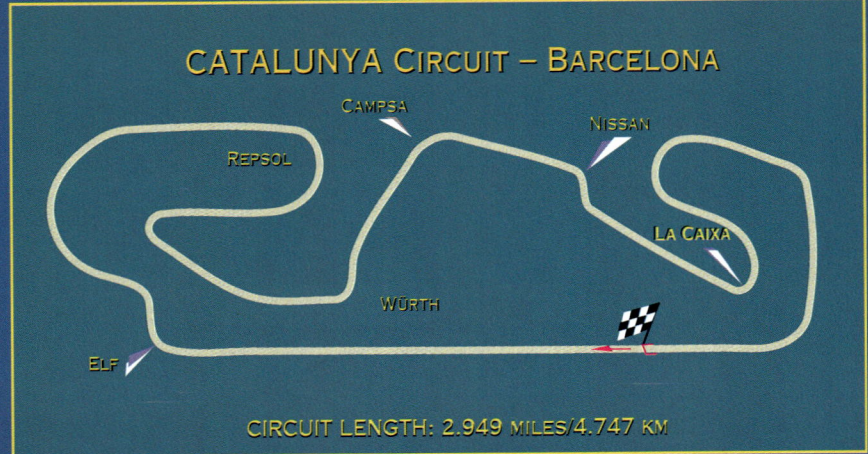

CATALUNYA CIRCUIT – BARCELONA
CIRCUIT LENGTH: 2.949 MILES/4.747 KM

Race weather: Dry, warm, sunny

Place	Driver	Nat.	No.	Entrant	Car/Engine	Laps	Time/Retirement	Speed (mph/km/h)
1	Damon Hill	GB	0	Rothmans Williams Renault	Williams FW16-Renault RS6 V10	65	1h 36m 14.374s	119.530/192.366
2	Michael Schumacher	D	5	Mild Seven Benetton Ford	Benetton B194-Ford Zetec-R V8	65	1h 36m 38.540s	119.032/191.565
3	Mark Blundell	GB	4	Tyrrell	Tyrrell 022-Yamaha OX10A V10	65	1h 37m 41.343s	117.757/189.512
4	Jean Alesi	F	27	Scuderia Ferrari	Ferrari 412T1 041 V12	64		
5	Pierluigi Martini	I	23	Minardi Scuderia Italia	Minardi M193B-Ford HB V8	64		
6	Eddie Irvine	GB	15	Sasol Jordan	Jordan 194-Hart 1035 V10	64		
7	Olivier Panis	F	26	Ligier Gitanes Blondes	Ligier JS39B-Renault RS6 V10	63		
8	Eric Bernard	F	25	Ligier Gitanes Blondes	Ligier JS39B-Renault RS6 V10	62		
9	Alessandro Zanardi	I	11	Team Lotus	Lotus 107C-Mugen Honda ZA5C V10	62		
10	David Brabham	AUS	31	MTV Simtek Ford	Simtek S941-Ford HB V8	61		
11	Martin Brundle	GB	8	Marlboro McLaren Peugeot	McLaren MP4/9-Peugeot A6 V10	59	Transmission	
	J.J. Lehto	SF	6	Mild Seven Benetton Ford	Benetton B194-Ford Zetec-R V8	53	Engine	
	Mika Häkkinen	SF	7	Marlboro McLaren Peugeot	McLaren MP4/9-Peugeot A6 V10	48	Engine	
	Johnny Herbert	GB	12	Team Lotus	Lotus 109-Mugen Honda ZA5C V10	41	Spun off	
	Rubens Barrichello	BR	14	Sasol Jordan	Jordan 194-Hart 1035 V10	39	Engine	
	Christian Fittipaldi	BR	9	Footwork Ford	Footwork FA15-Ford HB V8	35	Engine	
	David Coulthard	GB	2	Rothmans Williams Renault	Williams FW16-Renault RS6 V10	32	Electrics	
	Bertrand Gachot	F	34	Pacific Grand Prix Ltd	Pacific PR01-Ilmor 2175A V10	32	Wing mount	
	Gerhard Berger	A	28	Scuderia Ferrari	Ferrari 412T1 041 V12	27	Gearbox	
	Gianni Morbidelli	I	10	Footwork Ford	Footwork FA15-Ford HB V8	24	Fuel Filter	
	Heinz-Harald Frentzen	D	30	Broker Sauber Mercedes	Sauber C13-Mercedes-Benz V10	21	Gearbox	
	Erik Comas	F	20	Tourtel Larrousse F1	Larrousse LH94-Ford HB V8	19	Gearbox	
	Ukyo Katayama	J	3	Tyrrell	Tyrrell 022-Yamaha OX10A V10	16	Engine	
	Michele Alboreto	I	24	Minardi Scuderia Italia	Minardi M193B-Ford HB V8	4	Engine	
	Paul Belmondo	F	33	Pacific Grand Prix Ltd	Pacific PR01-Ilmor 2175A V10	2	Spun off	
DNS	Olivier Beretta	F	19	Tourtel Larrousse F1	Larrousse LH94-Ford HB V8	0	Engine failure on parade lap	
–	Andrea Montermini	I	31	MTV Simtek Ford	Simtek S941-Ford HB V8		Injured in free practice, Saturday	

Fastest lap: Schumacher, on lap 18, 1m 25.155s, 124.698 mph/200.683 km/h.
Lap record: Michael Schumacher (F1 Benetton B193B-Ford V8), 1m 20.989s, 131.113 mph/211.006 km/h (1993)
All cars used Goodyear tyres

QUALIFYING 1

Michael Schumacher	1m 23.426s
Mika Häkkinen	1m 24.580s
Damon Hill	1m 24.716s
Jean Alesi	1m 24.957s
Heinz-Harald Frentzen	1m 25.115s
Pierluigi Martini	1m 25.502s
J.J. Lehto	1m 25.587s
Mark Blundell	1m 25.863s
Rubens Barrichello	1m 25.990s
Erik Comas	1m 26.097s
Gerhard Berger	1m 26.121s
Eddie Irvine	1m 26.368s
Michele Alboreto	1m 26.595s
Martin Brundle	1m 26.614s
Ukyo Katayama	1m 27.017s
David Coulthard	1m 27.428s
Gianni Morbidelli	1m 27.459s
Christian Fittipaldi	1m 27.631s
Olivier Panis	1m 27.872s
Olivier Beretta	1m 28.011s
Eric Bernard	1m 28.289s
Alessandro Zanardi	1m 30.379s
David Brabham	1m 30.797s
Andrea Montermini	1m 31.111s
Paul Belmondo	1m 31.750s
Bertrand Gachot	1m 34.318s
Johnny Herbert	1m 59.009s

Friday afternoon
Dry, warm, sunny

QUALIFYING 2

Michael Schumacher	1m 21.908s
Damon Hill	1m 22.559s
Mika Häkkinen	1m 22.660s
J.J. Lehto	1m 22.983s
Rubens Barrichello	1m 23.594s
Jean Alesi	1m 23.700s
Gerhard Berger	1m 23.715s
Martin Brundle	1m 23.763s
David Coulthard	1m 23.782s
Ukyo Katayama	1m 23.969s
Mark Blundell	1m 23.981s
Heinz-Harald Frentzen	1m 24.254s
Eddie Irvine	1m 24.930s
Michele Alboreto	1m 24.996s
Gianni Morbidelli	1m 25.018s
Erik Comas	1m 25.050s
Olivier Beretta	1m 25.161s
Pierluigi Martini	1m 25.247s
Olivier Panis	1m 25.577s
Eric Bernard	1m 25.766s
Christian Fittipaldi	1m 26.084s
Johnny Herbert	1m 26.397s
Alessandro Zanardi	1m 27.685s
David Brabham	1m 28.151s
Bertrand Gachot	1m 28.873s
Paul Belmondo	1m 30.657s
Andrea Montermini	no time

Saturday afternoon
Dry, cool, cloudy

WARM-UP

J.J. Lehto	1m 23.834s
Michael Schumacher	1m 23.925s
Mika Häkkinen	1m 24.616s
David Coulthard	1m 24.737s
Jean Alesi	1m 25.136s
Ukyo Katayama	1m 25.160s
Damon Hill	1m 25.352s
Martin Brundle	1m 25.464s
Gerhard Berger	1m 25.792s
Christian Fittipaldi	1m 25.806s
Eddie Irvine	1m 25.814s
Pierluigi Martini	1m 26.140s
Heinz-Harald Frentzen	1m 26.378s
Rubens Barrichello	1m 26.380s
Gianni Morbidelli	1m 26.471s
Olivier Panis	1m 26.647s
Olivier Beretta	1m 26.699s
Mark Blundell	1m 26.781s
Erik Comas	1m 27.066s
Michele Alboreto	1m 27.151s
Eric Bernard	1m 27.154s
David Brabham	1m 28.398s
Alessandro Zanardi	1m 29.070s
Johnny Herbert	1m 29.293s
Bertrand Gachot	1m 30.711s
Paul Belmondo	1m 32.131s

Sunday morning
Dry, warm, sunny

FASTEST LAPS

Driver	Time	Lap
Michael Schumacher	1m 25.155s	18
Mika Häkkinen	1m 25.872s	29
Damon Hill	1m 25.874s	17
Martin Brundle	1m 26.233s	33
J.J. Lehto	1m 26.346s	38
Eddie Irvine	1m 26.580s	40
Ukyo Katayama	1m 26.658s	15
Rubens Barrichello	1m 26.863s	31
David Coulthard	1m 26.983s	10
Mark Blundell	1m 27.468s	14
Erik Comas	1m 27.533s	14
Jean Alesi	1m 27.558s	9
Gerhard Berger	1m 27.614s	11
Christian Fittipaldi	1m 28.002s	27
Gianni Morbidelli	1m 28.032s	23
Heinz-Harald Frentzen	1m 28.279s	17
Pierluigi Martini	1m 28.610s	58
Johnny Herbert	1m 28.901s	38
Olivier Panis	1m 29.118s	39
Eric Bernard	1m 29.233s	34
Michele Alboreto	1m 29.880s	4
Alessandro Zanardi	1m 30.493s	9
David Brabham	1m 30.558s	13
Bertrand Gachot	1m 31.557s	28
Paul Belmondo	1m 35.061s	2

All results and data © FIA 1994

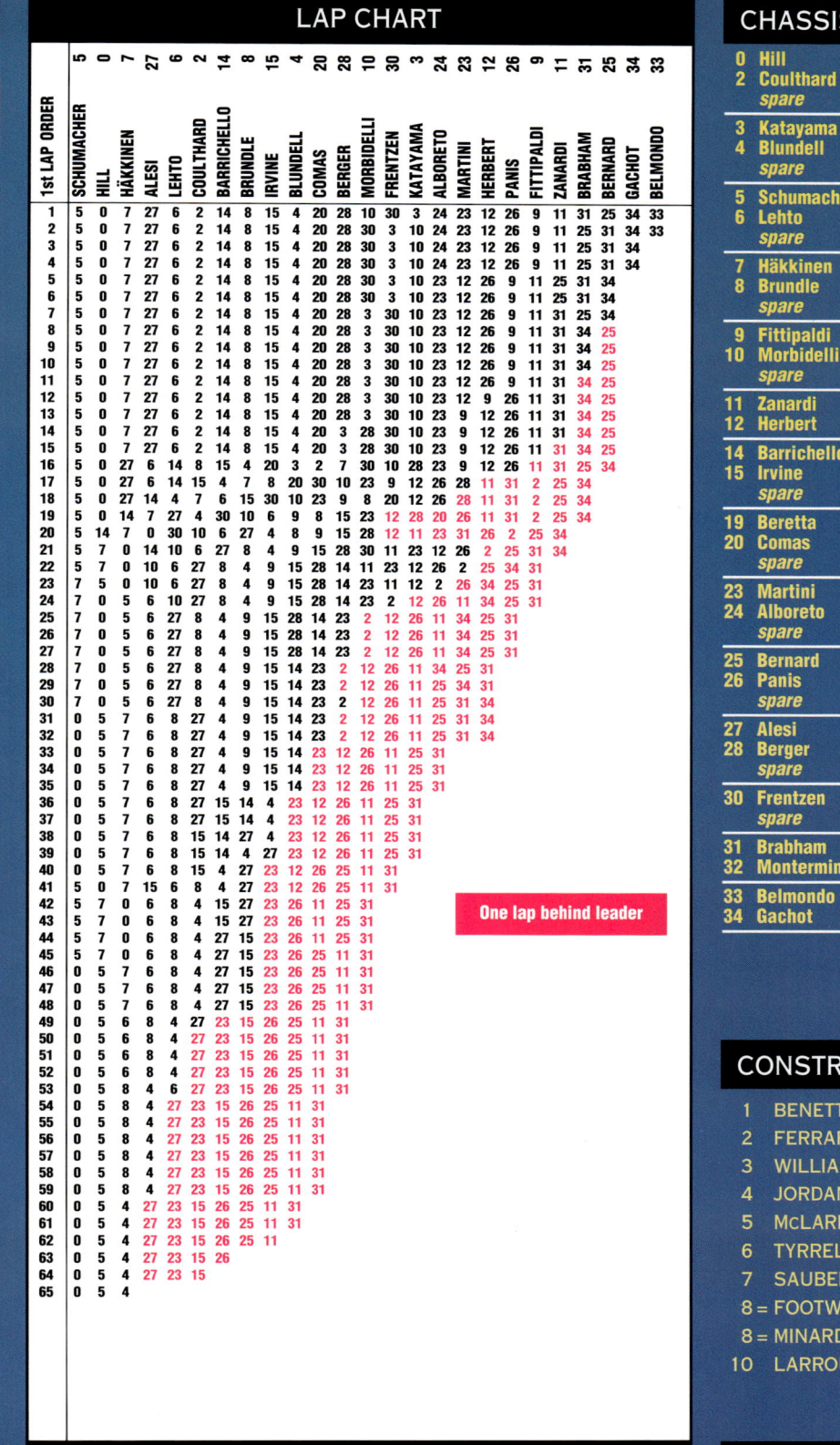

WORLD CHAMPIONSHIP • ROUND 6

CANADIAN GRAND PRIX

SCHUMACHER
HILL
ALESI
BERGER
COULTHARD
LEHTO

After stumbling with transmission problems in Spain, Michael Schumacher regained his vice-like grip on the World Championship battle with a familiarly dominant display in Montreal. The German driver's Benetton B194-Ford was in a class of its own throughout the entire weekend, taking pole position from Jean Alesi's Ferrari in the second qualifying session before leading the race from start to finish, unflustered by what seemed inconsequential challenges from Williams and Ferrari once the contest got under way. Eventually it was Damon Hill who battled through to take second place for Williams ahead of the Ferraris of Jean Alesi and Gerhard Berger, while young Scot David Coulthard scored the first points of his F1 career with fifth at the wheel of the other Williams FW16. In addition to the introduction of another tranche of technical changes, the Canadian GP was also marked by the installation of a temporary first-gear chicane on one of the fastest sections of the Circuit Gilles Villeneuve as a means of keeping lap speeds in check.

Taking centre stage. Michael Schumacher jumps for joy as his dominance of the 1994 World Championship continues unabated. Five wins from six starts leaves his closest rivals Damon Hill and Jean Alesi waiting in the wings.

Heike de Vries

CANADIAN GRAND PRIX

Diary

Ferrari reveals plans to field extensively revised version of its 412T1 in the French Grand Prix at Magny-Cours.

The Grand Prix Drivers' Association announces its recommendations for safety improvements at both Spa and Monza. A chicane at the famous Eau Rouge corner on the Belgian circuit and alterations to the Lesmo right-handers at the Italian GP venue are on the agenda.

McLaren Cars announces that it will open an exclusive showroom devoted solely to its £530,000 F1 supercar in London's Park Lane.

Paul Tracy scores his first Indy Car win of the season with his Penske-Ilmor at Detroit.

ENTRY AND PRACTICE

The capacity of the Grand Prix teams to make imaginative interpretations of the F1 technical regulations was demonstrated at Montreal when another chapter in the complicated 1994 World Championship story was opened. For this was the race at which the teams had to accommodate the latest helping of FIA-inspired rule changes designed to slow the cars even further, namely the adoption of pump fuel and a requirement that the ram effect of the engine airboxes be eliminated.

In addition, the minimum weight limit was boosted by 10 kg to 515 kg. This was described by Williams Technical Director Patrick Head as 'a cynical change – if anybody thinks it's safer, they must have a screw loose.' Being forced to position a 10 kg moulded block of lead beneath the fuel tanks of the FW16s unquestionably offended his engineering sensibilities!

Most teams conformed with the requirement to reduce ram effect by cutting exit slats in their airboxes, thereby retaining their invaluable function as billboards for those indispensable sponsors. However, the general consensus was that Ferrari's side-mounted exit slats were rather on the small side, raising inevitable speculation that Maranello had retained some measure of ram induction for its V12 engines.

Such uncharitable conclusions gained strength after Jean Alesi managed to post fastest time in Friday's first qualifying session, although the team attributed this upsurge in performance to recent aerodynamic changes enhancing the Ferrari 412T1's already promising form.

An intensive stint in the British Aerospace wind tunnel at Filton, near Bristol, had resulted in the cars taking to the track at Montreal with distinctively reshaped, square-cut radiator ducting. This facilitated the use of revised nose wings for enhanced front-end grip and, although neither Alesi nor Gerhard Berger felt the cars were particularly easy to drive, they wound up first and fourth at the end of that crucial first session, a real morale-booster for the famous Italian team.

A good time on the first day at the Circuit Gilles Villeneuve can be crucially important. At the height of the Canadian summer there is the very real worry that increased ambient temperatures on the second day may result in slower times, although this can be offset, to some degree, by the fact that the dusty track surface becomes progressively cleaner as the cars run on it.

In addition, safety concerns had seen the Canadian track emasculated by the installation of a tight, temporary first-gear chicane just before the fast ess-bend immediately after the old, open F1 pits which were last used in 1987. This had the effect of significantly slowing the cars through one of the most potentially hazardous sections of the circuit, although they were pretty well back up to maximum speed again by the time they arrived in the braking zone for the equally acrobatic ess-bend immediately before the present pit complex.

Taking an untypical second place on Friday was Michael Schumacher's hitherto-untouchable Benetton B194. The World Championship leaders came to Canada with several modifications to try, most notably a new underbody section and a revised rear wing which imitated the Williams FW16 style by having a V-profile lower plane.

By the end of the first free practice session, Schumacher hadn't had sufficient time to evaluate the new underfloor; neither was he totally convinced about the merits of the new wing, switching back to a standard-specification rear aerofoil in time for first qualifying.

There was much debate over precisely how much power loss resulted from the change to pump fuel and alterations to the airboxes. Ford, Ilmor and Hart estimated it at around 25–30 bhp – Cosworth's Martin Walters adding that, in the case of the Ford Zetec-R, it was 4.4 per cent at 200 mph, translating into 32 bhp.

Ferrari, on the other hand, claimed to have lost 70 bhp, although Berger was a little sceptical about this estimate, putting it close to 50 bhp. Either way, after some particularly vociferous complaints – most notably from McLaren boss Ron Dennis – the Ferrari team was asked to add an additional exit vent at the rear, the feeling now gaining momentum that the Prancing Horse really was gaining a measurable benefit from its side-vent set-up.

On Saturday, Schumacher slightly revised his Benetton's chassis set-up and took pole position, trading a little aerodynamic downforce for extra speed on the straight. That enabled him to get down to a 1m 26.178s, a mere 0.1s inside Alesi's Friday best. The Frenchman, celebrating his 30th birthday, tried everything he knew to match the Benetton, but failed even to equal his personal best from the first session.

'In those conditions, I just couldn't improve,' he shrugged. His teammate Berger was plagued by rear-end problems on Friday, but a change of rear dampers went some way towards improving things, allowing him to vault forward to a final third place on Saturday afternoon, even though the Austrian reported he still wasn't totally happy with his car's handling.

Alesi's fall from pole position was seen by some as evidence of Ferrari's airbox advantage in the first session, but Maranello team director Jean Todt contemptuously dismissed such speculation. 'As to the rumours flying around some of the English teams who seem to have a grudge against us, I cannot accept their comments,' he said firmly.

'Ferrari are complying with the regulations here in Montreal, as they always have done and always will do. To say that our air intake, which was seen and approved by the FIA on Thursday, does not comply with the regulations, or that we are using special fuel, is only the reaction of people who refuse to believe that we are competitive again. As a gesture of goodwill, and under no obligation, we put another hole in the airbox of the 412T1, and, as all could see, this made no difference.'

In the Williams camp, David Coulthard's second Friday run had been spoiled when his FW16 stuck in fifth gear. That left the young Scot in tenth place overnight, but once the second session began he really piled on the pressure to make one wonder about the need to sign up Nigel Mansell on a 'guest driver' basis, as all the paddock rumour suggested was to happen.

Coulthard managed fourth-fastest time on his first run the following day to close right onto Hill's tail, then made a terrific effort to take third place with a 1m 27.111s – a full 1.4 seconds faster than he had managed the previous afternoon.

Damon duly responded with a 1m 27.103s, then consolidated his position with a 1m 27.094s. Berger was next into his stride, bumping the Williams duo back to fourth and fifth in the final order. Even so, it was an excellent showing from both Frank's men, who really seemed to be making some positive progress with the difficult-to-drive FW16.

'The car was a bit better,' said Damon. 'We've improved a little, but it's a bit like trying to get blood out of a stone, if you like. It's a question of working very hard to find small gains all the time, but we're just not making a big breakthrough.

'In fact, you begin to wonder whether it's possible. There's no magic wand, and it doesn't feel like a bad car. But we're not producing the lap times, although I feel a lot more comfortable and confident than I did before Barcelona.'

As usual, Coulthard remained calm and unruffled about the whole affair. 'I'm obviously pretty happy to be fifth on the grid,' he smiled, 'but I don't think I'll be trying to make up three places on the first lap like I did in Spain. The first corner looks pretty tricky, so it will just be a case of trying to get round it without any problems.'

In sixth and eighth places, after excellent showings, the Jordan 194-Harts of Rubens Barrichello and Eddie Irvine were split by Mika Häkkinen's McLaren MP4/9. Both the Jordan lads had a difficult time on Friday, suffering with electrical problems caused by faulty wiring looms in addition to malfunctioning clutch master cylinders. Their first qualifying session was also disrupted by vaporisation of the pump fuel which they were using for the first time. Happily, they made a big improvement on the second day.

Their optimism was not shared by Häkkinen and Martin Brundle, both of whom bemoaned a lack of straight-line speed, Montreal not being a circuit to suit the modestly powerful Peugeot V10 engines. Häkkinen was also very upset when he ran over and killed a small marmot during Saturday's practice session.

Brundle, who could only qualify 12th, was further frustrated by a crankcase pressurisation problem which gave the McLaren crew a few nervous moments at the start of second qualifying. But his Peugeot engine at least managed to stay in one piece for both his timed runs.

Over in the Tyrrell camp, Ukyo Katayama had finished Friday's first qualifying session in an excellent 8th place, but things began to go wrong on Saturday morning. The Japanese suffered a major engine failure under braking for the new chicane, the session being red-flagged to a halt while the resultant oil slick was cleared from the racing line.

That at least enabled the team to retrieve Ukyo's car and make a start on installing a fresh J2-spec Yamaha V10 in time for the afternoon, a task

151

CANADIAN GRAND PRIX

Michael Schumacher tightened his stranglehold on the 1994 season with another commanding victory. The young German maestro started from pole position and his Benetton-Ford led all the way to the chequered flag.

which was completed in under 70 minutes after a heroic effort on the part of the team's mechanics.

Katayama failed to improve after spinning into the gravel at the first corner, but his Friday time was good enough for ninth place on the grid. That was still four places ahead of a frustrated Mark Blundell, the Englishman finding half a second in final qualifying despite complaining of poor grip.

Heinz-Harald Frentzen posted a respectable tenth place in the Sauber, slotting in ahead of Gianni Morbidelli's Footwork, but Andrea de Cesaris, freshly inducted into the Hinwil squad to substitute for the recovering Karl Wendlinger, just couldn't come to grips with the C13's handling. The Italian was very disappointed to end up in 14th place on the grid for his 200th Grand Prix, some 14 years after his F1 debut on this very circuit at the wheel of an Alfa Romeo.

Using the latest Minardi M194 for the first time in serious action, Pierluigi Martini bagged 15th place ahead of Christian Fittipaldi's Footwork FA15, the Brazilian frustrated at his inability to work out a chassis set-up which would yield any worthwhile grip throughout the two days of qualifying.

In 17th place, Johnny Herbert's Lotus 109 was benefiting from a test session at Snetterton the previous week during which it was found that a revised undertray offered a really worthwhile performance improvement. Herbert still complained that the new Lotus lacked grip, but it was definitely a step in the right direction and the team was extremely encouraged as a result.

By contrast, Alessandro Zanardi could only manage 23rd place with the older type 107C, but there was a definite glimmer of optimism about the team's mood for the first time this year. Splitting the two Lotus drivers were Michele Alboreto's Minardi M194, Olivier Panis's Ligier, which survived a spin in front of J.J. Lehto's Benetton, the bewildered Lehto himself and the Larrousse-Fords of Erik Comas and Olivier Beretta.

The grid was completed by Eric Bernard's Ligier, the Frenchman never having worked out a decent chassis set-up, David Brabham's Simtek, which was troubled by gear selection problems in the final session, and the ponderous Pacific PR01 of Bertrand Gachot. His unfortunate team-mate Paul Belmondo failed to qualify.

RACE

The race morning warm-up yielded something of a surprise with Martin Brundle 0.8s ahead of the field with the McLaren-Peugeot, raising the Englishman's hopes – falsely, as things turned out. Team-mate Mika Häkkinen sampled both his race car and the spare, the latter suffering from locking brakes, while Berger also swapped back and forth between race car and spare, as did Lehto in the Benetton camp, the Finn opting to race the spare B194.

For Schumacher, the start went precisely to plan as he eased into an immediate lead going into the first corner. Alesi edged out the fast-starting Berger for second place, almost putting the furious Austrian on the grass as he did so, while Coulthard got the jump on Hill. By the end of the opening lap, it was all over bar the shouting. Schumacher came through 1.7 seconds ahead of the Frenchman's Ferrari, with Berger and the Williams duo making it a tight four-way contest over second place.

Already a gap was opening up to Barrichello in sixth place, the Brazilian running ahead of Häkkinen, Irvine and Morbidelli. Coming up to the final chicane at the end of lap four, Brundle was running a lowly 13th when his McLaren's engine just died on him. 'I tried to flick the ignition switch a few times, but it was no use,' he shrugged. The MP4/9 rolled to a halt for good just at the start of the pit wall, leaving Peugeot to speculate that he had suffered a problem with the alternator/fuel pump drive.

With five laps completed Schumacher was 4.5 seconds clear of the pack, seemingly in another world to any other competitor on the track. Alesi had opened a slight gap to Berger, despite the fact he was running a heavier fuel load and planning to make just a single pit stop. Gerhard was clearly in trouble. 'The car was quite good in the warm-up,' he later reported, 'but in the race it was less well balanced and difficult to drive. I had to fight like mad to stay ahead of all those behind me.'

This was pretty obvious to the Williams duo, Coulthard clambering all over the Austrian in the slow corners within a few laps of the start, while Hill could only watch in frustration from fifth place.

After a bout of close wheel-to-wheel jousting, Hill finally squeezed ahead of Coulthard on lap nine after the young Scot was firmly told to make way for his senior colleague. Damon then set off after Berger and two laps later was right up onto the tail of the Ferrari. Even so, it took some determined work on the Englishman's part before Gerhard finally relinquished third place on lap 15.

Hill later admitted that he had been somewhat frustrated to be boxed in behind Coulthard. 'I was a little cheesed off, actually,' he said, 'because I knew I could go quicker. But I'm not complaining, because even if I'd been able to get ahead earlier than I did, I don't think I would have been able to catch Michael.'

Damon then became a little more thoughtful about Coulthard's performance when he was confronted with a specific question. 'I'll have a word with him,' he replied. 'I understand the nature of F1, and the fact that there's no love lost between teammates, but on the other hand this is supposed to be a team effort.'

Williams's new boy, who gradually fell back through the pack until he was in sixth place on lap 17, later admitted that he had pushed a little too hard in the opening stages, cooking his tyres, and also lost some feeling in his right foot, which made life difficult. Yet he was not apologetic to Hill.

'I don't think I was holding up Damon,' he said firmly. 'I got into the first corner before him and I felt I was entitled to race my way. I am also disappointed that he spoke to the press about it before he spoke to me.'

Further back, there had been some trouble when Zanardi overtook Lehto's Benetton at the new chicane, a misdemeanour for which the Lotus driver was rewarded with a stop-go penalty. Frentzen spun off as early as lap six, while Häkkinen made his first refuelling stop on lap 18, dropping from seventh to 12th, but quickly hauling back to the edge of the points-scoring positions.

On lap 21, Barrichello's fifth-placed Jordan made its first refuelling stop, dropping to ninth, while a lap later Berger was in for a 7.1-second stop, dropping to seventh, and on lap 23 Irvine – now sixth – came in and dropped to 14th. Both Jordan drivers were grappling with problems caused by the ECU controlling the semi-auto gearbox downchange mechanism and having quite a struggle as a result.

By lap 29, Schumacher was cruising round a comfortable 13.7 seconds ahead of Alesi, and when the Frenchman made an 11.4s refuelling stop on lap 31 Hill was able to move his Williams into second place. Two laps later, as a few fleeting spots of rain brushed the circuit to the accompaniment of thunder and lightning over downtown Montreal, Damon made his refuelling stop, leaving Schumacher with a 51-second advantage. That enabled him to make an unhurried single 10.4s refuelling stop at the end of lap 40, resuming still with half a minute in hand over the best-placed Williams.

Now the race settled down again with Hill vainly bringing every effort to bear to close on the leading Benetton, but to no avail. Alesi was an apprehensive third, increasingly hampered by problems changing from fourth to third gear, while Berger was fourth, but with Häkkinen's fine-handling McLaren carving yards out of his tenuous advantage under braking for every corner.

Mansell return monopolises paddock speculation

A whirlwind of speculation over Nigel Mansell's much-rumoured return to Williams on a 'guest driver' basis held the Montreal paddock in thrall for much of the Canadian Grand Prix weekend. The tipsters were confidently predicting that the 1992 World Champion would soon confirm a £4 million deal to race in four Grands Prix, starting at Magny-Cours on 3 July, when his prior commitments to the Newman-Haas Indy Car team allowed.

Mansell was due to fly to England immediately after the Detroit Indy Car race, raising speculation that he would finalise the deal with Frank Williams on a visit which was also scheduled to involve him in continued negotiations related to his proposed purchase of the Woodbury golf and country club near Exeter. This was all set against a backdrop of further gossip suggesting that Mansell had already told Carl Haas he wished to be released from his current contract which extended through to the end of 1995.

Certainly, Mansell was finding life difficult as reigning Indy Car champion, his Lola-Ford consistently outclassed by the dominant rival Penske-Ilmors. He had also infuriated the US racing establishment with his outspoken criticism of the Indy 500 organisers following his collision with backmarker Dennis Vitolo in the Memorial Day classic. Subsequently, Mansell found himself the focal point of boos and catcalls from the grandstands when he went out to practise at Milwaukee the following weekend.

Haas was apparently prepared to allow Mansell a one-off drive in the French Grand Prix, but insisted that any further F1 outings for the Englishman must wait until after the end of the Indy Car season. That would theoretically also permit Mansell to drive in the European Grand Prix at Jerez, plus the Japanese and Australian races.

At a press conference following practice at Detroit, Mansell deftly deflected speculation about his future. He confirmed that he would fulfil all his commitments with Newman-Haas to the end of the season and denied that he would be racing in the British Grand Prix at Silverstone, rightly pointing out that it clashed with the Indy Car round at Cleveland.

The driving force behind a proposed Mansell return to the F1 firmament proved to be Renault, the Williams team's engine partner believing that the Englishman's high profile would be just the tonic required to revitalise the team's efforts in the wake of Ayrton Senna's death. The Williams management, however, seemed more cautious. More specifically, recalling the tense circumstances of Mansell's departure from the F1 scene less than two years earlier, some team members seemed ambivalent to the point of hostility.

Martin Brundle summed it up nicely. 'It will be great for F1 and for the British fans if Nigel comes back,' he remarked, 'although I think he might have a few surprises.

'I'm also looking forward to his explanation as to why F1 was so bad when he left at Monza, 1992, and why it's so good now!'

Gianni Morbidelli *(left)* had climbed to fourth place in the Footwork-Ford when gearbox failure dashed his hopes of recording his first finish of the season.

Below left: Andrea de Cesaris's first race for Sauber as a stand-in for the injured Karl Wendlinger was the 200th of his eventful Grand Prix career.

Still bearing the scars – perhaps psychological as well as physical – of his pre-season testing crash at Silverstone, J.J. Lehto *(below)* picked up sixth place after Fittipaldi's disqualification.

Driving with a cool assurance that did little to endear him to his title-chasing team-mate, David Coulthard *(bottom)* took the Williams to a fifth-place finish in only his second Grand Prix.

CANADIAN GRAND PRIX

Although the Finn's Peugeot V10 was clearly out-gunned by the Ferrari V12 out of the corners, this finely balanced dispute looked set to continue all the way to the chequered flag, although Gerhard just managed to keep ahead after making his second refuelling stop on lap 44, a lap after the McLaren driver had done likewise.

On lap 41, meanwhile, Irvine's race had come to an abrupt end when he lost control trying to lap Zanardi's Lotus on the final ess-bend before the pits and hit the concrete wall.

'I was pushing too hard to get a run at him on the straight and I guess I must have got too close and lost downforce because suddenly the back end was gone,' explained Eddie. It was quite a smart impact, damaging the Jordan's right-rear suspension, but Irvine climbed out unhurt.

By lap 45 the order was Schumacher, Hill, Alesi, Morbidelli, Berger – who had made his second stop a lap earlier – Häkkinen, Barrichello, Coulthard, Blundell, Fittipaldi and Lehto. Katayama's Tyrrell had been running tenth in the opening stages when the Japanese driver had a quick spin on a tight left-hander on the return leg of the circuit.

Ukyo then spin-turned the Tyrrell in spectacular fashion, almost colliding with a couple of rivals as he momentarily ran against the traffic flow, a particularly risky manoeuvre by any standards. This incident damaged a brake cooling duct which left him experiencing braking problems thereafter. Eventually the Tyrrell snapped away from him and he spun off for good at the same point on lap 45.

On the same lap Erik Comas also stormed into the pits to retire from the race for less conventional reasons. Without a speed-limiter fitted, the Frenchman twice found his Larrousse exceeding the pit lane limit and received a couple of stop-go penalties as a result. On the second occasion he flounced away from the car in a temper, although officially his retirement reason was given as a clutch malfunction. 'A shit weekend and a shit race,' he remarked eloquently.

With 19 laps to go, Morbidelli's excellent run came to an end when his Footwork suffered gearbox failure, Beretta went out with engine trouble on lap 58 and then Häkkinen's McLaren ground to a standstill with another Peugeot breakage seven laps from home while he was running in fifth place.

'The engine developed a misfire and then failed one lap later,' he shrugged. A leak in the air-valve mechanism was officially blamed for the failure, the first time such a problem had cropped up during the season.

No such dramas touched Schumacher, however, and the Benetton team leader duly reeled off the last few laps to win by 39.6 seconds from the hard-trying Hill. In the dying moments of the race, Alesi's Ferrari began stuttering ominously, the Frenchman going into the last lap with his mount jammed in third gear. But he was still comfortably ahead of a less-than-satisfied Berger, who was frustrated by his car's poor handling all afternoon.

Coulthard finished a steady fifth to take his first-ever championship points, the Scot admitting that his foot trouble disappeared after his refuelling stop. Christian Fittipaldi was initially credited with sixth place, but post-race scrutineering revealed his Footwork to be fractionally below the 515 kg minimum weight limit, so he was excluded and the place was inherited by Lehto.

Barrichello had been within a second of Fittipaldi in the closing stages of the race but spun on the last lap, throwing away what could have been a championship point. His gearbox problems caused the Jordan to stick intermittently in sixth gear, a fault which contributed to an involuntary trip through the pit lane at the end of lap 52, and to his pirouette at the hairpin last time round.

Herbert ended the day in eighth place ahead of Martini and Blundell, the sole surviving Tyrrell driver also spinning on the last lap while embroiled in the Fittipaldi/Lehto/Barrichello battle for sixth. Alboreto was 11th, with the steady Ligiers of Panis and Bernard leading home Brabham's Simtek. Zanardi's delayed Lotus was classified 15th despite an engine failure on lap 63.

Basking in the afterglow of his victory, Michael Schumacher confidently predicted that the intensity of F1 competition would hot up during the second part of the season. He also enthusiastically looked forward to the much-touted return of Nigel Mansell.

'He might be trouble, but that's what we're here for!' he said confidently. On the strength of what we saw in Montreal, however, it looked as though it might take more than Mansell to stem Benetton's apparently relentless advance towards the title crown.

155

FIA FORMULA ONE WORLD CHAMPIONSHIP ROUND 6

GRAND PRIX DU CANADA
MONTREAL 10-12 JUNE 1994

MONTREAL – GILLES VILLENEUVE CIRCUIT
CIRCUIT LENGTH: 2.752 MILES/4.430 KM

Race weather: Overcast, brief shower mid-race

Place	Driver	Nat.	No.	Entrant	Car/Engine	Laps	Time/Retirement	Speed (mph/km/h)
1	Michael Schumacher	D	5	Mild Seven Benetton Ford	Benetton B194-Ford Zetec-R V8	69	1h 44m 31.887s	109.512/176.243
2	Damon Hill	GB	0	Rothmans Williams Renault	Williams FW16-Renault RS6 V10	69	1h 45m 11.547s	108.824/175.136
3	Jean Alesi	F	27	Scuderia Ferrari	Ferrari 412T1 041 V12	69	1h 45m 45.275s	108.245/174.205
4	Gerhard Berger	A	28	Scuderia Ferrari	Ferrari 412T1 041 V12	69	1h 45m 47.496s	108.207/174.144
5	David Coulthard	GB	2	Rothmans Williams Renault	Williams FW16-Renault RS6 V10	68		
6	J.J. Lehto	SF	6	Mild Seven Benetton Ford	Benetton B194-Ford Zetec-R V8	68		
7	Rubens Barrichello	BR	14	Sasol Jordan	Jordan 194-Hart 1035 V10	68		
8	Johnny Herbert	GB	12	Team Lotus	Lotus 109-Mugen Honda ZA5C V10	68		
9	Pierluigi Martini	I	23	Minardi Scuderia Italia	Minardi M194-Ford HB V8	68		
10	Mark Blundell	GB	4	Tyrrell	Tyrrell 022-Yamaha 0X10A V10	67	Spun off	
11	Michele Alboreto	I	24	Minardi Scuderia Italia	Minardi M194-Ford HB V8	67		
12	Olivier Panis	F	26	Ligier Gitanes Blondes	Ligier JS39B-Renault RS6 V10	67		
13	Eric Bernard	F	25	Ligier Gitanes Blondes	Ligier JS39B-Renault RS6 V10	66		
14	David Brabham	AUS	31	MTV Simtek Ford	Simtek S941-Ford HB V8	65		
15	Alessandro Zanardi	I	11	Team Lotus	Lotus 107C-Mugen Honda ZA5C V10	62	Engine	
	Mika Häkkinen	SF	7	Marlboro McLaren Peugeot	McLaren MP4/9-Peugeot A6 V10	61	Engine	
	Olivier Beretta	F	19	Tourtel Larrousse F1	Larrousse LH94-Ford HB V8	57	Engine	
	Gianni Morbidelli	I	10	Footwork Ford	Footwork FA15-Ford HB V8	50	Gearbox	
	Bertrand Gachot	F	34	Pacific Grand Prix Ltd	Pacific PR01-Ilmor 2175A V10	47	Engine	
	Erik Comas	F	20	Tourtel Larrousse F1	Larrousse LH94-Ford HB V8	45	Clutch	
	Ukyo Katayama	J	3	Tyrrell	Tyrrell 022-Yamaha 0X10A V10	44	Spun off	
	Eddie Irvine	GB	15	Sasol Jordan	Jordan 194-Hart 1035 V10	40	Spun off	
	Andrea de Cesaris	I	29	Broker Sauber Mercedes	Sauber C13-Mercedes-Benz V10	24	Engine	
	Heinz-Harald Frentzen	D	30	Broker Sauber Mercedes	Sauber C13-Mercedes-Benz V10	5	Spun off	
	Martin Brundle	GB	8	Marlboro McLaren Peugeot	McLaren MP4/9-Peugeot A6 V10	3	Engine	
DQ	Christian Fittipaldi	BR	9	Footwork Ford	Footwork FA15-Ford HB V8	68	Underweight	
DNQ	Paul Belmondo	F	33	Pacific Grand Prix Ltd	Pacific PR01-Ilmor 2175A V10			

Fastest lap: Schumacher, on lap 31, 1m 28.927s, 111.937 mph, 180.147 km/h.
Lap record: Michael Schumacher (F1 Benetton B193B-Ford V8), 1m 21.500s, 121.591 mph, 195.681 km/h (1993).
All cars used Goodyear tyres

QUALIFYING 1

Jean Alesi	**1m 26.277s**
Michael Schumacher	1m 26.820s
Mika Häkkinen	**1m 27.616s**
Gerhard Berger	1m 27.625s
Ukyo Katayama	**1m 27.827s**
Damon Hill	1m 28.011s
Heinz-Harald Frentzen	1m 28.048s
Martin Brundle	1m 28.451s
Rubens Barrichello	1m 28.612s
David Coulthard	1m 28.636s
Gianni Morbidelli	1m 28.730s
Eddie Irvine	1m 28.843s
Mark Blundell	1m 29.108s
Christian Fittipaldi	1m 29.493s
Olivier Panis	1m 29.530s
J.J. Lehto	1m 29.581s
Michele Alboreto	1m 29.597s
Erik Comas	1m 29.653s
Pierluigi Martini	1m 29.691s
Andrea de Cesaris	1m 29.793s
Johnny Herbert	1m 30.063s
Eric Bernard	1m 30.806s
Olivier Beretta	1m 31.167s
Alessandro Zanardi	1m 31.698s
David Brabham	1m 32.376s
Bertrand Gachot	**1m 32.838s**
Paul Belmondo	1m 33.291s

Friday afternoon
Dry, hot, sunny

QUALIFYING 2

Michael Schumacher	**1m 26.178s**
Jean Alesi	1m 26.319s
Gerhard Berger	**1m 27.059s**
Damon Hill	1m 27.094s
David Coulthard	1m 27.211s
Rubens Barrichello	1m 27.554s
Eddie Irvine	1m 27.780s
Mika Häkkinen	1m 27.851s
Ukyo Katayama	1m 27.953s
Heinz-Harald Frentzen	**1m 27.977s**
Gianni Morbidelli	1m 27.989s
Martin Brundle	**1m 28.197s**
Mark Blundell	1m 28.579s
Andrea de Cesaris	1m 28.694s
Pierluigi Martini	1m 28.847s
Christian Fittipaldi	1m 28.882s
Johnny Herbert	1m 28.889s
Michele Alboreto	1m 28.903s
Olivier Panis	1m 28.950s
J.J. Lehto	1m 28.993s
Erik Comas	**1m 29.039s**
Olivier Beretta	1m 29.403s
Alessandro Zanardi	1m 30.160s
Eric Bernard	1m 30.493s
David Brabham	1m 31.632s
Bertrand Gachot	1m 32.877s
Paul Belmondo	1m 33.006s

Saturday afternoon
Dry, hot, sunny

WARM-UP

Martin Brundle	1m 27.664s
Gerhard Berger	1m 28.401s
Jean Alesi	1m 28.491s
Rubens Barrichello	1m 28.588s
Damon Hill	1m 28.669s
David Coulthard	1m 28.735s
Andrea de Cesaris	1m 28.819s
Mark Blundell	1m 28.857s
Ukyo Katayama	1m 28.931s
Michael Schumacher	1m 29.079s
Gianni Morbidelli	1m 29.319s
Christian Fittipaldi	1m 29.348s
Mika Häkkinen	1m 29.421s
Johnny Herbert	1m 29.539s
Pierluigi Martini	1m 29.961s
Heinz-Harald Frentzen	1m 30.013s
Michele Alboreto	1m 30.126s
Olivier Beretta	1m 30.245s
Olivier Panis	1m 30.521s
Eddie Irvine	1m 30.957s
J.J. Lehto	1m 31.569s
Bertrand Gachot	1m 31.585s
Alessandro Zanardi	1m 31.824s
Erik Comas	1m 31.874s
Eric Bernard	1m 32.088s
David Brabham	1m 36.207s

Sunday morning
Dry, hot, cloudy

FASTEST LAPS

Driver	Time	Lap
Michael Schumacher	1m 28.927s	31
Damon Hill	1m 28.962s	56
Gerhard Berger	1m 29.142s	58
Jean Alesi	1m 29.260s	58
Mark Blundell	1m 29.369s	54
Mika Häkkinen	1m 29.512s	34
Gianni Morbidelli	1m 29.698s	39
Rubens Barrichello	1m 29.757s	65
David Coulthard	1m 29.966s	55
Ukyo Katayama	1m 30.079s	31
Erik Comas	1m 30.194s	11
J.J. Lehto	1m 30.374s	33
Eddie Irvine	1m 30.626s	21
Christian Fittipaldi	1m 30.700s	58
Heinz-Harald Frentzen	1m 30.796s	4
Johnny Herbert	1m 30.865s	14
Olivier Panis	1m 31.109s	65
Andrea de Cesaris	1m 31.187s	19
Michele Alboreto	1m 31.221s	66
Olivier Beretta	1m 31.451s	21
Pierluigi Martini	1m 31.587s	66
Alessandro Zanardi	1m 31.588s	6
Eric Bernard	1m 31.703s	6
Martin Brundle	1m 31.759s	3
David Brabham	1m 31.804s	6
Bertrand Gachot	1m 32.041s	6

All results and data © FIA 1994

STARTING GRID

No.	Driver	Team	Time
5	SCHUMACHER	Benetton	1m 26.178s
27	ALESI	Ferrari	1m 26.277s
28	BERGER	Ferrari	1m 27.059s
0	HILL	Williams	1m 27.094s
2	COULTHARD	Williams	1m 27.211s
14	BARRICHELLO	Jordan	1m 27.554s
7	HÄKKINEN	McLaren	1m 27.616s
15	IRVINE	Jordan	1m 27.780s
3	KATAYAMA	Tyrrell	1m 27.827s
30	FRENTZEN	Sauber	1m 27.977s
10	MORBIDELLI	Footwork	1m 27.989s
8	BRUNDLE	McLaren	1m 28.197s
4	BLUNDELL	Tyrrell	1m 28.579s
29	DE CESARIS	Sauber	1m 28.694s
23	MARTINI	Minardi	1m 28.847s
9	FITTIPALDI	Footwork	1m 28.882s
12	HERBERT	Lotus	1m 28.889s
24	ALBORETO	Minardi	1m 28.903s
26	PANIS	Ligier	1m 28.950s
6	LEHTO	Benetton	1m 28.993s
20	COMAS	Larrousse	1m 29.039s
19	BERETTA	Larrousse	1m 29.403s
11	ZANARDI	Lotus	1m 30.160s
25	BERNARD	Ligier	1m 30.493s
31	BRABHAM	Simtek	1m 31.632s
34	GACHOT	Pacific	1m 32.838s

NON-STARTERS

DNQ	33 BELMONDO	Pacific	1m 33.006s

LAP CHART

1st LAP ORDER	5 SCHUMACHER	27 ALESI	28 BERGER	2 COULTHARD	0 HILL	14 BARRICHELLO	7 HÄKKINEN	15 IRVINE	10 MORBIDELLI	3 KATAYAMA	30 FRENTZEN	4 BLUNDELL	8 BRUNDLE	9 FITTIPALDI	12 HERBERT	29 DE CESARIS	19 BERETTA	23 MARTINI	24 ALBORETO	11 ZANARDI	6 LEHTO	20 COMAS	26 PANIS	31 BRABHAM	25 BERNARD	34 GACHOT
1	5	27	28	2	0	14	7	15	10	3	30	4	8	9	12	29	19	23	24	11	6	20	26	31	25	34
2	5	27	28	2	0	14	7	15	10	3	30	4	8	9	12	29	19	23	24	11	6	20	26	31	25	34
3	5	27	28	2	0	14	7	15	10	3	30	4	8	9	12	29	19	23	24	11	6	20	26	31	25	34
4	5	27	28	2	0	14	7	15	10	3	30	4	9	12	29	19	23	24	11	6	20	26	31	25	34	
5	5	27	28	2	0	14	7	15	10	3	30	4	9	12	29	19	23	24	11	6	20	26	31	25	34	
6	5	27	28	2	0	14	7	15	10	3	4	9	12	29	19	23	24	11	20	6	26	31	25	34		
7	5	27	28	2	0	14	7	15	10	3	4	9	12	29	19	23	24	20	6	11	26	31	25	34		
8	5	27	28	2	0	14	7	15	10	3	4	9	12	29	19	23	24	20	6	11	26	31	25	34		
9	5	27	28	0	2	14	7	15	10	3	4	9	12	29	19	23	24	20	6	11	26	31	25	34		
10	5	27	28	0	2	14	7	15	10	3	4	9	12	29	19	23	20	24	6	11	26	25	34	31		
11	5	27	28	0	2	14	7	15	10	3	4	9	12	29	19	23	20	24	6	11	26	25	34	31		
12	5	27	28	0	2	14	7	15	10	3	4	9	12	29	19	20	23	6	24	11	26	25	34	31		
13	5	27	28	0	2	14	7	15	10	3	4	9	12	29	19	20	23	6	24	11	26	25	34	31		
14	5	27	28	0	2	14	7	15	10	3	4	9	12	29	19	20	23	6	24	26	11	25	34	31		
15	5	27	0	28	2	14	7	15	10	3	9	12	29	19	20	4	23	6	24	26	25	34	31	11		
16	5	27	0	28	2	14	7	15	10	3	9	12	29	19	20	23	4	6	24	26	25	34	31	11		
17	5	27	0	28	14	2	7	15	10	3	9	29	19	20	23	4	12	6	24	26	25	34	31	11		
18	5	27	0	28	14	2	10	15	9	29	19	7	23	4	6	12	24	26	20	25	3	34	31	11		
19	5	27	0	28	14	2	10	15	9	29	19	7	4	23	6	12	24	26	20	25	3	34	31	11		
20	5	27	0	28	14	2	10	15	9	19	7	4	23	6	12	24	29	26	20	25	3	31	11	34		
21	5	27	0	28	2	10	15	9	14	19	7	4	23	6	12	24	29	26	20	3	25	11	31	34		
22	5	27	0	2	10	15	9	28	14	7	4	19	23	6	12	24	29	26	20	3	11	31	25	34		
23	5	27	0	10	2	9	28	14	7	4	15	19	23	6	12	24	29	20	26	3	11	31	25	34		
24	5	27	0	2	9	28	14	7	4	10	19	6	23	15	12	24	29	20	26	3	11	31	25	34		
25	5	27	0	2	9	28	14	7	4	10	19	6	23	15	12	24	20	3	26	11	31	25	34			
26	5	27	0	2	9	28	14	7	4	10	6	19	23	15	12	24	20	3	26	11	31	25	34			
27	5	27	0	2	9	28	14	7	4	10	6	19	23	15	12	24	3	20	26	11	31	25	34			
28	5	27	0	2	9	28	14	7	4	10	6	19	23	15	12	24	3	26	20	11	31	25	34			
29	5	27	0	2	9	28	14	7	4	10	6	19	23	15	12	24	3	26	20	11	31	25	34			
30	5	27	0	2	9	28	14	7	4	10	6	23	15	12	24	3	19	26	20	11	31	25	34			
31	5	0	27	2	9	28	7	14	4	10	6	23	15	12	24	3	19	26	20	11	31	25	34			
32	5	0	27	2	9	28	7	14	10	6	23	15	12	4	24	3	19	26	20	11	31	25	34			
33	5	0	27	2	9	28	7	14	10	6	15	12	4	3	24	23	19	26	20	11	25	31	34			
34	5	0	27	9	28	7	14	10	6	2	15	12	4	3	24	23	19	26	20	11	25	31	34			
35	5	0	27	9	28	7	14	10	2	15	12	4	6	3	24	23	19	26	20	11	25	31	34			
36	5	0	27	28	7	14	10	9	2	15	12	4	3	6	24	23	19	26	20	11	25	31	34			
37	5	0	27	28	7	14	10	2	9	15	12	4	3	6	24	23	19	26	20	11	25	31	34			
38	5	0	27	28	7	14	10	2	9	15	12	4	3	6	24	23	19	26	20	11	25	31	34			
39	5	0	27	28	7	14	10	2	9	15	12	4	6	3	23	19	26	24	20	11	25	31	34			
40	5	0	27	28	7	14	10	2	9	15	4	12	6	23	3	19	24	26	20	11	25	31	34			
41	5	0	27	28	7	14	10	2	9	4	12	6	23	19	3	24	26	20	11	25	31	34				
42	5	0	27	28	7	14	10	2	9	4	12	6	23	19	3	24	26	20	11	25	31	34				
43	5	0	27	28	14	10	7	2	9	4	6	12	23	19	3	24	26	20	11	25	31	34				
44	5	0	27	14	10	28	7	2	4	9	6	12	23	3	19	24	26	20	11	25	31	34				
45	5	0	27	10	28	7	14	2	4	9	6	12	23	19	24	26	20	11	25	31	34					
46	5	0	27	10	28	7	14	2	4	9	6	12	23	19	24	26	11	25	31	34						
47	5	0	27	10	28	7	14	2	4	9	6	12	23	19	24	26	11	25	31	34						
48	5	0	27	10	28	7	14	2	4	9	6	12	23	19	24	26	11	25	31							
49	5	0	27	10	28	7	14	2	4	9	6	12	23	19	24	26	11	25	31							
50	5	0	27	28	7	14	2	4	9	6	10	12	23	19	24	26	11	25	31							
51	5	0	27	28	7	14	2	9	6	4	12	23	19	24	26	11	25	31								
52	5	0	27	28	7	2	14	9	6	4	12	23	19	24	26	11	25	31								
53	5	0	27	28	7	2	9	14	6	4	12	23	19	24	26	11	25	31								
54	5	0	27	28	7	2	9	14	6	4	12	23	19	24	26	11	25	31								
55	5	0	27	28	7	2	9	6	14	4	12	23	19	24	26	11	25	31								
56	5	0	27	28	7	2	9	6	14	4	12	23	19	24	26	11	25	31								
57	5	0	27	28	7	2	9	6	14	4	12	23	19	24	26	11	25	31								
58	5	0	27	28	7	2	9	6	14	4	12	23	24	26	11	25	31									
59	5	0	27	28	7	2	9	6	14	4	12	23	24	26	11	25	31									
60	5	0	27	28	7	2	9	6	14	4	12	23	24	26	11	25	31									
61	5	0	27	28	7	2	9	6	14	4	12	23	24	26	11	25	31									
62	5	0	27	28	2	9	6	14	4	12	23	24	26	11	25	31										
63	5	0	27	28	2	9	6	14	4	12	23	24	26	25	31											
64	5	0	27	28	2	9	6	14	4	12	23	24	26	25	31											
65	5	0	27	28	2	9	6	14	4	12	23	24	26	25	31											
66	5	0	27	28	2	9	14	6	4	12	23	24	26	25												
67	5	0	27	28	2	9	14	6	4	12	23	24	26													
68	5	0	27	28	2	9	6	14	12	23																
69	5	0	27	28																						

One lap behind leader

RACE DISTANCE: 69 LAPS, 189.934 MILES/305.670 KM

CHASSIS LOG BOOK

0	Hill	Williams FW16/3
2	Coulthard	Williams FW16/4
	spare	Williams FW16/5
3	Katayama	Tyrrell 022/2
4	Blundell	Tyrrell 022/1
	spare	Tyrrell 022/3
5	Schumacher	Benetton B194/5
6	Lehto	Benetton B194/4
	spare	Benetton B194/3
7	Häkkinen	McLaren MP4/9/6
8	Brundle	McLaren MP4/9/4
	spare	McLaren MP4/9/5
9	Fittipaldi	Footwork FA15/4
10	Morbidelli	Footwork FA15/5
	spare	Footwork FA15/1
11	Zanardi	Lotus 107C/3
12	Herbert	Lotus 109/1
14	Barrichello	Jordan 194/2
15	Irvine	Jordan 194/5
	spare	Jordan 194/3
19	Beretta	Larrousse LH94/2
20	Comas	Larrousse LH94/1
	spare	Larrousse LH94/3
23	Martini	Minardi M194/5
24	Alboreto	Minardi M194/1
	spare	Minardi M193B/3
25	Bernard	Ligier JS39B/6
26	Panis	Ligier JS39B/4
	spare	Ligier JS39B/2
27	Alesi	Ferrari 412T1/154
28	Berger	Ferrari 412T1/153
	spare	Ferrari 412T1/149
29	de Cesaris	Sauber C13/4
30	Frentzen	Sauber C13/3
	spare	Sauber C13/1
31	Brabham	Simtek S941/2
33	Belmondo	Pacific PR01/1
34	Gachot	Pacific PR01/2

CONSTRUCTORS' CUP

1	BENETTON-FORD	57
2	FERRARI	32
3	WILLIAMS-RENAULT	25
4	JORDAN-HART	11
5	McLAREN-PEUGEOT	10
6	TYRRELL-YAMAHA	8
7	SAUBER-MERCEDES	6
8 =	FOOTWORK-FORD	3
8 =	MINARDI-FORD	3
9	LARROUSSE-FORD	1

FOR THE RECORD

First Grand Prix points
David Coulthard

200th Grand Prix start
Andrea de Cesaris

100th Grand Prix start
Pierluigi Martini

50th Grand Prix start
Erik Comas

DRIVERS' POINTS

1	SCHUMACHER	56
2	HILL	23
3=	BERGER	13
3=	ALESI	13
5	BARRICHELLO	7
6=	LARINI	6
6=	BRUNDLE	6
8=	BLUNDELL	4
8=	HÄKKINEN	4
8=	KATAYAMA	4
8=	WENDLINGER	4
12=	DE CESARIS	3
12=	FITTIPALDI	3
14=	MARTINI	2
14=	FRENTZEN	2
14=	COULTHARD	2
17=	ALBORETO	1
17=	IRVINE	1
17=	COMAS	1
17=	LEHTO	1

WORLD CHAMPIONSHIP • ROUND 7

FRENCH GRAND PRIX

SCHUMACHER
HILL
BERGER
FRENTZEN
MARTINI
DE CESARIS

Nigel Mansell returned to the Formula 1 stage in France, making a 'guest appearance' at the wheel of a Rothmans Williams FW16. He had been offered the drive in what was widely regarded as an effort to restore some of the star quality which many people – apparently including Renault, who had bankrolled the exercise at a reputed cost of £1 million – felt had been sorely missing from Grand Prix racing ever since Ayrton Senna's tragic death at Imola. In terms of media attention, it was a rip-roaring success, but it didn't prevent Michael Schumacher from running away with the seventh round of the World Championship in his Benetton B194-Ford, although Damon Hill gave him a good run for his money in the early stages, the Englishman having beaten Mansell to pole position in a sensational head-to-head confrontation between the two Williams drivers in second qualifying. Gerhard Berger's Ferrari 412T1B took third place after Mansell retired with transmission problems on lap 46, leaving the Saubers of Heinz-Harald Frentzen and Andrea de Cesaris to finish fourth and sixth, sandwiching Pierluigi Martini's Minardi.

Nigel Mansell was inevitably the centre of attention for journalists and photographers alike. The expensively hired Indy Car star's much-heralded return to the Grand Prix arena was to end disappointingly when he was forced to abandon his Williams-Renault with engine problems halfway through the race.

FRENCH GRAND PRIX

> **Diary**
>
> *Former Ferrari manager Cesare Fiorio is appointed Sporting Director of the Benetton-owned Ligier team.*
>
> *Plans to revive the Austrian Grand Prix at a totally rebuilt Österreichring for 1995 receive the endorsement of Styrian politician Gerhard Hirschmann, the man bidding to bring the Winter Olympics to Graz in 2002.*
>
> *Sam Hanks, winner of the 1957 Indy 500, dies at the age of 79.*
>
> *Riccardo Patrese tests AMG Mercedes C-class racer on the short circuit at Hockenheim in anticipation of a possible future DTM programme.*

ENTRY AND PRACTICE

The feverish excitement swirling round Nigel Mansell's return to the F1 scene engendered a mood of expectancy which, with a peculiar irony, could almost have been calculated to result in disappointment. On the face of it, nothing but a glorious return to pole position after an 18-month absence from the F1 fold could do justice to the hype which preceded Mansell's arrival in the paddock at Magny-Cours. With this in mind, it was perhaps inevitable that there should be a sense of anti-climax when the former World Champion only managed seventh-fastest time in Friday's first qualifying session.

On the face of it, the return of the 1992 title holder – four times a winner of the French GP – seemed in no way to have altered the existing F1 status quo. Michael Schumacher's Benetton B194 set fastest time in that first session ahead of Gerhard Berger's revised Ferrari 412T1B and the Williams FW16 of Mansell's running mate Damon Hill. Nothing new there.

In fact, many people were quick to take his Friday performance as proof that Mansell's one-race deal would not provide the instant fix necessary to boost the Williams team's performance to the point where they could get on terms with Schumacher and Benetton. More tellingly, it served as a reminder that a guest appearance in such an intensely competitive environment requires more preparation than the 60-lap stint on the Brands Hatch Indy circuit which Mansell had undertaken – in front of several thousand adoring fans – the previous Tuesday.

As things turned out, however, first impressions were to prove slightly misleading. Those who believed that Mansell would be content to return to F1 in the role of an also-ran were to be proved dramatically incorrect in their assessment of the situation.

'I had a trouble-free practice and, for the first day, I am very pleased,' said Mansell, putting an upbeat gloss on a performance which saw him record a quickest lap 0.8s slower than Hill's sister car.

'There's a lot left in me and the car. I don't think we can win here as the combination of Schumacher and the Benetton looks unbeatable. But Damon is doing a fantastic job, getting the best from a car which does do some strange things which I'm not used to!

'I feel I have just got to settle in and see what I can do tomorrow, because I feel optimistic that I can go a lot better. A Grand Prix car is certainly more nervous than an Indy car and, with the tyres only giving maximum grip for a single lap in qualifying, I have to become used to that again.'

Mansell also stressed that his commitment was, for the moment, purely a one-off arrangement. 'I have come into the team to give some fresh input which might help improve the car,' he added. 'I hope Damon can challenge for the lead, but I would have no problem at all in waving him past if I found myself in that lovely situation.'

On Friday Jean Alesi's Ferrari set fourth-fastest time ahead of Martin Brundle's McLaren MP4/9, which benefited from the revised-specification 'Evolution 2' Peugeot V10 engine. By contrast, Brundle's team-mate Mika Häkkinen had a disappointing day, losing valuable time while an oil leak was staunched, but was optimistic that he would join the tightly packed bunch jostling for position behind Schumacher the following day.

As the Williams team's regular driver, holding second place in the drivers' championship table, Damon Hill's attention was firmly focused on the yawning 33-point deficit separating him from Schumacher. 'I feel strongly that my championship hopes should be given serious priority,' he said firmly, referring to Mansell's appearance on the scene. 'I have tried to keep everything in perspective and I think Nigel is going to have a lot to think about tonight in preparation for tomorrow. He's been a witness to the true situation, namely that the car is a bit difficult.'

Apart from Schumacher's domination on the first day, and the media attention surrounding the Williams team's efforts, Ferrari looked set to play a central role at Magny-Cours with the heavily revised 'B' version of its 412T1.

Engineer Gustav Brunner had overseen significant alterations to the original John Barnard design, including revised front wings, much shorter side pods and two-piece aerodynamic deflectors positioned behind the front wheels. One of the principal improvements yielded by these changes was a welcome significant reduction in oil and water temperatures. Further development, including the new 75-degree V12 engine and a weight-saving titanium-cased gearbox, were not far behind in the development pipeline.

The revised car had first been tried by Jean Alesi at Fiorano at the end of the previous week, followed by a more extensive test at Paul Ricard on the Tuesday prior to the French race. On this occasion Alesi was joined by Berger and comparative tests with the standard car revealed the new version to offer considerably enhanced development potential.

In first qualifying, both Ferraris looked strong. Twenty minutes into the session, Alesi popped up in second place on the timing screens, a mere 0.7s slower than Schumacher, only to straight-line one of the gravel traps. That excursion not only ripped off the right-hand aerodynamic deflectors, but also damaged the undertray, resulting in a prolonged pit stop for repairs. Later in the session Berger, who had looked tidier than his team-mate at the same point on the circuit, duplicated the manoeuvre – but not before he had pushed ahead of Hill and Alesi to post second-fastest time overnight.

On Friday night, the Williams mechanics made significant changes to the FW16 chassis set-up. They also installed the higher-revving, latest-spec Renault RS6B V10s into both cars and, from the start of the Saturday morning free practice session, both Hill and Mansell were suddenly trading fastest times at the head of the field.

In the afternoon the weather remained relatively cool and overcast for second qualifying, promising significantly quicker times than had been achieved in the sweltering conditions which had prevailed the previous day. Moreover, there were two other key factors to consider as the final grid order unfolded.

Firstly, Schumacher had damaged the underside of his Benetton and lost 45 minutes of crucial setting-up time during the morning after locking rear brakes had pitched him off the track. The German also had a subsequent spin, which he admitted was his own fault.

Secondly, Mansell had effectively lost one of his weekend's allocation of seven sets of tyres when one of the Goodyears he'd used on Friday picked up a deep cut on its tread. That meant he was one tyre short of three fresh sets for the balance of the weekend, whereas Hill had his three unused sets intact.

Schumacher's Friday best of 1m 17.085s was soon under assault. Alesi got close on 1m 17.205s, but then Michael went on the offensive, improving to 1m 17.063s. Eleven minutes into the session Mansell was the first to break the 1m 17s barrier with a 1m 16.987s.

At 13.25 came potentially the most serious incident of the weekend. Jos Verstappen, replacing J.J. Lehto, who was being 'rested' from the Benetton squad, lost control of his B194 coming through the final right-hander, slamming smartly into the pit wall with an impact that ripped off both the car's left-hand wheels, one wayward rim demolishing the McLaren team's timing monitors. The tattered wreckage slithered to a halt virtually at the feet of a rather taken-aback Damon Hill!

Out came the red flag to halt the session while the debris was cleared up and the damaged Benetton removed. After a ten-minute delay, Hill went out in an effort to topple Mansell from pole. It was gripping stuff!

At the first timing split, Damon was 0.017s quicker, then 0.043s quicker at the second split, stopping the clocks at 1m 16.609s. Fastest! Then Berger moved up to second with a 1m 16.959s in the Ferrari, only to be immediately displaced by Schumacher, who posted a 1m 16.912s.

With just over 20 minutes left, Mansell pulled a 1m 16.359s out of the bag. It looked like the last word: pole position on his return to F1 after more than a year away. Then, with 15 minutes to go, Damon – who had been frustrated to find his Williams fitted with two fifth gears early in the session – went out on his second run. But it looked as though his efforts might be in vain. At his first try, he clipped the inside kerb at the first right-hander after the pits, throwing the Williams off-line and effectively ruining the lap.

'I'd got a bit fired up because of that gearbox problem early in the session,' he admitted. 'The boys were working away to correct it and the pressure was building up. The first run put me on provisional pole, then Nigel went and beat it by three-tenths. I was starting to get a bit anxious by then, particularly as my second run didn't work very well.'

Correctly judging that the track conditions might be a little quicker right at the end of the session, Damon then came in and waited until making his final bid with five minutes left. 'The last run was beautiful, a bit desperate at times, but exciting. The track remained fairly constant, but perhaps it was a bit difficult at the end,' he admitted in tones which reflected his unbridled relief.

This final flourish – which included

159

With the outcome of the races all too often being settled during the pit stops and not out on the track, the TV cameras were obliged to make the most of every incident. There was no shortage of drama in France, including Zanardi's spectacular retirement in the Lotus *(above)* and Jean Alesi's equally lurid indiscretion. After spinning his Ferrari, the Frenchman rejoined the circuit, only to eliminate himself and the Jordan of an innocent Rubens Barrichello in a moment's carelessness *(bottom right)*.

In a bid to curb speeds, holes had been cut in the cars' airboxes to prevent them fulfilling their intended purpose of forcing air into the engines under pressure – as on the Williams *(below)*. They were still effective as billboards, though.

Pierluigi Martini *(bottom)* picked up more useful points for Minardi with fifth place.

FRENCH GRAND PRIX

riding the kerb precariously out of the final corner – left Hill celebrating the third pole position of his career with a 1m 16.282s. Mansell was second, with Schumacher off the front row for the first time so far this season, Benetton's boy blaming his loss of time in the morning for his failure to make sufficient progress just when he needed it most.

Clearly, Mansell was pretty satisfied with his first F1 qualifying sessions since the 1992 Australian GP, even though the expression on his face immediately after Hill posted his pole-winner suggested that he would really have liked to have done even better.

Both Ferrari drivers had improved on their Friday times to clinch fourth and fifth places in the final order, Alesi easing ahead of his team-mate, who was disappointed that the set-up change he made immediately prior to the final run failed to yield the performance boost he was looking for.

Eddie Irvine and Rubens Barrichello proved well matched with their Jordans, lining up in sixth and seventh places ahead of the luckless Verstappen. Irvine had a brand-new chassis at his disposal while Rubens tried a revised front wing first assessed at the Silverstone test. Ninth was Häkkinen, disappointed that he hadn't managed to squeeze more from the promising Evolution 2 Peugeot engine in his McLaren.

'We didn't have a perfect balance,' said Mika, who had lost time on Saturday morning with gearchange and throttle problems. 'But I am optimstic things will be better tomorrow.' Martin Brundle was even more disappointed with his eventual 12th place, separated from his team-mate by the Saubers of Heinz-Harald Frentzen and Andrea de Cesaris. 'In the end, I just couldn't get the car to work on this circuit,' he shrugged.

Olivier Panis did a good job in the Ligier JS39B to qualify 13th ahead of Ukyo Katayama, the Japanese driver once again displaying capable form in the Tyrrell-Yamaha. Ukyo believed that he could have been quicker had he not made a mistake on his first run, caught the red flag on his second, been balked by Morbidelli's Footwork on his third and then encountered more traffic on his fourth.

Even so, he was satisfied to be ahead of Mark Blundell, the Englishman unhappy with the handling of his 022 as he battled to an eventual 17th place behind Eric Bernard's Ligier and Pierluigi Martini's Minardi.

Further back, there were no significant surprises, although neither Christian Fittipaldi nor Gianni Morbidelli seemed able to make much sense of their Footworks' handling and were much further down than one would have expected. Christian, a lowly 18th, suffered a broken driveshaft on Friday morning and was frustrated by an overall shortage of grip, while Morbidelli was a rather bemused 22nd, reporting that his FA15 felt easy to drive yet just wasn't returning the times.

There was a glimmer of hope from Lotus once more, Johnny Herbert's 109 lining up in 19th place ahead of Erik Comas and Michele Alboreto. Herbert had been 12th fastest in the Friday morning session, but a change of dampers made the front end much too sensitive for his liking. Alessandro Zanardi was four places further back, having been plagued by excessive oversteer in the second Lotus 109 to be finished, while David Brabham's Simtek was 24th, the Australian briefly experimenting with a new semi-automatic gearbox which was eventually shelved due to hydraulic problems.

Olivier Beretta's Larrousse shared the final row of the grid with Simtek's new recruit, Jean-Marc Gounon, with the Pacific-Ilmors of Bertrand Gachot and Paul Belmondo both failing to make the cut. Bertrand was troubled by handling instability, possibly attributable to a lack of chassis stiffness, while his team-mate suffered an engine failure on both days.

RACE

In the race morning warm-up Schumacher was fractionally quicker than Alesi, Mansell, Verstappen and Hill, but the World Championship leader was not happy with the balance of his Benetton B194. By contrast, Alesi was extremely optimistic, but Mansell had reservations about the handling of his Williams and made some set-up changes before the race. It was to prove an unfortunate experiment, as things transpired.

Just before the start Mansell's car was diagnosed as suffering from a slight leak from the oil catch tank – which looked more serious than it was – and Hill was jokingly warned by Patrick Head not to worry if he saw a smoke haze from the back of his team-mate's car. Damon, needless to say, had absolutely no intention of seeing the back of his team-mate's car . . .

With the billiard-smooth track

161

surface at the Circuit de Nevers definitely enhancing the Williams's performance, allied to the fact that Schumacher was back on the second row, a closer than usual contest was confidently anticipated. Unfortunately, Michael buried those hopes in the first few seconds after the starting lights blinked to green.

'I made the second-best start I have made all year,' said Hill. 'I was pleased with it, but Michael just beat me to the first corner – he was going past me at one hell of a rate!' The Benetton shot through the gap between the Williams duo to consolidate a 0.9s advantage over Damon's Williams by the end of the opening lap.

Schumacher's nifty getaway served to strengthen paddock gossip that, well, perhaps there was something a little too perfect about the Benetton B194's starts. An illegal traction control system, said some, but Schumacher himself firmly scotched such ungenerous speculation once the race was over.

'I caught exactly the right moment to go as the red disappeared,' he explained. 'I saw Damon bog down a little, but my start was perfect. We've done a lot of development work on a new clutch.'

Such candour about matters technical was not altogether appreciated by the team's Technical Director Ross Brawn. 'We modify it ourselves to give ideal conditions for the start and it has a progressive feel,' he added by way of elaboration. 'We've had them all season.'

Mansell ran third from lap one, harried by Alesi, with Berger fifth ahead of Irvine, Frentzen, Häkkinen, Barrichello and Brundle. Second time round Schumacher's advantage had expanded to 1.2 seconds, stretching to 1.5s at the end of lap three. But then Hill steadied the gap and began to fight back, chipping away at the Benetton's advantage, reducing it first to 1.3 seconds, then 1.2s again. Thereafter Schumacher's lead never grew to more than 1.1s through to the end of lap 21 when they, along with Gerhard Berger's now third-placed Ferrari, made their first routine refuelling stops together.

Mansell had his hands full fending off Alesi from the word go. Within a few laps he found that those chassis set-up changes he'd made after the warm-up left him battling excessive oversteer. He made an early refuelling stop on lap 18 when he also took the chance to fit differently pressured tyres and remove the tail flaps from the nose wings in an attempt to improve things. He resumed in sixth place, only to be beset with acute understeer, and was back in for freshly pressured tyres – without bothering to refuel – at the end of lap 29. This went some way towards reducing the understeer, but did not eliminate it totally.

Meanwhile, Alesi, who had momentarily moved into third place when Mansell made his first stop, came into the pits on lap 19 for a quick 8.0-second refuelling stop which dropped him to fifth. Thus, by lap 22, the order was Schumacher, now 3.5 seconds ahead of Hill and pulling away, Barrichello, Alesi, Mansell and Berger.

This was the point at which Benetton beat Williams on strategy. In opting for three refuelling stops, Schumacher was able to enjoy a decisive performance advantage during

FRENCH GRAND PRIX

Although the Williams-Renaults filled the front row of the grid, Michael Schumacher *(left)* reasserted his authority in the race, scoring his sixth win in seven starts, though Damon Hill ran the Benetton-Ford much closer at Magny-Cours than he had elsewhere.

Ecclestone plays key role in Mansell return

FIA Vice-President and F1 Constructors' Association President Bernie Ecclestone played a leading role in negotiating with Carl Haas for the necessary contractual release which enabled Nigel Mansell to guest for the Williams team at Magny-Cours.

'It is incredible to have the opportunity as a guest driver for just this one race,' acknowledged Mansell at the pole winner's press conference. 'I want to thank the Newman-Haas and Williams teams, and also Formula 1 supremo Bernie Ecclestone, for making this weekend happen. I wasn't privy to the meetings, but it is sensational that they were able to get me here for this guest appearance.'

Mansell's presence at the Circuit de Nevers raised speculation that he had also been approached to drive in the final three races of the season at Jerez (16 October), Suzuka (6 November) and Adelaide (13 November) as part of a deal which would see him being paid a total of £4 million by Renault for the four races, including France. It was also being rumoured that Mansell wanted the last three races linked to a firm option to drive for the Williams squad in 1995 on a full-time basis, a proposed deal which reputedly had the support of the French national car maker.

Ecclestone admitted that the television viewing figures for the French Grand Prix were up. 'I sincerely hope we'll see him back once his Indy programme is finished,' he added.

'I was surprised that he got on with the programme as quickly as he did. He motivated the team and he motivated Damon. It also proved that the car was not up to it and Damon got his backside kicked. One thing is for sure, if Nigel hadn't been there, Damon would not have done the time he did on Saturday.

'But at Silverstone we will see a different Damon. He will be more confident and prepared to take charge. And the team will be more prepared to listen.'

Prophetic words, indeed.

---

the second phase of the race. 'The balance on my second set of tyres didn't seem to be as good,' admitted Damon, 'and Michael suddenly seemed to make a lot of ground, but I didn't know then that he was planning another fuel stop. Really, they probably beat us on strategy there, because I was pushing very hard and didn't understand why he was still pulling away.'

In the opening stages Irvine's Jordan had run in sixth place, but then Barrichello went by and Eddie found himself having to keep a watchful eye on Frentzen's Sauber, which was now looming large in his mirrors. Then came the disappointing McLarens, Häkkinen leading Brundle, with Verstappen's Benetton pressing Martin hard.

Midway round lap 11, Verstappen got inside Brundle after the McLaren driver made a slight mistake and the two cars touched. Unknown to the Dutchman, his front wing had been damaged, so when he arrived at the final ess-bend before the pits he found himself ploughing straight across the gravel trap. With his B194's nose section well shredded, Jos was at least able to steer straight into the pit lane.

Despite his having caught his team unawares, the mechanics quickly changed the nose section, despatching him back into the race in last place, now one lap down. Unfortunately, Verstappen survived only until lap 26, when he flew off the road into the sand trap on the fast right-hander immediately after the pits.

Irvine had dropped out a lap earlier. 'Nobody got past me but Rubens and it was looking good until the gearbox started playing up at the hairpin,' said Eddie. 'It wouldn't change down, so I had to go round the corner in fifth. I tried about four times to change the gear, but it just went into neutral. Then suddenly it flicked into gear and went bang!'

The first retirement had been Zanardi, who had parked the Lotus on lap 21 after a merry blaze had taken hold in the engine bay.

By lap 30 Schumacher was 7.6 seconds ahead of Hill, with Alesi third from Berger, Barrichello and Mansell. On lap 36 Alesi made a second refuelling stop in 6.3s, then Schumacher came in for a 7.0s top-up at the end of lap 38, handing Hill the initiative. Damon still had to make his second stop, of course, and when he pulled in for a 7.7s service at the end of lap 45 the Benetton was able to surge back into the lead, where it remained for the rest of the afternoon.

On lap 42, Alesi pulled a really wayward stunt. He spun on the tight ess-bend before the pits, but in his efforts to spin-turn the Ferrari back into the race he managed to collect Barrichello's Jordan, eliminating both cars on the spot.

Rubens was aghast with disappointment. 'He just didn't measure the distance between us,' he said in disbelief. 'I am so disappointed, because today I really believed we could finish on the podium.'

That promoted Mansell to fourth, which became third at the end of lap 45 when Berger's Ferrari made its second refuelling stop, Gerhard just failing to get out of the pit lane ahead of the Williams, which swept by into the fast left/right beyond the pits. Not that Mansell was destined to go much further. At the end of the long back straight he coasted to a halt with a transmission pump drive failure.

Both the McLarens had a dismal afternoon. Brundle was running in seventh place when he felt that there was something not quite right with his engine from about lap 27. Three laps later, it expired spectacularly, a major failure triggered by a cracked oil/water heat exchanger. 'It was a shame,' shrugged Martin, 'because I was clawing my way back through the field quite nicely and felt comfortable with the car until the problems started.'

Häkkinen had worked his way through to fourth with 23 laps to go after a race in which he had continued to battle the chassis balance problems which had beset him throughout qualifying. After his second refuelling stop, he noticed the engine temperatures rise alarmingly, simultaneously suffering a loss of power. The engine expired in a spectacular sheet of flame soon afterwards and the MP4/9 rolled to a halt out on the circuit.

That left Frentzen fourth from Ukyo Katayama's Tyrrell, Christian Fittipaldi's Footwork, Pierluigi Martini's Minardi and de Cesaris. Unfortunately Fittipaldi picked up a slow puncture, almost certainly on the debris scattered by the Alesi/Barrichello episode, and his handling began to deteriorate badly, dropping him out of the points by the finish.

The Tyrrell team also had a disappointing afternoon. Katayama fought his way up to fifth before spinning at the Adelaide hairpin and stalling his engine on lap 54. Mark Blundell, weighed down by a heavy fuel load for a one-stop run, made a bad start and later had a faulty pneumatic compressor pipe stick his gearbox in fifth. The resultant pit stop to rectify the problem cost him three laps, so he wound up a distant tenth at the finish.

Hill eventually took the chequered flag some 12.6 seconds behind Schumacher as the Benetton driver clinched his sixth win in seven races. By then, Mansell and his wife Rosanne were *en route* to the nearby Nevers aerodrome where their private jet was already warming up its engines in preparation for the journey to Exeter, where they would stop overnight before continuing to Florida the following day.

Berger finished third ahead of Frentzen, Martini and de Cesaris, whose sixth place ensured that the Sauber team got both its cars home in the top six for the first time in its brief career. Herbert was seventh, followed by the luckless Fittipaldi, with Jean-Marc Gounon's Simtek ninth ahead of the delayed Blundell, the Englishman's Tyrrell being the final car circulating at the finish.

Mansell hadn't won on his comeback outing, indeed he hadn't finished. But the general consensus was that his presence in the Williams line-up had forced Hill to dig deeper into his personal resources and raise the standard of his game to dramatic effect.

Schumacher may have won again, but there was only another seven days to wait before Damon Hill would demonstrate what he had learned from the pressure at Magny-Cours.

163

FIA FORMULA ONE WORLD CHAMPIONSHIP ROUND 7

GRAND PRIX DE FRANCE

MAGNY-COURS 1-3 JULY 1994

CIRCUIT DE NEVERS – MAGNY-COURS
CIRCUIT LENGTH: 2.654-MILES/4.271 KM

RACE WEATHER: HOT, DRY, SUNNY

Place	Driver	Nat.	No.	Entrant	Car/Engine	Laps	Time/Retirement	Speed (mph/km/h)
1	Michael Schumacher	D	5	Mild Seven Benetton Ford	Benetton B194-Ford Zetec-R V8	72	1h 38m 35.704s	115.709/186.216
2	Damon Hill	GB	0	Rothmans Williams Renault	Williams FW16-Renault RS6 V10	72	1h 38m 48.346s	115.462/185.819
3	Gerhard Berger	A	28	Scuderia Ferrari	Ferrari 412T1B 041 V12	72	1h 39m 28.469s	114.685/184.569
4	Heinz-Harald Frentzen	D	30	Sauber Mercedes	Sauber C13-Mercedes-Benz V10	71		
5	Pierluigi Martini	I	23	Minardi Scuderia Italia	Minardi M194-Ford HB V8	70		
6	Andrea de Cesaris	I	29	Sauber Mercedes	Sauber C13-Mercedes-Benz V10	70		
7	Johnny Herbert	GB	12	Team Lotus	Lotus 109-Mugen Honda ZA5C V10	70		
8	Christian Fittipaldi	BR	9	Footwork Ford	Footwork FA15-Ford HB V8	70		
9	Jean-Marc Gounon	F	32	MTV Simtek Ford	Simtek S941-Ford HB V8	68		
10	Mark Blundell	GB	4	Tyrrell	Tyrrell 022-Yamaha 0X10A V10	67		
11	Erik Comas	F	20	Tourtel Larrousse F1	Larrousse LH94-Ford HB V8	66	Engine	
	Ukyo Katayama	J	3	Tyrrell	Tyrrell 022-Yamaha 0X10A V10	53	Spun off	
	Mika Häkkinen	SF	7	Marlboro McLaren Peugeot	McLaren MP4/9-Peugeot A6 V10	48	Engine	
	Nigel Mansell	GB	2	Rothmans Williams Renault	Williams FW16-Renault RS6 V10	45	Transmission	
	Jean Alesi	F	27	Scuderia Ferrari	Ferrari 412T1B 041 V12	41	Collision with Barrichello	
	Rubens Barrichello	BR	14	Sasol Jordan	Jordan 194-Hart 1035 V10	41	Collision with Alesi	
	Eric Bernard	F	25	Ligier Gitanes Blondes	Ligier JS39B-Renault RS6 V10	40	Transmission	
	Olivier Beretta	F	19	Tourtel Larrousse F1	Larrousse LH94-Ford HB V8	36	Engine	
	Martin Brundle	GB	8	Marlboro McLaren Peugeot	McLaren MP4/9-Peugeot A6 V10	29	Engine	
	Gianni Morbidelli	I	10	Footwork Ford	Footwork FA15-Ford HB V8	28	Collision with Panis	
	Olivier Panis	F	26	Ligier Gitanes Blondes	Ligier JS39B-Renault RS6 V10	28	Collision with Morbidelli	
	David Brabham	AUS	31	MTV Simtek Ford	Simtek S941-Ford HB V8	28	Gearbox	
	Jos Verstappen	NL	6	Mild Seven Benetton Ford	Benetton B194-Ford Zetec-R V8	25	Spun off	
	Eddie Irvine	GB	15	Sasol Jordan	Jordan 194-Hart 1035 V10	24	Gearbox	
	Michele Alboreto	I	24	Minardi Scuderia Italia	Minardi M194-Ford HB V8	21	Engine	
	Alessandro Zanardi	I	11	Team Lotus	Lotus 109-Mugen Honda ZA5C V10	20	Fire	
DNQ	Bertrand Gachot	F	34	Pacific Grand Prix Ltd	Pacific PR01-Ilmor 2175A V10			
DNQ	Paul Belmondo	F	33	Pacific Grand Prix Ltd	Pacific PR01-Ilmor 2175A V10			

Fastest lap: Hill, on lap 4, 1m 19.678s, 119.316 mph/192.022 km/h.
Lap record: Nigel Mansell (F1 Williams FW14B-Renault V10), 1m 17.070s, 123.355 mph, 198.521 km/h (1992).
All cars used Goodyear tyres

QUALIFYING 1

Michael Schumacher	1m 17.085s
Gerhard Berger	1m 17.441s
Damon Hill	1m 17.539s
Jean Alesi	1m 17.855s
Martin Brundle	1m 18.112s
Rubens Barrichello	1m 18.326s
Nigel Mansell	1m 18.340s
Jos Verstappen	1m 18.669s
Mika Häkkinen	1m 19.041s
Eric Bernard	1m 19.292s
Heinz-Harald Frentzen	1m 19.318s
Eddie Irvine	1m 19.463s
Olivier Panis	1m 19.697s
Ukyo Katayama	1m 19.969s
Mark Blundell	1m 20.001s
Pierluigi Martini	1m 20.084s
Michele Alboreto	1m 20.097s
Johnny Herbert	1m 20.108s
Alessandro Zanardi	1m 20.122s
Andrea de Cesaris	1m 20.145s
Erik Comas	1m 20.596s
Gianni Morbidelli	1m 20.707s
Christian Fittipaldi	1m 20.801s
Olivier Beretta	1m 21.964s
David Brabham	1m 22.527s
Jean-Marc Gounon	1m 23.264s
Bertrand Gachot	1m 24.048s
Paul Belmondo	1m 24.637s

Friday afternoon
Dry, hot, sunny

QUALIFYING 2

Damon Hill	1m 16.282s
Nigel Mansell	1m 16.359s
Michael Schumacher	1m 16.707s
Jean Alesi	1m 16.954s
Gerhard Berger	1m 16.959s
Eddie Irvine	1m 17.441s
Rubens Barrichello	1m 17.482s
Jos Verstappen	1m 17.645s
Mika Häkkinen	1m 17.768s
Heinz-Harald Frentzen	1m 17.830s
Andrea de Cesaris	1m 17.866s
Martin Brundle	1m 18.031s
Olivier Panis	1m 18.044s
Ukyo Katayama	1m 18.192s
Eric Bernard	1m 18.236s
Pierluigi Martini	1m 18.248s
Mark Blundell	1m 18.381s
Christian Fittipaldi	1m 18.568s
Johnny Herbert	1m 18.715s
Erik Comas	1m 18.811s
Michele Alboreto	1m 18.890s
Gianni Morbidelli	1m 18.936s
Alessandro Zanardi	1m 19.006s
David Brabham	1m 19.771s
Olivier Beretta	1m 19.863s
Jean-Marc Gounon	1m 21.829s
Bertrand Gachot	1m 21.952s
Paul Belmondo	1m 23.004s

Saturday afternoon
Dry, hot, muggy

WARM-UP

Michael Schumacher	1m 18.743s
Jean Alesi	1m 18.759s
Nigel Mansell	1m 18.821s
Jos Verstappen	1m 19.159s
Damon Hill	1m 19.305s
Eric Bernard	1m 19.505s
Rubens Barrichello	1m 19.591s
Gerhard Berger	1m 19.654s
Martin Brundle	1m 19.730s
Pierluigi Martini	1m 20.045s
Heinz-Harald Frentzen	1m 20.088s
Eddie Irvine	1m 20.136s
Olivier Panis	1m 20.451s
Gianni Morbidelli	1m 20.717s
Christian Fittipaldi	1m 20.843s
Michele Alboreto	1m 20.856s
Alessandro Zanardi	1m 21.071s
Erik Comas	1m 21.079s
Mika Häkkinen	1m 21.171s
Andrea de Cesaris	1m 21.201s
Olivier Beretta	1m 21.214s
Mark Blundell	1m 21.520s
Ukyo Katayama	1m 21.603s
Johnny Herbert	1m 21.925s
David Brabham	1m 22.063s
Jean-Marc Gounon	1m 22.123s

Sunday morning
Dry, hot, sunny

FASTEST LAPS

Driver	Time	Lap
Damon Hill	1m 19.678s	4
Michael Schumacher	1m 19.753s	3
Jean Alesi	1m 20.220s	3
Nigel Mansell	1m 20.242s	4
Gerhard Berger	1m 20.659s	3
Rubens Barrichello	1m 20.762s	11
Jos Verstappen	1m 21.536s	25
Mika Häkkinen	1m 21.829s	37
Martin Brundle	1m 21.992s	23
Eddie Irvine	1m 22.007s	8
Heinz-Harald Frentzen	1m 22.080s	4
Andrea de Cesaris	1m 22.121s	13
Ukyo Katayama	1m 22.493s	10
Olivier Panis	1m 22.625s	14
Pierluigi Martini	1m 22.740s	57
Johnny Herbert	1m 22.763s	9
Christian Fittipaldi	1m 22.852s	9
Erik Comas	1m 23.037s	14
Eric Bernard	1m 23.195s	9
Gianni Morbidelli	1m 23.299s	4
Mark Blundell	1m 23.368s	34
Alessandro Zanardi	1m 23.558s	13
Michele Alboreto	1m 23.676s	5
Olivier Beretta	1m 23.739s	4
David Brabham	1m 23.920s	5
Jean-Marc Gounon	1m 24.351s	6

All results and data © FIA 1994

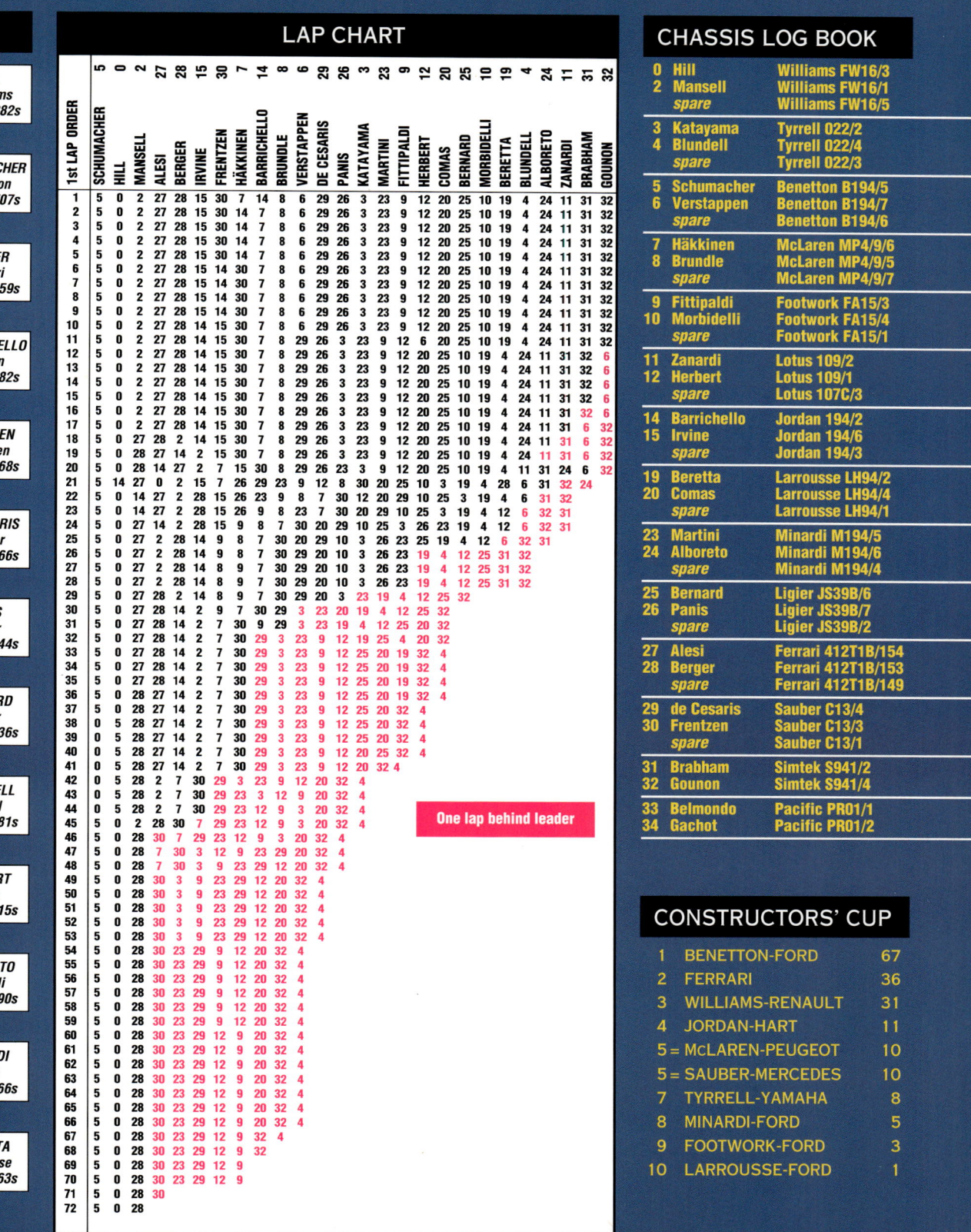

WORLD CHAMPIONSHIP • ROUND 8

BRITISH GRAND PRIX

| HILL |
| ALESI* |
| HÄKKINEN* |
| BARRICHELLO* |
| COULTHARD* |
| KATAYAMA* |
| *SCHUMACHER DSQ |

Damon Hill may have received a welcome leg-up on the way towards a memorable victory in the British Grand Prix, but the common consensus was that he might have got the better of Michael Schumacher even without it. Starting from pole position for the second time in eight days, Damon's Williams FW16 led Schumacher's Benetton B194 from the start and, although the German vaulted ahead after the first refuelling stops, the outcome of this Silverstone epic remained finely balanced until the World Championship leader ran into big trouble. Having breached the regulations by overtaking during each of the two pre-race parade laps, he then consistently ignored the black flag calling him in for a five-second 'stop-go' penalty while his team management argued the toss in provocative style with the race officials. In the end, Schumacher came in to take his punishment, finishing a distant second to a delighted Hill, who celebrated the second anniversary of his F1 debut in overwhelmingly memorable style. Third place fell to Jean Alesi's Ferrari 412T1B, with Mika Häkkinen taking fourth place, the Finn's McLaren-Peugeot just pipping Rubens Barrichello's Jordan-Hart in a sprint for the timing line after the two cars had collided at the final corner.

This one's for the family. Damon Hill lovingly cradles the trophy presented to the winner of the British Grand Prix – a race which his illustrious father Graham never managed to win.

BRITISH GRAND PRIX

> **Diary**
>
> *The permit to hold the 1994 Italian Grand Prix is suspended by the CSAI due to circuit safety worries at Monza.*
>
> *Carlo Chiti, the former Ferrari and Alfa Romeo F1 engineer, dies of a heart attack at the age of 70.*
>
> *Al Unser Jr scores his fifth Indy Car win of the season for Penske at Cleveland, beating Nigel Mansell's Newman-Haas Lola-Ford into second place.*
>
> *Gerhard Berger backs the prospect of a revival of the Austrian Grand Prix.*
>
> *One-time Ferrari F1 team manager Cesare Fiorio appointed Sporting Director of Ligier.*
>
> *Sam Hanks, winner of the 1957 Indy 500, dies at the age of 79.*

ENTRY AND PRACTICE

The reaction of the Silverstone authorities to the spate of F1 disasters earlier in the year was a model of prudent responsibility. Even before the dreadful accident to Lotus driver Pedro Lamy, whose Mugen-engined 107C had somersaulted into the spectator area at Bridge while evaluating technical changes just prior to the Spanish GP in May, Silverstone Circuits had planned to bring forward a £2.5 million programme of safety improvements originally in the pipeline for 1995.

The consequence was an intensive 19-day spurt of civil engineering which resulted in the track being transformed in time for a three-day test session just prior to the French Grand Prix. Copse, Stowe and Priory Corners were extensively reprofiled, a new chicane was installed at Abbey Curve and run-off areas at several other points were extended. Although on paper it might have appeared that the famous Northamptonshire track had been depressingly emasculated, the drivers felt that the venue retained much of its former appeal and unique character, while at the same time taking a significant step forward in terms of safety.

Although there was no Nigel Mansell on hand as a crowd-puller – Britain's most celebrated F1 expatriate having returned, for the moment, to his Indy Car exile with a race at Cleveland – both Damon Hill and David Coulthard arrived at Silverstone confident that their FW16s could give Michael Schumacher's Benetton more than a fleeting run for its money. Yet they were to find their resilience tested almost to breaking point as they battled to stay among the leaders during what proved to be a dramatically close first qualifying session.

A glance down the official timing sheets might have suggested that it was business as usual with Schumacher's Benetton emerging decisively quickest during that first hour-long blast. Moreover, with the steadily improving Ferrari 412T1Bs of Gerhard Berger and Jean Alesi next up, the fourth and sixth places achieved by Hill and Coulthard respectively looked distinctly average by Williams standards.

Yet a peek behind the scenes revealed high-speed spins for both Williams drivers, a sticking wheel nut which cost Coulthard over half an hour in the pits, and a lurid technical malfunction on Hill's car which deprived him of almost the entire morning's free practice session, so vital to the task of working out the best chassis settings for qualifying.

Hill's dramatic setback occurred only seconds after he accelerated out of the pits for the first time. Braking gently for Becketts, he was shocked to see his Williams's front wheels both wobble alarmingly and found himself skating to a halt to the accompaniment of flailing front suspension wishbones.

Stunned with disbelief, Damon climbed out to find that both top wishbones had apparently come undone from their rearward mounting on the side of the monocoque. As Hill walked back to the pits, he met Patrick Head, who was just strolling into the paddock, having been held up in the local traffic. Damon stopped to impart the news, a wake-up call which the Williams Technical Director could probably have done without!

There were inevitably some red faces within the team's pit garage. The failure was officially attributed to a 'car assembly problem' and resulted in Damon losing most of the session while the FW16 was first retrieved and then had its front suspension totally rebuilt before it was once again ready for action.

Hill was obviously as shaken as the team by this failure, but moved quickly to reassert his total confidence in the Williams operation.

'I was shocked, and also saddened as well,' he said, 'because it's not the sort of thing you expect to have happen. I know it's not good for the team to have something like this happen, and it's certainly not good for the confidence of the driver.

'Although this was a bit of a glitch, I've done a lot of miles for Williams and have absolute 100 per cent confidence in the team and the integrity of their workmanship. And I think I proved my belief in everybody at Williams by getting in and going as fast as I did immediately afterwards.

'It was a very unusual situation indeed. The only thing to do was to get on and recover. I spent most of first qualifying playing catch-up. As a result, I was over-driving a little bit, which would account for the spin I had at Club Corner.

'On my second run I settled down a bit in an effort to get a clearer track, but I don't think I've got tangled up with so many cars in one run all year, so it didn't work. But I believe it's got the potential to be on the front row, so if it's dry tomorrow I'll be out to prove it.'

This last remark was to be one of the most prophetic observations of the entire weekend. Meanwhile Coulthard, who was resuming his role as second driver following Mansell's guest outing in the previous weekend's French GP, was lucky not to make contact with the barrier when he spun at 170 mph going into the Bridge right-hander.

'I went into Bridge almost flat out, but when I hit the bumps, the car sat down at the rear, dug in at the front, and I was going backwards almost before I realised I'd got it wrong,' shrugged the young Scot.

'I had time to think that I was going to end up pretty sore, but thankfully I didn't hit anything. It's an uncomfortable feeling when you're going backwards, not in control of the car. It all happened so quickly that I thought "what went wrong?" rather than "am I scared?" '

Splitting the Williams duo in fifth place at the end of the first day was the impressive Heinz-Harald Frentzen's Sauber-Mercedes, with the Jordan-Harts of Rubens Barrichello and Eddie Irvine close behind in seventh and eighth.

However, the real eye-opener had been the form of the Ferraris, particularly the efforts of Gerhard Berger, who, together with the rest of the team, had not seen the revised track layout before arriving at Silverstone on the Thursday prior to the race. Gerhard's efforts to acquaint himself with the circuit changes were thwarted by engine failure on the first lap of the Friday morning session, a fact which made his overnight second place ahead of Jean Alesi all the more remarkable.

Thus the first day's qualifying ended with Hill and Coulthard lagging behind, and keen to emphasise that Ferrari's apparent upsurge in form was due to Williams's default rather than their own particular merit.

Both Williams FW16 had used the higher-revving Renault RS6B V10s on Friday and would retain these units for second qualifying. Over in the Maranello camp, Berger and Alesi would similarly benefit from the installation of the latest 75-degree type 043 V12 engines for second qualifying, although the cars would revert to earlier-spec 65-degree units for Sunday's race. In addition, the Ferraris were fitted with weight-saving titanium gearbox casings for the first time at this race, supplementing the 412T1's mid-season aerodynamic revamp.

Schumacher's fastest lap on Friday had been a 1m 26.323s, and although conditions were warmer on Saturday morning the second day's qualifying times were destined to be significantly quicker.

Barrichello opened proceedings with a storming 1m 26.745s, the Brazilian briefly moving up into fourth place. Then Mark Blundell emphasised just how much quicker conditions had become by posting a 1m 27.067s, followed by a 1m 26.920s, although this would eventually only be good enough for a distant 11th overall.

At 13.07, Hill went out on his first run and proved as good as his word. The British hero stormed round in 1m 26.733s to move onto the front row alongside Schumacher. But no sooner had the cheers from the grandstands subsided than Alesi popped up with the second-quickest time to knock Hill back onto the second row. Then Berger grabbed pole by 0.7s and, momentarily, there was a Ferrari 1-2 at the front of the pack.

A few moments later Alesi, who was still fighting excessive oversteer, slid up the escape road at Priory. Fortunately, he had sufficient presence of mind to keep the engine running and spin-turned his way back onto the circuit.

Then Schumacher went out for his first run. It yielded a convincing 1m 25.526s, good enough to return the German to the top of the list, but the Benetton was sliding all over the track on the tight infield section before the startline – the section where the B194's superb handling definitely conferred a significant performance edge.

There was a slight flurry of activity at the Luffield 1 right-hander when Olivier Panis spun his Ligier to avoid Michele Alboreto's Minardi, which had swapped ends a few seconds earlier. Then at 13.35 both Berger and Hill went out for their second runs. Gerhard was 0.6s inside Schumacher's best by the time he reached Club Corner on what should have been a storming pole winner, but the Austrian was badly balked by Mika Häkkinen's McLaren, which he found wandering in the middle of the circuit a couple of corners before the startline.

Fuming with indignation, Gerhard eased off immediately to conserve his tyres. Then he went for it again in a big way. Hill, meanwhile, was just raising cheers from the stands with a 1m 25.169s – the fastest so far – when Ferrari number 28 burst into view at the far end of Woodcote

167

BRITISH GRAND PRIX

to stop the clocks, and raise the stakes, with a 1m 24.980s.

It was the first sub-1m 25s lap of the weekend. Now the question was whether Schumacher could come back with a quicker time. And had Damon got anything else left?

At 13.44, Michael pointed the Benetton B194 out onto the circuit and rattled off a 1m 25.169s, which gave him second place. Then, with seven minutes left, Berger accelerated out of the pit lane once more. What followed was a gigantic anticlimax. To the amazement and sheer disbelief of everybody watching, Gerhard slid into the retaining wall on the left-hand side of the track as he steered out onto the circuit. It was such an astonishing lapse as to be almost unbelievable!

With the left-front wheel rim broken, he limped slowly round, intent on making it back to the pits. He almost achieved that objective, spinning to an ignominious and final halt at Brooklands, only two corners away from sanctuary.

'It really was a shame as the car was simply super,' shrugged Berger philosophically.

Surely that was the end of the action? Not a bit of it. Summoning up every ounce of commitment, Damon went out for a final, nerve-racking, *banzai* effort. In a re-run of his pole lap at Magny-Cours, he stopped the clock at 1m 24.960s – a couple of hundredths inside Berger's best.

'Nigel Mansell claimed that being on your home ground lifts you, that it's worth a second a lap,' he beamed, 'and I don't think he's far wrong. Believe me, it was very, very emotional in the car. My heart was in my mouth watching the others – although not as much as when I was out on my best lap!'

Schumacher headed out onto the circuit once more right at the end of the session and reduced his time to within three-thousandths of Damon's best, later admitting that he had made a slight mistake a couple of corners from the end of the lap. Thus, after a thrilling battle, Hill had taken pole position for the second time in as many weeks. Berger would line up alongside Alesi on the second row, the Austrian clearly hoping for great things come the race.

All this jousting for top times rather overshadowed the fact that Mika Häkkinen had finally qualified his McLaren MP4/9 in fifth place. After two days spent wrestling with clutch problems, everything clicked into place during that final hour and he

Peparations for practice at Silverstone range from the simple adjustment of a mirror by the driver *(right)* to the full attention of the engineering team *(below)* tending Barrichello's Sasol Jordan-Hart.

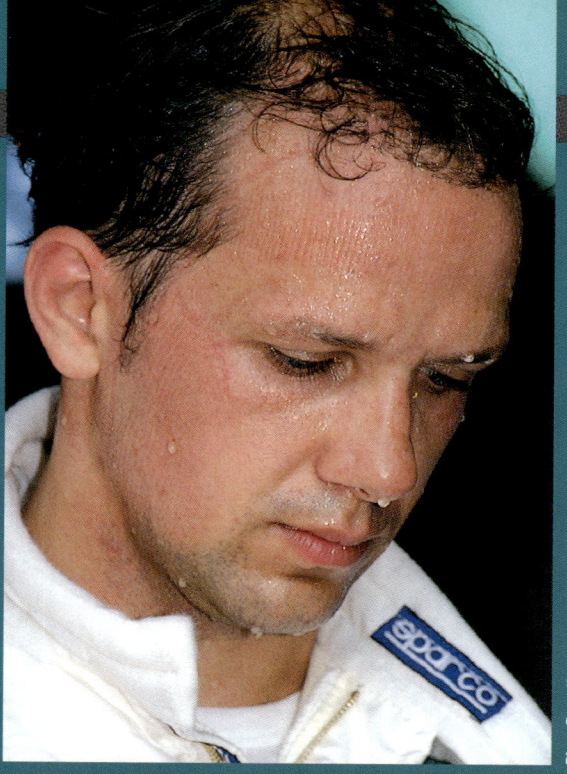
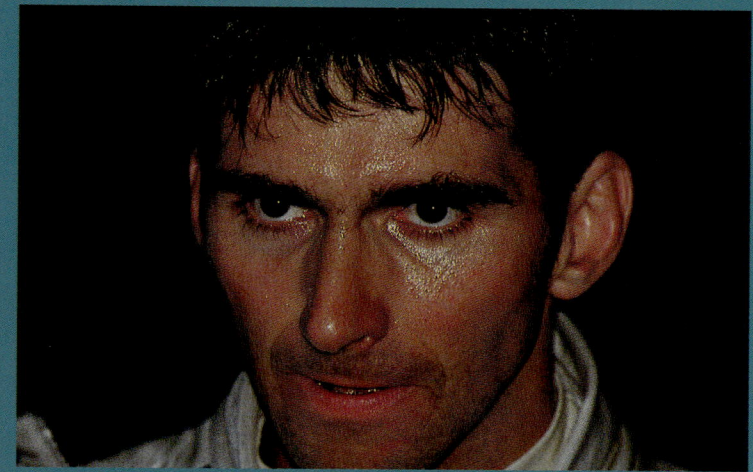

Top: Sweating it out at opposite ends of the grid, Jean-Marc Gounon and Damon Hill both show the strain of qualifying.

Jean Alesi *(above)* ponders Ferrari's progress, which saw the Italian cars battling for pole position on Saturday.

had two good clear runs, lining up four places ahead of team-mate Martin Brundle, who had no complaints about the performance of his machine.

Barrichello qualified sixth after an excellent showing with the Jordan 194, but Eddie Irvine – who benefitted from a Hart development engine on the second day in recognition of the fact that this was his home Grand Prix – didn't get the best out of his fresh V10 and wound up a disappointing 12th.

Irvine, candid as ever, confessed that he was probably over-driving. 'I think "too much effort, not enough finesse" pretty well sums it up,' he said honestly. 'All in all, it was a pretty poor performance.'

Coulthard was also very disappointed not to have bettered seventh place in the final line-up, never quite working out an ideal chassis balance until he was on his last set of tyres. 'Then I was balked by a couple of slower cars,' he admitted. 'Without that, I might have got one or two places further up, but not right there with the quick times.'

Katayama was an outstanding eighth, having consistently got the better of Blundell in the battle of the Tyrrells. But Frentzen was possibly the most disappointed man of all, dropping from fifth to 13th after the electronics controlling his Sauber's semi-auto gearbox went haywire in the second session and the change mechanism developed a mind of its own. Frentzen switched to de Cesaris's sister car right at the end of the session, but the Italian's C13 didn't have the right set-up and he just couldn't improve.

Tenth place fell to Jos Verstappen's Benetton, the Dutchman spinning off on his third lap of first qualifying. That dropped him from a momentary sixth to an overnight 16th, and after Schumacher led him round during Saturday morning's free practice he improved by a dramatic 2.3 seconds on the second day.

The next three places were filled by disappointed faces in the form of Blundell, Irvine and Frentzen, but Pierluigi Martini was delighted to line up 14th in the Minardi, one place ahead of Panis, who had taken over team-mate Eric Bernard's car to set his best time after that earlier contretemps with Alboreto. Gianni Morbidelli had a minor off-track excursion with the Footwork which kept the Italian down in 16th place, ahead of Alboreto, de Cesaris and Alessandro Zanardi, the fastest of the Lotus runners.

Struggling with a lack of mechanical grip, Zanardi at least had the consolation of qualifying a couple of places ahead of his team-mate Johnny Herbert, the Lotus 109s separated by a disappointed Christian Fittipaldi, whose Footwork lost an exhaust tailpipe out on the circuit during Friday qualifying, causing an electrical fire with consequent dire effects on the gearchange hydraulics. He was 15th overnight, but dropped five places on the second day, complaining of poor grip.

Behind Herbert came Erik Comas's Larrousse, separated from Olivier Beretta's sister car by Bernard's Ligier, while the Simtek duo of David Brabham and Jean-Marc Gounon were the last to make the cut. Brabham was hampered by fuel pressure problems on Friday, then scrambled a gearchange at Bridge, which cost him crucial fractions on his best Saturday lap. Finally, gearbox problems dogged the performance of the Pacific PR01s, ensuring that Bertrand Gachot and Paul Belmondo failed to qualify.

RACE

The first clash between competitors and officialdom on race day came when Berger was fined $10,000 for exceeding the pit lane speed limit during the warm-up, although the Austrian was unconcerned by the penalty. 'Ferrari had a new speed-limiter and I told them, "OK, I'll do it, but if it doesn't work it's your problem, not mine," he explained. 'It didn't – and they can pay the fine!'

Hill, who was starting from the fourth pole position of his career, could not believe his eyes as Schumacher accelerated several lengths ahead of his Williams on the run down to Copse Corner at the start of the parade lap. This was a clear breach of the regulations which strictly forbid overtaking, yet Schumacher duplicated this infringement when a second parade lap was necessary after Coulthard stalled his engine on the grid and the initial start was aborted.

Pumped up with adrenalin after overcoming Schumacher in qualifying, Hill out-dragged the Benetton when the green light was finally given, reaching Copse Corner decisively ahead. 'I was almost craning my neck to see where Michael was as we went into the first corner,' he explained, 'because I thought he might be tucked into my blind spot. But I turned in anyway, and found that I was ahead.'

Damon completed the opening lap 0.8s ahead of the Benetton with Berger third ahead of Barrichello, Alesi and Verstappen. Coulthard had been obliged to start at the back of the grid following his earlier lapse, while Brundle's McLaren had not even got off the line, its Peugeot V10 expiring in a huge spurt of oil smoke and flame even before the start had been given. As if all this weren't enough, Irvine's Jordan had suffered a rare failure of its Hart V10 engine when it lost oil pressure midway round the second parade lap.

Coulthard was soon in more trouble. The Scot overtook four cars on the run down to Copse, only to spin and drop to the tail of the field, and had to start his recovery all over

BRITISH GRAND PRIX

Leader Damon Hill gets out of shape at the revised Abbey Corner. Although Schumacher's 'stop-go' penalty ultimately decided the race in Hill's favour, many observers felt that, on this occasion, the Williams had the upper hand.

Sealed with a kiss. A tender moment between David Coulthard and girlfriend Andrea Murray snatched amidst the hurly-burly of qualifying.

again. Meanwhile Blundell made a storming getaway, despite the fact that Brundle's McLaren ignited immediately in front of him, and was seventh by Stowe. Then the Tyrrell's throttle jammed open on him coming into the Abbey chicane and he lost a lot of places, completing the first lap in 15th position.

With light fuel loads reflecting their two-stop race strategy, in the opening stages Hill and Schumacher simply sprinted away from the rest of the pack, running in tight formation at the head of the field, barely a second apart. Berger, who was planning a single stop, dropped seven seconds in the first five laps, with Barrichello, Alesi, Verstappen and Häkkinen all following in a well-ordered group close behind.

On the fifth lap, Zanardi's Lotus, which had started from the pit lane after a problem was diagnosed with a throttle butterfly on its Mugen Honda V10, also succumbed to engine failure out on the circuit. A lap later Morbidelli's Footwork, which had been running in tenth place behind Frentzen, began misfiring with all the symptoms of fuel pick-up problems. The Italian came straight into the pits and retired with a split fuel line. Then on lap 12 de Cesaris's Sauber retired from 15th place with a failure of its new air-valve Mercedes V10.

Hill led commandingly to lap 15 when he made his first refuelling stop, resuming in third place behind Berger and Schumacher. Three laps later it was the German's turn to make a 7.6-second first refuelling stop, picking up the threads of the battle behind Berger but ahead of Hill.

Damon's first stop had coincided with his catching a group of slower cars, so it seemed well timed. Consequently, he was a little disappointed that the Benetton team leader had slipped ahead by the time things settled down after their stops, but at least Berger's presence in the lead took the edge off Schumacher's pace and Hill was soon able to haul up on him.

BRITISH GRAND PRIX

Indecent exposure. Martin Brundle's McLaren-Peugeot expired in big way on the starting grid *(right)*, which only added to the embarrassment of the uneasy Anglo-French alliance.

Below right: Flags declaring allegiance to the stars add colour to the sun-drenched race day crowd.

Far right: Mika Häkkinen and Rubens Barrichello battled so intensely for fourth and fifth places that they eventually tangled within sight of the finish.

Bottom right: Flavio Briatore was to come off second best in his dispute with authority on this occasion.

At the end of lap 22, Gerhard duly made his refuelling stop, so now Schumacher was in front, leading Hill by a little more than half a second. But trouble was by now brewing for the German driver as a result of his rule infringement on the parade laps. When the leaders were on lap 13 it had been announced by the stewards that Schumacher would receive a five-second penalty for his misdemeanours, but it was not, apparently, made clear to the Benetton management what form this punishment would take.

They claimed they had thought that the five seconds would simply be added to his elapsed race time, so Schumacher pressed on – even in the face of a black flag, shown together with his race number at the start/finish line at the end of laps 21 and 22.

Strictly speaking, any driver shown the black flag must stop at his pit at the end of the following lap but, while race officials debated the matter with the Benetton crew, Schumacher stayed out. Not until the end of lap 27 did he finally come in to receive a five-second 'stop-go' penalty, resuming in second place, now over 20 seconds behind Hill's leading Williams.

At the end of lap 38 both Hill and Schumacher made their second refuelling stops, rejoining 17 seconds apart at the head of the field. By this stage Berger was no longer part of the equation, having slowed and stopped with engine trouble six laps earlier.

At this point Damon was bracing himself to repel a dramatic counter-attack from the championship points leader, but Michael was by now troubled by a slight gearchange problem which was causing him to lock his rear tyres intermittently under hard braking.

To the delight of the crowd, Hill thus ran out an emotional winner by 18.7 seconds from the disappointed Schumacher, who at least had the wit to keep his inner frustration to himself at the post-race press conference.

'A pity all of this happened, because I think we would have continued our fight,' he said thoughtfully. 'But congratulations to Damon and Williams. They ran a good race.'

Hill was obviously in a seventh heaven of delight as he stepped forward to accept his winner's trophy from the Princess of Wales.

'I feel that everything in my life has come together to this point,' said Damon emotionally. 'If you believe in destiny, then I honestly believe I was destined to win this race. I feel superb. It's the best day of my life. Like a dream!

'I had a lot of motivation here this weekend, not least because my father never won this race. I feel that this has completed a little hole in my father's record. Obviously his [Schumacher's] penalty was a godsend to us, but even without it I think it would have been a close race – a real titanic battle, in fact, right to the end.'

Alesi's Ferrari benefited from the retirement of Berger to finish third, with Mika Häkkinen just squeezing home to claim fourth place for the McLaren-Peugeot squad despite being pitched into the gravel trap at the final corner after a brush with Barrichello's pursuing Jordan.

Rubens, failing to appreciate that this was the final lap, limped slowly into the pit lane with damaged suspension. That allowed Häkkinen, having been pushed out of the gravel trap by willing hands, to trip the timing beam a second before Rubens did the same in the pit lane entrance!

Sixth place fell to Coulthard, the second Williams stuck in sixth gear in the closing stages. Having un-lapped himself from Hill, the Scot fell back behind the winner again a couple of laps from the finish. That was particularly unfortunate for, given an extra lap, Coulthard could almost certainly have capitalised on the Häkkinen/Barrichello collision and moved ahead to fourth place.

Frentzen lost seventh place to Katayama in a last-lap spin, the Sauber being followed home by Jos Verstappen's Benetton, Fittipaldi, Martini and Johnny Herbert. The Ligiers of Panis and Bernard ran steadily to finish 13th and 14th, Olivier losing time with a pit visit to rectify a vibrating nose cone, while Bernard found himself snagging the throttle pedal whenever he went for the brake, a less than satisfactory performance accessory on a circuit of this nature!

Olivier Beretta's Larrousse and the two Simteks completed the list of finishers, Gounon and Brabham spending much of the afternoon immersed in their own private battle.

After the race, the stewards imposed a $25,000 dollar fine on Schumacher and the Benetton team 'for not having a full knowledge and understanding of the F1 rules and the need for their meticulous application'. However, this was only the start of a rough ride for the World Championship leaders. Their problems were by no means over. In fact, they had only just begun.

FIA gets heavy with Benetton

The looks on the faces of Flavio Briatore and Tom Walkinshaw as they strolled from the race stewards' office at the end of the British Grand Prix radiated a degree of smug self-satisfaction which turned out to be dramatically misplaced. The team had been fined $25,000 but Schumacher had kept his second place and no doubt they hoped that would be the end of the matter.

Although the Benetton team management freely admitted that it 'messed up' in terms of interpreting the nature of the five-second penalty imposed on Schumacher, it countered by rightly pointing out that the stewards did not notify the team of the penalty within the 15-minute timescale laid down by the regulations.

However, the FIA was to see no merit in such a tacit plea for leniency. A few days after the British Grand Prix, the governing body announced that it would convene a special meeting of the World Motor Sports Council in Paris on 26 July – only three days before the start of practice for Schumacher's home GP at Hockenheim.

Schumacher and Benetton would be summoned for a further inquest into the events at Silverstone. In addition, Rubens Barrichello and Mika Häkkinen would be asked to explain why they had breached the rule requiring any driver involved in an incident to receive the stewards' permission to leave the circuit. Damon Hill was requested to attend to answer charges that he had stopped on the slowing-down lap to collect a celebratory Union flag – thus infringing the rule requiring all cars to proceed to *parc fermé* without stopping – and Silverstone Clerk of the Course Pierre Aumonier was required to give his account of the whole sorry episode.

The outcome was explosive. Schumacher was excluded from the results of the British Grand Prix and received a two-race ban, but immediately appealed in order to race at Hockenheim; Benetton was fined $500,000 for failing to obey the instructions of race officials; Barrichello and Häkkinen received a one-race suspended ban and Aumonier had his Clerk of the Course superlicence suspended for a year, while the RAC MSA was requested to instigate a detailed review of the British GP organisation. Only Hill was acquitted when it was proved to the FIA's satisfaction that, although he did collect a Union flag on the slowing-down lap, his Williams FW16 merely slowed to walking pace and did not in fact stop.

However, there was more, much more, to come. The FIA cast a further shadow over Schumacher's World Championship aspirations when it announced that Benetton was one of three teams found 'to have a computer system capable of breaching the regulations'.

It was a revelation destined to open the floodgates on yet another weekend of controversy, innuendo, doubt and abject self-justification as the teams headed for Hockenheim and the first race to be held under the 10 mm stepped undertray technical regulations.

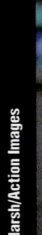

FIA FORMULA ONE WORLD CHAMPIONSHIP ROUND 8

BRITISH GRAND PRIX
SILVERSTONE 8–10 JULY 1994

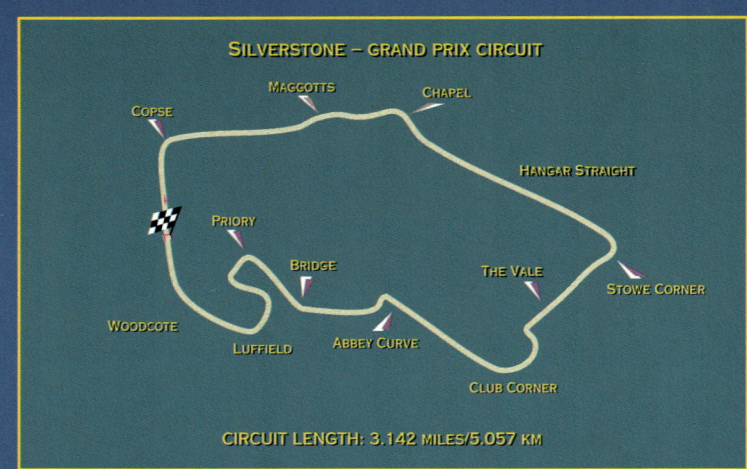

RACE WEATHER: Hot, dry, sunny

Place	Driver	Nat.	No.	Entrant	Car/Engine	Laps	Time/Retirement	Speed (mph/km/h)
1	**Damon Hill**	GB	0	Rothmans Williams Renault	Williams FW16-Renault RS6 V10	60	1h 30m 03.640s	125.606/202.143
*2	**Michael Schumacher**	D	5	Mild Seven Benetton Ford	Benetton B194-Ford Zetec-R V8	60	1h 30m 22.418s	125.171/201.443
3	**Jean Alesi**	F	27	Scuderia Ferrari	Ferrari 412T1B 041 V12	60	1h 31m 11.768s	124.042/199.626
4	**Mika Häkkinen**	SF	7	Marlboro McLaren Peugeot	McLaren MP4/9-Peugeot A6 V10	60	1h 31m 44.299s	123.309/198.447
5	**Rubens Barrichello**	BR	14	Sasol Jordan	Jordan 194-Hart 1035 V10	60	1h 31m 45.391s	123.284/198.407
6	**David Coulthard**	GB	2	Rothmans Williams Renault	Williams FW16-Renault RS6 V10	59		
7	Ukyo Katayama	J	3	Tyrrell	Tyrrell 022-Yamaha OX10A V10	59		
8	Heinz-Harald Frentzen	D	30	Sauber Mercedes	Sauber C13-Mercedes-Benz V10	59		
9	Jos Verstappen	NL	6	Mild Seven Benetton Ford	Benetton B194-Ford Zetec-R V8	59		
10	Christian Fittipaldi	BR	9	Footwork Ford	Footwork FA15-Ford HB V8	58		
11	Pierluigi Martini	I	23	Minardi Scuderia Italia	Minardi M194-Ford HB V8	58		
12	Johnny Herbert	GB	12	Team Lotus	Lotus 109-Mugen Honda ZA5C V10	58		
13	Olivier Panis	F	26	Ligier Gitanes Blondes	Ligier JS39B-Renault RS6 V10	58		
14	Eric Bernard	F	25	Ligier Gitanes Blondes	Ligier JS39B-Renault RS6 V10	58		
15	Olivier Beretta	F	19	Tourtel Larrousse F1	Larrousse LH94-Ford HB V8	58		
16	David Brabham	AUS	31	MTV Simtek Ford	Simtek S941-Ford HB V8	57		
17	Jean-Marc Gounon	F	32	MTV Simtek Ford	Simtek S941-Ford HB V8	57		
	Michele Alboreto	I	24	Minardi Scuderia Italia	Minardi M194-Ford HB V8	48	Engine	
	Gerhard Berger	A	28	Scuderia Ferrari	Ferrari 412T1B 041 V12	32	Engine	
	Mark Blundell	GB	4	Tyrrell	Tyrrell 022-Yamaha OX10A V10	20	Gearbox	
	Erik Comas	F	20	Tourtel Larrousse F1	Larrousse LH94-Ford HB V8	12	Engine	
	Andrea de Cesaris	I	29	Sauber Mercedes	Sauber C13-Mercedes-Benz V10	11	Engine	
	Gianni Morbidelli	I	10	Footwork Ford	Footwork FA15-Ford HB V8	5	Fuel pipe	
	Alessandro Zanardi	I	11	Team Lotus	Lotus 109-Mugen Honda ZA5C V10	4	Engine	
	Martin Brundle	GB	8	Marlboro McLaren Peugeot	McLaren MP4/9-Peugeot A6 V10	0	Engine	
DNS	Eddie Irvine	GB	15	Sasol Jordan	Jordan 194-Hart 1035 V10	0	Engine failure on parade lap	
DNQ	Bertrand Gachot	F	34	Pacific Grand Prix Ltd	Pacific PR01-Ilmor 2175A V10			
DNQ	Paul Belmondo	F	33	Pacific Grand Prix Ltd	Pacific PR01-Ilmor 2175A V10			

Fastest lap: Hill, on lap 11, 1m 27.100s, 129.875 mph/209.014 km/h (record for revised circuit).
Lap record for old circuit: Damon Hill (F1 Williams FW15C-Renault V10), 1m 22.515s, 141.674 mph/228.002 km/h (1993).
All cars used Goodyear tyres   * Schumacher subsequently disqualified and placings of other finishers adjusted accordingly

All results and data © FIA 1994

QUALIFYING 1

Michael Schumacher	1m 26.323s
Gerhard Berger	1m 26.738s
Jean Alesi	1m 26.891s
Damon Hill	1m 26.894s
Heinz-Harald Frentzen	**1m 27.284s**
David Coulthard	1m 27.698s
Rubens Barrichello	1m 27.890s
Eddie Irvine	1m 27.890s
Ukyo Katayama	1m 27.936s
Mika Häkkinen	1m 27.983s
Gianni Morbidelli	1m 28.159s
Martin Brundle	1m 28.224s
Mark Blundell	1m 28.510s
Pierluigi Martini	1m 28.517s
Christian Fittipaldi	1m 28.816s
Jos Verstappen	1m 29.142s
Alessandro Zanardi	1m 29.240s
Johnny Herbert	1m 29.268s
Olivier Panis	1m 29.381s
Michele Alboreto	1m 29.403s
Olivier Beretta	1m 29.971s
Andrea de Cesaris	1m 30.034s
Eric Bernard	1m 30.058s
Erik Comas	1m 30.274s
Jean-Marc Gounon	1m 31.225s
David Brabham	1m 31.437s
Bertrand Gachot	**1m 31.496s**
Paul Belmondo	1m 34.631s

Friday afternoon
Dry, hot, sunny

QUALIFYING 2

Damon Hill	**1m 24.960s**
Michael Schumacher	1m 24.963s
Gerhard Berger	1m 24.980s
Jean Alesi	1m 25.541s
Mika Häkkinen	1m 26.268s
Rubens Barrichello	1m 26.271s
David Coulthard	1m 26.337s
Ukyo Katayama	1m 26.414s
Martin Brundle	1m 26.768s
Jos Verstappen	1m 26.841s
Mark Blundell	1m 26.920s
Eddie Irvine	1m 27.065s
Pierluigi Martini	1m 27.522s
Olivier Panis	1m 27.785s
Gianni Morbidelli	1m 27.886s
Michele Alboreto	1m 28.100s
Andrea de Cesaris	1m 28.212s
Alessandro Zanardi	1m 28.225s
Christian Fittipaldi	1m 28.231s
Heinz-Harald Frentzen	1m 28.231s
Johnny Herbert	1m 28.340s
Erik Comas	1m 28.519s
Eric Bernard	1m 28.955s
Olivier Beretta	1m 29.299s
David Brabham	1m 30.690s
Jean-Marc Gounon	1m 30.722s
Bertrand Gachot	1m 31.877s
Paul Belmondo	1m 32.507s

Saturday afternoon
Dry, hot, sunny

WARM-UP

David Coulthard	1m 26.674s
Michael Schumacher	1m 26.928s
Damon Hill	1m 26.941s
Mark Blundell	1m 27.489s
Ukyo Katayama	1m 27.622s
Mika Häkkinen	1m 27.736s
Gerhard Berger	1m 27.770s
Eddie Irvine	1m 27.840s
Rubens Barrichello	1m 27.874s
Jean Alesi	1m 27.921s
Jos Verstappen	1m 28.003s
Michele Alboreto	1m 28.540s
Olivier Panis	1m 28.804s
Martin Brundle	1m 29.184s
Olivier Beretta	1m 29.223s
Erik Comas	1m 29.302s
Christian Fittipaldi	1m 29.312s
Heinz-Harald Frentzen	1m 29.665s
Gianni Morbidelli	1m 29.704s
Alessandro Zanardi	1m 29.704s
Johnny Herbert	1m 29.895s
Andrea de Cesaris	1m 30.320s
Eric Bernard	1m 30.397s
David Brabham	1m 31.188s
Pierluigi Martini	1m 31.759s
Jean-Marc Gounon	1m 32.223s

Sunday morning
Dry, hot, sunny

FASTEST LAPS

Driver	Time	Lap
Damon Hill	1m 27.100s	11
Michael Schumacher	1m 27.335s	8
David Coulthard	1m 27.889s	7
Gerhard Berger	1m 28.603s	18
Mark Blundell	1m 28.655s	13
Jean Alesi	1m 29.181s	23
Rubens Barrichello	1m 29.197s	11
Mika Häkkinen	1m 29.406s	24
Ukyo Katayama	1m 29.556s	8
Heinz-Harald Frentzen	1m 29.695s	26
Jos Verstappen	1m 29.876s	8
Olivier Panis	1m 29.993s	8
Gianni Morbidelli	1m 30.587s	4
Christian Fittipaldi	1m 30.683s	26
Eric Bernard	1m 30.769s	41
Michele Alboreto	1m 31.136s	17
Olivier Beretta	1m 31.253s	22
Pierluigi Martini	1m 31.481s	7
Johnny Herbert	1m 31.711s	8
Erik Comas	1m 31.741s	12
Andrea de Cesaris	1m 32.368s	9
David Brabham	1m 32.986s	15
Jean-Marc Gounon	1m 33.127s	14
Alessandro Zanardi	1m 34.266s	4

STARTING GRID

Pos	No	Driver	Team	Time
1	0	HILL	Williams	1m 24.960s
2	5	SCHUMACHER	Benetton	1m 24.963s
3	28	BERGER	Ferrari	1m 24.980s
4	27	ALESI	Ferrari	1m 25.541s
5	7	HÄKKINEN	McLaren	1m 26.268s
6	14	BARRICHELLO	Jordan	1m 26.271s
7	2	COULTHARD	Williams	1m 26.337s
8	3	KATAYAMA	Tyrrell	1m 26.414s
9	8	BRUNDLE	McLaren	1m 26.768s
10	6	VERSTAPPEN	Benetton	1m 26.841s
11	4	BLUNDELL	Tyrrell	1m 26.920s
12	15	IRVINE	Jordan	1m 27.065s
13	30	FRENTZEN	Sauber	1m 27.284s
14	23	MARTINI	Minardi	1m 27.522s
15	26	PANIS	Ligier	1m 27.785s
16	10	MORBIDELLI	Footwork	1m 27.886s
17	24	ALBORETO	Minardi	1m 28.100s
18	29	DE CESARIS	Sauber	1m 28.212s
19	11	ZANARDI	Lotus	1m 28.225s
20	9	FITTIPALDI	Footwork	1m 28.231s
21	12	HERBERT	Lotus	1m 28.340s
22	20	COMAS	Larrousse	1m 28.519s
23	25	BERNARD	Ligier	1m 28.955s
24	19	BERETTA	Larrousse	1m 29.299s
25	31	BRABHAM	Simtek	1m 30.690s
26	32	GOUNON	Simtek	1m 30.722s

NON-STARTERS

- DNQ — 34 GACHOT Pacific 1m 31.496s
- DNQ — 33 BELMONDO Pacific 1m 32.507s

LAP CHART

1st LAP ORDER	0 HILL	5 SCHUMACHER	28 BERGER	14 BARRICHELLO	27 ALESI	6 VERSTAPPEN	7 HÄKKINEN	3 KATAYAMA	30 FRENTZEN	10 MORBIDELLI	26 PANIS	29 DE CESARIS	23 MARTINI	12 HERBERT	4 BLUNDELL	2 ALBORETO	9 FITTIPALDI	20 COMAS	31 BRABHAM	25 BERNARD	19 BERETTA	2 COULTHARD	32 GOUNON	11 ZANARDI
1	0	5	28	14	27	6	7	3	30	10	26	29	23	12	4	2	9	20	31	25	19	2	32	11
2	0	5	28	14	27	6	7	3	30	10	26	4	23	12	29	9	2	20	19	31	25	11	32	
3	0	5	28	14	27	6	7	3	30	10	26	4	23	29	12	24	9	20	19	31	25	11	32	
4	0	5	28	14	27	6	7	3	30	10	26	4	23	12	29	24	9	20	19	31	11	25	32	
5	0	5	28	14	27	6	7	3	30	26	4	2	23	12	29	9	20	19	31	25	32			
6	0	5	28	14	27	6	7	3	30	26	4	2	23	12	29	9	20	19	31	25	32			
7	0	5	28	14	27	6	7	3	30	26	4	2	23	12	29	9	20	24	19	25	31	32		
8	0	5	28	14	27	6	7	3	30	26	4	2	23	12	29	9	20	24	19	25	31	32		
9	0	5	28	14	27	6	7	3	26	4	2	23	12	29	9	20	24	19	25	31	32			
10	0	5	28	14	27	6	7	3	26	4	2	23	12	29	9	20	24	19	25	31	32			
11	0	5	28	14	27	6	7	3	4	2	26	30	23	12	9	20	24	19	25	31	29	32		
12	0	5	28	14	27	6	7	3	4	2	26	30	23	12	9	24	25	19	31	32				
13	0	5	28	14	27	6	7	3	4	2	26	30	23	12	9	24	25	19	31	32				
14	0	5	28	14	27	6	7	3	4	2	30	26	23	12	9	24	25	19	31	32				
15	5	0	28	14	27	6	7	3	4	2	30	26	23	12	9	24	25	19	31	32				
16	5	28	0	14	27	6	7	3	2	4	30	23	12	26	9	24	25	19	31	32				
17	5	28	0	14	27	6	7	3	2	4	30	23	12	26	9	24	25	19	31	32				
18	28	5	0	14	27	6	7	3	30	2	4	23	12	26	9	24	19	31	32	25				
19	28	5	0	14	27	7	6	30	3	2	23	12	26	9	24	19	25	31	32					
20	28	5	0	14	7	6	30	3	2	23	12	26	9	24	25	32	31	4						
21	28	5	0	27	7	14	6	3	2	12	9	24	26	19	25	32	31							
22	5	0	28	27	7	14	30	3	2	6	23	12	9	24	19	26	25	32	31					
23	5	0	27	7	28	14	30	3	2	6	23	12	9	24	19	26	25	32	31					
24	5	0	27	7	28	14	30	2	3	6	23	12	9	24	26	19	25	32	31					
25	5	0	27	7	28	14	30	2	3	6	23	9	12	24	26	19	25	32	31					
26	5	0	27	7	28	14	30	2	3	6	9	23	12	24	26	19	25	32	31					
27	0	5	27	28	14	7	30	2	3	6	9	24	23	12	26	25	19	32	31					
28	0	27	5	7	28	14	30	2	3	6	9	24	23	12	26	25	19	32	31					
29	0	5	27	7	14	2	3	6	30	24	23	12	26	25	19	32	31							
30	0	5	28	27	14	7	2	3	6	30	24	9	23	12	26	19	25	31	32					
31	0	5	28	27	14	7	2	3	6	30	24	9	23	12	25	26	19	31	32					
32	0	5	14	27	7	2	3	6	28	9	23	12	26	24	25	19	31	32						
33	0	5	14	27	7	2	3	6	30	9	23	12	26	24	25	19	31	32						
34	0	5	14	27	7	2	3	6	30	9	23	12	26	24	25	19	31	32						
35	0	5	14	27	7	2	3	6	30	9	23	12	24	25	19	26	31	32						
36	0	5	14	27	7	2	3	6	30	9	23	12	24	25	19	26	31	32						
37	0	5	14	27	7	2	3	6	30	9	23	12	24	25	26	19	31	32						
38	0	5	14	27	7	2	3	6	30	9	23	12	24	26	25	19	32	31						
39	0	5	14	27	7	2	6	30	3	9	23	12	24	26	25	19	32	31						
40	0	5	14	27	7	2	6	30	3	9	23	12	24	26	25	19	31	32						
41	0	5	14	27	7	6	30	2	3	9	23	12	24	26	25	19	31	32						
42	0	5	27	7	14	30	2	3	6	9	23	12	24	26	19	25	32	31						
43	0	5	27	7	14	2	30	3	6	9	23	12	24	26	19	25	32	31						
44	0	5	27	7	14	2	30	3	6	9	23	12	24	26	19	25	32	31						
45	0	5	27	7	14	2	30	3	6	9	23	12	24	26	19	25	32	31						
46	0	5	27	7	14	2	30	3	6	9	23	12	24	26	19	25	32	31						
47	0	5	27	7	14	2	30	3	6	9	23	12	24	26	19	25	32	31						
48	0	5	27	7	14	2	30	3	6	23	12	26	19	25	32	31								
49	0	5	27	7	14	2	30	3	6	23	12	26	19	25	32	31								
50	0	5	27	7	14	2	30	3	6	23	12	26	19	25	31	32								
51	0	5	27	7	14	2	30	3	6	23	12	26	19	25	31	32								
52	0	5	27	7	14	2	30	3	6	23	12	26	19	25	31	32								
53	0	5	27	7	14	2	30	3	6	23	12	26	19	25	31	32								
54	0	5	27	7	14	2	30	3	6	23	12	26	19	25	31	32								
55	0	5	27	7	14	2	30	3	6	23	12	26	19	25	31	32								
56	0	5	27	7	14	2	30	3	6	23	12	26	19	25	31	32								
57	0	5	27	7	14	2	30	3	6	23	12	26	19	25	31	32								
58	0	5	27	7	14	2	30	3	6	23	12	26	25	19										
59	0	5	27	7	14	2	3	30	6															
60	0	5	27	7	14																			

One lap behind leader (shown in red in original)

Race distance: 60 laps, 188.536 miles/303.420 km

At a special meeting of the FIA World Motor Sports Council in Paris on 26 July, Michael Schumacher was disqualified from the British Grand Prix. The positions of the other finishers were adjusted accordingly and the Constructors' Cup and Drivers' World Championship points tables amended.

CHASSIS LOG BOOK

No	Driver	Chassis
0	Hill	Williams FW16/5
2	Coulthard	Williams FW16/1
spare		Williams FW16/3
3	Katayama	Tyrrell 022/2
4	Blundell	Tyrrell 022/4
spare		Tyrrell 022/3
5	Schumacher	Benetton B194/5
6	Verstappen	Benetton B194/6
spare		Benetton B194/4
7	Häkkinen	McLaren MP4/9/6
8	Brundle	McLaren MP4/9/5
spare		McLaren MP4/9/7
9	Fittipaldi	Footwork FA15/3
10	Morbidelli	Footwork FA15/4
spare		Footwork FA15/1
11	Zanardi	Lotus 109/2
12	Herbert	Lotus 109/1
spare		Lotus 107C/3
14	Barrichello	Jordan 194/2
15	Irvine	Jordan 194/6
spare		Jordan 194/3
19	Beretta	Larrousse LH94/2
20	Comas	Larrousse LH94/4
spare		Larrousse LH94/1
23	Martini	Minardi M194/5
24	Alboreto	Minardi M194/1
spare		Minardi M194/4
25	Bernard	Ligier JS39B/6
26	Panis	Ligier JS39B/7
spare		Ligier JS39B/2
27	Alesi	Ferrari 412T1B/154
28	Berger	Ferrari 412T1B/153
spare		Ferrari 412T1B/149
29	de Cesaris	Sauber C13/4
30	Frentzen	Sauber C13/3
spare		Sauber C13/1
31	Brabham	Simtek S941/2
32	Gounon	Simtek S941/4
33	Belmondo	Pacific PR01/1
34	Gachot	Pacific PR01/2

CONSTRUCTORS' CUP

Pos	Team	Points
1	BENETTON-FORD	73
2	WILLIAMS-RENAULT	42
3	FERRARI	40
4=	McLAREN-PEUGEOT	13
4=	JORDAN-HART	13
6	SAUBER-MERCEDES	10
7	TYRRELL-YAMAHA	8
8	MINARDI-FORD	5
9	FOOTWORK-FORD	3
10	LARROUSSE-FORD	1

DRIVERS' POINTS

Pos	Driver	Points
1	SCHUMACHER	72
2	HILL	39
3=	BERGER	17
3=	ALESI	17
5	BARRICHELLO	9
6	HÄKKINEN	7
7=	LARINI	6
7=	BRUNDLE	6
9	FRENTZEN	5
10=	BLUNDELL	4
10=	DE CESARIS	4
10=	WENDLINGER	4
10=	KATAYAMA	4
15=	MARTINI	3
15=	FITTIPALDI	3
17=	COULTHARD	1
17=	LEHTO	1
17=	ALBORETO	1
17=	IRVINE	1
17=	COMAS	1

WORLD CHAMPIONSHIP • ROUND 9

GERMAN GRAND PRIX

BERGER
PANIS
BERNARD
FITTIPALDI
MORBIDELLI
COMAS

GERMAN GRAND PRIX

Gerhard Berger totally dominated the German Grand Prix at Hockenheim, starting from pole position and leading every lap to put Ferrari back in the winner's circle for the first time in almost four years. Yet it was a horrifying pit lane conflagration involving Jos Verstappen's Benetton B194 which grabbed the headlines across the world on the morning after the race. Unjustly, this deflected attention from the Austrian's flawless performance, a thoroughly deserved reward for the Maranello team's intensive 1994 technical development programme and an endorsement of the management expertise brought to bear on the company over the previous 12 months by its Sporting Director, Jean Todt. In the early stages of the race Berger had to fend off a strong challenge from Germany's national hero, Michael Schumacher, but when the Benetton wilted with engine failure, the Ferrari had an easy run through to the chequered flag. A couple of multiple collisions between the grid and the first corner accounted for no fewer than 11 of the 26 starters, leaving the well-drilled Ligier duo, Olivier Panis and Eric Bernard, to finish second and third. Verstappen and his Benetton refuelling crew were indeed fortunate to escape with superficial burns when spilt fuel ignited the Dutchman's car from stem to stern during its first scheduled stop at the end of lap 15. Although it was seen by many as a damning indictment of the entire refuelling concept, the sport's masters seemed worryingly unconcerned about the whole episode, pointing to the efficient manner in which the blaze had been extinguished rather than pondering the wisdom of introducing such a hazardous strategy in the first place.

ENTRY AND PRACTICE

By the end of the first day's qualifying at Hockenheim, things didn't look too good for Michael Schumacher and the Benetton team. The partnership assumed a slightly beleaguered air after the German had been pushed back into third place in the provisional grid order, Damon Hill setting the early pace on the daunting high-speed circuit through the pine forests near Heidelberg.

Schumacher's participation in his home Grand Prix had remained in doubt until less than 48 hours before the first qualifying session. Finally, on the Wednesday prior to the race, an appeal against the two-race suspension imposed by the FIA for ignoring the black flag at Silverstone was formally lodged, allowing the German to race in front of his fellow-countrymen.

In the aftermath of the FIA's decision, and before the appeal was lodged, there had been some potentially ugly scenes brewing in the torrid summer sun. German racing 'fans' threatened to set fire to the tinder-dry pine forests in the event of Schumacher not competing in his home race. Even more ominously, Hill – the Benetton driver's closest rival in the championship points stakes – found himself the subject of death threats over the GP weekend and was accorded a police escort to and from the circuit.

The German Grand Prix was the first race to be held under revised F1 technical regulations which demanded a 10 mm stepped floor beneath the cars, intended to reduce aerodynamic downforce and slash cornering speeds in the interests of safety. Most cars were fitted with sheets of a wooden composite material called Jabroc beneath their undertrays in order to comply with the new regulations, but there was obvious concern as to how the stewards might police the rule which stipulated no more than a 10 per cent wear margin in terms of surface depth for the 'plank' during the course of the event. However, if there was obvious evidence of accident damage to the undertray, the stewards could rely on an alternative provision – namely, that the plank retained at least 90 per cent of its original weight – as a yardstick of conformity.

As far as the circuit was concerned, the final chicane on the return leg had been tightened significantly, and would now be taken in fourth gear. It had been renamed after Ayrton Senna in what was regarded by many as something of a questionable tribute to the late Brazilian star, and the same could be said of the decision to lend Jim Clark's name to the first chicane on the outward leg.

A formal ceremony was held to rename the latter chicane, attended by Jimmy's sister, Mattie Calder, and her husband Alec. Sadly, no members of the Senna family were present for the naming of the other corner.

Hill's Williams-Renault had lapped 0.6s faster than Gerhard Berger's Ferrari to take the provisional pole on Friday. 'It's good, but my normal cautiousness is creeping in, so I don't want to count any chickens before they're hatched,' he said. He was also sufficiently shrewd to realise that his car's performance on the first day might not fully reflect the overall competitive canvas, bearing in mind that both his main rivals – Benetton and Ferrari – had experienced their fair share of troubles.

'This lap time won't stand as fastest tomorrow if the conditions are the same,' he predicted, 'so we must keep working to improve the car. We made some improvements at last week's Silverstone test and I think those are showing up here, which means that what we've learned is translating from one circuit to another – and that is crucial.'

The FW16s appeared for this race in 'B' specification, indicating a revised aerodynamic package including significantly shortened side pods which allowed space for longer vertical deflectors, and were powered throughout the weekend by the slightly higher-revving RS6B versions of the Renault V10 first used in second qualifying at Magny-Cours.

Schumacher's third-fastest time on the first day resulted from the team attempting to help Jos Verstappen after the Dutchman damaged his own car beyond immediate repair in a spin on oil dropped by Berger's expiring Ferrari during the Friday morning free practice session.

Having taken over Michael's B194 after the German driver's first run, Verstappen promptly spun off at the Ostkurve on his first lap, leaving neither driver with an operational car for the balance of the session. Schumacher thus wound up just ahead of Jean Alesi's Ferrari, David Coulthard's Williams-Renault, the McLaren-Peugeot of Mika Häkkinen and Mark Blundell's Tyrrell-Yamaha.

Verstappen was highly embarrassed

Below: In a simple ceremony attended by the late World Champion's sister, Jim Clark is remembered at the memorial stone erected at the site of his fatal accident in 1968.

In the doldrums. Johnny Herbert *(right)* was increasingly disaffected with his lot in a Lotus team which had sadly long since lost the mystique it enjoyed in the glory days of the Sixties and Seventies.

Lukas Gorys

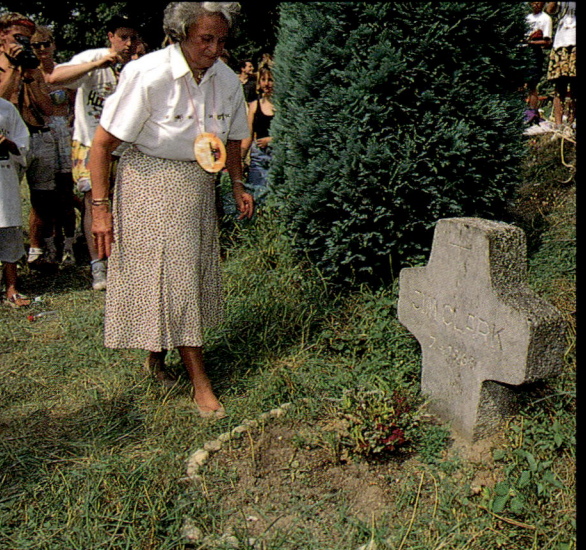

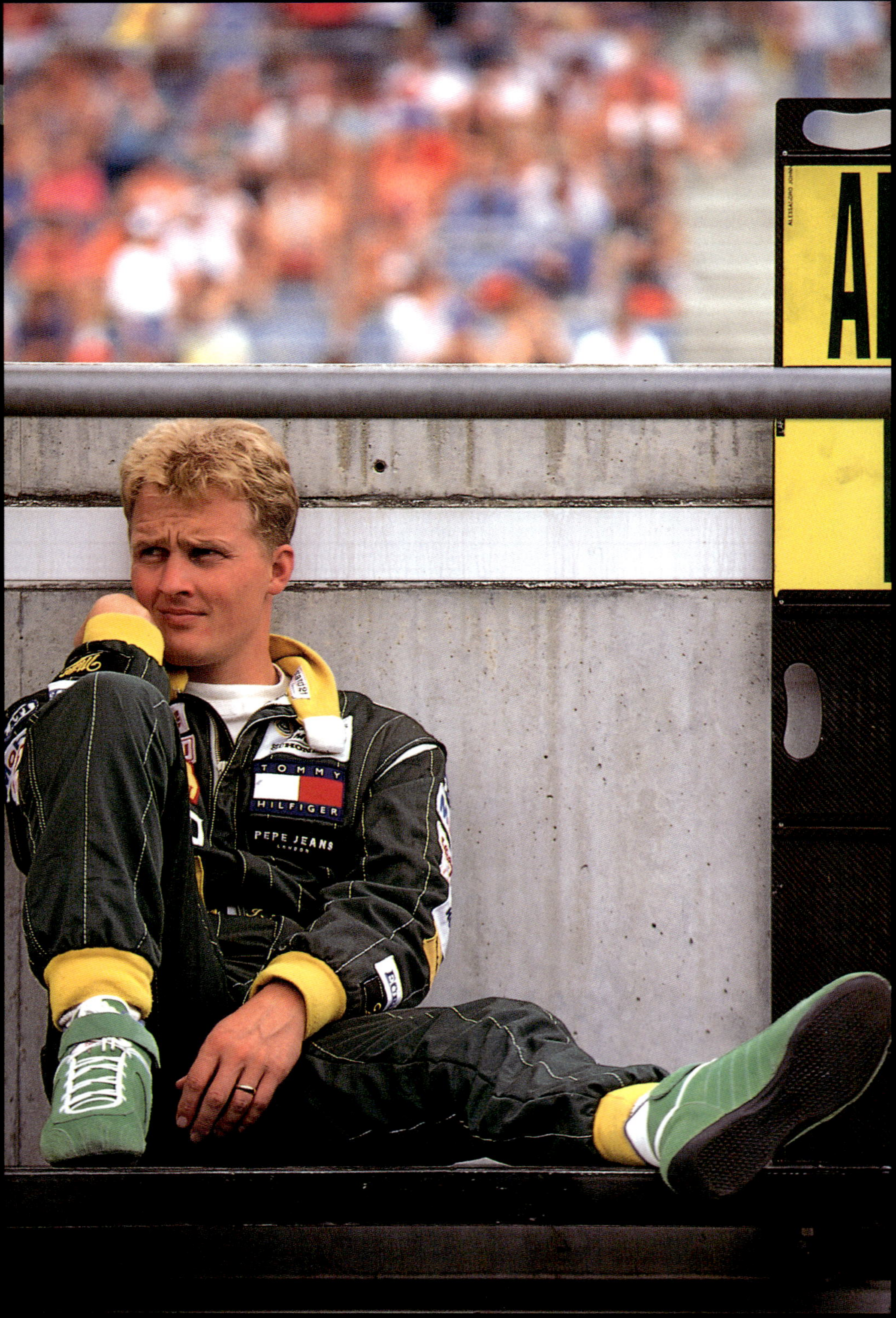

GP Photo/Peter Nygaard

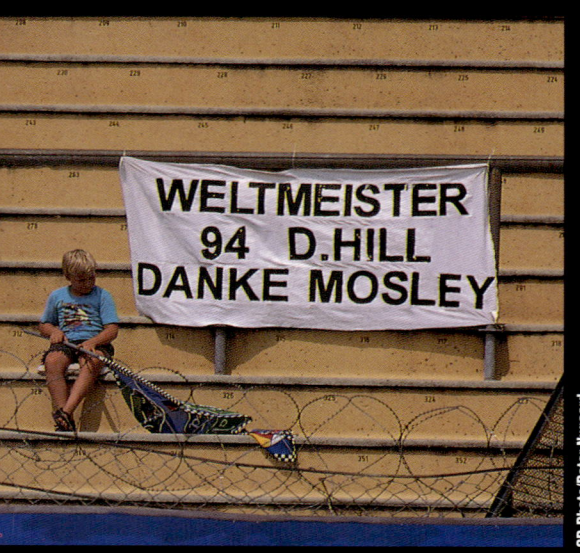

Not surprisingly, partisan messages from the Hockenheim tribunes accuse FIA President Max Mosley of tilting the championship battle in favour of Damon Hill.

Michael Schumacher *(right)* has his say on the controversial race at Silverstone and its aftermath, which saw him given a two-race ban for ignoring the black flag.

LAT Photographic

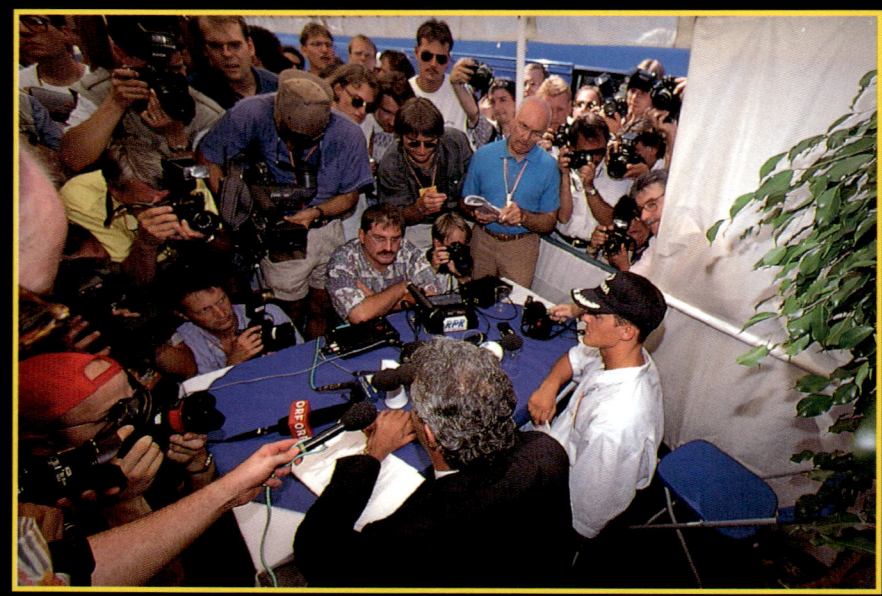

by blotting his copybook at the wheel of Schumacher's machine. 'I took it very easy through the first corner, as, above all, I didn't want to crash the car of the man leading the World Championship,' he explained. 'The handling was very good, but when I went through the second chicane, I suddenly spun into the gravel!'

Both Ferraris had started the day fitted with 65-degree type 041 V12 engines, but Berger's exploded spectacularly on Friday morning as he came past the pits, coating the rear tyres with lubricant and sending Gerhard straight into the gravel trap at the first corner. Even though the marshals were quick to display their warning flags, in addition to Verstappen, the resultant slick also claimed Bertrand Gachot's Pacific, Eddie Irvine's Jordan, Eric Bernard's Ligier and Michele Alboreto's Minardi – although the Italian just managed to extricate his M194 and kept going.

Apparently to maintain parity of equipment between its two drivers, Ferrari decided to fit both its cars with the latest type 043 V12s for Friday qualifying, a protracted change which took longer than usual as various ancillary components also had to be replaced to accommodate the wider 75-degree unit. The Ferrari team claimed that the decision to change both engines was taken, since Gerhard needed a replacement anyway, because the weather forecast for Saturday looked rather less favourable. In reality, it looked like a strategy to head off any possible complaints from Alesi!

As a result, Berger only got out in the closing moments of qualifying, posting fastest time before pulling off at the end of the pit straight when he felt his engine going off song. Alesi, meanwhile, fitted fresh tyres in such a rush prior to his last run that there was not sufficient time to refuel, with the result that although Jean started his final lap 20 seconds before the chequered flag came out his mount spluttered to a halt out on the circuit.

On Saturday the Maranello twins shrugged aside these niggling problems to display their anticipated fast-circuit form. After the session was briefly interrupted by the red flag to retrieve Mika Häkkinen's McLaren, which had speared into the tyre barrier on the exit of the right-hander leading out of the stadium, Alesi set the pace in storming style.

He pushed to the front of the pack with a 1m 44.012s, then immediately experienced a nasty fright when the rear bodywork and engine cover flew off his Ferrari at high speed on the straight just before the third chicane.

'I just saw a shadow in my mirrors and didn't know that I'd lost part of the bodywork,' he later explained. 'But they quickly told me over the radio what had happened and when I went into the next corner the car felt very light and I almost lost it.'

A few moments later, Berger topped his team-mate's best with a 1m 43.582s. It not only threw pole position beyond reach, but guaranteed the first all-Ferrari front row since Mansell and Prost qualified 1-2 for the 1990 Portuguese GP at Estoril.

Hill, meanwhile, tried everything he knew to get on terms with the Italian cars, but simply couldn't improve on a third-place start. 'We changed the car a little bit following the morning session,' he shrugged, 'but I'm afraid we've rather stood still. Yesterday Michael didn't get all his laps in, and Ferrari was in trouble, so perhaps this was a more representative indication of the current status quo.

'Even so, I'm confident we've got a satisfactory race set-up. This race is hard on engines and I think we'll be in good shape for tomorrow's race.'

Coulthard was similarly disappointed over his inability to better sixth overall, splitting the two very impressive Tyrrell-Yamahas of Ukyo Katayama and Blundell. 'Like Damon, I changed my car slightly after this morning's session in an effort to improve the handling,' he explained. 'I had oversteer this morning and I'm afraid I still had it this afternoon. It's made life difficult on the exit from the chicanes, overheating the rear tyres slightly to the point that, when I got round to the stadium section, I was struggling for grip.'

Schumacher was left simply to do his best in front of his home crowd, eventually taking a solid fourth place on the grid. Disappointing, perhaps, but, in truth, it was always likely to be. Ironically, in view of his appeal, if Schumacher was going to be defeated, it was most likely to be at Hockenheim, where the long straights tipped the scales in favour of the more powerful multi-cylinder engines from Ferrari and Renault.

'Under the circumstances, I am very happy to be one-tenth away from Damon on Saturday,' said Michael. 'I know he was 0.8s faster than me yesterday – but that was because Jos parked my car somewhere and I was unable to do my second run!' A spectacular spin coming into the stadium on Saturday morning served to remind Michael's fans just how hard he was trying.

After his problems on the first day, Verstappen never quite got into the swing of things. No matter what adjustments were made to his B194, it continued to yaw unpredictably from oversteer to understeer. He languished in a bewildered, slightly dejected 19th place in the final order.

By contrast, over in the Tyrrell camp there was much rejoicing after

Benetton battles rumour and innuendo

As if there were not enough problems for the Benetton team to grapple with on the circuit at Hockenheim, controversy and innuendo continued to envelop the World Championship leaders on the F1 political stage. The latest development was the publication by the FIA of a dossier of technical information outlining in some detail the evidence against the Benetton team which had recently been examined by the sport's governing body in connection with the control systems allegedly used on the B194.

In particular, the document contained a seeming litany of Benetton's repeated prevarication when asked to furnish detailed information about their on-board computer systems. In that connection, both Benetton and McLaren had been fined $100,000 at the previous week's FIA World Council meeting for failing to make available their computer 'source codes'.

The FIA also revealed that its F1 Technical Delegate, Charlie Whiting, was in no doubt that Michael Schumacher's car was equipped with an illegal 'launch control' facility during the ill-starred San Marino Grand Prix on 1 May.

'This is a system which, when armed, allows the driver to initiate the start with a single action,' said the FIA report. 'The system will control the clutch, gearshift and engine speed fully automatically to a predetermined pattern.'

The FIA statement continued: 'Benetton stated that this system is used only during testing. Benetton further stated that "it [the system] can only be switched on by recompilation of the code." This means recompilation of the source code. Detailed analysis by LDRA [the company commissioned by the FIA which specialises in analysis, verification and validation of computer software] experts revealed this statement was untrue. "Launch control" could in fact be switched on using a lap-top personal computer connected to the gearbox control unit.

'When confronted with this information, the Benetton representatives conceded that it was possible to switch on the launch control using a lap-top PC, but indicated that the availability of this feature of the software came as a surprise to them.

'In order to enable "launch control", a particular menu with ten options has to be selected on the PC screen. "Launch control" is not visibly listed as an option. The menu was so arranged that, after ten items, nothing further appeared. If, however, the operator scrolled down the menu beyond the tenth listed option, to option 13, launch control can be enabled, even though this is not visible on the screen. No satisfactory explanation was offered for this apparent attempt to conceal the feature.'

In addition, it was pointed out that the driver had to work through a particular sequence of gearshift paddle positions, as well as clutch and throttle pedal positions, in order to activate the system. The implication here was that the driver would have to be a willing accomplice in the event of the system being employed.

Such systems are clearly illegal under the 1994 F1 Technical Regulations, but Benetton insisted that they were used only during testing. However, Whiting passed his report to the FIA, noting that he was not satisfied that Schumacher's car had conformed with the rules at Imola.

However, the World Council decided that 'the best evidence' was that Benetton did not use the automatic start system at that race. Nevertheless, in making public such a detailed dossier on the matter only three days after the ruling, Benetton's continuing discomfort was virtually guaranteed.

However, Michael Schumacher was absolutely firm in his response on the matter. 'Under no circumstances would Benetton, Ford, Cosworth or myself knowingly operate outside of the 1994 FIA F1 regulations. Such an action is inconceivable as it would bring into question the integrity of all parties.'

This robust defence was mirrored by the team's Technical Director, Ross Brawn. 'On the subject of the engine calibration menu, the title "launch control" had been removed from that because our software is used by many engineers, not just the person who has written the software,' he explained.

'Once we understood that these features were not going to be legal, it was removed from the menu so that other engineers using the menu wouldn't initiate it accidentally. There was never any attempt made to conceal it. It was made very clear to LDRA that there was a launch control option within the software.'

That, for the moment, seemed to be that. Benetton now looked forward to the hearing of Schumacher's appeal against his two-race suspension during the week immediately following the Belgian Grand Prix at Spa. As the transporters left Hockenheim, it seemed hardly possible that there was even more controversy to come.

Yet another potential area of conflict would be revealed during the week after Hockenheim when FIA representatives attended the Benetton factory at Enstone to examine the refuelling rig which had been used on Verstappen's car at the fateful pit stop.

Benetton was still not yet out of the wood. Not by any means.

GERMAN GRAND PRIX

While the tail-end runners are in the process of eliminating themselves, a late-braking Mika Häkkinen is causing mayhem at the front of the field as his McLaren spears across the track. The Finn not only put himself in the barrier, but also triggered a chain-reaction which accounted for Mark Blundell, Eddie Irvine, Rubens Barrichello and Heinz-Harald Frentzen.

Katayama produced his best-ever qualifying performance to line up fifth ahead of Coulthard. More than that, it was the best qualifying position ever for a Japanese F1 driver, Ukyo making the very best use of the Tyrrell 022 in its revised stepped-undertray configuration.

'I am so happy that it is difficult to express my feelings,' admitted Ukyo. 'Everyone has worked so hard this year and it is a great reward.' In reality, as Harvey Postlethwaite explained, both Katayama and seventh-placed Blundell were reaping the rewards of a steady development programme, enhanced performance from Yamaha's J2 version of the V10 engine and a productive three-day Silverstone test prior to the race.

In the McLaren camp, the weekend began on a note of hopeful anticipation that the the incorporation of revised-specification piston rings might have successfully eliminated the crankcase pressurisation problems which had recently bedevilled the Peugeot V10s. As things transpired, the French engines ran pretty reliably throughout qualifying. With effect from this race, the two McLaren drivers had swapped engineers, with Steve Hallam transferring to Martin Brundle's MP4/9 and Giorgio Ascanelli – who in 1993 worked on Senna's car – moving across to take charge of Mika Häkkinen's mount.

Häkkinen was a moderately content sixth overall on the first day, dropping to eighth after crashing his race car on the first lap of second qualifying. Despite hurting his right thumb, he went straight back to the pits and took over Brundle's car after the Englishman had finished his own runs.

Pressure of time meant that only the bare minimum of cockpit changes could be made to accommodate Mika and although the Finn managed to squeeze in two runs he failed to improve on his Friday best. Brundle managed to trim his time by 0.4s but that still left him trailing in a disappointed 13th, splitting the Ligier JS39Bs of Olivier Panis and Eric Bernard, the French team now operating under the high-profile command of former Ferrari competitions manager Cesare Fiorio and using Renault's RS6A-spec V10 for the first time.

Heinz-Harald Frentzen was moderately satisfied with ninth place, although this was, perhaps, hardly the *tour de force* anticipated by Mercedes-Benz. With Sauber unable to test at Hockenheim or Monza (its nominated test track) prior to the event, most of the team's immediate preparations for the German race had been carried out at Paul Ricard and Mugello.

The latest version of the Ilmor-made Mercedes V10, incorporating pneumatic valvegear and modified camshafts, was available for this race. Andrea de Cesaris was up to his old tricks again, spinning into a guard rail on Saturday morning, and then proved unable to work out a decent chassis balance. He set 18th-fastest time, totally confused as to why the C13 seemed unable to reproduce its recent promising Mugello testing form.

Rubens Barrichello spent most of the weekend fighting off a nasty bout of flu caught while back home in Brazil during the week prior to the FIA World Council hearing in Paris. On Saturday morning, he lost a lot of time when his Hart V10 began smoking ominously and needed to be changed. In the afternoon, the best the Brazilian could manage was 11th, one place behind his team-mate Eddie Irvine. By contrast, Johnny Herbert at last had something to smile about, albeit weakly perhaps, as he qualified 15th with the Lotus 109 on a circuit which allowed its heavy, six-year-old Mugen Honda V10 to demonstrate its undoubted power.

Johnny commented that the 109 was understeering excessively but, despite an engine failure in Friday qualifying, was generally not bad. Alessandro Zanardi complained of a similar handling imbalance, traced to a broken diffuser bracket on Friday, and just failed to make the top 20 by a single place the following afternoon.

Gianni Morbidelli was the quicker of the Footwork drivers in 16th place, immediately ahead of teammate Christian Fittipaldi, who lost time with gearbox trouble on Saturday morning, with de Cesaris and Verstappen squeezing in ahead of Pierluigi Martini's 20th-placed Minardi, which ended Saturday qualifying in a gravel trap.

Erik Comas's Larrousse lined up in 22nd place ahead of Alboreto, the Italian veteran troubled by a succession of minor problems but content with the performance of Minardi's new semi-automatic gearchange. Olivier Beretta was 24th for Larrousse, while the Simtek team was struggling to make up ground after David Brabham had rolled his S941 at Stowe during the previous week's Silverstone test, the driver thankfully emerging unhurt although the car was quite badly damaged.

Brabham qualified 25th in the rebuilt machine, despite fluffing a gearchange on his best lap, while Jean-Marc Gounon scraped in last, complaining of a down-on-power engine. Lack of straightline speed was also a major handicap for the Pacifics of Paul Belmondo and Bertrand Gachot, and both were consigned to their familiar positions as non-qualifiers.

RACE

Schumacher posted the fastest time in the warm-up from Berger, Hill, Coulthard and a confident Brundle, but Alesi was left way down in 17th place with an engine problem on his Ferrari. For a while it looked as though he would have to take the spare car, still fitted with an earlier-spec 65-degree V12, for the start but eventually he stayed in his race car. It wouldn't be long before he was questioning the wisdom of deciding against the switch.

Berger made a superb getaway from pole position, Alesi tucking in behind him only for the second-place Ferrari's engine to expire within the first mile. Thus, as they hurtled down towards the first chicane it was Katayama's Tyrrell which momentarily held second place after the Japanese driver had made a brilliant start from the third row.

Schumacher was third ahead of Hill, but behind them everything went wrong almost from the moment the starting light blinked to green. To begin with, at the back of the grid, Andrea de Cesaris collided with Michele Alboreto and Alessandro Zanardi, eliminating Sauber, Minardi and Lotus on the spot.

Simultaneously, going into the first corner, Mika Häkkinen's McLaren tried to rocket down the inside close to the pit wall, squeezing Coulthard's Williams against Blundell's Tyrrell. Then there was chaos as Häkkinen suddenly found himself snapping broadside and shooting across the nose of his rivals to plunge into the barrier on the outside of the corner. As he did so, he left the rest of the pack scattering in all directions.

As Blundell also speared off the road, both Jordans found themselves with nowhere to go but into the gravel, along with Frentzen's Sauber, which was clipped by the departing Tyrrell. Also eliminated were Pierluigi Martini's Minardi and Johnny Herbert in the other Lotus-Honda, which was clipped by Martin Brundle's McLaren right on the exit of the right-hander.

'I got off the line well,' explained Herbert, 'and I passed Brundle as we got away, but he came back up the inside of me to repass. I decided to keep on the outside line, but he just carried on running on his own line and there was nowhere left to go.'

Lotus team chief Peter Collins was furious. 'You would have thought that after 200 Grands Prix he [de Cesaris] would know how not to cause an accident at the start of the race. Equally, the television shows Brundle blatantly driving Johnny off the circuit, which I find totally unacceptable.'

At the end of the day it would be Häkkinen who shouldered the blame

Sporting Pictures (UK) Ltd

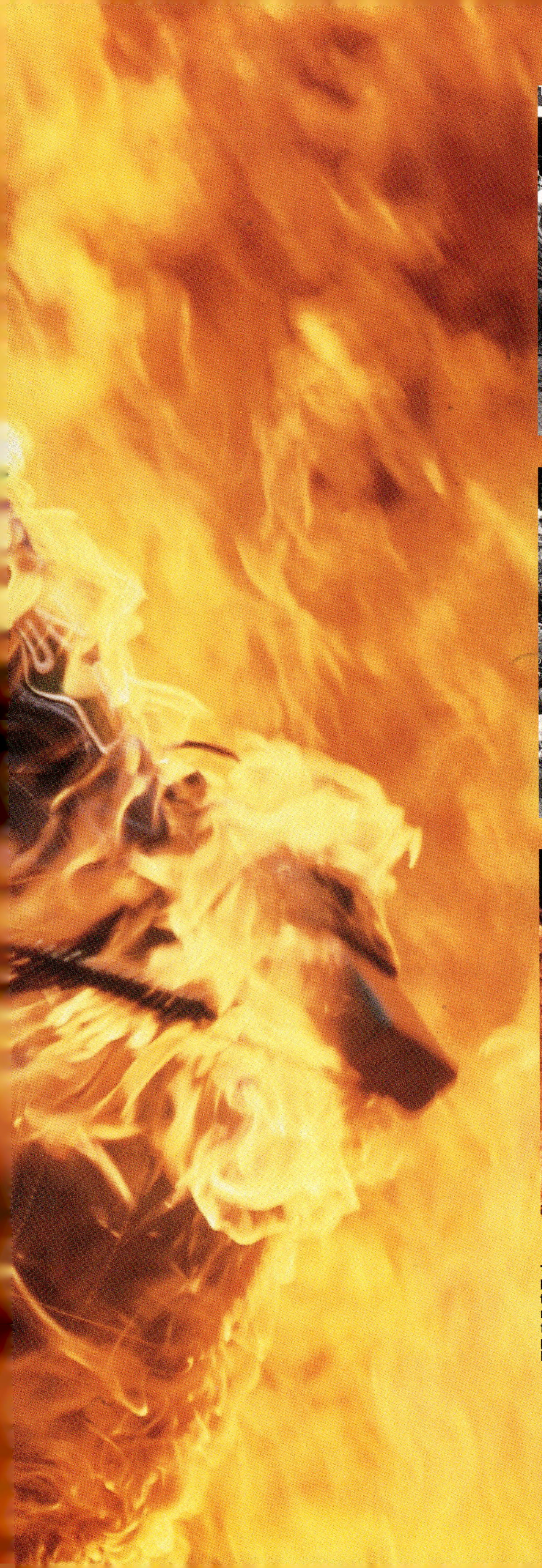

LAT Photographic

Diana Burnett

Diana Burnett

Sporting Pictures (UK) Ltd

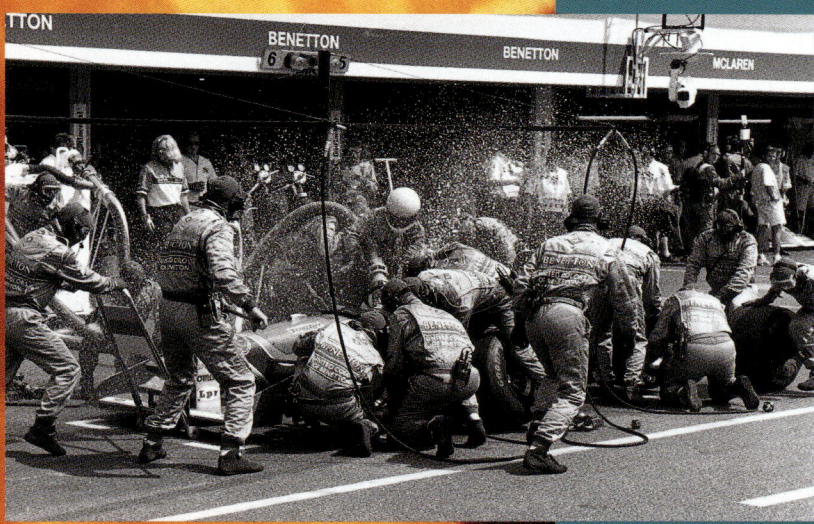

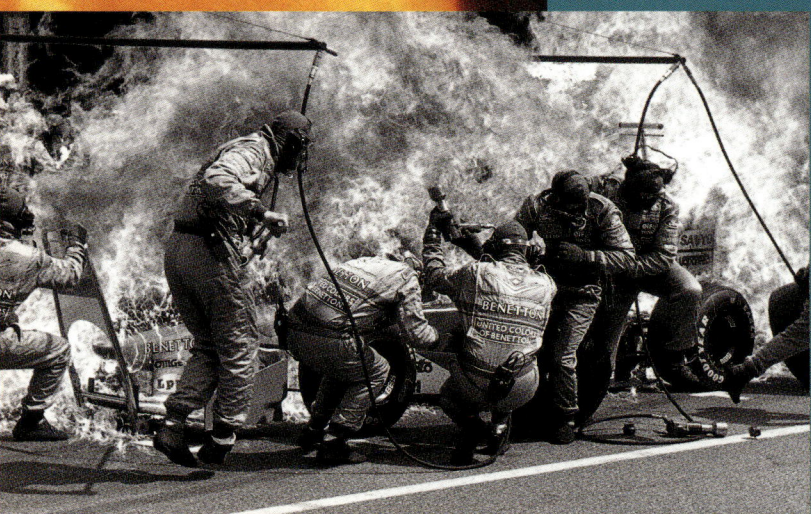

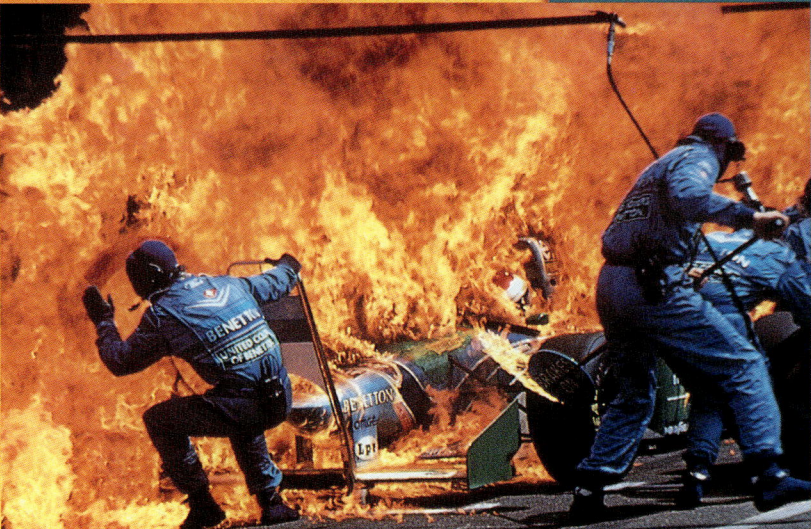

The full horror of the pit lane fire at Hockenheim is graphically displayed in this sequence of photos. Miraculously neither Jos Verstappen (seen enveloped in flames in his car above) nor the Benetton pit crew were seriously harmed, but it had been a lucky escape for all concerned.

GERMAN GRAND PRIX

With nearly half the field eliminated on the opening lap, it was the Ligiers which picked up the pieces. The French-blue cars of Olivier Panis *(below)* and Eric Bernard *(right)* took second and third places respectively, marking the first podium visit for the team since 1986.

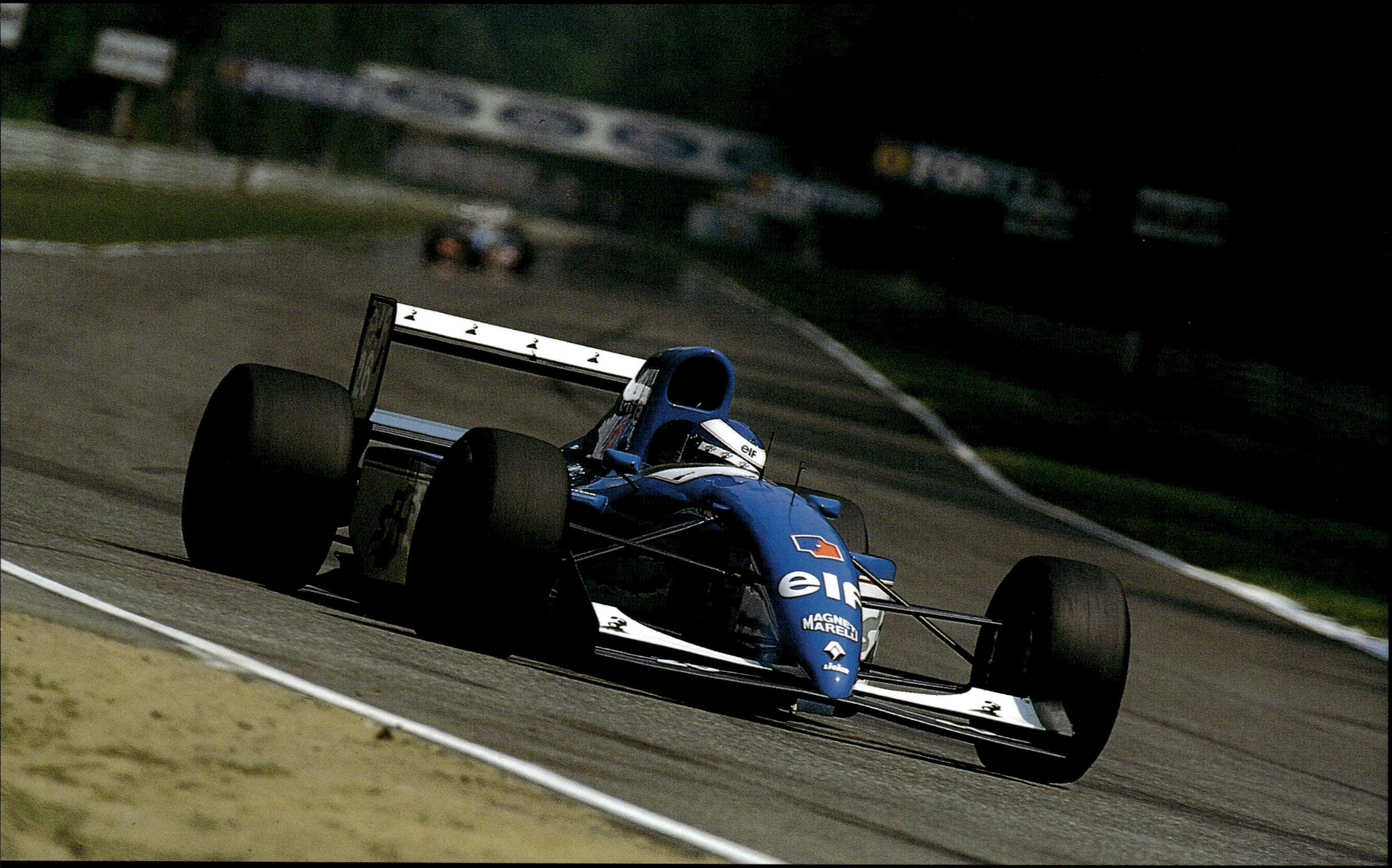

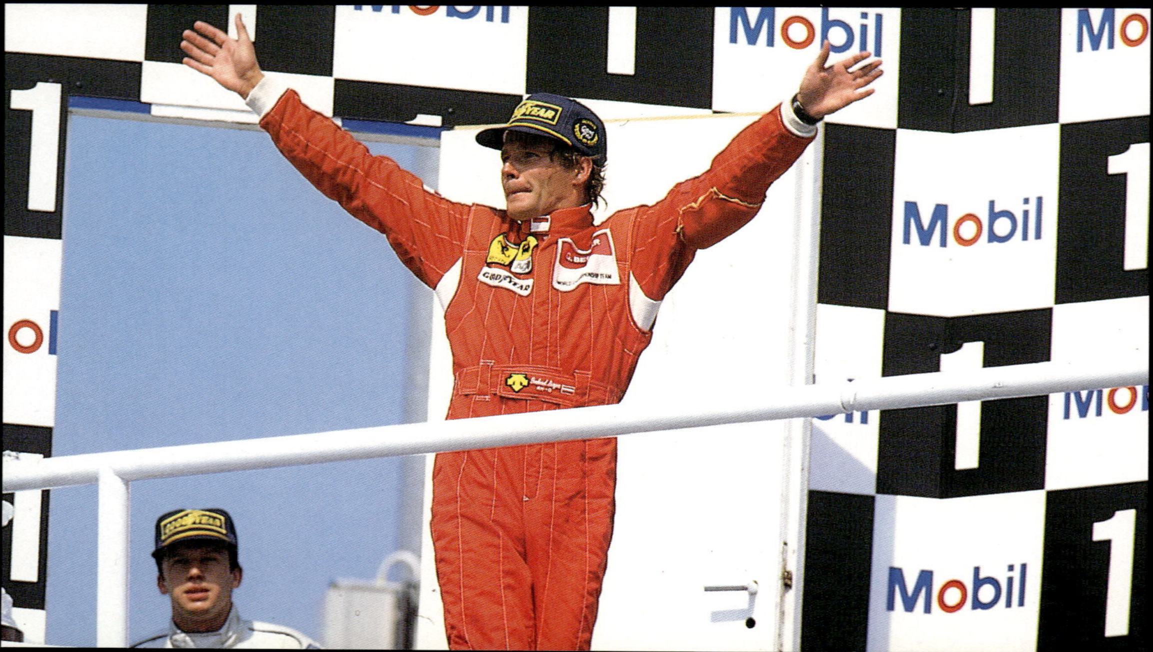

In through the out door. Winner Gerhard Berger, a veteran in terms of podium visits, strides on to take his applause. Olivier Panis, however, seems apprehensive about taking his bow.

GERMAN GRAND PRIX

A near-deserted Hockenheim stadium after Michael Schumacher's stunning run of success had come (albeit temporarily) to an end – to the huge disappointment of the now departed crowd.

for triggering the first-corner pile-up. The Finn was already racing under a suspended one-race ban imposed by the FIA World Council for a rule infringement at Silverstone and, following a protracted stewards' inquiry, this was now activated, with the result that Mika would miss the Hungarian Grand Prix.

Later, Alboreto, Zanardi and de Cesaris would also receive one-race bans, suspended for three races, for breaching Article 66 of the FIA regulations and leaving the circuit after an accident without the consent of the appropriate officials.

Back on the track, meanwhile, the race continued. Going into the third chicane, Schumacher dived inside Katayama to take second place and Hill followed him through, believing that the Tyrrell driver had also seen him and would give him the necessary racing room. Not so. Ukyo slammed the door, the two cars made contact and Damon was left limping towards the pits with a bent steering arm.

'I missed a golden opportunity today,' shrugged Hill, correctly assuming a portion of the blame. 'Katayama turned in, but I should have been ready for him. Frank Williams expects perfection and I don't think he will exactly be congratulating me. Perhaps if I had been more patient, I could have won the race.'

All this mayhem left the fans watching a somewhat depleted field. Berger led through at the end of the opening lap by 0.3s from Schumacher, then there was a huge gap back to Katayama, Panis, Verstappen, Bernard and the Footworks of Morbidelli and Fittipaldi.

A few moments later came the embarrassing sight of both Williams FW16Bs trailing into the pit lane. Coulthard arrived first for a replacement nose section while Hill had to wait his turn for a new steering arm to be fitted. The young Scot was bristling.

'What he [Häkkinen] did was totally unacceptable, weaving around like that,' he said later. 'It's not right that he should be involved in these sort of incidents when he's got a suspended ban hanging over his head.'

After that, Coulthard's car ran quite well at the tail of the field, running 12th when the Scot came in for his first refuelling stop at the end of lap 16. Unfortunately a short-circuit from one of the wheel speed sensors sent the electronics haywire, the gearbox jammed in

> **Diary**
>
> *Porsche confirms that it has built a V10 Formula 1 engine as a design exercise, but denies there are any plans to race it within the foreseeable future.*
>
> *The Jordan team bids to use the 3-litre version of the all-conquering Ford Zetec-R F1 engine in 1995.*
>
> *Italian F3000 exponent Massimiliano Papis is signed as Lotus test driver.*
>
> *Top Indy Car contender Robby Gordon signs a two-year extension to his deal with Derrick Walker's team through to the end of 1997.*

sixth and he retired after another single lap.

Berger, meanwhile, was giving Schumacher a demonstration of the new Ferrari V12's potential. The Austrian was really flying, and although Michael tried a couple of inside dives at the third chicane, there was no way Gerhard was allowing him past.

'I knew I was intending to stop only once,' Berger later explained, reflecting on the way in which Schumacher clung to his tail in the early stages. The Benetton, by contrast, was scheduled for a two-stop run, which certainly made things seem promising for the Maranello brigade.

The crowd loved it. Cheering madly, they were no doubt anticipating a historic home victory for their hero if the Ferrari didn't last the distance. On lap 12, Schumacher came in for his first refuelling stop, resuming in fourth place behind the two Ligiers and about 22 seconds behind Berger. He was soon back up to second, but Gerhard wasn't easing his pace. Then all hell let loose in the pit lane.

Verstappen was running in fifth place at the end of lap 15 when he came in for what should have been a routine refuelling stop. However, a malfunction of the refuelling system resulted in fuel continuing to flow once the hose was uncoupled from the car.

Television viewers around the world had just time to register that fuel was suddenly splashing all over the side of the Benetton before the car erupted in a horrifying fireball, scattering the mechanics in all directions as the driver remained momentarily trapped at the heart of the conflagration, frantically waving his arms.

It was the nightmare scenario everybody had anticipated ever since in-race refuelling had been reintroduced at the start of the season. Thankfully, extinguishers were immediately deployed to snuff out the blaze, by which time Verstappen had successfully vacated the cockpit. The Dutch driver and five mechanics were taken first to the circuit medical centre, and later to hospital for treatment to localised facial burning, two being kept in overnight as a precaution.

By any standards, it was an extremely fortunate escape for all concerned and one which catapulted the controversial topic of refuelling back to the top of the motor racing safety agenda. On a positive note, it was also a convincing endorsement of the high standard of safety equipment which is taken for granted on the contemporary motor racing scene. All those involved in the Hockenheim drama were wearing triple-layer flameproof overalls and protective headgear, and the fire was swamped by light water foam delivered from a huge reservoir of extinguishant which the regulations demand be stationed in each pit.

Only four laps after this near-disaster, Schumacher's Benetton began to slow, to the accompaniment of groans of disappointment from the crowd. Michael reported that the engine suddenly seemed to lose power, but the team's Technical Director Ross Brawn attributed the problem to a malfunction in the throttle mechanism, discreetly covering up for what appeared to be a rare Cosworth breakage. Either way, at the end of lap 20 Schumacher's race was run, and large sections of the crowd made tracks for the exit.

Berger was now effectively handed the race on a plate, immediately coming in to refuel at the end of lap 20 as soon as he was radioed that Schumacher was slowing. Under no pressure, and mindful of the near-disaster to Verstappen, the Ferrari pit crew didn't rush their task. Gerhard was stationary for 16.3 seconds while around 150 litres of Agip were taken aboard, more than sufficient to last him through to the finish.

From then on, once he had got back into his rhythm, he was able to dictate the pace of the race. In his wake, there were precious few cars left to run into trouble. Katayama had retired with six laps completed after throttle problems caused him to spin, and although Hill was storming round as quickly as ever at the tail of the field his early slip had cost him two laps and left him with no realistic prospect of collecting even a single championship point.

Once Schumacher had retired, Panis and Bernard moved into second and third places, the two Frenchmen thereafter having trouble-free runs and profiting from the misfortunes of those eliminated in the first-lap drama.

Brundle's McLaren ran as high as sixth place before retiring with yet another Peugeot engine failure, while both Simteks also failed to last the distance. Brabham dropped from ninth place with clutch failure after 37 laps, while Gounon stopped with gearbox failure two laps later.

In the closing stages Berger experienced a pronounced vibration through the steering, possibly caused by him picking up debris on his tyres. 'I pressed hard for two or three laps to try cleaning them up,' he explained, 'but in the closing stages I cut the revs and simply took things easy on the machinery.'

The two Ligier lads appeared on the rostrum in a slightly self-conscious frame of mind, almost as if they didn't quite understand how they had got there, while the Footworks of Fittipaldi and Morbidelli had equally fortuitous runs to take fourth and fifth places. Comas and Beretta continued the Noah's Ark formation by bringing their Larrousse LH94s home in sixth and seventh, ahead of Hill. The sole surviving Williams had been consistently quick throughout the afternoon, setting second-fastest race lap to his team-mate Coulthard.

After the race, Gerhard was obviously suffused with delight. He referred to his satisfaction in ending Ferrari's barren spell since 1990, Maranello's longest-ever absence from the victory circle since the start of the official World Championship in 1950.

It was only a shame that such a popular success should be overshadowed by Verstappen's refuelling fire. In that connection, everybody breathed a collective sigh of relief that the consequences had not been more serious. But, for Benetton, there was still more conflict looming on the horizon.

FIA FORMULA ONE WORLD CHAMPIONSHIP ROUND 9

GROSSER PREIS VON DEUTSCHLAND

HOCKENHEIM
29-31 JULY 1994

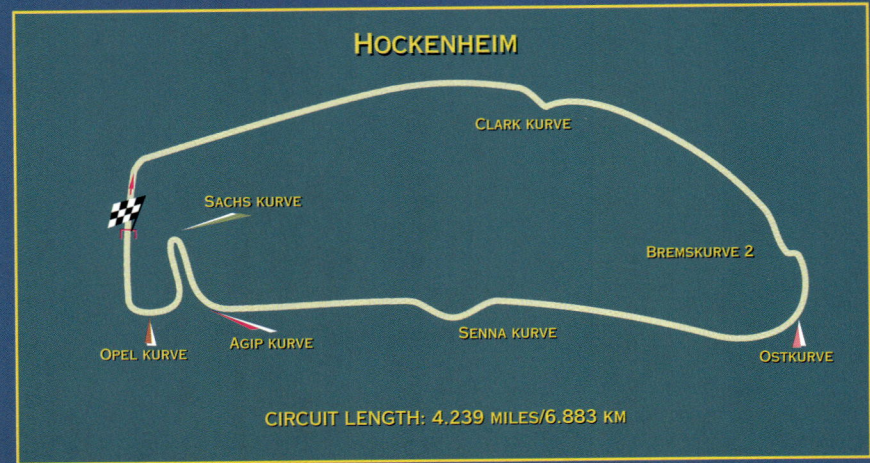

Race weather: Hot, some cloud

Place	Driver	Nat.	No.	Entrant	Car/Engine	Laps	Time/Retirement	Speed (mph/km/h)
1	Gerhard Berger	A	28	Scuderia Ferrari	Ferrari 412T1B 043 V12	45	1h 22m 37.272s	139.359/224.278
2	Olivier Panis	F	26	Ligier Gitanes Blondes	Ligier JS39B-Renault RS6A V10	45	1h 23m 32.051s	137.826/221.816
3	Eric Bernard	F	25	Ligier Gitanes Blondes	Ligier JS39B-Renault RS6A V10	45	1h 23m 42.314s	137.550/221.365
4	Christian Fittipaldi	BR	9	Footwork Ford	Footwork FA15-Ford HB V8	45	1h 23m 58.881s	137.099/220.641
5	Gianni Morbidelli	I	10	Footwork Ford	Footwork FA15-Ford HB V8	45	1h 24m 07.816s	136.849/220.239
6	Erik Comas	F	20	Tourtel Larrousse F1	Larrousse LH94-Ford HB V8	45	1h 24m 22.717s	136.450/219.595
7	Olivier Beretta	F	19	Tourtel Larrousse F1	Larrousse LH94-Ford HB V8	44		
8	Damon Hill	GB	0	Rothmans Williams Renault	Williams FW16B-Renault RS6B V10	44		
	Jean-Marc Gounon	F	32	MTV Simtek Ford	Simtek S941-Ford HB V8	39	Gearbox	
	David Brabham	AUS	31	MTV Simtek Ford	Simtek S941-Ford HB V8	37	Clutch	
	Michael Schumacher	D	5	Mild Seven Benetton Ford	Benetton B194-Ford Zetec-R V8	20	Engine	
	Martin Brundle	GB	8	Marlboro McLaren Peugeot	McLaren MP4/9-Peugeot A6 V10	19	Engine	
	David Coulthard	GB	2	Rothmans Williams Renault	Williams FW16B-Renault RS6B V10	17	Electrics	
	Jos Verstappen	NL	6	Mild Seven Benetton Ford	Benetton B194-Ford Zetec-R V8	15	Fire	
	Ukyo Katayama	J	3	Tyrrell	Tyrrell 022-Yamaha 0X10A V10	6	Throttle	
	Mark Blundell	GB	4	Tyrrell	Tyrrell 022-Yamaha 0X10A V10	0	Accident	
	Mika Häkkinen	SF	7	Marlboro McLaren Peugeot	McLaren MP4/9-Peugeot A6 V10	0	Accident	
	Alessandro Zanardi	I	11	Team Lotus	Lotus 109-Mugen Honda ZA5C V10	0	Accident	
	Johnny Herbert	GB	12	Team Lotus	Lotus 109-Mugen Honda ZA5C V10	0	Accident	
	Rubens Barrichello	BR	14	Sasol Jordan	Jordan 194-Hart 1035 V10	0	Accident	
	Eddie Irvine	GB	15	Sasol Jordan	Jordan 194-Hart 1035 V10	0	Accident	
	Pierluigi Martini	I	23	Minardi Scuderia Italia	Minardi M194-Ford HB V8	0	Accident	
	Michele Alboreto	I	24	Minardi Scuderia Italia	Minardi M194-Ford HB V8	0	Accident	
	Jean Alesi	F	27	Scuderia Ferrari	Ferrari 412T1B 043 V12	0	Electrics	
	Andrea de Cesaris	I	29	Sauber Mercedes	Sauber C13-Mercedes-Benz V10	0	Accident	
	Heinz-Harald Frentzen	D	30	Sauber Mercedes	Sauber C13-Mercedes-Benz V10	0	Accident	
DNQ	Paul Belmondo	F	33	Pacific Grand Prix Ltd	Pacific PR01-Ilmor 2175A V10			
DNQ	Bertrand Gachot	F	34	Pacific Grand Prix Ltd	Pacific PR01-Ilmor 2175A V10			

Fastest lap: Coulthard, on lap 11, 1m 46.211s, 143.700 mph/231.264 km/h.
Lap record: Michael Schumacher (Benetton B193B-Ford V8), 1m 41.859s, 150.060 mph/241.498 km/h (1993 on unrevised track).
All cars used Goodyear tyres

All results and data © FIA 1994

QUALIFYING 1

Damon Hill	1m 44.026s
Gerhard Berger	1m 44.616s
Michael Schumacher	1m 44.875s
Jean Alesi	1m 45.272s
David Coulthard	1m 45.477s
Mika Häkkinen	1m 45.487s
Mark Blundell	1m 45.814s
Eddie Irvine	1m 45.911s
Rubens Barrichello	1m 45.962s
Heinz-Harald Frentzen	1m 46.488s
Ukyo Katayama	1m 46.534s
Martin Brundle	1m 46.644s
Christian Fittipaldi	1m 47.150s
Eric Bernard	1m 47.531s
Alessandro Zanardi	1m 47.678s
Andrea de Cesaris	1m 47.745s
Gianni Morbidelli	1m 47.814s
Pierluigi Martini	1m 47.831s
Olivier Panis	1m 47.925s
Michele Alboreto	1m 48.402s
Johnny Herbert	1m 48.621s
Olivier Beretta	1m 48.681s
Erik Comas	1m 48.770s
Jean-Marc Gounon	1m 50.361s
David Brabham	1m 50.685s
Paul Belmondo	1m 51.916s
Bertrand Gachot	1m 52.839s
Jos Verstappen	40m 34.495s

Friday afernoon
Dry, hot, sunny

QUALIFYING 2

Gerhard Berger	1m 43.582s
Jean Alesi	1m 44.012s
Damon Hill	1m 44.131s
Michael Schumacher	1m 44.268s
Ukyo Katayama	1m 44.718s
David Coulthard	1m 45.146s
Mark Blundell	1m 45.474s
Mika Häkkinen	1m 45.878s
Heinz-Harald Frentzen	1m 45.893s
Rubens Barrichello	1m 45.939s
Eddie Irvine	1m 45.942s
Olivier Panis	1m 46.165s
Martin Brundle	1m 46.218s
Eric Bernard	1m 46.290s
Johnny Herbert	1m 46.630s
Gianni Morbidelli	1m 46.817s
Christian Fittipaldi	1m 47.102s
Andrea de Cesaris	1m 47.235s
Jos Verstappen	1m 47.316s
Pierluigi Martini	1m 47.402s
Alessandro Zanardi	1m 47.425s
Erik Comas	1m 48.229s
Michele Alboreto	1m 48.295s
David Brabham	1m 48.870s
Olivier Beretta	1m 48.875s
Jean-Marc Gounon	1m 49.204s
Paul Belmondo	1m 51.122s
Bertrand Gachot	1m 51.292s

Saturday afternoon
Dry, hot, sunny

WARM-UP

Michael Schumacher	1m 46.642s
Gerhard Berger	1m 46.721s
Damon Hill	1m 46.770s
David Coulthard	1m 46.996s
Martin Brundle	1m 47.126s
Eddie Irvine	1m 47.281s
Mika Häkkinen	1m 47.398s
Ukyo Katayama	1m 47.480s
Mark Blundell	1m 47.535s
Gianni Morbidelli	1m 48.050s
Rubens Barrichello	1m 48.146s
Jos Verstappen	1m 48.195s
Heinz-Harald Frentzen	1m 48.351s
Johnny Herbert	1m 48.448s
Andrea de Cesaris	1m 48.604s
Christian Fittipaldi	1m 48.940s
Jean Alesi	1m 49.145s
Pierluigi Martini	1m 49.273s
Alessandro Zanardi	1m 49.290s
Eric Bernard	1m 49.344s
Erik Comas	1m 49.355s
Michele Alboreto	1m 49.810s
Olivier Panis	1m 49.959s
Olivier Beretta	1m 50.345s
Jean-Marc Gounon	1m 51.283s
David Brabham	1m 51.396s

Sunday morning
Dry, hot, sunny

FASTEST LAPS

Driver	Time	Lap
David Coulthard	1m 46.211s	11
Damon Hill	1m 46.303s	9
Michael Schumacher	1m 47.103s	17
Gerhard Berger	1m 47.544s	12
Martin Brundle	1m 48.329s	11
Jos Verstappen	1m 49.219s	12
Olivier Panis	1m 49.253s	11
Eric Bernard	1m 49.459s	8
Ukyo Katayama	1m 49.966s	4
Gianni Morbidelli	1m 49.981s	12
Christian Fittipaldi	1m 49.982s	13
Erik Comas	1m 50.409s	9
Olivier Beretta	1m 50.466s	12
Jean-Marc Gounon	1m 52.023s	17
David Brabham	1m 52.364s	18

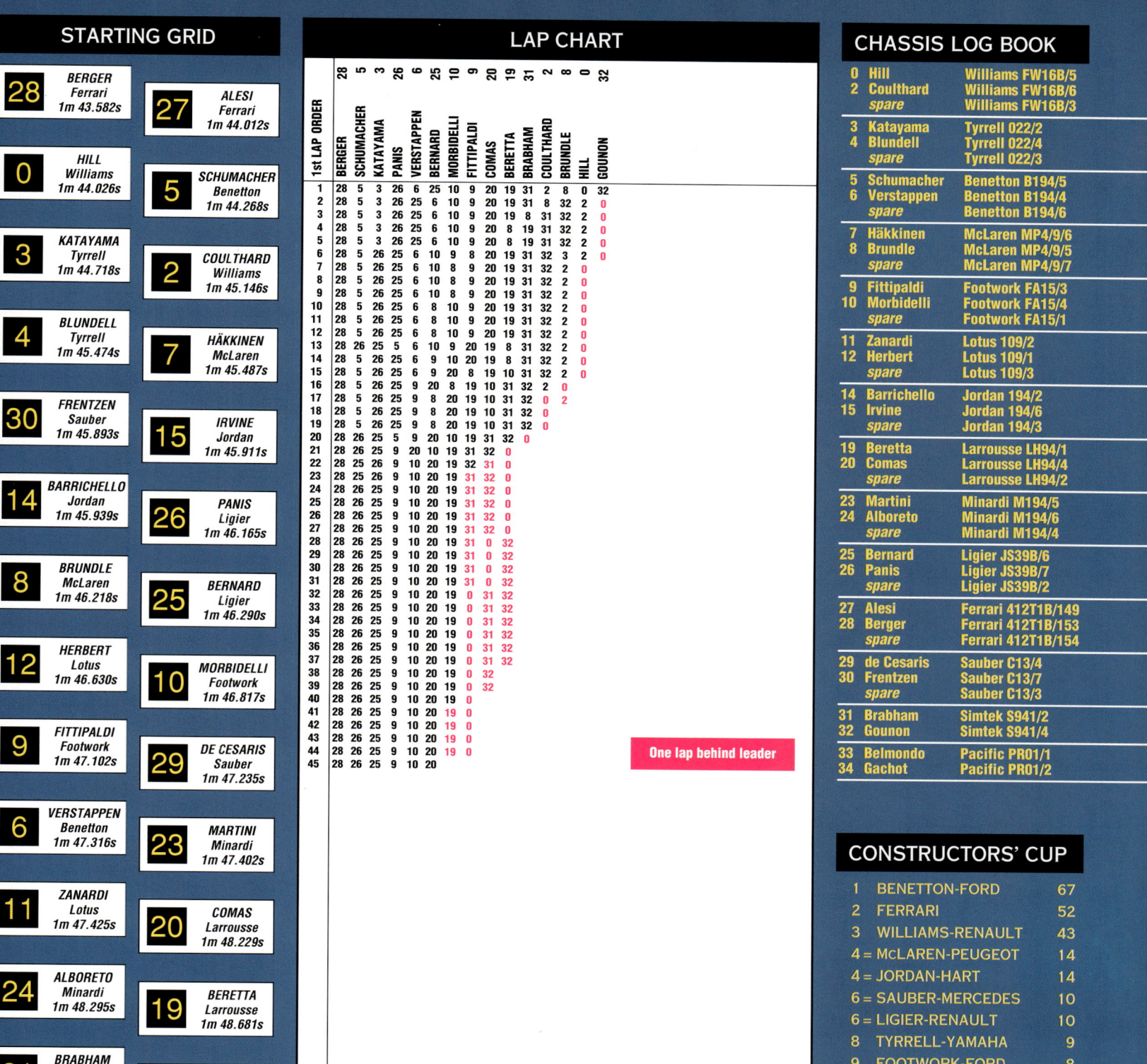

WORLD CHAMPIONSHIP • ROUND 10

HUNGARIAN GRAND PRIX

SCHUMACHER
HILL
VERSTAPPEN
BRUNDLE
BLUNDELL
PANIS

From the moment Michael Schumacher's Benetton swept round the outside of Damon Hill's Williams at the first corner of the race, the outcome of the Hungarian Grand Prix was never in doubt. However, in terms of tactics, the German star's seventh win of the season was one of his most accomplished. Schumacher was the firm pre-race favourite but a strategy which embraced three refuelling stops gave him an even more decisive edge over Hill's pursuing FW16B, the Londoner stopping only twice and losing far too much time bogged down in traffic as a consequence. Apart from restoring Schumacher to his winning ways after a two-race interregnum, the Hungaroring also yielded the best result yet for Benetton's wild and unpolished number two driver Jos Verstappen, who moved up to third place on the last lap when Martin Brundle's McLaren-Peugeot ground to a halt with alternator failure.

After the nightmare of Hockenheim, a podium finish was just the fillip Jos Verstappen needed. *Above:* The young Dutchman pulls into the garage reserved for the top three cars to be congratulated by winner Michael Schumacher and Benetton team boss Flavio Briatore. Meanwhile Damon Hill *(left)* took second place to keep his World Championship dream alive.

ENTRY AND PRACTICE

As Michael Schumacher set the pace during first qualifying at the Hungaroring, the F1 community was preoccupied with other matters. The race at the tortuous track near Budapest was taking place at the end of a week when it seemed as though the World Championship would finally be robbed of Monza after the Italian Grand Prix, scheduled for 11 September, had been formally removed from the F1 calendar.

The Italian Automobile Club had been unable to offer the required assurances that major safety improvements would be instigated for this year's race. Such work would, in the assessment of the organisers, involve the destruction of over one hundred trees, a course of action fiercely opposed by the influential environmental lobby in the regional government.

FIA President Max Mosley confirmed that the sport's governing body was now seeking an alternative venue at which to stage a replacement race. Germany's new Nürburgring and Donington Park, venue for the 1993 European Grand Prix, had been mentioned as possible candidates for the apparently vacant date.

There were, of course, two key factors to be kept in mind when considering this whole affair. The first was that nobody believed, even in their wildest dreams, that the Italian Grand Prix *would* be scrapped. Correctly, it was anticipated that a compromise would be reached. Italian Prime Minister Silvio Berlusconi intervened barely 24 hours after the FIA originally announced its cancellation to ensure that the oldest Grand Prix on the calendar would continue.

However, the second factor was that, wherever a race took place on 11 September, nobody expected Michael Schumacher to be taking part in it. The World Championship points leader still had to serve a two-race ban for ignoring the black flag at Silverstone. With his appeal against this sentence due to be heard at the end of August, the German driver had already mentally wiped the Italian and Portuguese events from his personal diary.

Thus the Benetton team leader had every incentive to win the Hungarian GP in a bid to strengthen his position in the points table. To that end, he started as he meant to continue by finishing the first session 0.2s ahead of his main rival, Damon Hill, the Williams number one in turn 0.7s in front of his team-mate David Coulthard.

'I must say that it's very nice to be back at the front,' said Schumacher. 'After all the problems the team has had recently, this is the best answer we can give to everyone.' Both Hill and Coulthard punctuated their sessions by spinning off the circuit, but while Hill confined his excursion to the slowing-down lap Coulthard's departure into a gravel trap was more permanent.

'I spun on the "in" lap because I was talking to the pits on the radio and just lost concentration,' explained Damon. 'I'm a little disappointed, because I felt I was having to work too much, but I'm on the front row, so I'm not too despondent. Traffic is a problem here, but given our improving form, I think Michael will have his plate full!'

Coulthard admitted that the task of acquainting himself with the Hungaroring was demanding every ounce of his concentration. 'On the whole, it's not the most enjoyable circuit, but it is certainly a challenging one,' he said. 'It is very difficult to learn – if you could image that your brain could breathe, a lap round here is as if you are holding your breath!

'As for the accident, I just made a mistake on the corner before the speed trap – I wanted to be quickest through there!'

Fourth place on the first day was well earned by Martin Brundle's McLaren MP4/9, the King's Lynn driver then having to relinquish his car to Philippe Alliot after the Frenchman spun off early in the session. Alliot, the McLaren team's Peugeot-supported test driver, was standing in for Mika Häkkinen after the Finn had received a one-race suspension for causing the first-corner multiple collision in the German Grand Prix.

By the end of Friday, the car shared by Brundle and Alliot was beginning to feel slightly down on power. Subsequent detailed examination revealed a slight loss of compression on one cylinder, requiring the installation of a fresh Peugeot V10 in time for Saturday morning. Alliot was clearly taking some time to become re-accustomed to the business of competitive F1 action and there is no doubt that, had it not been for the Peugeot link, Ron Dennis would never even have given him the time of day.

On Saturday morning, Hill managed to produce fastest time in the free practice session, just pipping Schumacher and Coulthard. Michael's Benetton lost a lot of time in the pits while the team carried out what was described as a suspension set-up change. As a result, he ran out of time and was unable to mount a counter-attack before the chequered flag was shown. Closer investigation revealed that the team had had an unexpected problem adjusting the suspension cross-weighting on Schumacher's car.

In the afternoon Schumacher had a quick spin on the second corner beyond the pits, openly admitting that he had made a mistake. 'My foot caught the brake pedal rather than the throttle,' he explained. 'That left me out on the dirty, wide line, and when that happens you've got no choice but to spin!'

However, Michael recovered from this setback to take pole position, with Hill more than half a second slower. The German paid tribute to the set-up work carried out by his team-mate Jos Verstappen during the morning session. It was just a shame that the Dutchman was unable to benefit from his own endeavours, having spun off into a tyre barrier early in the second qualifying session and damaged the rear of his Benetton beyond immediate repair. That slip dropped him to 12th in the final grid order.

Hill explained that he didn't manage to get clear laps on either of his first two runs and wasn't totally satisfied with his car's set-up. Coulthard consolidated his third place with a 1m 20.205s early in the session before spinning off again and hitting a tyre barrier on the downhill, outward leg of the circuit.

'I took it a little easy on my "out" lap as I didn't want to get held up in traffic,' he explained. 'As a result, I didn't warm up my rear tyres sufficiently and the car snapped away from me over a bump. It is just a shame that the barrier was in the way!'

Even so, it was an excellent effort for the young Scot to have gained third place on the grid – his best-ever qualifying position – for only his fifth Grand Prix.

Meanwhile, Ferrari came to the Hungaroring fully realising that the track's topography would stack the cards against a repeat of Gerhard Berger's Hockenheim success. On Friday, neither Berger nor Jean Alesi could work out a decent chassis balance, but the Austrian measurably improved this aspect of the car in second qualifying.

He qualified in a satisfactory fourth place, but reported that the V12 engine displayed poor throttle response out of the corners. By contrast, Jean Alesi was simply lost as far as chassis set-up was concerned, complaining that his car was bouncing around

---

Benetton called to account over refuelling irregularities

As if the lucky escape experienced by Jos Verstappen and the Benetton mechanics at Hockenheim were not disturbing enough in itself, the World Championship leaders found themselves plunged into even more controversy after the German Grand Prix when the team was summoned to appear before the World Motor Sport Council on 19 October to face a charge of having breached the F1 Technical Regulations.

Following a detailed examination of the refuelling rig used on Verstappen's car at Hockenheim, Intertechnique, the makers of the equipment, made a detailed report to the FIA. The governing body then made the following statement:

'The fuel spillage was caused by the fuel valve failing to close properly.

'The valve was slow to close due to the presence of a foreign body.

'The foreign body is believed to have reached the valve because a filter designed to eliminate the risk had been deliberately removed.'

However, the team countered by saying that Benetton Formula, having concluded the filter was unnecessary, removed it only with the full knowledge and permission of F1 Technical Delegate Charlie Whiting. According to Benetton, this permission was given on the afternoon of Thursday 28 July – the day before first qualifying at Hockenheim – to Benetton team manager Joan Villadelprat in the presence of Technical Director Ross Brawn. Needless to say, this allegation was robustly denied by both Whiting and the FIA.

Moreover, Benetton went very much on the defensive by producing an independent, specially commissioned report which identified significant design shortcomings in the FIA-approved refuelling rigs.

Produced by Accident and Failure Technical Analysis Ltd (AFTA), a specialist concern based in Camberley, Surrey, the report pointed to the risk of misalignment between the refuelling hose and the car and concluded that '[the system] lacks the integrity required in this sort of application'.

The report also emphasised that the Formula 1 motor racing environment inevitably created a conflict between speed and safety, making the challenge of refuelling an entirely different proposition from other forms of refuelling:

'With pressure refuelling, unlike gravity refuelling, in which the operator can normally see and have direct, immediate control over the flow of the fuel, no emergency action can be taken by the refueller if a problem arises and, indeed, he is only fully conscious of the problem when it is too late to take action.

'Clearly the present system is normally very fast, and consistent fast refuelling relies to a certain extent on luck,' concluded the document.

Rival teams regarded the report, however valid, as an irrelevance designed to deflect attention from the fact that Benetton would have been able to increase their refuelling flow rate by about 12.5 per cent by omitting the filter.

Benetton's position was not enhanced by claiming that 'the filter was introduced part way through the year in response to problems teams were having with debris entering the valve and the car.' A letter from Intertechnique, advising the teams that the new filter should be included, was written as early as 24 February, more than a month before the first race of the season.

However, that Intertechnique had been alerted to possible problems with their refuelling gear was made clear when engineers from the company arrived at the Hungaroring and began changing parts of the valves supplied to several other teams.

'We believe that the most likely cause of the Hockenheim fire was a faulty part in the Intertechnique refuelling valve,' continued the AFTA report. 'All of the same parts removed from the fuel valves of six different F1 teams had been found to have five times the operating clearance of the same part removed from Jos Verstappen's fuel rig.'

On the face of it, the wait until October for the charges against Benetton to be examined by the World Motor Sport Council seemed excessive. A final adjudication on this issue was clearly a matter of considerable urgency and it came as no surprise at all when the governing body announced it would reschedule the hearing for the Wednesday before the Italian Grand Prix, just over three weeks after the Hungarian race.

Despite worn shock absorbers, Mark Blundell eventually picked up fifth place for Tyrrell-Yamaha. *Left:* He leads Martin Brundle's McLaren in mid-race.

Below: Bare cheek! The hot weather encouraged light clothing but none perhaps so skimpy as this.

On the edge. Gerhard Berger's Ferrari *(bottom left)* kicks up the dirt in qualifying.

McLaren test driver Philippe Alliot, whose claims to a place in the team had been championed by Peugeot, at last had a chance to return to Grand Prix racing. In the event, the Frenchman (replacing the suspended Häkkinen for one race only) was no more than a midfield runner before engine maladies brought about his withdrawal.

HUNGARIAN GRAND PRIX

all over the place. He was dreadfully disappointed to end up a distant 13th overall.

Despite several spins over the two days of qualifying, Ukyo Katayama did a consistently impressive job to line up fifth in his Tyrrell-Yamaha. Mark Blundell was down in 11th, not complaining of any mechanical problems, but perhaps more acutely aware than ever of the impressive manner in which his Japanese team-mate has taken the initiative this season.

Brundle wound up sixth in the final grid order for McLaren, but his second qualifying session was not without its problems. He spun and stalled on the second corner after the pits, coming to rest with the car still in gear, and when the marshals attempted to move the MP4/9, they could not fathom out how to operate the external gearchange re-set control. The regulations decree that this control can only be activated by officials – not the driver – so the red flag came out while the car was removed. On his second run, Martin was plagued by traffic and locking brakes, so he did well to get onto the third row. Alliot, as expected, was well off the pace and faded to 14th in the final order.

Eddie Irvine again did a reliable job to qualify his Jordan-Hart seventh ahead of Heinz-Harald Frentzen's Sauber and the very promising Olivier Panis in the fast-improving Ligier JS39B. However, Rubens Barrichello damaged his Jordan's undertray, losing sufficient time to prevent him bettering tenth overall.

Pierluigi Martini lined up in 15th place, the Italian doing extremely well bearing in mind he was grappling to familiarise himself with his Minardi's newly installed semi-automatic gearchange. Languishing in 16th and 17th places, Christian Fittipaldi and Andrea de Cesaris were both deeply depressed about the poor handling of their Footwork and Sauber respectively, while Eric Bernard lost time with a gearbox problem in second qualifying and could manage only 18th place, the Ligier-Renault lining up ahead of Gianni Morbidelli's Footwork, Michele Alboreto's Minardi and the Larrousse of Erik Comas.

In the Lotus-Mugen camp, the type 109 was simply hopelessly outclassed on a circuit where its Japanese V10 engine did not have a straight worth the name on which to stretch its legs. Neither Alessandro Zanardi (22nd) nor Johnny Herbert (24th) could do anything to improve the situation and they finished the afternoon in an extremely dejected state of mind. For Herbert, in particular, the whole experience so sapped his morale that he began to think in terms of abandoning F1 altogether. 'I would rather race seriously in the British Touring Car Championship than just make up the numbers in F1,' he admitted.

David Brabham split the two Lotus men after a good showing with his Simtek S941, 23rd place being the best-ever qualifying position for the small Banbury-based team. Unfortunately, while Brabham was quite heartened by this showing, team-mate Jean-Marc Gounon had a persistent handling problem with his car, obliging the team to strip it down for a detailed check-over on the evening prior to the race. The Frenchman was a second slower than Olivier Beretta, who joined him on the last row of the grid, but comfortably ahead of the outclassed Pacific-Ilmors of Bertrand Gachot and Paul Belmondo.

RACE

Hill had been worried about his race set-up during the warm-up session on Sunday morning, in which he could manage only fifth-fastest time, but he made an absolutely terrific start to nose ahead of Schumacher as the pack sprinted for the first right-hander. But Michael knew full-well that if he took the outside line – just as Eddie Irvine had done on the first corner of the previous year's Japanese Grand Prix – he would be able to regain the advantage. He did just that, squeezing Damon in towards the apex, and the Benetton catapulted out of the corner ahead, on the outside and perfectly positioned to take the best line into the following left-hander.

Going into the second corner, the Jordan team found both its cars eliminated on the first lap for the second successive race. Irvine was running in fifth when Katayama attempted to run round the outside of his 194 going into the tricky, downhill left-hander – just as Barrichello aimed for the inside.

Inevitably, there just wasn't sufficient room for all three cars and they touched. The incident marked the end of the race for three drivers all of whom could have been expected to produce a decent performance in this gruelling event. Slightly less than two hours later, they were speculating

191

HUNGARIAN GRAND PRIX

Diary

Ferrari Sporting Director Jean Todt denies rumours that Nigel Mansell might rejoin the famous Italian team in 1995.

Williams concludes negotiations with Renault for continuation of engine supply arrangement for a further three seasons, 1995-97.

The Rahal-Hogan Indy Car team confirms that it will part company with its engine supplier, Honda, for 1995 after a series of consistently disappointing performances.

Indianapolis Motor Speedway chief Tony George announces new 1996 engine rules for the proposed breakaway Indy Racing League.

Ferrari team adviser Niki Lauda breaks three ribs in jet-ski accident off Ibiza.

Right: **Michael Schumacher eases his Benetton-Ford to yet another convincing victory as Martin Brundle unlaps himself in the McLaren-Peugeot. The unlucky Englishman was to suffer alternator failure on the last lap which dropped him from third place to fourth.**

After the dizzy heights of the podium at Hockenheim, Olivier Panis was back in more familiar midfield territory at the Hungaroring but earned another valuable point for the resurgent Ligier team.
Below: **The Frenchman leads David Coulthard and Heinz-Harald Frentzen.**

that they might indeed have all finished in the points!

At the end of the opening lap Schumacher was 0.97s ahead of Hill, with Coulthard third from Berger, Brundle and Olivier Panis's Ligier, the Frenchman having jumped the start but got away without penalty. In an incredible seventh place was Jean Alesi's Ferrari, the Frenchman having made up six places on his starting position after an amazing getaway from the seventh row.

For the first few laps, Hill steadied the gap to the leading Benetton, although the two leaders quickly began to ease away from Coulthard. By lap four the gap between the two Williams-Renaults was 4.4 seconds, and two laps later it was 6.9 seconds. It had expanded to 8.7s by lap eight and to 12.06s by lap ten. As the leading bunch settled down, a good battle began to brew up over sixth place, Panis coming under increasing pressure from Alesi as Frentzen, Verstappen and Blundell also moved in on the Ligier.

Midway round lap 13, Alesi pulled off an astonishingly audacious overtaking manoeuvre to get ahead of Panis, slipping inside the Ligier on a tricky medium-speed left-hander where passing had previously been regarded as a near-impossibility. Once clear of the French machine, he quickly began to close the gap on Brundle's fifth-placed McLaren.

Schumacher was 6.9 seconds ahead of Hill when he brought the Benetton in for a quick 7.5-second refuelling stop at the end of lap 17. He got back into the race only 16.6 seconds behind the Williams, and was now in a position to press home his advantage when Damon made the first of his two refuelling stops.

Hill was just over 11 seconds ahead when he made a 10.6-second stop at the end of lap 25, which dropped him back into second place ahead of Berger. In the meantime, Brundle had been in at the end of lap 19, dropping from fifth to 11th, and Coulthard called at his pit a lap later, the Williams slipping from third to sixth. But as all the front-runners completed their first pit stops, the leading positions settled down again.

Further back, Alliot's return to the F1 fold came to a halt at the end of lap 21 when his McLaren was signalled into the pits after the Peugeot engineers noticed that the engine temperature was rising ominously. He was running in 12th place at the time with the intention of completing the race with a single refuelling stop.

Although Hill was reluctant to criticise the Williams race strategy, a two-stop schedule simply did not work in the team's favour. Whether due to the lighter fuel load resulting from a three-stop strategy, more audacious driving or his Benetton's nimble handling in traffic, Schumacher sliced through the backmarkers far more decisively than his Williams rival.

Between laps 25 and 30, Hill lost an enormous 16 seconds to Schumacher. Lap times among the leading runners fluctuated wildly as slower cars got in their way. It was enormously frustrating for the quick men, but on the other hand you could see the problems faced by those being lapped. Once a car got off the racing line, the tyres picked up so much debris that it would take two or three further laps before they had cleaned up again.

By the end of lap 30, Schumacher and Hill were separated by half a minute, with Berger third ahead of Coulthard, Mark Blundell's Tyrrell-Yamaha and Brundle. Gerhard stopped for fuel at the end of lap 32, dropping back to seventh, leaving Brundle fourth from Alesi and Verstappen, Blundell immediately pulling in for his sole refuelling stop at the end of lap 33.

Schumacher made a second 8.1-second stop for fuel and tyres at the end of lap 37, resuming 15 seconds ahead of Hill, an advantage which the Williams driver had trimmed back to 12.1 seconds by the end of lap 42. But Schumacher was 16.1 seconds to the good by the end of lap 50, one lap before Hill, Alesi and Verstappen – running second, third and fourth – all came in for their second refuelling stops.

Coulthard, who had made his second stop at the end of lap 48, now moved back into third place. Hill was now around 45 seconds adrift of the leading Benetton, giving Schumacher plenty of leeway when it came to his third refuelling stop at the end of lap 58. He resumed 29.3 seconds ahead of Hill and the race was effectively over.

'The car was very good today,' said Schumacher after the race, 'although the circuit conditions changed quite a lot. Normally it gets faster as a coating of rubber goes down, but this time it got slower. But definitely the car was in good shape and I was pretty pleased with it.

'Three refuelling stops was certainly the right strategy, otherwise I wouldn't be here. In the beginning, there was pressure from Damon, but then, because of our different strategies, I managed to pull ahead.'

Hill frankly conceded that, prior to the race, he had suspected Benetton would go for a three-stop strategy. 'I kept the pressure on him up to a point, but then he started to slip

away and it became apparent that he was in fact going to stop three times.

'Then I pushed hard, thinking we were in with a chance, but in the traffic you just lose huge chunks. I found when I had fuller tanks I was not able to pass some people on the straight, so that was something of a failing with our strategy. My car behaved fantastically; I was really happy with its balance, but I just wasn't able to match the pace.

'Some people were particularly unco-operative, but it was the same for Michael too. He drove a fantastic race – this was always going to be a good one for Benetton – but I would say that the championship is not over yet!'

Hill's second place saved the day for Williams after his team-mate Coulthard crashed on lap 60 while running in a strong third place, albeit under increasing pressure from Brundle's McLaren.

'I just lost control of the car on the exit of a third-gear right-hander,' shrugged the young Scot. 'I don't know why. Maybe I touched a bump, but the next thing I knew I was spinning backwards into a barrier. The track conditions were very bad.'

That seemingly left Brundle a clear run through to the remaining place on the podium, but about seven laps from the finish he noticed his engine temperature begin to rise alarmingly. With a couple of laps to go all the warning lights came on in the cockpit, the MP4/9 finally grinding to a halt with alternator failure on the very last lap.

Ironically, Martin would not have been robbed of his seemingly secure third place had Schumacher not slowed dramatically in the closing stages, allowing the Englishman to unlap himself. As it was, Jos Verstappen took the place after his most convincing performance to date.

'There was no reason for me to push hard,' reflected Schumacher, 'so I was happy to let Martin by. Then I began to wonder how far behind Jos was and the team told me it was about nine seconds.

'Obviously, if they both unlapped themselves, they would have to do one more lap, to go the full distance, so I slowed right down to let Jos through too. It wasn't that I wanted anything to happen to Martin, but it gave Jos the chance to pick up a position if it did. And that was how it worked out!'

Behind Verstappen, Brundle was classified fourth ahead of Blundell's Tyrrell, which just managed to fend off Panis's Ligier by 0.1s in a frantic sprint to the chequered flag. After the second refuelling stop, Blundell was troubled by worn shock absorbers which made his car's ride over the bumps particularly lively and he was worried that Panis's team-mate Eric Bernard, who was running in front of them, a lap down, might attempt to influence the outcome of the contest.

Neither Ferrari made it to the finish. Alesi was holding fifth place ahead of Verstappen on lap 59 when he retired with gearbox troubles, while Berger lasted until five laps from the end. Then also running fifth, and closing on Verstappen, he rolled to a halt when his V12's pneumatic air valve system began to leak.

Michele Alboreto thus finished seventh for Minardi ahead of Larrousse duo Comas and Beretta, the latter hampered by discomfort from a wrenched shoulder sustained when he removed a tear-off visor from the front of his helmet. Tenth was Bernard's Ligier with David Brabham a gallant 11th despite suffering from severe stomach cramps from about one-quarter distance. Berger was classified 12th, ahead of Alessandro Zanardi and Christian Fittipaldi, who had stopped with gearbox trouble after 69 laps.

For Schumacher, his Hungaroring success represented a welcome return to the top spot on the rostrum for the first time since the French Grand Prix at Magny-Cours. Yet, despite this victory, Benetton still had many problems to deal with over the next few weeks which threatened to compromise the team's title aspirations.

FIA FORMULA ONE WORLD CHAMPIONSHIP ROUND 10

HUNGARIAN GRAND PRIX
BUDAPEST
12-14 AUGUST 1994

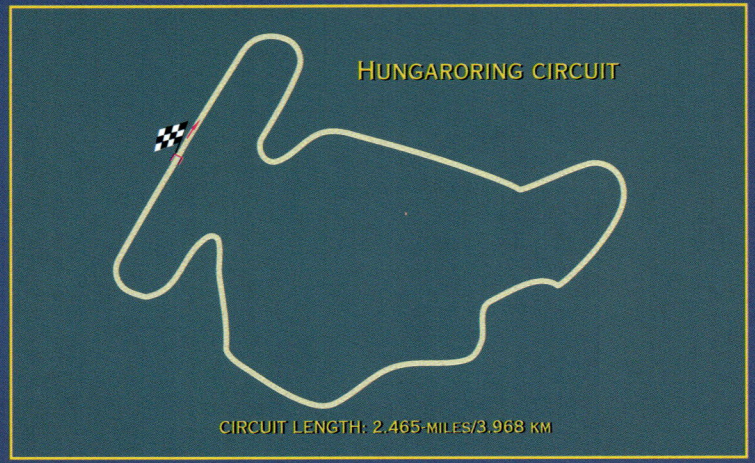

HUNGARORING CIRCUIT
CIRCUIT LENGTH: 2.465 MILES/3.968 KM

RACE WEATHER: HOT, DRY, SUNNY

Place	Driver	Nat.	No.	Entrant	Car/Engine	Laps	Time/Retirement	Speed (mph/km/h)
1	Michael Schumacher	D	5	Mild Seven Benetton Ford	Benetton B194-Ford Zetec-R V8	77	1h 48m 00.185s	105.470/169.193
2	Damon Hill	GB	0	Rothmans Williams Renault	Williams FW16B-Renault RS6B V10	77	1h 48m 21.012s	105.132/169.193
3	Jos Verstappen	NL	6	Mild Seven Benetton Ford	Benetton B194-Ford Zetec-R V8	77	1h 49m 10.514s	104.337/167.915
4	Martin Brundle	GB	8	Marlboro McLaren Peugeot	McLaren MP4/9-Peugeot A6 V10	76	Engine	
5	Mark Blundell	GB	4	Tyrrell	Tyrrell 022-Yamaha OX10A V10	76		
6	Olivier Panis	F	26	Ligier Gitanes Blondes	Ligier JS39B-Renault RS6A V10	76		
7	Michele Alboreto	I	24	Minardi Scuderia Italia	Minardi M194-Ford HB V8	75		
8	Erik Comas	F	20	Tourtel Larrousse F1	Larrousse LH94-Ford HB V8	75		
9	Olivier Beretta	F	19	Tourtel Larrousse F1	Larrousse LH94-Ford HB V8	75		
10	Eric Bernard	F	25	Ligier Gitanes Blondes	Ligier JS39B-Renault RS6A V10	75		
11	David Brabham	AUS	31	MTV Simtek Ford	Simtek S941-Ford HB V8	74		
12	Gerhard Berger	A	28	Scuderia Ferrari	Ferrari 412T1B 043 V12	72	Engine	
13	Alessandro Zanardi	I	11	Team Lotus	Lotus 109-Mugen Honda ZA5C	72		
14	Christian Fittipaldi	BR	9	Footwork Ford	Footwork FA15-Ford HB V8	69	Gearbox	
	David Coulthard	GB	2	Rothmans Williams Renault	Williams FW16B-Renault RS6B V10	59	Accident	
	Jean Alesi	F	27	Scuderia Ferrari	Ferrari 412T1B 043 V12	58	Gearbox	
	Pierluigi Martini	I	23	Minardi Scuderia Italia	Minardi M194-Ford HB V8	58	Spun off	
	Heinz-Harald Frentzen	D	30	Sauber Mercedes	Sauber C13-Mercedes-Benz V10	39	Gearbox	
	Johnny Herbert	GB	12	Team Lotus	Lotus 109-Mugen Honda ZA5C V10	34	Electrics	
	Andrea de Cesaris	I	29	Sauber Mercedes	Sauber C13-Mercedes-Benz V10	30	Collision with Morbidelli	
	Gianni Morbidelli	I	10	Footwork Ford	Footwork FA15-Ford HB V8	30	Collision with de Cesaris	
	Philippe Alliot	F	7	Marlboro McLaren Peugeot	McLaren MP4/9-Peugeot A6 V10	21	Engine	
	Jean-Marc Gounon	F	32	MTV Simtek Ford	Simtek S941-Ford HB V8	9	Handling	
	Ukyo Katayama	J	3	Tyrrell	Tyrrell 022-Yamaha OX10A V10	0	Accident	
	Rubens Barrichello	BR	14	Sasol Jordan	Jordan 194-Hart 1035 V10	0	Accident	
	Eddie Irvine	GB	15	Sasol Jordan	Jordan 194-Hart 1035 V10	0	Accident	
DNQ	Bertrand Gachot	F	34	Pacific Grand Prix Ltd	Pacific PR01-Ilmor 2175A V10			
DNQ	Paul Belmondo	F	33	Pacific Grand Prix Ltd	Pacific PR01-Ilmor 2175A V10			

Fastest lap: Schumacher, on lap 5, 1m 20.881s, 109.743 mph/176.615 km/h.
Lap record: Nigel Mansell (F1 Williams FW14B-Renault V10), 1m 18.308s, 113.349 mph/182.418 km/h (1992).
All cars used Goodyear tyres.

All results and data © FIA 1994

QUALIFYING 1

Michael Schumacher	1m 19.479s
Damon Hill	1m 19.700s
David Coulthard	1m 20.395s
Martin Brundle	1m 20.819s
Gerhard Berger	1m 21.009s
Jos Verstappen	**1m 21.141s**
Jean Alesi	1m 21.280s
Eddie Irvine	1m 21.406s
Rubens Barrichello	1m 21.498s
Mark Blundell	1m 21.731s
Ukyo Katayama	1m 21.877s
Heinz-Harald Frentzen	1m 22.268s
Gianni Morbidelli	**1m 22.311s**
Christian Fittipaldi	1m 22.375s
Michele Alboreto	1m 22.379s
Erik Comas	1m 22.754s
Philippe Alliot	1m 22.915s
Olivier Panis	1m 23.244s
Eric Bernard	1m 23.269s
Johnny Herbert	1m 23.306s
Alessandro Zanardi	1m 23.361s
Andrea de Cesaris	1m 23.573s
David Brabham	1m 24.181s
Pierluigi Martini	1m 24.440s
Olivier Beretta	1m 24.645s
Bertrand Gachot	1m 26.521s
Jean-Marc Gounon	1m 26.678s
Paul Belmondo	1m 28.334s

Friday afternoon
Dry, warm, overcast

QUALIFYING 2

Michael Schumacher	1m 18.258s
Damon Hill	1m 18.824s
David Coulthard	1m 20.205s
Gerhard Berger	1m 20.219s
Ukyo Katayama	1m 20.232s
Martin Brundle	1m 20.629s
Eddie Irvine	1m 20.698s
Heinz-Harald Frentzen	1m 20.858s
Olivier Panis	1m 20.929s
Rubens Barrichello	1m 20.952s
Mark Blundell	1m 20.984s
Jean Alesi	1m 21.206s
Philippe Alliot	1m 21.498s
Pierluigi Martini	1m 21.837s
Christian Fittipaldi	1m 21.873s
Andrea de Cesaris	1m 21.946s
Eric Bernard	1m 22.038s
Michele Alboreto	1m 22.379s
Erik Comas	1m 22.487s
Alessandro Zanardi	1m 22.513s
David Brabham	1m 22.614s
Johnny Herbert	1m 22.705s
Olivier Beretta	1m 22.899s
Jean-Marc Gounon	1m 24.191s
Bertrand Gachot	1m 24.908s
Paul Belmondo	1m 26.275s
Gianni Morbidelli	1m 30.262s
Jos Verstappen	9m 03.939s

Saturday afternoon
Dry, hot, sunny

WARM-UP

Michael Schumacher	1m 20.502s
David Coulthard	1m 21.321s
Martin Brundle	1m 21.376s
Gerhard Berger	1m 21.557s
Damon Hill	1m 21.615s
Heinz-Harald Frentzen	1m 21.672s
Ukyo Katayama	1m 21.974s
Rubens Barrichello	1m 22.045s
Olivier Panis	1m 22.061s
Jos Verstappen	1m 22.217s
Eddie Irvine	1m 22.325s
Christian Fittipaldi	1m 22.354s
Andrea de Cesaris	1m 22.447s
Michele Alboreto	1m 22.592s
Pierluigi Martini	1m 22.644s
Jean Alesi	1m 22.750s
Philippe Alliot	1m 22.778s
Gianni Morbidelli	1m 22.804s
Eric Bernard	1m 23.307s
Mark Blundell	1m 23.355s
Erik Comas	1m 23.539s
Johnny Herbert	1m 23.582s
Alessandro Zanardi	1m 24.101s
Olivier Beretta	1m 24.390s
David Brabham	1m 24.484s
Jean-Marc Gounon	1m 25.898s

Sunday morning
Dry, hot, sunny

FASTEST LAPS

Driver	Time	Lap
Michael Schumacher	1m 20.881s	5
Damon Hill	1m 21.520s	6
David Coulthard	1m 22.471s	12
Gerhard Berger	1m 22.490s	5
Martin Brundle	1m 22.739s	45
Jos Verstappen	1m 23.021s	45
Jean Alesi	1m 23.023s	44
Olivier Panis	1m 23.466s	5
Heinz-Harald Frentzen	1m 23.509s	7
Michele Alboreto	1m 23.697s	44
Christian Fittipaldi	1m 23.909s	63
Mark Blundell	1m 23.964s	25
Erik Comas	1m 24.012s	43
Olivier Beretta	1m 24.130s	21
Pierluigi Martini	1m 24.146s	28
Eric Bernard	1m 24.442s	57
Philippe Alliot	1m 24.609s	15
Andrea de Cesaris	1m 24.686s	15
Gianni Morbidelli	1m 24.704s	17
David Brabham	1m 25.137s	12
Alessandro Zanardi	1m 25.151s	60
Johnny Herbert	1m 25.850s	9
Jean-Marc Gounon	1m 26.616s	5

STARTING GRID

Pos	No	Driver	Team	Time
1	5	SCHUMACHER	Benetton	1m 18.258s
2	0	HILL	Williams	1m 18.824s
3	2	COULTHARD	Williams	1m 20.205s
4	28	BERGER	Ferrari	1m 20.219s
5	3	KATAYAMA	Tyrrell	1m 20.232s
6	8	BRUNDLE	McLaren	1m 20.629s
7	15	IRVINE	Jordan	1m 20.698s
8	30	FRENTZEN	Sauber	1m 20.858s
9	26	PANIS	Ligier	1m 20.929s
10	14	BARRICHELLO	Jordan	1m 20.952s
11	4	BLUNDELL	Tyrrell	1m 20.984s
12	6	VERSTAPPEN	Benetton	1m 21.141s
13	27	ALESI	Ferrari	1m 21.206s
14	7	ALLIOT	McLaren	1m 21.498s
15	23	MARTINI	Minardi	1m 21.837s
16	9	FITTIPALDI	Footwork	1m 21.873s
17	29	DE CESARIS	Sauber	1m 21.946s
18	25	BERNARD	Ligier	1m 22.038s
19	10	MORBIDELLI	Footwork	1m 22.311s
20	24	ALBORETO	Minardi	1m 22.379s
21	20	COMAS	Larrousse	1m 22.487s
22	11	ZANARDI	Lotus	1m 22.513s
23	31	BRABHAM	Simtek	1m 22.614s
24	12	HERBERT	Lotus	1m 22.705s
25	19	BERETTA	Larrousse	1m 22.899s
26	32	GOUNON	Simtek	1m 24.191s

NON-STARTERS

- DNQ — 34 GACHOT, Pacific, 1m 24.908s
- DNQ — 33 BELMONDO, Pacific, 1m 26.275s

LAP CHART

1st Lap Order	SCHUMACHER 5	HILL 0	COULTHARD 2	BERGER 28	BRUNDLE 8	PANIS 26	ALESI 27	FRENTZEN 30	VERSTAPPEN 6	BLUNDELL 4	MARTINI 23	ALLIOT 7	DE CESARIS 29	ALBORETO 24	COMAS 20	MORBIDELLI 10	BRABHAM 31	BERNARD 25	HERBERT 12	FITTIPALDI 9	BERETTA 19	GOUNON 32	ZANARDI 11
1	5	0	2	28	8	26	27	30	6	4	23	7	29	24	20	10	31	25	12	9	19	32	11
2	5	0	2	28	8	26	27	30	6	4	23	7	29	24	20	10	31	25	12	9	19	32	11
3	5	0	2	28	8	26	27	30	6	4	23	7	29	24	20	10	31	12	25	9	19	32	11
4	5	0	2	28	8	26	27	30	6	4	23	7	29	24	20	10	31	12	25	9	19	32	11
5	5	0	2	28	8	26	27	30	6	4	23	7	29	24	20	10	31	12	25	9	19	32	11
6	5	0	2	28	8	26	27	30	6	4	23	7	29	24	20	10	31	12	25	9	19	32	11
7	5	0	2	28	8	26	27	30	6	4	23	7	29	24	20	10	31	12	25	9	19	32	11
8	5	0	2	28	8	26	27	30	6	4	23	7	29	24	20	10	31	12	25	9	19	32	11
9	5	0	2	28	8	26	27	30	6	4	23	7	29	24	20	10	31	12	25	9	19	32	11
10	5	0	2	28	8	26	27	30	6	4	23	7	29	24	20	10	31	12	25	9	19	32	11
11	5	0	2	28	8	26	27	30	6	4	23	7	29	24	20	10	31	12	25	9	19	32	11
12	5	0	2	28	8	26	27	30	6	4	23	7	29	24	20	10	31	12	25	9	19	32	11
13	5	0	2	28	8	26	27	30	6	4	23	7	29	24	20	10	31	12	25	9	19	32	11
14	5	0	2	28	8	26	27	30	6	4	23	7	29	24	20	10	31	12	25	9	19	32	11
15	5	0	2	28	8	26	27	30	6	4	23	7	29	24	20	10	31	12	25	9	19	32	11
16	5	0	2	28	8	26	27	30	6	4	23	7	29	24	20	10	31	12	25	9	19	32	11
17	0	5	28	8	26	27	30	6	4	23	7	24	10	31	12	25	9	19	29	20	11		
18	0	5	28	8	26	27	30	6	4	23	7	24	10	31	12	25	9	19	29	20	11		
19	0	5	2	28	27	26	30	6	4	23	8	24	10	31	12	9	29	20	25	19	11		
20	0	5	2	28	26	30	6	4	23	8	7	24	10	12	9	29	20	25	19	11			
21	0	5	28	26	2	30	6	4	23	8	24	7	12	9	29	20	10	25	19	11			
22	0	5	28	27	26	2	30	6	4	23	8	24	31	12	9	20	29	10	19	11			
23	0	5	28	27	26	2	30	6	4	23	8	24	31	12	9	20	29	10	19	11			
24	0	5	28	27	26	2	30	4	6	23	8	24	31	12	9	20	29	10	25	19	11		
25	0	5	28	26	2	30	4	6	23	8	7	24	31	12	9	20	10	25	19	11			
26	0	5	28	26	2	4	26	23	7	24	20	12	9	20	10	25	19	11					
27	5	0	28	2	4	8	26	27	6	23	24	20	12	9	20	10	25	19	11				
28	5	0	28	2	4	8	27	26	6	23	24	12	9	20	10	25	19	11					
29	5	0	28	2	4	8	27	6	26	23	24	12	9	20	10	25	19	11					
30	5	0	28	2	4	8	27	6	26	30	24	9	20	29	10	25	19	31	11				
31	5	0	28	2	4	8	27	6	26	23	24	12	9	20	25	19	31	11					
32	5	0	28	2	4	8	27	6	26	23	24	12	9	20	25	19	31	11					
33	5	0	2	8	27	6	26	23	4	24	12	9	20	25	19	31	11						
34	5	0	2	8	27	6	28	23	4	24	12	9	20	25	19	31	11						
35	5	0	2	8	27	6	26	4	23	24	9	20	25	19	31	11							
36	5	0	2	8	27	6	26	4	23	24	9	20	25	19	31	11							
37	5	0	2	8	27	6	26	30	4	24	20	25	19	9	11								
38	5	0	2	8	27	6	26	30	4	24	20	19	31	9	25	11							
39	5	0	2	8	27	6	26	30	23	4	24	20	19	31	9	25	11						
40	5	0	2	8	27	6	26	23	4	24	20	19	31	9	11								
41	5	0	2	8	27	6	26	23	4	24	20	9	19	25	11								
42	5	0	2	8	27	6	26	28	4	24	20	9	19	25	11								
43	5	0	2	8	27	6	26	23	4	24	20	19	25	11									
44	5	0	2	8	27	6	26	23	4	24	19	25	11										
45	5	0	2	8	27	6	26	23	4	24	19	25	11										
46	5	0	2	8	27	6	26	28	23	4	24	19	25	11									
47	5	0	2	27	8	6	26	28	23	4	19	25	11										
48	5	27	2	6	26	28	23	4	19	25	11												
49	5	0	27	2	6	28	23	4	19	25	11												
50	5	0	27	6	2	28	4	26	23	24	20	19	25	11									
51	5	0	27	6	2	28	4	26	24	20	9	19	25	31	11								
52	5	0	2	27	6	28	4	26	24	20	9	19	25	31	11								
53	5	0	2	27	6	28	4	26	24	20	9	19	25	31	11								
54	5	0	2	27	6	28	4	26	24	20	9	19	25	31	11								
55	5	0	2	27	6	28	4	26	24	20	9	19	25	31	11								
56	5	0	2	27	6	28	4	26	24	20	9	19	25	31	11								
57	5	0	2	27	6	28	4	26	24	20	9	19	25	31	11								
58	5	0	2	27	6	28	4	26	24	20	9	19	25	31	11								
59	5	0	6	28	4	26	24	20	9	19	25	31	11										
60	5	0	6	28	4	26	24	20	9	19	25	31	11										
61	5	0	6	28	4	26	24	20	9	19	25	31	11										
62	5	0	6	28	4	26	24	20	19	25	31	11											
63	5	0	6	28	4	26	24	20	19	25	31	11											
64	5	0	8	6	28	4	26	24	20	19	25	31	11										
65	5	0	8	6	28	4	26	24	20	19	25	31	11										
66	5	0	8	6	28	4	26	24	20	19	25	31	11										
67	5	0	8	6	28	4	26	24	20	19	25	31	11										
68	5	0	8	6	28	4	26	24	20	19	25	31	11										
69	5	0	8	6	28	4	26	24	20	19	25	31	11										
70	5	0	8	6	28	4	26	24	20	19	25	31	11										
71	5	0	8	6	28	4	26	24	19	25	31	11											
72	5	0	8	6	28	4	26	24	19	25	31	11											
73	5	0	8	6	4	26	24	20	19	25	31												
74	5	0	8	6	4	26	24	20	19	25	31												
75	5	0	8	6	4	26	24	20	19	25													
76	5	0	6	4	26																		
77	5	0	6																				

One lap behind leader (shown in pink)

RACE DISTANCE: 77 LAPS, 189.850 MILES / 305.536 KM

Points tables subject to outcome of appeal by Benetton and Michael Schumacher

CHASSIS LOG BOOK

No	Driver	Chassis
0	Hill	Williams FW16B/5
2	Coulthard	Williams FW16B/6
	spare	Williams FW16B/3
3	Katayama	Tyrrell 022/2
4	Blundell	Tyrrell 022/4
	spare	Tyrrell 022/3
5	Schumacher	Benetton B194/8
6	Verstappen	Benetton B194/6
	spare	Benetton B194/4
7	Alliot	McLaren MP4/9/4
8	Brundle	McLaren MP4/9/6
	spare	McLaren MP4/9/7
9	Fittipaldi	Footwork FA15/3
10	Morbidelli	Footwork FA15/2
	spare	Footwork FA15/1
11	Zanardi	Lotus 109/2
12	Herbert	Lotus 109/1
	spare	Lotus 107C/3
14	Barrichello	Jordan 194/2
15	Irvine	Jordan 194/6
	spare	Jordan 194/5
19	Beretta	Larrousse LH94/1
20	Comas	Larrousse LH94/4
	spare	Larrousse LH94/2
23	Martini	Minardi M194/5
24	Alboreto	Minardi M194/6
	spare	Minardi M194/4
25	Bernard	Ligier JS39B/6
26	Panis	Ligier JS39B/7
	spare	Ligier JS39B/2
27	Alesi	Ferrari 412T1B/154
28	Berger	Ferrari 412T1B/153
	spare	Ferrari 412T1B/149
29	de Cesaris	Sauber C13/5
30	Frentzen	Sauber C13/7
	spare	Sauber C13/3
31	Brabham	Simtek S941/2
32	Gounon	Simtek S941/4
33	Belmondo	Pacific PR01/1
34	Gachot	Pacific PR01/2

CONSTRUCTORS' CUP

Pos	Team	Points
1	BENETTON-FORD	81
2	FERRARI	52
3	WILLIAMS-RENAULT	49
4	McLAREN-PEUGEOT	17
5	JORDAN-HART	14
6=	LIGIER-RENAULT	11
6=	TYRRELL-YAMAHA	11
8	SAUBER-MERCEDES	10
9	FOOTWORK-FORD	8
10	MINARDI-FORD	5
11	LARROUSSE-FORD	2

FOR THE RECORD

First Grand Prix points
Jos Verstappen

DRIVERS' POINTS

Pos	Driver	Points
1	SCHUMACHER	76
2	HILL	45
3	BERGER	27
4	ALESI	19
5	BARRICHELLO	10
6	BRUNDLE	9
7	HÄKKINEN	8
8	PANIS	7
9=	BLUNDELL	6
9=	FITTIPALDI	6
12=	LARINI	5
12=	FRENTZEN	5
14=	KATAYAMA	4
14=	BERNARD	4
14=	COULTHARD	4
14=	DE CESARIS	4
14=	MARTINI	4
14=	VERSTAPPEN	4
14=	WENDLINGER	4
20=	COMAS	2
20=	MORBIDELLI	2
22=	ALBORETO	1
22=	IRVINE	1
22=	LEHTO	1

WORLD CHAMPIONSHIP • ROUND 11

BELGIAN GRAND PRIX

HILL*
HÄKKINEN*
VERSTAPPEN*
COULTHARD*
BLUNDELL*
MORBIDELLI*
*SCHUMACHER dsq

Michael Schumacher and the Benetton team were sent reeling by another body-blow when they were stripped of their dominant victory in the Belgian Grand Prix following hours of deliberation in the scrutineering bay after the race. Schumacher had finished the afternoon having apparently extended his World Championship lead to a near-unassailable 35 points over Damon Hill, whose Williams had trailed him home in second place by almost 14 seconds. Yet just over five hours later that margin was slashed to a mere 21 points as the German driver became the first competitor to fall foul of F1's recently implemented 10 mm stepped undertray rules. That handed Hill his third win of the season ahead of Mika Häkkinen's McLaren MP4/9 and the other Benetton B194 of Jos Verstappen, which sailed through postrace scrutineering without a hitch. Once again, Williams's new recruit David Coulthard returned an outstandingly impressive performance, running ahead of Hill in second place for many laps before a wobbling rear wing caused his FW16B to be called in for a precautionary check. He eventually finished fourth ahead of Mark Blundell's Tyrrell-Yamaha and Gianni Morbidelli's Footwork after Schumacher's exclusion.

Putting a brave face on it. A crushing win for Michael Schumacher that extended the German's World Championship lead to 35 points left runner-up Damon Hill *(right)* with little real cause for celebration. Five hours later, however, the Benetton driver was disqualified, the victory was awarded to Hill and the position looked a lot more promising.

BELGIAN GRAND PRIX

Schumacher and Benetton: the latest crisis

Michael Schumacher and the Benetton team were well satisfied with their achievement in winning the Belgian Grand Prix so decisively, and when the stewards finally announced the German driver's exclusion from the race — more than five hours after the chequered flag had fallen — their response was one of total disbelief.

The winning Benetton was excluded because the 10 mm skidblock beneath the car — manufactured from a wood-composite material called Jabroc — was worn to a minimum of 7.4 mm at one point a short distance behind the leading edge of the block. This, contended the FIA, was consistent with repeated contact against the track surface and was not — as Benetton argued — a result of Schumacher's lap 19 spin on the plunging Pouhon left-hander.

The regulations relating to the stepped undertrays, introduced for the German Grand Prix, enable the race stewards to disregard the 10 per cent wear rule if they are satisfied that the damage was sustained in an accident. In that event, they can fall back on a requirement that the skidblock retain 90 per cent of its original weight, which the Benetton 'plank' conformed with on this occasion.

However, although the stewards accepted that there was transverse damage to the rear end of the skidblock, which they accepted could have been sustained when the Benetton spun over the kerb, they refused to accept that the main area of damage was caused by this incident. Moreover, they also claimed that the kerb concerned was completely smooth, a view disproved by Benetton at the subsequent appeal hearing.

Benetton's Technical Director Ross Brawn energetically denied that the team had been cheating, even though this was the Ford works team's fourth brush with the rulemakers so far in 1994.

'This is my third season with Benetton,' he said indignantly. 'I don't think it has ever been guilty of any infringement. Why didn't we do any cheating last year? We don't suddenly start cheating, particularly with the performance advantage and the driver we've got.'

Two days after the Belgian Grand Prix, Schumacher had more bad news when the FIA International Court of Appeal upheld his two-race ban for ignoring the black flag at Silverstone. He would be forced to sit out the Italian and Portuguese races — while the FIA now prepared to adjudicate on Benetton's alleged tampering with the refuelling equipment and its appeal against the Spa disqualification in the week immediately preceding the Monza event.

ENTRY AND PRACTICE

Brazilian prodigy Rubens Barrichello rounded off Friday's first qualifying session for the Belgian Grand Prix at Spa with a perfectly judged final run on a rapidly drying track to gain what seemed likely to be no more than a temporary pole position. Gambling on a late change from rain tyres to slicks at precisely the right moment, Barrichello — currently the youngest driver in the F1 game — edged out championship points leader Michael Schumacher's Benetton. It was a brilliant piece of strategic opportunism on the part of the Jordan squad and Rubens handled the tricky conditions to perfection on what remained one of the most demanding circuits in the business, despite its temporary emasculation by the incorporation of a slow chicane at the classic Eau Rouge corner.

Uncharacteristically, Schumacher had a quick spin as he struggled to match Barrichello's time, blaming himself for incorrectly adjusting the brake balance on his B194, but still finished the first day a couple of tenths clear of Damon Hill's Williams FW16B, with the other Jordan of Eddie Irvine in fourth place. Barrichello then firmly crossed his fingers, hoping that the heavy showers forecast for the rest of the weekend would keep conditions wet for Saturday's second qualifying.

'This was a nice surprise,' he admitted. 'If it's dry on Saturday, I may not stay on pole, so I'm just going to pray tonight that lots of rain comes!'

As things transpired, Barrichello's wishes would be granted. Torrential rain continued to douse the Belgian circuit for most of Saturday morning and, although it had eased by the start of second qualifying, there seemed little hope that the surface would dry out sufficiently for anybody to improve. It didn't, allowing Barrichello to take the first pole position of his brief F1 career, achieved in only his second season — a distinction matching that of his hero Ayrton Senna, to whose memory he dedicated his own efforts.

It was also the first pole position for the Jordan team and only the second for engine supplier Brian Hart. (Nine years earlier, Teo Fabi had qualified the Toleman TG185-Hart turbo fastest for the German Grand Prix held at the new Nürburgring.)

The weather conditions were certainly working against Damon Hill, who had been hoping for a crack at pole position, conceding that time could be running out for his own World Championship challenge.

'This is quite a critical weekend for me,' he confessed. 'I'm relying on perfect results in the next three races, so I really don't have much room to manoeuvre.

'Schumacher will be working hard to beat me. But it's now or never for me as far as the championship is concerned. It's long odds, but not so long that you wouldn't risk some money on it!

'Today, Jordan chose the right route. They gambled, and it paid off. But I think I would have been quicker if I hadn't lost a lot of time when I came up behind Verstappen, who was going slowly on slicks, at Blanchimont. That was really the difference.'

Damon also had his reservations about the changes to Eau Rouge. 'Well, we asked to have Eau Rouge made safer,' he admitted, 'and the drivers requested a chicane until safety at that point can be improved on a long-term basis.

'The chicane is OK, but I preferred the old Eau Rouge. However, I don't know whether the risk factor has been reduced that much because now you come down the hill and brake absolutely straight towards the barrier. So your line into Eau Rouge is changed a bit — which is not necessarily safer.'

However, the frantic last-minute scramble for quick times worked against Hill's team-mate David Coulthard, the young Scot having posted fastest time when the track surface was at its wettest. Coulthard, who viewed the race as the latest round in his battle to keep the Williams drive for 1995 in the face of Nigel Mansell's challenge, ended up a disappointed seventh.

'I was quite happy as I was quickest when the conditions were really wet,' he explained. 'During the damp in the morning I'd experienced a bit more understeer than I would have liked, but we continued to work on the front end and things got slightly better. I didn't get a run on the drying surface towards the end because I stalled at the end of the pit lane when I went out on slicks. It's all a little disappointing.'

Both Williams FW16Bs were fitted with further-revised versions of the Renault RS6B V10 engines which offered slightly increased top-end power, a valuable factor on a circuit where consistent flat-out running in top gear is a crucial component of a competitive lap time.

Ferrari's Jean Alesi also held fastest time early in the session, but the Frenchman rounded off the day on a sour note, furiously accusing Martin Brundle of balking him badly on what he'd hoped would be his quickest lap. Alesi, running on slicks, caught Brundle's McLaren as the two cars braked for La Source hairpin. Going down the hill towards the new chicane, Alesi drew alongside the McLaren, but Martin edged him out and kept ahead as they set out up the long climb to Les Combes. Alesi eventually plucked up sufficient courage to move off the dry line and squeeze past under braking for the tricky right-hander. He then paid Brundle back by holding up the McLaren on the long descent to Blanchimont.

After the session Alesi was absolutely simmering with indignation and stormed down to the McLaren pit for a confrontation with his rival. His candour startled everybody who heard the ensuing exchange. Apart from berating Martin for getting in his way, Jean offered the view that the English driver had been included in the McLaren line-up only because Ron Dennis couldn't get anybody else — and expressed the hope that this would change in 1995, and that the team would sign somebody with real talent.

Brundle wasn't to be provoked. 'Alesi was shouting bad words in bad English,' he shrugged. 'We've had our run-ins before, at Brazil — where we crashed — and at Imola two years ago. After those incidents he said he was going to kill me. He is a hot-head.'

Alesi justified his behaviour thus: 'I don't think Martin Brundle's actions were correct, so I went to tell him so personally as I think these things should be discussed face to face.'

In reality, Ferrari had much more competitive potential bottled up at Spa than might have been discerned from the team's performance on Friday. At the point when the track surface was beginning to dry out, Gerhard Berger still had six laps in hand and was heading to the pits to change onto slicks when his V12 expired spectacularly in a ball of flame due to an oil leak. He pulled off out on the circuit and found himself down in 11th place as a result.

The Ferraris had been equipped not only with a revised rear wing, but also with new rear suspension geometry which had proved very promising during preliminary tests at Fiorano. Alesi eventually set the fastest time in Saturday's wet session, although this was still four seconds away from Barrichello's pole-winner. The Frenchman never switched to slicks, although Gerhard did so right at the end of the session, to no effect.

Hill, who had to be content with third place on the grid behind Schumacher, reckoned that only another ten minutes would have been needed for a dry line to emerge. 'It was very

BELGIAN GRAND PRIX

critical,' said Damon. 'By the end of the session conditions were perhaps as they were about ten minutes from the end of Friday's session. When you've got 20 or so cars going round, it certainly dries out quickly. But somebody dropped some oil at Les Combes and I nearly went off on my slowing-down lap.'

Irvine remained an excellent fourth in the final order ahead of Alesi, Verstappen and Coulthard. In eighth place was Mika Häkkinen's McLaren MP4/9, the Finn having tried a slightly more powerful development version of the Peugeot A6 V10 on Friday morning only for the new unit to lose its oil pressure after just a few laps.

Ninth was Heinz-Harald Frentzen's Sauber, ahead of Pierluigi Martini's Minardi M194, the Italian machine featuring revised, shorter side pods which had been tested with some promise at Mugello. 'Piero' was quite happy with the chassis balance on Friday and, although he lost time with a gearchange hydraulic problem, he emerged eight places ahead of his disappointed team-mate Michele Alboreto, who was unable to work out a decent chassis balance.

The unpredictable conditions at least enabled Mark Blundell to out-qualify his Tyrrell-Yamaha team-mate Ukyo Katayama. Mark got tangled up in traffic, but still managed to set 12th-fastest time, while Ukyo unfortunately spun on his first flying lap as the track began to dry out and found himself down in 23rd place. Blundell had a problem with the throttle kicker mechanism down-changing through the gearbox on Friday morning, and his best lap during the afternoon was spoiled negotiating Alboreto's Minardi and a spinning Larrousse.

Brundle lined up 13th after his little confrontation with Alesi, just ahead of the Footwork of Gianni Morbidelli, the Italian receiving a three-race ban, suspended for three races, and a $10,000 fine for ignoring yellow flags during Friday qualifying. Then came Andrea de Cesaris in the Sauber, which the Italian complained was cutting out at low revs on Friday, followed by Ligier twins Eric Bernard and Olivier Panis, Alboreto and Philippe Alliot.

Alliot had replaced Olivier Beretta in the Larrousse line-up for this one race, the McLaren test driver innocently inquiring why the Ford-engined car didn't have an automatic upchange facility like the MP4/9 he'd driven at the Hungaroring. It was a remark which would return to haunt McLaren over the weeks to come. Once the FIA got wind of it!

Christian Fittipaldi had to endure a nerve-racking Friday night after his Footwork suffered an engine failure on its very first lap and it looked as though he might fail to qualify. In the event, he managed to scrape into the race with the 24th-fastest time overall after displaying just the right balance of restraint and forcefulness on the slippery track surface during the second session – to the acute disappointment of Pacific driver Bertrand Gachot, who found himself pushed back into the ranks of the non-qualifiers as a result.

Over in the Lotus camp, the mood was a little more optimistic after Johnny Herbert had tested the long-awaited new Mugen Honda V10 at Silverstone the previous week. It wasn't available to be raced at Spa, but the fact that Johnny had gone 2.5 seconds faster than he'd ever managed with the current engine at least provided a glimmer of light at the end of the tunnel on which to focus. The team was hoping that it would be able to race the new engine for the first time at Monza, where its reputed 16 kg weight saving was expected to give the Lotus 109 a more realistic chance to unlock its potential.

In the meantime, Herbert had to be content with 20th place ahead of David Brabham's Simtek, Erik Comas's Larrousse, Katayama, Fittipaldi and Jean-Marc Gounon in the second Simtek. It was Brabham's best qualifying position of the season to date, but Gounon still didn't feel happy with his car, although he couldn't put his finger on precisely where the problem lay.

Belgian Philippe Adams joined Herbert in the Lotus team for this race, his presence reputedly secured by a $500,000 sponsorship deal which also included the Portuguese and European GPs. The local touring car hot-shot celebrated his graduation to the senior formula by spinning into the pit barrier barely half an hour into Friday morning's free practice session. His car was duly repaired, but there was more fun and games in the pit lane when representatives of companies Adams had claimed were his sponsors arrived to refute such suggestions and energetically demanded that he remove all such identification from his car and his overalls!

Adams eventually claimed the last place on the grid, the Pacific PR01s

The two days of practice at Spa-Francorchamps were held in wet conditions which helped Rubens Barrichello take the first pole position of his F1 career – much to the joy of Eddie Jordan *(far left)*.

Left: Shelter from the storm. Martin Brundle and Jean Alesi became involved in a wheel-to-wheel battle during qualifying. Neither driver was willing to sacrifice his chance of improving his time and the angry Ferrari driver was less than charitable about the phlegmatic Englishman's abilities afterwards.

Above: When the sun eventually broke through it gave the photographers the opportunity to capture some stunning photos such as this shot of Mika Häkkinen's McLaren-Peugeot, beautifully highlighting the chassis's sculptured form.

BELGIAN GRAND PRIX

The continuing wave of safety-inspired circuit revisions saw Eau Rouge emasculated by a chicane which obliged the first-lap field *(right)* to file through in line astern. Happily plans are in place to return the corner to its former majesty in time for the 1995 race.

of Gachot and Paul Belmondo again failing to qualify. Both cars had revised cooling systems and aerodynamics for this race, Gachot reckoning he might have made the cut had his Ilmor V10 not lost its oil pressure at the end of the decisive first qualifying session, just when the track was drying out.

RACE

The forecasts promised better weather for Sunday morning, but it didn't look that way at first light. The roads were still glistening ominously and a heavy mist hung over the pine forests around the circuit. In the warm-up, Coulthard was fastest for much of the time on a circuit now progressively – and thankfully – drying out. Right at the end of the session Schumacher went considerably quicker, but Hill ploughed off into a gravel trap and Häkkinen crashed quite heavily exiting the 'bus stop' chicane, damaging his McLaren's nose and front suspension, although the car was still repairable for the race.

Worried that his Benetton might be running a little too low, and ever mindful of the implications of excessive wear to the wood-composite stepped undertray, Schumacher asked for the ride height of his B194 to be raised ever so slightly – by about 0.5 mm – before the start of the race.

Barrichello and Jordan opted for a one-stop strategy, so the pole position car was running a heavier fuel load than its immediate rivals, but the young Brazilian still managed to scrabble into the braking area at La Source in the lead when the starting lights flickered to green. Schumacher took an immediate second place with Alesi's Ferrari barnstorming up the inside of Hill, inside front wheel locked, to take third place into the first turn.

Barrichello kept ahead down into the Eau Rouge chicane, but Schumacher surged past into the lead as they approached Les Combes, taking every opportunity to make good his escape on the plunge down to Blanchimont while Alesi was blocked in behind the Jordan. At the end of the opening lap, Michael's Benetton slammed through 2.4 seconds ahead of Alesi, the Ferrari having neatly outbraked Barrichello as they came up to the 'bus stop' for the first time.

Jean was still second next time round, but as he accelerated across

the line his Ferrari's exhaust note suddenly changed, heralding another major V12 failure, and he pulled off for good just beyond La Source. 'What can I say?' shrugged Alesi. 'Once again things went wrong for me on a day where the car seemed really good. Everything happens to me. Now I will have a few days' holiday at home before concentrating on preparations for the Italian GP. I want to do better at Monza...'

It was midway round lap three before Hill pulled past Barrichello into second place, by which time Schumacher was 10.4 seconds ahead and it seemed to be all over bar the shouting. Coulthard was now running a strong third with Häkkinen fourth, and before long Frentzen's Sauber was challenging Barrichello for fifth.

Meanwhile, there had been a close call between the two slowest drivers in the race on lap four when Gounon spun his Simtek at Eau Rouge and Adams had been forced to brake to a halt to avoid the Frenchman. Both continued, but Frentzen was eliminated when he goofed at the same point seven laps later, spinning his Sauber and getting it beached over the high kerb, its rear wheels clawing the air clear of the ground.

By lap 11 – quarter-distance – Schumacher was 16.8 seconds ahead of Hill, who duly came in for his first refuelling stop (8.2s) next time round, dropping to fourth. Coulthard made a 9.3s stop on lap 13, resuming in third place behind Barrichello but ahead of Damon, then Schumacher came in for a 7.6s stop at the end of lap 14, retaining his lead with the Jordan still in second place.

Berger, another to opt for a single-stop strategy, was running in seventh on the 12th lap when his Ferrari's engine expired spectacularly as he braked for the 'bus stop'. He was too late to aim for the pit lane, but he didn't want to end up parking his machine in a dangerous position, so he swerved across the grass with the intention of rejoining the pit lane further along. Unfortunately, Brundle's McLaren was at that time using the conventional route into the pits for a refuelling stop and the two cars came close to colliding. Berger later collected a suspended one-race ban for his behaviour.

'When I realised what had happened, I headed for the pit lane as I did not want to leave the car in a dangerous place,' explained Gerhard. 'I indicated by putting my hand in the air, but I had not realised that a McLaren was right behind me, at an angle that made it difficult for me to see in my mirrors. I did this with good intentions, but I admit that it was dangerous.'

Meanwhile, further down the field, Katayama's performance had been electrifying, the Japanese driver displaying great panache as he made up for his disappointment in qualifying. Ukyo was 20th at the end of the first lap, but had soared through to ninth by the time he made his first refuelling stop at the end of lap 14, only to spin off when the engine seized five laps after he rejoined.

On lap 18 Barrichello made what was scheduled to be his sole refuelling stop, the Jordan 194 remaining stationary for 12.2 seconds and eventually resuming the chase behind Schumacher, Coulthard, Hill and Häkkinen. Two laps later the Brazilian got slightly off-line on the double-apex downhill Pouhon left-hander – which had claimed Adams a few laps earlier – and careered across the gravel trap before coming to rest against the tyre wall.

On lap 19, Schumacher's Benetton had suddenly got away from him at the same spot, snapping into a quick 360-degree spin, its rear wheels apparently climbing the outside kerb, the German immediately continuing. The effect on his lead was hardly measurable, but the episode was destined to have far-reaching effects which would stretch way beyond this late-summer afternoon in Belgium.

'I was using a line which I had also

BELGIAN GRAND PRIX

Left: The massed ranks of race fans and Formula 1 personnel gathered at Spa thought they had witnessed a decisive victory for Michael Schumacher, and most had set out on the long journey home before finding out that this was not in fact the case. An unsatisfactory outcome to the weekend's work for all concerned.

Belgian ex-F3 contender Philippe Adams *(bottom)* bought a ride in the financially stricken Lotus team and scraped onto the grid as the final qualifier. He lasted 15 laps before spinning out of the race.

Diary

NASCAR front-runner Ernie Irvan critically injured in practice accident at Michigan International Speedway.

Ferrari reaffirms commitment to F1 refuelling in 1995 and '96.

Benetton secures three-year deal with Renault for supply of powerful V10 engines, commencing in 1995. The Ligier team, recently acquired by Benetton boss Flavio Briatore, has used Renault engines since 1992.

Michael Andretti hospitalised overnight after 170 mph accident while testing the Ganassi team's Reynard-Ford at the Nazareth one-mile oval.

been using in the rain,' explained Schumacher, 'and at the beginning it worked out very well because there was no rubber on the circuit and you could choose whatever line you wanted.

'But then during the race there were people using a different line and it was getting dirtier and dirtier on the line I was using. Just one time it was too much: I couldn't turn in and I had to let the car go. I knew I was going to go over the kerbs and I thought I would also go into the gravel, but then one rear wheel went onto the grass and I did a three-sixty.

'Fortunately I didn't flat-spot [the tyres] too much, but I am sure something went wrong on the car because my steering wheel was pulling to the right and I couldn't drive as I had been doing before.'

By lap 22, half-distance, Schumacher was 17.2 seconds ahead of Coulthard with Damon only 0.8s further back. By lap 26 David had cut the Benetton's advantage to 15.4s, and it was down to 13.6s by the time the two Williams-Renaults made their second stops. Hill came in on lap 28, Coulthard a lap later and the Scot again got out just ahead of his more experienced team-mate. Schumacher also made his second stop on lap 28 and, two laps later, Coulthard was just 9.6s adrift.

Then David began to drop away very slightly. The gap was 10.5 seconds on lap 31 and 10.7s on lap 32, but then came back down to 10.1s on lap 33 and 8.9s on lap 34. Hill felt able to go quicker, but there was no way Coulthard was going to give way unless instructed to do so by the team.

Finally the matter was resolved when Patrick Head, having closely scrutinised Coulthard's progress on the pit lane television monitor, concluded that his FW16B's rear wing was wobbling ominously. At the end of lap 37, with only seven to go, David was called in for a routine inspection.

As the Williams rolled to a halt, Head dropped down beneath the wing and detected that the right-hand wing support mounting on the gearbox casing had broken. Thinking on his feet, Patrick immediately signalled Coulthard back into the race, satisfied that the aerodynamic download would keep the mounting in place while the car was running. 'A marginal decision', he frankly admitted much later.

Hill was now free to take a run at Schumacher's Benetton and really

began to pile on the pressure. Häkkinen had moved up to third place ahead of Verstappen's Benetton, Mark Blundell's Tyrrell and the delayed Coulthard. But Damon felt a little hard done by.

'In my view, the team should have acted sooner,' said Hill, who had taken a slight gamble with his race set-up and opted to run slightly less downforce than Coulthard. 'I let them know my feelings over the radio, and they replied, yes, they understood what I was saying. But nothing happened.

'Once I got past him, I was able to run much quicker because I was not in dirty air. But ultimately it's Frank and Patrick's team and they are quite entitled to run it in their way.'

The Williams management didn't act because they didn't believe that Damon was close enough. 'If he had been really hassling him, then there would have been no question, we would have asked David to let him by,' explained Patrick Head. 'But Frank and I discussed it and we really didn't think Damon was.'

Hill now piled on the pressure, setting the fastest lap with three to run, but Schumacher was still nearly 14 seconds ahead as he took the chequered flag.

'I had set my hopes on winning,' said Damon immediately after climbing from his car, 'but Michael just drove a fantastic race and beat us again, so I have to congratulate him and Benetton. I think we put up a good defence, but second is not really good enough to brighten the outlook for the championship.'

Häkkinen came home in third after wrestling with a slight brake balance problem on his McLaren MP4/9. By contrast, Martin Brundle had climbed from 13th to fifth place by lap 25 when he dropped a wheel over a kerb at Les Combes and smacked into the guard rail quite hard. This was an unfortunate lapse on a weekend when McLaren boss Ron Dennis had publicly expressed an interest in Rubens Barrichello.

Verstappen was fourth with Coulthard climbing to fifth at the end after inadvertently tapping Blundell's Tyrrell-Yamaha into a spin at La Source with four laps to go. After rejoining the race following his rear wing check, overheating hydraulics had caused Coulthard's transmission to jam in fourth gear and he had insufficient engine retardation as a result.

'Mark has every right to be very angry,' acknowledged David, 'but I went over to apologise to him immediately after the race.' Blundell took what appeared to be the final championship point ahead of Gianni Morbidelli's Footwork, which profited from the late-race retirement of Irvine's Jordan after an alternator problem flattened the 194's battery four laps from home. Eddie was eventually classified 13th.

Olivier Panis and Pierluigi Martini were next up, with Michele Alboreto within half a second of his Minardi team-mate as they took the chequered flag. Bernard's Ligier was 11th ahead of Gounon in the sole surviving Simtek, David Brabham having spun out of the race when he lost a rear wheel one lap after his second refuelling stop.

Five hours later came the latest blow to Michael Schumacher's World Championship aspirations. After exhaustive investigation, consideration and debate, the stewards announced that the winning Benetton was being excluded after a report from FIA Technical Delegate Charlie Whiting showed that the car's wood-composite skidblock – which forms the stepped undertray – had exceeded the 10 per cent wear margin permitted by the regulations.

As a result, Damon Hill, who was by now on a flight from Brussels back to London, found himself confirmed as winner of the Belgian Grand Prix, with the other finishers also gaining one place in the official classification.

FIA FORMULA ONE WORLD CHAMPIONSHIP ROUND 11

GRAND PRIX DE BELGIQUE

SPA-FRANCORCHAMPS
26-28 AUGUST 1994

Spa-Francorchamps — Circuit Length: 4.350 miles/7.001 km

Race weather: Dry, warm, cloudy

Place	Driver	Nat.	No.	Entrant	Car/Engine	Laps	Time/Retirement	Speed (mph/km/h)
1	Damon Hill	GB	0	Rothmans Williams Renault	Williams FW16B-Renault RS6B V10	44	1h 28m 47.170s	129.360/208.170
2	Mika Häkkinen	SF	7	Marlboro McLaren Peugeot	McLaren MP4/9-Peugeot A6 V10	44	1h 29m 38.551s	128.120/206.181
3	Jos Verstappen	NL	6	Mild Seven Benetton Ford	Benetton B194-Ford Zetec-R V8	44	1h 29m 57.623s	127.670/205.453
4	David Coulthard	GB	2	Rothmans Williams Renault	Williams FW16B-Renault RS6B V10	44	1h 30m 32.957s	126.840/204.116
5	Mark Blundell	GB	4	Tyrrell	Tyrrell 022-Yamaha OX10A V10	43		
6	Gianni Morbidelli	I	10	Footwork Ford	Footwork FA15-Ford HB V8	43		
7	Olivier Panis	F	26	Ligier Gitanes Blondes	Ligier JS39B-Renault RS6A V10	43		
8	Pierluigi Martini	I	23	Minardi Scuderia Italia	Minardi M194-Ford HB V8	43		
9	Michele Alboreto	I	24	Minardi Scuderia Italia	Minardi M194-Ford HB V8	43		
10	Eric Bernard	F	25	Ligier Gitanes Blondes	Ligier JS39B-Renault RS6A V10	42		
11	Jean-Marc Gounon	F	32	MTV Simtek Ford	Simtek S941-Ford HB V8	42		
12	Johnny Herbert	GB	12	Team Lotus	Lotus 109-Mugen Honda ZA5C V10	41		
13	Eddie Irvine	GB	15	Sasol Jordan	Jordan 194-Hart 1035 V10	40	Alternator	
	Christian Fittipaldi	BR	9	Footwork Ford	Footwork FA15-Ford HB V8	33	Engine	
	David Brabham	AUS	31	MTV Simtek Ford	Simtek S941-Ford HB V8	29	Accident	
	Andrea de Cesaris	I	29	Sauber Mercedes	Sauber C13-Mercedes-Benz V10	27	Sticking throttle	
	Martin Brundle	GB	8	Marlboro McLaren Peugeot	McLaren MP4/9-Peugeot A6 V10	24	Spun off	
	Rubens Barrichello	BR	14	Sasol Jordan	Jordan 194-Hart 1035 V10	19	Accident	
	Ukyo Katayama	J	3	Tyrrell	Tyrrell 022-Yamaha OX10A V10	18	Engine	
	Philippe Adams	B	11	Team Lotus	Lotus 109-Mugen Honda ZA5C V10	15	Spun off	
	Gerhard Berger	A	28	Scuderia Ferrari	Ferrari 412T1B 043 V12	11	Engine	
	Philippe Alliot	F	19	Tourtel Larrousse F1	Larrousse LH94-Ford HB V8	11	Engine	
	Heinz-Harald Frentzen	D	30	Sauber Mercedes	Sauber C13-Mercedes-Benz V10	10	Spun off	
	Erik Comas	F	20	Tourtel Larrousse F1	Larrousse LH94-Ford HB V8	3	Engine	
	Jean Alesi	F	27	Scuderia Ferrari	Ferrari 412T1B 043 V12	2	Engine	
DQ	Michael Schumacher	D	5	Mild Seven Benetton Ford	Benetton B194-Ford Zetec-R V8	44	1h 28m 33.508s	129.690/208.705
DNQ	Bertrand Gachot	F	34	Pacific Grand Prix Ltd	Pacific PR01-Ilmor 2175A V10			
DNQ	Paul Belmondo	F	33	Pacific Grand Prix Ltd	Pacific PR01-Ilmor 2175A V10			

Fastest lap: Hill, on lap 41, 1m 57.117s, 134.500 mph/215.200 km/h (record for revised circuit).
Lap record for old circuit: Alain Prost (F1 Williams FW15C-Renault V10), 1m 51.095s, 140.424 mph/225.990 km/h (1993).
All cars used Goodyear tyres

All results and data © FIA 1994

QUALIFYING 1

Rubens Barrichello	2m 21.163s
Michael Schumacher	2m 21.494s
Damon Hill	2m 21.681s
Eddie Irvine	2m 22.074s
Jean Alesi	2m 22.202s
Jos Verstappen	2m 22.218s
David Coulthard	2m 22.359s
Mika Häkkinen	2m 22.441s
Heinz-Harald Frentzen	2m 22.634s
Pierluigi Martini	2m 23.326s
Gerhard Berger	2m 23.895s
Mark Blundell	2m 24.048s
Martin Brundle	2m 24.117s
Gianni Morbidelli	2m 25.114s
Andrea de Cesaris	2m 25.695s
Eric Bernard	2m 26.044s
Olivier Panis	2m 26.079s
Michele Alboreto	2m 26.738s
Philippe Alliot	2m 26.901s
Johnny Herbert	2m 27.155s
David Brabham	2m 27.212s
Erik Comas	2m 28.156s
Ukyo Katayama	2m 28.979s
Jean-Marc Gounon	2m 31.755s
Philippe Adams	2m 33.885s
Bertrand Gachot	2m 34.582s
Paul Belmondo	2m 35.729s
Christian Fittipaldi	16m 56.162s

Friday afternoon
Wet, cool, overcast

QUALIFYING 2

Jean Alesi	2m 25.099s
Michael Schumacher	2m 25.501s
Damon Hill	2m 25.570s
David Coulthard	2m 27.180s
Heinz-Harald Frentzen	2m 28.026s
Mark Blundell	2m 28.164s
Jos Verstappen	2m 28.576s
Mika Häkkinen	2m 28.997s
Gerhard Berger	2m 29.391s
Ukyo Katayama	2m 29.925s
Andrea de Cesaris	2m 30.475s
Erik Comas	2m 30.524s
Pierluigi Martini	2m 30.896s
Christian Fittipaldi	**2m 30.931s**
Eric Bernard	2m 31.025s
Philippe Alliot	2m 31.350s
Gianni Morbidelli	2m 31.403s
Olivier Panis	2m 31.501s
Michele Alboreto	2m 32.286s
Johnny Herbert	2m 32.610s
Philippe Adams	2m 34.733s
Bertrand Gachot	2m 34.951s
Jean-Marc Gounon	2m 40.280s
David Brabham	2m 41.593s
Martin Brundle	no time
Rubens Barrichello	no time
Eddie Irvine	no time
Paul Belmondo	no time

Saturday afternoon
Wet, cool, overcast

WARM-UP

Michael Schumacher	2m 18.934s
David Coulthard	2m 21.953s
Gerhard Berger	2m 23.768s
Jos Verstappen	2m 24.027s
Jean Alesi	2m 24.110s
Martin Brundle	2m 24.613s
Erik Comas	2m 25.400s
Mika Häkkinen	2m 25.568s
Eddie Irvine	2m 25.658s
Olivier Panis	2m 26.013s
Mark Blundell	2m 26.055s
Rubens Barrichello	2m 26.462s
Johnny Herbert	2m 26.487s
Michele Alboreto	2m 26.636s
Heinz-Harald Frentzen	2m 27.425s
Ukyo Katayama	2m 27.983s
Gianni Morbidelli	2m 28.437s
Christian Fittipaldi	2m 28.674s
Eric Bernard	2m 29.928s
Damon Hill	2m 30.151s
Pierluigi Martini	2m 30.548s
Jean-Marc Gounon	2m 31.377s
Philippe Adams	2m 34.190s
David Brabham	2m 37.064s
Andrea de Cesaris	2m 38.506s
Philippe Alliot	6m 32.894s

Sunday morning
Drying, warm, overcast

FASTEST LAPS

Driver	Time	Lap
Damon Hill	1m 57.117s	41
Michael Schumacher	1m 57.198s	37
David Coulthard	1m 57.793s	36
Martin Brundle	1m 58.839s	24
Jos Verstappen	1m 59.001s	24
Mark Blundell	1m 59.031s	38
Mika Häkkinen	1m 59.359s	10
Olivier Panis	1m 59.502s	30
Rubens Barrichello	1m 59.527s	15
Heinz-Harald Frentzen	2m 00.068s	10
Eddie Irvine	2m 00.353s	29
Gerhard Berger	2m 00.372s	11
Ukyo Katayama	2m 00.531s	12
Johnny Herbert	2m 00.605s	17
Michele Alboreto	2m 01.209s	33
Gianni Morbidelli	2m 01.295s	39
Christian Fittipaldi	2m 01.653s	27
Pierluigi Martini	2m 02.298s	24
Jean Alesi	2m 02.587s	2
Eric Bernard	2m 02.665s	31
Andrea de Cesaris	2m 03.501s	19
Jean-Marc Gounon	2m 04.732s	24
David Brabham	2m 06.145s	10
Philippe Alliot	2m 06.157s	10
Philippe Adams	2m 06.759s	15
Erik Comas	2m 07.153s	3

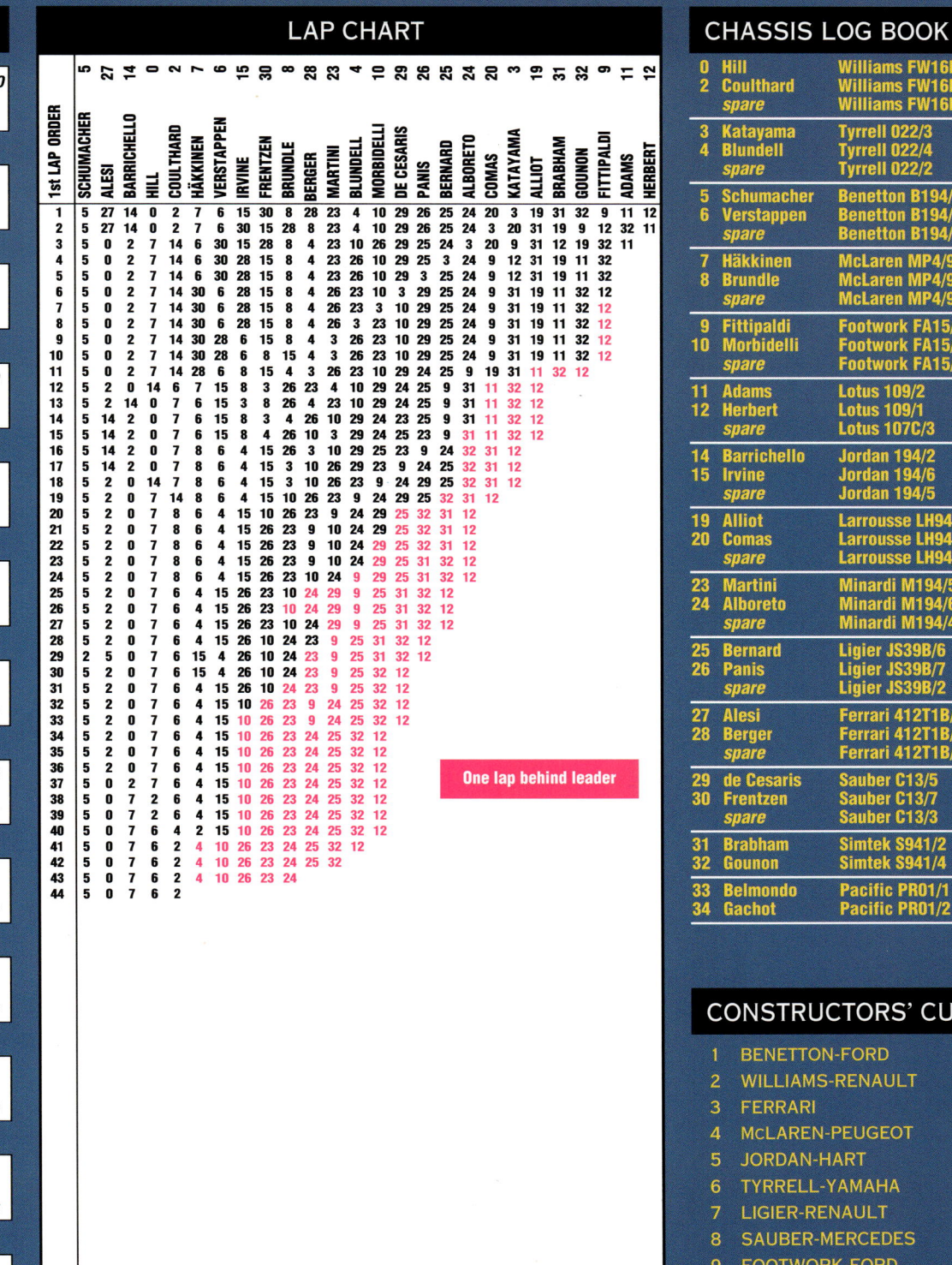

WORLD CHAMPIONSHIP • ROUND 12

ITALIAN GRAND PRIX

HILL
BERGER
HÄKKINEN
BARRICHELLO
BRUNDLE
COULTHARD

Ferrari's fans couldn't have been happier when second qualifying ended with an all-red front row for the Italian Grand Prix at Monza. But Damon Hill's post-practice prediction that Williams could well spoil their party come race day seemed to have been taken to heart by the *tifosi*. As things transpired, only 75,000 fans turned out to see Jean Alesi take a commanding lead, only to suffer a gearbox breakage at the first of his two scheduled refuelling stops, and Gerhard Berger pound home a gallant second in the spare Ferrari 412T1B, having emerged unscathed from a monumental accident in the Sunday morning warm-up. Thus Hill and his Williams-Renault emerged victorious from what was expected to be a close-fought confrontation, and Berger would have had to be content with third place had David Coulthard's FW16B not run out of fuel coming down to Parabolica on the last lap, allowing Mika Häkkinen to take the final place on the rostrum for McLaren. The sensation of qualifying had been Johnny Herbert, whose Lotus 109 was using the latest Mugen Honda engine for the first time, the Englishman lining up fourth and taking a momentary third place going into the first chicane before being spun off by Eddie Irvine's Jordan, the consequent multiple pile-up causing the race to be red-flagged. For the restart, Herbert had to take the spare car, which was fitted with one of the older engines, and failed to feature.

Once Jean Alesi had been forced into retirement, the way was clear for Damon Hill to capitalise on his opportunity to eat into the absent Michael Schumacher's 21-point World Championship lead. *Above:* Hill keeps an eye on team-mate David Coulthard, who lost a much-deserved second place when his Williams-Renault ran short of fuel on the last lap, dropping the young Scot back to sixth.

ITALIAN GRAND PRIX

Benetton wins one, loses one

It was good news and bad for the Benetton team when it appeared in front of the FIA World Council in Paris on the Wednesday prior to the Italian Grand Prix. The World Championship leaders escaped without penalty for the unauthorised removal of a filter in the refuelling rig used on Jos Verstappen's car at the German Grand Prix, but lost the appeal against Michael Schumacher's exclusion from victory in the Belgian race at Spa.

The World Council rejected the contention advanced on Benetton's behalf by eminent QC George Carman that excessive wear on the B194's wood-composite undertray had been caused by spinning over a kerb on lap 19 of the 44-lap race.

However, FIA President Max Mosley was quick to emphasise that Benetton had not 'got away' with the offence relating to the refuelling rig. The key point to remember, he explained, was that the team had pleaded guilty to the offence and offered a plea of mitigation.

'Their argument was that a filter was necessary only to clear the manufacturing debris from within the [refuelling] pipe, and that once the debris had gone, and there was obviously nothing further to be found in the filter, it was unnecessary and the filter could be removed,' he said.

'Now this was allegedly said, at a low level, between Intertechnique [the rig manufacturers] and the Larrousse team, and they did produce a letter from Larrousse saying this, and also a drawing from Intertechnique showing how the filter could be removed.

'At this point we could do one of two things. We cannot evoke something that may or may not have been said on television, or in a publication. We either had to accept the facts as put to us, or adjourn the entire proceedings to – in this case – 19 October [the next World Council meeting] to bring in Intertechnique, or, if we could get him there, Mr Walkinshaw, then examine every detail of the Larrousse/Intertechnique relationship, including the letter.

'We thought that in the interests of the sport, and in fairness to the other teams who wanted a decision, fairness generally would not be served by following that procedure.

'Once you had taken that decision, all you can consider are the matters that are placed in front of you. This we did and, just taking those factors into account, and being strictly legal and fair about it, we decided that they were guilty, but on the basis of the facts in front of us it would not be appropriate to impose a penalty.'

The FIA also took into account the fact that Benetton explained that it was a junior member of the team, understood to be team manager Joan Villadelprat, who removed the filter without consulting the team director. Moreover, at no time had the team attempted to conceal what it had done.

In addition, Benetton undertook to make 'substantial management changes' in order to ensure that such an occurrence would not happen again. Unconfirmed rumours suggested this would involve making Engineering Director Tom Walkinshaw the 'fall guy' for the whole unfortunate episode.

The World Council also found that the gearbox control device fitted to Mika Häkkinen's McLaren-Peugeot in the San Marino Grand Prix was in breach of the F1 technical regulations. The automatic upchange facility was not permissible, but the governing body was satisfied that McLaren had fitted it to the car believing it to be legal according to their interpretation of the rules. Such systems were banned from the Italian Grand Prix onwards and any similar downchange facility was specifically outlawed from the Portuguese race.

As far as 1995 was concerned, Mosley also announced proposed changes to the FIA statutes which would reinstate the competitor's right to go direct to the FIA Appeal Court, bypassing the Review Board which was introduced two years ago. It was also proposed that stewards could reconvene a meeting relating to any specific event should further evidence subsequently become available relating to any particular rule infringement.

Moreover, to eliminate the possibility of future race results hanging in the balance in the wake of scrutineering problems, teams would have to provide source codes for their engine management computers prior to the start of the new season. There will also be a 'DNA-style' comparative computer print-out made from the team's pre-season, baseline fuel specification to check against any samples taken at individual races.

ENTRY AND PRACTICE

Jean Alesi raised Ferrari's hopes of a home victory at Monza with a storming performance in first qualifying, the Frenchman successfully fighting off a strong challenge from the Williams-Renaults of Damon Hill and David Coulthard to post the fastest lap of the session. It was a characteristically spectacular effort from the Frenchman, rapturously received by the team's fervent supporters in the grandstands.

With World Championship points leader Michael Schumacher not a factor on this occasion – the Benetton driver sitting out the weekend after the confirmation of his two-race suspension – the 12th round of the title chase promised to see a straight fight between Ferrari and Williams at the historic Italian track set within the grounds of a former royal palace on the northern outskirts of Milan.

The race had been in doubt for some time after the conservationist movement had opposed the felling of trees deemed necessary to implement new safety provisions. Thankfully, a compromise was eventually reached which saw the run-off at the Curva Grande widened and the second Lesmo right-hander transformed into a third-gear turn rather than a flat-out blind.

Alesi's provisional pole position on the first day was achieved despite a dramatic spin over a high kerb at the first chicane which pitched his Ferrari into the air but resulted in only superficial damage. However, Hill thought things might have worked out differently had his Williams not jammed in fifth gear shortly before the end of the session.

'The Ferraris are going to be tough to beat,' he said, 'but, assuming it is dry on Saturday, I feel we have the car and the power to beat them to pole position.

'I quite like the modifications to the circuit and I don't think they have detracted from the feel of Monza – the second Lesmo is actually quite quick and good.'

Meanwhile, Coulthard, whose previous experience at Monza had extended to nothing more than a test session in a Formula 3000 car, displayed an insouciant confidence and maturity perfectly calculated to enhance his reputation at a time when his position in the Williams squad for 1995 seemed under threat from Nigel Mansell.

'I was quite happy, although I ran into a bit of traffic, and if I'd remained totally calm I might have been quicker,' explained the young Scot. 'With that in mind, I feel quite confident that I can get onto the front row tomorrow.

'As far as Nigel's return for the last three races of this season is concerned, I'm just concentrating on getting on with my job. I'm obviously disappointed that I've only got a couple more races this season, but in the end I'm 23 and he's 41, so perhaps I've got a longer-term future in F1!'

Gerhard Berger's Ferrari was fourth fastest on Friday, ahead of Mika Häkkinen's McLaren MP4/9, with Johnny Herbert making it three British drivers in the top six, revelling in the power and nimble handling of his Lotus 109 now that it was fitted with the long-awaited Mugen Honda ZA6C V10 engine for the first time.

'It's a nice feeling to be back in the limelight, although I wasn't sure I could still do it,' said Herbert. 'With the new car I'm able to push hard, despite a little understeer, and we haven't been able to do that for a long time.'

Less fortunate among the British brigade was Eddie Irvine, whose times in the Jordan 194 were disallowed after he exceeded the 12-lap maximum permitted in an official qualifying session.

On Saturday, Hill and Coulthard started out in an extremely confident mood. Yet Ferrari maintained the upper hand with Alesi continuing to dominate both the morning's untimed stint and the second qualifying session.

In slightly cooler conditions, Jean trimmed his Friday best of 1m 24.620s to 1m 23.844s. Berger, who had requested a slight change to his engine's electronic mapping, vaulted forward to take second on the grid with a 1m 23.978s after Coulthard and Hill had briefly held second and third places.

'This is a really special day, a great day after all my bad luck,' enthused Alesi. 'To score my first pole in a Ferrari, and at Monza, gives me enormous pleasure that is difficult to explain. All the testing we have done makes me confident and I have also found a good race set-up.'

The Williams duo stayed in their pit lane garage until just over five minutes from the end of the session before making their final bids for positions on the front row. But Hill just couldn't find that little bit extra, feeling that the Maranello brigade was now reaping the benefit of an intensive three-day test at Monza immediately prior to the race.

'We're still not 100 per cent where we want to be, but we're getting there,' said Berger optimistically. Hill, however, had a different prediction for race day. 'Given that Ferrari has been testing here for three days, I'd say we were going to spoil their party,' he said. Damon emerged in third place, with Coulthard dropping to fifth in the final grid order after his Renault V10 abruptly lost power, stranding him out on the circuit between the second Lesmo and the Variante Ascari.

This was a big disappointment for Williams, but at least it gave a welcome boost to Johnny Herbert's fortunes. Making the most of a car transformed by its new engine, the Englishman stormed through to take a momentary third place ahead of the Williams-Renaults before Hill pushed him back to fourth.

The Mugen Honda personnel were displaying a characteristically secretive attitude towards the new power unit, discouraging prying cameras from getting too close when the Lotus's engine cover was removed. But while Herbert was unquestionably impressed by the new engine, it was the fact that it was around 16 kg lighter than its predecessor – and sat fractionally lower in the chassis – which absolutely transformed the car's handling.

'With the old car, it felt as though it was trying to fall over itself in the corners,' said Herbert. 'Now this feels like a proper racing car again!

'This morning I had a bit of a problem with downchanges and didn't run new tyres, so this afternoon we incorporated a few little changes and it felt quite good. We got rid of the understeer I had yesterday, so I could push hard and drive properly. It responds well to changes, and the new brakes were very good too.'

Over in the McLaren camp, both Mika Häkkinen and Martin Brundle complained that their MP4/9s were struggling for chassis balance in the low-downforce aerodynamic trim required at Monza. This also tended to show up the power deficiency of the Peugeot V10 in a harsher light, but the Finn put a smile on everybody's face with a strong sixth place as the session neared its end.

He had set his time after borrowing his team-mate's car for his second run while a slight engine problem with his own machine was quickly rectified. But McLaren's satisfaction at the prospect of a third-row qualifying position was soon blown asunder. With barely a couple of minutes remaining before the chequered flag, Olivier Panis stormed through to take sixth place with the Ligier JS39B, a really terrific effort with which to round off a session which had started on a troubled note.

ITALIAN GRAND PRIX

> **Diary**
>
> *The day after the Italian Grand Prix, Team Lotus successfully applies to the High Court to be placed in administration, with accountants Neil Cooper and Nigel Ruddock of the London firm Robson Rhodes appointed as joint administrators.*
>
> *Williams receives an official reprimand for modifying a sleeve within its refuelling equipment to prevent the system leaking.*
>
> *Michael Schumacher linked with possible McLaren-Mercedes drive in 1996.*
>
> *Williams Touring Car Engineering established as part of a three-year deal to run Renault Lagunas in British Touring Car Championship.*

Early on, the Frenchman spun off and broke his Ligier's right-rear suspension, but he was able to prevent the Renault V10 from stalling and managed to limp back to the pits for repairs. He resumed only to take another equally lurid trip over the kerb exiting the Variante Ascari, but kept control to earn his eventual starting place on the third row.

The improving French cars clearly enjoyed Monza's long straights, team-mate Eric Bernard taking an encouraging 12th place overall. Brundle, however, could manage only 15th-fastest time.

Sauber was another team to have benefited from three days of pre-race preparation at Monza, this being the Swiss constructor's nominated test circuit. Despite battling with understeer throughout the two days of qualifying, Andrea de Cesaris lined up a very satisfied eighth in front of his home crowd, but Heinz-Harald Frentzen encountered rotten luck in the second session.

The impressive young German found his C13 yawing from understeer to oversteer and back to understeer again. This erratic handling caught him out at the Ascari chicane and he plunged off the road into the barrier. Thankfully, he emerged unhurt, but this unscheduled excursion left him trailing in a disappointed 11th.

Ninth place on the grid represented a fine effort by Eddie Irvine, but Rubens Barrichello encountered traffic on his first set of tyres and then complained of acute oversteer, not an ideal characteristic on such a fast circuit. The team changed his chassis set-up, but that left him grappling with violent understeer and he couldn't improve on 16th.

One of the stars of the show was Alessandro Zanardi, whose Lotus 109 was using the old Mugen Honda engine. The Italian, obviously fired up on his home turf, put in a remarkable performance to line up in 13th place.

'Although it's my best performance of the year I'm not as satisfied as I could have been because I had a problem with the brakes,' said 'Alex'. 'I was having to pump the pedal twice before every corner and, on my fourth lap, I thought I was doing a miracle time – and was two-tenths faster by the time I ran wide at the Ascari chicane!'

In the Benetton camp, meanwhile, it was clear that Michael Schumacher's presence was sorely missed. The constructors' championship leaders were left floundering on Friday, neither Jos Verstappen nor J.J. Lehto managing to work out a halfway decent set-up.

Schumacher likes his B194 set up like a kart, with the front end all 'pointy' and super-nervous, while the rear end is left to its own devices. Lehto simply couldn't come to terms with this, so his set-up was changed for Saturday morning, only for the beleaguered Finn to encounter an engine problem.

He ended up a dejected 20th fastest. 'I'm surprised I couldn't go any quicker and I really don't know what to say,' he shrugged. 'I'm suffering from lack of testing and it can only get better. But it's a long race, so you never know what might happen.'

Verstappen, on the other hand, improved to tenth despite hitting a camera which had fallen from another car. This lodged in one of the Benetton's side pods, causing damage to the radiator and undertray. 'After it was repaired there was not enough time to go out again,' said Jos, 'which was a pity, because there was more to come from the car.'

Gianni Morbidelli's Footwork was 17th ahead of Pierluigi Martini, the Minardi driver's M194 being converted back to manual gearchange trim after seemingly endless problems with the new semi-auto change had lost him most of Friday's qualifying session. Christian Fittipaldi's Footwork was 19th, ahead of Lehto, while Mark Blundell's Tyrrell 022 and Michele Alboreto's Minardi were next up, both having spun off the circuit during the final session.

'Today was not easy for me, starting this morning when we lost an engine after five laps,' explained Blundell. 'That meant we hadn't had enough time to evaluate the car, and none in qualifying configuration as we were running a heavy fuel load. I also used a different brake material for qualifying and anticipated it would produce more retardation.

'It didn't, so I couldn't reduce my speed sufficiently and went into the gravel at the second Lesmo.' At least his team-mate Ukyo Katayama had done reasonably well to qualify 14th, although it was not quite as strong a performance as the Japanese driver had hoped for.

'I don't understand what happened today,' said Ukyo. 'The balance of the car was as good as it had been this morning, and I pushed very hard, but didn't get the result I expected.'

Yannick Dalmas, who had taken over the second Larrousse driven at Spa by Philippe Alliot, broke his car's suspension with a spin over the kerb at the first chicane, but still qualified ahead of team-mate Erik Comas, the pair filling the penultimate row of the grid, with the two Simteks of Jean-Marc Gounon and David Brabham completing the line-up.

Once again, the two Pacifics failed to make the cut, Paul Belmondo crashing on Saturday morning and damaging the gearbox and monocoque of his PR01 beyond immediate repair, which meant he was unable to participate in second qualifying.

RACE

Ferrari's prospects suffered a major setback in the half-hour Sunday morning warm-up session when Berger locked his race car's rear brakes approaching the Variante Roggia, just after the Curva Grande, and spun heavily into the protective tyre barrier facing the guard rail. It was a huge impact and the situation appeared extremely worrying for a few minutes as safety crews lifted Berger from the cockpit and laid him on a stretcher.

Amazingly, those charged with the race organisation dithered for a full ten minutes before having the wit to display the red flag and bring the session to a close. This not only left Gerhard lying on the edge of the track literally feet away from other cars charging past at high speed, but also prevented the safety car bringing FIA Medical Delegate Professor Watkins to the scene of the accident. Most people regarded this as an unforgiveable failure on the part of the organisers.

Meanwhile, Alesi posted the fastest time ahead of Katayama, Coulthard and Blundell. Once it had been ascertained that Berger was not seriously injured, he was taken first to the circuit medical centre and then on to the local Monza hospital. There he was found to have strained his neck and went through quite a pantomime persuading the medical authorities that, come hell or high water, he was returning to the track and starting the race in the spare 412T1B. Gerhard, who had strained his neck the previous week in a road accident near the circuit, had plenty to say about the whole affair.

'You cannot leave somebody there with the cars continuing at 180 mph,' he insisted. 'And the guys removing my helmet need to be shown how to do it, because they just didn't have an idea. When I got to the hospital there were 25 doctors pulling me this way and that. One said we need to X-ray this, another we need to X-ray that. The whole thing was unbelievable, a big casino.'

Hill suffered a sticking throttle during the warm-up, then transferred to the spare FW16B immediately before the start after his race car developed an oil leak. Martin Brundle was another who had to make a last-minute switch, discovering a water pressure problem on his McLaren MP4/9, which also obliged him to switch to the team's spare. This had been set up for Häkkinen, and the McLaren lads worked miracles on the grid to change the cockpit adjustments to suit the Englishman.

At the green light Alesi barnstormed away into an immediate lead from Berger, with Herbert getting the jump on Hill to push the revised Lotus-Mugen into a glorious third place as the pack sprinted for the first chicane. But suddenly Eddie Irvine came hurtling down the outside in the Jordan, locked his brakes and couldn't prevent himself tapping Herbert into a spin over the chicane's high kerb.

In a split-second there were cars everywhere. Herbert suddenly found himself beached, facing in the direction from which he had come. Coulthard, Panis and Comas also became involved and the race was immediately red-flagged to a halt for the track to be cleared.

For Lotus, this would go down in the history books as a body-blow of almost terminal proportions. With the financially beleaguered team scheduled the following day to apply to be placed in administration under the protection of the High Court in London in order to fend off a planned winding-up order from Cosworth Engineering, a good result at Monza could have yielded a timely commercial boost.

All that was now in ruins, for while Coulthard, Panis and Irvine could all take over spare cars identical to the ones they had just damaged, Herbert's spare 109 was fitted with one of the earlier, painfully heavy Mugen Honda V10s. That meant he had no chance at the restart. He was not a happy man.

'Irvine has done far too much damage this year and should finally be properly penalised,' said Johnny firmly. 'F1 doesn't need drivers like this – one day there may be serious harm.'

Lotus boss Peter Collins was not so

Paul-Henri Cahier

Bryn Williams/Words & Pictures

Christine Lalla

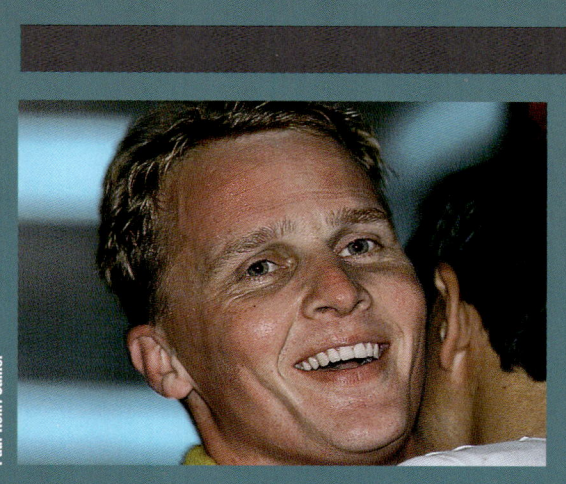

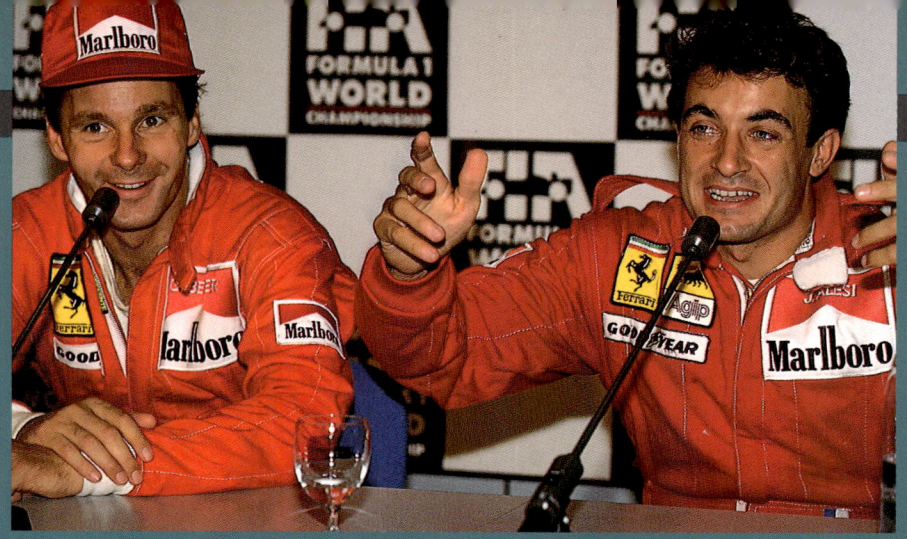

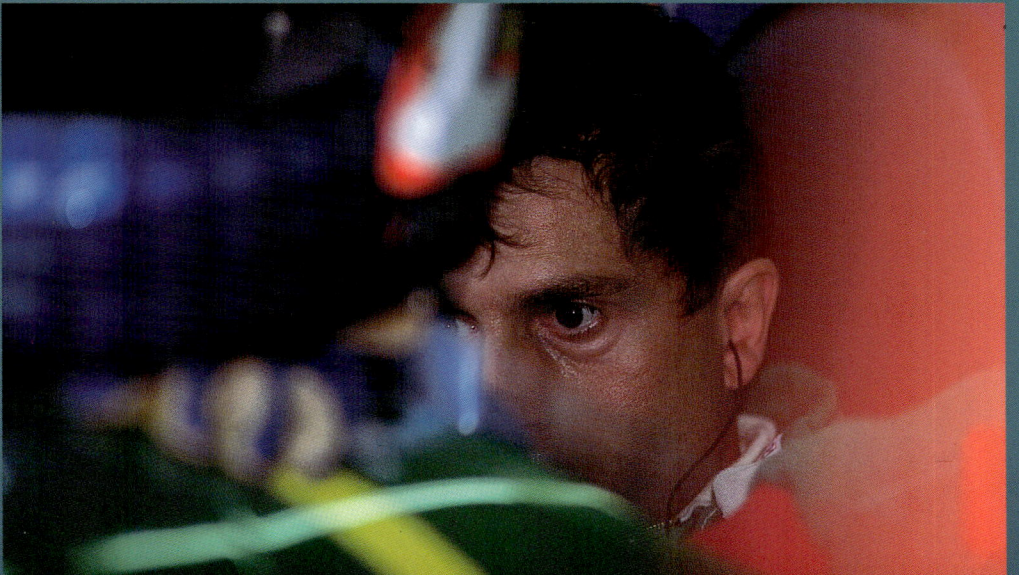

Top left: **Some comfort and joy at last for Johnny Herbert, who qualified fourth fastest with the help of the new Mugen Honda V10 fitted to his Lotus. Sadly Johnny was a victim of the by now customary first-lap multiple collision *(above)* which stopped the race.**

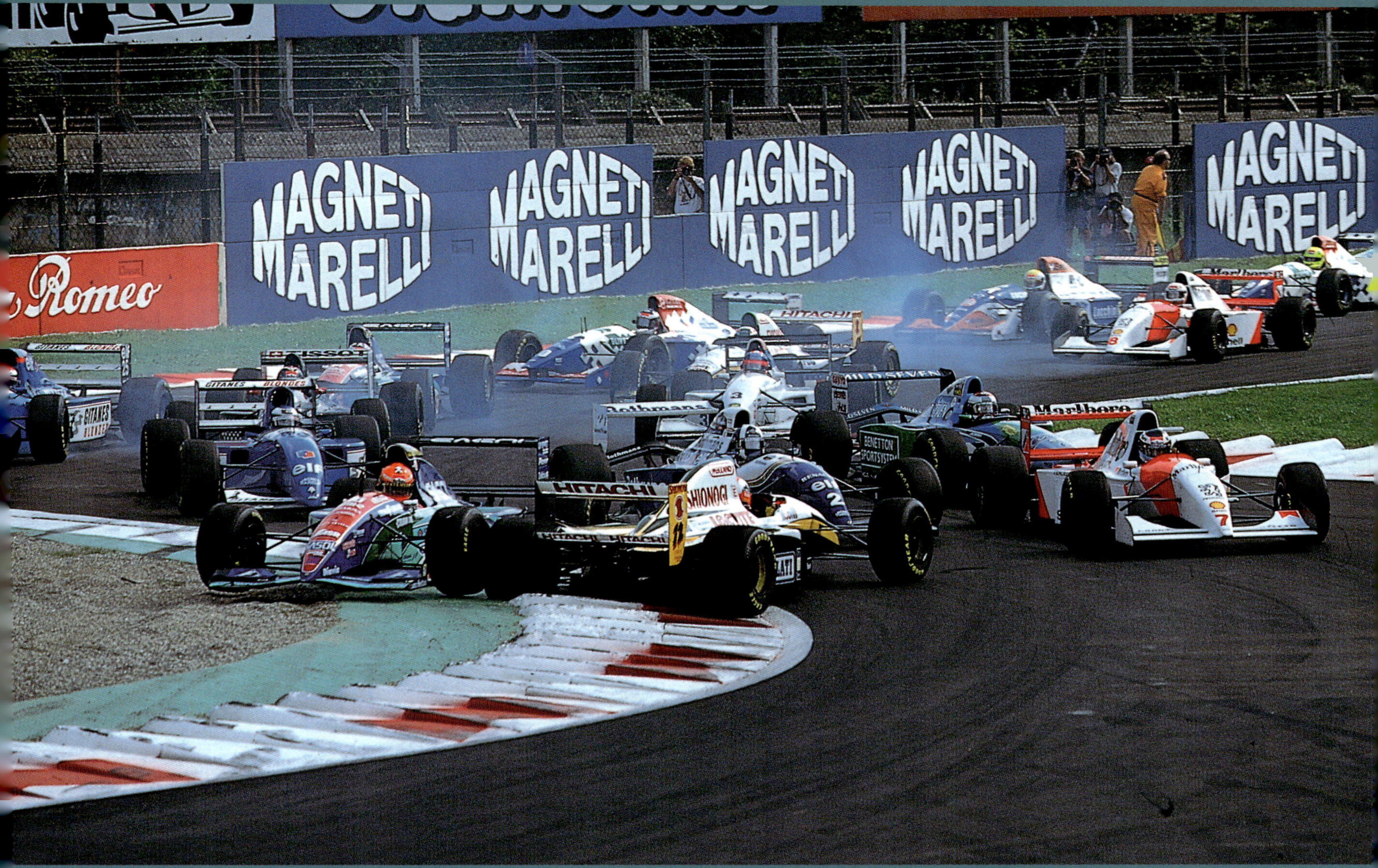

Top right: **Ferrari's practice form saw a buoyant Gerhard Berger and Jean Alesi fill the front row of the grid. Alesi *(right)* relishes the chance to talk about his first-ever pole position at the Saturday afternoon press conference.**

Yannick Dalmas *(left)* made a surprise return to the Grand Prix arena. His comeback after nearly four years away saw him out-qualify team-mate Erik Comas, but his race ended disappointingly when he spun out at the first chicane on lap 19.

complimentary. 'Irvine's three-race suspension at the beginning of the year was far too short,' he commented. 'His brain has obviously been removed and it is about time that his licence was too.' The words were too harsh, but you could understand his extreme frustration . . .

Coulthard took over Hill's repaired race car for the restart and everybody managed to get away cleanly at the second attempt. Alesi, who had opted to make two refuelling stops, went away from the grid like a rocket, completing the opening lap 1.2 seconds ahead of Berger, with Hill next up, then Coulthard, Häkkinen, Frentzen and Katayama. The opening lap had accounted for three retirements, Zanardi making contact with Verstappen, the impact puncturing one of the Lotus's rear tyres and pitching it into Morbidelli's Footwork.

Going into the second lap Berger locked up and straight-lined the sand trap at the first chicane, dropping him back into Hill's clutches and allowing Alesi to expand his advantage to 3.7s second time round. By lap three Katayama – who, like team-mate Blundell, was opting for a two-stop strategy to make up for his poor grid position – was through to sixth ahead of Frentzen, and the Japanese driver had vaulted past Häkkinen and closed in on Coulthard next time round.

Berger admitted that he had quite a lot of discomfort from his neck in the early part of the race and was hampered by the fact that he'd lost his best engine in the warm-up accident. But he worked hard to keep ahead of Hill in the opening stages, while Alesi tore away from the pack so decisively that he was almost ten seconds ahead with ten laps completed.

At the end of lap 12, Katayama made his first refuelling stop and was stationary for more than 12 seconds due to a sticking rear wheel nut, while Alesi came in two laps later. The Ferrari was stationary for 7.8 seconds, but when Jean went to accelerate back into the fray, his car lurched forward a few yards and ground to a stop. Alesi fiddled with the gearchange levers, the Ferrari crept forward a second time and then stopped again.

Trembling with fury, Alesi undid his seat harness and stormed away from the car. Once behind the pits, he hurled away the keys of his road Ferrari, climbed aboard an Alfa 164 and drove flat out all the way to his boat at Antibes, on the French Riviera, his pent-up anger such that he hurtled straight past Milan's Malpensa airport, where his own private jet was awaiting his pleasure . . .

Ferrari's official communiqué explained that Jean had retired with a transmission problem: 'He could not engage first gear and the Ferrari's gearbox will not select any other gear unless it starts in first.' This contention was subsequently rejected by John Barnard, who explained that Alesi had stripped the dogrings on first gear by selecting the ratio a millisecond before the clutch had properly engaged. 'If he'd just calmed down, let the revs drop back and engaged third, he could have probably got back into the race,' explained the Ferrari R&D director.

Almost unnoticed, Herbert's spare Lotus had rolled to a halt with alter-

ITALIAN GRAND PRIX

Despite his McLaren suffering from excessive oversteer, Martin Brundle (left) joined team-mate Mika Häkkinen in the top six at the finish, confirming that the Peugeot engine had found some welcome reliability.

Bottom: Ligier's Eric Bernard locks his brakes in his efforts to fend off the challenge of Mark Blundell. The Frenchman drove well after a delayed start to finish seventh, but brake trouble eventually accounted for the Tyrrell, which crashed out.

nator failure as Berger took over at the front of the field, inheriting a 1.1-second advantage over Hill which he gradually eased open to 2.3 seconds by the end of lap 20. Coulthard was a close third with a big gap back to Häkkinen, Frentzen, Barrichello, Brundle, de Cesaris, Fittipaldi, Martini and Katayama.

On lap 24 Berger came in for his sole refuelling stop, his Ferrari stationary for 12.3 seconds, but was delayed fractionally by Panis bringing the Ligier in to stop in the next pit. Hill came in next time round for a 12.3s halt, allowing Coulthard to lead for a lap until he came in on lap 26, then Häkkinen momentarily went ahead before he stopped at the end of lap 27.

All this ducking and diving left Coulthard in the lead, the Scot deferentially easing off on the startline straight at the end of lap 28 to let Damon ahead. Now the two Williams-Renaults began to ease confidently away from Berger, the surviving Ferrari hampered by excessive understeer immediately after his return to the race.

By this stage both Saubers had quit the fray with major piston failures on their 'super spec' Mercedes pneumatic-valve V10 engines, while Katayama and Blundell were storming through the pack to such great effect that they were running sixth and seventh by the end of lap 34, both in with a chance of championship points at the finish.

The first signs of trouble for the Tyrrells came midway round lap 39 when Blundell ran wide over the sand trap at Variante Ascari. Next time round he did exactly the same, this time far more dramatically, as one of the 022's new-spec carbon fibre brake discs exploded. Six laps later, the same fate befell Katayama and the Japanese driver spun wildly into the tyre barriers at the Curva Grande. Fortunately, neither driver came to any harm.

Over the last ten laps, Hill and Coulthard eased the pace very slightly, lapping in the 1m 29s bracket, allowing Berger, running about two seconds a lap faster, to close up. The Ferrari's understeer had all but disappeared by this stage and Gerhard was pushing hard, but the Williams duo seemed to have everything under control and went into the final lap running smoothly at the head of the field. Thus it was a cruel disappointment for Coulthard when his car ran out of fuel on the run down to Parabolica on the final lap and the Scot dropped to sixth place in the final results.

'I felt something amiss and tried to short-shift the gears, but unfortunately the engine died in the middle of Parabolica, and there just wasn't enough to carry me to the line,' shrugged Coulthard. 'It was a very comfortable, relaxed race.'

Closer examination revealed that the Renault engineers had failed to take into account the number of warm-up laps completed by the car, first by Hill and then by Coulthard. It should have been topped up further before the start, but wasn't.

For Hill, of course, it was a great day, just the result he so badly needed to begin his attempt to make inroads into the absent Schumacher's championship points lead. Without the German driver on hand, the effectiveness of Benetton's challenge had been neutered. After Verstappen's abrupt departure on the opening lap, Lehto had endless problems with the clutch, gearbox, electrics and speed-limiter – receiving a stop-go penalty as a result and trailing home ninth.

'I would have loved David to have been up there with me, as he played a big part in the weekend and deserved to be on the podium,' said Damon. 'In the race I was worried about Jean going away so much, but his advantage seemed to stabilise a bit, although I couldn't guarantee in my mind that he was planning a two-stop race.

'Gerhard seemed to get quicker as his fuel load came off and I was pushing very hard to stay in touch with him in the early stages. We passed him in the pits, which was very fortunate as it would have been more difficult to have passed him on the track!'

Berger was relaxed and happy with his second place. It had been a truly heroic performance after his accident during the warm-up, while David Coulthard's last-lap misfortune promoted Häkkinen's McLaren to third place ahead of Rubens Barrichello in the sole surviving Jordan, Eddie Irvine having retired with engine failure. The Ulsterman later received a one-race suspended ban for causing the first-corner collision which resulted in the race being stopped.

Häkkinen had made only one refuelling stop, while Brundle did an equally workmanlike job, battling excessive oversteer in Mika's spare MP4/9 to come home in fifth ahead of the luckless Coulthard. Eric Bernard finished seventh, leading home Comas, Lehto and Panis, who completed the procession of only ten classified finishers at the chequered flag.

Christian Fittipaldi's Footwork had succumbed to engine failure, David Brabham had a lucky escape when one of his Simtek's brake discs exploded and neither Minardi made it to the finish of the team's home Grand Prix, Alboreto wilting with gearbox problems while Martini spun into a sand trap.

Now it was off to Estoril, with Hill keeping his fingers firmly crossed and Coulthard hoping that his luck would change at long last in his final F1 race of the season prior to relinquishing the second Williams seat to the returning Nigel Mansell.

FIA FORMULA ONE WORLD CHAMPIONSHIP ROUND 12

GRAN PREMIO D'ITALIA MONZA
9-11 SEPTEMBER 1994

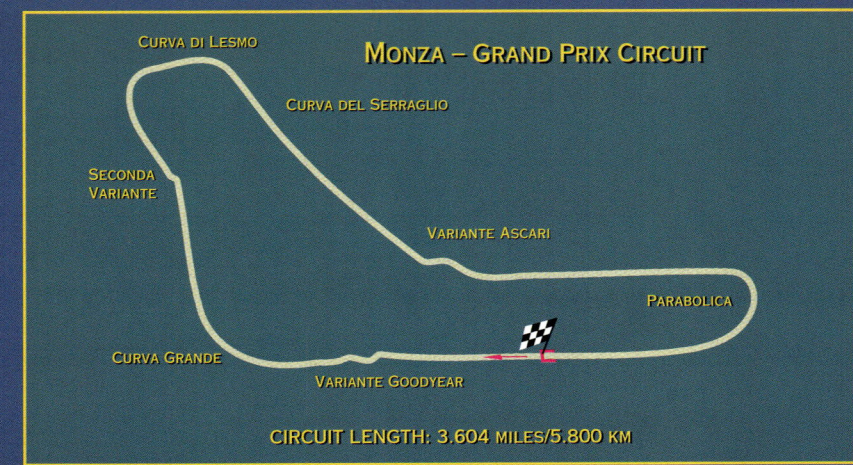

MONZA – GRAND PRIX CIRCUIT
CIRCUIT LENGTH: 3.604 MILES/5.800 KM

RACE WEATHER: Dry, warm, cloudy

Place	Driver	Nat.	No.	Entrant	Car/Engine	Laps	Time/Retirement	Speed (mph/km/h)
1	Damon Hill	GB	0	Rothmans Williams Renault	Williams FW16B-Renault RS6C V10	53	1h 18m 02.754s	146.850/236.322
2	Gerhard Berger	A	28	Scuderia Ferrari	Ferrari 412T1B 043 V12	53	1h 18m 07.684s	146.700/236.073
3	Mika Häkkinen	SF	7	Marlboro McLaren Peugeot	McLaren MP4/9-Peugeot A6 V10	53	1h 18m 28.394s	146.050/235.035
4	Rubens Barrichello	BR	14	Sasol Jordan	Jordan 194-Hart 1035 V10	53	1h 18m 53.388s	145.280/233.794
5	Martin Brundle	GB	8	Marlboro McLaren Peugeot	McLaren MP4/9-Peugeot A6 V10	53	1h 19m 28.329s	144.220/232.081
6	David Coulthard	GB	2	Rothmans Williams Renault	Williams FW16B-Renault RS6C V10	52	Out of fuel	
7	Eric Bernard	F	25	Ligier Gitanes Blondes	Ligier JS39B-Renault RS6A V10	52		
8	Erik Comas	F	20	Tourtel Larrousse F1	Larrousse LH94-Ford HB V8	52		
9	J.J. Lehto	SF	5	Mild Seven Benetton Ford	Benetton B194-Ford Zetec-R V10	52		
10	Olivier Panis	F	26	Ligier Gitanes Blondes	Ligier JS39B-Renault RS6A V10	51		
	David Brabham	AUS	31	MTV Simtek Ford	Simtek S941-Ford HB V8	46	Brakes	
	Ukyo Katayama	J	3	Tyrrell	Tyrrell 022-Yamaha 0X10A V10	45	Accident	
	Christian Fittipaldi	BR	9	Footwork Ford	Footwork FA15-Ford HB V8	43	Engine	
	Eddie Irvine	GB	15	Sasol Jordan	Jordan 194-Hart 1035 V10	41	Engine	
	Mark Blundell	GB	4	Tyrrell	Tyrrell 022-Yamaha 0X10A V10	39	Accident	
	Pierluigi Martini	I	23	Minardi Scuderia Italia	Minardi M194-Ford HB V8	30	Spun off	
	Michele Alboreto	I	24	Minardi Scuderia Italia	Minardi M194-Ford HB V8	28	Gearbox	
	Heinz-Harald Frentzen	D	30	Sauber Mercedes	Sauber C13-Mercedes-Benz V10	22	Engine	
	Andrea de Cesaris	I	29	Sauber Mercedes	Sauber C13-Mercedes-Benz V10	20	Engine	
	Jean-Marc Gounon	F	32	MTV Simtek Ford	Simtek S941-Ford HB V8	20	Transmission	
	Yannick Dalmas	F	19	Tourtel Larrousse F1	Larrousse LH94-Ford HB V8	18	Accident	
	Jean Alesi	F	27	Scuderia Ferrari	Ferrari 412T1B 043 V12	14	Gearbox	
	Johnny Herbert	GB	12	Team Lotus	Lotus 109-Mugen Honda ZA5C	13	Engine	
	Jos Verstappen	NL	6	Mild Seven Benetton Ford	Benetton B194-Ford Zetec-R V10	0	Puncture	
	Gianni Morbidelli	I	10	Footwork Ford	Footwork FA15-Ford HB V8	0	Collision with Zanardi	
	Alessandro Zanardi	I	11	Team Lotus	Lotus 109-Mugen Honda ZA5C V10	0	Collision with Morbidelli	
DNQ	Bertrand Gachot	F	34	Pacific Grand Prix Ltd	Pacific PR01-Ilmor 2175A V10			
DNQ	Paul Belmondo	F	33	Pacific Grand Prix Ltd	Pacific PR01-Ilmor 2175A V10			

Fastest lap: Hill, on lap 24, 1m 25.930s, 150.985 mph/242.988 km/h.
Lap record: Damon Hill (F1 Williams FW15C-Renault V10), 1m 23.575s, 155.241 mph/249.835 km/h (1993 on unrevised track).
All cars used Goodyear tyres.

All results and data © FIA 1994

QUALIFYING 1

Jean Alesi	1m 24.620s
Damon Hill	1m 24.734s
David Coulthard	1m 24.869s
Gerhard Berger	1m 24.915s
Mika Häkkinen	1m 26.004s
Johnny Herbert	1m 26.365s
Heinz-Harald Frentzen	1m 26.406s
Ukyo Katayama	1m 26.525s
Mark Blundell	**1m 26.574s**
Martin Brundle	1m 26.899s
Olivier Panis	1m 26.958s
Rubens Barrichello	1m 27.034s
Andrea de Cesaris	1m 27.188s
Jos Verstappen	1m 27.361s
Eric Bernard	1m 27.387s
J.J. Lehto	1m 27.611s
Alessandro Zanardi	1m 27.617s
Michele Alboreto	1m 27.623s
Christian Fittipaldi	1m 27.675s
Gianni Morbidelli	1m 27.939s
Yannick Dalmas	1m 29.528s
Jean-Marc Gounon	1m 29.594s
Erik Comas	1m 30.530s
David Brabham	1m 30.691s
Bertrand Gachot	1m 31.549s
Paul Belmondo	**1m 32.035s**
Pierluigi Martini	19m 42.320s
Eddie Irvine	no time

Friday afternoon
Dry, hot, sunny

QUALIFYING 2

Jean Alesi	**1m 23.844s**
Gerhard Berger	**1m 23.978s**
Damon Hill	**1m 24.158s**
Johnny Herbert	**1m 24.374s**
David Coulthard	**1m 24.502s**
Olivier Panis	**1m 25.455s**
Mika Häkkinen	**1m 25.528s**
Andrea de Cesaris	**1m 25.540s**
Eddie Irvine	**1m 25.568s**
Jos Verstappen	**1m 25.618s**
Heinz-Harald Frentzen	**1m 25.628s**
Eric Bernard	**1m 25.718s**
Alessandro Zanardi	**1m 25.733s**
Ukyo Katayama	**1m 25.889s**
Martin Brundle	**1m 25.933s**
Rubens Barrichello	**1m 25.946s**
Gianni Morbidelli	**1m 26.002s**
Pierluigi Martini	**1m 26.056s**
Christian Fittipaldi	**1m 26.337s**
J.J. Lehto	**1m 26.384s**
Mark Blundell	1m 26.697s
Michele Alboreto	**1m 26.832s**
Yannick Dalmas	**1m 27.846s**
Erik Comas	**1m 27.894s**
Jean-Marc Gounon	**1m 28.353s**
David Brabham	**1m 28.619s**
Bertrand Gachot	**1m 31.387s**
Paul Belmondo	no time

Saturday afternoon
Dry, hot, sunny

WARM-UP

Jean Alesi	1m 25.371s
Ukyo Katayama	1m 25.855s
David Coulthard	1m 25.858s
Mark Blundell	1m 26.080s
Gerhard Berger	1m 26.199s
Mika Häkkinen	1m 26.433s
Johnny Herbert	1m 26.526s
Damon Hill	1m 26.629s
Heinz-Harald Frentzen	1m 26.787s
Olivier Panis	1m 26.805s
Christian Fittipaldi	1m 27.047s
Rubens Barrichello	1m 27.332s
Gianni Morbidelli	1m 27.483s
Martin Brundle	1m 27.494s
Alessandro Zanardi	1m 27.531s
Jos Verstappen	1m 27.611s
Andrea de Cesaris	1m 27.629s
J.J. Lehto	1m 27.962s
Eric Bernard	1m 28.001s
Erik Comas	1m 28.154s
Michele Alboreto	1m 28.178s
Pierluigi Martini	1m 28.181s
Eddie Irvine	1m 28.388s
Yannick Dalmas	1m 29.998s
David Brabham	1m 30.028s
Jean-Marc Gounon	1m 33.919s

Sunday morning
Dry, hot, sunny

FASTEST LAPS

Driver	Time	Lap
Damon Hill	1m 25.930s	24
Jean Alesi	1m 26.279s	8
Gerhard Berger	1m 26.541s	17
David Coulthard	1m 26.607s	23
Olivier Panis	1m 26.630s	47
Mark Blundell	1m 26.663s	36
Ukyo Katayama	1m 26.702s	31
Mika Häkkinen	1m 27.432s	46
Rubens Barrichello	1m 27.449s	21
Eric Bernard	1m 27.488s	9
Heinz-Harald Frentzen	1m 27.786s	18
J.J. Lehto	1m 28.072s	13
Christian Fittipaldi	1m 28.133s	27
Martin Brundle	1m 28.185s	49
Eddie Irvine	1m 28.312s	19
Andrea de Cesaris	1m 28.411s	20
Pierluigi Martini	1m 28.473s	19
Erik Comas	1m 28.475s	24
Johnny Herbert	1m 28.871s	9
Michele Alboreto	1m 28.956s	12
Yannick Dalmas	1m 29.485s	10
David Brabham	1m 30.036s	12
Jean-Marc Gounon	1m 30.479s	17

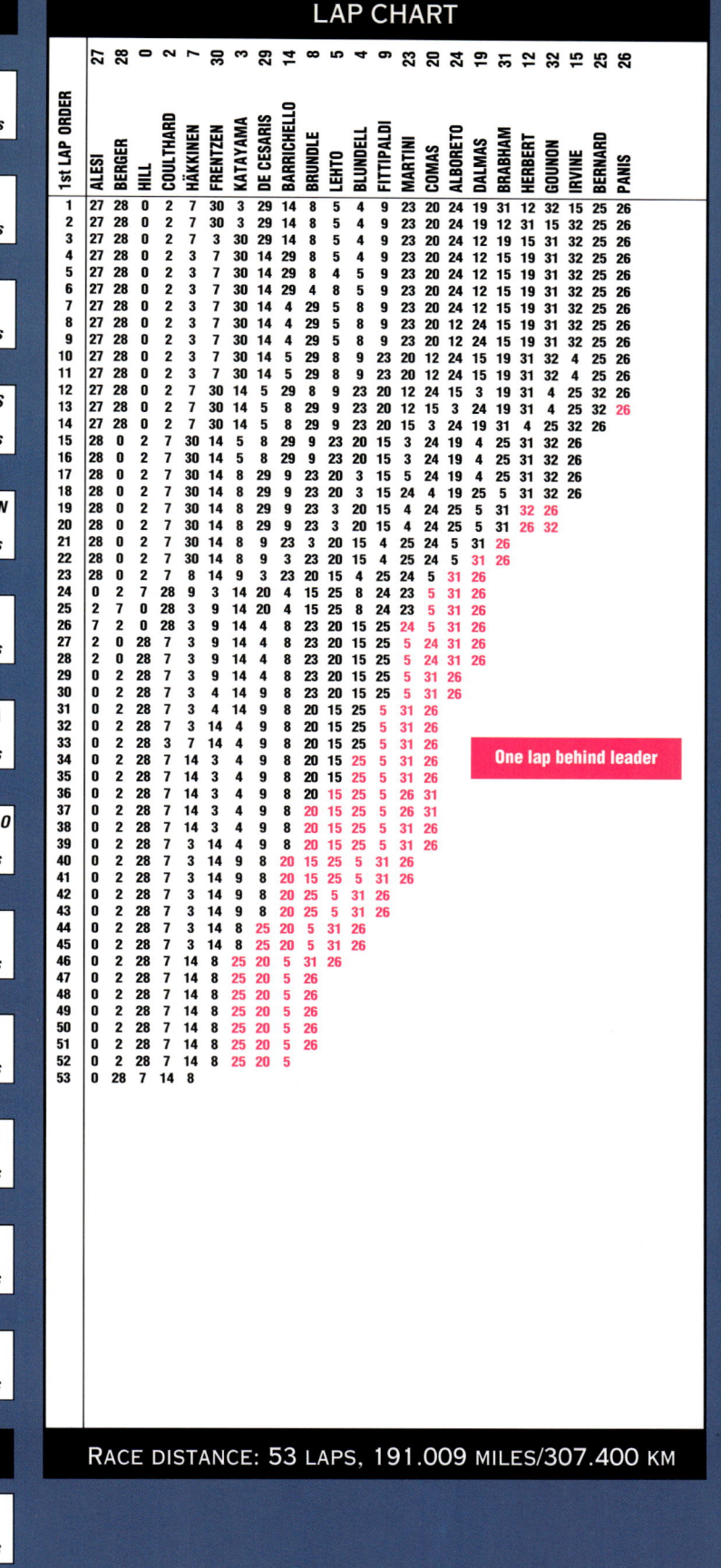

WORLD CHAMPIONSHIP • ROUND 13

PORTUGUESE GRAND PRIX

| HILL |
| COULTHARD |
| HÄKKINEN |
| BARRICHELLO |
| VERSTAPPEN |
| BRUNDLE |

Damon Hill took a giant, potentially crucial, stride towards the 1994 World Championship title with a superbly paced win in the Portuguese Grand Prix at Estoril, leading home his brilliant young team-mate David Coulthard in a decisive 1-2 for the Williams team, its first so far this season. In a delightful historic twist, it was the first 1-2 finish for British drivers since Damon's late father Graham beat the Frank Williams-owned Brabham driven by Piers Courage in the 1969 Monaco Grand Prix. It also made it harder than ever to understand why Williams should even consider meeting the $1 million a race fee reputedly required by Nigel Mansell for a full-time F1 return in 1995 when Coulthard, eighteen years his junior, had displayed such immense long-term potential in only eight outings with the Didcot team. With Michael Schumacher sitting out the second event of his two-race suspension, the Williams-Renault duo crossed the finishing line 0.6s apart after closing up into tight formation over the last few laps. They were almost 20 seconds ahead of Mika Häkkinen's third-placed McLaren-Peugeot, with the Jordan-Hart of Rubens Barrichello, Jos Verstappen's Benetton and Martin Brundle's McLaren completing the top six. It was a result which meant that Hill would go into the European GP at Jerez only one point behind Schumacher with three of the season's 16 races still to run.

Top right: Damon Hill escaped injury when his Williams overturned after tangling with Eddie Irvine's Jordan in practice.

Above: David Coulthard runs wide and Damon grabs his chance to take the lead as he tucks in behind the Larrousse of Erik Comas.

Right: After his disappointment at Monza, Coulthard savours his first visit to the podium as Mika Häkkinen dispenses the traditional hospitality.

The clock starts ticking for Team Lotus

At Estoril, Team Lotus was contesting its first race since being placed in administration by the High Court, thereby being guaranteed a breathing space from its debtors and heading off the prospect of a winding-up order from Cosworth Engineering, to whom it owed a minimum of £600,000 – a legacy of its 1992 and '93 seasons using Ford's customer HB V8 engine.

With approximately another £7 million owing to the controversial finance company, Landhurst Leasing, which itself was now in receivership, Lotus's debt was certainly running at a high level for such a relatively small company. Yet Neil Cooper, the London-based accountant from the firm Robson Rhodes who was appointed administrator the day after Johnny Herbert had started the Italian Grand Prix from a best-ever fourth place on the grid, was far from downcast over the possibility of salvaging the team which carries one of the most famous names in F1 history.

'It's a bit like the cavalry coming over the hill to the rescue,' he explained at Estoril. 'Simply a question of whether we can arrive in time. Under the administration procedure, I have to report back to the creditors within three months.

'In addition, the judge who granted the order has instructed me to produce a further report by 24 October as he is concerned about the need to begin expenditure on the new cars for the 1995 season.'

Several options are open to an administrator in these circumstances. The present board of directors could conceivably put together their own rescue package, the company's assets could be sold or, in a worst-case scenario, Team Lotus could effectively find itself being broken up and its assets dispersed.

As a parable for our times, Lotus's problems highlighted the economic conundrum facing many teams seeking to make their mark on the contemporary F1 scene. Its plight inevitably struck a chord with teams such as Simtek and Pacific, who are struggling to make progress from the lowest rung on the ladder of F1 achievement – not to mention several more established teams whose finances seemed to be more precarious than one might have concluded from an outside view.

ENTRY AND PRACTICE

Fresh from its disappointment at Monza, where second place was the best it could muster in front of its home crowd, Ferrari was determined to produce a worthwhile result at Estoril, where Alesi had led quite decisively in the opening stages 12 months before. Gerhard Berger duly set the pace in Friday's first qualifying session, posting a 1m 20.608s best – good enough, it transpired, to secure pole position for the Ferrari 412T1B.

The Austrian frankly admitted that he was slightly surprised to have emerged fastest, feeling that he was losing a lot of time in the absurdly tight first-gear chicane that had been introduced at the back of the circuit.

'On Saturday my car had a strange handling problem, which is why I kept running even though the track was slower than yesterday,' he explained. 'It is important that we solve this problem as I believe that, even in race trim, the Williams still has a small advantage over Ferrari. I don't agree with people who say I was lucky, as Hill's time was very close to mine, and I only missed pole by a whisker at Silverstone and Monza.

'If we have a problem, it is that, while we have enough power, we don't have enough torque.'

In the Williams camp, Damon Hill reckoned he might have taken a serious crack at pole position had it not been for a headwind on the start/finish straight during Saturday's second qualifying session. In fact, Damon could count himself pretty fortunate to be in a position to start the race at all. In the closing moments of Friday's hour-long qualifying session, Eddie Irvine's Jordan spun in front of him on the approach to the new chicane, triggering a highly dramatic sequence of events.

Hill attempted to slip by his rival, but the Williams's left-rear wheel rode over the pirouetting Jordan's left-rear and the FW16B was neatly flipped into the gravel trap on the outside of the circuit. Cool as a cucumber, Hill scrambled from beneath the upturned machine, hardly pausing to brush the gravel off his overalls before strolling back to the pit lane garage. Characteristically, Damon was pretty philosophical about the whole affair.

'What can you do?' he shrugged. 'Eddie lost control. He didn't do it deliberately. I could see him coming back across the track, but there was nowhere to go!

'It was the first time I've ever been upside down in a racing car. It may have looked pretty tame on television, but there is still 500 kg of racing car on top of you in such a situation!'

The Williams was then pretty badly knocked about by the marshals, who dropped it back onto its wheels and then dragged it away across the gravel, much to the detriment of its suspension, bodywork and aerofoils. By the time it was rebuilt for the following day, the monocoque and gearbox casing were pretty well the only original components to be recycled!

'It's typical, isn't it?' laughed Irvine. 'I spun once, and the guy who's trying to get the championship comes through and collects me. The luck of the Irish has never come my way!'

Although Hill could not top Berger's best, both he and team-mate David Coulthard improved their times on Saturday, making a lot of effort to reduce the touch of high-speed understeer which could be so potentially damaging in terms of front tyre wear come the race.

'On my third run, the tyres didn't quite come in like they had on the first and second sets,' said Hill. 'But on my second run I was ahead at the timing split, only to catch a Simtek. But I'm very confident for tomorrow.'

Coulthard would line up in third place on the grid, ahead of Mika Häkkinen's McLaren-Peugeot and Jean Alesi's Ferrari. The young Scot was naturally delighted to have equalled his previous best qualifying position in Hungary. 'On my first Saturday run I had a little bit of traffic,' he explained, 'then on my second run I touched a kerb at the first corner and had to come in.'

Alesi found himself struggling to work out a decent chassis balance, and his plight was made more acute when he lost much of the Saturday morning free practice session after an engine failure. That left Jean so frustrated that he did only six laps on Saturday before concluding that there was no realistic prospect of improving his time, the Frenchman returning to the pits in order to conserve his supply of tyres.

Häkkinen was pretty content with his time, only 0.64s away from pole position, the McLaren-Peugeots thriving at a circuit where top-end power is less of a priority. Mika and team-mate Martin Brundle, who qualified seventh, both did their best times in the more favourable conditions on Friday, the Englishman admitting he made a slight mistake on his best lap which cost him a few tenths.

Ukyo Katayama was understandably satisfied with sixth place in the Tyrrell-Yamaha. After the Friday morning free practice session, he changed his 022's set-up slightly, putting more downforce on the rear, and popped in his best time in the closing stages of first qualifying. That was just as well, because he was able to manage only a handful of laps on Saturday afternoon, frustrated by a throttle assembly problem which had almost stranded him out on the circuit. Team-mate Mark Blundell took 12th place on the strength of his Friday best, having been delayed slightly when Bertrand Gachot's Pacific spun after suffering an engine failure.

Rubens Barrichello had a trouble-free run to qualify eighth on Friday, and improved his time to hold his position the following day. Irvine, by contrast, suffered an engine failure on Friday morning, then had his celebrated brush with Hill and was held up by Erik Comas on his best qualifying lap the following day. As a result, the Ulsterman had to settle for a disappointing 13th place on the grid, despite managing to set sixth-fastest time on Saturday morning.

'I was very disappointed with my final position,' he admitted. 'The car and engine were much better today, but my best lap was ruined by traffic. I was two-tenths up at the first split, then I found Comas on my line coming into the new chicane.'

In the Sauber-Mercedes camp, Heinz-Harald Frentzen had a frustrating time on Friday when a differential problem caused him to stop after three laps, leaving him in 13th. Happily, on Saturday he improved by the best part of a second to vault forward into ninth place overall. Team-mate Andrea de Cesaris had two of his Friday runs ruined by Gianni Morbidelli's pirouetting Footwork and waved yellow flags, emerging an unhappy 17th fastest after virtually matching his time in slower conditions the following day.

Elsewhere, even allowing for Schumacher's absence, Benetton seemed to have lost the fine edge of their competitiveness. Hitherto, one of the B194's strongest cards had been its slow-speed handling, yet J.J. Lehto and Jos Verstappen were losing almost a second on the very slow new section alone.

The pair spent most of the weekend chasing a decent chassis set-up and Verstappen was the quicker of the two in tenth spot, with Lehto four places further back. 'We seemed to have too much downforce,' explained Lehto, 'and I struggled a bit during my first two runs. We then went back to settings tried during the morning but, on my third set, there was a lot of traffic. I think it would have been hard to break the 1m 22s barrier, but I am happy with the car in race trim. I think we'll be

215

PORTUGUESE GRAND PRIX

in better shape than we've been in qualifying.'

Olivier Panis was beset by poor grip on his Ligier JS39B, managing only 19th-fastest time on Friday. However, like team-mate Eric Bernard, he found more than a second the following day to line up 15th. Unfortunately Bernard's 1.3s improvement merely moved him from 23rd to 21st, so he was still pretty dismayed by the outcome.

Christian Fittipaldi, meanwhile, had been getting the best out of a new floor, differential and braking system on his Footwork FA15, qualifying a promising 11th as a result. Gianni Morbidelli looked set for a worthwhile improvement on 15th at the end of Friday's qualifying runs, but braking problems produced a succession of flat-spotted tyres and he eventually slipped to 16th in the final order.

Closely matched in 18th and 19th places were the Minardis of Pierluigi Martini and Michele Alboreto. Piero had missed much of Friday morning's session with a wiring loom problem, but set his qualifying time that afternoon – he failed to improve the following day, complaining that his engine felt down on power. Alboreto opted to use Minardi's hydraulic suspension system, unlike his team-mate, and also set his time on the first day. On Saturday afternoon he was hampered by a misfire and also strayed into a gravel trap due to a glitch in the car's semi-automatic gearchange system.

Lotus, now operating under the administration of the High Court in London, had a simply terrible weekend, a bitter disappointment after Johnny Herbert's terrific fourth place in qualifying at Monza. The Englishman started off with a major error of judgement, spinning off and stalling his engine on Friday, an inexplicable mistake which lost him the entire first qualifying session after he was excluded for receiving an illegal push-start, against the traffic, from some nearby marshals.

For the rest of the weekend Herbert grappled with rear suspension problems and never came close to unlocking the potential of the new Mugen Honda V10. He qualified 20th, with Philippe Adams putting the other 109 (still with the old-spec engine) on the back row of the grid, just ahead of Jean-Marc Gounon's Simtek.

This was not quite what the Lotus management had been hoping for, particularly under the watchful gaze of Neil Cooper, the team's administrator, who had made the trip to Portugal to help assess the likelihood of a rescue package.

Behind Herbert came Bernard, followed by the Larrousse LH94s of Comas and Yannick Dalmas, while David Brabham lined up 24th with the Simtek. 'We have tried everything with the car here,' said Brabham, 'truly maxed out, in fact. There doesn't seem to be any more to come and I certainly couldn't have tried harder. I guess we have to accept that with our weight and power penalties, and lack of an automatic gearbox, we're just not going to be much quicker.'

Languishing behind Adams and Gounon, neither Pacific made the cut. Bertrand Gachot had an engine problem on Friday and wasted time trying new uprights which then had to be replaced with the original components. Another engine problem on Saturday pitched him into a half-spin and wiped out any prospect of his qualifying. Paul Belmondo had engine problems on Saturday morning, requiring a fresh Ilmor V10, and a braking glitch in final qualifying.

RACE

Although Berger had been fastest in qualifying, Coulthard and Hill topped the timing sheets in the race morning warm-up and the Williams team was quietly confident that things would be just fine when the serious action of the day began. Third and fourth fastest were the McLarens of Häkkinen and Brundle, although neither seriously believed he would be a factor in the battle for front-running positions.

Even before the start, one contender was in trouble when Katayama's Tyrrell rolled to a halt on the parade lap just before the pits entrance. The Yamaha V10 had cut out midway round the lap, but the Japanese driver had successfully managed to restart it. Unfortunately it had then died a second time and he was pushed into the pit lane. Ukyo was eventually able to join in late, long after Gerhard Berger's Ferrari had led the sprint down to the first corner.

From his position on the left-hand side of the second row, Coulthard produced another of his excellent getaways, running round the outside of Hill to take an immediate second place. Everybody managed to negotiate the opening lap without undue drama, Berger leading the pack across the timing line 1.02 seconds

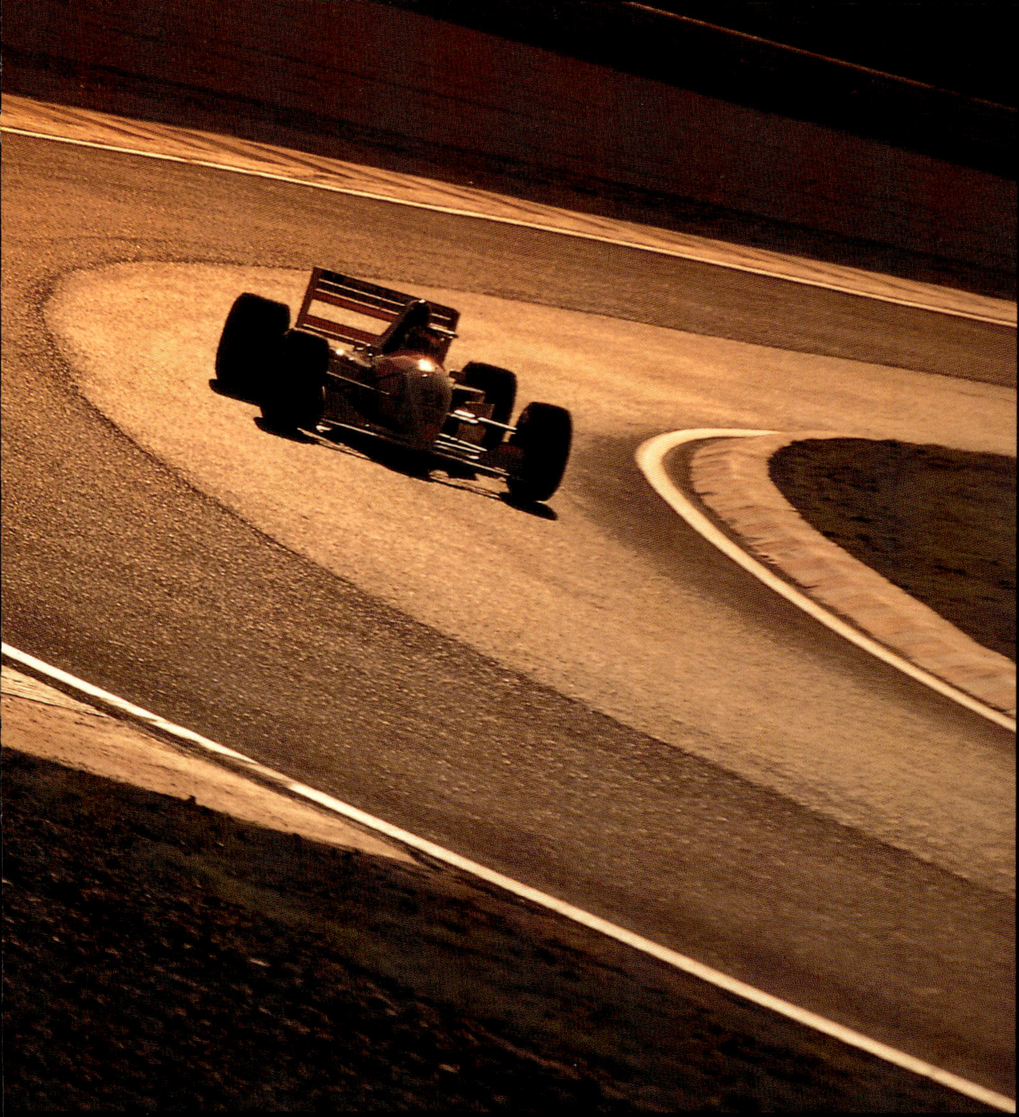

Bryn Williams/Words & Pictures

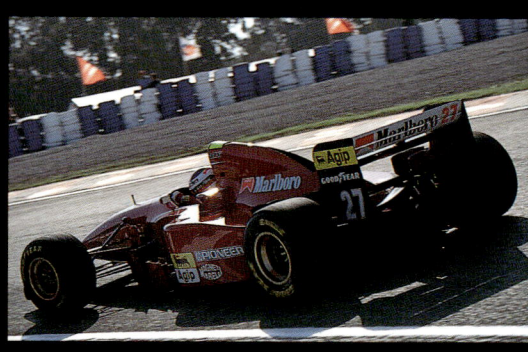

Bathed in warm autumn sunshine, Jean Alesi *(above)*, Mika Häkkinen *(left)* and David Coulthard get to grips with the twisty and undulating Estoril track. Coulthard and Häkkinen were bound for the podium, but Alesi eliminated himself from the race after colliding with David Brabham's Simtek.

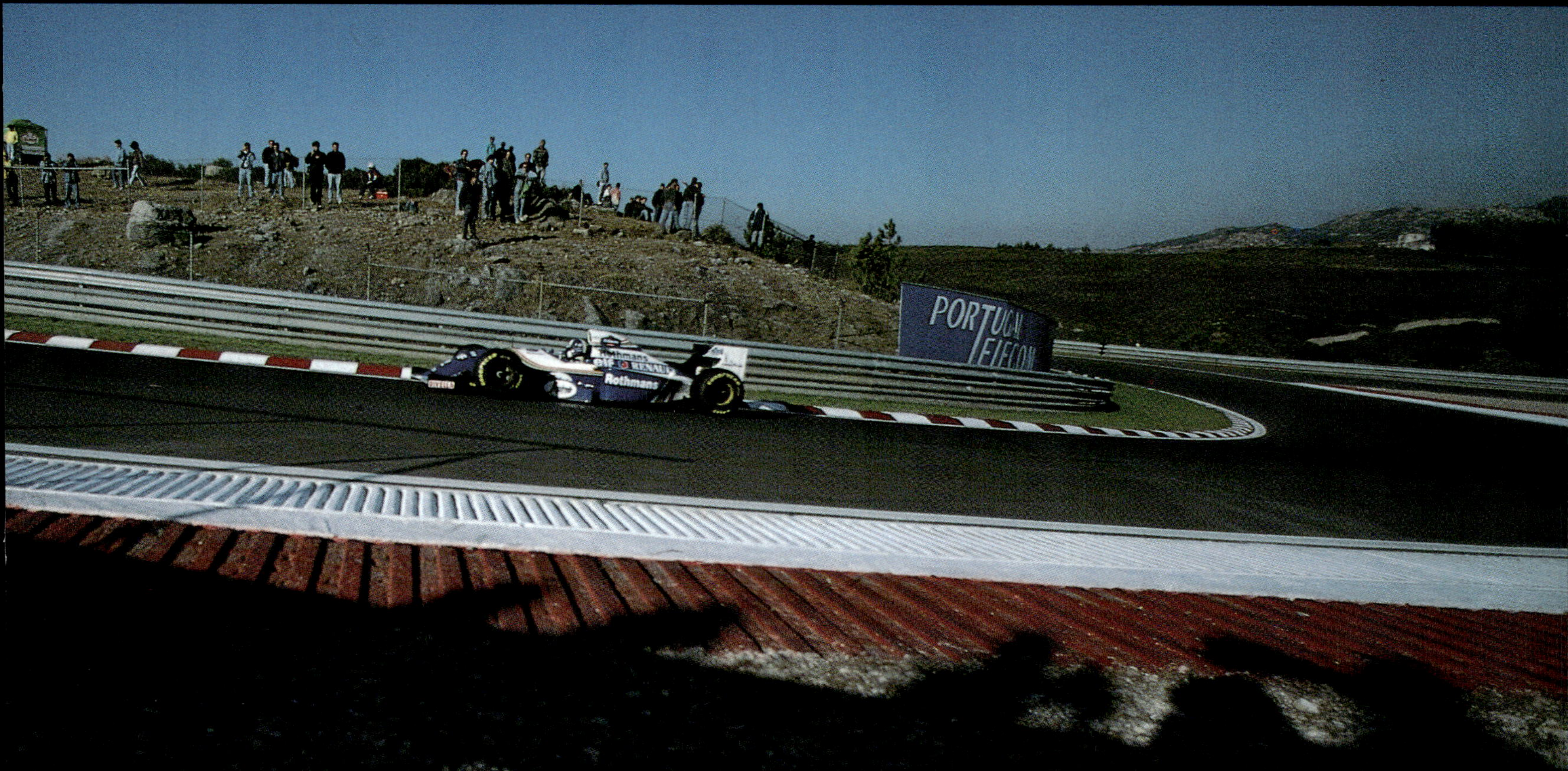

PORTUGUESE GRAND PRIX

Diary

Penske Indy Car star Paul Tracy attends the Portuguese GP as a spectator prior to testing a Benetton B194 during the week immediately after the race.

Ferrari comes close to withdrawing from Portuguese GP after receiving a $50,000 fine and a one-race ban – suspended for three races – after several of its mechanics kicked down a locked door trying to leave the Estoril circuit on the Friday evening before the race. The incident provoked the local police to draw their guns.

Christian Fittipaldi explores possibility of Indy Car season in 1995.

French Formula 3000 front-runner Franck Lagorce is signed as test driver by the Ligier team.

ahead of the young Scot. Hill was third with Alesi hanging on to the Williams as best he could. Then came Häkkinen, Barrichello, Frentzen, Verstappen and Brundle.

On the second lap Coulthard began to inch closer to the Ferrari. Over the next three laps Gerhard's advantage shrank from 1.08s to 1.004s, 0.6s and then 0.5s. By lap seven it was clear that David would like to get past, for Damon was also crowding him by this stage, but the two Williams drivers were saved the trouble of a close tussle with the Ferrari when Berger pulled off midway round the eighth lap, the gearchange hydraulic system having failed.

Hill later admitted that he was struggling slightly to keep pace with his younger team-mate in the opening phase of the race. Troubled by a touch too much oversteer, he was worried about rear tyre wear and by the end of lap 17 he was 5.5 seconds adrift.

Coulthard surrendered his advantage when he pulled into the pits for fuel and tyres a lap later, Damon making a fractionally quicker stop next time round. The Williams duo dropped to fourth and fifth places as Alesi briefly inherited the lead, pursued by Häkkinen and Barrichello, but this trio duly made their first refuelling stops over the next few laps, and by lap 27 the situation at the head of the field had stabilised once more, with Coulthard just ahead of Hill.

Then David suddenly found himself boxed in by Comas's Larrousse going into the first-gear infield hairpin. He went fractionally wide and Hill didn't hesitate for a moment, diving up the inside of his team-mate to take the lead.

'He got stuck behind some slower cars,' explained Hill, 'so I thought, well, I'm coming through – I just hope I have enough steering lock to get round.'

Coulthard freely conceded that he'd been caught on the hop. 'To be perfectly honest, Damon took me totally by surprise,' he admitted. 'He pulled a terrific overtaking manoeuvre and caught me asleep. I thought we'd agreed that we wouldn't be overtaking each other at that particular corner and he intended that should last through the race!

'If it had been anybody else, I would have defended my position.'

In fact, as others told it, at the pre-race drivers' briefing, Hill had voiced some concern about the state of that tight corner; understandably, of course, as this was the point at which Irvine had launched him into orbit on Friday. It was apparently agreed that the no-passing convention would only apply in the early stages of the race.

At the time the two Williams-Renaults swapped places at the head of the field, Heinz-Harald Frentzen was running in a splendid third place, having benefited thus far from

a one-stop strategy. Then, on lap 32, to the German driver's dismay, his transmission broke.

'I just can't believe it,' he shrugged. 'I'm sure that I had a very good chance to finish the race third. In the early stages I pushed very hard, but wasn't able to follow Barrichello and Häkkinen. On the other hand, I had no problem to keep Verstappen under control, and when all the drivers around me stopped as from lap 20 I knew how competitive our car was.

'Suddenly they showed me P3, and when I realised that Alesi could not pick up on time I was convinced I would score a fantastic result, because the balance of the car was perfect and the engine very good. But suddenly, there was no more traction.'

As far as the lead battle was concerned, from this point on Coulthard duly played a supporting role, but he never allowed Hill to become complacent. By lap 36 – half-distance – Damon had opened a 4.7s advantage over the second FW16B. Alesi was

Left: Midfield runners Blundell, Irvine, Panis, Verstappen, de Cesaris, Herbert and Morbidelli form an orderly queue through the absurdly tight new hairpin on the first lap.

Bottom left: Pierluigi Martini in the Minardi heads the Ligier of Eric Bernard. On a day when there were only nine retirements from a field of 26, reliability alone was not enough to earn them a worthwhile result.

now third, almost 20 seconds further back, ahead of Häkkinen, Barrichello and Verstappen.

Despite his brief spell in the lead, Alesi had a generally miserable afternoon. His Ferrari's set-up was such that its handling wasn't in the same class as Berger's, and he had a couple of lurid trips up the high kerb exiting the tricky second right-hander beyond the pits in his anxiety to keep pace in the opening stages.

His race eventually came to a spectacular end at the third turn, midway round lap 39. Still holding a distant third, he dived inside Brabham's Simtek to lap the slower car, the two machines made contact and pirouetted off into the gravel trap.

Brabham rightly emerged from his cockpit feeling pretty indignant about the whole affair, accusing Alesi of being excessively aggressive. For his part, Jean simply replied that Brabham had been paying insufficient attention to his mirrors. Objectively, though, it seemed from the touchlines that Alesi had started his overtaking move from too far back. The stewards' decision to give Brabham a one-race suspended ban for causing the incident ranked as one of the less comprehensible decisions in a season already not distinguished by a surfeit of logic . . .

Brabham, who had been punted out of the Monaco GP by Alesi in similar circumstances, certainly did not mince his words. 'I must say I was surprised to get hit, but when I turned around and saw that it was Jean Alesi, I wasn't surprised at all.

'Sometimes you think these top guys are a bit slow because they're all so cautious to make sure you have seen them coming. But not him!'

Coulthard made his second refuelling stop (8.7 seconds) at the end of lap 46 with Hill following suit (8.1s) next time round. Damon emerged 3.7s ahead and for the rest of the race the two Williams-Renaults toured steadily round at the front of the field, Häkkinen's third-placed McLaren being almost 20 seconds behind by the lap 50 mark.

Mika was handicapped by such a lack of power that he had great difficulty inching past even the slowest back-markers on the straight. For many laps it seemed as though Barrichello might mount a formidable challenge for third place, but Häkkinen had the upper hand in traffic and, although Rubens got to within 3.3 seconds at one point, the Finn had extended his cushion to just under eight seconds at the chequered flag.

Barrichello, in turn, came under threat from Verstappen's Benetton in the closing stages. The Dutchman had been seriously short of grip on his first set of tyres, so radioed the pit crew to reduce the pressures on the second set, a strategy which worked a treat after his first pit visit.

'After that, I managed better and better lap times and really got into the race,' said Jos. He dropped back slightly after a huge moment on the grass coming through the recently renamed Ayrton Senna right-hander coming onto the startline straight, but was still less than a couple of seconds behind the Jordan at the finish. Team-mate J.J. Lehto could claim no such vindication, dropping a wheel over a kerb and spinning into a gravel trap with 11 laps to go.

Brundle was sixth after making up for a bad start, while Blundell's Tyrrell-Yamaha looked set to make it a very close call for the final point when it suffered a major bottom-end engine failure, probably a broken crankshaft, with just under ten laps left to run. That completed a bad day for Tyrrell, as Katayama had stopped for good after 26 laps when the electronics went haywire again and he suddenly found himself unable to select any gears.

Irvine did well to finish seventh ahead of Fittipaldi's down-on-power Footwork, while Panis crossed the line in ninth place, only for his Ligier to fail the skidblock test and be disqualified from the results. That promoted Morbidelli to ninth ahead of Bernard and Herbert, the Lotus team leader again having a dismal time, grappling with a downshift problem which obliged him to use a left-foot braking technique in the closing stages of the contest. Closely matched Minardi teammates Pierluigi Martini and Michele Alboreto were next, two laps down.

Damon was over the moon with his third victory in as many races. 'I am absolutely, completely and utterly delighted with what was a really crucial win here today,' he admitted. 'We knew we had a good technical package and it was great to be able to finish the job. It is a terrific platform from which to launch an attack on the World Championship points lead at the next race.'

For Coulthard, who was less than a second behind at the chequered flag, it was an historic moment, his first podium finish achieved in only the eighth Grand Prix of his career. 'It's been a long time coming,' grinned the Scot. 'I was praying as I counted down each lap to the finish. I'd like to thank the team for the faith they have showed in putting me in the car when others might have selected a more experienced driver.'

As a footnote, it is worth mentioning that there was a good standard of mechanical reliability displayed at this race, with 17 of the 26 starters making it to the finish. But the standard of driving among the back-markers was certainly not as good as it might have been, and there were several close escapes as the faster cars picked their way through slower traffic.

FIA FORMULA ONE WORLD CHAMPIONSHIP ROUND 13

GRAN PREMIO DE PORTUGAL
ESTORIL
23-25 SEPTEMBER 1994

ESTORIL – GRAND PRIX CIRCUIT

CIRCUIT LENGTH: 2.725 MILES/4.360 KM

RACE WEATHER: DRY, WARM, CLOUDY

Place	Driver	Nat.	No.	Entrant	Car/Engine	Laps	Time/Retirement	Speed (mph/km/h)
1	Damon Hill	GB	0	Rothmans Williams Renault	Williams FW16B-Renault RS6C V10	71	1h 41m 10.165s	114.080/183.594
2	David Coulthard	GB	2	Rothmans Williams Renault	Williams FW16B-Renault RS6C V10	71	1h 41m 10.768s	114.070/183.578
3	Mika Häkkinen	SF	7	Marlboro McLaren Peugeot	McLaren MP4/9-Peugeot A6 V10	71	1h 41m 30.358s	113.800/183.144
4	Rubens Barrichello	BR	14	Sasol Jordan	Jordan 194-Hart 1035 V10	71	1h 41m 38.168s	113.560/182.757
5	Jos Verstappen	NL	6	Mild Seven Benetton Ford	Benetton B194-Ford Zetec-R V8	71	1h 41m 39.550s	113.530/182.709
6	Martin Brundle	GB	8	Marlboro McLaren Peugeot	McLaren MP4/9-Peugeot A6 V10	71	1h 42m 02.867s	113.100/182.017
7	Eddie Irvine	GB	15	Sasol Jordan	Jordan 194-Hart 1035 V10	70		
8	Christian Fittipaldi	BR	9	Footwork Ford	Footwork FA15-Ford HB V8	70		
9	Gianni Morbidelli	I	10	Footwork Ford	Footwork FA15-Ford HB V8	70		
10	Eric Bernard	F	25	Ligier Gitanes Blondes	Ligier JS39B-Renault RS6A V10	70		
11	Johnny Herbert	GB	12	Team Lotus	Lotus 109-Mugen Honda ZA6C V10	70		
12	Pierluigi Martini	I	23	Minardi Scuderia Italia	Minardi M194-Ford HB V8	69		
13	Michele Alboreto	I	24	Minardi Scuderia Italia	Minardi M194-Ford HB V8	69		
14	Yannick Dalmas	F	19	Tourtel Larrousse F1	Larrousse LH94-Ford HB V8	69		
15	Jean-Marc Gounon	F	32	MTV Simtek Ford	Simtek S941-Ford HB V8	67		
16	Philippe Adams	B	11	Team Lotus	Lotus 109-Mugen Honda ZA5C V10	67		
	Mark Blundell	GB	4	Tyrrell	Tyrrell 022-Yamaha 0X10A V10	61	Engine	
	J.J. Lehto	SF	5	Mild Seven Benetton Ford	Benetton B194-Ford Zetec-R V8	60	Spun off	
	Andrea de Cesaris	I	29	Sauber Mercedes	Sauber C13-Mercedes-Benz V10	54	Spun off	
	Jean Alesi	F	27	Scuderia Ferrari	Ferrari 412T1B 043 V12	38	Collision with Brabham	
	David Brabham	AUS	31	MTV Simtek Ford	Simtek S941-Ford HB V8	36	Collision with Alesi	
	Heinz-Harald Frentzen	D	30	Sauber Mercedes	Sauber C13-Mercedes-Benz V10	31	Gearbox	
	Erik Comas	F	20	Tourtel Larrousse F1	Larrousse LH94-Ford HB V8	27	Accident	
	Ukyo Katayama	J	3	Tyrrell	Tyrrell 022-Yamaha 0X10A V10	26	Gearbox	
	Gerhard Berger	A	28	Scuderia Ferrari	Ferrari 412T1B 043 V12	7	Transmission	
DQ	Olivier Panis	F	26	Ligier Gitanes Blondes	Ligier JS39B-Renault RS6A V10	70		
DNQ	Bertrand Gachot	F	34	Pacific Grand Prix Ltd	Pacific PR01-Ilmor 2175A V10			
DNQ	Paul Belmondo	F	33	Pacific Grand Prix Ltd	Pacific PR01-Ilmor 2175A V10			

Fastest lap: Coulthard, on lap 12, 1m 22.446s, 118.296 mph/190.379 km/h (record for revised circuit).
Lap record for old circuit: Damon Hill (F1 Williams FW15C-Renault V10), 1m 14.859s, 129.987 mph/209.193 km/h (1993).
All cars used Goodyear tyres.

QUALIFYING 1

Gerhard Berger	**1m 20.608s**
Damon Hill	1m 20.803s
David Coulthard	1m 21.120s
Mika Häkkinen	**1m 21.251s**
Jean Alesi	**1m 21.517s**
Ukyo Katayama	1m 21.590s
Martin Brundle	**1m 21.656s**
Rubens Barrichello	1m 21.839s
Mark Blundell	**1m 22.288s**
J.J. Lehto	1m 22.613s
Jos Verstappen	1m 22.614s
Christian Fittipaldi	1m 22.636s
Heinz-Harald Frentzen	1m 22.795s
Andrea de Cesaris	**1m 22.885s**
Gianni Morbidelli	1m 22.974s
Pierluigi Martini	**1m 23.243s**
Michele Alboreto	**1m 23.364s**
Eddie Irvine	1m 23.411s
Olivier Panis	1m 23.711s
Erik Comas	**1m 24.192s**
Yannick Dalmas	**1m 24.438s**
David Brabham	1m 24.527s
Eric Bernard	1m 25.039s
Philippe Adams	**1m 25.313s**
Jean-Marc Gounon	1m 25.686s
Bertrand Gachot	1m 27.960s
Paul Belmondo	1m 32.706s
Johnny Herbert	no time

Friday afternoon
Dry, warm, sunny

QUALIFYING 2

Damon Hill	**1m 20.766s**
David Coulthard	**1m 21.033s**
Mika Häkkinen	1m 21.700s
Rubens Barrichello	**1m 21.796s**
Gerhard Berger	1m 21.863s
Heinz-Harald Frentzen	**1m 21.921s**
Jos Verstapppen	**1m 22.000s**
Martin Brundle	1m 22.035s
Jean Alesi	1m 22.086s
Christian Fittipaldi	**1m 22.132s**
Eddie Irvine	**1m 22.294s**
J.J. Lehto	**1m 22.369s**
Olivier Panis	**1m 22.672s**
Gianni Morbidelli	**1m 22.756s**
Andrea de Cesaris	1m 22.888s
Mark Blundell	1m 22.971s
Johnny Herbert	**1m 23.408s**
Pierluigi Martini	1m 23.464s
Eric Bernard	**1m 23.699s**
Michele Alboreto	1m 24.186s
Erik Comas	1m 24.306s
David Brabham	**1m 24.514s**
Yannick Dalmas	1m 24.920s
Jean-Marc Gounon	**1m 25.649s**
Philippe Adams	1m 25.708s
Bertrand Gachot	**1m 27.385s**
Paul Belmondo	**1m 29.000s**
Ukyo Katayama	4m 03.441s

Saturday afternoon
Dry, warm, sunny

WARM-UP

David Coulthard	1m 21.442s
Damon Hill	1m 21.929s
Mika Häkkinen	1m 22.152s
Martin Brundle	1m 22.456s
Eddie Irvine	1m 22.567s
Rubens Barrichello	1m 22.606s
Gerhard Berger	1m 22.611s
Ukyo Katayama	1m 22.894s
Jean Alesi	1m 23.008s
Gianni Morbidelli	1m 23.242s
Olivier Panis	1m 23.380s
J.J. Lehto	1m 23.395s
Heinz-Harald Frentzen	1m 23.565s
Mark Blundell	1m 23.693s
Jos Verstappen	1m 23.717s
Christian Fittipaldi	1m 23.750s
Andrea de Cesaris	1m 23.872s
Eric Bernard	1m 23.979s
Johnny Herbert	1m 24.569s
Pierluigi Martini	1m 24.701s
Yannick Dalmas	1m 25.155s
Erik Comas	1m 25.155s
David Brabham	1m 25.508s
Jean-Marc Gounon	1m 25.860s
Michele Alboreto	1m 26.237s
Philippe Adams	1m 26.816s

Sunday morning
Dry, warm, sunny

FASTEST LAPS

Driver	Time	Lap
David Coulthard	1m 22.446s	12
Gerhard Berger	1m 22.935s	3
Damon Hill	1m 22.997s	10
Jean Alesi	1m 23.236s	3
Ukyo Katayama	1m 23.419s	4
Jos Verstappen	1m 23.702s	58
Rubens Barrichello	1m 23.806s	69
Mika Häkkinen	1m 23.819s	6
Eddie Irvine	1m 23.930s	61
Eric Bernard	1m 24.069s	7
Gianni Morbidelli	1m 24.275s	6
Martin Brundle	1m 24.325s	60
Heinz-Harald Frentzen	1m 24.550s	4
Mark Blundell	1m 24.564s	18
Christian Fittipaldi	1m 24.716s	5
J.J. Lehto	1m 24.728s	60
Johnny Herbert	1m 24.748s	3
Olivier Panis	1m 24.804s	42
Andrea de Cesaris	1m 25.568s	10
Pierluigi Martini	1m 25.690s	15
David Brabham	1m 25.760s	19
Jean-Marc Gounon	1m 26.212s	19
Yannick Dalmas	1m 26.288s	58
Michele Alboreto	1m 26.577s	39
Erik Comas	1m 26.786s	4
Philippe Adams	1m 27.082s	4

All results and data © FIA 1994

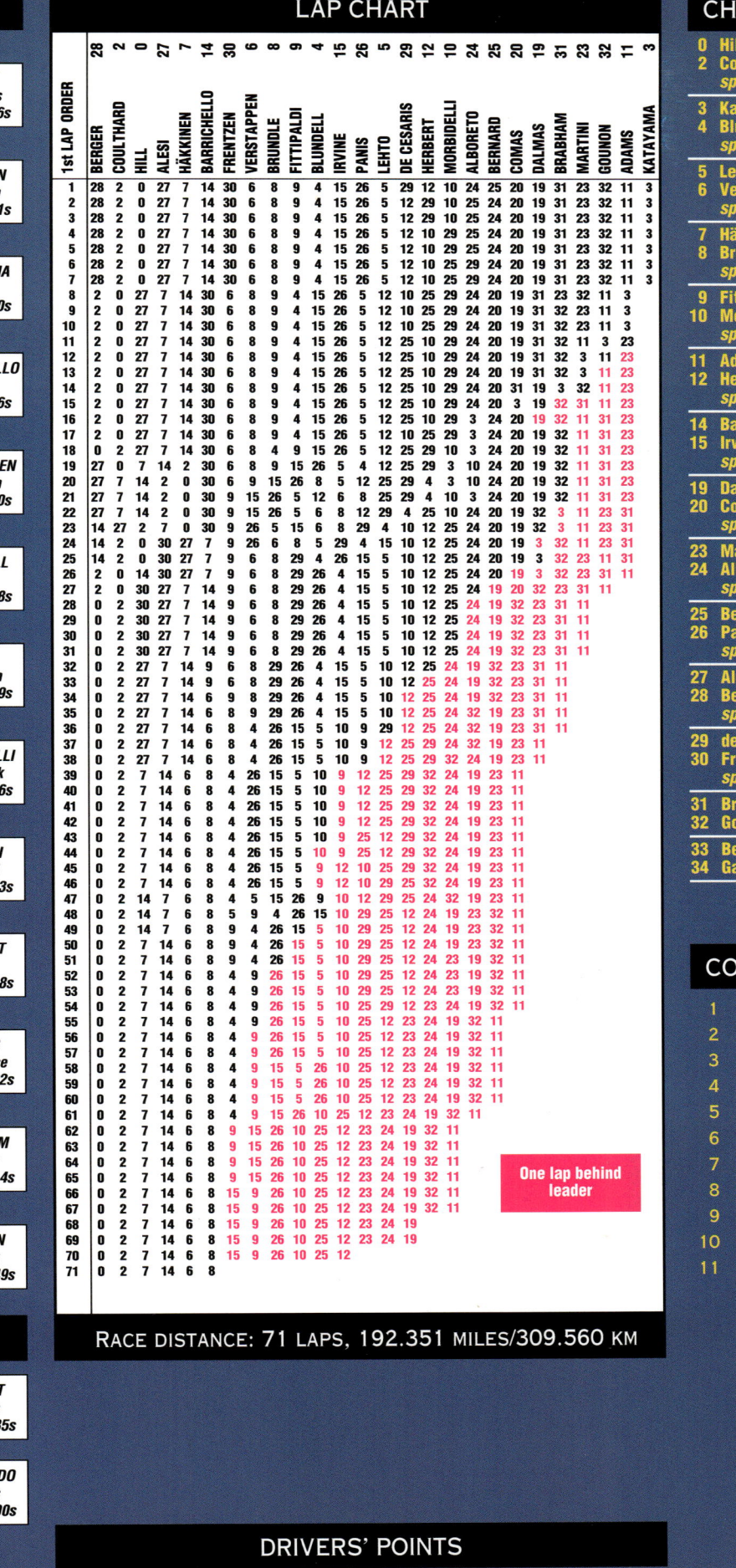

WORLD CHAMPIONSHIP • ROUND 14

GRAND PRIX of EUROPE

SCHUMACHER
HILL
HÄKKINEN
IRVINE
BERGER
FRENTZEN

Michael Schumacher returned from his two-race suspension to record a convincing victory that bolstered his chances of becoming the first German driver to win the World Championship.

Michael Schumacher demonstrated conclusively that his two-race suspension had in no way dulled his competitive edge as he decisively beat Damon Hill into second place in the European Grand Prix at Jerez, a success which extended his World Championship lead over the Englishman to five points with only two races remaining. However, the contest might well have been a lot closer than it ultimately proved, for Hill made a storming start from his second-place grid position to take an immediate lead at the green light, and ran ahead of Schumacher through to the first refuelling stops. At this point, the Englishman was dealt a frustrating hand when a malfunction with the Williams team's FIA-supplied refuelling rig led them to conclude that Hill's car had been short-changed by 13 litres, his pit crew duly compensating for this apparent problem by topping him up with an additional 14 litres at his second stop. In fact, the correct fuel load had been taken aboard, so Hill – who made only two pit stops to Schumacher's three – found himself running through the second half of the contest handicapped by an excessively heavy fuel load. Damon believed that this would have made a significant difference at the end of a day which saw him come home ahead of Mika Häkkinen's McLaren-Peugeot and the Jordan-Hart of Eddie Irvine. Returning World Champion Nigel Mansell had a disappointing race after qualifying respectably in third place. Having made a poor start, he had a brush with Barrichello's Jordan and eventually spun into a sand trap.

ENTRY AND PRACTICE

Damon Hill answered Michael Schumacher's outspoken criticism that he is not a world-class driver in the most convincing style possible by setting fastest time in the first qualifying session for the European GP at Jerez. Benefiting from the use of a special differential designed to reduce transmission power loss, which he had tested at Estoril the previous week, Hill stormed the Williams FW16B round the tortuous 2.75-mile circuit, last used to host the Spanish GP in 1990, 0.04s faster than Heinz-Harald Frentzen's Sauber-Mercedes on a track surface transformed into a skating rink by oil dropped when Ukyo Katayama's Tyrrell suffered a Yamaha engine failure early in the session.

It was an impressive opening salvo from the Londoner at the start of a crucial weekend as the title battle moved into its final phase with Hill only a single point behind Schumacher with three races left to run.

The Benetton team leader was left trailing in a disappointed third with Nigel Mansell marking his second guest outing of the year for Williams by posting a staggering sixth-fastest time behind the Jordan-Harts of Rubens Barrichello and Eddie Irvine.

'It's first blood to Williams, Renault and me,' observed Hill confidently. 'Now we must try to keep it up for the rest of the weekend. The real point is that today we established our superiority over Michael and Benetton. It's something for him to think about tonight, isn't it? Especially as he's got another German driver ahead of him as well. I should think that went down the wrong way!'

Damon also described Schumacher's remarks, made during the run-up to the race, as 'a pretty half-baked effort to try and destabilise me, but he'll have to do rather better than that.

'I would rather not drag the championship down in that way by trying to diminish the reputation of the opposition. I think that it's sad that, for too long, F1 has got itself into the situation where the two leading protagonists seemingly hate each other's guts.

'I think it is bad for the sport, bad for F1 and especially so in a season when we've lost a great champion in Ayrton Senna. I would prefer a clean, sporting fight for the last three races. I think Michael's remarks are ill-conceived and immature.'

Hill's performance also took the spotlight off Mansell's F1 return, although the former Indy Car champion seemed content to take second billing on this occasion. Looking lean and fit after an intensive programme of physical preparation, Mansell was relaxed and seemingly happy to be back in the F1 business for the first time since his outing at Magny-Cours.

'On my last set of tyres I thought I had made a slight improvement to the set-up of the car,' he noted, 'but I found two cars in the way on what I thought would be my best lap, so I'll just have to wait until tomorrow and be patient.'

Hill also had his hands full out on the circuit when Michele Alboreto, apparently annoyed when the Williams driver got in his way, drove into the FW16B and knocked its front suspension askew. Damon managed to get back to the pits, but was hard pressed to conceal his understandable indignation.

Even so, Hill's generally relaxed demeanour contrasted with Schumacher's rather tense mood at the end of the first day. 'I was certainly a little bit disappointed at the end of qualifying compared to how I was feeling this morning,' he admitted.

'The car didn't handle as well as it had in the morning and, when I went out, the track was slippery from the oil as well as stones which had been flicked onto the track at one corner. Even so, I thought I had a fair chance of taking [provisional] pole, but at the quick corner after the new chicane there was a Lotus going slowly on its way to the pits and I lost maybe one-tenth of a second.'

Subsequent inspection also revealed that Schumacher's car had a broken engine mounting bolt which could have contributed to the handling imbalance, and this was duly repaired overnight.

With hindsight, the oil slick dropped by Katayama's Tyrrell could be said to have distorted the outcome of first qualifying in Hill's favour. Yet the trend remained unchanged during Saturday morning's free qualifying session with Damon switching to a new set of tyres to turn a 1m 22.755s. That put him 0.755s ahead of Barrichello, Frentzen, Schumacher – still troubled by understeer – Irvine and Mansell.

Nigel didn't use fresh tyres, so remained very confident about his prospects for second qualifying. 'The car felt fine and, with new tyres worth about a second a lap, I feel confident we can get down into the low 1m 23s,' he predicted. As things turned out, this assessment was absolutely correct. In second qualifying he trimmed his best to 1m 23.392s, an achievement which, he said, 'gives me the best seat in the house' behind the front-row duo.

Second qualifying took place in slightly cooler conditions and proved a pretty electrifying affair. Barrichello set the ball rolling with a 1m 24.978s, vaulting to the head of the timing screens. Then Herbert went quickest with 1m 24.040s on his maiden outing for Ligier, the Englishman's contract having been bought from the Team Lotus administrators for a sum rumoured to be in the region of £850,000.

Mansell, Berger and Schumacher followed with fast times to head the list in quick succession. Michael's best of 1m 23.028s was a pretty impressive effort by any standards and, when Mark Blundell's Tyrrell and the Sauber of Andrea de Cesaris both crashed heavily, it looked as though dust and debris all over the track might put paid to any significant improvements.

Some 23 minutes into the session, Hill played what seemed to be his ace card. Having earlier been delayed by Paul Belmondo's wandering Pacific, Damon dramatically raised the stakes in the battle for pole with a 1m 22.892s. But Schumacher was equal to the challenge. Seven minutes later he slammed his Benetton round in 1m 22.762s and that was the end of the contest.

Hill counter-attacked gamely, but an impromptu trip over a gravel trap wiped out any chance of further improvement.

'It's obviously vital to be on the front row,' said Hill, 'and Michael has obviously helped himself there. Overtaking on this circuit is very difficult, so I suspect this will turn out to be a very tactical race. On my first run I seemed to develop a magnetic attraction for Belmondo, the second run was fine and, all told, the last one was a bit of a failure.'

Frentzen maintained the momentum of the Sauber challenge with a fine run to fourth overall, aided to the Swiss team's best-ever qualifying position by a new differential first tried at Spa, ahead of Barrichello and Berger in the Ferrari. Gerhard claimed that he'd squeezed every ounce of potential from the 412T1B, but poor Alesi locked up his front brakes and slid into a sand trap.

Given that Jean's preference in terms of car set-up is about as far from Gerhard's as it is possible to be, there was no point in the Frenchman borrowing his team-mate's machine. Consequently, he sat out the balance of the session and slipped to 16th in the final order.

The Maranello squad was evaluating a further-revised version of its type 043 engine, using longer inlet trumpets and offering more torque, and the cars also sported revised rear suspension. Berger ran comparative tests between the revised engine and the earlier-spec unit, and

Schumacher aims verbal barb at title rival Hill

In the run-up to the European Grand Prix, Michael Schumacher shocked the F1 fraternity with a vitriolic attack on his championship rival Damon Hill, an episode which those close to the German driver believed to be quite out of character.

Schumacher, who was returning to the F1 fray at Jerez after sitting out his two-race suspension, was scathing in his assessment of Hill's abilities, strongly implying he thought that both Nigel Mansell and David Coulthard were quicker. This verbal assault was delivered directly to the British daily press during testing at Estoril, where many concluded that Schumacher must have been encouraged by his advisers to indulge in such sledgehammer diplomacy.

'It was interesting to see the performance of Coulthard, who has shown himself to be very quick, but had to move over for Hill at both Monza and Estoril,' noted Schumacher waspishly. 'I've learned nothing about Damon's weaknesses, because he's never been under pressure. I have already known his weak points for some time.

'I think it is great for me that Nigel Mansell is coming to take the place of Coulthard, because that is going to put Hill under great pressure. I am also convinced that Mansell is not coming just to help Hill in these three races, but with the definite intention of proving he still has the speed.'

Refusing to be provoked, Hill brushed aside the German driver's remarks. 'That may be his perception of the situation,' he said firmly, 'but he's clutching at straws, really. I think I've already answered these questions a hundred times before.'

However, Damon confirmed that he had a great deal of respect for Schumacher. 'I would be pretty ignorant not to,' he said, 'but I have always worked on the premise that nobody is unbeatable. My dad beat Jim Clark, and it's examples like that which remind you that everyone puts their trousers on one leg at a time.

'It is too easy to be put off by the myth that one person is so much better than another. If I had accepted that, I would have given up a long time ago.'

223

Top: Jean Alesi and Gerhard Berger in the cockpits of their Ferraris.

Occasional Indy Car racer Mimmo Schiattarella *(above)* locks a wheel in practice. The Italian had replaced Jean-Marc Gounon in the second Simtek and made the grid as final qualifier.

Maintaining focus. Despite intense media pressure, Damon Hill *(right)* had to fix his mind on the task in hand.

GRAND PRIX OF EUROPE

Nigel Mansell's run of bad luck followed him across the Atlantic. Returning to Formula 1 for the final three races of the year, Nigel was predictably on the pace in qualifying but was soon out of contention in the race after tangling with Barrichello's Jordan. He eventually faced a long walk home *(centre left)* after spinning out on lap 48.

F3000 runner Hideki Noda *(left)* brought some much-needed finance to the Larrousse team, but his Grand Prix debut was to last a mere ten laps before he was sidelined with a jammed gearbox.

although he used the torquey version to qualify sixth he reverted to the regular unit for the race.

Over in the Ligier pit, Herbert was soon impressing everybody with his technical input. The English newcomer quickly dialled out much of the understeer which had slowed his JS39B on Friday and was delighted to qualify seventh. Olivier Panis, by contrast, still found himself struggling with poor front-end grip and lined up in 11th.

Yet, while Ligier felt upbeat and optimistic, the McLaren-Peugeot squad was having a difficult time. Mika Häkkinen was pretty frustrated with his MP4/9's lack of grip and admitted that much more work still needed to be done in order to improve the Peugeot V10's driveability, even though a further-uprated version of the French engine was available with more power. He did, however, restrain himself from saying that this wouldn't concern the team for very much longer . . .

Mika hurled his machine round like a man possessed, but the net result was ninth place, just behind Gianni Morbidelli's Footwork – not a state of affairs with which the Woking team was exactly familiar. Meanwhile, Martin Brundle, who was using a new chassis for this race, suffered badly with an apparent aerodynamic imbalance during the Saturday morning free practice session. The team thought it had cured the problem in time for second qualifying, but Martin continued to battle with such an acute lack of grip that he was unable to improve on 15th. 'I tried every kerb, every approach, but it was no good,' he shrugged. 'I suspect that something else may be wrong with the chassis.' McLaren retained power steering on both cars for this race.

Eddie Irvine lost some time correcting a slight damper problem on his Jordan, then picked up too much dirt on the tyres during his final run, dropping to tenth. Verstappen, grappling with seemingly insoluble oversteer, was 12th for Benetton ahead of Ukyo Katayama and the shaken Blundell, who was lucky to escape injury when a wayward front wheel brushed the side of his helmet as debris flew during the course of his pile-up.

Neither of the Tyrrell 022s seemed to be handling particularly well on this tight circuit and Katayama found himself balked on his final run by Simtek novice Domenico Schiattarella, who had taken over the second seat alongside David Brabham in place of Jean-Marc Gounon. Meanwhile, Mark's car had been pretty comprehensively destroyed so the Tyrrell mechanics set to and assembled him a totally new machine overnight in time for the race.

Behind Brundle and Alesi, Pierluigi Martini emerged as the faster Minardi runner ahead of the luckless de Cesaris, Christian Fittipaldi's Footwork and Michele Alboreto, who changed the chassis set-up on his Minardi for the final session only to find the track conditions had deteriorated by the time he went for a quick lap.

Just outside the top twenty were the Lotus 109s of Alessandro Zanardi and Eric Bernard, the former Ligier driver having effectively swapped seats with Herbert at short notice. The Frenchman began the weekend using the older Mugen Honda V10 engine, but the latest unit was installed in his car for the second day. Unfortunately, consistently poor chassis balance prevented either driver from even vaguely approaching the sort of form displayed at Monza, where Herbert had qualified fourth.

There were no further surprises in the remaining two rows of the grid, although Hideki Noda (the latest occupant of the Larrousse seat in which Olivier Beretta had started the season) and Schiattarella, the 1991 Italian F3 Championship runner-up, did respectably in preparation for their first GP outings. Erik Comas lined up in 23rd place but David Brabham, using a revised, lighter Simtek chassis, had qualified ahead of the two Larrousses, only to have his best lap on Saturday disallowed after he missed the pit lane weight-check red light in the hubbub following Blundell's accident. That dropped him two places to 25th. By contrast, neither Pacific made the field as usual, and the team's transporter was on its way back to England early on Sunday morning.

RACE

The race morning warm-up ended with Hill very happy, lapping 0.9s ahead of Schumacher's Benetton, while Mansell had a slight gearchange problem and took time off for a quick spin. In the McLaren camp, Brundle elected to take the spare car after discovering how much better it felt in the half-hour session, while the Jordan crew was having a busy time after Barrichello

225

GRAND PRIX OF EUROPE

Diary

Paddock rumours link top Indy Car team owner Roger Penske with the impending announcement of an F1 McLaren-Mercedes partnership for 1995. Jordan poised to inherit the Peugeot engine supply contract.

Jesus Gil, the mayor of Marbella, attends the European GP to examine the possibility of a street race at the Mediterranean resort at some point in the future.

Karl Wendlinger, who spent 19 days in a coma following his practice accident at Monaco, prepares to test a Sauber C13-Mercedes during the week immediately following the Jerez race in preparation for a possible comeback at Suzuka.

Keke Rosberg announces that he has formed his own team to contest the 1995 DTM, using Opel Calibra V6s. Reigning DTM champion Klaus Ludwig is to leave the Mercedes fold to partner the Finn.

Johnny Herbert found himself transferred from Lotus to Ligier and quickly established a good rapport with his new team, eventually bringing the Renault-powered car home in a steady eighth place.

Eddie Irvine *(below left)* confirmed his talent with an impressively mature display in the Jordan that earned him fourth place, his best result to date.

suffered a water leak on his race car, the Brazilian switching to the spare, which promptly lost oil pressure. In the grandstand immediately opposite the Williams pit hung a banner reading: 'Nige! We love you, but give Coulthard the keys!'

At the last minute Brundle was frustrated in his ambition to produce a decent race result when the spare MP4/9 sprung a water leak on the grid and he had to quickly change back to his unloved race chassis. As the starting lights turned green, Hill made an absolute peach of a start from second place on the grid to beat Schumacher in the sprint to the first right-hander. Mansell, meanwhile, got bogged down with excessive wheelspin and was passed on all sides.

At the end of the opening lap, Damon was 0.9s ahead of Schumacher, with a well-defined gap already opening to Frentzen, whose fuel-heavy Sauber was going through with a single stop. Barrichello was fourth from Berger, Mansell, Irvine, Herbert, Häkkinen and the rest of the pack. Both Noda and Katayama had stalled on the grid and were push-started after the field had departed.

This clearly looked like a two-horse race. With only three laps completed, Hill and Schumacher were covered by less than a second, but Frentzen was already 6.8 seconds back in third. Mansell had nipped past Berger on the second lap and harried Barrichello to such good effect that he was through to fourth ahead of the Jordan by lap six. On lap 12, however, Nigel allowed himself to be boxed in behind Noda's slowing Larrousse and Barrichello repassed him. (Noda retired with a jammed gearbox having completed ten laps – two more than Brundle, who had been posted as the first retirement of the afternoon with another Peugeot engine breakage.)

Soon afterwards, Mansell damaged the nose of his Williams when he brushed the Jordan's right-rear wheel as he made a bid to overtake. 'Nigel's race went wrong at that point,' explained Frank Williams. 'Immediately after that, he started losing about 30 yards through the fast right-hander leading onto the long straight, and knew he had a problem.'

Mansell came in at the end of lap 15 for a replacement nose section to be fitted, just as Schumacher made a 6.8-second refuelling stop – the first of three. Three laps later, Damon made the first of his two scheduled stops, at which point things began to go wrong for Williams.

Damon resumed in second place and at the end of lap 19 was 4.8 seconds behind Schumacher. He began to drift away, the gap extending to 7.3s by lap 26, but reckoned that as long as he kept within 20 seconds of the Benetton, he would very likely emerge the winner because Michael would lose at least that much time during his third refuelling stop.

Schumacher duly made his second stop on lap 33, the Benetton being stationary for 6.6 seconds, but Hill, who briefly retook the lead, was then somewhat surprised to find himself being called into the pits at the end of lap 35. Unknown to Damon, there had been a snag with the refuelling equipment with the result that he had apparently been short-changed by 13 litres at his first refuelling stop. An additional 14 litres was thus put in to compensate at this earlier-than-expected second refuelling stop and Damon set off in hot pursuit. Thereafter, however, his race fell apart.

Schumacher surged away to such good effect that he was 25.6 seconds ahead as the 40-lap mark approached. The race seemed to be unfolding in much the same way as the Hungarian GP had done, with Hill getting tangled up among the slower traffic which just seemed to melt out of the way when Schumacher arrived on the scene. Michael was thus able to make a leisurely 7.7-second final refuelling stop at the end of lap 52, keeping Hill over 14 seconds behind as he accelerated back into the battle.

'I can't always complain about the traffic,' Hill later admitted ruefully. 'I think we put up a good challenge, but Michael did a fantastic job and the team performed better than we did. Let me say that the strategy we chose today seemed to be the right one through to the first pit stop, as proved by the fact that I was ahead of Michael to that point, even though we were carrying a lot more fuel. But somewhere the strategy got lost.'

In fact, the first refuelling stop had upset Hill's prospects. The apparent glitch meant that Damon was forced to take on 95 litres of fuel at his second stop while Schumacher, who still had another stop in hand, only had about 55 litres in the Benetton. But in addition to driving a car which was around 50 kg heavier, Hill also had to do the second half of the race on one set of tyres, while Michael was able to change again at his final refuelling stop.

The reality, however, was even worse. At the initial fuel stop, the intended amount of fuel had in fact gone into the Williams, so, after the car was topped up with an extra 14 litres at its second stop, Hill was running with a 13-litre surplus in the second half of the race. Insiders at Williams may have calculated that Damon wouldn't have won in any event, that it was Schumacher's devastatingly consistent, quick laps immediately after the first refuelling stop which broke his challenge, but there is no doubt that he would have been a great deal closer than 25 seconds had it not been for this setback.

Mansell, meanwhile, had resumed in 22nd place and came in for tyres at the end of lap 42, by which time he had climbed to 14th. Three laps later he was back into the pits once again for a precautionary stop to check an apparent loose bolt on a front wing end plate. On lap 48, he spun off and finished his race with the Williams firmly embedded in the gravel.

'Nigel's last stop was due to a Williams team cock-up,' admitted Frank Williams. 'As he went back into the race after his second fuel stop, an eagle-eyed mechanic spotted that loose bolt securing the end plate. Under the circumstances, we had to call him back to check it out, because if one of those had flown off he might have had a big accident.'

Häkkinen enjoyed a bold, energetic race to third place, although Schumacher was not impressed with the way the McLaren driver defended himself from being lapped just prior to the Benetton driver's final refuelling stop. After a couple of laps' cut-and-thrust, the Benetton pit signalled that Michael should forget about lapping the Finn and come in for his final helping of fuel.

Frentzen hung on in third place all the way until lap 33 when he came in for his sole refuelling stop of the afternoon. He later admitted that this strategy had probably been a mistake, for the Sauber was at rest for 11.4 seconds, rejoining in seventh as a result.

With 15 laps to go, Häkkinen was third ahead of Irvine and Barrichello, the Jordan team seemingly on course for a generous portion of constructors' championship points. But five laps later, Rubens suddenly slowed with a left-rear puncture and struggled painfully into the pit lane for attention, losing a lap to finish the afternoon a disappointed 12th.

Irvine, who was indignant over the fact that Häkkinen had apparently got away with exceeding the pit lane speed limit as he resumed after his second refuelling stop – and thus just squeezed ahead of the Jordan as Eddie rejoined after his own second stop – took fourth place. The Ulsterman was only nine seconds away from his first podium finish after the most impressive performance of his Grand Prix career to date.

Berger wound up a hard-driving fifth ahead of Frentzen, while Katayama drove brilliantly after an overheating clutch on the parade lap had caused him to stall on the grid, finishing seventh just 0.1s behind the Sauber. That placed him ahead of a satisfied Herbert, the Englishman leading Panis over the line in tight formation to finish his debut outing for Ligier on a most satisfactory note. Johnny later explained that, following Panis's disqualification in Portugal, the team had taken a very conservative approach to the car's ride-height settings, raising it slightly before the start to avoid any unexpected wear to its wood-composite skidblock.

A disillusioned Alesi trailed home tenth ahead of Morbidelli, with Barrichello staying ahead of Mark Blundell's Tyrrell to the chequered flag. It was a hard race for Mark, who had not slept well following his accident the previous afternoon, and he did really well to keep going to the finish. Despite his exhaustion, he still managed to stay ahead of both Minardis, Zanardi's Lotus, Fittipaldi (who had been delayed by a pit stop to tend to slight nose damage early in the race), Bernard and Schiattarella, who kept out of trouble to finish his first Grand Prix.

For Hill, the outcome of the race was an enormous let-down after his pace in the opening stages. Yet for Mansell, things could hardly have gone worse. Events not only conspired to keep him away from the main contest of the day, but his failure to score any points meant that Williams dropped back behind Benetton in the constructors' points table.

In truth, it had not been the most absorbing of Grands Prix, but Schumacher had certainly reasserted his place as F1's man of the moment. Despite its problems in qualifying, the Benetton ran faultlessly throughout the race. Under the circumstances, Hill might have been forgiven if he had left Jerez coming to terms with the fact that his title bid now looked likely to end at Suzuka.

FIA FORMULA ONE WORLD CHAMPIONSHIP ROUND 14

GRAND PRIX OF EUROPE
JEREZ
14-16 OCTOBER 1994

RACE WEATHER: WARM, CLOUDY

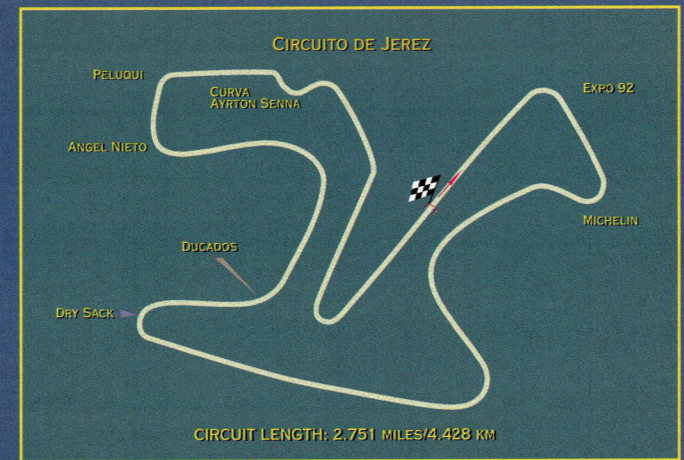

Circuito de Jerez — CIRCUIT LENGTH: 2.751 MILES/4.428 KM

Place	Driver	Nat.	No.	Entrant	Car/Engine	Laps	Time/Retirement	Speed (mph/km/h)
1	Michael Schumacher	D	5	Mild Seven Benetton Ford	Benetton B194-Ford Zetec-R V8	69	1h 40m 26.689s	114.070/183.578
2	Damon Hill	GB	0	Rothmans Williams Renault	Williams FW16B-Renault RS6C V10	69	1h 40m 51.378s	113.600/182.822
3	Mika Häkkinen	SF	7	Marlboro McLaren Peugeot	McLaren MP4/9-Peugeot A6 V10	69	1h 41m 36.337s	112.760/181.470
4	Eddie Irvine	GB	15	Sasol Jordan	Jordan 194-Hart 1035 V10	69	1h 41m 45.135s	112.600/181.212
5	Gerhard Berger	A	28	Scuderia Ferrari	Ferrari 412T1B 043 V12	68		
6	Heinz-Harald Frentzen	D	30	Sauber Mercedes	Sauber C13-Mercedes-Benz V10	68		
7	Ukyo Katayama	J	3	Tyrrell	Tyrrell 022-Yamaha 0X10A V10	68		
8	Johnny Herbert	GB	25	Ligier Gitanes Blondes	Ligier JS39B-Renault RS6A V10	68		
9	Olivier Panis	F	26	Ligier Gitanes Blondes	Ligier JS39B-Renault RS6A V10	68		
10	Jean Alesi	F	27	Scuderia Ferrari	Ferrari 412T1B 043 V12	68		
11	Gianni Morbidelli	I	10	Footwork Ford	Footwork FA15-Ford HB V8	68		
12	Rubens Barrichello	BR	14	Sasol Jordan	Jordan 194-Hart 1035 V10	68		
13	Mark Blundell	GB	4	Tyrrell	Tyrrell 022-Yamaha 0X10A V10	68		
14	Michele Alboreto	I	24	Minardi Scuderia Italia	Minardi M194-Ford HB V8	67		
15	Pierluigi Martini	I	23	Minardi Scuderia Italia	Minardi M194-Ford HB V8	67		
16	Alessandro Zanardi	I	12	Team Lotus	Lotus 109-Mugen Honda ZA6C V10	67		
17	Christian Fittipaldi	BR	9	Footwork Ford	Footwork FA15-Ford HB V8	66		
18	Eric Bernard	F	11	Team Lotus	Lotus 109-Mugen Honda ZA6C V10	66		
19	Domenico Schiattarella	I	32	MTV Simtek Ford	Simtek S941-Ford HB V8	64		
	Nigel Mansell	GB	2	Rothmans Williams Renault	Williams FW16B-Renault RS6C V10	47	Accident	
	David Brabham	AUS	31	MTV Simtek Ford	Simtek S941-Ford HB V8	42	Engine	
	Andrea de Cesaris	I	29	Sauber Mercedes	Sauber C13-Mercedes-Benz V10	37	Accelerator	
	Erik Comas	F	20	Tourtel Larrousse F1	Larrousse LH94-Ford HB V8	37	Electrics	
	Jos Verstappen	NL	6	Mild Seven Benetton Ford	Benetton B194-Ford Zetec-R V10	15	Spun off	
	Hideki Noda	J	19	Tourtel Larrousse F1	Larrousse LH94-Ford HB V8	10	Gearbox	
	Martin Brundle	GB	8	Marlboro McLaren Peugeot	McLaren MP4/9-Peugeot A6 V10	8	Engine	
DNQ	Bertrand Gachot	F	34	Pacific Grand Prix Ltd	Pacific PR01-Ilmor 2175A V10			
DNQ	Paul Belmondo	F	33	Pacific Grand Prix Ltd	Pacific PR01-Ilmor 2175A V10			

Fastest lap: Schumacher, on lap 17, 1m 25.040s, 116.429 mph/187.450 km/h (record for revised circuit).
Lap record for old circuit: Riccardo Patrese (F1 Williams FW13B-Renault V10), 1m 24.513s, 111.644 mph/179.674 km/h (1990).
All cars used Goodyear tyres.

All results and data © FIA 1994

QUALIFYING 1

Damon Hill	1m 24.137s
Heinz-Harald Frentzen	1m 24.184s
Michael Schumacher	1m 24.207s
Rubens Barrichello	1m 24.700s
Eddie Irvine	1m 24.794s
Nigel Mansell	1m 24.971s
Gerhard Berger	1m 25.079s
Jean Alesi	**1m 25.182s**
Mika Häkkinen	1m 25.275s
Olivier Panis	1m 25.384s
Andrea de Cesaris	**1m 25.407s**
Pierluigi Martini	1m 25.812s
Martin Brundle	1m 25.942s
Mark Blundell	1m 25.995s
Gianni Morbidelli	1m 26.048s
Christian Fittipaldi	1m 26.094s
Johnny Herbert	1m 26.241s
Ukyo Katayama	1m 26.304s
Michele Alboreto	1m 26.744s
Alessandro Zanardi	1m 26.973s
Erik Comas	1m 28.042s
Eric Bernard	1m 28.047s
David Brabham	1m 28.388s
Hideki Noda	1m 29.081s
Domenico Schiattarella	1m 30.069s
Bertrand Gachot	1m 30.099s
Paul Belmondo	1m 35.441s
Jos Verstappen	no time

Friday afternoon
Hot, dry, sunny

QUALIFYING 2

Michael Schumacher	**1m 22.762s**
Damon Hill	1m 22.892s
Nigel Mansell	1m 23.392s
Heinz-Harald Frentzen	1m 23.431s
Rubens Barrichello	1m 23.455s
Gerhard Berger	1m 23.677s
Johnny Herbert	1m 24.040s
Gianni Morbidelli	1m 24.079s
Mika Häkkinen	1m 24.122s
Eddie Irvine	1m 24.157s
Olivier Panis	1m 24.432s
Jos Verstappen	1m 24.643s
Ukyo Katayama	1m 24.738s
Mark Blundell	1m 24.770s
Martin Brundle	1m 25.110s
Pierluigi Martini	1m 25.294s
Andrea de Cesaris	1m 25.411s
Christian Fittipaldi	1m 25.427s
Michele Alboreto	1m 25.511s
Alessandro Zanardi	1m 25.557s
Eric Bernard	1m 25.595s
Erik Comas	1m 26.272s
Hideki Noda	1m 27.168s
David Brabham	1m 27.201s
Domenico Schiattarella	1m 27.976s
Bertrand Gachot	1m 29.488s
Paul Belmondo	1m 30.234s
Jean Alesi	1m 44.801s

Saturday afternoon
Dry, hot, sunny

WARM-UP

Damon Hill	1m 23.571s
Michael Schumacher	1m 24.402s
Nigel Mansell	1m 24.255s
Mika Häkkinen	1m 24.514s
Gerhard Berger	1m 24.538s
Eddie Irvine	1m 24.841s
Jean Alesi	1m 24.969s
Olivier Panis	1m 25.180s
Heinz-Harald Frentzen	1m 25.318s
Ukyo Katayama	1m 25.425s
Gianni Morbidelli	1m 25.482s
Rubens Barrichello	1m 25.492s
Martin Brundle	1m 25.503s
Jos Verstappen	1m 25.772s
Michele Alboreto	1m 25.916s
Johnny Herbert	1m 25.921s
Andrea de Cesaris	1m 25.950s
Christian Fittipaldi	1m 26.069s
Mark Blundell	1m 26.264s
Eric Bernard	1m 26.295s
Pierluigi Martini	1m 26.667s
Erik Comas	1m 26.702s
Alessandro Zanardi	1m 27.498s
David Brabham	1m 27.802s
Hideki Noda	1m 27.955s
Domenico Schiattarella	1m 29.206s

Sunday morning
Dry, hot, sunny

FASTEST LAPS

Driver	Time	Lap
Michael Schumacher	1m 25.040s	17
Rubens Barrichello	1m 25.529s	62
Damon Hill	1m 25.532s	10
Eddie Irvine	1m 26.259s	52
Jean Alesi	1m 26.410s	67
Nigel Mansell	1m 26.448s	36
Ukyo Katayama	1m 26.511s	59
Olivier Panis	1m 26.613s	59
Gerhard Berger	1m 26.629s	40
Gianni Morbidelli	1m 26.651s	54
Mika Häkkinen	1m 26.656s	50
Heinz-Harald Frentzen	1m 26.947s	56
Christian Fittipaldi	1m 27.030s	25
Johnny Herbert	1m 27.040s	63
Mark Blundell	1m 27.392s	42
Andrea de Cesaris	1m 27.635s	17
Erik Comas	1m 27.755s	7
Michele Alboreto	1m 27.952s	13
Jos Verstappen	1m 28.249s	15
Martin Brundle	1m 28.355s	7
Alessandro Zanardi	1m 28.467s	67
Pierluigi Martini	1m 28.551s	44
Eric Bernard	1m 29.147s	5
David Brabham	1m 29.307s	21
Hideki Noda	1m 30.525s	4
Domenico Schiattarella	1m 30.912s	51

STARTING GRID

- **5** SCHUMACHER, Benetton, 1m 22.762s
- **0** HILL, Williams, 1m 22.892s
- **2** MANSELL, Williams, 1m 23.392s
- **30** FRENTZEN, Sauber, 1m 23.431s
- **14** BARRICHELLO, Jordan, 1m 23.455s
- **28** BERGER, Ferrari, 1m 23.677s
- **25** HERBERT, Ligier, 1m 24.040s
- **10** MORBIDELLI, Footwork, 1m 24.079s
- **7** HÄKKINEN, McLaren, 1m 24.122s
- **15** IRVINE, Jordan, 1m 24.157s
- **26** PANIS, Ligier, 1m 24.432s
- **6** VERSTAPPEN, Benetton, 1m 24.643s
- **3** KATAYAMA, Tyrrell, 1m 24.738s
- **4** BLUNDELL, Tyrrell, 1m 24.770s
- **8** BRUNDLE, McLaren, 1m 25.110s
- **27** ALESI, Ferrari, 1m 25.182s
- **23** MARTINI, Minardi, 1m 25.294s
- **29** DE CESARIS, Sauber, 1m 25.407s
- **9** FITTIPALDI, Footwork, 1m 25.427s
- **24** ALBORETO, Minardi, 1m 25.511s
- **12** ZANARDI, Lotus, 1m 25.557s
- **11** BERNARD, Lotus, 1m 25.595s
- **20** COMAS, Larrousse, 1m 26.272s
- **19** NODA, Larrousse, 1m 27.168s
- **31** BRABHAM, Simtek, 1m 27.201s
- **32** SCHIATTARELLA, Simtek, 1m 27.976s

NON-STARTERS

- DNQ — **34** GACHOT, Pacific, 1m 29.488s
- DNQ — **33** BELMONDO, Pacific, 1m 30.234s

LAP CHART

1st LAP ORDER	0 HILL	5 SCHUMACHER	30 FRENTZEN	14 BARRICHELLO	28 BERGER	2 MANSELL	15 IRVINE	25 HERBERT	7 HÄKKINEN	10 MORBIDELLI	4 BLUNDELL	8 BRUNDLE	27 ALESI	26 PANIS	29 DE CESARIS	6 VERSTAPPEN	23 MARTINI	24 ALBORETO	20 COMAS	12 ZANARDI	11 BERNARD	31 BRABHAM	32 SCHIATTARELLA	3 KATAYAMA	19 NODA	9 FITTIPALDI
1	0	5	30	14	28	2	15	25	7	10	4	8	27	26	29	6	23	24	20	12	11	31	32	3	19	9
2	0	5	30	14	2	28	15	25	7	10	4	8	27	26	29	6	23	24	20	12	11	31	32	3	19	9
3	0	5	30	14	2	28	15	25	7	10	4	8	27	26	29	6	23	24	20	12	11	31	32	3	19	9
4	0	5	30	14	2	28	15	25	7	10	4	8	27	26	29	6	23	24	20	12	11	31	32	3	19	9
5	0	5	30	14	2	28	15	25	7	10	4	8	27	26	29	6	23	24	20	12	11	31	32	3	19	9
6	0	5	30	2	14	28	15	25	7	10	4	8	27	26	29	6	23	24	20	12	11	31	3	32	19	9
7	0	5	30	2	14	28	15	25	7	10	4	8	27	26	29	6	23	24	20	12	11	31	3	32	19	9
8	0	5	30	2	14	28	15	25	7	10	4	8	27	26	29	6	23	24	20	12	11	3	31	32	19	9
9	0	5	30	2	14	28	15	25	7	10	4	27	26	29	6	23	24	20	12	11	3	31	32	19	9	
10	0	5	30	2	14	28	15	25	7	10	4	27	26	29	6	23	24	20	12	11	3	31	32	19	9	
11	0	5	30	2	14	28	15	25	7	10	4	27	26	29	6	23	24	20	12	11	3	31	32	9		
12	0	5	30	14	2	28	15	25	7	10	4	27	26	29	6	23	24	20	12	3	11	31	32	9		
13	0	5	30	14	2	28	15	25	7	10	4	27	26	29	6	23	24	20	12	3	11	31	32	9		
14	0	5	30	14	2	28	15	25	7	10	4	27	26	29	6	23	24	20	3	12	11	31	32	9		
15	0	5	30	14	28	15	25	7	10	4	27	26	29	6	23	24	20	3	12	11	31	2	32	9		
16	0	5	30	14	28	15	25	7	10	27	26	29	20	3	23	4	12	11	24	31	2	32	9			
17	0	5	30	14	28	15	25	7	27	26	29	20	3	10	23	12	4	11	31	24	2	32	9			
18	5	0	30	14	15	7	27	26	28	20	3	25	10	23	12	4	29	11	24	2	31	32	9			
19	5	0	30	14	15	7	27	26	3	20	28	25	10	23	12	4	11	29	24	2	31	32	9			
20	5	0	30	14	15	7	26	3	28	25	27	10	23	12	4	11	29	20	24	2	31	32	9			
21	5	0	30	15	7	26	3	14	28	25	27	10	23	4	11	29	20	24	12	2	31	32	9			
22	5	0	30	15	7	26	28	14	25	27	10	3	23	4	11	29	20	24	12	2	31	9	32			
23	5	0	30	15	7	26	28	14	25	27	10	3	4	29	20	24	23	12	2	11	31	9	32			
24	5	0	30	15	7	28	14	25	26	27	10	3	4	29	20	24	23	2	12	11	31	9	32			
25	5	0	30	15	7	28	14	25	27	26	10	3	4	29	20	24	2	23	12	11	31	9	32			
26	5	0	30	7	15	28	14	25	27	26	10	3	4	29	20	24	2	23	12	11	31	9	32			
27	5	0	30	7	15	28	14	25	27	26	10	3	4	29	20	24	2	23	12	11	31	9	32			
28	5	0	30	7	15	28	14	25	27	26	10	3	4	29	20	24	2	23	12	11	31	9	32			
29	5	0	30	7	15	28	14	25	27	26	10	3	4	29	20	24	2	23	12	11	31	9	32			
30	5	0	30	7	15	28	14	25	27	26	10	3	4	29	20	24	2	23	12	11	31	9	32			
31	5	0	30	7	15	28	14	25	27	26	10	3	4	29	20	24	2	23	12	11	31	9	32			
32	5	0	30	7	15	28	14	25	27	26	10	3	4	29	20	2	24	23	12	11	31	9	32			
33	0	5	7	15	28	30	14	25	27	26	10	3	4	29	2	20	24	23	12	11	31	9	32			
34	0	5	7	15	28	14	30	25	26	27	10	3	4	29	2	20	23	12	24	11	31	9	32			
35	5	0	7	15	28	14	30	25	26	27	3	4	10	2	29	20	23	12	24	11	31	9	32			
36	5	0	7	15	28	14	30	25	26	27	3	4	10	2	29	20	23	12	24	11	31	9	32			
37	5	0	7	15	28	14	30	25	26	27	3	4	10	2	29	20	23	12	24	11	31	9	32			
38	5	0	7	15	28	14	30	25	26	27	3	4	10	2	23	12	24	11	31	9	32					
39	5	0	7	15	28	14	30	25	26	27	3	4	10	2	23	12	24	11	31	9	32					
40	5	0	7	15	28	14	30	25	26	27	4	3	10	2	23	12	24	11	9	31	32					
41	5	0	15	28	14	7	30	26	27	4	25	10	3	2	23	12	24	11	9	31	32					
42	5	0	15	14	7	28	30	26	27	4	10	3	25	2	23	12	24	11	9	31	32					
43	5	0	15	14	7	28	30	4	10	26	3	25	27	2	23	12	24	11	9	32						
44	5	0	15	14	7	28	30	4	10	3	25	26	27	2	23	24	12	11	9	32						
45	5	0	15	14	7	28	30	10	3	25	26	27	4	24	2	23	12	11	9	32						
46	5	0	15	14	7	28	30	10	3	25	26	27	4	24	2	23	12	9	11	32						
47	5	0	15	7	14	28	30	10	3	25	26	27	4	24	2	23	12	9	11	32						
48	5	0	15	7	14	28	30	10	3	25	26	27	4	24	23	12	9	11	32							
49	5	0	7	15	14	28	30	10	3	25	26	27	4	24	23	12	9	11	32							
50	5	0	7	15	14	28	30	10	3	25	26	27	4	24	23	12	9	11	32							
51	5	0	7	15	14	28	30	10	3	25	26	27	4	24	23	12	9	11	32							
52	5	0	7	15	14	28	30	3	25	26	27	10	4	24	23	12	9	11	32							
53	5	0	7	15	14	28	30	3	25	26	27	10	4	24	23	12	9	11	32							
54	5	0	7	15	14	28	30	3	25	26	27	10	4	24	23	12	9	11	32							
55	5	0	7	15	14	28	30	3	25	26	27	10	4	24	23	12	9	11	32							
56	5	0	7	15	14	28	30	3	25	26	27	10	4	24	23	12	9	11	32							
57	5	0	7	15	14	28	30	3	25	26	27	10	4	24	23	12	9	11	32							
58	5	0	7	15	14	28	30	3	25	26	27	10	4	24	23	12	9	11	32							
59	5	0	7	15	28	14	30	3	25	26	27	10	4	24	23	12	9	11	32							
60	5	0	7	15	28	30	3	25	26	27	10	4	14	24	23	12	9	11	32							
61	5	0	7	15	28	30	3	25	26	27	10	4	14	24	23	12	9	11	32							
62	5	0	7	15	28	30	3	25	26	27	10	4	14	24	23	12	9	11	32							
63	5	0	7	15	28	30	3	25	26	27	10	4	14	24	23	12	9	11	32							
64	5	0	7	15	28	30	3	25	26	27	10	4	14	24	23	12	9	11	32							
65	5	0	7	15	28	30	3	25	26	27	10	4	14	24	23	12	9	11								
66	5	0	7	15	28	30	3	25	26	27	10	4	14	24	23	12	9	11								
67	5	0	7	15	28	30	3	25	26	27	10	14	4	24	23	12										
68	5	0	7	15	28	30	3	25	26	27	10	14	4													
69	5	0	7	15																						

One lap behind leader

RACE DISTANCE: 69 LAPS, 189.848 MILES/305.532 KM

CHASSIS LOG BOOK

0 Hill	Williams FW16B/5
2 Mansell	Williams FW16B/6
spare	Williams FW16B/1
3 Katayama	Tyrrell 022/5
4 Blundell	Tyrrell 022/4
spare	Tyrrell 022/3
5 Schumacher	Benetton B194/8
6 Verstappen	Benetton B194/4
spare	Benetton B194/5
7 Häkkinen	McLaren MP4/9/4
8 Brundle	McLaren MP4/9/8
spare	McLaren MP4/9/6
9 Fittipaldi	Footwork FA15/3
10 Morbidelli	Footwork FA15/4
spare	Footwork FA15/1
11 Bernard	Lotus 109/3
12 Zanardi	Lotus 109/2
spare	Lotus 109/1
14 Barrichello	Jordan 194/3
15 Irvine	Jordan 194/6
spare	Jordan 194/5
19 Noda	Larrousse LH94/2
20 Comas	Larrousse LH94/4
spare	Larrousse LH94/1
23 Martini	Minardi M194/5
24 Alboreto	Minardi M194/6
spare	Minardi M194/4
25 Herbert	Ligier JS39B/6
26 Panis	Ligier JS39B/7
spare	Ligier JS39B/1
27 Alesi	Ferrari 412T1B/155
28 Berger	Ferrari 412T1B/154
spare	Ferrari 412T1B/151
29 de Cesaris	Sauber C13/5
30 Frentzen	Sauber C13/7
spare	Sauber C13/3
31 Brabham	Simtek S941/5
32 Schiattarella	Simtek S941/4
33 Belmondo	Pacific PR01/1
34 Gachot	Pacific PR01/2

CONSTRUCTORS' CUP

1	BENETTON-FORD	97
2	WILLIAMS-RENAULT	95
3	FERRARI	60
4	McLAREN-PEUGEOT	38
5	JORDAN-HART	23
6	TYRRELL-YAMAHA	13
7=	LIGIER-RENAULT	11
7=	SAUBER-MERCEDES	11
9	FOOTWORK-FORD	9
10	MINARDI-FORD	5
11	LARROUSSE-FORD	2

FOR THE RECORD

50th Grand Prix start
Michael Schumacher

First Grand Prix start
Domenico Schiattarella
Hideki Noda

DRIVERS' POINTS

1 SCHUMACHER	86
2 HILL	81
3 BERGER	35
4 HÄKKINEN	26
5 ALESI	19
6 BARRICHELLO	16
7 COULTHARD	14
8 BRUNDLE	12
9 VERSTAPPEN	10
10 BLUNDELL	8
11 PANIS	7
12= LARINI	6
12= FITTIPALDI	6
12= FRENTZEN	6
15 KATAYAMA	5
16= BERNARD	4
16= WENDLINGER	4
16= DE CESARIS	4
16= IRVINE	4
16= MARTINI	4
21 MORBIDELLI	3
22 COMAS	2
23= ALBORETO	1
23= LEHTO	1

WORLD CHAMPIONSHIP • ROUND 15

JAPANESE GRAND PRIX

HILL
SCHUMACHER
ALESI
MANSELL
IRVINE
FRENTZEN

'Well done, Damon.' Beaten into second place at Suzuka, Michael Schumacher is the first to shake his rival's hand after the race. The German's World Championship lead had been narrowed to a single point.

Damon Hill capitalised brilliantly on a tactical blunder by the Benetton team to outfox Michael Schumacher and win a rain-soaked, two-part Japanese Grand Prix by just over three seconds. It was a success which not only kept the World Championship battle open through to the following week's finale in Adelaide, but also went down as probably the best race of Hill's career. Under relentless pressure from Schumacher in the closing stages, the Williams driver knew he could not afford a single slip on the glass-like track surface and coped superbly as the German inched into his aggregate advantage as the final laps ticked away. The conditions had been next to impossible from the start, with the safety car being deployed to slow the field after only four laps when three cars crashed on the pit straight. The race was then red-flagged to a halt after 15 laps after Martin Brundle's McLaren spun off and injured a marshal. After the restart Schumacher found himself forced into making not one, but two refuelling stops after his team mistakenly gambled that the race would be called with full points awarded after 75 per cent of the scheduled distance, and the German couldn't quite make up the necessary ground. Hill's superb win was perfectly complemented by Nigel Mansell's dogged run to fourth place after a race-long battle with Jean Alesi's Ferrari, thus catapulting Williams back into a five-point lead at the head of the constructors' championship table going into the final race.

JAPANESE GRAND PRIX

Ayrton Senna was immensely popular in Japan and a moving ceremony on race morning, attended by members of the late champion's family, gave the huge Suzuka crowd an opportunity to pay their respects to their fallen hero.

ENTRY AND PRACTICE

Damon Hill's hopes of emulating his Williams team-mate Nigel Mansell's 1986 achievement in keeping the World Championship battle alive right to the end of the season looked even more precarious after the first qualifying session at Suzuka, where Michael Schumacher set the fastest time in confident and unruffled style. Eight years earlier, Mansell had been heading for the title in the Australian Grand Prix when one of his Williams-Honda's rear tyres disintegrated, throwing him out of control at almost 200 mph. Now, unless Hill could produce a truly momentous reversal of form, it seemed likely that his arch-rival would arrive triumphant in Adelaide the following week as the first German World Champion and the second-youngest driver in history to take the title.

The margin of Schumacher's domination may have looked slender at only 0.4s, but the timing sheets told only half the story. What they did not indicate was the fact that the Benetton driver achieved his time in five fewer laps than the Englishman and used only one set of tyres to Hill's two.

With the current F1 regulations permitting each competitor only seven sets of tyres for an entire Grand Prix weekend, Hill was now very much fighting a rearguard action to stay in contention. 'I'm certainly not sandbagging,' he said. 'Michael seems to be in good shape and I really expected us to be closer. Tomorrow I want to take pole position and I know it is possible, but Michael was very confident he could do that time and save his tyres.'

Hill's efforts could also have been thwarted by several other drivers keen to advance their own reputations irrespective of the implications for the championship. While Nigel Mansell and Benetton's new signing Johnny Herbert could be expected to give as much support as possible to Hill and Schumacher respectively, Sauber-Mercedes driver Heinz-Harald Frentzen, who set the third-fastest time on Friday, was firmly pursuing his own agenda.

Mansell performed steadily to claim fourth place on the overnight grid, explaining that he had been slightly held up in traffic when set for a lap only a tenth away from Schumacher's best. 'I had a very enjoyable afternoon,' he said. 'We are there or thereabouts and we have the potential to go quicker tomorrow. The only small difficulty I had was that I didn't have enough elbow room in the cockpit and I did one lap less than my allocation.

'Damon is doing a tremendous job. He's doing a really professional job and showing a lot of character. I went into the last two races of 1986 with a ten-point lead. Michael is only five points ahead now. He is quicker, but he hasn't got a comfortable margin. It's pretty good, but it's not comfortable.'

There were other less obvious signs of competition manifesting themselves within the Williams family as David Coulthard, the man who had had to step aside for Mansell prior to the European GP, was politely requested not to hang around the pit lane garage during the qualifying sessions. Mansell clearly felt more comfortable without Coulthard and his business manager, IMG's Tim Wright, in the immediate vicinity.

This was mere detail, of course. It was the manner in which Michael Schumacher had regained his competitive composure following a nerve-racking two-race ban which continued to impress everybody in the business.

'I am totally satisfied,' he said calmly after his exertions on Friday. 'The car has been nearly perfect from the first lap and there has been a good start to a weekend in which there is a lot of pressure. Now, let's say, the pressure is moving to someone else . . .'

Clearly, Damon Hill did not need the message spelled out in any further detail.

For Williams, the real problem was their cars' handling balance in slow-speed corners. That was particularly evident in the tight chicane before the pits. On two occasions during Friday qualifying, Mansell was 0.1s up on Schumacher at the timing split on the straight before the chicane, but then lost his advantage by the time he had negotiated the corner and crossed the start/finish line.

The Williams-Renaults were certainly improved for Saturday's untimed session, when Mansell raised the hopes of his many Japanese fans by setting fastest time. Unfortunately, the heavens then opened and the second qualifying session was ruined by heavy rain, Martin Brundle eventually posting fastest time for McLaren. There was, however, some consolation for Hill, who no longer had to worry about any possible shortage of dry-weather slick tyres on race day.

Johnny Herbert's return to the cockpit of a Benetton had effectively brought his F1 career round in a full circle. The Englishman had made his F1 debut in the 1989 Brazilian Grand Prix at the wheel of a Benetton-Ford and finished in an excellent fourth place. Unfortunately, at this point in his career he was still suffering the after-effects of the leg injuries he had sustained when he crashed his Formula 3000 Reynard at Brands Hatch the previous August. By the middle of the '89 season, he had been replaced at Benetton by Emanuele Pirro and, thereafter, took some time to get his Grand Prix career back on the rails.

Now he was back in a Benetton at a time when it was the most competitive car on the grid. He took fifth place in first qualifying but confessed that he was still trying too hard and not letting the times flow easily. Then, in the rain, he crashed quite heavily, at exactly the point which had claimed Mansell during practice in 1987, damaging the rear wing and suspension.

'The car was very good on my first run in the wet,' he shrugged. 'We made a few small changes to the race set-up which meant that I had a little more understeer than before. I got a wheel on the kerb and the car spun.'

Behind Herbert, Eddie Irvine did well to qualify sixth after a water pump needed replacing on his Jordan's Hart V10 engine. Unfortunately nothing went right for Rubens Barrichello, the Brazilian youngster eventually lining up tenth after an engine failure on Friday followed by a heavy accident in the rain on Saturday afternoon which caused the session to be red-flagged to a halt with 16 minutes left to run.

'I just aquaplaned off,' explained Rubens. 'I am extremely annoyed because it wasn't necessary and it hurts to see the car looking like that. There was not much I could do, though. I was a passenger.

'As I went off I was praying that I would not disappear [become unconscious] like I did last time. Imola was a bigger accident than this, but I was unconscious for about six minutes there.

'After this crash, I opened my eyes and found that I was still here, and I was very pleased about that!'

The Jordan's right-rear corner was pretty well destroyed in the impact, which also damaged the rear of the monocoque around the engine mountings. However, Chief Engineer Gary Anderson remained confident that the car was repairable and the mechanics settled down to what promised to be a long night.

Neither Ferrari driver could work out a decent chassis balance for an entire lap of Suzuka. Jean Alesi wound up seventh, with Berger trailing in 11th overall. Gerhard also tried a revised V12 engine, offering improved torque lower down the rev range, but could not reach any serious conclusion as to its merits.

In the dry conditions on Friday, the McLarens of Mika Häkkinen and Martin Brundle had proved quite difficult to drive, the Finn qualifying eighth with Martin right behind. But Brundle found a really good chassis set-up in the wet conditions and surprised his team-mate by setting the fastest time in the rain-hit second qualifying session, a fraction ahead of Frentzen's Sauber.

Admittedly, Häkkinen had lost a lot of time in the morning when a heat-exchanger breakage had caused a Peugeot engine failure, but the mechanics worked miracles to fit a replacement in little more than an hour and Mika was back on the track before the end of the untimed session. Nevertheless, he felt that the new engine was a little down on power and that did not help his position in the afternoon.

Gianni Morbidelli emerged in 12th place on the grid in the Footwork

231

JAPANESE GRAND PRIX

McLaren-Mercedes deal announced as Peugeot teams up with Jordan

Months of fevered speculation finally ended on 28 October 1994, when McLaren and Mercedes-Benz announced a long-term collaboration with the simple aim of dominating Formula 1. The deal, which will see McLaren switching from Peugeot to Mercedes-financed engines built by British specialists Ilmor Engineering, will involve a seven-figure investment by the legendary German car maker which made it clear that it is seeking a Honda-style domination of the Grand Prix scene.

The contract signalled the end of Mercedes' association with the Sauber team, which it had indirectly bankrolled during the course of the season after sponsorship from *Broker* magazine failed to materialise.

Commented Helmut Werner, the Chief Executive Officer of Mercedes-Benz AG: 'We had assumed a role which went beyond the original agreement in that in 1993 and '94, despite the shortage of sponsorship money, Sauber was supported by MB to an extent that enabled the team to compete in all races at a high technical level. This point has provided a sound basis for independent racing activities in 1995.'

However, Werner was at pains to point out that MB would not be adopting a strategy of financial overkill to its F1 involvement. 'The F1 and Indy Car partners [Penske Racing] finance the design, construction and entry of the racing cars with the funds provided by sponsors while Mercedes-Benz contribute the engines and, in F1, part of the development budget,' he insisted.

In that connection, it was announced that McLaren's ten-year association with Shell was to end, with Mobil – already connected with Mercedes in both Indy cars and the DTM – taking over as fuel and lubricant supplier.

However, Werner did make it clear that Mercedes were playing for high stakes. 'The objective of McLaren and Mercedes-Benz is to finish the 1995 season among the top four teams and thus prove their ability to win races,' he said.

Speculation that US racing mogul Roger Penske, whose Mercedes-engined Indy car won the 1994 Indy 500 race at its first attempt, would become involved with the McLaren team was specifically denied. Similarly, rumours that McLaren was in financial trouble were dismissed.

'In 1994 our financial performance will be the best we have ever achieved since 1984 when Ron [Dennis] and I joined forces,' said Mansour Ojjeh, Chairman of the TAG McLaren group.

'Thus, we are entering into an agreement with Mercedes-Benz from a position of great strength. Ron and I are keen racers, but we are first and foremost businessmen. We are proud of what we have achieved at McLaren and look forward to the future with delight.'

The dissolution of the McLaren-Peugeot partnership at the end of only a single year enabled the French engine supplier to conclude a deal with the Jordan team for 1995. Speaking at the launch of the Jordan-Peugeot partnership in Paris, only three days before the McLaren-Mercedes alliance was officially confirmed, Peugeot's Deputy General Manager Frédéric Saint-Geours made it clear that his company's objectives remained unchanged by the switch of teams.

'The aim was to get podium positions in 1994,' he asserted. 'We have achieved seven. For 1995 the ambition is to win our first victory and, the following season, to figure in the race for the world title.'

A delighted Eddie Jordan was naturally excited about the future prospects of his developing team. 'We are now responsible for the image of a worldwide motor manufacturer and that will produce a lot of pressure,' he acknowledged.

'The McLaren-Peugeots have finished fourth in this year's World Championship, so we must aim to beat that record next season. This year, Jordan has scored its first podium finish and its first pole position. No question, next year the onus is on us to win our first race.'

The field stream away in an eerie gloom with only the glare of fluorescent lights and splashes of dayglo red on the cars piercing the murk. Schumacher has the edge while Barrichello, Herbert, Hill, Frentzen and Alesi are spread across the track behind him.

Bottom left: Ferrari mechanics watch the action from the shelter of their pit garage.

Martin Brundle was one of many drivers to fall victim to the atrocious track conditions, his McLaren aquaplaning off the circuit and injuring a marshal before coming to rest *(bottom right)*.

ahead of the Tyrrells of Mark Blundell and a highly disappointed Ukyo Katayama, who apologised to his fans for not having qualified better for his home Grand Prix. Katayama had a slightly uprated Yamaha V10 available on Friday, but this failed at the end of the untimed session and the popular Japanese driver could not produce the sort of form he had hoped for in the first qualifying session.

'I made a big mistake on my last flying lap in the second Degner curve and I am sure it cost me a full second,' said Katayama regretfully. 'The balance of my car improved as compared to the morning session, but we still needed to do more work. And I must thank my mechanics for their great work in changing my engine [so quickly] after the morning session.'

It had been hoped that Karl Wendlinger would make his F1 return at Suzuka after completing a remarkable recovery from the serious injuries he sustained during practice at Monaco. However, after testing at Barcelona, the Austrian driver suffered severe neck pains and deferred to medical advice that he should not race for the time being. As a result, J.J. Lehto, who drove for Sauber in 1993, was recruited for the final two races of the season. The pleasant Finn played himself in carefully, qualifying 15th in the dry and then having two spins in the rain on Saturday.

Further back, Alessandro Zanardi did his usual excellent job for the Lotus-Mugen team, qualifying 17th, while new recruit Mika Salo showed commendable confidence and cool on his F1 debut in the second car. On Saturday he had alternator problems which caused the engine to cut out under hard braking, but still scraped in with one place to spare.

Hideki Noda was well satisfied to qualify in front of his home crowd, while Taki Inoue also made the field on his debut for Simtek – although he had a close shave on Saturday morning when he spun at the first right-hander beyond the pits. Michael Schumacher only just avoided colliding with him after locking up the brakes of his Benetton!

RACE

Carefully calculated dry-weather race strategies went out of the window as Sunday dawned to continued heavy rain and the promise of little respite throughout the day. Brundle repeated his Saturday performance by producing fastest time in the saturated warm-up session, 0.067s ahead of Mansell, with Frentzen and an optimistic Blundell next.

As the race's starting time approached, conditions seemed extremely marginal. Standing water was only a problem on one particular section of the circuit, but visibility would clearly be next to impossible in such heavy rain, just as it had been at Fuji 18 years before when the late James Hunt clinched his World Championship in the inaugural Japanese Grand Prix.

Nevertheless, the race got under way at its prescribed starting time. In gathering gloom lightened only by a fusillade of popping flashguns from the grandstands, Schumacher gently led the field round on its parade lap. At the back of the pack, fuel injection problems had delayed Hideki Noda's Larrousse, the Japanese novice being obliged to start from the pit lane after the rest of the field had departed.

At the green light, Schumacher fishtailed across in front of Hill's Williams to take the lead in a blatant piece of gamesmanship which looked a whole lot more dramatic on television than it really was. Damon, in fact, made a quite average getaway and, as the cars sprinted for the first right-hander, Frentzen's Sauber drew level with the Williams on the outside, but was forced to fall back in line.

All round that opening lap, Schumacher benefited from a clear view to pull out a 1.7-second lead over Hill as they slammed past the pits for the first time. Frentzen was still keeping up ahead of Herbert, Alesi, Mansell, Irvine, Brundle, Häkkinen and Berger, but on the second lap the young German indulged in a spot of autocrossing, much to the detriment of his Sauber's undertray, and dropped to sixth. His team-mate J.J. Lehto claimed the distinction of being the race's first retirement, failing to complete the opening lap after his Mercedes V10 abruptly broke.

Conditions had become really appalling by the end of lap three and, as Herbert came through in third place to start his fourth lap, he spun wildly on the straight just beyond the pits, knocking his Benetton's nose off against the left-hand barrier. Ukyo Katayama's Tyrrell and Taki Inoue's Simtek also ended their races at the same point, aquaplaning suddenly on the start/finish straight and slamming into the pit wall. By this stage the organisers had deployed the safety car in order to slow the field at the height of the downpour and the procession duly cruised round at a gentle pace as Katayama climbed from his Tyrrell and was helped away with minor bruising to his right leg.

JAPANESE GRAND PRIX

JAPANESE GRAND PRIX

Nigel Mansell was back on form in Japan. His chase of Jean Alesi's Ferrari *(left)* was thrillingly captured by the in-car cameras as the pair disputed third place.

Below left: **Damon Hill shows his emotions on the podium after a hard-earned victory that kept his title chances alive. Michael Schumacher *(left)* must now wait seven days for the championship to be decided at the final round.**

Diary

British F3 Champion Jan Magnussen impresses on his F1 test debut at Estoril at the wheel of a McLaren.

Team Lotus is sold by the court-appointed administrator to an as-yet unidentified consortium.

F3000 driver Gil de Ferran signs to drive for Jim Hall's Pennzoil-backed team at the wheel of a Reynard 95I-Mercedes in the 1995 PPG Indy Car World Series.

Mario and Michael Andretti set to team up in a Momo-backed Ferrari 333SP to contest the Daytona and Le Mans 24-hour events in 1995.

'When the tremendous rain started to fall on the third lap, I was pushing hard, but lost the car at the entry to the start/finish straight,' said Ukyo. 'There was so much water on the track, there was nothing I could do.'

The damaged Simtek and Tyrrell having been cleared from the track, at the end of lap nine the safety car was signalled aside and the battle resumed. Schumacher, who had been speeding up and slowing down abruptly in an effort to psyche out Hill during their spell behind the pace car, really got the jump on his Williams rival at the restart.

He came through 4.8 seconds ahead at the end of lap ten, with Alesi now third from Mansell, Frentzen and Brundle. Berger by now was in trouble, the prolonged period of low-speed running having triggered an electrical problem with his Ferrari. Gradually it lost cylinders to the point where Gerhard abandoned it out on the circuit midway round the 11th lap, feeling this was a safer option than limping home at low speed with every risk that he might be hit by another car in the restricted visibility.

At the same time, three more midfield contenders fell foul of the terrible conditions.

F1 debutant Franck Lagorce was grappling his way through the murk in 17th place when he was tapped into a spin from behind by Pierluigi Martini's Minardi. Martini also gyrated, but while David Brabham's Simtek dodged through unscathed, Michele Alboreto braked hard to avoid his team-mate and spun off in the second Minardi. It had not been a good day for the small Faenza firm.

On lap 14, Gianni Morbidelli's Footwork, running in eighth, crashed heavily at the second Degner curve. The impact ripped off both front wheels and suspension units, but the main monocoque did an excellent job in protecting the young Italian, who hopped out and walked away.

However, in order to move the marooned and crippled car, a caterpillar tractor had to be driven across from the edge of the gravel trap. The clean-up operation was in full swing, under the apparent protection of the yellow flags, when Brundle lost control next time round and his McLaren hurtled straight towards the tractor.

'I really thought that was the end for me,' admitted Martin. 'I just closed my eyes, not expecting to be able to open them. But at the last moment the car spun round a little further and I missed it.' Unfortunately he did not miss a luckless marshal, who unhappily sustained a broken leg, and the red flag was very properly shown at the end of the 15th lap.

As an ambulance was despatched to collect the marshal, the competing cars all assembled in front of the pits. Most of the drivers climbed out to stretch their legs and, of the leading contenders, only Hill remained firmly strapped into his cockpit, seemingly unwilling to break the thread of his concentration by vacating the car.

Just over 20 minutes later, the race was resumed with a rolling start over a balance of 37 laps. An aggregate result would be produced by combining the times for this second 'heat' with those of the first, positions for which were taken, in accordance with the rules, at the end of the penultimate lap prior to the red flag being shown – lap 13.

Hill wasn't being caught on the hop for a second time and was only two seconds behind Schumacher at the end of lap 14 on the road, although in fact 8.6s down on aggregate at this stage of what was destined to become an increasingly confusing contest. Alesi and Mansell were now locked together battling for third on the road, although in fact Jean began the second 'heat' with a 4.54s edge over the Williams driver from the first.

At the end of lap 18, Schumacher came into the pits for fuel and tyres, the Benetton remaining stationary for 8.0 seconds. That meant that on lap 19 Hill was 18.7s ahead on corrected times, opening this advantage to 21.7s, 24.0s (Michael dropping to third behind Alesi on lap 22), 26.3s, and 29.5s on the next four consecutive laps.

It was an absolute reversal of the situation we had seen at Jerez. Hill, his Williams now light on fuel, was taking advantage of the fact that Schumacher's car had 80 litres more fuel aboard, he was running in traffic and the visibility was appalling.

Schumacher's position was such that Hill made a 9.2s stop at the end of lap 25. The mechanic working on the right-rear found the wheel nut so firmly jammed that he just satisfied himself that the tyre's condition was satisfactory and Damon accelerated back into the fray with three new tyres and one of the originals!

The Williams still emerged ahead, its advantage slashed from 26.331s to a mere 1.9s over Alesi and 7.5s over Schumacher. Jean made his refuelling stop at the end of lap 29, leaving the Benetton team leader a clear run at Hill.

On lap 30 the gap was 5.386s, then 3.44s by lap 33 and finally 0.484s on lap 35, Michael retaking the lead by 1.1s on aggregate, but not on the road, next time round. It all seemed over bar the shouting, but, amazingly, that did not prove to be the case.

Further back in the field, Barrichello had long since retired with electrical problems affecting the gearchange mechanism, while Mark Blundell was running ninth on lap 27 when his engine failed.

'I am very disappointed because I knew I was competitive in the wet with fourth-quickest time in the warm-up,' he shrugged. 'I was playing it safe with the rain, but we were also very competitive in the race.'

At the end of lap 40, Schumacher came in for a second refuelling stop. This was very much a 'splash and dash' affair with only around 40 litres of fuel going in and a fresh set of tyres being fitted. Benetton had gambled that the filthy weather conditions would result in the race being flagged after 75 per cent of its distance, the minimum which would qualify for full championship points. But the weather conditions had improved slightly, the race would run its full course and they now found themselves in the unaccustomed position of fighting a rearguard action.

The last ten laps were positively electrifying. Schumacher went back into the race 14.5 seconds down and with everything to do. By lap 43 he was only 11.9s behind and in another two laps he had reduced the deficit to 8.35s. It was going all the way down to the wire with the pressure on Hill like never before, the Englishman driving as hard as he dared, knowing that any sort of mistake would effectively wipe out his chances of challenging for the World Championship.

Yet Damon never put a wheel wrong. Schumacher was only 5.2 seconds adrift by lap 48, then 4.22s, and going into the last lap the Benetton was 2.45s behind. But by then the game was up, Hill finishing with a spurt to take the chequered flag with 3.36s in hand. At a stroke, the World Championship contest had been transformed from a foregone conclusion to a spine-chilling finale in Adelaide with the two contestants a single point apart.

The conditions, particularly early in the race, had been absolutely appalling. 'The downpour was pretty sudden,' said Hill. 'You just couldn't see to drive down the straight. The car was squirming all over the road down the straight.

'In the closing stages, it was really just a question of taking as many risks as I could. He [Schumacher] was closing at quite a rate, and I knew that I just couldn't afford one mistake.

'This is the first time that Michael has been beaten fair and square all season. I put myself under a lot of pressure and, for that reason, I think this win is even more satisfying than the one I scored at Silverstone.'

Mansell, who had spent the entire afternoon nosing alongside, but never quite getting past, Alesi's Ferrari on the long straight leading back towards the chicane, finally found a gap and squeezed ahead on the final lap. Momentarily believing that he had secured a place on the podium, he punched the air furiously as he took the chequered flag, only to be reminded that Alesi was still ahead on aggregate.

'Anyone who finished deserved a medal,' grinned Mansell. 'For a few laps the conditions were even worse than at Adelaide in 1989 and '91.'

Eddie Irvine picked up fifth place, grappling with too much understeer once his Jordan switched to a second set of tyres, while Heinz-Harald Frentzen struggled home in sixth, the handling of his Sauber badly impaired after his off-track excursion on the second lap. Seventh was Häkkinen, disappointed as ever about the handling of his McLaren, ahead of Christian Fittipaldi's Footwork and Erik Comas in the Larrousse. F1 debutant Mika Salo drove with commendable confidence and precision, never once having put a wheel out of place all weekend, to finish tenth for Lotus.

Completing the list of finishers were Olivier Panis's Ligier JS39B, David Brabham's Simtek-Ford and the other Lotus 109 of Alessandro Zanardi, the Italian struggling home with a broken diffuser and undertray and no means of seeing behind him, the lenses in both rear-view mirrors having vibrated off long ago.

One race to go and everything to play for. Suddenly Schumacher looked slightly beleaguered. As Hill rightly said, the boot was now on the other foot. It would be a question of who cracked first in Adelaide.

FIA FORMULA ONE WORLD CHAMPIONSHIP ROUND 15

JAPANESE GRAND PRIX
SUZUKA
4-6 NOVEMBER 1994

Suzuka Racing Circuit

First Curve · S Curve · Degner Curve · Underpass · Chicane · Hairpin · Spoon Curve

CIRCUIT LENGTH: 3.641 MILES/5.859 KM

Race weather: Wet, cool, cloudy

Place	Driver	Nat.	No.	Entrant	Car/Engine	Laps	Time/Retirement	Speed (mph/km/h)
1	Damon Hill	GB	0	Rothmans Williams Renault	Williams FW16B-Renault RS6C V10	50	1h 55m 53.532s	94.321/151.796
2	Michael Schumacher	D	5	Mild Seven Benetton Ford	Benetton B194-Ford Zetec-R V8	50	1h 55m 56.897s	94.275/151.722
3	Jean Alesi	F	27	Scuderia Ferrari	Ferrari 412T1B 043 V12	50	1h 56m 45.577s	93.621/150.668
4	Nigel Mansell	GB	2	Rothmans Williams Renault	Williams FW16B-Renault RS6C V10	50	1h 56m 49.606s	93.567/150.581
5	Eddie Irvine	GB	15	Sasol Jordan	Jordan 194-Hart 1035 V10	50	1h 57m 35.639s	92.956/149.599
6	Heinz-Harald Frentzen	D	30	Sauber Mercedes	Sauber C13-Mercedes-Benz V10	50	1h 57m 53.395s	92.723/149.224
7	Mika Häkkinen	SF	7	Marlboro McLaren Peugeot	McLaren MP4/9-Peugeot A6 V10	50	1h 57m 56.517s	92.682/149.158
8	Christian Fittipaldi	BR	9	Footwork Ford	Footwork FA15-Ford HB V8	49		
9	Erik Comas	F	20	Tourtel Larrousse F1	Larrousse LH94-Ford HB V8	49		
10	Mika Salo	SF	11	Team Lotus	Lotus 109-Mugen Honda ZA6C V10	49		
11	Olivier Panis	F	26	Ligier Gitanes Blondes	Ligier JS39B-Renault RS6C V10	49		
12	David Brabham	AUS	31	MTV Simtek Ford	Simtek S941-Ford HB V8	48		
13	Alessandro Zanardi	I	12	Team Lotus	Lotus 109-Mugen Honda ZA6C V10	48		
	Mark Blundell	GB	4	Tyrrell	Tyrrell 022-Yamaha 0X10A V10	26	Electrics	
	Rubens Barrichello	BR	14	Sasol Jordan	Jordan 194-Hart 1035 V10	16	Electrics	
	Martin Brundle	GB	8	Marlboro McLaren Peugeot	McLaren MP4/9-Peugeot A6 V10	13	Accident	
	Gianni Morbidelli	I	10	Footwork Ford	Footwork FA15-Ford HB V8	13	Accident	
	Gerhard Berger	A	28	Scuderia Ferrari	Ferrari 412T1B 043 V12	10	Electrics	
	Franck Lagorce	F	25	Ligier Gitanes Blondes	Ligier JS39B-Renault RS6C V10	10	Spun off	
	Pierluigi Martini	I	23	Minardi Scuderia Italia	Minardi M194-Ford HB V8	10	Spun off	
	Michele Alboreto	I	24	Minardi Scuderia Italia	Minardi M194-Ford HB V8	10	Spun off	
	Johnny Herbert	GB	6	Mild Seven Benetton Ford	Benetton B194-Ford Zetec-R V8	3	Spun off	
	Ukyo Katayama	J	3	Tyrrell	Tyrrell 022-Yamaha 0X10A V10	3	Accident	
	Taki Inoue	J	32	MTV Simtek Ford	Simtek S941-Ford HB V8	3	Accident	
	Hideki Noda	J	19	Tourtel Larrousse F1	Larrousse LH94-Ford HB V8	0	Fuel Injection	
	J.J. Lehto	SF	29	Sauber Mercedes	Sauber C13-Mercedes-Benz V10	0	Engine	
DNQ	Bertrand Gachot	F	34	Pacific Grand Prix Ltd	Pacific PR01-Ilmor 2175A V10			
DNQ	Paul Belmondo	F	33	Pacific Grand Prix Ltd	Pacific PR01-Ilmor 2175A V10			

Fastest lap: Hill, on lap 24, 1m 56.597s, 112.502 mph/181.054 km/h.
Lap record: Nigel Mansell (F1 Williams FW14B-Renault V10), 1m 40.646s, 130.332 mph/209.749 km/h (1992).
All cars used Goodyear tyres.

All results and data © FIA 1994

QUALIFYING 1

Michael Schumacher	1m 37.209s
Damon Hill	1m 37.696s
Heinz-Harald Frentzen	1m 37.742s
Nigel Mansell	1m 37.768s
Johnny Herbert	1m 37.828s
Eddie Irvine	1m 37.880s
Jean Alesi	1m 37.907s
Mika Häkkinen	1m 37.998s
Martin Brundle	1m 38.076s
Rubens Barrichello	1m 38.533s
Gerhard Berger	1m 38.570s
Gianni Morbidelli	1m 39.030s
Mark Blundell	1m 39.266s
Ukyo Katayama	1m 39.462s
J.J. Lehto	1m 39.483s
Pierluigi Martini	1m 39.548s
Alessandro Zanardi	1m 39.721s
Christian Fittipaldi	1m 39.868s
Olivier Panis	1m 40.042s
Franck Lagorce	1m 40.577s
Michele Alboreto	1m 40.652s
Erik Comas	1m 40.978s
Hideki Noda	1m 40.990s
David Brabham	1m 41.659s
Mika Salo	1m 41.805s
Taki Inoue	1m 45.004s
Bertrand Gachot	1m 46.374s
Paul Belmondo	1m 46.629s

Friday afternoon
Dry, warm, sunny

QUALIFYING 2

Martin Brundle	1m 56.876s
Heinz-Harald Frentzen	1m 56.935s
Michael Schumacher	1m 57.128s
Damon Hill	1m 57.278s
Eddie Irvine	1m 57.760s
Mika Häkkinen	1m 58.204s
Jean Alesi	1m 58.610s
Gerhard Berger	1m 58.926s
Johnny Herbert	1m 59.729s
J.J. Lehto	1m 59.943s
Christian Fittipaldi	2m 00.084s
Olivier Panis	2m 00.575s
Nigel Mansell	2m 00.963s
Erik Comas	2m 01.035s
Mika Salo	2m 01.637s
Rubens Barrichello	2m 01.905s
Pierluigi Martini	2m 01.929s
Alessandro Zanardi	2m 02.077s
Michele Alboreto	2m 02.219s
Mark Blundell	2m 02.266s
Franck Lagorce	2m 02.780s
Ukyo Katayama	2m 04.187s
Hideki Noda	2m 05.354s
Gianni Morbidelli	2m 07.293s
David Brabham	2m 09.453s
Taki Inoue	no time
Paul Belmondo	no time
Bertrand Gachot	no time

Saturday afternoon
Cool, wet, cloudy

WARM-UP

Martin Brundle	1m 57.837s
Nigel Mansell	1m 57.904s
Heinz-Harald Frentzen	1m 58.279s
Mark Blundell	1m 58.914s
Damon Hill	1m 59.297s
Jean Alesi	1m 59.347s
Michael Schumacher	1m 59.431s
Eddie Irvine	1m 59.503s
Ukyo Katayama	2m 00.743s
Gerhard Berger	2m 00.762s
Erik Comas	2m 00.787s
Rubens Barrichello	2m 00.843s
J.J. Lehto	2m 01.231s
Olivier Panis	2m 01.532s
Gianni Morbidelli	2m 01.880s
Pierluigi Martini	2m 02.119s
Mika Häkkinen	2m 02.225s
Johnny Herbert	2m 02.298s
Michele Alboreto	2m 02.416s
Mika Salo	2m 03.045s
Alessandro Zanardi	2m 03.560s
David Brabham	2m 04.373s
Franck Lagorce	2m 04.374s
Hideki Noda	2m 06.814s
Christian Fittipaldi	2m 07.128s
Taki Inoue	2m 07.191s

Sunday morning
Wet, cool, cloudy

FASTEST LAPS

Driver	Time	Lap
Damon Hill	1m 56.597s	24
Michael Schumacher	1m 56.679s	44
Nigel Mansell	1m 57.912s	25
Eddie Irvine	1m 58.095s	31
Jean Alesi	1m 58.438s	24
Heinz-Harald Frentzen	1m 59.612s	19
Mika Häkkinen	1m 59.831s	24
Mark Blundell	2m 00.437s	20
Christian Fittipaldi	2m 00.456s	26
Erik Comas	2m 01.088s	40
Mika Salo	2m 01.811s	43
Olivier Panis	2m 02.413s	39
David Brabham	2m 03.105s	41
Alessandro Zanardi	2m 04.371s	26
Martin Brundle	2m 04.733s	13
Gianni Morbidelli	2m 06.206s	13
Rubens Barrichello	2m 07.632s	13
Gerhard Berger	2m 11.960s	2
Johnny Herbert	2m 12.194s	2
Ukyo Katayama	2m 16.655s	2
Pierluigi Martini	2m 19.252s	2
Franck Lagorce	2m 20.381s	2
Michele Alboreto	2m 21.689s	2
Taki Inoue	2m 21.978s	2

STARTING GRID

Pos	No	Driver	Team	Time
1	5	SCHUMACHER	Benetton	1m 37.209s
2	0	HILL	Williams	1m 37.696s
3	30	FRENTZEN	Sauber	1m 37.742s
4	2	MANSELL	Williams	1m 37.768s
5	6	HERBERT	Benetton	1m 37.828s
6	15	IRVINE	Jordan	1m 37.880s
7	27	ALESI	Ferrari	1m 37.907s
8	7	HÄKKINEN	McLaren	1m 37.998s
9	8	BRUNDLE	McLaren	1m 38.076s
10	14	BARRICHELLO	Jordan	1m 38.533s
11	28	BERGER	Ferrari	1m 38.570s
12	10	MORBIDELLI	Footwork	1m 39.030s
13	4	BLUNDELL	Tyrrell	1m 39.266s
14	3	KATAYAMA	Tyrrell	1m 39.462s
15	29	LEHTO	Sauber	1m 39.483s
16	23	MARTINI	Minardi	1m 39.548s
17	12	ZANARDI	Lotus	1m 39.721s
18	9	FITTIPALDI	Footwork	1m 39.868s
19	26	PANIS	Ligier	1m 40.042s
20	25	LAGORCE	Ligier	1m 40.577s
21	24	ALBORETO	Minardi	1m 40.652s
22	20	COMAS	Larrousse	1m 40.978s
23	19	NODA	Larrousse	1m 40.990s
24	31	BRABHAM	Simtek	1m 41.659s
25	11	SALO	Lotus	1m 41.805s
26	32	INOUE	Simtek	1m 45.004s

NON-STARTERS
- DNQ — 34 GACHOT Pacific 1m 46.374s
- DNQ — 33 BELMONDO Pacific 1m 46.629s

LAP CHART

1st LAP ORDER	SCHUMACHER	HILL	FRENTZEN	HERBERT	ALESI	MANSELL	IRVINE	BRUNDLE	HÄKKINEN	BERGER	MORBIDELLI	BLUNDELL	KATAYAMA	BARRICHELLO	PANIS	FITTIPALDI	ZANARDI	LAGORCE	COMAS	SALO	MARTINI	BRABHAM	ALBORETO	INOUE
	5	0	30	6	27	2	15	8	7	28	10	4	3	14	26	9	12	25	20	11	23	31	24	32
1	5	0	30	6	27	2	15	8	7	28	10	4	3	14	26	9	12	25	20	11	23	31	24	32
2	5	0	6	27	2	30	8	7	28	10	4	15	3	14	26	9	12	25	11	20	23	31	24	32
3	5	0	6	27	2	30	8	7	28	10	4	15	3	14	26	9	12	25	11	20	23	31	24	32
4	5	0	27	2	30	8	7	10	28	4	15	14	26	9	12	11	25	20	23	31	24			
5	5	0	27	2	30	8	7	10	28	4	15	14	26	9	12	11	25	20	23	31	24			
6	5	0	27	2	30	8	7	10	28	4	15	14	26	9	12	11	25	20	23	31	24			
7	5	0	27	2	30	8	7	10	28	4	15	14	26	9	12	11	25	20	23	31	24			
8	5	0	27	2	30	8	7	10	28	4	15	14	26	9	12	11	25	20	23	31	24			
9	5	0	27	2	30	8	7	10	28	4	15	14	26	9	12	11	25	20	23	31	24			
10	5	0	27	2	30	8	7	10	28	4	15	14	26	9	12	11	25	20	23	31	24			
11	5	0	27	2	30	8	7	10	4	15	14	26	9	12	11	20	31							
12	5	0	27	2	30	8	7	10	4	15	14	26	9	12	11	20	31							
13	5	0	27	2	30	8	7	10	4	15	14	26	9	12	11	20	31							
14	5	0	27	2	30	7	4	15	14	26	11	9	12	20	31									
15	5	0	27	2	30	7	4	15	14	9	26	12	11	20	31									
16	5	0	27	2	30	7	4	15	9	26	12	11	20	14	31									
17	5	0	27	2	30	7	4	15	9	26	12	11	20	31										
18	5	0	27	2	30	7	4	15	9	26	12	11	20	31										
19	0	5	27	2	30	7	4	15	26	20	12	11	31											
20	0	5	27	2	30	7	4	15	26	20	12	11	31											
21	0	5	27	2	7	4	30	15	26	20	12	11	31											
22	0	5	27	2	7	30	15	9	4	20	26	12	11	31										
23	0	27	5	2	7	15	30	9	4	20	26	12	11	31										
24	0	27	5	2	7	15	30	9	4	20	26	12	11	31										
25	0	27	5	2	7	15	30	9	4	20	26	12	11	31										
26	0	27	5	2	7	15	30	9	4	20	26	12	11	31										
27	0	27	5	2	7	15	30	9	20	26	12	11	31											
28	0	27	5	2	15	30	9	20	26	12	11	31												
29	0	27	5	2	15	30	9	20	26	12	11	31												
30	0	5	27	15	30	9	20	26	11	12	31													
31	0	5	27	15	7	30	20	9	26	11	12	31												
32	0	5	27	15	7	30	9	20	26	11	12	31												
33	0	5	27	15	7	30	9	20	26	11	12	31												
34	0	5	27	15	7	30	9	20	26	11	12	31												
35	0	5	27	15	7	30	9	20	26	11	12	31												
36	5	0	27	15	7	30	9	20	26	11	12	31												
37	5	0	27	15	7	30	9	20	26	11	12	31												
38	5	0	27	2	15	7	30	9	20	26	11	12	31											
39	5	0	27	2	15	7	30	9	26	11	12	31												
40	5	0	27	2	15	7	30	9	26	11	12	31												
41	0	5	27	2	15	7	30	9	20	26	11	12	31											
42	0	5	27	2	15	7	30	9	20	26	11	12	31											
43	0	5	27	2	15	7	30	9	20	26	11	12	31											
44	0	5	27	2	15	7	30	9	20	26	11	31	12											
45	0	5	27	2	15	7	30	9	20	26	11	31	12											
46	0	5	27	2	15	7	30	9	20	11	26	31	12											
47	0	5	27	2	15	30	7	9	20	11	26	31	12											
48	0	5	27	2	15	30	7	9	20	11	26	31	12											
49	0	5	27	2	15	30	7	9	20	11	26													
50	0	5	27	2	15	7																		

Race stopped on lap 15. Results taken at end of lap 13 and combined with those of 37-lap second part to produce aggregate result.

One lap behind leader

Race distance: 50 laps, 182.030 miles/292.950 km

CHASSIS LOG BOOK

No	Driver	Chassis
0	Hill	Williams FW16B/5
2	Mansell	Williams FW16B/6
spare		Williams FW16B/1
3	Katayama	Tyrrell 022/5
4	Blundell	Tyrrell 022/2
spare		Tyrrell 022/3
5	Schumacher	Benetton B194/8
6	Herbert	Benetton B194/4
spare		Benetton B194/5
7	Häkkinen	McLaren MP4/9/4
8	Brundle	McLaren MP4/9/8
spare		McLaren MP4/9/6
9	Fittipaldi	Footwork FA15/3
10	Morbidelli	Footwork FA15/4
spare		Footwork FA15/1
11	Salo	Lotus 109/1
12	Zanardi	Lotus 109/3
spare		Lotus 109/2
14	Barrichello	Jordan 194/3
15	Irvine	Jordan 194/6
spare		Jordan 194/5
19	Noda	Larrousse LH94/2
20	Comas	Larrousse LH94/4
spare		Larrousse LH94/1
23	Martini	Minardi M194/5
24	Alboreto	Minardi M194/6
spare		Minardi M194/2
25	Lagorce	Ligier JS39B/6
26	Panis	Ligier JS39B/7
spare		Ligier JS39B/1
27	Alesi	Ferrari 412T1B/155
28	Berger	Ferrari 412T1B/154
spare		Ferrari 412T1B/151
29	Lehto	Sauber C13/5
30	Frentzen	Sauber C13/7
spare		Sauber C13/3
31	Brabham	Simtek S941/5
32	Inoue	Simtek S941/4
33	Belmondo	Pacific PR01/1
34	Gachot	Pacific PR01/2

CONSTRUCTORS' CUP

Pos	Team	Pts
1	WILLIAMS-RENAULT	108
2	BENETTON-FORD	103
3	FERRARI	64
4	McLAREN-PEUGEOT	38
5	JORDAN-HART	25
6	TYRRELL-YAMAHA	13
7	SAUBER-MERCEDES	12
8	LIGIER-RENAULT	11
9	FOOTWORK-FORD	9
10	MINARDI-FORD	5
11	LARROUSSE-FORD	2

FOR THE RECORD

First Grand Prix start
- Mika Salo
- Franck Lagorce
- Taki Inoue

DRIVERS' POINTS

Pos	Driver	Pts
1	SCHUMACHER	92
2	HILL	91
3	BERGER	35
4	HÄKKINEN	26
5	ALESI	23
6	BARRICHELLO	16
7	COULTHARD	14
8	BRUNDLE	12
9	VERSTAPPEN	10
10	BLUNDELL	8
11=	PANIS	7
11=	FRENTZEN	7
13=	LARINI	6
13=	FITTIPALDI	6
13=	IRVINE	6
16	KATAYAMA	5
17=	BERNARD	4
17=	WENDLINGER	4
17=	DE CESARIS	4
17=	MARTINI	4
21=	MANSELL	3
21=	MORBIDELLI	3
23	COMAS	2
24=	ALBORETO	1
24=	LEHTO	1

WORLD CHAMPIONSHIP • ROUND 16

AUSTRALIAN GRAND PRIX

MANSELL
BERGER
BRUNDLE
BARRICHELLO
PANIS
ALESI

Back at the front. Nigel Mansell's win in Adelaide may have been inherited following the controversial Schumacher–Hill collision but it could not be denied that, after a largely moribund season in Indy Car racing, he had gone a long way in making his critics eat their words.

Below: The top three finishers and newly crowned World Champion Michael Schumacher wrap up proceedings at the final post-race press conference of the year.

Nigel Mansell returned to the F1 winner's circle in Adelaide for the first time since the 1992 Portuguese Grand Prix, picking up the threads of his partnership with the Williams-Renault team to push his career tally to 31 wins. Having qualified on pole position for only his fourth F1 race of the 1994 season, Mansell, running a two-refuelling-stop strategy, dropped to fifth after a mistake midway round the opening lap. By this time Michael Schumacher and Damon Hill, who had gone into this final race of the season only one point apart in their battle for the championship, were streaking away from the pack, locked into a terrific battle for the lead. With both men scheduled to make three refuelling stops, they were running on absolutely even terms for the first time all season and it was an exercise which proved that there was virtually nothing to choose between them. Sadly, their epic battle ended in a collision after Schumacher brushed a wall, came back onto the circuit, Hill went for the gap – and the Benetton lurched into his Williams. Schumacher was out on the spot, and only after Hill had limped back to the pits to discover that his car was irreparably damaged did Michael know he had become the first German World Champion in the contest's 45-season history.

AUSTRALIAN GRAND PRIX

Hill in contract dispute with Williams

Damon Hill went into the Australian GP weekend in dispute with the Williams team over what he regarded as its apparent lack of appreciation of his efforts.

Hill was irked that, under his current contract, which is essentially an extension of his original testing deal, he would continue to be paid a relatively modest retainer – estimated to be in the region of £300,000.

This is a mere fraction of what Mansell can expect if he eventually does a deal for a full-time return in 1995, as Renault would very much like him to do.

'I am pretty disgusted with some of the things that have gone on,' said Damon when he arrived in Adelaide the Wednesday before the race. 'I feel they have not contributed to making me feel that the team is behind me to win the championship.

'I have been in negotiation with the team about my contract. I do have a contract. They have taken up their option on my services for next year, but I reckon I am a lot better than my contract says I am. The dispute is about the team recognising what you feel yourself to be worth.

'I have won nine Grands Prix,' he continued. 'This year I have had to carry the role of number one driver in only my second season in F1. I'm one point off the championship lead with one race to go.'

Even before his performance on Sunday, it was almost inconceivable that Hill would not drive for Williams in 1995 and it seemed likely that, by taking such an apparently outspoken stance almost on the eve of the race, he was merely creating the sort of high-pressure situation which brings out the best in his driving.

It was speculated that in the unlikely event of Hill splitting with Williams – leaving a Mansell/Coulthard driver line-up – a deal with McLaren-Mercedes might be a possibility.

'The fact that Damon didn't make a mistake [at Suzuka] speaks volumes for his character,' said Ron Dennis enigmatically.

'[But] it doesn't seem to come across when he's out of the car and I think he's as frustrated by that as he is with anything else.

'He craves recognition. I think his placid character doesn't go with his results. If his character was slightly more vivacious or sparkling, perhaps he would be held in higher esteem.'

Perhaps so. Yet even Dennis admitted that he was pretty impressed at Hill's performance in the Adelaide race. Damon had certainly saved the best till last.

ENTRY AND PRACTICE

At the close of the first qualifying session for the Australian Grand Prix it looked as though Nigel Mansell might play a decisive role in helping his Williams team-mate Damon Hill win the World Championship, although it was not easy to envisage the form any tactical exercise mounted against points leader Michael Schumacher might take. Mansell set a storming pace to take what would prove to be the 32nd pole position of his career after heavy rain washed out Saturday's second qualifying session.

It was a characteristically exuberant performance from the 41-year-old, who had started the day by sliding into the pit lane wall at near-walking pace, slightly damaging the nose section of his car, during the morning free practice session. Mansell had his Williams FW16B tottering on the outer limits of adhesion – and sometimes beyond – for much of the qualifying session through the bumpy Adelaide streets and, in one particularly dramatic incident, narrowly avoided a major collision when Johnny Herbert's Benetton spun in front of him and came to rest right on the racing line on the exit of a tight left-hand corner.

'I just came round, threw the car sideways and locked up its brakes so I spun,' explained Mansell. 'There was no way I was going to hit him head-on because that would have risked my legs.

'The thing that threw me is that there were no waved yellow warning flags, only stationary yellow caution flags. I'm going to have a word with the Clerk of the Course about this later.

'That was a close moment and I was happy to be able to do a time after that. I gave myself one lap to settle down and then tried to give it the big effort, and it was just enough.'

Schumacher would line up in second place despite crashing heavily in the closing moments of Friday's first qualifying period. This rare lapse by the German had looked on the cards from the very start of the session.

Early on, Michael had allowed his Benetton to slide wide over a high kerb and he only just regained control before it hit the wall. It was the first indication that the pressure of the championship battle was beginning to get to the Benetton team leader, who would go into Sunday's race only one point ahead of Hill. Finally, he clipped a kerb at the 120 mph chicane beyond the pits and his car snapped wildly out of control, slamming tail-first into the tyre barrier on the left-hand side of the circuit, before spinning round and charging in head-on.

'On my second lap I over-drove a little,' said Schumacher, 'so I decided to cool my tyres, then go for a fast lap time, which obviously didn't work.

'I was concerned yesterday already about this chicane and I talked to the FIA to make some changes, particularly the first kerb on the left-hand side which has a very sharp edge, and if you touch it the car gets very unsettled and jumps to the right.

'They made the changes, but still not good enough. And I just pushed very hard and I spun.'

Ironically, Schumacher had inspected the circuit the previous day and asked the stewards to alter certain points, including these kerbs. 'They did something, but not enough,' he added ruefully.

The session was red-flagged to a halt with the Benetton's wheels and suspension components scattered all over the track. The B194 was badly damaged beyond immediate repair, although not written-off. However, rather than switch Schumacher to the spare for Saturday, the team would build up a totally new car overnight around a back-up monocoque.

Meanwhile Hill ended the first qualifying session trailing in third place with handling problems. 'I didn't seem to retain the handling balance that I had during the morning untimed session,' he said. 'I am quite disappointed, but by no means disheartened. It is good news that Nigel, who is being very helpful, wound up fastest rather than Michael!' Damon was also doing his best to concentrate on the job in hand after a tense couple of days during which he had been complaining about the terms of his contract with Williams for 1995.

As far as the championship mathematics were concerned, Hill faced the task of beating Schumacher, irrespective of whether Mansell ran away and won the race decisively. Damon simply had to score two points more than Michael in order to become World Champion.

Mika Häkkinen finished Friday's dry qualifying session having set fourth-fastest time in the McLaren MP4/9. 'The balance of the car is not 100 per cent,' he admitted, 'and the engine's rather sudden response makes it difficult to drive smoothly on a bumpy circuit like this.

'These problems are difficult to solve in a very short time, so I don't think we can really improve the driveability this weekend. This sudden response also means it is difficult to take care of the rear tyre wear.'

Häkkinen also caught the red flag for Schumacher's accident just as he was poised for a lap which he believed could have been slightly quicker than his previous best.

Further back, Martin Brundle was encountering the same problems as Hill. His MP4/9 had felt extremely good during the morning's free practice session, but then the balance seemed to slip away and he found himself battling too much understeer during qualifying. That dropped him to a disappointed ninth.

Fifth and sixth fastest on Friday were the Jordan 194-Harts of Rubens Barrichello and Eddie Irvine. The Brazilian admitted to a slight mistake on his best lap, but didn't believe he could have quite caught Häkkinen, while Irvine was lucky to survive a huge slide coming through the tricky right-hander onto the pit straight, coming within inches of hitting the concrete wall.

Johnny Herbert found himself in seventh place, admitting that he still did not feel quite at ease with the Benetton B194, while Jean Alesi was the fastest Ferrari driver in eighth place, both he and team-mate Gerhard Berger getting absolutely nowhere with their chassis set-up and despairing of a solution. The Austrian would start in 11th place.

The pressure switched to Hill in Saturday morning's free practice session, Damon spinning his Williams over a high kerb after locking his rear brakes. That meant he was sidelined through to the mid-session break when the FW16B was retrieved and dusted down, although by this time the rain had started to come down heavily.

This hardly mattered by the end of the afternoon, of course, since the wet conditions lingered, denying Damon any chance of making the front row of the grid.

Heinz-Harald Frentzen took tenth place on the grid for Sauber, frustrated by too much understeer, while team-mate J.J. Lehto had to be satisfied with 17th. The Finn found it difficult to work out a decent chassis balance, making a change between his two runs which produced an uncomfortably lively ride over the bumps.

Behind Berger, Olivier Panis did well to set 12th-fastest time, although he felt that his Ligier's chassis balance had deteriorated slightly since the morning, while Franck Lagorce proved much quicker on his second set of tyres to line up 20th. Both Ligier drivers were having their first experience of the Adelaide circuit.

The Tyrrell-Yamahas of Mark Blundell and Ukyo Katayama sandwiched Alessandro Zanardi's 14th-placed Lotus 109. Zanardi's effort was especially praiseworthy as the brakes didn't feel particularly effective, the bias moving dramatically towards the rear wheels 'because of the basic inefficiency with the fronts,' as he explained it.

Mika Salo, handling the second Lotus once again, complained of a little too much understeer and qualified an unobtrusive 22nd fastest on only his second Grand Prix outing.

Michele Alboreto claimed 16th spot with his Minardi M194, two places ahead of his team-mate Pierluigi Martini. In the dry, both men were happy with their chassis balance, but slow on the straight due to running too much downforce.

Lagorce's 20th-placed Ligier separated the Footworks of Christian Fittipaldi and Gianni Morbidelli. Christian tried an experimental differential on Friday. It failed. Meanwhile, Morbidelli was frustrated by an irksome handling imbalance. Too late, it was traced to a faulty damper and he was left trailing.

In 23rd place came the Larrousse of Hideki Noda, ahead of local favourite David Brabham's Simtek,

AUSTRALIAN GRAND PRIX

which had suffered a fuel pressure loss in Friday qualifying. Jean-Denis Deletraz, Larrousse's latest recruit, was next, while 'Mimmo' Schiattarella also made the cut, despite damaging his Simtek's front and rear suspension with a spin into the wall.

The Pacific team missed out once again, suffering one final frustration. Having failed to make the field on Friday, Bertrand Gachot posted a 1m 22.123s in Saturday's free practice. Had he repeated that in second qualifying, it would have been good enough for 24th on the grid. But the rain took care of that . . .

'Today is a great day, because I will never have to drive the Pacific PR01 again!' said Gachot on Saturday.

Schumacher was decisively fastest in the wet second qualifying session, but it was not so much the fact that he was 1.1s ahead of Hill as that he outpaced his team-mate Johnny Herbert by an amazing 3.085s which raised some cynical eyebrows.

Interestingly, at the post-practice press conference Schumacher seemed extremely nervous when asked why he periodically slowed right down out on the circuit, then accelerated hard away. No convincing explanation was offered. Was it just a wind-up to unnerve the opposition? Or did Benetton have something to hide?

As far as Williams team tactics were concerned, Mansell, fifth fastest in the wet session, claimed that he wanted to keep out of the championship battle between Schumacher and Hill. Did he rule out the possibility of blocking Michael?

'That is a disgraceful question beyond professionalism and I am not even going to answer it,' he told the startled interviewer . . .

RACE

Mansell was quickest in the race morning warm-up from Alesi, Schumacher and the McLarens of Brundle and Häkkinen. Hill was sixth, much happier with the dry-weather handling of his Williams, but slower than he expected from his car's feel. Going into the race, Schumacher decided on something of a gamble. Rightly anticipating that Hill would give him a really good run for his money, he took off some wing angle in an effort to enhance his straight-line speed.

It was a decision which would come within a whisker of costing him the World Championship.

Mansell had pledged to let the championship contenders get on with it and proved as good as his word. Tension ran high as the veteran of 185 Grand Prix starts led the pack round the parade lap to take up his place on pole position, facing the short sprint to the acrobatic first chicane.

On came the green light and Mansell was moving first. He feinted slightly as if to block Schumacher, but Michael had already catapulted alongside Nigel's Williams by the time they drew level with the pit exit. Mansell glanced in his mirrors, saw Hill following the Benetton through and neatly side-stepped out of the line of fire, allowing Damon to storm away in pursuit of Schumacher.

Michael was really hard on it all the way round that opening lap. By the time Benetton number five had slammed through the fast right-hander onto the Brabham Straight, it was already ten lengths ahead of Hill and pulling away. It looked like the same old season-long story.

Further back, Mansell had slid wide a couple of corners into the lap, dropping behind Häkkinen and Barrichello, while Herbert and Irvine had tangled at the first chicane, the Benetton number two finding himself pitched into a quick spin.

'I didn't get such a bad start,' said Johnny. 'Alesi got in front of me, but then I got him back after the first corner. I was trying to overtake Irvine, which I did, but then he decided, just as I was turning into the corner, that he was basically going to drive into me.'

At the end of the opening lap, Schumacher was a sensational 2.1 seconds ahead, but that was as good as it got. Hill was at last running the same three-stop refuelling strategy as his rival and second time round he was only 0.4s behind, not just hanging on grimly, but pressing hard. Suddenly, Schumacher realised that this wasn't going to be a pushover, not by any means.

Even allowing for the fact that most of the other cars were running a two-stop strategy, and were thus handicapped by a heavier fuel load in the early stages, Schumacher and Hill were blowing away the opposition like seldom before. Damon, in particular, was lapping within a few tenths of his third-place qualifying time and, with ten laps completed, there was an 18.3s gap back to Häkkinen's third-placed McLaren.

At the end of lap two, Mansell had outbraked Barrichello to take fourth place into the hairpin at the end of Brabham Straight, but immediately slid wide and was repassed by the Brazilian. On lap 15 he made it stick and next time round did the same to Häkkinen, but again ran wide, allowing Mika to retake the position.

By the end of lap 17 the order was Schumacher, Hill, then a huge gap back to Häkkinen, Mansell, Barrichello and Brundle – all running in close company – with Berger seventh.

Hill was continuing to subject Schumacher to relentless pressure and the atmosphere was absolutely electric when, by sheer coincidence, the Benetton and Williams came in together for the first of their three scheduled refuelling stops at the end of lap 18.

The German remained ahead as they resumed the battle but by now there were signs that Hill, in second place, was getting the upper hand. He was more decisive than Michael when it came to slicing a path through the slower traffic and Schumacher, grappling with a touch more oversteer than he would have liked – the legacy of reducing downforce at the last moment – increasingly looked up against it.

Sadly, Damon's title dreams would end in disaster midway round the race's 36th lap when he was pushed out of the race by Schumacher only seconds after the Benetton's rear suspension had been bent after striking a retaining wall.

Schumacher ran wide coming through a tight left-hander, but Hill did not witness his glancing impact with the wall, the Englishman emerging from the previous corner simply to see the Benetton coming off the grass.

'I thought, "Hello, you've slipped up there,"' said Hill later. 'But I thought his car was OK. Only when I later looked at the video was it clear that his right-rear suspension was pretty damaged and would have put him out of the race.

'Of course, it's easy if you want to look back in time. In retrospect, I would have let him go.'

As it was, with Schumacher apparently recovering, Hill saw his opportunity and dived for the inside going into the next right-hander. Schumacher lurched into him, the Benetton was pitched up onto two wheels and slithered into the tyre barrier on the outside of the circuit. Michael was out of the race. Hill limped back to the pits, hoping that his Williams could be repaired, but nothing could be done. The left-front top wishbone

The moments when the 1994 drivers' championship was decided. The sequence at the top shows Damon Hill being squeezed onto the kerb as Michael Schumacher firmly closes the door. The Benetton *(above)* is launched up onto two wheels and into retirement, but Hill's car was also eliminated with suspension damage after the Englishman had limped back to the pits in the hope of a repair.

Right: Schumacher watches subsequent proceedings from behind the debris fencing, not yet aware that the title is his.

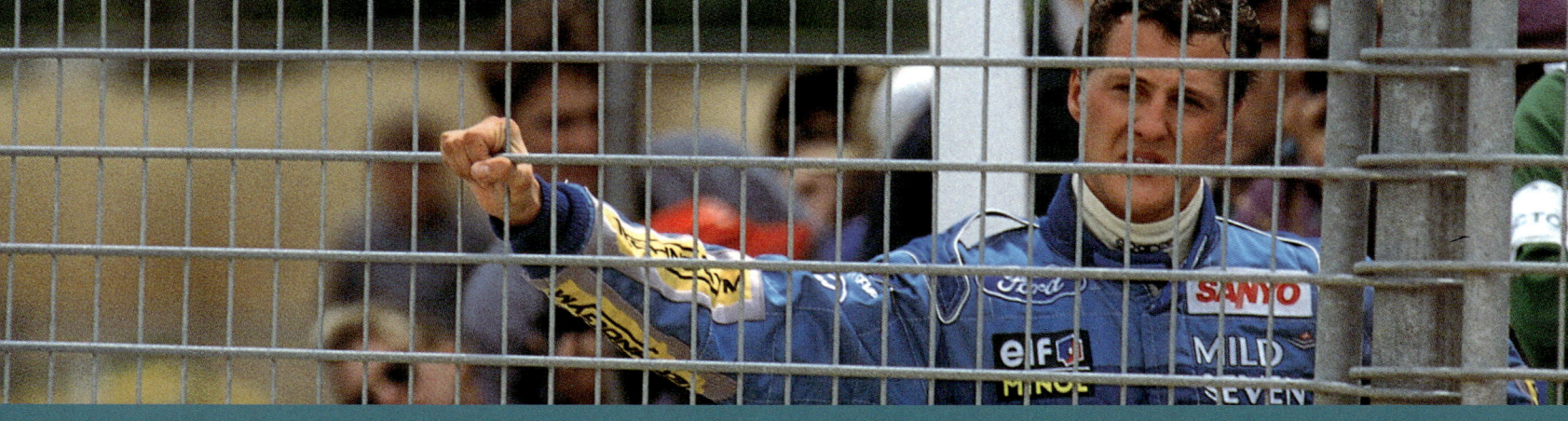

Nigel Snowdon

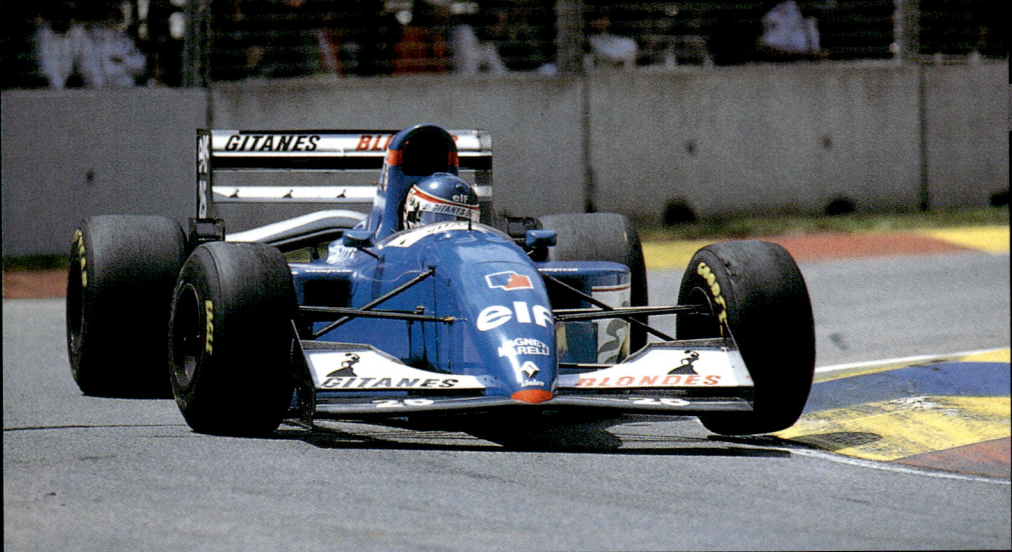

Despite a spin on the first lap Franck Lagorce *(left)* drove sensibly in his second Grand Prix to bring his Ligier-Renault into 11th place at the finish.

Below: Martin Brundle closed his season with McLaren-Peugeot with a distant third place. Very popular with the team, the vastly experienced Norfolk driver must wait to see if he remains part of the set-up next season.

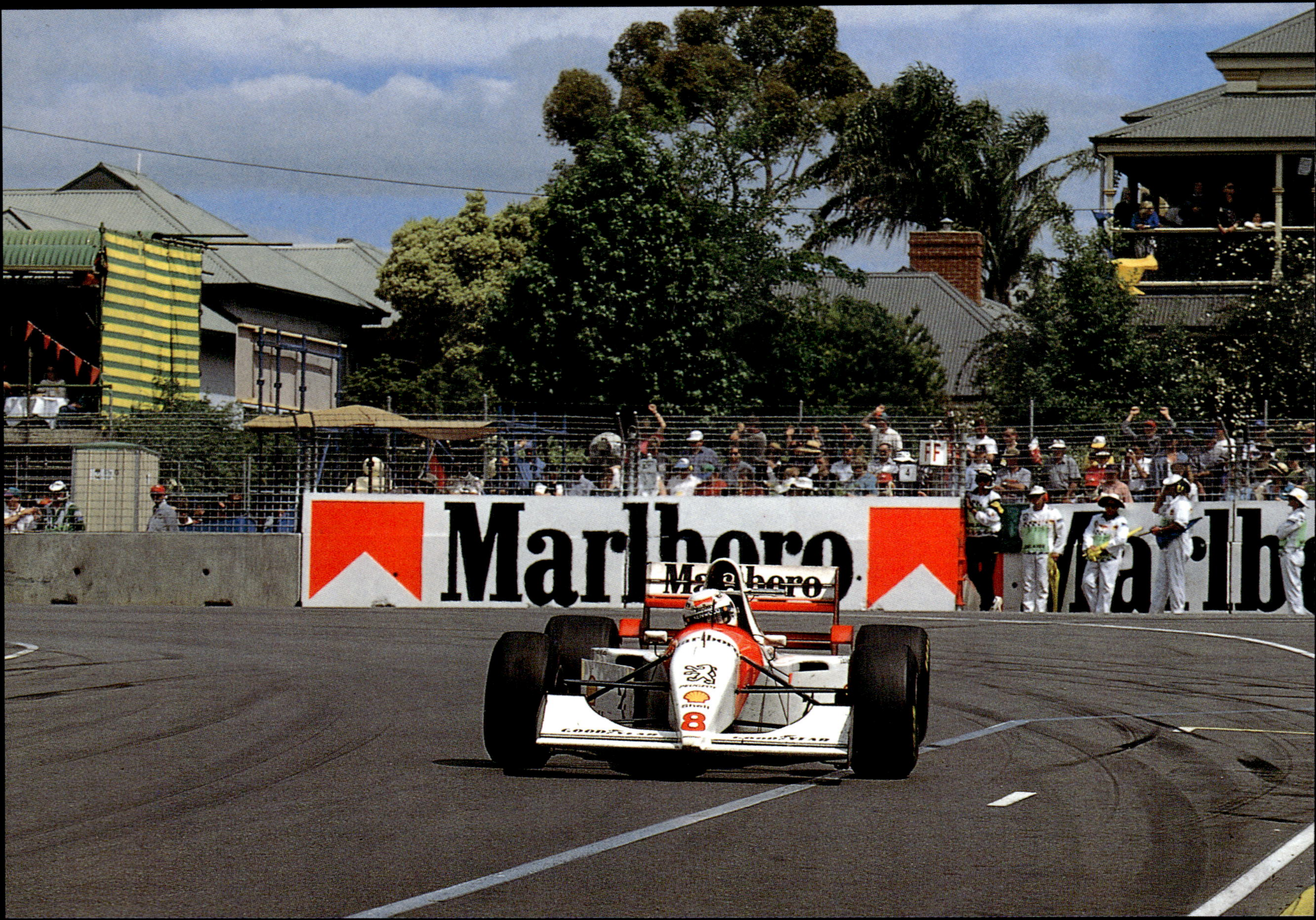

The spate of rent-a-drives continued to the season's end. Sometime F3000 racer Jean-Denis Deletraz secured a ride with Larrousse at the expense of Erik Comas, and ran slowly at the back of the field before retiring with gearbox maladies – though not before picking up a stop-go penalty for speeding in the pit lane!

Nigel Snowdon

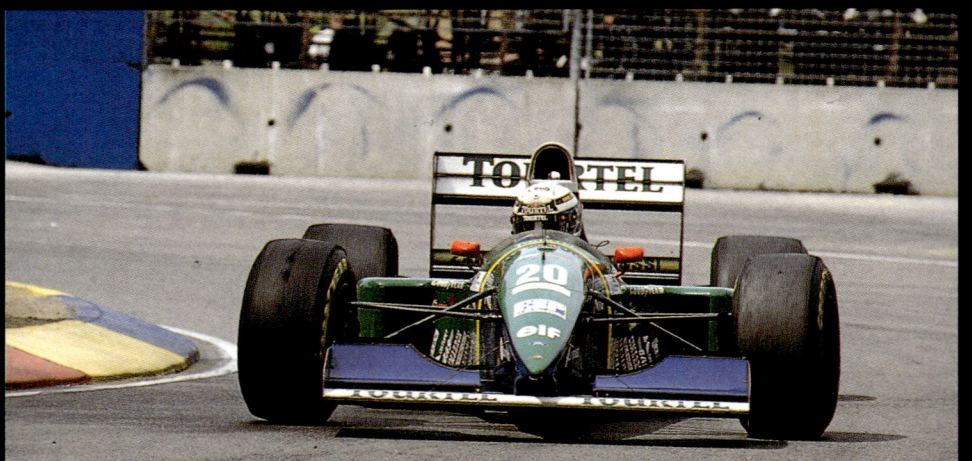

AUSTRALIAN GRAND PRIX

Diary

Bernie Ecclestone allegedly receives death threats from a group opposed to the running of the 1996 Australian Grand Prix on a new circuit in Melbourne's Albert Park.

Minardi close to finalising Honda engine supply deal for 1995.

Sauber confirms it will use works Ford 3-litre Zetec-R V8 engines in 1995.

David Coulthard poised to join McLaren for the 1995 season if Williams dispenses with his services.

had been bent beyond repair, leaving Hill a devastated loser and Schumacher the first German World Champion in the 45-year history of the contest.

For a few moments, Hill sat motionless in the cockpit, his brown eyes glowering ominously from the slit in his balaclava. Having composed himself, he climbed from the cockpit and walked straight to the Williams team office to telephone his wife Georgie in England.

'It was a bit of an empty feeling, but I think I gave him a good run for his money,' said Damon philosophically. 'He certainly was feeling the pressure, because he ended up falling off the road.

'I saw the opportunity and thought I had to go for it, but it didn't happen. I am afraid that is motor racing. Going into the last race with a one-point deficit to Michael was always going to put me in a position where I had everything to lose.

'But I think everyone in the Williams team deserves some sort of a medal this year, because we've been through a hell of a tough time, and to be here for the last race, fighting for the championship, was quite an achievement.'

Meanwhile, the German driver attempted to defuse what looked like a potentially awkward situation, dedicating his World Championship to the late Ayrton Senna and publicly apologising to Hill for making derogatory remarks about his ability just before the previous month's European Grand Prix.

'My car was difficult to drive throughout the race, because I was suffering from a lot of oversteer,' said Schumacher, 'but somehow I kept Damon behind me and found a way to increase the gap.

'After that I got caught out on a bump when the car stepped out and went sideways, and I caught it. Then I went over the grass and touched the wall, but continued.

'Then I just wanted to run into the corner, and suddenly saw Damon next to me and we just hit each other.'

Mansell now took the lead, only 4.5 seconds ahead of Berger, but the Austrian reduced this to 1.9s and was just 2.5s adrift when Nigel came in for his second refuelling stop at the end of lap 53.

Gerhard led until his own second stop at the end of lap 57 and some slick Ferrari pit work got him back into the fray with his advantage intact. Then Gerhard ran wide on a fast right-hander, allowing Mansell back through to the lead, where he stayed to win by 2.5 seconds after 81 laps.

Berger was extremely frustrated to have ended up with second place. His Ferrari was handling better than it had all season, but he had been short of tyres after flat-spotting one of his race sets in a spin during the morning warm-up. That meant that he had to change onto a used set at his second refuelling stop. 'It cost me half a second a lap in the closing stages,' he shrugged. 'And I was also pretty angry with Frentzen, who balked me very badly indeed.'

Third at the finish was Martin Brundle on what could well have been his final race with McLaren. He reported that his car felt perfectly balanced and got the upper hand over Häkkinen and Barrichello, both of whom received a ten-second stop-go penalty for speeding in the pits.

Mika's disappointing day came to a lurid end when he slammed off the road while running fourth with only four laps remaining, his McLaren MP4/9 veering left into the wall under braking for the hairpin at the end of Brabham Straight.

The accident quite badly damaged the MP4/9 and officially it was attributed to a possible braking problem. Later Brundle's power steering system failed on his slowing-down lap, causing his MP4/9 to turn sharp right very suddenly, fortunately without hitting the wall.

Barrichello did a solid job to finish fourth, his Jordan suffering from too much oversteer with a heavy fuel load, which briefly lost him the place to Häkkinen. It was a good result for the Jordan team on a day when Irvine had the bad luck, spinning off at the end of Brabham Straight when he locked his rear brakes.

Olivier Panis did well to finish fifth, but Jean Alesi, the only other front-runner pursuing a three-stop strategy, was absolutely fuming after taking the flag in sixth place, his efforts blunted by frustratingly long second and third pit visits.

Jean ran competitively in the opening stages of the race and was up to sixth when he made his first stop at the end of lap 17. By lap 36, he was up to third, but then stalled his engine at his second stop on lap 39, dropping back to ninth.

At his third stop on lap 59, he was further delayed when the reservoir for the V12 engine's pneumatic valvegear, which had shown signs of losing pressure on the telemetry, was charged up via its external connection. At the end of the afternoon he concluded that sixth place was a woefully inadequate reward when he might well have had a place on the podium and stormed away in a foul temper.

By any standards, it had been an incredible race. Hill had fought magnificently, lost gallantly and taken his defeat on the chin. Just as his father would have done.

'It was absolutely Damon's finest race,' said Patrick Head, Williams's Technical Director. 'He was a man on a mission and, had it not been for the accident, I have no doubts that he would have got the job done.'

Frank Williams added: 'Today we saw a new Damon. He reached a new level of performance and I am full of admiration for his achievement.'

Yet Schumacher, despite all his trials and tribulations throughout the season, had come out on top. Somehow that seemed right and proper. Just as, in many people's eyes, it was appropriate that Williams had clinched the constructors' title.

Bottom: Impromptu celebrations for Schumacher and his Benetton colleagues, but after the unsatisfactory Adelaide finale his coronation as champion was understandably a trifle muted.

FIA FORMULA ONE WORLD CHAMPIONSHIP ROUND 16

AUSTRALIAN GRAND PRIX
ADELAIDE
11-13 NOVEMBER 1994

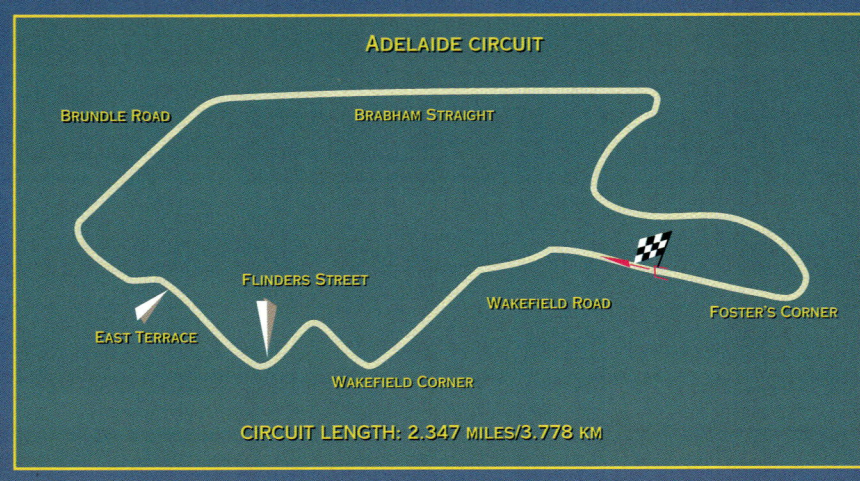

ADELAIDE CIRCUIT

CIRCUIT LENGTH: 2.347 MILES/3.778 KM

RACE WEATHER: WARM, DRY, SUNNY

Place	Driver	Nat.	No.	Entrant	Car/Engine	Laps	Time/Retirement	Speed (mph/km/h)
1	Nigel Mansell	GB	2	Rothmans Williams Renault	Williams FW16B-Renault RS6C V10	81	1h 47m 51.480s	105.834/170.323
2	Gerhard Berger	A	28	Scuderia Ferrari	Ferrari 412T1B 043 V12	81	1h 47m 53.991s	105.793/170.257
3	Martin Brundle	GB	8	Marlboro McLaren Peugeot	McLaren MP4/9-Peugeot A6 V10	81	1h 48m 43.967s	104.982/168.953
4	Rubens Barrichello	BR	14	Sasol Jordan	Jordan 194-Hart 1035 V10	81	1h 49m 02.010s	104.693/168.487
5	Olivier Panis	F	26	Ligier Gitanes Blondes	Ligier JS39B-Renault RS6C V10	80		
6	Jean Alesi	F	27	Scuderia Ferrari	Ferrari 412T1B 043 V12	80		
7	Heinz-Harald Frentzen	D	30	Sauber Mercedes	Sauber C13-Mercedes-Benz V10	80		
8	Christian Fittipaldi	BR	9	Footwork Ford	Footwork FA15-Ford HB V8	80		
9	Pierluigi Martini	I	23	Minardi Scuderia Italia	Minardi M193B-Ford HB V8	79		
10	J.J. Lehto	SF	29	Sauber Mercedes	Sauber C13-Mercedes-Benz V10	79		
11	Franck Lagorce	F	25	Ligier Gitanes Blondes	Ligier JS39B-Renault RS6C V10	79		
12	Mika Häkkinen	SF	7	Marlboro McLaren Peugeot	McLaren MP4/9-Peugeot A6 V10	76	Accident	
	Michele Alboreto	I	24	Minardi Scuderia Italia	Minardi M193B-Ford HB V8	69	Accident	
	Mark Blundell	GB	4	Tyrrell	Tyrrell 022-Yamaha OX10A V10	66	Accident	
	Jean-Denis Deletraz	CH	20	Tourtel Larrousse F1	Larrousse LH94-Ford HB V8	56	Gearbox	
	Mika Salo	SF	11	Team Lotus	Lotus 109-Mugen Honda ZA6C V10	49	Electrics	
	David Brabham	AUS	31	MTV Simtek Ford	Simtek S941-Ford HB V8	49	Engine	
	Alessandro Zanardi	I	12	Team Lotus	Lotus 109-Mugen Honda ZA6C V10	40	Throttle	
	Michael Schumacher	D	5	Mild Seven Benetton Ford	Benetton B194-Ford Zetec-R V8	35	Collision with Hill	
	Damon Hill	GB	0	Rothmans Williams Renault	Williams FW16B-Renault RS6C V10	35	Collision with Schumacher	
	Domenico Schiattarella	I	32	MTV Simtek Ford	Simtek S941-Ford HB V8	21	Gear selection	
	Ukyo Katayama	J	3	Tyrrell	Tyrrell 022-Yamaha OX10A V10	19	Spun off	
	Hideki Noda	J	19	Tourtel Larrousse F1	Larrousse LH94-Ford HB V8	18	Oil leak	
	Gianni Morbidelli	I	10	Footwork Ford	Footwork FA15-Ford HB V8	17	Oil leak	
	Eddie Irvine	GB	15	Sasol Jordan	Jordan 194-Hart 1035 V10	15	Spun off	
	Johnny Herbert	GB	6	Mild Seven Benetton Ford	Benetton B194-Ford Zetec-R V8	13	Gearbox	
DNQ	Paul Belmondo	F	33	Pacific Grand Prix Ltd	Pacific PR01-Ilmor 2175A V10			
DNQ	Bertrand Gachot	F	34	Pacific Grand Prix Ltd	Pacific PR01-Ilmor 2175A V10			

Fastest lap: Schumacher, on lap 29, 1m 17.140s, 109.613 mph/176.406 km/h.
Lap record: Damon Hill (F1 Williams FW15C-Renault V10), 1m 15.381s, 112.172 mph/180.523 km/h (1993).
All cars used Goodyear tyres.

All results and data © FIA 1994

QUALIFYING 1

Nigel Mansell	1m 16.179s
Michael Schumacher	1m 16.197s
Damon Hill	1m 16.830s
Mika Häkkinen	1m 16.992s
Rubens Barrichello	1m 17.537s
Eddie Irvine	1m 17.667s
Johnny Herbert	1m 17.727s
Jean Alesi	1m 17.801s
Martin Brundle	1m 17.950s
Heinz-Harald Frentzen	1m 17.962s
Gerhard Berger	1m 18.070s
Olivier Panis	1m 18.072s
Mark Blundell	1m 18.237s
Alessandro Zanardi	1m 18.331s
Ukyo Katayama	1m 18.411s
Michele Alboreto	1m 18.755s
J.J. Lehto	1m 18.806s
Pierluigi Martini	1m 18.957s
Christian Fittipaldi	1m 19.061s
Franck Lagorce	1m 19.153s
Gianni Morbidelli	1m 19.610s
Mika Salo	1m 19.844s
Hideki Noda	1m 20.145s
David Brabham	1m 20.442s
Jean-Denis Deletraz	1m 22.422s
Domenico Schiattarella	1m 22.529s
Paul Belmondo	1m 24.087s
Bertrand Gachot	7m 40.317s

Friday afternoon
Dry, hot, sunny

QUALIFYING 2

Michael Schumacher	1m 32.627s
Damon Hill	1m 33.792s
Gerhard Berger	1m 33.818s
Jean Alesi	1m 33.905s
Nigel Mansell	1m 33.988s
Gianni Morbidelli	1m 35.136s
Mika Häkkinen	1m 35.432s
Mark Blundell	1m 35.462s
Heinz-Harald Frentzen	1m 35.623s
Johnny Herbert	1m 35.712s
Christian Fittipaldi	1m 35.790s
Olivier Panis	1m 36.222s
J.J. Lehto	1m 36.245s
Martin Brundle	1m 36.246s
Pierluigi Martini	1m 36.257s
Michele Alboreto	1m 36.498s
Ukyo Katayama	1m 36.628s
Franck Lagorce	1m 37.393s
Rubens Barrichello	1m 37.610s
Alessandro Zanardi	1m 39.179s
Mika Salo	1m 43.071s
Jean-Denis Deletraz	1m 44.155s
Hideki Noda	1m 47.569s
Eddie Irvine	no time
David Brabham	no time
Domenico Schiattarella	no time
Paul Belmondo	no time
Bertrand Gachot	no time

Saturday afternoon
Wet, warm, cloudy

WARM-UP

Nigel Mansell	1m 16.377s
Jean Alesi	1m 16.866s
Michael Schumacher	1m 17.153s
Martin Brundle	1m 17.290s
Mika Häkkinen	1m 17.584s
Damon Hill	1m 17.643s
Rubens Barrichello	1m 17.694s
Ukyo Katayama	1m 17.945s
Eddie Irvine	1m 18.038s
Mark Blundell	1m 18.167s
Christian Fittipaldi	1m 18.188s
Olivier Panis	1m 18.227s
Heinz-Harald Frentzen	1m 18.234s
Pierluigi Martini	1m 18.242s
Johnny Herbert	1m 18.414s
Gerhard Berger	1m 18.480s
Gianni Morbidelli	1m 18.824s
Alessandro Zanardi	1m 18.852s
Mika Salo	1m 19.173s
Franck Lagorce	1m 19.269s
J.J. Lehto	1m 19.726s
Michele Alboreto	1m 19.748s
David Brabham	1m 20.425s
Domenico Schiattarella	1m 20.676s
Hideki Noda	1m 21.518s
Jean-Denis Deletraz	1m 22.324s

Sunday morning
Dry, hot, sunny

FASTEST LAPS

Driver	Time	Lap
Michael Schumacher	1m 17.140s	29
Damon Hill	1m 17.294s	20
Gerhard Berger	1m 18.094s	48
Nigel Mansell	1m 18.167s	52
Jean Alesi	1m 18.193s	34
Mika Häkkinen	1m 18.632s	66
Rubens Barrichello	1m 18.674s	60
Martin Brundle	1m 18.819s	76
Olivier Panis	1m 18.864s	60
Mark Blundell	1m 18.909s	56
Eddie Irvine	1m 18.932s	10
Heinz-Harald Frentzen	1m 19.346s	12
Christian Fittipaldi	1m 19.458s	47
Ukyo Katayama	1m 19.592s	10
Johnny Herbert	1m 19.658s	11
Alessandro Zanardi	1m 19.784s	11
J.J. Lehto	1m 20.159s	53
Mika Salo	1m 20.164s	41
Pierluigi Martini	1m 20.255s	54
Michele Alboreto	1m 20.338s	38
Franck Lagorce	1m 20.436s	40
David Brabham	1m 20.637s	14
Gianni Morbidelli	1m 20.771s	12
Hideki Noda	1m 21.961s	11
Domenico Schiattarella	1m 22.674s	16
Jean-Denis Deletraz	1m 23.929s	3

STARTING GRID

#	Driver	Team	Time
2	MANSELL	Williams	1m 16.179s
5	SCHUMACHER	Benetton	1m 16.197s
0	HILL	Williams	1m 16.830s
7	HÄKKINEN	McLaren	1m 16.992s
14	BARRICHELLO	Jordan	1m 17.537s
15	IRVINE	Jordan	1m 17.667s
6	HERBERT	Benetton	1m 17.727s
27	ALESI	Ferrari	1m 17.801s
8	BRUNDLE	McLaren	1m 17.950s
30	FRENTZEN	Sauber	1m 17.962s
28	BERGER	Ferrari	1m 18.070s
26	PANIS	Ligier	1m 18.072s
4	BLUNDELL	Tyrrell	1m 18.237s
12	ZANARDI	Lotus	1m 18.331s
3	KATAYAMA	Tyrrell	1m 18.411s
24	ALBORETO	Minardi	1m 18.755s
29	LEHTO	Sauber	1m 18.806s
23	MARTINI	Minardi	1m 18.957s
9	FITTIPALDI	Footwork	1m 19.061s
25	LAGORCE	Ligier	1m 19.153s
10	MORBIDELLI	Footwork	1m 19.610s
11	SALO	Lotus	1m 19.844s
19	NODA	Larrousse	1m 20.145s
31	BRABHAM	Simtek	1m 20.442s
20	DELETRAZ	Larrousse	1m 22.422s
32	SCHIATTARELLA	Simtek	1m 22.529s

NON-STARTERS

#	Driver	Team	Time
DNQ	33	BELMONDO Pacific	1m 24.087s
DNQ	34	GACHOT Pacific	7m 40.317s

LAP CHART

1st LAP ORDER	SCHUMACHER 5	HILL 0	HÄKKINEN 7	BARRICHELLO 14	MANSELL 2	ALESI 27	IRVINE 15	BRUNDLE 8	HERBERT 6	FRENTZEN 30	BERGER 28	PANIS 26	BLUNDELL 4	KATAYAMA 3	ZANARDI 12	ALBORETO 24	MARTINI 23	FITTIPALDI 9	MORBIDELLI 10	LAGORCE 25	SALO 11	NODA 19	BRABHAM 31	SCHIATTARELLA 32	DELETRAZ 20
1	5	0	7	14	2	27	15	8	6	30	28	26	4	3	12	29	24	23	9	10	25	11	19	31	32	20
2	5	0	7	14	2	27	15	8	6	30	28	26	4	3	12	29	24	23	9	10	25	11	19	31	32	20
3	5	0	7	14	2	27	15	8	6	30	28	26	4	3	12	29	24	23	9	10	25	11	19	31	32	20
4	5	0	7	14	2	27	15	8	30	28	26	4	12	3	29	24	9	10	11	25	31	19	32	20		
5	5	0	7	14	2	27	15	8	30	28	26	4	12	3	6	29	24	9	10	11	25	31	19	32	20	
6	5	0	7	14	2	27	15	8	30	28	26	4	3	12	6	29	24	9	10	11	25	31	19	32	20	
7	5	0	7	14	2	27	15	8	30	28	26	4	3	12	6	29	24	10	25	31	19	32	20			
8	5	0	7	14	2	27	15	8	30	28	26	4	3	12	6	29	24	10	25	31	19	32	20			

(Lap chart continues through lap 81. Race distance: 81 laps, 190.150 miles/306.018 km)

One lap behind leader (pink rows from lap ~10 onwards for trailing drivers)

CHASSIS LOG BOOK

#	Driver	Chassis
0	Hill	Williams FW16B/5
2	Mansell	Williams FW16B/6
	spare	Williams FW16B/1
3	Katayama	Tyrrell 022/5
4	Blundell	Tyrrell 022/2
	spare	Tyrrell 022/3
5	Schumacher	Benetton B194/8
6	Herbert	Benetton B194/4
	spare	Benetton B194/5
7	Häkkinen	McLaren MP4/9/4
8	Brundle	McLaren MP4/9/8
	spare	McLaren MP4/9/6
9	Fittipaldi	Footwork FA15/3
10	Morbidelli	Footwork FA15/4
	spare	Footwork FA15/1
11	Salo	Lotus 109/1
12	Zanardi	Lotus 109/3
	spare	Lotus 109/2
14	Barrichello	Jordan 194/3
15	Irvine	Jordan 194/6
	spare	Jordan 194/5
19	Noda	Larrousse LH94/2
20	Deletraz	Larrousse LH94/4
	spare	Larrousse LH94/1
23	Martini	Minardi M194/5
24	Alboreto	Minardi M194/6
	spare	Minardi M194/2
25	Lagorce	Ligier JS39B/6
26	Panis	Ligier JS39B/7
	spare	Ligier JS39B/1
27	Alesi	Ferrari 412T1B/155
28	Berger	Ferrari 412T1B/154
	spare	Ferrari 412T1B/151
29	Lehto	Sauber C13/5
30	Frentzen	Sauber C13/7
	spare	Sauber C13/3
31	Brabham	Simtek S941/5
32	Schiattarella	Simtek S941/4
33	Belmondo	Pacific PR01/1
34	Gachot	Pacific PR01/2

CONSTRUCTORS' CUP

Pos	Team	Pts
1	WILLIAMS-RENAULT	118
2	BENETTON-FORD	103
3	FERRARI	71
4	McLAREN-PEUGEOT	42
5	JORDAN-HART	28
6=	LIGIER-RENAULT	13
6=	TYRRELL-YAMAHA	13
8	SAUBER-MERCEDES	12
9	FOOTWORK-FORD	9
10	MINARDI-FORD	5
11	LARROUSSE-FORD	2

FOR THE RECORD

50th Grand Prix start
Gianni Morbidelli

First Grand Prix start
Jean-Denis Deletraz

DRIVERS' POINTS

Pos	Driver	Pts
1	SCHUMACHER	92
2	HILL	91
3	BERGER	41
4	HÄKKINEN	26
5	ALESI	24
6	BARRICHELLO	19
7	BRUNDLE	16
8	COULTHARD	14
9	MANSELL	13
10	VERSTAPPEN	10
11	PANIS	9
12	BLUNDELL	8
13	FRENTZEN	7
14=	LARINI	6
14=	FITTIPALDI	6
17	IRVINE	6
17	KATAYAMA	5
18=	BERNARD	4
18=	WENDLINGER	4
18=	DE CESARIS	4
18=	MARTINI	4
22	MORBIDELLI	3
23	COMAS	2
24=	ALBORETO	1
24=	LEHTO	1

1994 FIA WORLD CHAMPIONSHIP

Compiled by Nick Henry

Driver	Nationality	Date of birth	Car	Brazil	Pacific	San Marino	Monaco	Spain	Canada	France	Britain	Germany	Hungary	Belgium	Italy	Portugal	Europe	Japan	Australia	Points total
Michael Schumacher	D	3/1/69	Benetton-Ford	1f	1f	1f	1pf	2pf	1pf	1	DQ	R	1pf	DQ	–	–	1pf	2p	Rf	**92**
Damon Hill	GB	17/9/60	Williams-Renault	2	R	6f	R	1	2	2pf	1pf	8	2	1f	1f	1	2	1f	R	**91**
Gerhard Berger	A	27/8/59	Ferrari	R	2	R	3	R	4	3	R	1p	12	R	2	Rp	5	R	2	**41**
Mika Häkkinen	SF	28/9/68	McLaren-Peugeot	R	R	3	R	R	R	R	3	R	–	2	3	3	3	7	12*	**26**
Jean Alesi	F	11/6/64	Ferrari	3	–	–	5	4	3	R	2	R	R	R	Rp	R	10	3	6	**24**
Rubens Barrichello	BR	23/5/72	Jordan-Hart	4	3	DNS	R	R	7	R	4	R	R	Rp	4	4	12	R	4	**19**
Martin Brundle	GB	1/6/59	McLaren-Peugeot	R	R	8	2	11*	R	R	R	R	R	4*	R	5	6	R	3	**16**
David Coulthard	GB	27/3/71	Williams-Renault	–	–	–	–	R	5	–	5	Rf	R	R	4	6*	2f	–	–	**14**
Nigel Mansell	GB	8/8/53	Williams-Renault	–	–	–	–	–	–	R	–	–	–	–	–	–	R	4	1p	**13**
Jos Verstappen	NL	4/3/72	Benetton-Ford	R	R	–	–	–	–	R	8	R	3	3	R	5	R	–	–	**10**
Olivier Panis	F	2/9/66	Ligier-Renault	11	9	11	9	7	12	R	12	2	6	7	10	DQ	9	11	5	**9**
Mark Blundell	GB	8/4/66	Tyrrell-Yamaha	R	R	9	R	3	10	10	R	R	5	5	R	13	R	R	–	**8**
Heinz-Harald Frentzen	D	18/5/67	Sauber-Mercedes	R	5	7	DNS	R	R	4	7	R	R	R	R	R	6	6	7	**7**
Nicola Larini	I	19/3/64	Ferrari	–	R	2	–	–	–	–	–	–	–	–	–	–	–	–	–	**6**
Christian Fittipaldi	BR	18/1/71	Footwork-Ford	R	4	13*	R	R	DQ	8	9	4	14	R	R	8	17	8	8	**6**
Eddie Irvine	GB	10/11/65	Jordan-Hart	R	–	–	–	6	R	R	R	R	R	13	R	7	4	5	R	**6**
Ukyo Katayama	J	29/5/63	Tyrrell-Yamaha	5	R	5	R	R	R	R	R	6	R	R	R	R	7	R	R	**5**
Eric Bernard	F	26/8/64	Ligier-Renault	R	10	12	R	8	13	R	13	3	10	10	7	10	–	–	–	
			Lotus-Mugen Honda	–	–	–	–	–	–	–	–	–	–	–	–	–	18	–	–	**4**
Karl Wendlinger	A	20/12/68	Sauber-Mercedes	6	R	4	DNS	–	–	–	–	–	–	–	–	–	–	–	–	**4**
Andrea de Cesaris	I	31/5/59	Jordan-Hart	–	–	R	4	–	–	–	–	–	–	–	–	–	–	–	–	
			Sauber-Mercedes	–	–	–	–	R	6	R	R	R	R	R	R	R	R	–	–	**4**
Pierluigi Martini	I	23/4/61	Minardi-Ford	8	R	R	R	5	9	5	10	R	R	8	R	12	15	R	9	**4**
Gianni Morbidelli	I	31/1/68	Footwork-Ford	R	R	R	R	R	R	R	R	5	R	6	R	9	11	R	R	**3**
Erik Comas	F	28/9/63	Larrousse-Ford	9	6	R	10	R	R	R	R	6	8	R	8	R	R	9	–	**2**
Michele Alboreto	I	23/12/56	Minardi-Ford	R	R	R	6	R	R	R	R	R	7	9	R	13	14	R	R	**1**
J.J. Lehto	SF	31/1/66	Benetton-Ford	–	–	R	7	R	6	–	–	–	–	–	9	R	–	–	–	
			Sauber-Mercedes	–	–	–	–	–	–	–	–	–	–	–	–	–	–	R	10	**1**
Philippe Adams	B	19/11/69	Lotus-Mugen Honda	–	–	–	–	–	–	–	–	–	–	R	–	16	–	–	–	**0**
Philippe Alliot	F	27/7/54	McLaren-Peugeot	–	–	–	–	–	–	–	–	–	–	R	–	–	–	–	–	
			Larrousse-Ford	–	–	–	–	–	–	–	–	–	–	–	R	–	–	–	–	**0**
Paul Belmondo	F	23/4/63	Pacific-Ilmor	DNQ	DNQ	DNQ	R	R	DNQ	DNQ	DNQ	R	R	DNQ	DNQ	DNQ	DNQ	DNQ	DNQ	**0**
Olivier Beretta	F	23/11/69	Larrousse-Ford	R	R	R	8	R	R	14	7	9	–	–	–	–	–	–	–	**0**
David Brabham	AUS	5/9/65	Simtek-Ford	12	R	R	R	10	14	R	15	R	11	R	R	R	R	12	R	**0**
Yannick Dalmas	F	28/7/61	Larrousse-Ford	–	–	–	–	–	–	–	–	–	–	R	14	–	–	–	–	**0**
Jean-Denis Deletraz	CH	1/10/63	Larrousse-Ford	–	–	–	–	–	–	–	–	–	–	–	–	–	–	–	R	**0**
Bertrand Gachot	F	22/12/62	Pacific-Ilmor	R	DNQ	R	R	R	R	DNQ	DNQ	DNQ	DNQ	DNQ	DNQ	DNQ	DNQ	DNQ	DNQ	**0**
Jean-Marc Gounon	F	1/1/63	Simtek-Ford	–	–	–	–	–	–	9	16	R	R	11	R	15	–	–	–	**0**
Johnny Herbert	GB	27/6/64	Lotus-Mugen Honda	7	7	10	R	R	8	7	11	R	R	R	12	R	11	–	–	
			Ligier-Renault	–	–	–	–	–	–	–	–	–	–	–	–	–	8	–	–	
			Benetton-Ford	–	–	–	–	–	–	–	–	–	–	–	–	–	–	R	R	**0**
Taki Inoue	J	5/9/63	Simtek-Ford	–	–	–	–	–	–	–	–	–	–	–	–	–	R	–	–	**0**
Franck Lagorce	F	1/9/68	Ligier-Renault	–	–	–	–	–	–	–	–	–	–	–	–	–	–	R	11	**0**
Pedro Lamy	P	20/3/72	Lotus-Mugen Honda	10	8	R	11	–	–	–	–	–	–	–	–	–	–	–	–	**0**
Andrea Montermini	I	30/5/64	Simtek-Ford	–	–	–	–	DNS	–	–	–	–	–	–	–	–	–	–	–	**0**
Hideki Noda	J	7/3/69	Larrousse-Ford	–	–	–	–	–	–	–	–	–	–	–	–	–	R	R	R	**0**
Roland Ratzenberger	A	4/7/62	Simtek-Ford	DNQ	11	DNS	–	–	–	–	–	–	–	–	–	–	–	–	–	**0**
Mika Salo	SF	25/9/67	Lotus-Mugen Honda	–	–	–	–	–	–	–	–	–	–	–	–	–	–	10	R	**0**
Domenico Schiattarella	I	17/11/67	Simtek-Ford	–	–	–	–	–	–	–	–	–	–	–	–	19	–	–	R	**0**
Ayrton Senna	BR	21/3/60	Williams-Renault	Rp	Rp	Rp	–	–	–	–	–	–	–	–	–	–	–	–	–	**0**
Aguri Suzuki	J	8/9/60	Jordan-Hart	–	R	–	–	–	–	–	–	–	–	–	–	–	–	–	–	**0**
Alessandro Zanardi	I	23/10/66	Lotus-Mugen Honda	–	–	–	–	9	15	R	R	R	13	–	R	–	16	13	R	**0**

KEY

p	pole position	*	classified but not running at finish	DNS	did not start
f	fastest lap	R	retired	DNQ	did not qualify
		DQ	disqualified		

CAREER PERFORMANCES: 1994 DRIVERS

Driver	Nationality	Races	Championships	Wins	2nd places	3rd places	4th places	5th places	6th places	Pole positions	Fastest laps	Points
Philippe Adams	B	2	–	–	–	–	–	–	–	–	–	–
Michele Alboreto	I	194	–	5	9	9	10	8	6	2	5*	186.5
Jean Alesi	F	85	–	–	4	9	9	5	3	1	1	100
Philippe Alliot	F	109	–	–	–	–	1	5	–	–	–	7
Rubens Barrichello	BR	31	–	–	–	1	5	1	–	1	–	21
Paul Belmondo	F	7	–	–	–	–	–	–	–	–	–	–
Olivier Beretta	F	10	–	–	–	–	–	–	–	–	–	–
Gerhard Berger	A	163	–	9	15	14	18	8	8	10	16	307
Eric Bernard	F	45	–	–	–	1	1	–	3	–	–	10
Mark Blundell	GB	46	–	–	–	3	–	3	1	–	–	19
David Brabham	AUS	24	–	–	–	–	–	–	–	–	–	–
Martin Brundle	GB	131	–	–	2	6	6	11	7	–	–	83
Andrea de Cesaris	I	208	–	–	2	3	7	4	6	1	1	59
Erik Comas	F	59	–	–	–	–	1	5	–	–	–	7
David Coulthard	GB	8	–	–	1	–	1	2	1	–	2	14
Yannick Dalmas	F	23	–	–	–	–	–	1	–	–	–	2
Jean-Denis Deletraz	CH	1	–	–	–	–	–	–	–	–	–	–
Christian Fittipaldi	BR	40	–	–	–	–	3	1	1	–	–	12
Heinz-Harald Frentzen	D	15	–	–	–	–	1	1	2	–	–	7
Bertrand Gachot	F	36	–	–	–	–	–	1	3	–	1	5
Jean-Marc Gounon	F	9	–	–	–	–	–	–	–	–	–	–
Mika Häkkinen	SF	48	–	–	1	6	2	2	3	–	–	43
Johnny Herbert	GB	63	–	–	–	–	4	2	2	–	–	18
Damon Hill	GB	34	–	9	9	3	1	–	1	4	10	160
Taki Inoue	J	1	–	–	–	–	–	–	–	–	–	–
Eddie Irvine	GB	15	–	–	–	–	1	1	2	–	–	7
Ukyo Katayama	J	46	–	–	–	–	–	2	1	–	–	5
Franck Lagorce	F	2	–	–	–	–	–	–	–	–	–	–
Pedro Lamy	P	8	–	–	–	–	–	–	–	–	–	–
Nicola Larini	I	44	–	–	–	1	–	–	–	–	–	6
J.J. Lehto	SF	62	–	–	–	1	1	1	1	–	–	10
Nigel Mansell	GB	185	1	31	17	11	8	6	9	32	30	482
Pierluigi Martini	I	110	–	–	–	–	2	4	4	–	–	18
Andrea Montermini	I	–	–	–	–	–	–	–	–	–	–	–
Gianni Morbidelli	I	50	–	–	–	–	–	1	2	–	–	3.5
Hideki Noda	J	3	–	–	–	–	–	–	–	–	–	–
Olivier Panis	F	16	–	–	1	–	–	1	1	–	–	9
Roland Ratzenberger	A	1	–	–	–	–	–	–	–	–	–	–
Mika Salo	SF	2	–	–	–	–	–	–	–	–	–	–
Domenico Schiattarella	I	2	–	–	–	–	–	–	–	–	–	–
Michael Schumacher	D	52	1	10	10	7	3	1	2	6	15	201
Ayrton Senna	BR	161	3	41	23	16	7	6	3	65	19	614
Aguri Suzuki	J	59	–	–	–	1	–	–	3	–	–	7
Jos Verstappen	NL	10	–	–	–	2	–	1	–	–	–	10
Karl Wendlinger	A	35	–	–	–	–	3	1	3	–	–	14
Alessandro Zanardi	I	25	–	–	–	–	–	–	1	–	–	1

* includes fastest lap shared with Nelson Piquet at the 1984 GP of Europe.

QUALIFYING POSITIONS: 1994

	Driver	Attempts	Best	Worst	Average
1	Ayrton Senna	3	1	1	1.00
2	Michael Schumacher	14	1	3	1.79
3	Nigel Mansell	4	1	4	2.50
4	Damon Hill	16	1	4	2.69
5	David Coulthard	8	3	9	5.63
6	Jean Alesi	14	1	16	5.79
7	Gerhard Berger	16	1	17	5.81
8	Mika Häkkinen	15	2	9	6.27
9	Nicola Larini	2	6	7	6.50
10	Heinz-Harald Frentzen	15	3	12	8.73
11	Eddie Irvine	13	4	16	9.23
12	Rubens Barrichello	16	1	28	9.69
13	Jos Verstappen	10	6	19	10.60
14	Martin Brundle	16	6	18	10.81
15	Ukyo Katayama	16	5	23	11.25
16	Karl Wendlinger	3	7	19	12.00
17	Mark Blundell	16	7	21	12.56
18=	J.J. Lehto	8	4	20	14.00
18=	Gianni Morbidelli	16	6	22	14.00
20	Olivier Panis	16	6	22	15.44
21	Andrea de Cesaris	11	8	21	15.55
22	Pierluigi Martini	16	9	20	15.63
23	Christian Fittipaldi	16	6	24	16.25
24	Johnny Herbert	16	4	24	16.31
25	Philippe Alliot	2	14	19	16.50
26	Michele Alboreto	16	12	23	18.31
27	Eric Bernard	14	12	24	18.64
28	Alessandro Zanardi	10	13	23	19.60
29	Erik Comas	15	13	24	19.67
30=	Aguri Suzuki	1	20	20	20.00
30=	Franck Lagorce	2	20	20	20.00
32	Olivier Beretta	10	17	25	22.20
33	Pedro Lamy	4	19	24	22.25
34	Yannick Dalmas	2	23	23	23.00
35	Hideki Noda	3	23	24	23.33
36	Mika Salo	2	22	25	23.50
37	David Brabham	16	21	26	24.19
38	Jean-Denis Deletraz	1	25	25	25.00
39	Philippe Adams	2	25	26	25.50
40	Jean-Marc Gounon	7	25	26	25.71
41=	Taki Inoue	1	26	26	26.00
41=	Domenico Schiattarella	2	26	26	26.00
43	Roland Ratzenberger	3	26	27	26.33
44	Bertrand Gachot	16	23	28	26.44
45	Paul Belmondo	16	24	28	26.75
46	Andrea Montermini	1	27	27	27.00

UNLAPPED: 1994

Number of cars on same lap as leader

Grand Prix	Starters	at ¼ distance	at ½ distance	at ¾ distance	at full distance
Brazil	26	15	4	2	1
Pacific	26	10	4	2	2
San Marino	25	21	14	7	4
Monaco	24	9	6	3	3
Spain	26	19	10	6	3
Canada	26	23	9	6	4
France	26	23	8	3	3
Britain	26	15	10	6	5
Germany	26	13	7	7	3
Hungary	26	17	10	4	3
Belgium	26	20	13	7	5
Italy	26	22	13	8	5
Portugal	26	22	14	8	6
Europe	26	20	11	7	4
Japan	26	17	14	9	6
Australia	26	16	10	8	4

LAP LEADERS: 1994

Grand Prix	Michael Schumacher	Damon Hill	Gerhard Berger	Nigel Mansell	Ayrton Senna	Jean Alesi	David Coulthard	Mika Häkkinen	Nicola Larini	Rubens Barrichello
Brazil	50	–	–	–	21	–	–	–	–	–
Pacific	83	–	–	–	–	–	–	–	–	–
San Marino	35	–	9	–	5	–	–	4	5	–
Monaco	78	–	–	–	–	–	–	–	–	–
Spain	27	30	–	–	–	–	–	8	–	–
Canada	69	–	–	–	–	–	–	–	–	–
France	65	7	–	–	–	–	–	–	–	–
Britain	8	48	4	–	–	–	–	–	–	–
Germany	–	–	45	–	–	–	–	–	–	–
Hungary	68	9	–	–	–	–	–	–	–	–
Belgium	43	–	–	–	–	–	1	–	–	–
Italy	–	26	9	–	–	14	3	1	–	–
Portugal	–	45	7	–	–	4	12	–	–	3
Europe	50	19	–	–	–	–	–	–	–	–
Japan	23	27	–	–	–	–	–	–	–	–
Australia	35	–	10	36	–	–	–	–	–	–
Total	634	211	84	36	26	18	16	13	5	3
Percentage	60.6	20.2	8.0	3.4	2.5	1.7	1.5	1.2	0.5	0.3

RETIREMENTS: 1994

Number of cars to have retired

Grand Prix	Starters	at ¼ distance	at ½ distance	at ¾ distance	at full distance
Brazil	26	7	13	13	14
Pacific	26	6	10	15	
San Marino	25	4	8	10	13
Monaco	24	4	7	12	13
Spain	26	3	10	14	16
Canada	26	2	3	8	12
France	26	–	8	15	16
Britain	26	6	7	8	9
Germany	26	12	16	16	18
Hungary	26	4	8	9	14
Belgium	26	3	8	11	13
Italy	26	3	9	12	17
Portugal	26	1	4	6	9
Europe	26	3	3	7	7
Japan	26	9	12	13	13
Australia	26	5	9	12	14

POINTS & PERCENTAGES
Compiled by DAVID HAYHOE

FORMULA 3000 REVIEW

CROWNED JULES

by Simon Arron

Just over halfway through the FIA European Formula 3000 Championship, the title battle appeared to have been reduced to a two-horse race. Gil de Ferran and Franck Lagorce had swapped the series lead since it commenced at Silverstone in May; each had taken two wins; Lagorce's second victory, at Hockenheim, had given him a two-point advantage. With just three races to go, Jean-Christophe Boullion, known to all and sundry by the nickname 'Jules', was fully 19 points adrift of Lagorce, and apparently out of the reckoning.

In a bizarre transformation, however, the highly rated Frenchman, one of the most popular pre-season favourites, went on to win all three. As Lagorce and de Ferran stumbled their way through the championship's closing stages, Boullion completed a most extraordinary recovery to become the fourth French F3000 champion, and the tenth in all.

If the manner of his success was ultimately startling, the fact that he should actually take the title was not. At Silverstone, he had been the second-fastest man on the circuit, although he was unable to convert a poor qualifying performance into points. At Pau, he was a modest fourth. He was unquestionably the quickest driver at both Barcelona and Enna, only to commit costly errors. Enna, in truth, was not his fault. He crashed during qualifying as there were a couple of marshals standing in the middle of the track. Having to choose between them and the tyre wall, he chose the latter. And yet still the Sicilian circuit continues to be included in the calendar; it has already been confirmed for 1995.

Just as it appeared that the pressure was putting an irreparable strain on the relationship between Boullion and his team, DAMS, the most successful in F3000 history, he put in a strong showing to finish second to Lagorce at Hockenheim. He struck perhaps the most stunning psychological blow in the following race at Spa, however, where his maiden F3000 victory, in the 100th FIA Championship race, was preceded by an overtaking manoeuvre of stunning audacity. Although Boullion himself played it down, the way he plunged around the outside of Lagorce, at the daunting Blanchimont kink, and in the wet to boot, was one of the motor racing season's unsung moments of heroism.

As his crusade gained momentum, his main adversaries faltered.

Lagorce showed crass judgement at Spa, pitting for slicks at a stage of the race when the track was still far too damp. It cost him a certain top-four finish. De Ferran, meanwhile, had recovered magnificently from a first-lap spin in Belgium to finish fifth. Already a majestic victor at both Pau and Enna, Paul Stewart Racing's team leader was in front again at Estoril, but only for a couple of minutes. Lagorce's team-mate Emmanuel Clérico pitched him into the gravel, and it was little consolation that Lagorce himself later made a fundamental error while lying third. Although the two of them still jointly led the series, Boullion's second win took him to within a point, with just one race to go.

Magny-Cours was always likely to favour the French — Lagorce's team, Apomatox, is based there — and so it proved. De Ferran and Vincenzo Sospiri, who still had an outside title chance thanks to his consistent points scoring, were well down the grid.

Lagorce and Boullion, meanwhile, shared the front row . . . Lagorce led, made a small mistake on the eighth lap, and Boullion pounced. They finished 1-2, and that was enough to swing the title Boullion's way. It was a cruel blow to Apomatox, which has lived in DAMS's shadow for so long. Both teams were

248

formed in 1989, since when DAMS has won three titles. Lagorce brought Apomatox its first victories this year, but he and the team were well aware that they should have done much more than that.

Ultimately, that erroneous pit stop at Spa proved more costly than anyone could have imagined.

At least Lagorce had the consolation of a late-season F1 debut with Ligier, for whom he will serve, at the very least, as test driver in 1995. Boullion, meanwhile, is tipped to graduate to F1 along with DAMS, assuming team principal Jean-Paul Driot raises the cash.

De Ferran, meanwhile, has committed himself to three years of Indy Car racing with Jim Hall's team. That is as clear an indication as any of just how hard decent F1 drives are to come by in this day and age, even for those who show obvious signs of ability. Cerebral and aggressive in equal measure, de Ferran's decision will be F1's loss, America's gain.

Although Sospiri, a far better racer than he was a qualifier, eventually took fourth in the championship, and de Ferran's PSR team-mate Didier Cottaz took fifth (thanks to two podium finishes), the only other race winner was Massimiliano Papis, who absolutely marmalised the opposition in Barcelona, though he might have been made to fight had Boullion not stalled at the start. As it was, this proved to be a real flash in the pan. At other races, the likeable Italian's performance graph looked like a cross-setion of the Pyrenees. And he was usually at a loss to explain his inconsistency. It was noticeable that team-mate Fabrizio de Simone's strongest showing came at Barcelona, too, as Mythos chalked up an impressive 1-2.

Cottaz apart, there were promising performances from French newcomers Guillaume Gomez and Emmanuel Clérico. Gomez twice finished on the podium, while Clérico proved that he has lots more to offer the sport than film-star looks. There were mistakes at Hockenheim and Estoril, and he could easily have won in Portugal, but mostly he was the victim of an unfortunate series of engine problems which never afflicted team-mate Lagorce.

Italian F3 Champion Christian Pescatori offered several clues to his ultimate potential, though a year-old Durango Reynard wasn't the best tool for the job, while Britain's brightest hope, Oliver Gavin, ran into financial difficulties halfway through the season. Gavin was one of the few to use a Lola chassis, but though the Huntingdon marque occasionally showed well in races – notably in the hands of Nordic Racing's Marc Goossens – it too often started at a disadvantage, having failed to make as much use of new tyres in qualifying as the Reynards always seemed able to do. Since entering F3000 in 1988, Reynard has now failed to provide the championship-winning car only once.

Other rookies who emerged with credit were 18-year-old Brazilian Tarso Marques and Wim Eyckmans, who achieved respectable results with a car run by his own small family team. Of the older guard, Hideki Noda's improvement in form was sufficiently dramatic to have carried him into F1, with Larrousse, within two weeks of the season ending...

The best advertisement for F3000 was, undoubtedly, David Coulthard. Second in the opening race at Silverstone, the Scot was whisked into F1 and the realms of national celebrity in the wake of the tragic events at Imola. How much longer F3000 can go on producing drivers of such obvious talent remains to be seen, for 1995 marks the final season under the existing regulations.

In 1996, the FIA intends to introduce a series for identical chassis and engines, albeit similar in concept to the current Formula 3000. Its precise form and name have yet to be determined, but it seems certain that the proposal will be accepted.

Opposite page: Quiet and unassuming off the track, Jean-Christophe Boullion won the F3000 title with a driving style that was both forceful and direct. He snatched the crown at the death after a late-season charge and now looks towards Formula 1.

Gil de Ferran *(above left)* won two rounds in the Paul Stewart Racing Reynard but managed only third place in the championship. The Brazilian now heads west to take up the new challenge of Indy Car racing with Jim Hall's team.

Though very fast, Franck Lagorce *(bottom)* made a number of errors which ultimately cost him the championship. The single-minded Frenchman did, however, have the consolation of a Grand Prix debut for Ligier at Suzuka.

FORMULA THREE REVIEW

HEIR APPARENT

by Andrew Benson

'Jan Magnussen', said Jackie Stewart after the Dane had won the British Formula 3 Championship for Paul Stewart Racing in the most dominant fashion ever achieved, 'is one of the most talented young men to come along since Ayrton Senna, and maybe the most talented.'

It may seem a trifle inflated to speak of a man just past his 21st birthday in such exalted terms, and it is true that not all the drivers who shine in F3 go on to be successful in Formula 1. But the ease and style with which Magnussen reduced his rivals to bit players in the strongest British F3 field for years gave every indication of a great talent starting to flower.

His 14 wins from 18 races in the world's toughest F3 series smashed the previous record of 12 victories out of 20 attempts, which was set by Senna in 1983. Magnussen didn't dominate all the races, and he had to fight very hard indeed to hold back pursuers in three or four of them. But the truth is that even when he was threatened he always looked to have the race under control.

Magnussen has all the qualities a top-line driver needs: incredible feel; blinding pace on cold tyres; fearlessness; an ability to improvise like few others; and a supreme level of confidence. 'This year,' he said, reflecting on his success, 'when I sat down before a race, I could never imagine myself not winning it. And when I didn't, it was entirely my own fault.'

Like Senna in 1983, Magnussen had a worrying wobble mid-season. In three races in a row – two in Britain, and one the Marlboro Masters international invitation race – he crashed, through over-confidence, and an absolute refusal to be denied the lead for a minute longer than necessary. The occasional flaw in his make-up as a driver seems to be a fallibility and impatience when challenging for the lead.

Ironically, the first of those three races gave him the opportunity to demonstrate just why people are now raving about his talent. At the British Grand Prix meeting in July, Magnussen started fourth after misjudging his qualifying run, and at the first corner of the race was caught out by the braking points of his rivals; he cannoned into the back of Ricardo Rosset, breaking one side of his front wing. Somehow, with massively reduced front downforce, he managed to stick to the back of the leading pack until two-thirds distance, and even held fastest lap at one stage.

'I'd told the guys to prepare for a pit stop,' said his engineer at Paul Stewart Racing, Bruce Jenkins, 'and then I looked at the stop-watch at the end of the first lap, and I thought it must be wrong. But then it happened again and again. Eventually the front tyres started to wear out. He'd pushed so hard by the end of the race that they were completely bald. It should have been impossible to drive at that speed, but he'd just got even more pumped up by it, because he was annoyed by the fact that he'd made the mistake at the start.'

At the next race, at Snetterton, he crashed while trying to take the lead from Rosset around the outside of the fifth-gear first corner, when he could have passed the Brazilian with ease two corners later. But so convinced was he that the move was possible that he tried it again in testing the following day. The PSR crew had their hearts in their mouths as they watched their driver dive for the outside again, but he made it – just to prove a point to himself.

The season quickly fell into a pattern, with Magnussen taking a front-row qualifying position, usually pole, making a great start, and driving a blinding first three laps to pull out a lead. From there, he could control the race at will, and did.

He is easy on his equipment, and pulled off some outstanding overtaking moves. With one race to go, only a single question remained about his ability: was he as fast in the wet as in the dry? Conditions at that final round were about as bad as they ever get at a race track, with near-torrential rain rendering the circuit treacherous, and visibility virtually non-existent. But as rivals spun the race away around him, Magnussen won with nonchalant ease. A McLaren test contract is his reward for a brilliant season.

What made it all the more impressive was that this was the most competitive British F3 field since the late Eighties. All year, lap times were extremely close, but, all year, Magnussen stayed one step ahead of the game.

There were more than 20 Class A runners throughout the season, and back in March it looked likely that as many as ten of them could win races. As it turned out, only Magnussen, Vincent Radermecker, Rosset and Dario Franchitti did so, although Gareth Rees and Jérémie Dufour should have.

Franchitti, Magnussen's team-mate at PSR, started off well enough with a dominant win in the first round, helped by the fact that Magnussen had shunted his car heavily in practice. But after that Franchitti faded badly. PSR was again the outstanding team, and most of what few problems it had came Dario's way, but his confidence was shot to pieces by Magnussen's unrelenting excellence. There were a couple of other occasions where he could have beaten his team-mate, but on the whole it was a bit like the days when Gerhard Berger and Senna were team-mates at McLaren. Franchitti could match Magnussen for pace on occasion, but the consistency was just not there.

The same could be said of Radermecker. He and the West Surrey Racing team had high hopes for the season, but they lost ground in the early races chasing a set-up. After

FORMULA THREE REVIEW

Opposite page: Jan Magnussen is congratulated by Jackie Stewart after yet another 1994 victory. Driving a Paul Stewart Racing Dallara, the 21-year-old Dane won a record 14 races out of 18 to take the British championship and earn an F1 testing contract with McLaren.

Tipped as a likely title contender, Vincent Radermecker *(left)* was left trailing in Magnussen's wake. The Belgian did score two wins for West Surrey Racing, including a victory in the high-profile British GP support race.

Bottom: The experienced Jörg Müller was crowned German F3 Champion.

that the Belgian was consistently quick. He eventually won two races, one at the all-important British GP meeting, and took a well-deserved second place in the championship. But while Radermecker is a charming man out of the car, he seems to grow horns in it, and pulled off a couple of very scary moves, particularly when he pushed Magnussen onto the grass at 120 mph at the first double-header race, at Brands Hatch in April, denying the Dane another victory, and when he forced Dufour either to brake or to collide with the pit wall on the run down to the first corner at the British GP meeting.

Rees took a brilliant victory at the prestigious Marlboro Masters, but incredibly failed to win in his national championship. He had to wait until mid-season for a car with a set-up he felt comfortable with, and from then on he was always a factor, but it never quite came together for a win. His best chances were at Thruxton in May and Silverstone at the end of August. Both times he was delayed enough at the start from a front-row grid position to make a win out of the question, and at Silverstone he stalled, before fighting back brilliantly from 22nd to fifth. If only . . .

The last of the consistent pacesetters was Dufour, who had become very good indeed by the end of the season, and the Fortec team – as well as 1993 F3 Champion Kelvin Burt, whom it employed as driver coach – deserve great credit for turning him around from an 18-year-old who thought he knew everything to someone who listened and learnt from the experience of others. By the end of the season he was, with Magnussen, Radermecker and Rees, consistently one of the four quickest drivers in the championship.

Of the rest, Rosset took his sole win at Snetterton, which he knows like the back of his hand, but never really looked like winning elsewhere, although he was always on the pace in the top six or so.

Scott Lakin was extremely impressive on a tiny budget with the Intersport team in the first half of the year, and he, too, looked set to win a race before long. Sadly, two crashes within three races mid-season and he had to withdraw.

Marcos Gueiros, by contrast, was probably the disappointment of the season. The twice Brazilian F3 Champion had been right on the pace at the end of 1993, and was expected to be a championship contender as 1994 dawned. But he seemed to find it impossible to overtake. It was true that the Spiess-tuned Vauxhall engine was not the force it had been in 1993, but it was certainly not as bad as Gueiros occasionally made it look – as Italian Champion Giancarlo Fisichella proved when he came to Britain for a one-off race at the Grand Prix. He was quicker than Gueiros and Edenbridge team-mate Luiz Garcia throughout, and finished an impressive fourth.

Class B was won at a canter by Duncan Vercoe, who faced opposition only from a handful of gentlemen drivers.

Despite the wealth of talent on show, the spectator figures remained woefully low. In an attempt to improve things, the F3 Association introduced double-header races for the first time. In general it was agreed that double-headers were a nice idea, and they will make up two-thirds of next season's races. But those who run F3 are kidding themselves if they think that their introduction will do any more than keep the teams' travel costs down. Crowd figures were generally as pitiful at the twin-race meetings as at single ones.

For years, F3 has needed promotion, and it still does. The organising clubs do little to help, and now that the BBC has pulled out of the series and it has no terrestrial TV deal, crowd figures at circuits must be boosted. Team managers must be – should be – ruing their failure to get F3 onto the TOCA British touring car package at the end of 1992. That would seem to be the only real way of guaranteeing crowds – that and an increase in power to make the racing more spectacular than soporific.

Despite that, engines were not the issue they had been in previous years, with the Mugen Honda, the Spiess Vauxhall/Opel, and the Fiat very evenly matched, while the HKS Mitsubishi had come on in leaps and bounds by the end of the season. The Mugen, though, after some intensive development over the winter, was probably the strongest of the lot: it dominated the British Championship, and won the Marlboro Masters. Only the Renault engine, on the French company's return to F3 after a 15-year absence, disappointed, its talented drivers Pedro de la Rosa and Ivan Arias relegated to mid-teens grid positions by the unit's lack of torque and flexibility. Whether Renault intended to stay in F3 remained in the balance as this review was written.

Chassis choice was even simpler. Unless you drove for the works TOM'S Toyota team in Japan, you needed a Dallara to be competitive, so completely had the Italian company dominated the category in 1993. In Britain, Ralt attempted to make a comeback, but its 94C was terrible over bumps and the team was under-financed. It withdrew after four races. Former F1 racer Teddy Pilette, meanwhile, produced a car with a suspension of fearsome complexity. It had one race in Germany before the end of the year, but was woefully off the pace.

The German series retained its position as the number two championship to Britain, and was won by Jörg Müller, a veteran of five seasons of F3. Sascha Maassen, who has four years behind him, was expected to set the pace for the crack WTS team, but was disappointing, and particularly exasperated his team by failing to get the hang of starts. He was beaten in the championship by the impressive Alexander Wurz, and WTS team-mate Ralf Schumacher, who looks promising, if not possessing the same raw talent as his brother Michael. Argentinian Norberto Fontana also shone.

The French and Italian series had a rough time, although the driving standard clearly remains high in both. The Italian championship was in crisis by the end of the season, with leading teams pulling out, citing lack of media interest and promotion. As this review went to press, a rescue package was being worked on by its organisers, and those of the ailing Italian GT series. The championship was dominated by Fisichella, while Lucas Rangoni and Riccitelli, and Gianantonio Pacchioni also won fairly regularly.

The French, recognising problems before they became too serious, ran their series for 1993 cars to keep costs down, and saw a great showdown between the late-1993 pacesetter Christophe Tinseau, who missed a race after being knocked down by a getaway car from a burglary, and novice Jean-Philippe Belloc, who came out on top after beating Tinseau in a straight fight in the final round.

TOM'S once again dominated in Japan, with German Michael Krumm taking its heavily funded works effort to a second consecutive title. But by the end of the year, the man to beat was British refugee Warren Hughes, in the rapidly improving HKS-powered Dallara.

F3 moves into a new era in 1995, with stepped-floor regulations, like those in F1, replacing the current flat-bottom rules, and a four-race European Championship providing added interest – which is a great idea, as long as costs can be contained. But as the year motor racing lost Ayrton Senna slips into the history books, the pervading memory from F3 will be centred on one man. It's still too early to say ultimately how good Jan Magnussen is, but it will be fascinating to see whether he can fulfil his incredible promise in the more rarefied atmosphere of Formula 1.

251

SPORTS CAR RACING REVIEW

GREEN SHOOTS OF RECOVERY

by Adam Cooper

It seems unlikely that international sports car racing will ever again reach the level of factory involvement and star driver participation of 1988-91. But there were some signs in 1994 that, at the very least, reports of its demise have been exaggerated.

The old Group C turbo machines and 3.5-litre 'two-seat F1 cars' are now consigned to history, and instead progress is being made on two fronts. In Europe and Japan GT racing is slowly but surely taking hold, while in America classic open prototypes survive in the form of IMSA's new World Sports Car class. These cars may yet have a significant future in Europe, especially at Le Mans.

As in 1993, Le Mans charted its own course, free of any FIA restrictions. The wonderful Peugeot and Toyota atmo cars were gone, but, for one final time, the Group C machines they superseded were allowed back. It was just as well, for they provided a thrilling contest which was as good as any of recent years.

The Group C cars were handicapped both by flat-bottom aerodynamics and by turbo restrictors. The most significant entries came from the local Courage team, a long-time stalwart with its Porsche-powered cars, and from the privateer SARD and Trust Toyota outfits from Japan. There was also a 962 spyder for Derek Bell, making his 24th and last Le Mans start.

There were few other serious cars in the prototype ranks, but two Trojan horses lurked on the GT entry list. Porsche returned with a full factory effort, and a pair of subtly modified 962s. They were supposedly based on a road car developed and homologated by former private entrant Jochen Dauer, and were duly entered as 'Dauer 962LMs'.

They were not as driver-friendly as pukka 962s of previous years, but nor could they be in any way compared with the rest of the large and varied production-based GT entry. To show how serious the Stuttgart effort was, one car was handled by Hans Stuck, Danny Sullivan and Thierry Boutsen, and the other by Yannick Dalmas, Hurley Haywood and Mauro Baldi. Nothing was left to chance.

The Courage effort faded early, and we were left with a superb battle between the Porsches and the two private Toyotas. Trust's entry, anchored by Bob Wollek, fell out of contention with transmission problems. But the SARD car, crewed by Eddie Irvine, Mauro Martini and Jeff Krosnoff, kept up the pace. Through the night the lead swapped around as the Porsches hit problems and the Toyota lost ground with overly conservative brake disc changes.

The Toyota looked set to win, but in the 23rd hour the gear linkage broke. Somehow Krosnoff fudged it and got the car back to the pits, and after proper repairs Jordan star Irvine resumed for a brilliant final charge. He overhauled second-place Boutsen at the start of the last lap, but the Dalmas/Haywood/Baldi car was out of reach. It was the third Le Mans win in 17 years for veteran Haywood, and the second for Dalmas after his Peugeot triumph in 1992.

Fourth place went to the works Nissan IMSA team of Clayton Cunningham, which brought along a pair of its superb 300ZX 'silhouette' GTS cars. These had already won outright at both Daytona and Sebring after the fragile WSC machines broke.

All this took attention away from the true GT cars, which formed the bulk of the entry. With the FIA not taking a lead, GT racing had been boosted by the efforts of the Paris-based BPR organisation, led by Porsche customer liaison man Jurgen Barth.

BPR set up a series of races – definitely not an official championship – at circuits such as Montlhéry, Paul Ricard, Jarama and Spa. They also took a squad of cars to a Suzuka round of the expanding Japanese series, and put on the first international event in China on the Zhuhai street circuit in November.

The cars which contested these races formed the heart of the Le Mans GT field, which was notable for its variety. Alongside the expected Porsches, Venturis, Lotus Esprits and Ferraris were Dodge Vipers, factory-backed Honda NSXs, a Callaway Corvette, a de Tomaso, an Alpine and even a magnificent Bugatti.

The other races, mostly of four-hour duration, proved to be successful, attracting increasing interest as the year went on. Victories were shared between Porsche, Venturi and Ferrari, while GT drivers included ex-F1 stars like Jean-Pierre Jarier, Jacques Laffite, René Arnoux and Olivier Grouillard, who enjoyed the low-key events.

During the year more and more interesting GT projects were announced. Most were from smaller manufacturers, although Toyota had an exotic Supra running in Japan. Jaguar XJ220s and McLaren F1s are expected to be seen next year, in private hands.

As yet there are no plans for a pukka FIA championship, and the races will continue to be one-offs. As

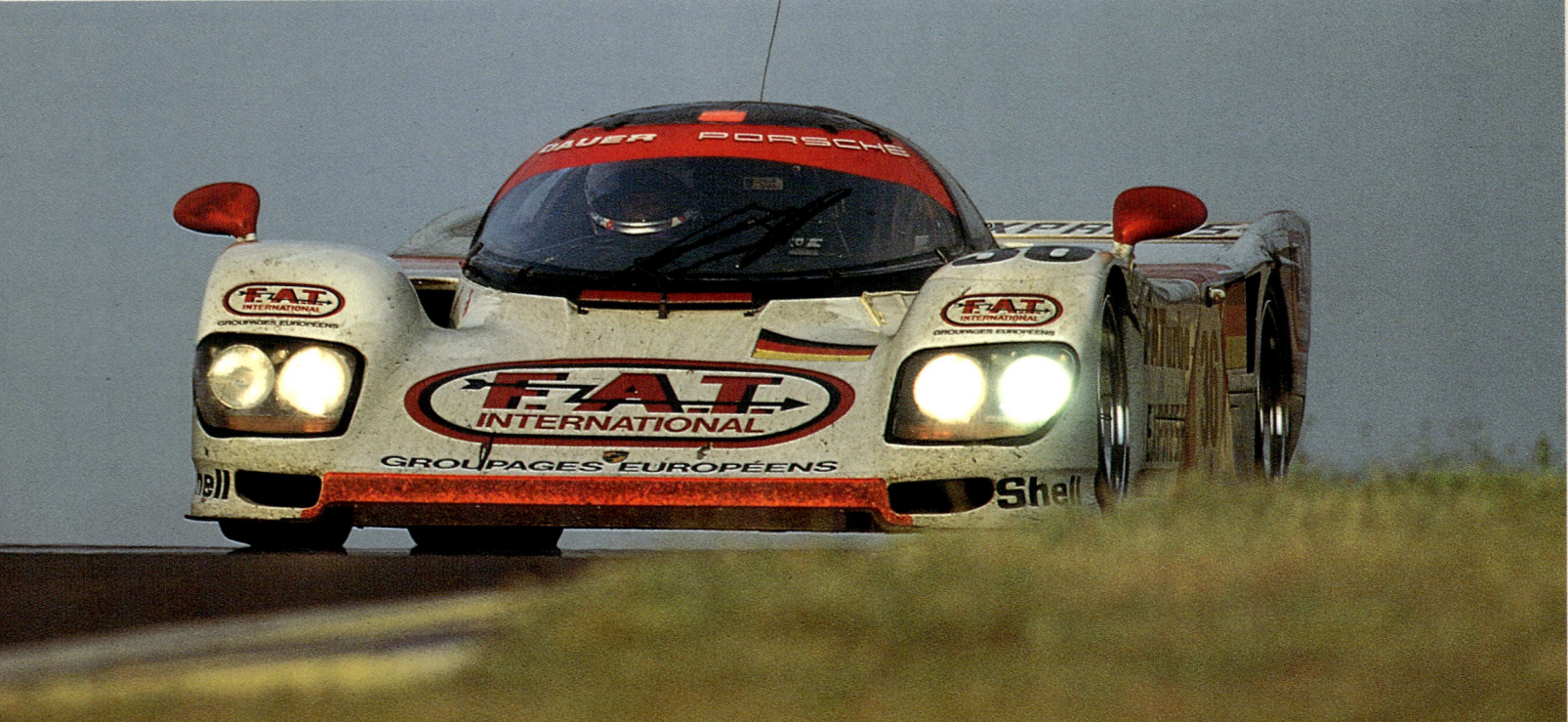

Colin McMaster/Words & Pictures

Bell's last chime

Five-times Le Mans winner Derek Bell finally rounded off his 24-year love affair with the French classic in 1994 with a third-place finish in the world's most famous endurance race at the wheel of a Gulf Oils-backed Kremer Porsche K8.

The 51-year-old Englishman had first raced at the Sarthe in 1970 when he shared a works Ferrari 512M with the late Ronnie Peterson. On that occasion they retired, but Bell would be back the following year at the wheel of a Gulf Porsche 917 and would eventually win the race for the first time in a Ford V8-powered Gulf Mirage in 1975, sharing with Jacky Ickx.

As a member of the factory Porsche team, Bell went on to win at Le Mans again in 1981, '82, '86 and '87. In 1985 and '86 he won the World Sports Car Championship and he was awarded the MBE in 1986 for his services to motor racing.

Having aimed for a full-time F1 career in the late 1960s after a suitably successful apprenticeship on the European F2 Championship trail, Derek was recruited to the Ferrari Grand Prix line-up in the summer of 1968. Unfortunately the famous Maranello team was struggling at the time, weighed down by financial problems and barely a year away from its takeover by Fiat.

Derek's single-seater credibility never fully recovered from this failure, but he went on to carve a niche as one of the best endurance drivers in the business, and one of the sport's most gregarious and popular personalities.

A.H.

more cars appear, both BPR and the Le Mans organisers will face the problem of oversubscribed entry lists; at this year's 24 Hours run-of-the-mill Porsches were turned away in favour of the more interesting cars.

Meanwhile in the USA IMSA's World Sports Car class made steady progress. Harking back to CanAm days, the rules called for flat-bottom, open two-seaters. Engines had to be production-based; turbos were not allowed at first, but that has been relaxed for 1995.

Most competitors used either old GTP cars with the lids cut off, or new cars based on revisions of the existing designs; Spice proved the most popular choice. But the saviour of the category was the arrival of Ferrari. Entrant Gianpiero Moretti and the North American importer persuaded Maranello to build its first proper sports racer for 21 years. Designed by Tony Southgate, the 333SP was a sensational car. Up to five were soon seen in action, with the factory keeping close tabs on them.

However, controversy surrounded the red machines. Rivals wondered just when they'd see the F1-derived V12 in a production car, while arguments raged about rev limits. When IMSA tried to introduce one to trim the V12's power, Ferrari successfully defeated the sanctioning body.

Nevertheless, at some circuits the less advanced Chevy and Oldsmobile-equipped machines could outrun the high-tech Italian cars. In fact the championship was won by the consistent Wayne Taylor, who never actually won a race in his underpowered Kudzu-Mazda.

With the door now open for turbos, Porsche has a WSC car under development, and other manufacturers are taking a look at the category. At the end of the year Courage revealed a new contender, built to a very high standard and penned by an ex-Peugeot 905 designer.

The French car is aimed as much at Le Mans as Daytona. Fortunately, IMSA has worked closely with the Automobile Club de l'Ouest to establish common regulations, and WSC cars should be out in force in next year's 24 Hours, in 'LM Prototype' guise. For the time being, that will be their only opportunity to race outside the USA, which rather reduces the prospects of European teams investing in the new machinery.

This will be the first time since 1973 that Ferrari has gone to the Sarthe with a chance of overall victory. Hopefully that will add much-needed magic to the event, and help to bring the fans in . . .

Opposite page: The GT entry list at Le Mans featured two factory-backed Porsche 962s, supposedly derived from a road car developed by Jochen Dauer. One of them, crewed by seasoned campaigners Yannick Dalmas, Hurley Haywood and Mauro Baldi, snatched overall victory from a privately entered Group C Toyota.

True GT cars, such as the Dodge Viper *(above centre)* made up the bulk of the field at Le Mans.

Ferrari returned to sports car racing with the Tony Southgate-designed 333SP which appeared in North America's IMSA championship. This shot of the example handled by Gianpiero Moretti and Eliseo Salazar at Watkins Glen evokes memories of the halcyon days of the early Seventies.

BRITISH TOURING CAR CHAMPIONSHIP REVIEW

THEY CAME, THEY THEY CONQUERED

SAW,

by Laurence Foster

After conquering the DTM in 1993, Alfa Corse set their sights on the British Touring Car Championship in 1994. Greatly underrated former F1 driver Gabriele Tarquini led their assault and, despite the controversy that surrounded the team's reading of the rule book, the quiet Italian proved a worthy champion.

Having Gabriele Tarquini and the crack Alfa Corse team competing in the British Touring Car Championship, so they said, would vividly demonstrate the competitiveness of the world's best 2-litre touring car series.

How? Well, quite simply by making the Italian visitors look ordinary – maybe even a little bit out of their depth – against the battle-hardened squads from Ford, Vauxhall, BMW and the rest. Proof, if proof were needed, that the BTCC led the way.

In practice, however, their presence merely showed that Alfa Corse, the Alfa Romeo 155 TS Silverstone and ex-Formula 1 driver Tarquini were the best team, car and driver combination anywhere in the touring car world.

The 1994 BTCC was totally dominated by the blood-red machine and its blindingly quick driver. Right from the off, they set the pace and called the shots. It was almost as if Alfa Corse was the home team and the rest were the wide-eyed visitors. If the Italians *were* floundering on the steep learning curve of the opening races, it certainly didn't show.

But the season wasn't just dominated by Alfa on the track, it was also dominated by their actions, their presence and their mystique off it. Whichever way one looked at it, it was an Alfa Romeo year.

The man at the centre of the cult of Alfa was Tarquini. Affable, polite and eminently patient out of his car – to the point where it was difficult to believe he'd ever been near the ivory towers of an F1 paddock – the 32-year-old Italian was the benchmark by which the others were judged once in it.

Alfa began its season with a debut victory at a bitingly cold and gale-lashed Thruxton. It was a harsh welcome for Tarquini and his Turin-based Alfa Corse mechanics, but not just in a meteorological sense. Alfa had been clever – Alfa had read the rules and interpreted them as close to the wind as anyone had ever sailed, and the opposition didn't like it. Like what? The fact that Alfa had homologated a car with a couple of pieces of what looked like Meccano stuck in a lump of foam rubber in the boot.

Incredibly, when removed from the boot and stuck on its lid, those few little pieces of metal proved the catalyst to a vitriolic and damaging war of words, protests, and eventually actions, that would run for almost half of the season. The pieces raised the Alfa's rear wing, moving it into cleaner air and increasing its effectiveness. It was perfectly legal within the homologation procedure, but it was something the opposition had never contemplated doing – or in some cases, shouldn't that be never *thought* of doing? – itself. It just wasn't cricket, old boy.

After a double victory for Tarquini at the next round, Brands Hatch, the natives were restless. For Snetterton, the FIA had acted and banned 'add-on' parts for events it sanctioned. It invited governing bodies of the various national championships to follow suit and, sure enough, the RAC took up the offer.

The cars appeared for the first time with their rear wings clipped at Snetterton, the fourth round of the series. And the winner? Tarquini. Back to the drawing board for everyone else...

Hence, at Silverstone, the target of the opposition's rancour shifted from the rear of the car to the front and its moveable front splitter. The argument was that the splitter was illegal when pulled out.

The case for the prosecution? Well, it needed rivets to secure it, but these are surely 'add-on' parts. Nevertheless, Alfa raced under appeal and Tarquini duly notched up his fifth win of the season.

With the distinct danger of making it sound like the 1994 BTCC was one continual manure fight, one must now go on to the events at Oulton Park, the race when the phoney war ended and the metaphorical manure really *did* fly.

The appeal against the pushed-out front splitter had been upheld, and in Cheshire Alfa Corse was asked to qualify and race with them pushed in. Alfa Corse refused and went home. It was a genuine shock, but one that made both sides pull back from whatever the next brink was. Peace was declared – Alfa could run with its splitter out until the beginning of July, but would have to race with it pushed in afterwards.

The saddest thing about the whole sorry business was that it merely disguised the real truth of the matter – that Tarquini and Alfa could have won those races anyway, probably even towing a caravan, such was the out-of-the-box strength of the overall package in the opening rounds.

As a swan-song for the extended splitter, Tarquini took his sixth and seventh wins around the Brands Hatch Grand Prix circuit, then entered the fallow stretch of his season.

BRITISH TOURING CAR CHAMPIONSHIP REVIEW

Vauxhall's fortunes were placed in the capable hands of Ray Mallock Engineering this year but the Cavalier was no longer a front-runner and lead driver John Cleland *(right)* had to settle for a single victory.

Below: Paul Radisich pushes his Ford Mondeo to the limit – and beyond. The spirited Kiwi's dogged pursuit of Tarquini was destined to end in disappointment.

But that was hardly due to (yawn) a lack of splitters and high wings on the Alfa. Instead it was down to wings and splitters on other cars, plus a small matter of 50 kg.

On 1 July, not only did Alfa push its splitter in, but Renault and BMW gained a rear wing each, while the rear-wheel drive cars (the BMWs) shed 50 kg of their original 100 kg weight penalty. The status quo was suddenly, and significantly, altered.

OK, other cars had already won races during the season: Paul Radisich and his Ford Mondeo ended Tarquini's early-season winning streak with a win at Silverstone when Tarquini was involved in an accident; Alain Menu won for Renault in the race that Alfa boycotted at Oulton Park, and John Cleland scored an easy double for Vauxhall at Donington on a weekend when Alfa had trouble keeping its engines in a single piece. But on those occasions, Alfa had always had an alibi to explain itself. Now, the revised weights and aerodynamic packages from the opposition meant Alfa were actually being beaten in a straight fight.

At the race supporting the British Grand Prix – the first run to the controversial revised weights – 1993 British Touring Car Champion Jo Winkelhock took BMW's first win of the season, but was chased hard by Tarquini on badly fading tyres in one of his most impressive drives of the season.

That race was also memorable for the startline shunt that saw a dozen cars off into the Copse gravel. It was sod's law that, of all the places to start behaving badly, the BTCC chose the highest-profile race of the season.

Three weeks later, the circus moved north of the border, to Knockhill in Fife, and, for the first time, the Alfas were genuinely struggling, unable to ride the kerbs. Steve Soper's BMW and Menu's Renault took a win apiece, but Tarquini could only qualify eighth. In the first race, the Italian's fortunes took a further dive when he was punted into a multiple barrel roll by Tim Harvey's Renault.

The double-zero score from Knockhill had suddenly brought Tarquini back briefly into the sights of his closest pursuer, Radisich, with the season entering its final stretch. But on the championship's second visit to Oulton Park, Tarquini again sailed over the horizon and just out of sight with a third place, behind winner Winkelhock and runner-up Menu, as Radisich failed to finish.

After that, the return to the happy hunting ground of Brands – the circuit on which Alfa built the foundations of its championship – brought the Alfa driver a brace of second places as Radisich again enjoyed miserable fortunes.

Clinching the championship would now be a formality, but Tarquini wanted more and, at Silverstone's penultimate meeting, he did it in style, coming second, behind Harvey, in the first race to get the formalities over and done with, before taking his eighth win of the season in race two. What made the feat even more impressive was the fact that Tarquini

CLEAN SWEEP FOR MICHELIN PILOTS

Victory in the 1994 British Touring Car Championship has shown there's no beating Michelin tyres.

It was Michelin tyres that gave Alfa Romeo its grip on the overall Championship title and Michelin-shod cars took the first three places in the driver, manufacturer and team competitions as well as the top two privateer positions.

For the record, here's how Michelin-shod cars set the pace:

- 🏁 50 podium places from the 63 possible
- 🏁 14 wins, 19 second and 17 third places
- 🏁 8 clean sweeps of 1st, 2nd and 3rd
- 🏁 11 pole positions from the 14 possible
- 🏁 15 of the 21 fastest laps
- 🏁 17 wins out of 21 rounds in the Total Privateers Cup

And Michelin tyres are unbeatable on the road. The Michelin Pilot range of high performance tyres provides the same level of excellence for drivers of luxury, executive and sports cars.

Find out which Pilot tyre suits your car and your style of driving. Call Michelin free on 0800 591 859.

MAKE SURE IT'S A MICHELIN

SPAWNED THE BEAST

PRIMERA eGT

BRITISH TOURING CAR CHAMPIONSHIP REVIEW

The Renault Lagunas *(right)* enjoyed a strong second half to the season. The French manufacturer is hoping that the expertise of the Williams F1 team will boost its title aspirations in 1995.

A 50 kg mid-season weight reduction helped return BMW to winning ways. Steve Soper *(below)* was an occasional visitor to the BTCC.

was suffering from a debilitating virus and swollen glands that had laid him low and snuffed out his normal ebullience in the days leading up to the race.

Tarquini's team-mate, Giampiero Simoni, made it nine wins from 21 races for Alfa Corse at the Donington Park finale. It rounded off a year in which Alfa Romeo also won the manufacturers' title and Alfa Corse the team prize. Without any doubt, they came, they saw, they conquered . . . .

Hopefully, given the perspective afforded by hindsight, people will remember those wins and Tarquini's championship for what they were – the results of a driver and a team totally on top of their art and not the easy products of some canny homologation moves.

Going back to the misguided pre-season belief that Alfa Romeo were setting themselves up to be lambs to the slaughter, the majority of voters had plumped for Ford to be leading the wolf pack.

Ford and its Kiwi revelation Paul Radisich had stunned the BTCC regulars during a half-season of competition in 1993 that culminated in victory for Radisich's Mondeo at the inaugural FIA Touring Car Challenge at Monza against the cream of Europe – including Alfa Corse.

An intensive off-season of testing and development, including swapping the original spoilered GSi model for the extra cooling possibilities of the Ghia, pointed to the Andy Rouse-developed cars taking up where they'd left off.

But in reality, Ford, like everyone else, struggled. However, all credit to Radisich; not once did he give up in his pursuit of Tarquini.

Halfway through the season, a veritable shed-full of second places, plus that solitary win at Silverstone, kept his title hopes alive. But a late-season spate of non-finishes and non-scores – including an endorsement-attracting red-mist moment at the August Bank Holiday Monday Brands Hatch meeting – terminally blunted his challenge and finally ended it altogether at Silverstone's penultimate round.

Almost as frustrating for Radisich was the fact that his plucky challenge failed to bag him the runner-up spot in the final standings either. Instead, Alain Menu and Renault hit the sort of second-half form that pulled them bang into the frame.

It had been a strange start to the season for Renault, with a homologation gaffe rendering the rear spoiler ineligible on its brand-new Laguna after a winter spent testing in that configuration. Nevertheless, the car showed promise, including pole on the Silverstone national circuit and Menu's victory from pole at the Oulton Park race boycotted by Alfa.

As well as having the car pretty well sorted chassis-wise for the second half of the campaign, Renault finally got its wings from 1 July. Two further wins – one apiece for Menu and Tim Harvey – marked the car out as one to watch in the future.

But anything Renault did in the second half of the season was somewhat overshadowed by the staggering BMW renaissance that yielded five wins in the last ten races, with Winkelhock taking four and Steve Soper, juggling the BTCC with Japanese commitments, bagging the fifth. The 100 kg weight penalty applied to rear-wheel drive cars proved a millstone in the early rounds, but the 50 kg reduction, allied to BMW's homologation of a wing and air dam, turned the 318i into an almost invincible force during the late-summer races.

To Alfa's relief, the weight-break also gave the paddock grumblers a new target – the Munich marque.

BRITISH TOURING CAR CHAMPIONSHIP REVIEW

The RAC *Auto Trader* British Touring Car Championship has attracted major manufacturers in remarkable numbers, and their presence has done much to increase the series' prestige. Nissan *(right)*, Peugeot *(centre right)* and Volvo *(bottom right)* all played their part in making it another exciting season.

The weight issue basically divided the teams into two camps: those who agreed with the 50 kg reduction, i.e. BMW, and those who didn't, i.e. the rest . . .

John Cleland and Vauxhall completed the list of eight different winners. The Vauxhall Sport official factory tag had been switched from Dave Cook Racing to Ray Mallock Engineering and at times Cleland and the team seemed puzzled by the complexity of Mallock's design for the venerable Cavalier 16v.

Cleland's day in the sun came at Donington's June double-header when a combination of durable Dunlops and a perfect set-up on the Cavalier made it *the* combination to have.

Patrick Watts and Peugeot came closest to making it nine different winners. The 405 Mi16 was one of the most powerful cars in the series – a relative term in the evenly matched, rev-limited 2-litre formula – and at times in the early going looked like the only car capable of hanging on to the Alfa. As it was, the bespectacled Watts had to be content with four podium visits and a rocketing reputation.

The number of works teams in the 1994 BTCC rose to a staggering ten, with Volvo and its unique estate joining Alfa as the other new boys.

The Volvo 850 estate was gradually improved as the season wore on, progressing well beyond mere novelty status. But its handling never quite reached the standards of its engine or its leading driver, Rickard Rydell, and the Tom Walkinshaw Racing-run operation is likely to shift to a more conventional saloon for 1995. The crowd-pleasing aspect may be somewhat reduced, but expect the car to be well on the pace in its second season.

Completing the BTCC's factory

VOLVO goes racing

Racing a Volvo? You must be mad. And it's an estate car as well? Words fail me. These were the sort of reactions provoked by the launch of the Volvo 850 Racing Team in the British Touring Car Championship last autumn. But both on and off the track the first third of this initial three-year programme has been a huge success.

VOLVO'S 850 ESTATE racers have proved they've got what it takes in the world's most competitive touring car racing series and have received an enormous amount of media coverage. Those who simply thought of Volvo as a safe way to shift the wife, kids and dogs are being made ever more aware that the 850 is exciting – a great driver's car.

The reasons for the birth of the race project are complex. Senior Vice President Martin Rybeck felt that a return to competition–Volvo's last major international racing campaign in the European Touring Car Championship finished in 1986– would boost 850 sales, improve the brand image and have beneficial effects to Volvo internally, both in technical development and providing new motivation for staff.

PHOTO: SUTTON PHOTOGRAPHIC

ADVERTISEMENT FEATURE

ADVERTISEMENT FEATURE

ABOVE: Three generations of Volvo Competition cars—the Amazon rally car of the Sixties in forest action, the 240 Turbo leading the pack at Silverstone in the Eighties, and the 850 estate about to embark on Volvo's 1994 British Touring Car Championship campaign.

Although the Volvo image had become very safety-oriented by the early '90s the company does have an illustrious competition history. Initially the success came in rallying. Well-known drivers like Tom Trana, Ewy Rosquist and Joginder Singh put Volvo on the map, driving the PV444s, 544s and Amazons. Trana won the RAC Rally two years running in 1963 and '64 with PV544s and in the late '50s and early '60s Volvo netted six European championships and twice won the manufacturers' class of the World Rally Championship. Per-Inge Walfriddson–another star works Volvo rally driver–won the 1980 European Rallycross Championship at the wheel of a 343 Turbo.

The biggest project though was the assault on the European Touring Car Championship–then run to the extremely complicated Group A rules. Using 240 Turbos Volvo entered the championship in 1983 and two years later Italian Gianfranco Brancatelli and Swede Thomas Lindstrom won the championship in 240s prepared by the Swiss expert Rudi Eggenberger. Further success followed in 1986, with Volvo taking three outright race wins. But at the end of the year the decision was made to pull out of racing. A 740 Turbo had been assessed and found quicker than the 240, but the board felt that racing was not the right image for their range-topper.

Rybeck's desire to see the company back in competition soon led him to the burgeoning 2-litre touring car formula, pioneered in the BTCC and now spreading worldwide. He soon became convinced that the 850 would be competitive, but the board wanted a little more. So the first estate racer was built. Rybeck had recruited a variety of old hands from the now defunct Volvo competition department and in their spare time they designed and built parts for a test car. It was built up on a red five-door estate shell by Steffanson Automotive, a local firm which had taken over some of the duties of the competition department, supplying parts to privateers and keeping in touch with developments at the FIA, the sport's governing body.

The 'red car', as it became known, showed that the project could work. Areas of doubt were cleared up–the car could be built down to the weight limit, initial power output from the five-cylinder engine was promising and wind tunnel work proved that an estate body would certainly present no disadvantages...

It was time for the next step. Volvo design chief Peter Horbury had been chatting to an old colleague–Ian Callum–who was now

ABOVE: Volvo's racing design study, the 'red car'– the link between the road car range and this year's racers. Photo: Norman Lomax/BBC Top Gear Magazine.

ON THE ROAD

The Volvo 850 has always been highly-rated and much of the praise that has been heaped on it is for qualities which until recently have not been considered Volvo territory.

Words like 'fast', 'lively', 'agile', and even 'fun' have all been applied to the 850 range which boasts five different five-cylinder engines from the 143bhp 2-litre to the 10 and 20-valve 2.5 litre and the turbocharged 2.3-litre powerhouses. With these great motors allied to its excellent chassis it's no wonder that the 850 has won more international awards than any other car.

From the 2-litre to the T5-R all versions are well respected, but it's the sporting versions that have stunned road-testers and played a major role in changing the way we look at current Volvos. The 220bhp T5 is super-quick, but still relatively discreet, so if you really want to play at being Rickard Rydell, the car to have is the outrageous new T5-R. Available only in a very bright yellow or black, the T5-R's turbocharged 2.3-litre engine puts out a full 240bhp and with its charismatic BTCC-look alloy wheels it is never going to be mistaken for sensible down-to-earth family transport. But of course like all the other 850s it can easily play that role too. With the 850 you really can have your cake and eat it too.

MAIN PIC: Former Grand Prix driver and Le Mans winner Jan Lammers was recruited to help spearhead Volvo's racing return.

BELOW: The Volvo 850–more motoring awards than any other car.

working for Tom Walkinshaw at TWR. Talks soon became more serious and in early 1993 TWR– whose illustrious history includes a spell as one of Volvo's biggest rivals in the ETC battles of the '80s and running Jaguar's Le Mans sports car efforts– was commissioned to do an indepth feasibility study.

In October a deal was announced. TWR would design, build and race 850s in the BTCC and the initial deal was for three years. Already rumours that Volvo was contemplating racing an estate were about and the Volvo and TWR marketing teams skillfully exploited the confusion to gain further publicity- it was the start of a year's outstanding success on the marketing side. 'The red car was a good red herring for us,' said TWR Racing's Marketing and Communications Manager Andy King. 'People got to hear about it and we were able to take advantage of that, but it was really just a test car and the decision about four–door or five–door was taken later.'

Suppliers were not contacted until after the launch in mid-October and the cars were designed and built in double quick time. At the Stockholm Motor Show in February TWR and Volvo were still ostensibly hedging their bets, displaying both estate and saloon show cars and the real race car did not actually turn a wheel until late March–the first race was April 4!

The decision to run the estate car was marketing-led. It was clear that the five-door would generate considerably more publicity and Volvo sells a far greater proportion of estates than most manufacturers– estates accounting for around half of all 850 sales in the UK. But, as Walkinshaw was always ready to point out, the idea was to win races so any advantage shown in either body-shape would be important. Aerodynamically the estate had some distinct advantages; notably it generates less lift than the four-door. That is because the step down from roof to boot on the saloon creates turbulence and therefore slightly more lift. The estate would be more stable at high speed and in quick corners.

ADVERTISEMENT FEATURE

RIGHT: Volvo chose Tom Walkinshaw Racing to build and run the 850 in BTCC, with a firm belief that their teamwork will bring success over the three–year programme.

BELOW: The ideal co-driver for an estate car!

ABOVE: The cockpit of the 850 racer with Rickard Rydell preparing for the start, in what is regarded as the world's foremost touring car series– the British Touring Car Championship.

Racing the estate proved to be a master-stroke. In terms of column inches in the press Volvo has been right up there behind the cars which dominated the racing in the BTCC–Alfa Romeo, BMW, Ford. What's more a high proportion of the articles on Volvo included pictures. The marketing push run by TWR for Volvo has linked well with the international nature of the project. The BTCC has a distinct international profile, with TV coverage right around the world–North America was the only notable gap, but that will be filled for 1995. Guests from 16 countries, including Japan, Lithuania and Australia as well as more obvious European nations, have been entertained by Volvo 850 Racing at BTCC rounds this year and with journalists included in most groups media coverage and enthusiasm within Volvo's offshoots has been generated far and wide.

When the estate racer was first rumoured, there was a tendency for it to be treated as a novelty item. Early artists' impressions in the press included dog-guards and the jokes came thick and fast–the basis for the programme, it was claimed, was simply a translation error–Volvo's board had thought it was sanctioning an entry in the British Towing Car Championship. The team played along and at the season's third meeting produced a pair of life-size stuffed dogs to accompany drivers Rickard Rydell and Jan Lammers on the parade lap.

But there was seldom any doubt about quite how serious the whole project was. The past records of both Volvo and TWR were enough to convince most and any remaining sceptics were brought into line when Rydell qualified third at Snetterton, just five weeks after the racer had first turned a wheel. Overall the season's results did not quite match the team's ambitious pre-season aim, to get onto the podium before the end of the year, but fifth places for each of the two drivers were no mean feat in this most competitive series. Despite the severe lack of development time between races–two weeks in almost every case–great progress was made and the car's potential is there for all to see.

Now with a full winter's testing behind them before the team moves into the second of the three years already planned for the project, instead of the couple of days they had this year, who would bet against the 850s in '95. There is still huge potential in the 850, whereas many of the opposition's cars are nearing the end of their development. And when real success arrives in the BTCC we can expect 850s to appear in other series around the world.

But will it be estates again or saloons in 1995? Keep guessing. The decision will not be made until the FIA issues its rules on the aerodynamic spoilers which all cars will be allowed in '95. If the new regulations don't damage the estate's aerodynamics we might all be scrabbling round for new estate car jokes in '95. But it's more likely that their speed will put that sort of thing firmly into the background and the Volvo 850 will be generating all that newsprint simply because it's winning.

EUROPEAN TOURING CAR REVIEW

by Peter Nygaard

TWO-SPEED EUROPE

Touring car racing maintained its healthy progress on two fronts in 1994. While Germany's *Deutsche Tourenwagen Meistershchaft* (DTM) enjoyed another successful season with the prototype-like, and prototype-expensive, Class 1 rules for 2.5-litre V6 cars, the less expensive Class 2 for 2-litre machines continued to conquer the rest of the world.

Following a relatively weak 1993 season, when only Alfa Romeo and Mercedes built cars to the new Class 1 rules, the DTM flourished in 1994. Opel joined Alfa Romeo and Mercedes and, suddenly, the DTM was once again competing with Britain's BTCC for the distinction of being the world's best saloon car series.

While Alfa and Opel, who had debuted their stunning four-wheel drive Calibra at the final round of the '93 series at Hockenheim, both relied on heavily modified versions of the models they had used the previous year, Mercedes had a brand-new Class 1 challenger ready for 1994. Having entered a modified 190E in 1993, Mercedes' first all-new Class 1 car was based on the new C-class production model. The 2.5-litre V6 engine was derived from the V8 used in the E- and S-class saloons and produced more than 400 bhp at close to 12,000 rpm.

In a high-tech series like the DTM, where lap times are reduced by several seconds from year to year, it was not surprising that the new Mercedes proved superior to the older cars from Alfa Romeo and Opel once its teething problems had been solved. The evergreen Klaus Ludwig, now 44, who had scored Mercedes' first championship triumph in 1992, regained the DTM crown with a consistent season that saw him win three races and score points in 19 rounds out of 20.

Ludwig, who was driving for the AMG team, is one of the very few drivers in the DTM able to run at the front even with the maximum ballast of 50 kg in the car. This, combined with his reliable driving and a certain amount of good fortune that allowed him to survive minor collisions with rivals, saw Ludwig take the title at the penultimate round at Singen.

Before the season, Zakspeed Mercedes' Jörg van Ommen had been regarded as a solid team player and the perfect back-up for the more established Mercedes stars. All that changed in 1994, with van Ommen finishing second to Ludwig in the championship after an impressive double win at the short Nürburgring in September. The Zakspeed driver also won the Gold Cup, which, in addition to the 20 DTM races, also included the four non-championship events at Mugello and Donington.

Van Ommen's team-mate, 1986 champion Kurt Thiim, was formidable in single-car qualifying, taking pole position at four of the ten DTM meetings and both non-championship events. However, he was often unlucky in the races, and the quiet Dane had to settle for fifth in the championship with two wins.

AMG's Bernd Schneider was the unlucky hero of the DTM in 1994, leading several races but only winning twice and usually retiring with mechanical problems. His team-mate Roland Asch was the best-placed Mercedes driver in 1993, but had to settle for sixth this year with a couple of second places. The sixth Mercedes works driver, rapid lady Ellen Lohr, was a disappointment and her best result was a third place.

Alfa Romeo had dominated the DTM during their 1993 debut season and were expected to continue the trend this year, at least in the early-season races until the new Mercedes was sorted. Alfa Corse's Alessandro Nannini started the programme with three wins from the first four races and looked likely to pick up the torch from 1993 champion Nicola Larini. But the Mercedes became a winner sooner than expected, and while Nannini had a strong first half to the season, the second half proved disappointing, culminating in a couple of mistakes under pressure at Singen which cost him all hope of the title.

Reigning champion Larini's season was just the opposite of his team-mate's. He was drafted into the Ferrari F1 team to replace the injured Jean Alesi for the Pacific and San Marino GPs and had difficulty switching from F1 to the DTM every other week. He regained confidence in the second half of the year and actually took third place from Nannini in the closing stages of the season. The third Alfa Corse entry was handled by the young and inexperienced Stefano Buttiero for much of the year, his machine effectively acting as an unofficial T-car for his faster colleagues. Former F1 driver Stefano Modena took it over at the end of the season, impressing greatly with two wins, two second places and a pole position.

Germany's Schübel Engineering ran three works Alfas for Christian Danner, Giorgio Francia and new recruit Kris Nissen. Somewhat surprisingly, Nissen quickly established himself as the fastest Schübel entry, and took a popular win at the Norisring.

Opel, with three works Calibras for Keke Rosberg, Manuel Reuter and 'John Winter', was the most popular make in the 1994 DTM as far as the fans were concerned. While Alfa was very much The Foreigner and Mercedes The Upper Class, Opel was the only marque with which the enormous crowds could easily identify. The Calibra was challenging for the lead on several occasions, with Rosberg and Reuter evenly matched, but 'John Winter' was usually outpaced. However, the spectacular Calibra was also unreliable and Opel's only win of 1994 came in one of the non-championship races at Donington, where Reuter was declared the winner after Nannini had been disqualified.

Uwe Alzen, the talented Mercedes privateer who actually enjoyed some backing from the factory, won the Privateers' Cup in a 1993 Class 1 Mercedes 190E.

The DTM aims at becoming more international next year, with races planned in Italy, Great Britain, France, Finland and Portugal. At the same time, cost-saving rules like a limit on engine revs and a ban on active suspension will be introduced, but despite these measures, the DTM is still on shaky ground. With only three manufacturers involved, the withdrawal of only one could kill the series.

The 1994 season saw the popular 2-litre Class 2 cars having their own championship in Germany for the first time but, despite strong support from the manufacturers, the ADAC *Tourenwagen Cup* was not in the same class as the DTM. As the leading German organisers are all running their events within the established DTM framework, some of the eight rounds of the *Tourenwagen Cup* were held at second-class venues like Wunstorf (dropped by the DTM this year) and the Salzburgring.

Nevertheless, the series produced some great racing between works teams from BMW, Audi, Ford and Nissan, featuring stars like Johnny Cecotto, Joachim Winkelhock and Altfrid Heger (BMW), Emanuele Pirro, Hans Stuck and Frank Biela (Audi), Ivan Capelli (Nissan), and Thierry Boutsen and Markus Oestreich (Ford). Biela's Audi dominated the first half of the season, but after a new rear spoiler was homologated for the BMW mid-season, Cecotto put in a strong final spurt to take the title ahead of Biela, Pirro, Heger and Oestreich.

In Italy's *Superturismo* series for Class 2 cars, Pirro was even more successful. The ex-F1 driver was dropped by BMW at the end of 1993, but enjoyed sweet revenge by taking the Italian title for Audi. Alfa Romeo, with star names like Modena and Antonio Tamburini, started the season with a flourish and Tamburini eventually took second place behind Pirro in the championship. Peugeot's Fabrizio Giovanardi was third, while BMW had a disappointing season with Roberto Ravaglia only fourth in the final standings, the experienced Venetian taking his first wins only after the BMW 318's ballast was reduced in late July.

In France, Peugeot, Opel and BMW fought for the *Supertoursime* title until the last round at Ledenon. Peugeot finally took the title thanks to Laurent Aïello, while Opel's leading driver, the experienced Alain Cudini, was runner-up ahead of BMW's Yvan Muller. Like all the other leading touring car series in Europe, the French championship featured former Grand Prix drivers, but interestingly this contest also had two 1994 GP exponents in the shape of Yannick Dalmas (Peugeot) and Jean-Marc Gounon (BMW), who finished fourth and fifth respectively.

Japan's strong touring car championship also adopted the Class 2 regulations for 1994, and immediately attracted respected names like Britain's Steve Soper and the Schintzer BMW team. Soper fought hard with Toyota drivers Tom Kristensen and Masanori Sekiya all year, local hero Sekiya taking the title at the final double-header meeting at Fuji after Kristensen hit trouble.

Japan was one of the very few countries not to send drivers to the FIA Touring Car World Cup at Donington in October, which was won once again by New Zealand's Paul Radisich in a Ford Mondeo, while Germany took national honours thanks to the efforts of Winkelhock, Stuck and Oestreich.

On the endurance front, BMW was dominant with an almost incredible Spa 24 Hours grand slam in which they took the first eight places, led by Roberto Ravaglia, Thierry Tassin and Alexander Burgstaller. In the Nürburing 24 Hours, Karl-Heinz Wlazik, Frank Katthöfer and Fred Rosterg took a somewhat surprising win in an ultra-reliable Group N M3.

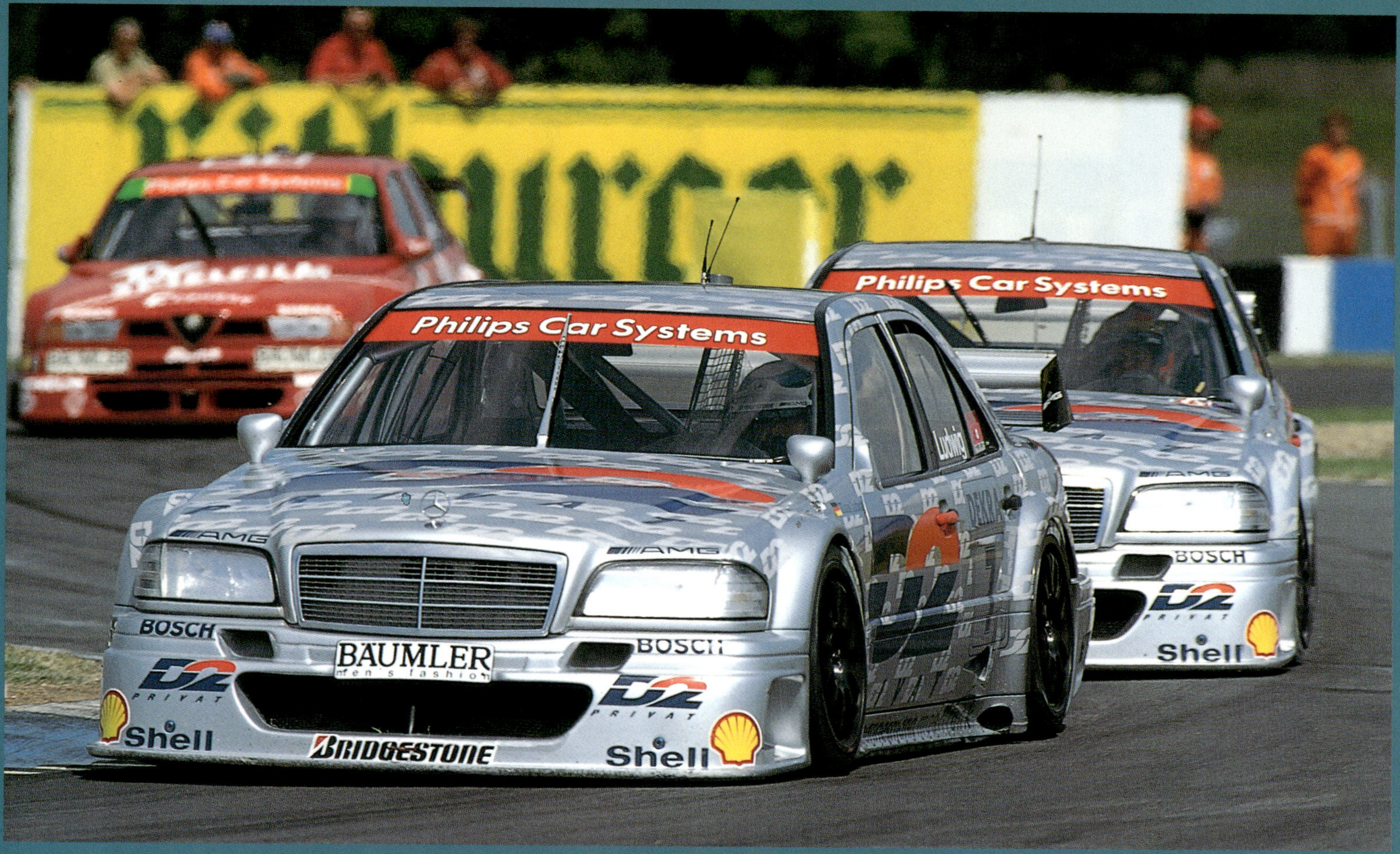

Colin McMaster/Words & Pictures

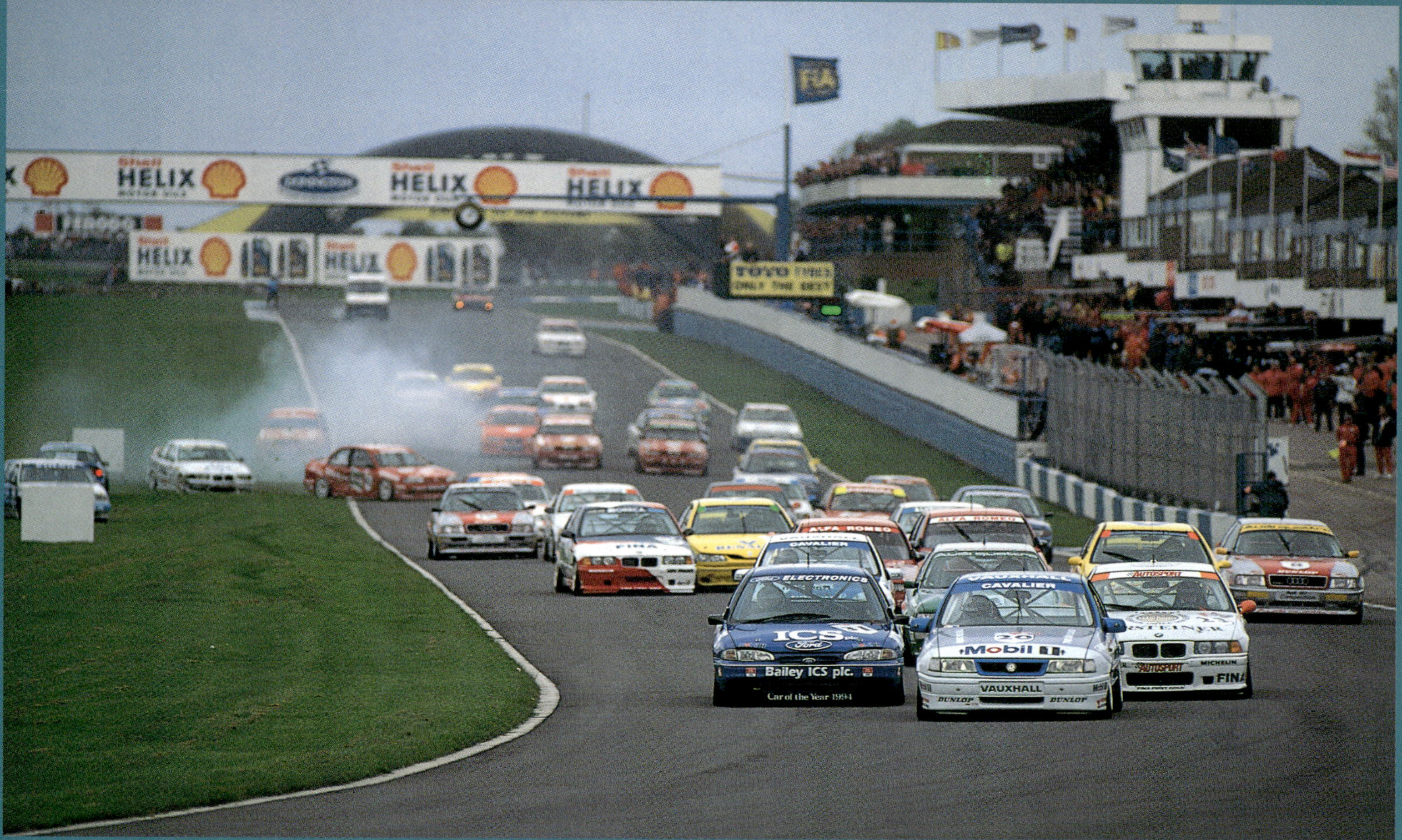

Mark Bothwell/ Bothwell Photographic

Top: **Klaus Ludwig used all his vast experience to claim the DTM crown once more in the AMG Mercedes. It was a major surprise when he revealed at season's end that he would be driving an Opel in 1995.**

The FIA World Cup for 2-litre touring cars was staged at Donington Park this year and attracted a strong international field. A multiple startline accident among the midfield runners brought out the red flag. Up at the front, Ford, Vauxhall and BMW dispute the lead going into Redgate Corner.

EUROPEAN TOURING CAR REVIEW

Above: Klaus Ludwig is now one of racing's veterans, but his consistency and racecraft gave him the DTM title.

Kurt Thiim *(right)* was often the quickest driver in qualifying, but the Dane enjoyed little luck in the races.

Alfa's Alessandro Nannini *(far right)* seemed to lose his way as the year wore on and it was DTM new boy Stefano Modena who posed the greatest threat to Mercedes at season's end.

Keke Rosberg *(below)* had the fans cheering with his swashbuckling style in the Opel, but no wins came the ex-World Champion's way.

EUROPEAN TOURING CAR REVIEW

Although Alfa Corse made a strong start to the DTM campaign, with Alessandro Nannini *(left)* winning three of the first four rounds, they were eventually outpaced by the new C-class Mercedes as the season developed.

Below: Jörg van Ommen put in some scintillating performances in the Zakspeed car to finish runner-up in the DTM and also took the Gold Cup, which included the non-championship races in Italy and England.

Paul Radisich *(above right)* again took the individual honours in the FIA World Cup at the wheel of the Ford Mondeo, but top-ten finishes for Joachim Winkelhock (BMW), Markus Oestreich (Ford) and Hans Stuck in an Audi *(right)* gave the Nations' Cup title to Germany.

Left: Manuel Reuter endured a largely frustrating DTM season in the Opel Calibra. He was often let down by the car when well placed to challenge but at least had the satisfaction of winning a non-championship race, albeit only after the disqualification of Nannini's Alfa.

KEEPING THE CUSTOMER SATIS

AMERICAN RACING REVIEW

Automobile racing continues to grow by leaps and bounds in America. Almost nine million spectators bought tickets in 1994 to watch the 16 PPG Indy Car World Series rounds, 31 NASCAR Winston Cup races and 18 NHRA Winston Drag Racing series races that are the élite events of a vast panorama of American motor sport. There are more than eight hundred race tracks across the continental USA and hundreds of thousands of competition licence holders in all the many disciplines. And for the first time in more than two decades new superspeedways are being built. Bob Bahre built New Hampshire International Speedway five years ago, while Ralph Sanchez is building an oval/road course complex just outside Miami, and Roger Penske and Cary Agajanian are behind separate superspeedways planned for completion in greater Los Angeles in late 1995 or early '96.

NASCAR's well-conceived and well-managed Winston Cup 'stock car' championship continues to command the largest overall numbers in trackside attendance and domestic television viewers. The Winston Cup championship draws more than four million spectators, with a steady stream of new races coming onboard in recent years and in the immediate years ahead. Indy Car racing also continues to set attendance records at most rounds of the PPG Cup. More than three million people paid to see this season's races, and crowds and starting fields get bigger and stronger every year.

In NASCAR, Dale Earnhardt established himself as one of stock car racing's greatest drivers by winning his seventh Winston Cup title, equalling the record for championships established in stock cars by Richard Petty and in Indy cars by A.J. Foyt. Earnhardt beat Rusty Wallace to the crown, as he did in 1993, doing it by being consistently competitive rather than blindingly fast. Earnhardt won four races to Wallace's eight and led only half as many laps as his rival, but he was there in second and third more frequently than Wallace and made it to the finish more times as well. And no fewer than ten other drivers won at least one Winston Cup race in 1994. The competitive depth of NASCAR's fields remains unprecedented in motor sport.

There was tragedy in NASCAR this year as well. Veteran Neil Bonnett and rookie Rodney Orr were both killed in February while practising for the season-opening Daytona 500. Bonnett had come out of retirement to race again and was deeply mourned by the racing community. He and Earnhardt were close friends and after winning his seventh title at North Carolina Motor Speedway in October, Earnhardt dedicated the championship to Bonnett. And in August, Ernie Irvan was badly injured in a head-on collision with the wall at Michigan International Speedway. Irvan was Earnhardt's closest championship challenger at the time and looked like giving the reigning champion a real run for his money until his accident. Unconscious for a week and with his life in danger for a few days, Irvan has since begun a remarkable recovery and hopes to race again in 1995.

After a dream rookie season in 1993, Nigel Mansell learned some hard lessons about American racing in general and Indy Car racing in particular in 1994. Mansell failed to win a race and was a tremendous disappointment in the second half of the season, pulling out of two races and fading in the end to finish a lacklustre eighth in the PPG Cup championship. It was one of the weakest Indy Car championship defences in memory.

Mansell was not only comprehensively blown off by Roger Penske's three-car superteam of Al Unser Jr, Emerson Fittipaldi and Paul Tracy. He was also frequently outpaced by Michael Andretti, Robby Gordon and Rookie of the Year Jacques Villeneuve, and was involved in a long series of incidents, accidents and strategic mistakes under the yellows. Meanwhile, Penske swept to the PPG Cup championship, with Al Jr winning eight races, including the 78th Indy 500, and team-mates Fittipaldi and Tracy bringing the team's tally up to a record 12 wins as well as finishing second and third in the championship. In the eighty-year history of Indy Car racing, no team has been so dominant.

by Gordon Kirby

AMERICAN RACING REVIEW

Previous pages: Whether it's Indy Car racing at Phoenix or a NASCAR round at Bristol, the American spectator can expect to enjoy non-stop action.

Right: Marlboro Team Penske dominated the PPG Indy Car World Series and Al Unser Jr took the drivers' crown with eight victories at the wheel of car number 31. Unser was ably supported by team-mates Emerson Fittipaldi *(bottom)* and Paul Tracy, who raised the team's victory tally to a record-breaking 12 from 16 races.

PENSKE ALL THE WAY

After a slightly slow start at Surfers Paradise in March it was Team Penske all the way. Fittipaldi was a close second to Michael Andretti in Australia but back on home turf at Phoenix two weeks later Fittipaldi and Unser finished 1-2 for Penske before Unser and the team embarked on a remarkable winning streak.

Al Jr won three in a row – at Long Beach (for a record fifth time), Indianapolis and Milwaukee – before being knocked out of the lead by team-mate Paul Tracy in Detroit. Tracy won that race but Unser bounced back to take victory at Portland and Cleveland, rounding out a run of seven successive wins for the team. Al Jr put the championship on ice with another three-race streak later in the summer at Mid-Ohio, New Hampshire and Vancouver.

Al's tally of eight wins equalled Michael Andretti's modern PPG Cup record from 1991 but fell short of the all-time record of ten wins held jointly by A.J. Foyt (1964) and father Al Sr (1970). However, Penske's total of 12 wins (three by Tracy, one by Fittipaldi) was a record for an Indy Car team and included no fewer than five 1-2-3 sweeps, while the red and white cars led 1584 laps, an astonishing 76 per cent of the total!

Although this was Penske's ninth Indy Car title, it was the first for the team in six years, since Danny Sullivan won six races and the championship in 1988. Penske himself says he believes that hiring Al Jr and deciding to run three cars in 1994 were the key moves in bringing his team the PPG Cup title.

'I think the key element in the 1994 season', commented Penske, 'really was that in the beginning there was a lot of doubt by everyone if we could succeed in running a three-car team with any success, based on the strength of the other organisations like Newman-Haas and Rahal-Hogan. That in itself gave the team incentive. It gave our team members the incentive to show that we could run three cars. We'd run three cars before and we'd successfully run a two-car team for many years. But with the calibre of people that we had, we knew we could be at the top with three cars.

'The drivers have been very open in their communication,' Penske went on, 'and that's been very beneficial. One day one of them might have the set-up and the other guy might not have it. Well, on race day there was absolute parity. All three drivers have had an opportunity to have what we think is the best car. That proved to be successful every weekend.'

Even Penske struggles for words to describe what Al Jr has brought to the team. 'The hiring of Al Unser has been very, uh, what can you say?' said Penske, searching for the right comment. 'It rewarded the team a lot more than I think I ever really expected. Al is a great driver. That's why we hired him. But to see his tenacity and his commitment to the sport just so focused, I think that energised the team and the other drivers. For me it just completed the question that it was the right move. Absolutely it was the right move for us and if you talk to Al I think he feels the same way.'

Penske also takes pains to credit chief designer Nigel Bennett. 'Nigel doesn't get a lot of notoriety in this whole equation but he has again produced a great car,' noted Penske. 'Not a good car but a great car. The '88 car was good and last year's car was great too. We just didn't get it together last year. I think that this year's car has been great and the ability for the race engineers to communicate with the drivers has been the best that I've seen in a long time.

'And we've got the preparation. When you look at our reliability, we had an engine failure with Al in Toronto and we broke a few engines at Michigan, but so did everyone else. If you were running up front there, everybody dropped out. And we had two gearbox failures at Long Beach and another at Laguna and some electronic problems at the first race in Australia.

'So we've had reliability, a great car and great drivers and it all came together. But as I tell people, it's a point in time. You don't think that because you did well this year it automatically gives you an open book for '95 because there are some very good teams out there. Newman-Haas will be strong with Michael and Tracy. I think that with the Mercedes engine, Rahal-Hogan will be a great team. And there are guys like young Villeneuve in Barry Green's team. It's gonna be tough.'

Penske also points out the major role played by Ilmor, both in squeezing more power out of the four-cam 2.65-litre Ilmor D and in producing the Indy 500-winning, single-cam 3.4-litre Mercedes-Benz V8. 'When we got to Milwaukee I felt our power was much better than people had

Tony Di Zinno

Steve Swope

Michael C. Brown

spirit

power

victory

Left: Paul Tracy burns rubber on his way out of the pits. The young Canadian ended the season in a blaze of glory, winning the final two rounds of the PPG Cup championship, and had a successful F1 test at Estoril for Benetton. Next season he moves to Newman-Haas – where he will be joined by Michael Andretti – to challenge the Penske domination.

Roger Penske's inspired decision to commission the single-cam Ilmor-built Mercedes V8 for Indianapolis was rewarded with a runaway Brickyard win for Al Unser Jr *(below left)*.

indicated at the start of the season. If you read the newspapers it seemed like we were 100 horsepower short,' quipped Penske.

PENSKE & MERCEDES

Penske says Unser's win at Indianapolis in his team's first appearance with Mercedes-Benz was the most important of the year if not his entire racing career. 'I would say, if you talk about one victory that had more riding on it than anything else, that was it,' concedes Penske. 'You know, our reputation was on the line. Could we go out there, sit on the pole and win the race when people thought you had won it when you hadn't even unloaded yet? It was a great win. It was disappointing for Emerson and Paul but it was a great win for the team.'

At Indianapolis, Penske took advantage of USAC's foolish equivalency rules to outpower the rest of the field but he was particularly gratified to see his team run so strongly following Indianapolis after reverting to the more standard four-cam Ilmor engines.

'As Al came on and we started to get that momentum coming out of Indy, the real good news was everyone was somewhat negative on us because of the single-cam Mercedes engine at Indy but then to come right back and show it was drivers, it was car, it was team and it was engine on a level playing field. We probably had more of an advantage in some cases after Indianapolis than we did at Indy.'

Unser was outpaced in practice at Indianapolis by Fittipaldi but a quirk of the qualifying rules at The Speedway and hot, windy weather on Sunday allowed Al to take the pole, the first time he has done so at Indianapolis. For him, winning at Long Beach was one thing but taking the pole at the Brickyard was something else again. He began to believe in the reality of his championship dream.

'I didn't have the car exactly the way that I wanted it at Indianapolis,' noted Al. 'But the only one that was really outrunning me was Emerson, who had been with the team for quite a while. I was still learning to work with the engineers and it still wasn't right. But then we drew an early number and we qualified on Saturday.

'And Emerson had to qualify on Sunday because he drew a late number. He was the faster guy but then

Sunday was a totally different day and he couldn't get the speed in those conditions to take the pole away from me. It was then that I started to feel that the good Lord is smiling on me, that we were having good fortune with the win at Long Beach and now the pole at Indy.'

In the race, Fittipaldi and Unser ran away from the field although Al stalled when trying to leave the pits, losing time during his first stop. With less than fifty miles to go Fittipaldi lapped Unser, but Al repassed in traffic, and then Fittipaldi lost it and hit the wall while running hard in Unser's slipstream. Al remembers that victory as proof of the strength of the Penske team.

'That's when I knew for sure this is the strongest team I've ever been with. I was still making mistakes 'cause I messed up that first pit stop again. My third race in a row that I can't get out of the pits on the first stop but we still came out winners.'

At Milwaukee the next weekend Al was superb, soundly beating Fittipaldi and Tracy, who finished second and third for the team's first clean sweep of the top three places. Junior says his car handled better at Milwaukee than in any other race in 1994.

'The next few races I had the confidence in myself and in the team, and the team started to have confidence in me, that I could get it out of the pits. Milwaukee was the first race where I got it out of the pits on the first pit stop. I told 'em, "If I can get out of the pits on the first pit stop, there ain't gonna be no looking back." I had the car working the best there it's ever been. We had a good race with Emerson but we had him covered. It was wonderful.

'That was where [engineer] Terry Satchell and I started working pretty good with each other. I was starting to mix in with the team, with the mechanics really well, and starting to have confidence within myself on this race team. I think that was kind of like the turning point in the year where I knew I had a legitimate shot at the championship. I had Lady Luck helping me out and as long as Lady Luck kept helping me out we were for sure going to do it because I've got the strongest team.'

And so it was. Even a bout of food poisoning at Vancouver in September couldn't faze Al. He was forced to sit out Friday's practice and qualifying, the first time he had missed a day in his career. He came back weakly the next day for a few practice laps and a handful of qualifying laps, enough to start eighth. And in the race he drove steadily, keeping his head while all around were losing theirs.

Al came through to win for the second year in a row in Vancouver, driving away from Robby Gordon and Michael Andretti from the final restart on the bumpy, narrow little street track. That was an iron-man performance, a demonstration of real championship mettle which enabled him to wrap up the title the following weekend with two races to go by finishing a strong second to first-time winner Jacques Villeneuve.

Team-mates Fittipaldi and Tracy did their part to achieve the team's idealised goal of sweeping the championship. Fittipaldi was second in points, as he was in '93. Tracy was third, also as he was in '93. Between Penske's three drivers the team had no fewer than 29 top-three finishes, comprising twelve wins, nine second places and eight thirds.

Fittipaldi scored his only win of the year in style at Phoenix in April, beating Al Jr after Tracy crashed. At Indianapolis he was superb all month and looked to have the race in his pocket when he crashed while trying to lap Unser with less than twenty laps to go. Somehow, Emerson never recovered. His best chance at winning in the rest of the season came at New Hampshire, where he took the pole and led the opening laps but blistered his right-front tyre. He came back to finish third right behind Unser and Tracy in their fiercest three-way battle to the flag of the year. Fittipaldi's record for the season shows one win, four second places and five thirds as well as two poles.

Tracy's year started slowly but ended on a high note. He had electrical problems and a first-lap incident in Australia. At Phoenix he crashed through no fault of his own while leading, then had transmission trouble and spun at Long Beach. He crashed in practice at Indianapolis, ruining Penske's dream of sweeping the front row for Mercedes. Nor did he finish the 500 (for the third year in a row), dropping out of the race with a split exhaust header. Tracy didn't win until Detroit in June and that was after he'd run into the tail of Unser as they worked traffic.

In the end it was a good year for Paul, however, as he had far fewer incidents than in 1993 and finished by winning the last two races of the year, in command both times. He also enjoyed a fine F1 test with Benetton in September. Tracy's record shows three wins, two second places and three thirds as well as four poles. With Penske cutting back to two cars for 1995, Tracy has joined Newman-Haas with Michael Andretti, which should be quite a combination. Penske has an option to buy Tracy back in '96 and for the 25-year-old Canadian the future looks boundless.

REYNARD ARRIVES!

Best of the rest was Michael Andretti, who finished fourth in PPG Cup points driving Chip Ganassi's Reynard-Ford. Michael started the year in magnificent style, winning in Australia. It was a great way for him to return to Indy cars after a rough

AMERICAN RACING REVIEW

Michael Andretti returned to Indy Car racing in Chip Ganassi's Reynard and scored a season-opening win at Surfers Paradise *(far left)*, but was surprisingly uncompetitive at several races.

A bright new star. Canada's Jacques Villeneuve *(left)* was undoubtedly Rookie of the Year.

Nigel Mansell *(below)* in the traditional car-and-driver pose at Indianapolis. The defending PPG Cup champion had a disappointing year with Newman-Haas and was happy to return to Grand Prix racing (and the winner's circle) at season's end.

year in F1 and it was a truly memorable way for Adrian Reynard's company to make its competitive debut in Indy cars.

Thereafter, however, reality set in. Michael endured a very difficult year, qualifying outside the top ten in half the races. There were a few bright moments, including another street-fighting win in Toronto in July, but by the beginning of June Michael had already agreed to return to his 'home' – Newman-Haas Racing – for 1995-97.

Ganassi ran a second programme for Brazilian F1 refugee Mauricio Gugelmin, who frequently impressed in qualifying. Gugelmin is a very competent driver and fine gentleman who will continue with Ganassi in 1995. Teamed with Andretti's talented and bright replacement, Bryan Herta, he could be quite effective.

Reynards were raced by four other teams – Forsythe-Green, Hall Racing, Galles International and Hayhoe Racing. Barry Green's operation was clearly the best of these as the former Galles and Kraco team manager proved his worth as an owner-operator. With the shy but brilliantly talented Jacques Villeneuve at the wheel, Green's outfit soon emerged as the most consistently competitive of all the Reynard-equipped teams.

Jacques (pronounced 'Shak', remember) was a superb second at Indianapolis and scored the first win of his Indy Car career at Elkhart Lake in September, beating the Penskes in a straight fight. A runaway winner of IndyCar's Jim Trueman Rookie of the Year award, Villeneuve also stole sixth place in PPG Cup points from Nigel Mansell by finishing an aggressive third in the season finale at Laguna Seca. A gleamingly outstanding rookie year.

Driven by Teo Fabi, Jim Hall's Reynard finished ninth in the championship. It was Fabi's second year with Hall and by mid-season it was clear the two would part company for '95. Ironically, Fabi was more competitive in the season's second half but never made the podium. Adrian Fernandez occasionally impressed in Rick Galles's Reynard but the team threw away a couple of good chances, running out of fuel in Vancouver when a podium finish looked possible. Nevertheless, the Fernandez-Galles combination showed steady improvement and may be a factor in '95. Jimmy Vasser drove Jim Hayhoe's Reynard but seemed to lack utterly for either luck or reliability.

As Reynard made its mark in Indy cars, Lola struggled. The only Lola victory in 1994 was Scott Goodyear's win in the great Michigan 500 endurance race. The quasi-factory Newman-Haas team suffered its worst season on record, failing to win a single race, as Derrick Walker's growing team and driver Robby Gordon proved to be the most effective Lola representatives. Gordon finished fifth in the PPG Cup points table thanks to a strong second in Vancouver and third places at Long Beach and Detroit, street circuits all. He was also on the pole in Toronto and Vancouver. Walker has switched to Reynard chassis for 1995 and, with more money available, Robby will be trying as hard as ever to score that first win.

BYE, BYE NIGE

'Last year was the honeymoon,' commented a veteran Newman-Haas mechanic at the midsummer Michigan 500. 'This year, right from the start, it's been the divorce.' Indeed. Nigel Mansell's interest in Indy Car racing faded as the year wore on. It was disappointing that he showed so little fight, this man known in some parts of the world as *'Il Leone'*. Apart from a few early-season visits to the podium, Mansell was barely heard from in 1994. His best finish in the season's second half was seventh and he eventually faded to eighth in the points behind both young Villeneuve and Raul Boesel.

What happened? Mansell's year started poorly when he was outduelled by Michael Andretti and then spun and stalled in the Australian season-opener. He qualified and finished third at Phoenix, lapped by the Penskes of Fittipaldi and Unser, and spent the early part of the race battling with young rookie Jacques Villeneuve, who was making his second Indy Car start!

At Long Beach, Mansell was a distant second to Unser after Tracy and Fittipaldi hit trouble, and then came the month of May at Indianapolis, where his season began to unravel. He was never particularly quick at The Speedway, qualifying eighth and then getting knocked out of the race by Dennis Vitolo. Mansell was entirely a victim of Vitolo's stupidity but his uncharitable, almost surly comments on television when he emerged from the mandatory trip to the medical centre lost him a lot of fans and respect in America.

At Milwaukee the following weekend he was fifth, destroyed by the Penske's team's first 1-2-3 but beaten also by Michael Andretti and just barely holding off Robby Gordon. Mansell was on the pole in Detroit the next week but was quickly passed by Unser, Tracy and Fittipaldi before hitting the Brazilian in the tail in traffic and clouting the tyre barriers. He was fifth again at Portland behind the Penske trio and young Gordon, who beat him on the last lap. Mansell then went to Magny-Cours for his mid-season re-acquaintance with Formula 1 and when he returned his attitude had clearly changed. He was a distant second to Unser at Cleveland the weekend after Magny-Cours but thereafter his season simply fell apart.

Convinced that he had an Ecclestone-backed F1 deal for 1995, Mansell refused to test for Newman-Haas any more and also argued privately and publicly with team-mate Andretti. In fact he had two incidents with Mario, one in qualifying at Cleveland and a more serious one at New Hampshire in August in which both Newman-Haas cars were eliminated from the race. Then in Vancouver in September, Mansell tried a *banzai* last-lap, last-turn move on Fittipaldi, taking both of them out and ending Emerson's last hopes of beating Unser to the championship.

Then there was the matter of the two races in which Mansell simply gave up rather than plug on to the finish for points. In Toronto in July, Mansell was hit in the back by Michael Andretti as they battled for the lead. The impact punctured one

AMERICAN RACING REVIEW

of Mansell's rear tyres and after losing a lap in the pits he pulled in to quit. He did the same on the Nazareth oval in September when his car became wildly tail-happy in the race. In the last eight races of the year Mansell's best finish was seventh at Mid-Ohio in August. By the time he helicoptered out of Laguna Seca after the last race of the season and headed back to F1, many people in the Indy Car paddock had forgotten that Mansell was ever there.

Mario Andretti's 'Arrivederci' season also had its difficulties, although he never once thought of pulling out of a race. That kind of thing would never have entered Mario's mind. It was particularly disappointing to watch his car fail him in both the Indianapolis and Michigan 500s, where he had a genuine shot at winning.

Mario's best finish of his final year in Indy cars was a very competitive third in the Australian season-opener, the last time he would stand with son Michael on the podium. At Laguna Seca's season finale he was running a good seventh, ahead of Mansell, when his engine quit running with just four laps to go, ending a thirty-year career in Indy cars. Mario Andretti will always be remembered as one of Indy Car racing's greatest drivers.

Raul Boesel beat Mansell into seventh in the points with a strong drive to second place in the season finale. Boesel had a handful of other good races and was on the front row again at Indianapolis in his third year with Dick Simon's Lola-Ford team. Near the end of the year Raul signed with Rahal-Hogan for 1995, hoping to find victory lane at least once in his career.

Three-times PPG Cup champion Bobby Rahal gambled on the future with Honda and had decided by mid-season that the gamble wasn't worth it. Lack of horsepower meant he was never remotely competitive in any oval races. His best race came at Toronto's street circuit were he was second with a great-handling car. He was also third at Indianapolis, driving a rented Penske-Ilmor after failing to qualify his own Lola-Honda. With Mercedes-powered Lolas in 1995 and the very experienced Boesel replacing Mike Groff, Rahal-Hogan should win races and possibly challenge for the championship. Honda's plans for the Indy Car scene in 1995 were unknown at the time of writing, although it appeared the Japanese manufacturer might focus on testing rather than racing.

Arrivederci, Mario

Mario Andretti retired from Indy Car racing at the end of the season after 31 years. Acknowledged as one of the most versatile drivers in the history of motor racing, he won four Indy Car championships as well as the 1978 Formula 1 World Championship with Lotus, and also won races in stock cars (the 1967 Daytona 500) and long-distance sports car events, racing for the Ford and Ferrari factory teams. The tally of Andretti's Indy Car achievements is particularly impressive. He holds the records for pole positions (66), laps led (7587) and races started (407), and is second only to A.J. Foyt in race wins with 52 to Foyt's 67.

As 53-year-old Andretti considers his future in the sport and the possibility of becoming a team owner, he says he'll be staying in touch with the Indy Car scene. 'I don't want to jump into it just for the sake of doing it. I want to do it right and that means giving myself a break before attacking the project. But I don't think I'll be too far away. I think I'll be very close. I'll probably go to most of the testing this winter with Michael, try to stay on top of things. I think that will be very important.'

And of course, he still has unfinished business at Le Mans, one of the few prizes missing from his trophy room. The way he's talking, it sounds as if he'll drive a factory Ferrari at Daytona and Le Mans in 1995. 'If my plans to race at the Daytona and Le Mans 24-hour races come together I'll be doing quite a bit of testing in the fall and winter in preparation for Daytona. So, there goes the vacation!'

Mario refutes any talk that he's been unlucky throughout his career. 'A lot of people have said I'm unlucky. But the thing is, no way you could say I'm unlucky. I think I'm very lucky. If you look at my career and what I've been spared and the opportunities that I've had. I've been lucky in a lot of ways, believe me.'

Andretti also wants to make it clear where he stands in regard to Tony George's 1996 plans for his own Indy Car series called the Indy Racing League. 'I'm happy to report that I leave the state of Indy Car racing in very good hands with Andrew Craig and IndyCar. It's probably enjoying the best moments in its history, no question. It's definitely in good hands, and with all the young talent that we have on board there's a lot of depth in the field. I think the future of the PPG Indy Car World Series is very bright and very strong. I just wish Tony George would understand that.'

Another American racing legend retired in 1994. Drag racer Don Prudhomme is the same age as Andretti and has achieved just about as much in all of drag racing's major categories. Prudhomme announced at season's end that he will continue to run his own team in 1995 and beyond. As a driver he was competitive to the end, winning four races in 1994 and finishing second in the NHRA's Top Fuel category. Prudhomme wasn't kidding when he called his retirement season 'The Final Strike Tour'!

TONY GEORGE & THE IRL

Sixteen years ago the Indy Car team owners of the time broke away from USAC to form CART – Championship Auto Racing Teams. There were separate CART and USAC series in 1979 with Rick Mears winning the inaugural CART title and A.J. Foyt taking the last semi-reputable USAC championship. Now, in 1996, we may see a repeat of 1979 with two competing Indy Car championships. Indianapolis Motor Speedway president Tony George, grandson of USAC founder Tony Hulman, announced that starting in 1996 he will run his own Indy Car series to be called the Indy Racing League. George and his hand-picked IRL Commissioner Jerry Hauer are trying to recruit tracks to run IRL races in 1996 after 15 of the tracks currently running PPG Indy Car World Series events signed long-term contracts during the summer of '94 with CART – or IndyCar, as the organisation is now known.

Despite Indy Car racing's continued growth in crowds, competitors and general media coverage, George has been vocally unhappy with IndyCar's structure and operating style since he ascended to the IMS's presidency five years ago. In 1992 and '93 he had a temporary seat on a revised IndyCar board of directors but never saw eye to eye with the team owners and resigned at the end of 1993. George is now determined to go his own way with his own series, with USAC acting as the rule-makers and officials.

Few people believe the IRL will succeed because the PPG Cup series has grown so steadily over the past 16 years and become very strong. There's been plenty of political infighting among the team owners, to be sure, resulting in a series of different presidents and chairmen. When George resigned from the IndyCar board last winter, following the departure of IndyCar's latest and least effective chairman, Bill Stokkan, it looked like he might have been playing his cards well. IndyCar was fortunate, however, to be approached by Andrew Craig as a candidate for the vacant job. Once installed, Craig quickly took control, showing lots of energy and a hands-on style.

A former amateur F3 and sports car racer, Craig is an Englishman who has worked for the past ten years selling Olympic and World Cup soccer sponsorships with the Swiss-based sports marketing company ISL. Craig was able in 1994 to rally IndyCar's team owners together and sign critical long-term contracts with most of the current PPG Cup tracks or venues. In the meantime George has been slow to pull together rules, tracks, sponsors or the identity of any top driver or team that might compete in the IRL. In 1995, quite obviously, everyone will be watching keenly to see how all this posturing plays itself out.

PERFORMANCE FRICTION

NASCAR Winston Cup
Hanes 500
Martinsville, Virginia
September 25, 1994

FINISH	PADS	FINISH	PADS
1 R.Wallace	PFC	19 M.Waltrip	PFC
2 Earnhardt	PFC	20 Spencer	PFC
3 Elliot	PFC	21 Andretti	PFC
4 K.Wallace	PFC	22 Nemechek	PFC
5 Jarrett	PFC	23 Stricklin	PFC
6 Schrader	PFC	24 Petty	PFC
7 Marlin	PFC	25 Rudd	PFC
8 Gant	PFC	26 Sacks	PFC
9 Musgrave	PFC	27 Teague	PFC
10 D.Waltrip	PFC	28 M.Wallace	PFC
11 Gordon	PFC	29 Mast	PFC
12 Grissom	PFC	30 B.Bodine	PFC
13 Hamilton	PFC	31 B.Labonte	PFC
14 T.Labonte	PFC	32 Trickle	PFC
15 Shepherd	PFC	33 T.Bodine	PFC
16 Martin	PFC	34 Speed	PFC
17 Cope	PFC	35 W.Burton	PFC
18 G.Bodine	PFC	36 J.Burton	PFC

IndyCar World Series
Bank of America 300
Laguna Seca, California
October 9, 1994

FINISH	PAD	FINISH	PAD
1 Tracy	PFC	16 Zampredi	PFC
2 Boesel	PFC	17 Johnstone	PFC
3 Villeneuve	PFC	18 Freon	PFC
4 Fittipaldi	PFC	19 Ma.Andretti	PFC
5 Fabi	PFC	20 Unser Jnr	PFC
6 Luyendyk	PFC	21 Sharp	PFC
7 Fernandez	PFC	22 Gugelmin	PFC
8 Mansell	PFC	23 Matsushita	PFC
9 Montermini	PFC	24 Greco	PFC
10 Dobson	PFC	25 Cheever	PFC
11 Ribbs	PFC	26 Vasser	PFC
12 Johansson	PFC	27 Goodyear	PFC
13 Gordon	PFC	28 Mi.Andretti	PFC
14 Smith	PFC	29 Rahal	PFC
15 Groff	PFC		

EVERY NASCAR TEAM AND EVERY
INDYCAR TEAM SELECTED
CARBON METALLIC® BRAKE PADS
MANUFACTURED BY
PERFORMANCE FRICTION CORP...

WHAT BRAKE PAD DO YOU SELECT?

CALL FOR INFORMATION ON OUR NEW Z RATED STREET PADS

THE POWER TO STOP THE BEST

PERFORMANCE FRICTION CORP.
83 CARBON METALLIC HIGHWAY, PO BOX 819, CLOVER, SC 29710-0819, U.S.A.
(800)521-8874 - (803)222-2141 - FAX (803)222-2144

AMERICAN RACING REVIEW

Right: Battle of the Giants. Dale Earnhardt heads Rusty Wallace as the pair fight for the Winston Cup title. The 1994 season gave Earnhardt (seen below with his wife Theresa) a record-equalling seventh championship success.

THE MIGHTY EARNHARDT

There are no such political games in NASCAR, where Bill France Jr remains firmly in control of the organisation which his father founded in 1949. Bill Jr has run NASCAR since 1972. His key right-hand man for the past ten years has been Les Richter, who has taken semi-retirement this past year to take over Roger Penske's new California Speedway, scheduled for business in 1996. Richter has been replaced by Mike Helton, who has been a driver and track manager and worked beside Richter throughout 1994, learning the ropes of overseeing the

running of all Winston Cup races. Technical chief Gary Nelson joined NASCAR four years ago after establishing himself as one of stock car racing's top crew chiefs. NASCAR has therefore moved into a third, younger generation of management, all within the same stable, dictatorial structure established by the late Bill France Sr.

In company with series sponsor Winston cigarettes (R.J. Reynolds owns the brand), NASCAR has grown steadily over the last twenty years. With the coming of cable television and the all-sports network ESPN in 1980, NASCAR began to take off. Its close, populist racing worked as well on TV as it does at trackside. In recent years most NASCAR tracks have had to build new grandstands to accommodate the demand for tickets with almost every race sold out.

In 1994, NASCAR made its debut at Indianapolis with the inaugural running on 6 August of the Brickyard 400. This was the first time since 1911 that any race other than the Indianapolis 500 had taken place at the hallowed Indianapolis Motor Speedway and it was a great triumph for NASCAR. The place was sold out months in advance and the race was won by 23-year-old Jeff Gordon, who had spent his teenage years living in the Indianapolis region racing midgets and sprint cars.

The Winston Cup championship is more popular than ever, therefore. A fine measure of the series' strength is the fact that *Winston Cup Scene*, the weekly newspaper covering strictly the Winston Cup and second division Busch Grand National series, sells no fewer than 110,000 copies every week. It is the largest-circulation English language racing weekly in the world, which helps explain why Dale Earnhardt is reputed to make as much as $7 million per year from the sale of Earnhardt souvenirs and clothing. In this department, 43-year-old Earnhardt is the world's best-paid driver, perhaps the best measure of all of NASCAR's popularity.

Earnhardt has won his most recent Winston Cup championships not by being the fastest driver in most races but by being the most persistent and consistent. NASCAR's points system puts an absolute premium on finishing races in the top ten and avoiding even a small number of DNFs, and on these counts Earnhardt has soundly beaten primary rival Rusty Wallace in each of the past two years. In 1994, his 11th year with Richard Childress's outstanding Chevrolet team, Earnhardt won four races, only half as many as Wallace. But he had seven seconds and six third places compared to Wallace's three second places and a single third-place finish. He also failed to finish just three races while Wallace fell out of five, either crashing or blowing engines.

Having equalled Richard Petty's record of seven championships, and won four of them in the last five years, Earnhardt shows no signs of retiring. He could well continue to race for another five or even ten years in the best tradition of American race drivers. It's unlikely he will ever approach Petty's all-time record of 200 career wins (Earnhardt has 63 wins) but the younger of the two North Carolinians may set an unbeatable record of his own for championships.

Wallace was eventually placed third in the championship despite winning more races and leading more laps than anyone else for the

AMERICAN RACING REVIEW

The serious accident which befell Ernie Irvan *(right)* in mid-season was yet another dreadful blow to the Robert Yates team. Thankfully Irvan is on the road to recovery and hopes to return to the track next season.

Young Jeff Gordon *(far right)* won the inaugural Brickyard 400 at Indianapolis and established himself as a future championship contender.

Firestone/Patrick Racing Indy Car test driver Scott Pruett took the TransAm title in a Chevrolet Camaro *(below right)*.

Englishman Steve Robertson *(bottom right)* gave Tasman Motorsports its second successive Indy Lights crown.

second season running. Wallace, 38, won the Winston Cup title with drag racer Raymond Beadle's team in 1989 and started Penske South in partnership with Roger Penske at the end of 1990. In the last two years Wallace has won 18 races with Penske South and in '94 he led 2142 laps, more than a fifth of the season and more than twice as many as Earnhardt. The team also made a successful switch in 1994 from General Motors brand Pontiac to Ford and stands as the most likely operation to stop Earnhardt and Childress winning an unprecedented eighth title in 1995.

IRVAN INJURED

The other team capable of winning the championship is Robert Yates's Ford team which came close with Davey Allison in 1992 and was challenging again in '93 when Allison was killed in a helicopter crash. Ernie Irvan was signed to replace Allison, running the last nine races of the 1993 season and winning two of them. In '94, Irvan got off to a fast start, finishing a strong second in the Daytona 500 and winning the third and fourth races of the year at Richmond and Atlanta. By the middle of the season Irvan and Yates's team were locked in a close championship battle with Earnhardt, running well clear at that point of Wallace.

At the high-banked, 2.0-mile Michigan International Speedway in August, however, Irvan crashed heavily while practising, the apparent victim of a tyre failure. He hit the wall head-on, fracturing his skull and collapsing his lungs. Irvan was unconscious for a week before making a steady comeback. He was a spectator at the last few races of the year, fighting a vision problem but vowing to be back in 1995. In the meantime, Yates says he'll run a car for Irvan whenever he's ready but at the time of writing was trying to hire Dale Jarrett to be his regular driver in '95.

The next most competitive Winston Cup driver in recent years has been Mark Martin with Jack Roush's Ford team. The Martin-Roush combination finished second in the championship in 1990 and third in 1989 and '93. This year Martin could usually be counted on to run strongly up front and pipped Wallace to second place with a win in the final round. There were too many DNFs (eight), however, and not enough wins (two) for him to challenge for the championship.

Rick Hendrick's three-car team of Chevrolets won two of the year's biggest races (the Brickyard 400 and Charlotte 600) with young phenomenon Jeff Gordon, who was in only his second season on the circuit. Gordon was eighth in the championship and should develop into a title contender in the next year or two. Former champion (1984) Terry Labonte joined Hendrick, replacing Ricky Rudd, and was more competitive than in years, winning three races and frequently challenging for victory. Good guy Ken Schrader completed his seventh season with Hendrick, failing to win a race for the third successive year but finishing fourth in the championship through consistent results.

After four years with Hendrick's multi-car outfit, Rudd left to start his own team in 1994. Taking sponsor Tide with him and opting to run Fords, Rudd showed he was up to the double job of being an owner-driver. He won his first race in that capacity at Daytona in July and finished fifth in the Winston Cup points table in a very successful first season.

Sixth in the championship behind Schrader and Rudd and ahead of Labonte was veteran Morgan Shepherd. In his third year with the Wood Brothers' Fords, 53-year-old Shepherd was second at Atlanta in the spring and third in two more races but was unable to win a race as he did in 1993. However, the good Morgan will be back in '95 after a throughly respectable season.

Junior Johnson's pair of Fords driven by former champion Bill Elliott and up-and-comer Jimmy Spencer were surprisingly uncompetitive in many races, although Elliott managed to win one race and the sometimes wild Spencer won twice. In his third year with Johnson's team Elliott was able to eke out tenth place in the championship before going off to restart his own family team with brother Ernie. Elliott won 31 races between 1984 and '89 and the '88 Winston Cup title with the family team and hopes to rekindle that kind of success again in 1995. Spencer was far too hot and cold and finished way down the points table but continues with Johnson in '95.

Three-times (1981, '82 and '85) champion Darrell Waltrip finished ninth in points in his fourth year with his own Chevrolet-equipped team. At 47, Waltrip hasn't won a race in two years.

Other drivers who were able to win in 1994 included Geoff Bodine, Sterling Marlin and Dale Jarrett. Bodine equalled Irvan's season-high tally of five poles and won three races but had far too many DNFs to come close to making the top ten in points. Marlin and Jarrett had their moments but nothing more.

Bodine was the top driver to run the season on Hoosier tyres, enjoying a close relationship with the comparatively small racing tyre manufacturer. Hoosier competed against Goodyear in NASCAR in 1988 and '89 and returned this year with Bodine and a handful of other teams. Occasionally, Hoosier's tyres worked to fine effect but it was often clear that Goodyear had the best tyre for the race.

Tyre wars are always dangerous and many people blamed NASCAR's latest tyre battle for Irvan's accident. In the wake of the February deaths of Neil Bonnett and Rodney Orr and Irvan's subsequent injuries, NASCAR determined to make some detail rule changes for 1995. The weight minimum has been cut by 100 lb to 3400 lb in an effort to reduce impact velocities in accidents. New specifications for the central roof bar in the roll cage require it to be mounted to the right side of the driver's head. Roof flaps, in use at most superspeedways in 1994 to help keep cars on the ground when they spin, will now be required at all races.

It seems probable that in 1996 tyre widths will be reduced and the currently unrestricted engine compression ratio will be established at 9:1. As ever, NASCAR moves slowly, steadily and inevitably following a carefully considered plan. The FIA could learn much from Bill France and NASCAR.

OTHER MAJOR 1994 RESULTS

Compiled by David Hayhoe

FIA International Formula 3000 Championship

BRDC INTERNATIONAL TROPHY, Silverstone Grand Prix Circuit, Towcester, Northamptonshire, Great Britain, 2 May. Round 1. 38 laps of the 3.247-mile/5.226-km circuit, 123.386 miles/198.571 km.
1 Franck Lagorce, F (Reynard 94D-Cosworth AC), 1h 01m 56.79s, 119.509 mph/192.331 km/h.
2 David Coulthard, GB (Reynard 94D-Cosworth AC), 1h 02m 00.89s.
3 Gil de Ferran, BR (Reynard 94D-Zytek Judd KV), 1h 02m 04.31s.
4 Vincenzo Sospiri, I (Reynard 94D-Cosworth AC), 1h 02m 37.98s.
5 Hideki Noda, J (Reynard 94D-Cosworth AC), 1h 02m 39.77s.
6 Didier Cottaz, F (Reynard 94D-Zytek Judd KV), 1h 02m 40.65s.
7 Massimiliano Papis, I (Reynard 94D-Zytek Judd KV), 1h 02m 41.18s; **8** 'Jules' Boullion, F (Reynard 94D-Cosworth AC), 1h 02m 41.64s; **9** Jordi Gene, E (Lola T94/50-Cosworth AC), 1h 02m 58.80s; **10** Oliver Gavin, GB (Lola T94/50-Cosworth AC), 1h 02m 59.43s; **11** Guillaume Gomez, F (Reynard 94D-Cosworth AC), 1h 02m 59.72s; **12** Kenny Brack, S (Reynard 94D-Zytek Judd KV), 1h 03m 00.45s; **13** Tarso Marques, BR (Reynard 94D-Cosworth AC), 1h 03m 15.85s; **14** Jérôme Policand, F (Reynard 94D-Cosworth DFV), 37 laps; **15** Taki Inoue, J (Reynard 94D-Cosworth AC), 37; **16** Fabrizio de Simone, I (Reynard 94D-Zytek Judd KV), 36; **17** Severino Nardozi, I (Reynard 93D-Cosworth AC), 35; **18** Nicolas Leboissetier, F (Reynard 94D-Cosworth DFV), 32 (DNF – electrics); **19** Emmanuel Clérico, F (Reynard 94D-Cosworth AC), 22 (DNF – oil pressure); **20** Marc Goossens, B (Lola T94/50-Cosworth AC), 21 (DNF – spin); **21** Christian Pescatori, I (Reynard 93D-Cosworth AC), 20; **22** Pedro Diniz, BR (Reynard 94D-Cosworth AC), 14 (DNF – wheel nut); **23** Robbie Stirling, CDN (Lola T93/50-Zytek Judd KV), 12 (DNF – clutch); **24** Wim Eyckmans, B (Reynard 93D-Cosworth AC), 9 (DNF – engine); **25** Paolo delle Piane, I (Reynard 94D-Cosworth AC), 5 (DNF – accident).
Fastest race lap: Lagorce, 1m 36.67s, 120.919 mph/194.600 km/h.
Fastest qualifying lap: Lagorce, 1m 33.83s, 124.578 mph/200.490 km/h.
Did not start: Mikke van Hool, B (Reynard 93D-Zytek Judd KV).
Championship points: 1 Lagorce, 9; **2** Coulthard, 6; **3** de Ferran, 4; **4** Sospiri, 3; **5** Noda, 2; **6** Cottaz, 1.

54th GRAND PRIX AUTOMOBILE DE PAU, Circuit de Pau, France, 23 May. Round 2. 71 laps of the 1.715-mile/2.760-km circuit, 121.764 miles/195.960 km.
1 Gil de Ferran, BR (Reynard 94D-Zytek Judd KV), 1h 25m 39.27s, 85.294 mph/137.268 km/h.
2 Vincenzo Sospiri, I (Reynard 94D-Cosworth AC), 1h 25m 44.74s.
3 Didier Cottaz, F (Reynard 94D-Zytek Judd KV), 1h 25m 51.12s.
4 'Jules' Boullion, F (Reynard 94D-Cosworth AC), 1h 25m 52.83s.
5 Franck Lagorce, F (Reynard 94D-Cosworth AC), 1h 26m 23.34s.
6 Guillaume Gomez, F (Reynard 94D-Cosworth AC), 70 laps.
7 Christian Pescatori, I (Reynard 93D-Cosworth AC), 70; **8** Jérôme Policand, F (Reynard 94D-Cosworth DFV), 70; **9** Jordi Gene, E (Lola T94/50-Cosworth AC), 70; **10** Fabrizio de Simone, I (Reynard 94D-Zytek Judd KV), 69; **11** Patrick Crinelli, I (Lola T94/50-Zytek Judd KV), 45 (DNF – accident); **12** Massimiliano Papis, I (Reynard 94D-Zytek Judd KV), 32 (DNF – accident); **13** Emmanuel Clérico, F (Reynard 94D-Cosworth AC), 32 (DNF – accident); **14** Tarso Marques, BR (Reynard 94D-Cosworth AC), 30 (DNF – accident); **15** Mikke van Hool, B (Reynard 93D-Zytek Judd KV), 25 (DNF – suspension); **16** Taki Inoue, J (Reynard 94D-Cosworth AC), 19 (DNF – suspension); **17** Hideki Noda, J (Reynard 94D-Cosworth AC), 16 (DNF – spin); **18** Marc Goossens, B (Lola T94/50-Cosworth AC), 15 (DNF – oil leak); **19** Allan McNish, GB (Reynard 94D-Cosworth AC), 7 (DNF – accident); **20** Nicolas Leboissetier, F (Reynard 94D-Cosworth DFV), 1 (DNF – accident); **21** Pedro Diniz, BR (Reynard 94D-Cosworth AC), 1 (DNF – hit wheel).
Fastest race lap: Sospiri, 1m 11.39s, 86.482 mph/139.179 km/h.
Fastest qualifying lap: de Ferran, 1m 09.63s, 88.668 mph/142.697 km/h.
Did not start: Paolo delle Piane, I (Reynard 94D-Cosworth AC), driver injury; Kenny Brack, S (Reynard 94D-Zytek Judd KV), did not qualify; Severino Nardozi, I (Reynard 93D-Cosworth AC), did not qualify; Oliver Gavin, GB (Lola T94/50-Zytek Judd), did not qualify.
Championship points: 1 de Ferran, 13; **2** Lagorce, 11; **3** Sospiri, 9; **4** Coulthard, 6; **5** Cottaz, 5; **6** Boullion, 3.

FIA INTERNATIONAL FORMULA 3000 CHAMPIONSHIP, Circuit de Catalunya, Montmelo, Barcelona, Spain, 28 May. Round 3. 41 laps of the 2.950-mile/4.747-km circuit, 120.936 miles/194.627 km.
1 Massimiliano Papis, I (Reynard 94D-Zytek Judd KV), 1h 05m 41.393s, 110.460 mph/177.769 km/h.
2 Fabrizio de Simone, I (Reynard 94D-Zytek Judd KV), 1h 06m 04.825s.
3 Vincenzo Sospiri, I (Reynard 94D-Cosworth AC), 1h 06m 05.302s.
4 Jordi Gene, E (Lola T94/50-Cosworth AC), 1h 06m 13.991s.
5 Franck Lagorce, F (Reynard 94D-Cosworth AC), 1h 06m 15.529s.
6 Marc Goossens, B (Lola T94/50-Cosworth AC), 1h 06m 27.295s.
7 Didier Cottaz, F (Reynard 94D-Zytek Judd KV), 1h 06m 28.129s; **8** Guillaume Gomez, F (Reynard 94D-Cosworth AC), 1h 06m 28.522s; **9** Christian Pescatori, I (Reynard 93D-Cosworth AC), 1h 06m 36.333s; **10** Pedro Diniz, BR (Reynard 94D-Cosworth AC), 1h 06m 56.321s; **11** Kenny Brack, S (Reynard 94D-Zytek Judd KV), 1h 07m 06.618s; **12** Mikke van Hool, B (Reynard 93D-Zytek Judd KV), 1h 07m 08.876s; **13** Taki Inoue, J (Reynard 94D-Cosworth AC), 40 laps; **14** Gil de Ferran, BR (Reynard 94D-Zytek Judd KV), 35 laps (DNF – fuel fire); **15** Wim Eyckmans, B (Reynard 93D-Cosworth AC), 30 (DNF – gearbox); **16** Jérôme Policand, F (Reynard 94D-Cosworth DFV), 25 (DNF – accident); **17** Patrick Crinelli, I (Lola T94/50-Zytek Judd KV), 24 (DNF – driver fatigue); **18** Severino Nardozi, I (Reynard 93D-Cosworth AC), 22 (DNF – driver gave up); **19** Oliver Gavin, GB (Lola T94/50-Cosworth AC), 10 (DNF – accident); **20** 'Jules' Boullion, F (Reynard 94D-Cosworth AC), 10 (DNF – accident); **21** Emmanuel Clérico, F (Reynard 94D-Cosworth AC), 6 (DNF – engine); **22** Hideki Noda, J (Reynard 94D-Cosworth AC), 5 (DNF – accident); **23** Paolo delle Piane, I (Reynard 94D-Cosworth AC), 12 (DNF – disqualified).
Fastest race lap: Boullion, 1m 34.639s, 112.203 mph/180.572 km/h.
Fastest qualifying lap: Papis, 1m 30.889s, 116.832 mph/188.023 km/h.
Did not start: Tarso Marques, BR (Reynard 94D-Cosworth AC), accident during practice.
Championship points: 1= de Ferran, 13; **1=** Lagorce, 13; **1=** Sospiri, 13; **4** Papis, 9; **5=** Coulthard, 6; **5=** de Simone, 6.

32nd GRAN PREMIO del MEDITERRANEO, Ente Autodromo di Pergusa, Enna-Pergusa, Catania, Sicily, Italy, 17 July. Round 4. 40 laps of the 3.076-mile/4.950-km circuit, 123.031 miles/198.000 km.
1 Gil de Ferran, BR (Reynard 94D-Zytek Judd KV), 57m 41.731s, 127.946 mph/205.909 km/h.
2 Franck Lagorce, F (Reynard 94D-Cosworth AC), 57m 52.357s.
3 Hideki Noda, J (Reynard 94D-Cosworth AC), 57m 55.845s.
4 Massimiliano Papis, I (Reynard 94D-Zytek Judd KV), 58m 13.860s.
5 Jérôme Policand, F (Reynard 94D-Cosworth DFV), 58m 19.358s.
6 Christian Pescatori, I (Reynard 93D-Cosworth AC), 58m 24.122s.
7 Marc Goossens, B (Lola T94/50-Cosworth AC), 58m 35.804s; **8** Paolo delle Piane, I (Reynard 93D-Cosworth AC), 58m 41.497s; **9** Didier Cottaz, F (Reynard 94D-Zytek Judd KV), 58m 52.095s; **10** Guillaume Gomez, F (Reynard 94D-Cosworth AC), 58m 52.277s; **11** Kenny Brack, S (Reynard 94D-Zytek Judd KV), 58m 53.989s; **12** Tarso Marques, BR (Reynard 94D-Cosworth AC), 58m 41.027s*; **13** Taki Inoue, J (Reynard 94D-Cosworth AC), 39 laps; **14** 'Jules' Boullion, F (Reynard 94D-Cosworth AC), 39; **15** James Taylor, GB (Reynard 94D-Cosworth AC), 37; **16** Vincenzo Sospiri, I (Reynard 94D-Cosworth AC), 22 (DNF accident); **17** Emmanuel Clérico, F (Reynard 94D-Cosworth AC), 20 (DNF – suspension); **18** Pedro Diniz, BR (Reynard 94D-Cosworth AC), 9 (DNF – accident); **19** Nicolas Leboissetier, F (Reynard 94D-Cosworth DFV), 6 (DNF – accident); **20** Norio Matsubara, BR (Lola T94/50-Zytek Judd KV), 5 (DNF – accident); **21** Oliver Gavin, GB (Lola T94/50-Zytek Judd KV), 1 (DNF throttle cable); **22** Mikke van Hool, B (Reynard 93D-Zytek Judd KV), 0 (DNF – clutch); **23** Fabrizio de Simone, I (Reynard 94D-Zytek Judd KV), 0 (DNF – accident).
** includes 1-minute penalty for jumping the start.*
Fastest race lap: Pescatori, 1m 25.157s, 130.028 mph/209.261 km/h.
Fastest qualifying lap: Lagorce, 1m 24.159s, 131.570 mph/211.742 km/h.
Did not start: Severino Nardozi, I (Reynard 93D-Cosworth AC), did not qualify.
Championship points: 1 de Ferran, 22; **2** Lagorce, 19; **3** Sospiri, 13; **4** Papis, 12; **5=** Coulthard, 6; **5=** Noda, 6; **5=** de Simone, 6.

FIA INTERNATIONAL FORMULA 3000 CHAMPIONSHIP, Hockenheimring, Heidelberg, Germany, 30 July. Round 5. 29 laps of the 4.240-mile/6.823-km circuit, 122.949 miles/197.867 km.
1 Franck Lagorce, F (Reynard 94D-Cosworth AC), 58m 07.686s, 126.908 mph/204.239 km/h.
2 'Jules' Boullion, F (Reynard 94D-Cosworth AC), 58m 15.484s.
3 Gil de Ferran, BR (Reynard 94D-Zytek Judd KV), 58m 28.089s.
4 Vincenzo Sospiri, I (Reynard 94D-Cosworth AC), 58m 38.724s.
5 Marc Goossens, B (Lola T94/50-Cosworth AC), 58m 46.652s.
6 Wim Eyckmans, B (Reynard 94D-Cosworth AC), 58m 55.587s.
7 Jérôme Policand, F (Reynard 94D-Cosworth DFV), 58m 56.576s; **8** Christian Pescatori, I (Reynard 93D-Cosworth AC), 59m 01.188s; **9** Kenny Brack, S (Reynard 94D-Zytek Judd KV), 59m 11.806s; **10** Tarso Marques, BR (Reynard 94D-Cosworth AC), 59m 21.338s; **11** Didier Cottaz, F (Reynard 94D-Zytek Judd KV), 59m 22.125s; **12** Taki Inoue, J (Reynard 94D-Cosworth AC), 59m 23.136s; **13** Mikke van Hool, B (Reynard 93D-Zytek Judd KV), 59m 33.010s; **14** Fabrizio de Simone, I (Reynard 94D-Zytek Judd KV), 1h 00m 05.428s; **15** Emmanuel Clérico, F (Reynard 94D-Cosworth AC), 28 laps; **16** Severino Nardozi, I (Reynard 93D-Cosworth AC), 27; **17** Hideki Noda, J (Reynard 94D-Cosworth AC), 24 (DNF – engine); **18** Massimiliano Papis, I (Reynard 94D-Zytek Judd KV), 21 (DNF – accident); **19** Pedro Diniz, BR (Reynard 94D-Cosworth AC), 20 (DNF – accident); **20** James Taylor, GB (Reynard 94D-Cosworth AC), 17 (DNF – accident); **21** Guillaume Gomez, F (Reynard 94D-Cosworth AC), 16 (DNF – accident); **22** Nicolas Leboissetier, F (Reynard 94D-Cosworth DFV), 4 (DNF – accident); **23** Paolo delle Piane, I (Reynard 93D-Cosworth AC), 1 (DNF – accident); **24** Oliver Gavin, GB (Lola T94/50-Cosworth AC), 0 (DNF – clutch).
Fastest race lap: Lagorce, 1m 59.278s, 127.958 mph/205.929 km/h.
Fastest qualifying lap: Gomez, 1m 55.880s, 131.711 mph/211.968 km/h.
Championship points: 1 Lagorce, 28; **2** de Ferran, 26; **3** Sospiri, 16; **4** Papis, 12; **5** Boullion, 9; **6=** Coulthard, 6; **6=** Noda, 6; **6=** de Simone, 6.

FIA INTERNATIONAL FORMULA 3000 CHAMPIONSHIP, Circuit de Spa-Francorchamps, Stavelot, Belgium, 27 August. Round 6. 27 laps of the 4.350-mile/7.001-km circuit, 117.456 miles/189.027 km.
1 'Jules' Boullion, F (Reynard 94D-Cosworth AC), 1h 11m 34.525s, 98.461 mph/158.457 km/h.
2 Didier Cottaz, F (Reynard 94D-Zytek Judd KV), 1h 11m 51.464s.
3 Kenny Brack, S (Reynard 94D-Zytek Judd KV), 1h 12m 12.698s.
4 Guillaume Gomez, F (Reynard 94D-Cosworth AC), 1h 12m 22.004s.
5 Gil de Ferran, BR (Reynard 94D-Zytek Judd KV), 1h 12m 26.967s.
6 Fabrizio de Simone, I (Reynard 94D-Zytek Judd KV), 1h 12m 38.048s.
7 Hideki Noda, J (Reynard 94D-Cosworth AC), 1h 12m 39.759s; **8** Tarso Marques, BR (Reynard 94D-Cosworth AC), 1h 12m 46.253s; **9** Pedro Diniz, BR (Reynard 94D-Cosworth AC), 1h 12m 48.168s; **10** Christian Pescatori, I (Reynard 93D-Cosworth AC), 1h 13m 00.873s; **11** Massimiliano Papis, I (Reynard 94D-Zytek Judd KV), 1h 13m 09.627s; **12** Jérôme Policand, F (Reynard 94D-Cosworth DFV), 1h 13m 31.258s; **13** Franck Lagorce, F (Reynard 94D-Cosworth AC), 1h 14m 09.070s; **14** Taki Inoue, J (Reynard 94D-Cosworth AC), 26 laps; **15** Elton Julian, USA (Lola T94/50-Zytek Judd KV), 26; **16** Severino Nardozi, I (Reynard 93D-Cosworth AC), 26; **17** Wim Eyckmans, B (Reynard 94D-Cosworth AC), 26; **18** Paolo delle Piane, I (Reynard 93D-Cosworth AC), 19 (DNF – generator); **19** Nicolas Leboissetier, F (Reynard 94D-Cosworth DFV), 10 (DNF – accident); **20** Marc Goossens, B (Lola T94/50-Cosworth AC), 4 (DNF – accident); **21** James Taylor, GB (Reynard 94D-Cosworth AC), 2 (DNF – differential); **22** Mikke van Hool, B (Reynard 93D-Zytek Judd KV), 2 (DNF – brakes); **23** Emmanuel Clérico, F (Reynard 93D-Cosworth AC), 0 (DNF – accident); **24** Vincenzo Sospiri, I (Reynard 94D-Cosworth AC), 0 (DNF – accident).
Fastest race lap: Marques, 2m 32.388s, 102.769 mph/165.391 km/h (record).
Fastest qualifying lap: Lagorce, 2m 07.685s, 122.652 mph/197.389 km/h.
Championship points: 1= Lagorce, 28; **1=** de Ferran, 28; **3** Boullion, 18; **4** Sospiri, 16; **5** Papis, 12; **6** Cottaz, 11.

FIA INTERNATIONAL FORMULA 3000 CHAMPIONSHIP, Circuito do Estoril, Portugal, 23 September. Round 7. 44 laps of the 2.709-mile/4.360-km circuit, 119.204 miles/191.840 km.
1 'Jules' Boullion, F (Reynard 94D-Cosworth AC), 1h 08m 11.419s, 104.886 mph/168.798 km/h.
2 Vincenzo Sospiri, I (Reynard 94D-Cosworth AC), 1h 08m 32.879s.
3 Guillaume Gomez, F (Reynard 94D-Cosworth AC), 1h 08m 35.054s.
4 Pedro Diniz, BR (Reynard 94D-Cosworth AC), 1h 08m 37.572s.
5 Didier Cottaz, F (Reynard 94D-Zytek Judd KV), 1h 08m 38.358s.
6 Kenny Brack, S (Reynard 94D-Zytek Judd KV), 1h 08m 40.463s.
7 Emmanuel Clérico, F (Reynard 94D-Cosworth AC), 1h 08m 41.114s; **8** Franck Lagorce, F (Reynard 94D-Cosworth AC), 1h 08m 59.898s; **9** Taki Inoue, J (Reynard 94D-Cosworth AC), 1h 09m 15.069s; **10** Nicolas Leboissetier, F (Reynard 94D-Cosworth DFV), 1h 09m 20.397s; **11** Mikke van Hool, B (Reynard 94D-Zytek Judd KV), 1h 09m 20.911s; **12** Tarso Marques, BR (Reynard 94D-Cosworth AC), 1h 09m 38.843s; **13** Massimiliano Papis, I (Reynard 94D-Zytek Judd KV), 43 laps; **14** Elton Julian, USA (Lola T94/50-Zytek Judd KV), 43; **15** James Taylor, GB (Reynard 94D-Cosworth AC), 43; **16** Hideki Noda, J (Reynard 94D-Cosworth AC), 43 (DNF – spin); **17** Jérôme Policand, F (Reynard 94D-Zytek Judd KV), 41; **18** Christian Pescatori, I (Reynard 93D-Cosworth AC), 27 (DNF – spin); **19** Fabrizio de Simone, I (Reynard 94D-Zytek Judd KV), 23 (DNF – electrics); **20** Marc Rostan, F (Lola T94/50-Zytek Judd KV), 15 (DNF – electrics); **21** Paolo delle Piane, I (Reynard 94D-Cosworth AC), 9 (DNF – electrics); **22** Paulo Carcasci, BR (Lola T94/50-Cosworth AC), 8 (DNF – electrics); **23** Gil de Ferran, BR (Reynard 94D-Zytek Judd KV), 2 (DNF – accident); **24** Marc Goossens, B (Lola T94/50-Cosworth AC), 0 (DNF – puncture); **25** Wim Eyckmans, B (Reynard 94D-Cosworth AC), 0 (DNF – electrics).
Fastest race lap: Clérico, 1m 31.193s, 106.949 mph/172.118 km/h.
Fastest qualifying lap: Clérico, 1m 28.852s, 109.767 mph/176.653 km/h.
Did not start: Severino Nardozi, I (Reynard 93D-Cosworth AC), did not qualify.
Championship points: 1= Lagorce, 28; **1=** de Ferran, 28; **3** Boullion, 27; **4** Sospiri, 22; **5** Cottaz, 13; **6** Papis, 12.

FIA INTERNATIONAL FORMULA 3000 CHAMPIONSHIP, Circuit de Nevers, Magny-Cours, France, 2 October. Round 8. 48 laps of the 2.641-mile/4.250-km circuit, 126.760 miles/204.000 km.
1 'Jules' Boullion, F (Reynard 94D-Cosworth AC), 1h 10m 41.298s, 107.593 mph/173.155 km/h.
2 Franck Lagorce, F (Reynard 94D-Cosworth AC), 1h 10m 45.661s.
3 Guillaume Gomez, F (Reynard 94D-Cosworth AC), 1h 10m 53.138s.
4 Tarso Marques, BR (Reynard 94D-Cosworth AC), 1h 11m 51.018s.
5 Vincenzo Sospiri, I (Reynard 94D-Cosworth AC), 1h 11m 56.800s.
6 Massimiliano Papis, I (Reynard 94D-Zytek Judd KV), 1h 12m 03.743s.
7 Didier Cottaz, F (Reynard 94D-Zytek Judd KV), 1h 13m 00.576s*; **8** Paolo delle Piane, I (Reynard 94D-Cosworth AC), 47 laps; **9** Christian Pescatori, I (Reynard 93D-Cosworth AC), 47; **10** Kenny Brack, S (Reynard 94D-Zytek Judd KV), 47; **11** Hideki Noda, J (Reynard 94D-Cosworth AC), 47; **12** Nicolas Leboissetier, F (Reynard 94D-Cosworth DFV), 47; **13** Elton Julian, USA (Lola T94/50-Zytek Judd KV), 46; **14** Marc Rostan, F (Lola T94/50-Zytek Judd KV), 45; **15** Severino Nardozi, I (Reynard 93D-Cosworth AC), 43; **16** Emmanuel Clérico, F (Reynard 94D-Cosworth AC), 31 (DNF – engine); **17** Wim Eyckmans, B (Reynard 94D-Cosworth AC), 30 (DNF – electrics); **18** Pedro Diniz, BR (Reynard 94D-Cosworth AC), 28 (DNF – accident); **19** Taki Inoue, J (Reynard 94D-Cosworth AC), 26 (DNF – accident); **20** Jérôme Policand, F (Reynard 94D-Zytek Judd KV), 19 (DNF – accident); **21** Marc Goossens, B (Lola T94/50-Cosworth AC), 0 (DNF – accident); **22** Gil de Ferran, BR (Reynard 94D-Zytek Judd KV), 0 (DNF – accident); **23** Fabrizio de Simone, I (Reynard 94D-Zytek Judd KV), 0 (DNF – accident); **24** Mikke van Hool, B (Reynard 94D-Zytek Judd KV), 0 (DNF – accident).
** includes 1-minute penalty for jumping the start.*
Fastest race lap: Lagorce, 1m 27.211s, 109.011 mph/175.437 km/h.
Fastest qualifying lap: Lagorce, 1m 37.332s, 97.676 mph/157.194 km/h.
Did not start: James Taylor, GB (Reynard 94D-Cosworth AC), did not qualify.

Final championship points

1	'Jules' Boullion, F	36
2	Franck Lagorce, F	34
3	Gil de Ferran, BR	28
4	Vincenzo Sospiri, I	24
5=	Didier Cottaz, F	13
5=	Massimiliano Papis, I	13

7 Guillaume Gomez, F, 12; **8** Fabrizio de Simone, I, 7; **9=** David Coulthard, GB, 6; **9=** Hideki Noda, J, 6; **11** Kenny Brack, S, 5; **12=** Pedro Diniz, BR, 3; **12=** Jordi Gene, E, 3; **12=** Tarso Marques, BR, 3; **12=** Marc Goossens, B, 3; **16** Jérôme Policand, F, 2; **17=** Wim Eyckmans, B, 1; **17=** Christian Pescatori, I, 1.

British Formula 3 Championship

BRITISH FORMULA 3 CHAMPIONSHIP, Silverstone Club Circuit, Towcester, Northamptonshire, Great Britain, 27 March. Round 1. 25 laps of the 1.649-mile/2.654-km circuit, 41.225 miles/66.345 km.
1 Dario Franchitti, GB (Dallara F394-Mugen Honda), 23m 29.76s, 105.273 mph/169.421 km/h.
2 Scott Lakin, GB (Dallara F393-Mugen Honda), 23m 32.06s.

3 Jan Magnussen, DK (Dallara F393-Mugen Honda), 23m 34.98s.
4 Gareth Rees, GB (Dallara F394-Mugen Honda), 23m 36.12s.
5 Steven Arnold, GB (Dallara F394-Mugen Honda), 23m 36.69s.
6 Vincent Radermecker, B (Dallara F394-Mugen Honda), 23m 37.68s.
7 Jérémie Dufour, F (Dallara F394-Vauxhall), 23m 41.48s; 8 Marcos Gueiros, BR (Dallara F394-Mugen Honda), 23m 44.17s; 9 Ricardo Rosset, BR (Dallara F394-Mugen Honda), 23m 46.60s; 10 Gualter Salles, BR (Dallara F394-Mugen Honda), 23m 47.30s.
Fastest race lap: Radermecker, 55.60s, 106.770 mph/171.829 km/h.
Class B winner: Duncan Vercoe, GB (Dallara F393-Vauxhall), 24m 04.40s.
Fastest qualifying lap: Franchitti, 55.31s, 107.330 mph/172.730 km/h.
Championship points. Class A: 1 Franchitti, 20; 2 Lakin, 15; 3 Magnussen, 12; 4 Rees, 10; 5 Arnold, 8; 6 Radermecker, 7. **Class B:** 1 Vercoe, 21; 2 Gray Hedley, GB, 15; 3 Steve Allen, GB, 12.

BRITISH FORMULA 3 CHAMPIONSHIP, Donington Park Grand Prix Circuit, Derbyshire, Great Britain, 10 April. Round 2. 20 laps of the 2.500-mile/4.023-km circuit, 50.000 miles/80.467 km.
1 Jan Magnussen, DK (Dallara F394-Mugen Honda), 30m 33.68s, 98.163 mph/157.978 km/h.
2 Luiz Garcia Jr, BR (Dallara F394-Vauxhall), 30m 36.03s.
3 Dario Franchitti, GB (Dallara F394-Mugen Honda), 30m 36.35s.
4 Scott Lakin, GB (Dallara F393-Mugen Honda), 30m 43.15s.
5 Gareth Rees, GB (Dallara F394-Mugen Honda), 30m 44.50s.
6 Steven Arnold, GB (Dallara F394-Mugen Honda), 30m 57.42s.
7 Dino Morelli, GB (Dallara F394-Fiat), 31m 03.01s; 8 Brian Cunningham, USA (Dallara F394-Mugen Honda), 31m 03.33s; 9 Stephen Watson, ZA (Dallara F394-Mugen Honda), 31m 07.64s; 10 Ricardo Rosset, BR (Dallara F394-Mugen Honda), 31m 07.99s.
Fastest race lap: Garcia Jr, 1m 30.56s, 99.382 mph/159.939 km/h (record).
Class B winner: Duncan Vercoe, GB (Dallara F393-Vauxhall), 31m 42.81s.
Fastest qualifying lap: Magnussen, 1m 30.15s, 99.834 mph/160.667 km/h.
Championship points. Class A: 1= Franchitti, 32; 1= Magnussen, 32; 3 Lakin, 25; 4 Rees, 18; 5 Garcia Jr, 16; 6 Arnold, 14. **Class B:** 1 Vercoe, 42; 2 Hedley, 30; 3 Paul Dawson, GB, 22.

BRITISH FORMULA 3 CHAMPIONSHIP, Brands Hatch Indy Circuit, Dartford, Kent, Great Britain, 24 April. Round 3. 15 laps of the 1.204-mile/1.938-km circuit, 18.054 miles/29.055 km.
1 Jan Magnussen, DK (Dallara F394-Mugen Honda), 10m 49.23s, 100.109 mph/161.111 km/h.
2 Vincent Radermecker, B (Dallara F394-Mugen Honda), 10m 50.33s.
3 Gareth Rees, GB (Dallara F394-Mugen Honda), 10m 51.33s.
4 Jérémie Dufour, F (Dallara F394-Mugen Honda), 10m 51.89s.
5 Marcos Gueiros, BR (Dallara F394-Vauxhall), 10m 52.06s.
6 Ricardo Rosset, BR (Dallara F394-Mugen Honda), 10m 53.00s.
7 Jamie Spence, GB (Dallara F394-Mugen Honda), 10m 53.75s; 8 Warren Hughes, GB (Ralt 94C-TOM'S Toyota), 10m 57.02s; 9 Gualter Salles, BR (Dallara F394-Mugen Honda), 10m 59.87s; 10 Luiz Garcia Jr, BR (Dallara F394-Vauxhall), 11m 00.06s.
Fastest race lap: Magnussen, 42.48s, 102.000 mph/164.153 km/h.
Class B winner: Duncan Vercoe, GB (Dallara F393-Vauxhall), 11m 05.42s.
Fastest qualifying lap: Magnussen, 41.93s, 103.338 mph/166.306 km/h.

BRITISH FORMULA 3 CHAMPIONSHIP, Brands Hatch Indy Circuit, Dartford, Kent, Great Britain, 24 April. Round 4. 15 laps of the 1.204-mile/1.938-km circuit, 18.054 miles/29.055 km.
1 Vincent Radermecker, B (Dallara F394-Mugen Honda), 12m 52.20s, 84.168 mph/135.455 km/h.
2 Gareth Rees, GB (Dallara F394-Mugen Honda), 12m 52.78s.
3 Jérémie Dufour, F (Dallara F394-Mugen Honda), 12m 53.10s.
4 Jan Magnussen, DK (Dallara F394-Mugen Honda), 12m 53.26s.
5 Marcos Gueiros, BR (Dallara F394-Vauxhall), 12m 53.55s.
6 Jamie Spence, GB (Dallara F394-Mugen Honda), 12m 55.26s.
7 Brian Cunningham, USA (Dallara F394-Mugen Honda), 12m 56.12s; 8 Duncan Vercoe, GB (Dallara F393-Vauxhall), 12m 59.01s (1st Class B); 9 Pedro de la Rosa, E (Dallara F394-Renault), 13m 00.00s; 10 Ricardo Rosset, BR (Dallara F394-Mugen Honda), 13m 00.33s.
Fastest race lap: Dufour, 42.48s, 102.000 mph/164.153 km/h.
Pole position: Magnussen.
Championship points. Class A: 1 Magnussen, 63; 2 Rees, 45; 3 Radermecker, 42; 4 Franchitti, 32; 5 Dufour, 27; 6 Lakin, 25. **Class B:** 1 Vercoe, 84; 2 Hedley, 54; 3 Dawson, 40.

BRITISH FORMULA 3 CHAMPIONSHIP, Silverstone Club Circuit, Towcester, Northamptonshire, Great Britain, 2 May. Round 5. 12 laps of the 1.649-mile/2.654-km circuit, 19.788 miles/31.846 km.
1 Jan Magnussen, DK (Dallara F394-Mugen Honda), 11m 22.13s, 104.433 mph/168.068 km/h.
2 Vincent Radermecker, B (Dallara F394-Mugen Honda), 11m 22.64s.
3 Marcos Gueiros, BR (Dallara F394-Vauxhall), 11m 23.20s.
4 Scott Lakin, GB (Dallara F393-Mugen Honda), 11m 23.72s.
5 Dino Morelli, GB (Dallara F394-Fiat), 11m 25.48s.
6 Ricardo Rosset, BR (Dallara F394-Mugen Honda), 11m 26.59s.
7 Gareth Rees, GB (Dallara F394-Mugen Honda), 11m 28.37s; 8 Brian Cunningham, USA (Dallara F394-Mugen Honda), 11m 32.78s; 9 Luiz Garcia Jr, BR (Dallara F394-Vauxhall), 11m 34.20s; 10 Jamie Spence, GB (Dallara F394-Mugen Honda), 11m 38.61s.
Fastest race lap: Lakin, 55.91s, 106.178 mph/170.877 km/h.
Class B winner: Duncan Vercoe, GB (Dallara F393-Vauxhall), 11m 42.49s.
Fastest qualifying lap: Magnussen, 55.45s, 107.059 mph/172.294 km/h.

BRITISH FORMULA 3 CHAMPIONSHIP, Silverstone Club Circuit, Towcester, Northamptonshire, Great Britain, 2 May. Round 6. 12 laps of the 1.649-mile/2.654-km circuit, 19.788 miles/31.846 km.
1 Jan Magnussen, DK (Dallara F394-Mugen Honda), 11m 22.03s, 104.448 mph/168.093 km/h.
2 Scott Lakin, GB (Dallara F393-Mugen Honda), 11m 22.41s.
3 Vincent Radermecker, B (Dallara F394-Mugen Honda), 11m 22.88s.
4 Ricardo Rosset, BR (Dallara F394-Mugen Honda), 11m 23.29s.
5 Marcos Gueiros, BR (Dallara F394-Vauxhall), 11m 23.53s.
6 Dino Morelli, GB (Dallara F394-Fiat), 11m 25.69s.
7 Brian Cunningham, USA (Dallara F394-Mugen Honda), 11m 26.38s; 8 Jamie Spence, GB (Dallara F394-Mugen Honda), 11m 27.49s; 9 Gareth Rees, GB (Dallara F394-Mugen Honda), 11m 27.78s; 10 Dario Franchitti, GB (Dallara F394-Mugen Honda), 11m 28.43s.
Fastest race lap: Franchitti, 55.54s, 106.885 mph/172.015 km/h (record).
Class B winner: Duncan Vercoe, GB (Dallara F393-Vauxhall), 11m 30.89s.
Pole position: Magnussen.
Championship points. Class A: 1 Magnussen, 103; 2 Radermecker, 69; 3= Rees, 51; 3= Lakin, 51; 5 Gueiros, 39; 6 Franchitti, 34. **Class B:** 1 Vercoe, 126; 2 Hedley, 74; 3 Dawson, 64.

BRITISH FORMULA 3 CHAMPIONSHIP, Brands Hatch Grand Prix Circuit, Dartford, Kent, Great Britain, 8 May. Round 7. 17 laps of the 2.600-mile/4.184-km circuit, 44.200 miles/71.133 km.
1 Jan Magnussen, DK (Dallara F394-Mugen Honda), 23m 20.62s, 113.607 mph/182.832 km/h.
2 Dario Franchitti, GB (Dallara F394-Mugen Honda), 23m 20.73s.
3 Vincent Radermecker, B (Dallara F394-Mugen Honda), 23m 21.16s.
4 Marcos Gueiros, BR (Dallara F394-Vauxhall), 23m 21.60s.
5 Scott Lakin, GB (Dallara F393-Mugen Honda), 23m 27.00s.
6 Gareth Rees, GB (Dallara F394-Mugen Honda), 23m 27.29s.
7 Gualter Salles, BR (Dallara F394-Mugen Honda), 23m 29.09s; 8 Dino Morelli, GB (Dallara F394-Fiat), 23m 31.03s; 9 Brian Cunningham, USA (Dallara F394-Mugen Honda), 23m 34.52s; 10 Steven Arnold, GB (Dallara F393-Mugen Honda), 23m 35.42s.
Fastest race lap: Jérémie Dufour, F (Dallara F394-Mugen Honda), 1m 20.83s, 115.799 mph/186.360 km/h (record).
Class B winner: Piers Hunnisett, GB (Bowman BC4-Mugen Honda), 24m 13.08s.
Fastest qualifying lap: Lakin, 1m 20.56s, 116.187 mph/186.984 km/h.
Championship points. Class A: 1 Magnussen, 123; 2 Radermecker, 81; 3 Lakin, 59; 4 Rees, 57; 5= Gueiros, 49; 5= Franchitti, 49. **Class B:** 1 Vercoe, 126; 2 Hedley, 86; 3 Dawson, 64.

BRITISH FORMULA 3 CHAMPIONSHIP, Thruxton Circuit, Andover, Hampshire, Great Britain, 30 May. Round 8. 17 laps of the 2.356-mile/3.792-km circuit, 40.052 miles/64.457 km.
1 Jan Magnussen, DK (Dallara F394-Mugen Honda), 19m 59.40s, 120.216 mph/193.469 km/h.
2 Dario Franchitti, GB (Dallara F394-Mugen Honda), 20m 00.45s.
3 Gareth Rees, GB (Dallara F394-Mugen Honda), 20m 00.72s.
4 Scott Lakin, GB (Dallara F393-Mugen Honda), 20m 01.89s.
5 Jérémie Dufour, F (Dallara F394-Mugen Honda), 20m 02.32s.
6 Ricardo Rosset, BR (Dallara F394-Mugen Honda), 20m 09.45s.
7 Marcos Gueiros, BR (Dallara F394-Vauxhall), 20m 14.65s; 8 Gualter Salles, BR (Dallara F394-Mugen Honda), 20m 15.91s; 9 Stephen Watson, ZA (Dallara F394-Mugen Honda), 20m 17.54s; 10 Steven Arnold, GB (Dallara F393-Mugen Honda), 20m 23.60s.
Fastest race lap: Franchitti, 1m 09.57s, 121.915 mph/196.203 km/h (record).
Class B winner: Duncan Vercoe, GB (Dallara F393-Vauxhall), 20m 24.34s.
Fastest qualifying lap: Warren Hughes, GB (Dallara F394-Fiat), 1m 09.43s, 122.160 mph/196.598 km/h.
Championship points. Class A: 1 Magnussen, 143; 2 Radermecker, 81; 3= Lakin, 69; 3= Rees, 69; 5 Franchitti, 65; 6 Gueiros, 53. **Class B:** 1 Vercoe, 146; 2 Hedley, 98; 3 Steve Allen, GB, 66.

BRITISH FORMULA 3 CHAMPIONSHIP, Oulton Park Circuit, Tarporley, Cheshire, Great Britain, 4 June. Round 9, 15 laps of the 2.776-mile/4.468-km circuit, 41.640 miles/67.013 km.
1 Jan Magnussen, DK (Dallara F394-Mugen Honda), 25m 34.52s, 97.688 mph/157.213 km/h.
2 Gareth Rees, GB (Dallara F394-Mugen Honda), 25m 34.52s.
3 Jérémie Dufour, F (Dallara F394-Mugen Honda), 25m 34.97s.
4 Vincent Radermecker, B (Dallara F394-Mugen Honda), 25m 36.16s.
5 Ricardo Rosset, BR (Dallara F394-Mugen Honda), 25m 36.52s.
6 Jamie Spence, GB (Dallara F393-Fiat), 25m 36.75s.
7 Marc Gene, E (Dallara F394-HKS Mitsubishi), 25m 37.38s; 8 Dino Morelli, GB (Dallara F394-Fiat), 25m 37.77s; 9 Brian Cunningham, USA (Dallara F394-Mugen Honda), 25m 39.11s; 10 Luiz Garcia Jr, BR (Dallara F394-Vauxhall), 25m 39.46s.
Fastest race lap: Magnussen, 1m 33.68s, 106.678 mph/171.682 km/h (record).
Class B winner: Chris Clark, GB (Dallara F393-Fiat), 25m 47.23s.
Fastest qualifying lap: Magnussen, 1m 33.13s, 107.308 mph/172.696 km/h.
Championship points. Class A: 1 Magnussen, 164; 2 Radermecker, 91; 3 Rees, 84; 4 Lakin, 69; 5 Franchitti, 65; 6 Gueiros, 53. **Class B:** 1 Vercoe, 163; 2 Hedley, 110; 3 Clark, 80.

BRITISH FORMULA 3 CHAMPIONSHIP, Donington Park Grand Prix Circuit, Derbyshire, Great Britain, 25 June. Round 10. 17 laps of the 2.500-mile/4.023-km circuit, 42.500 miles/68.397 km.
1 Jan Magnussen, DK (Dallara F394-Mugen Honda), 25m 54.91s, 98.398 mph/158.356 km/h.
2 Gareth Rees, GB (Dallara F394-Mugen Honda), 25m 55.55s.
3 Dario Franchitti, GB (Dallara F394-Mugen Honda), 25m 56.07s.
4 Marcos Gueiros, BR (Dallara F394-Vauxhall), 25m 56.52s.
5 Ricardo Rosset, BR (Dallara F394-Mugen Honda), 25m 59.54s.
6 Vincent Radermecker, B (Dallara F394-Mugen Honda), 26m 00.61s.
7 Jérémie Dufour, F (Dallara F394-Mugen Honda), 26m 01.08s; 8 Luiz Garcia Jr, BR (Dallara F394-Vauxhall), 26m 10.99s; 9 Brian Cunningham, USA (Dallara F394-Mugen Honda), 26m 18.97s; 10 Jamie Spence, GB (Dallara F394-Fiat), 26m 23.50s.
Fastest race lap: Rosset, 1m 30.80s, 99.119 mph/159.516 km/h.
Class B winner: Duncan Vercoe, GB (Dallara F393-Vauxhall), 27m 09.53s.
Steve Allen, GB (Dallara F393-Mugen Honda) finished first in Class B in 27m 06.52s, but was disqualified due to car being underweight.
Fastest qualifying lap: Magnussen, 1m 30.04s, 99.956 mph/160.863 km/h.
Championship points. Class A: 1 Magnussen, 184; 2 Rees, 99; 3 Radermecker, 97; 4 Franchitti, 77; 5 Lakin, 69; 6 Gueiros, 63. **Class B:** 1 Vercoe, 184; 2 Hedley, 125; 3 Dawson, 86.

BRITISH FORMULA 3 CHAMPIONSHIP, Silverstone Grand Prix Circuit, Towcester, Northamptonshire, Great Britain, 9 July. Round 11. 15 laps of the 3.142-mile/5.057-km circuit, 47.130 miles/75.848 km.
1 Vincent Radermecker, B (Dallara F394-Mugen Honda), 27m 15.44s, 103.745 mph/166.961 km/h.
2 Jérémie Dufour, F (Dallara F394-Mugen Honda), 27m 16.20s.
3 Gareth Rees, GB (Dallara F394-Mugen Honda), 27m 22.74s.
4 Giancarlo Fisichella, I (Dallara F393-Opel), 27m 23.16s.
5 Marcos Gueiros, BR (Dallara F394-Vauxhall), 27m 28.08s.
6 Dario Franchitti, GB (Dallara F394-Mugen Honda), 27m 29.02s.
7 Jan Magnussen, DK (Dallara F394-Mugen Honda), 27m 29.47s; 8 Luiz Garcia Jr, BR (Dallara F394-Vauxhall), 27m 38.62s; 9 Steven Arnold, GB (Dallara F394-Mugen Honda), 27m 46.92s; 10 Christian Horner, GB (Dallara F394-Mugen Honda), 27m 49.19s.
Fastest race lap: Dufour, 1m 47.89s, 104.840 mph/168.724 km/h.
Class B winner: Duncan Vercoe, GB (Dallara F393-Vauxhall), 27m 56.49s.
Fastest qualifying lap: Radermecker, 1m 46.69s, 106.019 mph/170.622 km/h.
Championship points. Class A: 1 Magnussen, 188; 2 Radermecker, 117; 3 Rees, 111; 4 Franchitti, 83; 5 Gueiros, 71; 6 Lakin, 69. **Class B:** 1 Vercoe, 184; 2 Hedley, 125; 3 Dawson, 86.

BRITISH FORMULA 3 CHAMPIONSHIP, Snetterton Circuit, Norfolk, Great Britain, 24 July. Round 12. 25 laps of the 1.952-mile/3.141-km circuit, 48.800 miles/78.537 km.
1 Ricardo Rosset, BR (Dallara F394-Mugen Honda), 28m 31.74s, 102.632 mph/165.171 km/h.
2 Vincent Radermecker, B (Dallara F394-Mugen Honda), 28m 32.32s.
3 Gualter Salles, BR (Dallara F394-Mugen Honda), 28m 33.73s.
4 Marcos Gueiros, BR (Dallara F394-Vauxhall), 28m 34.38s.
5 Jérémie Dufour, F (Dallara F394-Mugen Honda), 28m 36.03s.
6 Steven Arnold, GB (Dallara F394-Mugen Honda), 28m 46.83s.
7 Jamie Spence, GB (Dallara F394-Fiat), 28m 49.83s; 8 Marc Gene, E (Dallara F394-HKS Mitsubishi), 28m 52.28s; 9 Luiz Garcia Jr, BR (Dallara F394-Vauxhall), 28m 53.83s; 10 Dario Franchitti, GB (Dallara F394-Mugen Honda), 28m 54.22s.
Fastest race lap: Rosset, 1m 07.28s, 104.447 mph/168.091 km/h.
Class B winner: Gray Hedley, GB (Dallara F393-Mugen Honda), 24 laps.
Fastest qualifying lap: Rosset, 1m 06.08s, 106.344 mph/171.144 km/h.
Championship points. Class A: 1 Magnussen, 188; 2 Radermecker, 132; 3 Rees, 111; 4 Franchitti, 84; 5 Gueiros, 81; 6 Dufour, 76. **Class B:** 1 Vercoe, 205; 2 Hedley, 155; 3 Dawson, 110.

BRITISH FORMULA 3 CHAMPIONSHIP, Pembrey Circuit, Llanelli, Great Britain, 21 August. Round 13. 17 laps of the 1.456-mile/2.343-km circuit, 24.752 miles/39.834 km.
1 Jan Magnussen, DK (Dallara F394-Mugen Honda), 15m 11.52s, 97.757 mph/157.324 km/h.
2 Vincent Radermecker, B (Dallara F394-Mugen Honda), 15m 11.72s.
3 Dario Franchitti, GB (Dallara F394-Mugen Honda), 15m 13.87s.
4 Ricardo Rosset, BR (Dallara F394-Mugen Honda), 15m 16.20s.
5 Gareth Rees, GB (Dallara F394-Mugen Honda), 15m 16.63s.
6 Christian Horner, GB (Dallara F394-Mugen Honda), 15m 22.00s.
7 Dino Morelli, GB (Dallara F394-Fiat), 15m 22.36s; 8 Gualter Salles, BR (Dallara F394-Mugen Honda), 15m 23.86s; 9 Duncan Vercoe, GB (Dallara F393-Vauxhall), 15m 25.93s (1st Class B); 10 Marc Gene, E (Dallara F394-HKS Mitsubishi), 15m 26.55s.
Fastest race lap: Franchitti, 52.88s, 99.123 mph/159.522 km/h.
Fastest qualifying lap: Radermecker, 52.02s, 100.761 mph/162.160 km/h.

BRITISH FORMULA 3 CHAMPIONSHIP, Pembrey Circuit, Llanelli, Great Britain, 21 August. Round 14. 20 laps of the 1.456-mile/2.343-km circuit, 29.120 miles/46.864 km.
1 Jan Magnussen, DK (Dallara F394-Mugen Honda), 17m 52.19s, 97.774 mph/157.352 km/h.
2 Dario Franchitti, GB (Dallara F394-Mugen Honda), 17m 53.04s.
3 Ricardo Rosset, BR (Dallara F394-Mugen Honda), 17m 53.55s.
4 Gareth Rees, GB (Dallara F394-Mugen Honda), 17m 54.54s.
5 Vincent Radermecker, B (Dallara F394-Mugen Honda), 17m 58.94s.
6 Dino Morelli, GB (Dallara F394-Fiat), 18m 00.39s.
7 Gualter Salles, BR (Dallara F394-Mugen Honda), 18m 01.35s; 8 Duncan Vercoe, GB (Dallara F393-Vauxhall), 18m 01.79s (1st Class B); 9 Christian Horner, GB (Dallara F394-Mugen Honda), 18m 02.59s; 10 Marc Gene, E (Dallara F394-HKS Mitsubishi), 18m 03.33s.
Fastest race lap: Radermecker, 52.97s, 98.954 mph/159.251 km/h.
Pole position: Magnussen.
Championship points. Class A: 1 Magnussen, 228; 2 Radermecker, 156; 3 Rees, 129; 4 Franchitti, 112; 5 Rosset, 92; 6 Gueiros, 82. **Class B:** 1 Vercoe, 247; 2 Hedley, 167; 3 Dawson, 135.

BRITISH FORMULA 3 CHAMPIONSHIP, Silverstone Club Circuit, Towcester, Northamptonshire, Great Britain, 29 August. Round 15. 15 laps of the 1.642-mile/2.643-km circuit, 24.630 miles/39.638 km.
1 Jan Magnussen, DK (Dallara F394-Mugen Honda), 14m 24.69s, 102.543 mph/165.027 km/h.
2 Marcos Gueiros, BR (Dallara F394-Vauxhall), 14m 26.64s.
3 Ricardo Rosset, BR (Dallara F394-Mugen Honda), 14m 27.26s.
4 Jérémie Dufour, F (Dallara F394-Mugen Honda), 14m 27.87s.
5 Gareth Rees, GB (Dallara F394-Mugen Honda), 14m 30.65s.
6 Vincent Radermecker, B (Dallara F394-Mugen Honda), 14m 31.24s.
7 Gualter Salles, BR (Dallara F394-Mugen Honda), 14m 34.60s; 8 Dino Morelli, GB (Dallara F394-Fiat), 14m 35.99s; 9 Luiz Garcia Jr, BR (Dallara F394-Vauxhall), 14m 36.48s; 10 Marc Gene, E (Dallara F394-HKS Mitsubishi), 14m 43.64s.
Fastest race lap: Rees, 56.73s, 104.199 mph/167.692 km/h.
Class B winner: Duncan Vercoe, GB (Dallara F393-Vauxhall), 14m 46.39s.
Fastest qualifying lap: Magnussen, 56.23s, 105.125 mph/169.183 km/h.

BRITISH FORMULA 3 CHAMPIONSHIP, Silverstone Club Circuit, Towcester, Northamptonshire, Great Britain, 29 August. Round 16. 15 laps of the 1.642-mile/2.643-km circuit, 24.630 miles/39.638 km.
1 Jan Magnussen, DK (Dallara F394-Mugen Honda), 14m 24.99s, 102.508 mph/164.970 km/h.
2 Ricardo Rosset, BR (Dallara F394-Mugen Honda), 14m 27.18s.
3 Gareth Rees, GB (Dallara F394-Mugen Honda), 14m 28.00s.
4 Dino Morelli, GB (Dallara F394-Fiat), 14m 29.72s.
5 Marcos Gueiros, BR (Dallara F394-Vauxhall), 14m 30.07s.
6 Vincent Radermecker, B (Dallara F394-Mugen Honda), 14m 30.62s.
7 Jérémie Dufour, F (Dallara F394-Mugen Honda), 14m 31.11s; 8 Dario Franchitti, GB (Dallara F394-Mugen Honda), 14m 35.41s; 9 Marc Gene, E (Dallara F394-HKS Mitsubishi), 14m 35.96s; 10 Luiz Garcia Jr, BR (Dallara F394-Vauxhall), 14m 42.75s.
Fastest race lap: Dufour, 56.70s, 104.199 mph/167.692 km/h.
Class B winner: Duncan Vercoe, GB (Dallara F393-Vauxhall), 14m 46.60s.
Pole position: Magnussen.
Championship points. Class A: 1 Magnussen, 268; 2 Radermecker, 168; 3 Rees, 150; 4 Rosset, 119; 5 Franchitti, 115; 6 Gueiros, 105. **Class B:** 1 Vercoe, 289; 2 Hedley, 187; 3 Dawson, 135.

BRITISH FORMULA 3 CHAMPIONSHIP, Thruxton Circuit, Andover, Hampshire, Great Britain, 11 September. Round 17. 20 laps of the 2.356-mile/3.792-km circuit, 47.120 miles/75.832 km.
1 Jan Magnussen, DK (Dallara F394-Mugen Honda), 23m 43.47s, 119.168 mph/191.782 km/h.
2 Vincent Radermecker, B (Dallara F394-Mugen Honda), 23m 44.36s.
3 Ricardo Rosset, BR (Dallara F394-Mugen Honda), 23m 44.67s.
4 Jérémie Dufour, F (Dallara F394-Mugen Honda), 23m 45.13s.
5 Dario Franchitti, GB (Dallara F394-Mugen Honda), 23m 48.13s.
6 Gareth Rees, GB (Dallara F394-Mugen Honda), 23m 49.46s.
7 Dino Morelli, GB (Dallara F394-Fiat), 23m 56.59s; 8 Luiz Garcia Jr, BR (Dallara F394-Vauxhall), 23m 57.81s; 9 Marcos Gueiros, BR (Dallara F394-Vauxhall), 23m 57.95s; 10 Marc Gene, E (Dallara F394-HKS Mitsubishi), 24m 03.47s.
Fastest race lap: Dufour, 1m 10.18s, 120.855 mph/194.497 km/h.

Class B winner: Thomas Erdos, BR (Dallara F393-Vauxhall), 24m 10.41s.
Fastest qualifying lap: Radermecker, 1m 09.83s, 121.461 mph/195.472 km/h.
Championship points. Class A: 1 Magnussen, 288; **2** Radermecker, 183; **3** Rees, 156; **4** Rosset, 131; **5** Franchitti, 123; **6** Gueiros, 107. **Class B: 1** Vercoe, 289; **2** Hedley, 202; **3** Dawson, 145.

BRITISH FORMULA 3 CHAMPIONSHIP, Silverstone Grand Prix Circuit, Towcester, Northamptonshire, Great Britain, 2 October. Round 18. 12 laps of the 3.142-mile/5.057-km circuit, 37.704 miles/60.679 km.
1 Jan Magnussen, DK (Dallara F394-Mugen Honda), 26m 03.08s, 86.838 mph/139.752 km/h.
2 Gareth Rees, GB (Dallara F394-Mugen Honda), 26m 07.03s.
3 Dino Morelli, GB (Dallara F394-Fiat), 26m 17.65s.
4 Dario Franchitti, GB (Dallara F394-Mugen Honda), 26m 19.56s.
5 Brian Cunningham, USA (Dallara F394-Mugen Honda), 26m 34.03s.
6 Gualter Salles, BR (Dallara F394-Mugen Honda), 26m 38.00s.
7 Marc Gene, E (Dallara F394-HKS Mitsubishi), 26m 38.28s; **8** Pedro de la Rosa, E (Dallara F394-Renault), 26m 42.61s; **9** Stephen Watson, ZA (Dallara F394-Mugen Honda), 26m 44.38s; **10** Fabiano Belletti, I (Dallara F393-Mugen Honda), 26m 52.88s.
Fastest race lap: Jérémie Dufour, F (Dallara F394-Mugen Honda), 2m 07.22s, 88.911 mph/143.088 km/h.
Class B winner: Thomas Erdos, BR (Dallara F393-Fiat), 27m 05.41s.
Fastest qualifying lap: Vincent Radermecker, B (Dallara F394-Mugen Honda), 1m 51.54s, 101.409 mph/163.203 km/h.

Final championship points
Class A

1	Jan Magnussen, DK	308
2	Vincent Radermecker, B	183
3	Gareth Rees, GB	171
4	Dario Franchitti, GB	133
5	Ricardo Rosset, BR	132
6	Marcos Gueiros, BR	107

7 Jérémie Dufour, F, 103; **8** Scott Lakin, GB, 69; **9** Dino Morelli, GB, 63; **10** Gualter Salles, BR, 39; **11** Luiz Garcia Jr, BR, 34; **12** Brian Cunningham, USA, 29; **13** Jamie Spence, GB, 25; **14** Steven Arnold, GB, 24; **15** Marc Gene, E, 19; **16=** Christian Horner, GB, 10; **16=** Giancarlo Fisichella, I, 10; **18** Stephen Watson, ZA, 7; **19** Pedro de la Rosa, E, 6; **20** Warren Hughes, GB, 3; **21** Fabiano Belletti, I, 1.

Class B

1	Duncan Vercoe, GB	289
2	Gray Hedley, GB	202
3	Paul Dawson, GB	145
4	Steve Allen, GB	113
5	Chris Clark, GB	80
6	Johnny Mowlem, GB	45

7 Thomas Erdos, BR, 41; **8** Zak Brown, USA, 39; **9** Nigel Greensall, GB, 27; **10** Piers Hunnisett, GB, 21; **11** Alex Postan, GB, **16**; **12** David Campana, I, 15; **13** Jean Clermont, CDN, 12; **14=** Tim Pearson, GB, 8; **14=** Costas Lazarakis, GR, 8; **16** Jonathan Williams, GB, 6; **17** Bobby Verdon-Roe, GB, 1.

French Formula 3 Championship

COUPES DE PAQUES, Circuit Automobile Paul Armagnac, Nogaro, France, 3 April. Round 1. 21 laps of the 2.259-mile/3.636-km circuit, 47.445 miles/76.356 km.
1 David Dussau, F (Dallara F393-Opel), 35m 08.64s, 81.002 mph/130.360 km/h.
2 Christophe Tinseau, F (Dallara F393-Opel), 35m 10.50s.
3 Jean-Philippe Belloc, F (Dallara F393-Fiat), 35m 35.49s.
4 Alexandre Janoray, F (Dallara F393-Opel), 35m 37.56s.
5 Jesse Bouhet, F (Dallara F393-Fiat), 35m 52.91s.
6 Nicolas Minassian, F (Dallara F393-Fiat), 36m 12.52s.
7 Benjamin Roy, F (Dallara F393-Fiat), 36m 13.44s; **8** Thierry Glas, F (Dallara F393-Fiat), 36m 46.83s; **9** Eric Alberto, F (Dallara F393-Opel), 36m 56.41s; **10** Laurent Redon, F (Dallara F393-Fiat), 20 laps.
Fastest race lap: Dussau, 1m 38.91s, 82.231 mph/132.338 km/h.
Championship points: 1 Dussau, 16; **2** Tinseau, 12; **3** Belloc, 10; **4** Janoray, 8; **5** Bouhet, 6; **6** Minassian, 5.

COUPES DE PRINTEMPS, Circuit de Ledènon, Nimes, France, 17 April. Round 2. 24 laps of the 1.957-mile/3.150-km circuit, 46.976 miles/75.600 km.
1 Jean-Philippe Belloc, F (Dallara F393-Fiat), 32m 36.02s, 86.457 mph/139.139 km/h.
2 Alexandre Janoray, F (Dallara F393-Opel), 32m 40.87s.
3 David Dussau, F (Dallara F393-Opel), 32m 42.48s.
4 Jean-Claude de Castelli, F (Dallara F393-Seymaz Honda), 32m 54.02s.
5 Laurent Pareyre, F (Dallara F393-Opel), 32m 55.01s.
6 Eric Alberto, F (Dallara F393-Opel), 33m 06.11s.
7 Nicolas Minassian, F (Dallara F393-Fiat), 33m 06.33s; **8** Laurent Redon, F (Dallara F393-Fiat), 33m 17.45s; **9** Steeve Hiesse, F (Dallara F393-Fiat), 33m 18.02s; **10** Thierry Glas, F (Dallara F393-Fiat), 33m 39.49s.
Fastest race lap: Belloc, 1m 20.52s, 87.510 mph/140.834 km/h.
Championship points: 1= Dussau, 26; **1 =** Belloc, 26; **3** Janoray, 20; **4** Tinseau, 12; **5** Minassian, 9; **6** de Castelli, 8.

FRENCH FORMULA 3 CHAMPIONSHIP, Circuit de Pau, France, 22 May. Round 3. 28 laps of the 1.715-mile/2.760-km circuit, 48.020 miles/77.280 km.
1 Christophe Tinseau, F (Dallara F393-Opel), 35m 43.55s, 80.647 mph/129.788 km/h.
2 Jean-Claude de Castelli, F (Dallara F393-Seymaz Honda), 35m 46.54s.
3 David Dussau, F (Dallara F393-Opel), 35m 47.43s.
4 Jean-Philippe Belloc, F (Dallara F393-Fiat), 36m 10.78s.
5 Alexandre Janoray, F (Dallara F393-Opel), 36m 18.70s.
6 Jesse Bouhet, F (Dallara F393-Fiat), 36m 19.89s.
7 Laurent Redon, F (Dallara F393-Fiat), 36m 34.16s; **8** Eric Alberto, F (Dallara F393-Opel), 36m 40.86s; **9** Benjamin Roy, F (Dallara F393-Fiat), 36m 43.51s; **10** Jean-Bernard Bouvet, F (Dallara F392-Volkswagen), 36m 54.26s.
Fastest race lap: Tinseau, 1m 15.41s, 81.872 mph/131.760 km/h.
Championship points: 1 Dussau, 36; **2** Belloc, 34; **3** Tinseau, 28; **4** Janoray, 26; **5** de Castelli, 20; **6** Bouhet, 11.

GRAND PRIX DIJON-BOURGOGNE, Circuit de Dijon-Prenois, Fontaine-les-Dijon, France, 5 June. Round 4. 20 laps of the 2.361-mile/3.800-km circuit, 47.224 miles/76.000 km.
1 Jean-Claude de Castelli, F (Dallara F393-Seymaz Honda), 25m 16.91s, 112.075 mph/180.367 km/h.
2 Alexandre Janoray, F (Dallara F393-Opel), 25m 17.50s.
3 Laurent Pareyre, F (Dallara F393-Opel), 25m 30.52s.
4 Jesse Bouhet, F (Dallara F393-Fiat), 25m 34.56s.
5 David Dussau, F (Martini MK67-Opel), 25m 38.71s.
6 Jean-Philippe Belloc, F (Dallara F393-Fiat), 25m 40.50s.
7 Christophe Tinseau, F (Dallara F393-Opel), 25m 41.70s; **8** Steeve Hiesse, F (Dallara F393-Fiat), 25m 42.09s; **9** Nicolas Minassian, F (Dallara F393-Fiat), 25m 49.21s; **10** Benjamin Roy, F (Dallara F393-Fiat), 25m 52.98s.
Fastest race lap: Tinseau, 1m 14.89s, 113.505 mph/182.668 km/h.
Championship points: 1 Dussau, 42; **2** Belloc, 39; **3** Janoray, 38; **4** de Castelli, 35; **5** Tinseau, 33; **6** Bouhet, 19.

FRENCH FORMULA 3 CHAMPIONSHIP, Circuit du Val de Vienne, Le Vigeant, France, 26 June. Round 5. 24 laps of the 2.334-mile/3.757km circuit, 56.028 miles/90.168 km.
1 Jean-Philippe Belloc, F (Dallara F393-Fiat), 39m 17.37s, 85.561 mph/137.698 km/h.
2 David Dussau, F (Dallara F393-Opel), 39m 18.62s.
3 Elton Julian, USA (Dallara F393-Opel), 39m 26.21s.
4 Christophe Tinseau, F (Dallara F393-Opel), 39m 36.06s.
5 Claude Dégremont, F (Elise-Fiat), 39m 36.53s.
6 Jesse Bouhet, F (Dallara F393-Fiat), 39m 37.12s.
7 Laurent Redon, F (Dallara F393-Fiat), 39m 44.45s; **8** Laurent Pareyre, F (Dallara F393-Opel), 39m 56.98s; **9** Steeve Hiesse, F (Dallara F393-Fiat), 40m 02.94s; **10** Philippe Sinault, F (Dallara F393-Fiat), 40m 05.53s.
Fastest race lap: Dussau, 1m 37.16s, 86.498 mph/139.205 km/h.
Championship points: 1 Dussau, 55; **2** Belloc, 54; **3** Tinseau, 41; **4** Janoray, 38; **5** de Castelli, 35; **6** Bouhet, 24.

TROPHEES JEAN BERNIGAUD, Circuit de Nevers, Magny-Cours, France, 3 July. Round 6. 21 laps of the 2.641-mile/4.250-km circuit, 55.457 miles/89.250 km.
1 Jean-Philippe Belloc, F (Dallara F393-Fiat), 34m 34.08s, 96.258 mph/154.912 km/h.
2 Christophe Tinseau, F (Dallara F393-Opel), 34m 34.79s.
3 David Dussau, F (Dallara F393-Opel), 34m 38.75s.
4 Alexandre Janoray, F (Dallara F393-Opel), 34m 53.16s.
5 Elton Julian, USA (Dallara F393-Fiat), 35m 01.15s.
6 Nicolas Minassian, F (Dallara F393-Fiat), 35m 01.89s.
7 Jean-Claude de Castelli, F (Dallara F393-Seymaz Honda), 35m 11.93s; **8** Laurent Redon, F (Dallara F393-Fiat), 35m 13.22s; **9** Eric Alberto, F (Dallara F393-Opel), 35m 16.48s; **10** Benjamin Roy, F (Dallara F393-Fiat), 35m 19.58s.
Fastest race lap: Janoray, 1m 37.32s, 97.688 mph/157.213 km/h.
Championship points: 1 Belloc, 69; **2** Dussau, 65; **3** Tinseau, 53; **4** Janoray, 47; **5** de Castelli, 39; **6** Bouhet, 24.

FRENCH FORMULA 3 CHAMPIONSHIP, Circuit Croix-en-Ternois, France, 17 July. Round 7. 40 laps of the 1.181-mile/1.900-km circuit, 47.224 miles/76.000 km.
1 Christophe Tinseau, F (Dallara F393-Opel), 34m 27.67s, 82.222 mph/132.323 km/h.
2 Jean-Claude de Castelli, F (Dallara F393-Seymaz Honda), 34m 32.25s.
3 Jean-Philippe Belloc, F (Dallara F393-Fiat), 34m 32.90s.
4 Nicolas Minassian, F (Dallara F393-Fiat), 34m 46.40s.
5 Benjamin Roy, F (Dallara F393-Fiat), 34m 53.35s.
6 Laurent Pareyre, F (Dallara F393-Opel), 34m 54.02s.
7 Franck Guibbert, F (Dallara F393-Fiat), 34m 54.64s; **8** Alexandre Janoray, F (Dallara F393-Opel), 34m 55.24s; **9** Jesse Bouhet, F (Dallara F393-Fiat), 34m 57.46s; **10** Laurent Redon, F (Dallara F393-Fiat), 34m 57.73s.
Fastest race lap: Tinseau, 51.03s, 83.288 mph/134.039 km/h.
Championship points: 1 Belloc, 79; **2** Tinseau, 69; **3** Dussau, 65; **4** de Castelli, 51; **5** Janoray, 50; **6** Bouhet, 26.

FRENCH FORMULA 3 CHAMPIONSHIP, Circuit ASA Paul Ricard, Le Beausset, France, 24 July. Round 8. 22 laps of the 2.361-mile/3.800-km circuit, 51.947 miles/83.600 km.
1 Jean-Philippe Belloc, F (Dallara F393-Fiat), 30m 16.79s, 102.933 mph/165.655 km/h.
2 Christophe Tinseau, F (Dallara F393-Opel), 30m 21.99s.
3 David Dussau, F (Dallara F393-Opel), 30m 23.56s.
4 Laurent Redon, F (Dallara F393-Fiat), 30m 24.76s.
5 Jesse Bouhet, F (Dallara F393-Fiat), 30m 26.78s.
6 Benjamin Roy, F (Dallara F393-Fiat), 30m 31.52s.
7 Nicolas Minassian, F (Dallara F393-Fiat), 30m 33.17s; **8** Jean-Claude de Castelli, F (Dallara F393-Seymaz Honda), 30m 38.35s; **9** Eric Alberto, F (Dallara F393-Opel), 30m 38.84s; **10** Alexandre Janoray, F (Dallara F393-Opel), 30m 39.21s.
Fastest race lap: Belloc, 1m 22.02s, 103.638 mph/166.789 km/h.
Championship points: 1 Belloc, 95; **2** Tinseau, 81; **3** Dussau, 75; **4** de Castelli, 54; **5** Janoray, 51; **6** Bouhet, 32.

52nd GRAND PRIX D'ALBI, Circuit d'Albi, France, 4 September. Round 9. 23 laps of the 2.206-mile/3.551-km circuit, 50.749 miles/81.673 km.
1 Christophe Tinseau, F (Dallara F393-Opel), 27m 47.67s, 109.552 mph/176.307 km/h.
2 Nicolas Minassian, F (Dallara F393-Fiat), 27m 48.51s.
3 Jean-Philippe Belloc, F (Dallara F393-Fiat), 27m 58.68s.
4 Steeve Hiesse, F (Dallara F393-Fiat), 27m 59.76s.
5 David Dussau, F (Dallara F393-Opel), 28m 14.32s.
6 Franck Guibbert, F (Dallara F393-Fiat), 28m 18.55s.
7 Didier Andre, F (Dallara F393-Fiat), 28m 33.10s; **8** Laurent Pareyre, F (Dallara F393-Opel); **9** Philippe Sinault, F (Dallara F393-Fiat), 23m 39.79s; **10** Claude Dégremont, F (Elise-Fiat), 28m 57.14s.
Fastest race lap: Minassian, 1m 11.57s, 110.987 mph/178.616 km/h.
Championship points: 1 Belloc, 105; **2** Tinseau, 96; **3** Dussau, 81; **4** de Castelli, 54; **5** Janoray, 51; **6** Minassian 41.

COUPES D'AUTOMNE, Circuit Le Mans-Bugatti, France, 18 September. Round 10. 17 laps of the 2.753-mile/4.430-km circuit, 46.795 miles/75.310 km.
1 Alexandre Janoray, F (Dallara F393-Opel), 28m 36.45s, 98.146 mph/157.951 km/h.
2 Jean-Philippe Belloc, F (Dallara F393-Fiat), 28m 41.03s.
3 Christophe Tinseau, F (Dallara F393-Opel), 28m 41.49s.
4 Jean-Claude de Castelli, F (Dallara F393-Seymaz Honda), 28m 46.29s.
5 David Dussau, F (Dallara F393-Opel), 28m 53.81s.
6 Franck Guibbert, F (Dallara F393-Fiat), 28m 54.53s.
7 James Ruffier, F (Dallara F393-Fiat), 28m 55.18s; **8** Nicolas Minassian, F (Dallara F393-Fiat), 28m 55.51s; **9** Laurent Pareyre, F (Dallara F393-Opel), 28m 56.28s; **10** Laurent Redon, F (Dallara F393-Fiat), 29m 07.78s.
Fastest race lap: Janoray, 1m 39.49s, 99.604 mph/160.297 km/h.
Championship points: 1 Belloc, 117; **2** Tinseau, 106; **3** Dussau, 87; **4** Janoray, 67; **5** de Castelli, 62; **6** Minassian, 44.

FRENCH FORMULA 3 CHAMPIONSHIP, Circuit de Nevers, Magny-Cours, France, 2 October. Round 11. 21 laps of the 2.641-mile/4.250-km circuit, 55.457 miles/89.250 km.
1 Jean-Philippe Belloc, F (Dallara F393-Fiat), 33m 46.22s, 98.532 mph/158.571 km/h.
2 Christophe Tinseau, F (Dallara F393-Opel), 33m 47.93s.
3 Alexandre Janoray, F (Dallara F393-Opel), 33m 53.07s.
4 Jean-Claude de Castelli, F (Dallara F393-Seymaz Honda), 33m 58.30s.
5 David Dussau, F (Dallara F393-Opel), 33m 58.65s.
6 Laurent Pareyre, F (Dallara F393-Opel), 34m 07.59s.
7 Nicolas Minassian, F (Dallara F393-Fiat), 34m 13.85s; **8** Franck Guibbert, F (Dallara F393-Fiat), 34m 19.96s; **9** Steeve Hiesse, F (Dallara F393-Fiat), 34m 27.69s; **10** Jean-Bernard Bouvet, F (Dallara F393-Volkswagen), 34m 38.59s.
Fastest race lap: Belloc, 1m 35.94s, 99.093 mph/159.475 km/h.

Final championship points (best 9 results)

1	Jean-Philippe Belloc, F	120 (133)
2	Christophe Tinseau, F	113 (118)
3	David Dussau, F	87 (93)
4	Alexandre Janoray, F	77
5	Jean-Claude de Castelli, F	70
6	Nicolas Minassian, F	48

7 Laurent Pareyre, F, 34; **8** Jesse Bouhet, F, 32; **9** Laurent Redon, F, 25; **10** Benjamin Roy, F, 19; **11=** Steeve Hiesse, F, 17; **11=** Franck Guibbert, F, 17; **13** Elton Julian, USA, 16; **14** Eric Alberto, F, 14; **15** Claude Dégremont, F, 7; **16=** Didier Andre, F, 4; **16=** Thierry Glas, F, 4; **16=** James Ruffier, F, 4; **19** Philippe Sinault, F, 3; **20** Jean-Bernard Bouvet, F, 2.

German Formula 3 Championship

GERMAN FORMULA 3 CHAMPIONSHIP, Omloop van Zolder, Hasselt, Belgium, 9 April. Round 1. 15 laps of the 2.606-mile/4.194-km circuit, 39.090 miles/62.910 km.
1 Jörg Müller, D (Dallara F394-Fiat), 23m 48.18s, 98.535 mph/158.577 km/h.
2 Sascha Maassen, D (Dallara F394-Opel), 23m 54.84s.
3 Ralf Schumacher, D (Dallara F394-Opel), 23m 55.66s.
4 Alexander Wurz, A (Dallara F394-Opel), 23m 57.11s.
5 Pedro Couceiro, P (Dallara F394-Opel), 23m 57.46s.
6 Christian Abt, D (Dallara F394-Opel), 24m 03.96s.
7 Andreas Reiter, A (Dallara F394-Fiat), 24m 04.98s; **8** Frederico Viegas, P (Dallara F394-Opel), 24m 08.14s; **9** Olivier Tichy, A (Dallara F393-Volkswagen), 24m 10.24s (1st Class II); **10** Christian Menzel, D (Dallara F393-Opel), 24m 10.66s.
Fastest race lap: Maassen, 1m 34.13s, 99.668 mph/160.399 km/h.
Championship points: 1 Müller, 20; **2** Maassen, 15; **3** Schumacher, 12; **4** Wurz, 10; **5** Couceiro, 8; **6** Abt, 6.

GERMAN FORMULA 3 CHAMPIONSHIP, Hockenheimring, Heidelberg, Germany, 23 April. Round 2. 23 laps of the 1.639-mile/2.638-km circuit, 37.701 miles/60.674 km.
1 Alexander Wurz, A (Dallara F394-Opel), 23m 22.11s, 96.800 mph/155.784 km/h.
2 Pedro Couceiro, P (Dallara F394-Opel), 23m 23.32s.
3 Ralf Schumacher, D (Dallara F394-Opel), 23m 26.53s.
4 Jörg Müller, D (Dallara F394-Fiat), 23m 30.27s.
5 Philipp Peter, A (Dallara F394-Fiat), 23m 32.50s.
6 Johnny Hauser, CH (Dallara F394-Mugen Honda), 23m 32.91s.
7 Andreas Reiter, A (Dallara F394-Fiat), 23m 33.87s; **8** Roberto Colciago, I (Dallara F394-Fiat), 23m 34.88s; **9** Frederico Viegas, P (Dallara F394-Opel), 23m 35.51s; **10** Christian Abt, D (Dallara F394-Opel), 23m 38.83s.
Fastest race lap: Sascha Maassen, D (Dallara F394-Opel), 59.85s, 98.597 mph/158.677 km/h.
Class II winner: Olivier Tichy, A (Dallara F393-Volkswagen), 23m 47.00s.

GERMAN FORMULA 3 CHAMPIONSHIP, Hockenheimring, Heidelberg, Germany, 24 April. Round 3. 23 laps of the 1.639-mile/2.638-km circuit, 37.701 miles/60.674 km.
1 Alexander Wurz, A (Dallara F394-Opel), 23m 23.19s, 96.725 mph/155.664 km/h.
2 Pedro Couceiro, P (Dallara F394-Opel), 23m 27.75s.
3 Jörg Müller, D (Dallara F394-Fiat), 23m 28.29s.
4 Philipp Peter, A (Dallara F394-Fiat), 23m 30.48s.
5 Roberto Colciago, I (Dallara F394-Fiat), 23m 35.47s.
6 Christian Abt, D (Dallara F394-Opel), 23m 35.91s.
7 Frederico Viegas, P (Dallara F394-Opel), 23m 36.31s; **8** Norberto Fontana, RA (Dallara F394-Opel), 23m 36.70s; **9** Ralf Schumacher, D (Dallara F394-Opel), 23m 37.45s; **10** Sascha Maassen, D (Dallara F394-Opel), 23m 39.59s.
Fastest race lap: Wurz, 1m 00.30s, 97.861 mph/157.493 km/h.
Class II winner: Thomas Winkelhock, D (Dallara F393-Opel), 23m 43.32s.
Championship points: 1 Wurz, 50; **2** Müller, 42; **3** Couceiro, 38; **4** Schumacher, 26; **5** Peter, 18; **6** Maassen, 16.

GERMAN FORMULA 3 CHAMPIONSHIP, Nürburgring, Nürburg/Eifel, Germany, 7 May. Round 4. 14 laps of the 2.822-mile/4.542-km circuit, 39.512 miles/63.588 km.
1 Jörg Müller, D (Dallara F394-Fiat), 22m 26.55s, 105.635 mph/170.002 km/h.
2 Pedro Couceiro, P (Dallara F394-Opel), 22m 29.58s.
3 Alexander Wurz, A (Dallara F394-Opel), 22m 29.82s.
4 Sascha Maassen, D (Dallara F394-Opel), 22m 38.07s.
5 Christian Menzel, D (Dallara F393-Opel), 22m 39.63s (1st Class II).
6 Massimiliano 'Max' Angelelli, I (Dallara F394-Volkswagen), 22m 41.42s.
7 Klaus Graf, D (Dallara F393-Opel), 22m 43.01s; **8** Arnd Meier, D (Dallara F393-Opel), 22m 44.79s; **9** Katsumi Yamamoto, J (Dallara F393-Opel), 22m 45.68s; **10** Frederico Viegas, P (Dallara F394-Opel), 22m 52.60s.
Fastest race lap: Wurz, 1m 34.90s, 107.062 mph/172.299 km/h.

GERMAN FORMULA 3 CHAMPIONSHIP, Nürburgring, Nürburg/Eifel, Germany, 8 May. Round 5. 14 laps of the 2.822-mile/4.542-km circuit, 39.512 miles/63.588 km.
1 Jörg Müller, D (Dallara F394-Fiat), 22m 17.79s, 106.326 mph/171.116 km/h.
2 Pedro Couceiro, P (Dallara F394-Opel), 22m 18.11s.
3 Alexander Wurz, A (Dallara F394-Opel), 22m 18.47s.
4 Klaus Graf, D (Dallara F393-Opel), 22m 26.55s (1st Class II).
5 Frederico Viegas, P (Dallara F394-Opel), 22m 28.90s.
6 Christian Menzel, D (Dallara F393-Opel), 22m 30.03s.
7 Massimiliano 'Max' Angelelli, I (Dallara F394-Volkswagen), 22m 30.59s; **8** Ralf Schumacher, D (Dallara F394-Opel), 22m 30.81s; **9** Norberto Fontana, RA (Dallara F394-Opel), 22m 32.87s; **10** Patrick Berhardt, D (Dallara F394-Volkswagen), 22m 35.10s.
Fastest race lap: Schumacher, 1m 34.34s, 107.697 mph/173.322 km/h.
Championship points: 1 Müller, 82; **2** Wurz, 74; **3** Couceiro, 68; **4** Schumacher, 29; **5** Maassen, 26; **6=** Viegas, 18; **6=** Peter, 18.

GERMAN FORMULA 3 CHAMPIONSHIP, Wunstorf Airfield Circuit, Hanover, Germany, 11 June. Round 6. 12 laps of the 3.138-mile/5.050-km circuit, 37.655 miles/60.600 km.
1 Norberto Fontana, RA (Dallara F394-Opel), 20m 09.61s, 112.068 mph/180.356 km/h.
2 Ralf Schumacher, D (Dallara F394-Opel), 20m 10.62s.
3 Arnd Meier, D (Dallara F393-Opel), 20m 11.11s (1st Class II).
4 Sascha Maassen, D (Dallara F394-Opel), 20m 15.66s.

5 Pedro Couceiro, P (Dallara F394-Opel), 20m 16.39s.
6 Frederico Viegas, P (Dallara F394-Opel), 20m 27.93s.
7 Massimiliano 'Max' Angelelli, I (Dallara F394-Volkswagen), 20m 29.44s; **8** Philipp Peter, A (Dallara F394-Fiat), 20m 32.11s; **9** Olivier Tichy, A (Dallara F393-Volkswagen), 20m 32.43s; **10** Manuel Giao, P (Dallara F394-Opel), 20m 34.00s.
Fastest race lap: Maassen, 1m 39.50s, 113.533 mph/182.714 km/h.

GERMAN FORMULA 3 CHAMPIONSHIP, Wunstorf Airfield Circuit, Hanover, Germany, 12 June. Round 7. 12 laps of the 3.138-mile/5.050-km circuit, 37.655 miles/60.600 km.
1 Jörg Müller, D (Dallara F394-Fiat), 20m 14.79s, 111.590 mph/179.587 km/h.
2 Pedro Couceiro, P (Dallara F394-Opel), 20m 18.10s.
3 Frederico Viegas, P (Dallara F394-Opel), 20m 19.49s.
4 Sascha Maassen, D (Dallara F394-Opel), 20m 20.13s.
5 Philipp Peter, A (Dallara F394-Fiat), 20m 25.25s.
6 Alexander Wurz, A (Dallara F394-Opel), 20m 25.71s.
7 Massimiliano 'Max' Angelelli, I (Dallara F394-Volkswagen), 20m 27.58s; **8** Norberto Fontana, RA (Dallara F394-Opel), 20m 28.10s; **9** Manuel Giao, P (Dallara F394-Opel), 20m 30.09s; **10** Klaus Graf, D (Dallara F394-Opel), 20m 30.79s.
Fastest race lap: Müller, 1m 39.55s, 113.476 mph/182.622 km/h.
Class II winner: Arnd Meier, D (Dallara F393-Opel), 20m 36.31s.
Championship points: **1** Müller, 102; **2** Couceiro, 91; **3** Wurz, 80; **4** Maassen, 46; **5** Schumacher, 44; **6** Viegas, 36.

GERMAN FORMULA 3 CHAMPIONSHIP, Norisring, Nürnberg, Germany, 25 June. Round 8. 26 laps of the 1.429-mile/2.300-km circuit, 37.158 miles/59.800 km.
1 Jörg Müller, D (Dallara F394-Fiat), 22m 48.03s, 97.782 mph/157.365 km/h.
2 Sascha Maassen, D (Dallara F394-Opel), 22m 49.29s.
3 Philipp Peter, A (Dallara F394-Opel), 22m 52.30s.
4 Alexander Wurz, A (Dallara F394-Opel), 22m 57.49s.
5 Norberto Fontana, RA (Dallara F394-Opel), 22m 58.82s.
6 Marco Werner, D (Dallara F394-Fiat), 23m 03.25s.
7 Michael Graf, D (Dallara F394-Opel), 23m 06.28s; **8** Christian Abt, D (Dallara F394-Opel), 23m 06.51s; **9** Thomas Winkelhock, D (Dallara F393-Opel), 23m 08.48s (1st Class II); **10** Christian Menzel, D (Dallara F393-Opel), 23m 10.55s.
Fastest race lap: Abt, 51.73s, 99.458 mph/160.062 km/h.

GERMAN FORMULA 3 CHAMPIONSHIP, Norisring, Nürnberg, Germany, 26 June. Round 9. 26 laps of the 1.429-mile/2.300-km circuit, 37.158 miles/59.800 km.
1 Philipp Peter, A (Dallara F394-Opel), 22m 39.98s, 98.361 mph/158.296 km/h.
2 Jörg Müller, D (Dallara F394-Fiat), 22m 41.61s.
3 Alexander Wurz, A (Dallara F394-Opel), 22m 44.24s.
4 Pedro Couceiro, P (Dallara F394-Opel), 22m 45.31s.
5 Sascha Maassen, D (Dallara F394-Opel), 22m 45.50s.
6 Christian Abt, D (Dallara F394-Opel), 22m 51.49s.
7 Massimiliano 'Max' Angelelli, I (Dallara F394-Volkswagen), 22m 53.72s; **8** Marco Werner, D (Dallara F394-Fiat), 22m 53.95s; **9** Manuel Giao, P (Dallara F394-Opel), 22m 56.87s; **10** Ralf Schumacher, D (Dallara F394-Opel), 22m 57.96s.
Fastest race lap: Couceiro, 51.61s, 99.689 mph/160.434 km/h.
Class II winner: Thomas Winkelhock, D (Dallara F393-Opel), 22m 58.60s.
Championship points: **1** Müller, 137; **2** Wurz, 102; **3** Couceiro, 101; **4** Maassen, 69; **5** Peter, 61; **6** Schumacher, 45.

GERMAN FORMULA 3 CHAMPIONSHIP, Diepholz Airfield Circuit, Osnabruck, Germany, 23 July. Round 10. 23 laps of the 1.690-mile/2.720-km circuit, 38.873 miles/62.560 km.
1 Jörg Müller, D (Dallara F394-Fiat), 23m 21.30s, 99.660 mph/160.719 km/h.
2 Ralf Schumacher, D (Dallara F394-Opel), 23m 22.34s.
3 Alexander Wurz, A (Dallara F394-Opel), 23m 36.15s.
4 Patrick Berhardt, D (Dallara F394-Volkswagen), 23m 27.85s.
5 Philipp Peter, A (Dallara F394-Opel), 23m 28.71s.
6 Massimiliano 'Max' Angelelli, I (Dallara F394-Volkswagen), 23m 40.23s.
7 Tim Bergmeister, D (Dallara F393-Opel), 23m 42.83s (1st Class II); **8** Marco Werner, D (Dallara F394-Fiat), 23m 43.55s; **9** Andre Fibier, D (Dallara F393-Opel), 23m 46.73s; **10** Olivier Tichy, A (Dallara F393-Volkswagen), 23m 53.43s.
Fastest race lap: Bernhardt, 59.95s, 101.492 mph/163.336 km/h.

GERMAN FORMULA 3 CHAMPIONSHIP, Diepholz Airfield Circuit, Osnabruck, Germany, 24 July. Round 11. 22 laps of the 1.690-mile/2.720-km circuit, 37.183 miles/59.840 km.
1 Jörg Müller, D (Dallara F394-Fiat), 22m 23.75s, 99.866 mph/160.316 km/h.
2 Ralf Schumacher, D (Dallara F394-Opel), 22m 24.58s.
3 Alexander Wurz, A (Dallara F394-Opel), 22m 28.19s.
4 Philipp Peter, A (Dallara F394-Fiat), 22m 29.12s.
5 Massimiliano 'Max' Angelelli, I (Dallara F394-Volkswagen), 22m 29.70s.
6 Andreas Reiter, A (Dallara F394-Fiat), 22m 30.89s.
7 Christian Abt, D (Dallara F394-Opel), 22m 33.32s; **8** Sascha Maassen, D (Dallara F394-Opel), 22m 36.77s; **9** Patrick Berhardt, D (Dallara F394-Volkswagen), 22m 39.22s; **10** Frederico Viegas, P (Dallara F394-Opel), 22m 45.14s.
Fastest race lap: Reiter, 1m 00.18s, 101.104 mph/162.712 km/h.
Class II winner: Andre Fibier, D (Dallara F393-Opel), 22m 39.55s.
Championship points: **1** Müller, 177; **2** Wurz, 126; **3** Couceiro, 101; **4** Peter 79; **5** Schumacher, 75; **6** Maassen, 74.

GERMAN FORMULA 3 CHAMPIONSHIP, Nürburgring, Nürburg/Eifel, Germany, 20 August. Round 12. 13 laps of the 2.822-mile/4.542-km circuit, 36.689 miles/59.046 km.
1 Norberto Fontana, RA (Dallara F394-Opel), 20m 46.17s, 105.990 mph/170.575 km/h.
2 Ralf Schumacher, D (Dallara F394-Opel), 20m 46.78s.
3 Alexander Wurz, A (Dallara F394-Opel), 20m 47.31s.
4 Sascha Maassen, D (Dallara F394-Opel), 20m 49.80s.
5 Christian Abt, D (Dallara F394-Opel), 20m 51.29s.
6 Jörg Müller, D (Dallara F394-Fiat), 20m 51.58s.
7 Philipp Peter, A (Dallara F394-Opel), 21m 01.70s; **8** Martin Koene, NL (Dallara F394-Opel), 21m 02.27s; **9** Andre Fibier, D (Dallara F393-Opel), 21m 04.03s (1st Class II); **10** Manuel Giao, P (Dallara F394-Opel), 21m 10.07s.
Fastest race lap: Schumacher, 1m 34.79s, 107.186 mph/172.499 km/h.

GERMAN FORMULA 3 CHAMPIONSHIP, Nürburgring, Nürburg/Eifel, Germany, 21 August. Round 13. 14 laps of the 2.822-mile/4.542-km circuit, 39.512 miles/63.588 km.
1 Norberto Fontana, RA (Dallara F394-Opel), 22m 20.16s, 106.138 mph/170.813 km/h.
2 Alexander Wurz, A (Dallara F394-Opel), 22m 20.57s.
3 Ralf Schumacher, D (Dallara F394-Opel), 22m 21.18s.
4 Sascha Maassen, D (Dallara F394-Opel), 22m 21.52s.
5 Jörg Müller, D (Dallara F394-Fiat), 22m 23.83s.
6 Christian Abt, D (Dallara F394-Opel), 22m 36.49s.
7 Philipp Peter, A (Dallara F394-Opel), 22m 41.70s; **8** Andre Fibier, D (Dallara F393-Opel), 22m 42.18s (1st Class II); **9** Martin Koene, NL (Dallara F394-Opel), 22m 42.48s; **10** Manuel Giao, P (Dallara F394-Opel), 22m 43.07s.
Fastest race lap: Wurz, 1m 34.78s, 107.197 mph/172.517 km/h.
Championship points: **1** Müller, 191; **2** Wurz, 153; **3=** Schumacher, 102; **3=** Couceiro, 102; **5** Maassen, 94; **6** Peter, 87.

GERMAN FORMULA 3 CHAMPIONSHIP, Avus Circuit, Berlin, Germany, 3 September. Round 14. 24 laps of the 1.640-mile/2.640-km circuit, 39.370 miles/63.360 km.
1 Jörg Müller, D (Dallara F394-Fiat), 22m 00.56s, 107.327 mph/172.727 km/h.
2 Ralf Schumacher, D (Dallara F394-Opel), 22m 02.01s.
3 Norberto Fontana, RA (Dallara F394-Opel), 22m 05.36s.
4 Alexander Wurz, A (Dallara F394-Opel), 22m 17.06s.
5 Christian Abt, D (Dallara F394-Opel), 22m 17.39s.
6 Sascha Maassen, D (Dallara F394-Opel), 22m 17.85s.
7 Pedro Couceiro, P (Dallara F394-Opel), 22m 22.20s; **8** Philipp Peter, A (Dallara F394-Opel), 22m 23.01s; **9** Arnd Meier, D (Dallara F393-Opel), 22m 28.81s (1st Class II); **10** Massimiliano 'Max' Angelelli, I (Dallara F394-Volkswagen), 22m 28.98s.
Fastest race lap: Müller, 54.18s, 108.998 mph/175.415 km/h.

GERMAN FORMULA 3 CHAMPIONSHIP, Avus Circuit, Berlin, Germany, 4 September. Round 15, 23 laps of the 1.640-mile/2.640-km circuit, 37.730 miles/60.720 km.
1 Jörg Müller, D (Dallara F394-Fiat), 21m 05.00s, 107.373 mph/172.800 km/h.
2 Norberto Fontana, RA (Dallara F394-Opel), 21m 06.80s.
3 Alexander Wurz, A (Dallara F394-Opel), 21m 15.62s.
4 Sascha Maassen, D (Dallara F394-Opel), 21m 16.58s.
5 Christian Abt, D (Dallara F394-Opel), 21m 17.14s.
6 Pedro Couceiro, P (Dallara F394-Opel), 21m 29.44s.
7 Massimiliano 'Max' Angelelli, I (Dallara F394-Volkswagen), 21m 30.97s; **8** Marco Werner, D (Dallara F394-Fiat), 21m 31.97s; **9** Rudi Melkus, D (Dallara F394-Opel), 21m 37.06s; **10** Arnd Meier, D (Dallara F393-Opel), 21m 40.24s (1st Class II).
Fastest race lap: Müller, 54.10s, 109.159 mph/175.674 km/h.
Championship points: **1** Müller, 231; **2** Wurz, 175; **3** Schumacher, 117; **4** Couceiro, 112; **5** Maassen, 110; **6** Fontana, 103.

GERMAN FORMULA 3 CHAMPIONSHIP, Singen Circuit, Germany, 17 September. Round 16. 22 laps of the 1.740-mile/2.800-km circuit, 38.276 miles/61.600 km.
1 Ralf Schumacher, D (Dallara F394-Opel), 27m 41.55s, 82.932 mph/133.466 km/h.
2 Jörg Müller, D (Dallara F394-Fiat), 27m 42.17s.
3 Sascha Maassen, D (Dallara F394-Opel), 27m 42.80s.
4 Christian Abt, D (Dallara F394-Opel), 27m 55.66s.
5 Alexander Wurz, A (Dallara F394-Opel), 27m 56.75s.
6 Arnd Meier, D (Dallara F393-Opel), 28m 04.82s (1st Class II).
7 Christian Menzel, D (Dallara F393-Opel), 28m 08.45s; **8** Massimiliano 'Max' Angelelli, I (Dallara F394-Volkswagen), 28m 08.57s; **9** Philipp Peter, A (Dallara F394-Fiat), 28m 10.54s; **10** Marco Werner, D (Dallara F394-Fiat), 28m 11.01s.
Fastest race lap: Müller, 1m 14.36s, 84.231 mph/135.557 km/h.

GERMAN FORMULA 3 CHAMPIONSHIP, Singen Circuit, Germany, 18 September. Round 17. 22 laps of the 1.740-mile/2.800-km circuit, 38.276 miles/61.600 km.
1 Jörg Müller, D (Dallara F394-Fiat), 27m 53.05s, 82.362 mph/132.548 km/h.
2 Ralf Schumacher, D (Dallara F394-Opel), 28m 03.70s.
3 Alexander Wurz, A (Dallara F394-Opel), 28m 15.08s.
4 Massimiliano 'Max' Angelelli, I (Dallara F394-Volkswagen), 28m 18.15s.
5 Sascha Maassen, D (Dallara F394-Opel), 28m 18.82s.
6 Philipp Peter, A (Dallara F394-Fiat), 28m 20.89s.
7 Arnd Meier, D (Dallara F393-Opel), 28m 26.60s (1st Class II); **8** Christian Menzel, D (Dallara F393-Opel), 28m 27.09s; **9** Andre Fibier, D (Dallara F393-Opel), 28m 30.99s; **10** Tim Bergmeister, D (Dallara F393-Opel), 28m 33.74s.
Fastest race lap: Müller, 1m 14.71s, 83.836 mph/134.922 km/h.
Championship points: **1** Müller, 266; **2** Wurz, 195; **3** Schumacher, 152; **4** Maassen, 130; **5** Couceiro, 112; **6** Peter, 98.

GERMAN FORMULA 3 CHAMPIONSHIP, Hockenheimring, Heidelberg, Germany, 8 October. Round 18. 9 laps of the 4.235-mile/6.815-km circuit, 38.112 miles/61.335 km.
1 Jörg Müller, D (Dallara F394-Fiat), 19m 46.10s, 115.675 mph/186.161 km/h.
2 Norberto Fontana, RA (Dallara F394-Opel), 19m 49.52s.
3 Pedro Couceiro, P (Dallara F394-Opel), 19m 51.10s.
4 Sascha Maassen, D (Dallara F394-Opel), 19m 51.44s.
5 Philipp Peter, A (Dallara F394-Fiat), 19m 53.25s.
6 Massimiliano 'Max' Angelelli, I (Dallara F394-Volkswagen), 19m 58.54s.
7 Alexander Wurz, A (Dallara F394-Opel), 19m 59.88s; **8** Marco Werner, D (Dallara F394-Fiat), 20m 00.90s; **9** Christophe Tinseau, F (Dallara F394-Opel), 20m 03.65s; **10** Andreas Reiter, A (Dallara F394-Fiat), 20m 04.03s.
Fastest race lap: Ralf Schumacher, D (Dallara F394-Opel), 2m 09.38s, 117.829 mph/189.627 km/h.
Class II winner: Oliver Tichy, A (Dallara F393-Volkswagen), 20m 04.50s.

GERMAN FORMULA 3 CHAMPIONSHIP, Hockenheimring, Heidelberg, Germany, 9 October. Round 19. 9 laps of the 4.235-mile/6.815-km circuit, 38.112 miles/61.335 km.
1 Alexander Wurz, A (Dallara F394-Opel), 19m 51.26s, 115.174 mph/185.355 km/h.
2 Sascha Maassen, D (Dallara F394-Opel), 19m 52.10s.
3 Pedro Couceiro, P (Dallara F394-Opel), 19m 56.43s.
4 Philipp Peter, A (Dallara F394-Fiat), 19m 57.04s.
5 Andreas Reiter, A (Dallara F394-Fiat), 19m 57.44s.
6 Ralf Schumacher, D (Dallara F394-Opel), 19m 57.74s.
7 Jörg Müller, D (Dallara F394-Fiat), 19m 58.88s; **8** Massimiliano 'Max' Angelelli, I (Dallara F394-Volkswagen), 19m 59.36s; **9** Marco Werner, D (Dallara F394-Fiat), 19m 59.59s; **10** Christophe Tinseau, F (Dallara F394-Opel), 19m 59.87s.
Fastest race lap: Schumacher, 2m 09.73s, 117.511 mph/189.116 km/h.
Class II winner: Tim Bergmeister, D (Dallara F393-Opel), 20m 05.24s.

Final championship points

1	Jörg Müller, D	290
2	Alexander Wurz, A	219
3	Ralf Schumacher, D	158
4	Sascha Maassen, D	155
5	Pedro Couceiro, P	136
6	Norberto Fontana, RA	118

7 Philipp Peter, A, 116; **8** Christian Abt, D, 66; **9** Massimiliano 'Max' Angelelli, I, 63; **10** Frederico Viegas, P, 38; **11** Arnd Meier, D, 28; **12** Andreas Reiter, A, 26; **13** Christian Menzel, D, 23; **14** Marco Werner, D, 22; **15** Klaus Graf, D, 14; **16** Patrick Berhardt, D, 13; **17** Roberto Colciago, I, 11; **18** Manuel Giao, P, 9; **19** Johnny Hauser, CH, 7; **20** Martin Koene, NL, 6.

Italian Formula 3 Championship

ITALIAN FORMULA 3 CHAMPIONSHIP, Autodromo di Vallelunga, Rome, Italy, 26 March. Round 1. 26 laps of the 1.988-mile/3.200-km circuit, 51.698 miles/83.200 km.
1 Gianantonio Pacchioni, I (Dallara F393/4-Fiat), 30m 37.992s, 101.259 mph/162.960 km/h.
2 Giancarlo Fisichella, I (Dallara F394-Opel), 30m 39.39s.
3 Luca Rangoni, I (Dallara F393/4-Fiat), 30m 51.20s.
4 Gianluca Paglicci, I (Dallara F394-Fiat), 30m 57.03s.
5 Alberto Pedemonte, I (Dallara F394-Fiat), 30m 57.55s.
6 Federico Gemmo, I (Dallara F394-Fiat), 30m 58.09s.
7 Luca Riccitelli, I (Dallara F393/4-Fiat), 31m 00.08s; **8** Danilo Tomassini, I (Dallara F393-Fiat), 31m 03.52s; **9** Simone Rebai, I (Dallara F393/4-Fiat), 31m 04.24s; **10** Giovanni Gulinelli, I (Dallara F393/4-Fiat), 31m 06.88s.
Fastest race lap: Pacchioni, 1m 10.046s, 102.193 mph/164.463 km/h.
Fastest qualifying lap: Pacchioni, 1m 09.666s, 102.750 mph/165.360 km/h.

ITALIAN FORMULA 3 CHAMPIONSHIP, Autodromo di Vallelunga, Rome, Italy, 27 March. Round 2. 26 laps of the 1.988-mile/3.200-km circuit, 51.698 miles/83.200 km.
1 Gianantonio Pacchioni, I (Dallara F393/4-Fiat), 30m 49.352s, 100.637 mph/161.959 km/h.
2 Giancarlo Fisichella, I (Dallara F394-Opel), 30m 50.05s.
3 Luca Rangoni, I (Dallara F393/4-Fiat), 30m 56.39s.
4 Gianluca Paglicci, I (Dallara F394-Fiat), 31m 03.16s.
5 Luca Riccitelli, I (Dallara F393/4-Fiat), 31m 04.29s.
6 Maurizio Mediani, I (Dallara F394-Fiat), 31m 05.74s.
7 Danilo Tomassini, I (Dallara F393-Fiat), 31m 06.38s; **8** Alberto Pedemonte, I (Dallara F394-Fiat), 31m 06.86s; **9** Giovanni Gulinelli, I (Dallara F393/4-Fiat), 31m 08.04s; **10** Simone Rebai, I (Dallara F393/4-Fiat), 31m 15.38s.
Fastest race lap: Fisichella, 1m 10.565s, 101.441 mph/163.254 km/h.
Championship points: **1** Pacchioni, 40; **2** Fisichella, 30; **3** Rangoni, 24; **4** Paglicci, 20; **5** Riccitelli, 12; **6** Pedemonte, 11.

ITALIAN FORMULA 3 CHAMPIONSHIP, Ente Autodromo di Pergusa, Enna-Pergusa, Catania, Sicily, 9 April. Round 3. 18 laps of the 3.076-mile/4.950-km circuit, 55.364 miles/89.100 km.
1 Giancarlo Fisichella, I (Dallara F394-Opel), 29m 15.321s, 113.547 mph/182.736 km/h.
2 Luca Rangoni, I (Dallara F393/4-Fiat), 29m 18.11s.
3 Gianantonio Pacchioni, I (Dallara F393/4-Fiat), 29m 20.10s.
4 Luca Riccitelli, I (Dallara F393/4-Fiat), 29m 21.35s.
5 Rolando Galli, I (Dallara F393/4-Fiat), 29m 21.44s.
6 Maurizio Mediani, I (Dallara F394-Fiat), 29m 22.95s.
7 Gianluca Paglicci, I (Dallara F394-Fiat), 29m 27.17s; **8** Giovanni Gulinelli, I (Dallara F393/4-Fiat), 29m 23.39s; **9** Federico Gemmo, I (Dallara F394-Fiat), 29m 32.21s; **10** Alberto Scilla, I (Dallara F394-Fiat), 29m 40.92s.
Fastest race lap: Fisichella, 1m 36.292s, 114.992 mph/185.062 km/h.
Fastest qualifying lap: Pacchioni, 1m 35.970s, 115.378 mph/185.683 km/h.

ITALIAN FORMULA 3 CHAMPIONSHIP, Ente Autodromo di Pergusa, Enna-Pergusa, Catania, Sicily, 10 April. Round 4. 18 laps of the 3.076-mile/4.950-km circuit, 55.364 miles/89.100 km.
1 Giancarlo Fisichella, I (Dallara F394-Opel), 29m 02.931s, 114.354 mph/184.035 km/h.
2 Luca Riccitelli, I (Dallara F393/4-Fiat), 29m 05.69s.
3 Gianantonio Pacchioni, I (Dallara F393/4-Fiat), 29m 08.80s.
4 Rolando Galli, I (Dallara F393-Fiat), 29m 09.10s.
5 Oliver Martini, I (Dallara F393-Mugen Honda), 29m 16.19s.
6 Alberto Scilla, I (Dallara F394-Fiat), 29m 29.27s.
7 Federico Gemmo, I (Dallara F394-Fiat), 29m 29.50s; **8** Gianluca Paglicci, I (Dallara F394-Fiat), 29m 31.01s; **9** Danilo Tomassini, I (Dallara F393-Fiat), 29m 31.08s; **10** Michele Gasparini, I (Dallara F394-Fiat), 29m 33.13s.
Fastest race lap: Fisichella, 1m 35.967s, 115.382 mph/185.689 km/h.
Championship points: **1** Fisichella, 70; **2** Pacchioni, 64; **3** Rangoni, 39; **4** Riccitelli, 37; **5** Paglicci, 27; **6** Galli, 18.

ITALIAN FORMULA 3 CHAMPIONSHIP, Autodromo Riccardo Paletti, Varano, Parma, Italy, 24 April. Round 5. 41 laps of the 1.118-mile/1.800-km circuit, 45.857 miles/73.800 km.
1 Giancarlo Fisichella, I (Dallara F394-Opel), 31m 12.565s, 88.160 mph/141.880 km/h.
2 Gianantonio Pacchioni, I (Dallara F393/4-Fiat), 31m 19.75s.
3 Luca Rangoni, I (Dallara F393/4-Fiat), 31m 27.17s.
4 Michele Gasparini, I (Dallara F394-Fiat), 31m 32.78s.
5 Alberto Pedemonte, I (Dallara F394-Fiat), 31m 41.10s.
6 Giovanni Gulinelli, I (Dallara F394-Fiat), 31m 43.07s.
7 Federico Gemmo, I (Dallara F394-Fiat), 31m 44.00s; **8** Pietro Antonelli, I (Dallara F394-Fiat), 31m 44.90s; **9** Giorgio Tibaldo, I (Dallara F393-Fiat), 31m 51.26s; **10** Paolo Coloni, I (Dallara F393-Fiat), 31m 54.90s.
Fastest race lap: Fisichella, 45.133s, 89.214 mph/143.576 km/h.
Fastest qualifying lap: Fisichella, 44.734s, 90.010 mph/144.856 km/h.

ITALIAN FORMULA 3 CHAMPIONSHIP, Autodromo Riccardo Paletti, Varano, Parma, Italy, 25 April. Round 6. 41 laps of the 1.118-mile/1.800-km circuit, 45.857 miles/73.800 km.
1 Giancarlo Fisichella, I (Dallara F394-Opel), 31m 05.630s, 88.488 mph/142.408 km/h.
2 Gianantonio Pacchioni, I (Dallara F393/4-Fiat), 31m 10.28s.
3 Luca Rangoni, I (Dallara F393/4-Fiat), 31m 11.35s.
4 Danilo Rossi, I (Dallara F394-Fiat), 31m 12.14s.
5 Luca Riccitelli, I (Dallara F394-Fiat), 31m 16.61s.
6 Michele Gasparini, I (Dallara F394-Fiat), 31m 16.38s.
7 Maurizio Mediani, I (Dallara F394-Fiat), 31m 23.30s; **8** Paolo Ruberti, I (Dallara F394-Fiat), 31m 28.06s; **9** Federico Gemmo, I (Dallara F394-Fiat), 31m 30.24s; **10** Alberto Scilla, I (Dallara F394-Fiat), 31m 30.80s.
Fastest race lap: Fisichella, 44.904s, 89.669 mph/144.308 km/h.
Championship points: **1** Fisichella, 110; **2** Pacchioni, 94; **3** Rangoni, 63; **4** Riccitelli, 45; **5** Paglicci, 27; **6** Pedemonte, 19.

ITALIAN FORMULA 3 CHAMPIONSHIP, Autodromo Magione, Perugia, Italy, 28 May. Round 7. 34 laps of the 1.025-mile/1.650-km circuit, 34.859 miles/56.100 km.
1 Gianluca Paglicci, I (Dallara F394-Fiat), 27m 46.318s, 75.311 mph/121.201 km/h.
2 Luca Rangoni, I (Dallara F393/4-Fiat), 27m 47.26s.
3 Luca Riccitelli, I (Dallara F394-Fiat), 27m 50.10s.

4 Giovanni Gulinelli, I (Dallara F394-Fiat), 27m 51.57s.
5 Gianantonio Pacchioni, I (Dallara F393/4-Fiat), 27m 52.97s.
6 Maurizio Mediani, I (Dallara F394-Fiat), 27m 53.30s.
7 Federico Gemmo, I (Dallara F394-Fiat), 27m 59.88s; **8** Alberto Pedemonte, I (Dallara F394-Fiat), 28m 06.30s; **9** Paolo Ruberti, I (Dallara F394-Fiat), 28m 07.88s; **10** Rolando Galli, I (Dallara F393/4-Fiat), 28m 10.11s.
Fastest race lap: Mediani, 48.313s, 76.397 mph/122.948 km/h.
Fastest qualifying lap: Paglicci, 47.732s, 77.326 mph/124.445 km/h.

ITALIAN FORMULA 3 CHAMPIONSHIP, Autodromo Magione, Perugia, Italy, 29 May. Round 8. 34 laps of the 1.025-mile/1.650-km circuit, 34.859 miles/56.100 km.
1 Giancarlo Fisichella, I (Dallara F394-Opel), 27m 30.395s, 76.038 mph/122.371 km/h.
2 Gianluca Paglicci, I (Dallara F394-Fiat), 27m 30.72s.
3 Maurizio Mediani, I (Dallara F394-Fiat), 27m 41.84s.
4 Luca Rangoni, I (Dallara F393/4-Fiat), 27m 43.31s.
5 Oliver Martini, I (Dallara F393-Mugen Honda), 27m 47.74s.
6 Federico Gemmo, I (Dallara F394-Fiat), 27m 49.03s.
7 Gianantonio Pacchioni, I (Dallara F393/4-Fiat), 27m 54.00s; **8** Alberto Scilla, I (Dallara F394-Fiat), 27m 54.78s; **9** Danilo Rossi, I (Dallara F394-Fiat), 28m 00.19s; **10** Thomas Biagi, I (Dallara F394-Mugen Honda), 28m 00.97s.
Fastest race lap: Paglicci, 47.884s, 77.081 mph/124.050 km/h.
Championship points: **1** Fisichella, 130; **2** Pacchioni, 106; **3** Rangoni, 88; **4** Paglicci, 62; **5** Riccitelli, 57; **6** Mediani, 34.

ITALIAN FORMULA 3 CHAMPIONSHIP, Autodromo di Binetto, Bari, Italy, 11 June. Round 9. 42 laps of the 0.980-mile/1.577-km circuit, 41.156 miles/66.234 km.
1 Giancarlo Fisichella, I (Dallara F394-Opel), 30m 50.618s, 80.060 mph/128.845 km/h.
2 Luca Rangoni, I (Dallara F393/4-Fiat), 30m 51.22s.
3 Gianantonio Pacchioni, I (Dallara F393/4-Fiat), 30m 55.67s.
4 Thomas Biagi, I (Dallara F394-Mugen Honda), 31m 06.65s.
5 Michele Gasparini, I (Dallara F394-Fiat), 31m 07.74s.
6 Giovanni Gulinelli, I (Dallara F393/4-Fiat), 31m 11.63s.
7 Federico Gemmo, I (Dallara F394-Fiat), 31m 12.58s; **8** Luca Riccitelli, I (Dallara F393/4-Fiat), 31m 12.56s; **9** Maurizio Mediani, I (Dallara F394-Fiat), 31m 23.37s; **10** Alberto Scilla, I (Dallara F394-Fiat), 31m 23.81s.
Fastest race lap: Rangoni, 43.245s, 81.574 mph/131.280 km/h.
Fastest qualifying lap: Gianluca Paglicci, I (Dallara F394-Fiat), 43.115s, 81.820 mph/131.676 km/h.

ITALIAN FORMULA 3 CHAMPIONSHIP, Autodromo di Binetto, Bari, Italy, 12 June. Round 10. 25 laps of the 0.980-mile/1.577-km circuit, 24.498 miles/39.425 km.
Race stopped early due to rain. Half points awarded.
1 Gianluca Paglicci, I (Dallara F394-Fiat), 21m 32.853s, 68.214 mph/109.780 km/h.
2 Luca Rangoni, I (Dallara F393/4-Fiat), 21m 48.42s.
3 Giancarlo Fisichella, I (Dallara F394-Opel), 21m 54.10s.
4 Oliver Martini, I (Dallara F393-Mugen Honda), 21m 59.97s.
5 Maurizio Mediani, I (Dallara F394-Fiat), 22m 00.96s.
6 Michele Gasparini, I (Dallara F394-Fiat), 22m 25.60s.
7 Andrea Belluzzi, I (Dallara F394-Fiat), 24 laps; **8** Giorgio Tibaldo, I (Dallara F394-Fiat), 24; **9** Luca Riccitelli, I (Dallara F393/4-Fiat), 24; **10** Danilo Tomassini, I (Dallara F393/4-Fiat), 24.
Fastest race lap: Martini, 46.302s, 76.188 mph/122.612 km/h.
Championship points: **1** Fisichella, 156; **2** Pacchioni, 118; **3** Rangoni, 110.5; **4** Paglicci, 72; **5** Riccitelli, 61; **6** Mediani, 40.

LOTTERIA DI MONZA, Autodromo Nazionale di Monza, Milan, Italy, 25 June. Round 11. 16 laps of the 3.604-mile/5.800-km circuit, 57.663 miles/92.800 km.
1 Luca Rangoni, I (Dallara F393/4-Fiat), 29m 02.231s, 119.150 mph/191.754 km/h.
2 Giancarlo Fisichella, I (Dallara F394-Opel), 29m 03.03s.
3 Gianluca Paglicci, I (Dallara F394-Fiat), 29m 04.81s.
4 Danilo Rossi, I (Dallara F394-Fiat), 29m 08.17s.
5 Gianantonio Pacchioni, I (Dallara F393/4-Fiat), 29m 09.14s.
6 Maurizio Mediani, I (Dallara F394-Fiat), 29m 15.34s.
7 Luca Riccitelli, I (Dallara F393/4-Fiat), 29m 16.90s; **8** Giorgio Tibaldo, I (Dallara F394-Fiat), 29m 17.45s; **9** Pietro Antonelli, I (Dallara F393/4-Fiat), 29m 24.83s; **10** Oliver Martini, I (Dallara F393-Mugen Honda), 29m 29.33s.
Fastest race lap: Riccitelli, 1m 47.032s, 121.218 mph/195.082 km/h.
Fastest qualifying lap: Fisichella, 1m 46.691s, 121.606 mph/195.705 km/h.

LOTTERIA DI MONZA, Autodromo Nazionale di Monza, Milan, Italy, 26 June. Round 12. 16 laps of the 3.604-mile/5.800-km circuit, 57.663 miles/92.800 km.
1 Luca Riccitelli, I (Dallara F393/4-Fiat), 28m 57.586s, 119.469 mph/192.267 km/h.
2 Giancarlo Fisichella, I (Dallara F394-Opel), 28m 57.88s.
3 Maurizio Mediani, I (Dallara F394-Fiat), 29m 08.90s.
4 Giovanni Gulinelli, I (Dallara F394-Fiat), 29m 10.22s.
5 Giorgio Tibaldo, I (Dallara F394-Fiat), 29m 10.42s.
6 Pietro Antonelli, I (Dallara F393/4-Fiat), 29m 10.91s.
7 Federico Gemmo, I (Dallara F394-Fiat), 29m 11.41s; **8** Paolo Ruberti, I (Dallara F394-Fiat), 29m 12.15s; **9** Fabiano Belletti, I (Dallara F394-Opel), 29m 17.69s; **10** Michele Gasparini, I (Dallara F394-Fiat), 29m 18.37s.
Fastest race lap: Gasparini, 1m 46.910s, 121.357 mph/195.304 km/h.
Championship points: **1** Fisichella, 186; **2** Rangoni, 130.5; **3** Pacchioni, 126; **4** Riccitelli, 85; **5** Paglicci, 84; **6** Mediani, 58.

ITALIAN FORMULA 3 CHAMPIONSHIP, Autodromo di Vallelunga, Rome, Italy, 23 July. Round 13. 26 laps of the 1.988-mile/3.200-km circuit, 51.698 miles/83.200 km.
1 Giancarlo Fisichella, I (Dallara F394-Opel), 31m 20.693s, 98.960 mph/159.260 km/h.
2 Luca Riccitelli, I (Dallara F393/4-Fiat), 31m 21.58s.
3 Federico Gemmo, I (Dallara F394-Fiat), 31m 21.99s.
4 Gianluca Paglicci, I (Dallara F394-Fiat), 31m 22.70s.
5 Luca Rangoni, I (Dallara F393/4-Fiat), 31m 26.61s.
6 Maurizio Mediani, I (Dallara F394-Fiat), 31m 28.27s.
7 Paolo Ruberti, I (Dallara F393-Fiat), 31m 30.15s; **8** Roberto Colciago, I (Dallara F393/4-Fiat), 31m 32.23s; **9** Gianantonio Pacchioni, I (Dallara F393/4-Fiat), 31m 32.47s; **10** Fabrizio Gollin, I (Dallara F393/4-Fiat), 31m 32.91s.
Fastest race lap: Gemmo, 1m 11.552s, 100.042 mph/161.002 km/h.
Fastest qualifying lap: Fisichella, 1m 11.125s, 100.642 mph/161.968 km/h.

ITALIAN FORMULA 3 CHAMPIONSHIP, Autodromo di Vallelunga, Rome, Italy, 24 July. Round 14. 24 laps of the 1.988-mile/3.200-km circuit, 47.721 miles/76.800 km.
1 Luca Riccitelli, I (Dallara F393/4-Fiat), 30m 28.977s, 93.930 mph/151.166 km/h.
2 Federico Gemmo, I (Dallara F394-Fiat), 30m 36.66s.
3 Luca Rangoni, I (Dallara F393/4-Fiat), 30m 38.76s.
4 Gianantonio Pacchioni, I (Dallara F393/4-Fiat), 30m 42.88s.
5 Maurizio Mediani, I (Dallara F394-Fiat), 30m 47.69s.
6 Oliver Martini, I (Dallara F393-Mugen Honda), 30m 48.35s.
7 Paolo Ruberti, I (Dallara F394-Fiat), 30m 54.66s; **8** Giancarlo Fisichella, I (Dallara F394-Opel), 30m 54.98s; **9** Michele Gasparini, I (Dallara F394-Fiat), 30m 57.34s; **10** Alberto Scilla, I (Dallara F394-Fiat), 31m 01.43s.
Fastest race lap: Pacchioni, 1m 11.860s, 99.613 mph/160.312 km/h.
Championship points: **1** Fisichella, 209; **2** Rangoni, 150.5; **3** Pacchioni, 139; **4** Riccitelli, 120; **5** Paglicci, 94; **6** Mediani, 72.

ITALIAN FORMULA 3 CHAMPIONSHIP, Autodromo Internazionale del Mugello, Scarperia, Florence, Italy, 3 September. Round 15. 16 laps of the 3.259-mile/5.245-km circuit, 52.145 miles/83.920 km.
1 Gianluca Paglicci, I (Dallara F394-Fiat), 29m 01.919s, 107.768 mph/173.436 km/h.
2 Luca Riccitelli, I (Dallara F393/4-Fiat), 29m 03.61s.
3 Danilo Rossi, I (Dallara F394-Fiat), 29m 04.13s.
4 Giancarlo Fisichella, I (Dallara F394-Opel), 29m 04.37s.
5 Gianantonio Pacchioni, I (Dallara F393/4-Fiat), 29m 08.52s.
6 Michele Gasparini, I (Dallara F394-Fiat), 29m 09.58s.
7 Roberto Colciago, I (Dallara F393/4-Fiat), 29m 21.457s; **8** Roberto Carta, I (Dallara F394-Opel), 29m 21.900s; **9** Alberto Pedemonte, I (Dallara F394-Fiat), 29m 23.139s; **10** Rolando Galli, I (Dallara F393-Fiat), 29m 23.411s.
Fastest race lap: Rossi, 1m 47.366s, 109.278 mph/175.866 km/h.
Fastest qualifying lap: Paglicci, 1m 46.295s, 110.379 mph/177.638 km/h.

ITALIAN FORMULA 3 CHAMPIONSHIP, Autodromo Internazionale del Mugello, Scarperia, Florence, Italy, 4 September. Round 16. 14 laps of the 3.259-mile/5.245-km circuit, 45.627 miles/73.430 km.
Race scheduled for 16 laps, but reduced after two aborted starts.
1 Luca Riccitelli, I (Dallara F393/4-Fiat), 25m 19.069s, 108.131 mph/174.020 km/h.
2 Giancarlo Fisichella, I (Dallara F394-Opel), 25m 19.65s.
3 Danilo Rossi, I (Dallara F394-Fiat), 25m 20.25s.
4 Gianantonio Pacchioni, I (Dallara F393/4-Fiat), 25m 21.32s.
5 Michele Gasparini, I (Dallara F394-Fiat), 25m 22.17s.
6 Roberto Colciago, I (Dallara F393/4-Fiat), 25m 25.01s.
7 Rolando Galli, I (Dallara F393-Fiat), 25m 29.231s; **8** Maurizio Mediani, I (Dallara F394-Fiat), 25m 32.121s; **9** Luca Rangoni, I (Dallara F393/4-Fiat), 25m 37.606s; **10** Roberto Carta, I (Dallara F394-Opel), 25m 40.582s.
Fastest race lap: Rossi, 1m 47.045s, 109.606 mph/176.393 km/h.
Championship points: **1** Fisichella, 234; **2** Pacchioni, 157; **3** Riccitelli, 155; **4** Rangoni, 153.5; **5** Paglicci, 114; **6** Mediani, 77.

ITALIAN FORMULA 3 CHAMPIONSHIP, Autodromo Magione, Perugia, Italy, 8 October. Round 17. 36 laps of the 1.025-mile/1.650-km circuit, 36.909 miles/59.400 km.
1 Giancarlo Fisichella, I (Dallara F394-Opel), 29m 25.956s, 75.242 mph/121.090 km/h.
2 Michele Gasparini, I (Dallara F394-Fiat), 29m 29.29s.
3 Luca Rangoni, I (Dallara F393/4-Fiat), 29m 30.70s.
4 Giovanni Gulinelli, I (Dallara F393/4-Fiat), 29m 32.44s.
5 Luca Riccitelli, I (Dallara F393/4-Fiat), 29m 32.88s.
6 Gianantonio Pacchioni, I (Dallara F393/4-Fiat), 29m 33.46s.
7 Gianluca Paglicci, I (Dallara F394-Fiat), 29m 39.99s; **8** Thomas Biagi, I (Dallara F394-Mugen Honda), 29m 40.39s; **9** Alberto Pedemonte, I (Dallara F394-Fiat), 29m 48.10s; **10** Fabrizio Gollin, I (Dallara F393/4-Fiat), 29m 48.42s
Fastest race lap: Gasparini, 48.202s, 76.572 mph/123.231 km/h.
Fastest qualifying lap: Fisichella, 48.074s, 76.777 mph/123.560 km/h.

ITALIAN FORMULA 3 CHAMPIONSHIP, Autodromo Magione, Perugia, Italy, 9 October. Round 18. 36 laps of the 1.025-mile/1.650-km circuit, 36.909 miles/59.400 km.
1 Giancarlo Fisichella, I (Dallara F394-Opel), 29m 05.472s, 76.125 mph/122.511 km/h.
2 Luca Riccitelli, I (Dallara F393/4-Fiat), 29m 08.08s
3 Roberto Colciago, I (Dallara F393/4-Fiat), 29m 17.11s.
4 Gianluca Paglicci, I (Dallara F394-Fiat), 29m 17.70s.
5 Alberto Pedemonte, I (Dallara F394-Fiat), 29m 32.61s.
6 Maurizio Mediani, I (Dallara F394-Fiat), 29m 33.41s.
7 Fabrizio Gollin, I (Dallara F393/4-Fiat), 29m 33.91s; **8** Oliver Martini, I (Dallara F393-Mugen Honda), 29m 35.29s; **9** Gaston Mazzacane, I (Dallara F394-Opel), 29m 36.57s; **10** Andrea Belluzzi, I (Dallara F394-Fiat), 29m 37.41s.
Fastest race lap: Fisichella, 47.923s, 77.018 mph/123.948 km/h.
Championship points: **1** Fisichella, 274; **2** Riccitelli, 178; **3** Rangoni, 165.5; **4** Pacchioni, 163; **5** Paglicci, 130; **6** Mediani, 85.

ITALIAN FORMULA 3 CHAMPIONSHIP, Autodromo Santamonica, Misano Adriatico, Rimini, Italy, 21 October. Round 19. 20 laps of the 2.523-mile/4.060-km circuit, 50.455 miles/81.200 km.
1 Giancarlo Fisichella, I (Dallara F394-Opel), 29m 43.144s, 101.865 mph/163.935 km/h.
2 Roberto Colciago, I (Dallara F393/4-Fiat), 29m 43.991s.
3 Gianantonio Pacchioni, I (Dallara F393/4-Fiat), 29m 50.356s.
4 Andrea Boldrini, I (Dallara F393/4-Fiat), 29m 50.720s.
5 Gianluca Paglicci, I (Dallara F394-Fiat), 29m 51.832s.
6 Luca Riccitelli, I (Dallara F393/4-Fiat), 29m 54.385s.
7 Michele Gasparini, I (Dallara F394-Fiat), 29m 54.985s; **8** Giovanni Gulinelli, I (Dallara F393/4-Fiat), 30m 12.251s; **9** Gaston Mazzacane, I (Dallara F394-Opel), 30m 15.276s; **10** Thomas Biagi, I (Dallara F394-Mugen Honda), 30m 17.026s.
Fastest race lap: Colciago, 1m 27.940s, 103.275 mph/166.204 km/h.
Fastest qualifying lap: Fisichella, 1m 28.135s, 103.046 mph/165.836 km/h.

ITALIAN FORMULA 3 CHAMPIONSHIP, Autodromo Santamonica, Misano Adriatico, Rimini, Italy, 22 October. Round 20. 20 laps of the 2.523-mile/4.060-km circuit, 50.455 miles/81.200 km.
1 Andrea Boldrini, I (Dallara F393/4-Fiat), 30m 09.747s, 100.367 mph/161.525 km/h.
2 Giancarlo Fisichella, I (Dallara F394-Opel), 30m 20.590s.
3 Roberto Colciago, I (Dallara F393/4-Fiat), 30m 27.113s.
4 Gianantonio Pacchioni, I (Dallara F393/4-Fiat), 30m 28.771s.
5 Gianluca Paglicci, I (Dallara F394-Fiat), 30m 30.729s.
6 Luca Riccitelli, I (Dallara F393/4-Fiat), 30m 35.025s.
7 Luca Rangoni, I (Dallara F393-Fiat), 30m 42.646s; **8** Giovanni Gulinelli, I (Dallara F393/4-Fiat), 30m 44.020s; **9** Giorgio Tibaldo, I (Dallara F394-Fiat), 30m 50.320s; **10** Oliver Martini, I (Dallara F393-Mugen Honda), 30m 52.658s.
Fastest race lap: Boldrini, 1m 28.549s, 102.564 mph/165.061 km/h.

Final championship points

1	Giancarlo Fisichella, I	309
2	Luca Riccitelli, I	190
3	Gianantonio Pacchioni, I	185
4	Luca Rangoni, I	169.5
5	Gianluca Paglicci, I	146
6	Maurizio Mediani, I	85

7 Michele Gasparini, I, 64; **8** Federico Gemmo, I, 63; **9** Giovanni Gulinelli, I, 54; **10** Danilo Rossi, I, 46; **11** Alberto Pedemonte, I, 38; **12** Oliver Martini, I, 34; **13** Andrea Boldrini, I, 30; **14=** Roberto Colciago, I, 27; **14=** Rolando Galli, I, 27; **16** Giorgio Tibaldo, I, 16.5; **17** Paolo Ruberti, I, 16; **18** Thomas Biagi, I, 15; **19** Alberto Scilla, I, 13; **20** Pietro Antonelli, I, 11; **21** Danilo Tomassini, I, 9.5; **22** Fabrizio Gollin, I, 9; **23** Roberto Carta, I, 7; **24** Gastone Mazzacane, I, 5; **25** Andrea Belluzzi, I, 4; **26** Simone Rebai, I, 3; **27** Fabiano Belletti, I, 2; **28** Paolo Coloni, I, 1.

Major Non-Championship Formula 3 Results

1993 Results

The Macau and Fuji Formula 3 races were run after Autocourse 1993/94 went to press.

FIA F3 WORLD CUP, 40th MACAU GP, Circuito Da Guia, Macau, 22 November. 12 and 15 laps of the 3.801-mile/6.117-km circuit, 102.625 miles/165.159 km.
First heat stopped after an accident, and run over an aggregate of 1 and 11 laps.
1 Jörg Müller, D (Dallara F393-Fiat), 1h 02m 57.87s, 97.793 mph/157.383 km/h.
2 Tom Kristensen, DK (TOM'S 033F-Toyota), 1h 03m 23.77s.
3 Kelvin Burt, GB (Dallara F393-Mugen Honda), 1h 03m 30.31s.
4 Roberto Colciago, I (Dallara F393-Opel), 1h 03m 30.791s.
5 Massimiliano 'Max' Angelelli, I (Dallara F393-Opel), 1h 03m 39.59s.
6 Michael Krumm, D (Dallara F393-Opel), 1h 03m 49.42s.
7 Sascha Maassen, D (Dallara F393-Mugen Honda), 1h 03m 50.77s; **8** Oliver Gavin, GB (Dallara F393-Vauxhall), 1h 04m 28.25s; **9** Markus Liesner, USA (Dallara F393-Opel), 1h 04m 36.58s; **10** Christophe Tinseau, F (Dallara F393-Opel), 1h 04m 42.26s.
Fastest race lap: Rickard Rydell, S (TOM'S 033F-Toyota), 2m 17.40s, 99.588 mph/160.271 km/h (record).
Fastest qualifying lap: Müller, 2m 18.60s, 98.725 mph/158.883 km/h.

EURO-MACAU-FUJI CHALLENGE CUP, 4th INTERNATIONAL F3 LEAGUE, Fuji International Speedway, Japan, 28 November. 20 laps of the 2.777-mile/4.469-km circuit, 55.538 miles/89.380 km.
1 Tom Kristensen, DK (TOM'S 033F-Toyota), 29m 51.154s, 111.625 mph/179.643 km/h.
2 Roberto Colciago, I (Dallara F393-Opel), 29m 51.552s.
3 Massimiliano 'Max' Angelelli, I (Dallara F393-Opel), 29m 52.427s.
4 Oliver Gavin, GB (Dallara F393-Vauxhall), 29m 54.292s.
5 Warren Hughes, GB (Ralt 93C-Toyota), 30m 00.294s.
6 Michael Krumm, D (Dallara F393-Opel), 30m 03.097s.
7 Shinji Nakano, J (Dallara F393-Mugen Honda 393), 30m 03.814s; **8** Rickard Rydell, S (TOM'S 033F-Toyota), 30m 03.848s; **9** Hidetoshi Mitsusada, J (TOM'S 033F-Toyota), 30m 04.373s; **10** Christian Abt, D (Dallara F393-Opel), 30m 04.939s.
Fastest race lap: Vincenzo Sospiri, I (Dallara F393-TOM'S), 1m 28.675s, 112.736 mph/181.431 km/h.
Fastest qualifying lap: Colciago, 1m 28.611s, 112.817 mph/181.562 km/h.

1994 Results

36th GRAND PRIX DE MONACO FORMULA 3, Monte Carlo Circuit, Monaco, 14 May. 24 laps of the 2.068-mile/3.328-km circuit, 49.630 miles/79.872 km.
1 Giancarlo Fisichella, I (Dallara F394-Opel), 39m 06.16s, 76.154 mph/122.557 km/h.
2 Jörg Müller, D (Dallara F394-Fiat), 39m 07.86s.
3 Sascha Maassen, D (Dallara F394-Opel), 39m 13.12s.
4 Gianantonio Pacchioni, I (Dallara F393-Fiat), 39m 21.23s.
5 Massimiliano 'Max' Angelelli, I (Dallara F394-Volkswagen), 39m 22.05s.
6 Michael Krumm, D (Dallara F394-Opel), 39m 29.06s.
7 Philipp Peter, A (Dallara F394-Fiat), 39m 33.65s; **8** Luca Riccitelli, I (Dallara F393-Fiat), 39m 39.06s; **9** Oliver Martini, I (Dallara F394-Mugen Honda), 39m 39.71s; **10** Alexander Wurz, A (Dallara F394-Opel), 39m 40.34s.
Fastest race lap: Paolo Coloni, I (Dallara F394-Fiat), 1m 38.16s, 75.841 mph/122.054 km/h.
Fastest qualifying lap: Fisichella, 1m 34.23s, 79.004 mph/127.144 km/h.

4th MARLBORO MASTERS OF FORMULA 3, Circuit van Zandvoort, Holland, 7 August. 30 laps of the 1.565-mile/2.519-km circuit, 46.957 miles/75.570 km.
1 Gareth Rees, GB (Dallara F394-Mugen Honda), 36m 29.363s, 77.212 mph/124.261 km/h.
2 Jörg Müller, D (Dallara F394-Fiat), 36m 30.115s.
3 Sascha Maassen, D (Dallara F394-Opel), 36m 30.473s.
4 Philipp Peter, A (Dallara F394-Fiat), 36m 32.255s.
5 Norberto Fontana, RA (Dallara F394-Opel), 36m 35.150s.
6 Paolo Coloni, I (Dallara F394-Fiat), 36m 38.982s.
7 Roberto Colciago, I (Dallara F394-Fiat), 36m 41.176s; **8** Jérémie Dufour, F (Dallara F394-Mugen Honda), 36m 41.434s; **9** Giancarlo Fisichella, I (Dallara F394-Opel), 36m 42.153s; **10** Marcos Gueiros, BR (Dallara F394-Vauxhall), 36m 43.812s.
Fastest race lap: Maassen, 1m 01.509s, 91.610 mph/147.432 km/h.
Fastest qualifying lap: Müller, 1m 01.306s, 91.913 mph/147.920 km/h.

INTERNATIONAL FORMULA 3 CHALLENGE, Donington Park Grand Prix Circuit, Derbyshire, Great Britain, 16 October. 15 laps of the 2.500-mile/4.023-km circuit, 37.500 miles/60.350 km.
1 Christophe Tinseau, F (Dallara F393-Opel), 22m 18.61s, 100.851 mph/162.304 km/h.
2 Oliver Gavin, GB (Dallara F394-Vauxhall), 22m 24.63s.
3 Helio Castro Neves, BR (Dallara F394-Mugen Honda), 22m 25.92s.
4 Jamie Spence, GB (Dallara F394-Mugen Honda), 22m 32.70s.
5 Warren Hughes, GB (Dallara F394-TOM'S Toyota), 22m 36.42s.
6 Gualter Salles, BR (Dallara F394-Mugen Honda), 22m 38.44s.
7 Marc Gene, E (Dallara F394-HKS Mitsubishi), 22m 39.11s; **8** Laurent Redon, F (Dallara F394-Mugen Honda), 22m 42.09s; **9** Ralph Firman Jr, GB (Dallara F394-Mugen Honda), 22m 43.41s; **10** Jamie Davies, GB (Dallara F394-Vauxhall), 22m 43.62s.
Fastest race lap: Tinseau, 1m 28.01s, 102.261 mph/164.573 km/h (record)
Fastest qualifying lap: Pedro de la Rosa, E (Dallara F394-Mugen Honda), 1m 27.94s, 102.342 mph/164.704 km/h.

Result of Macau Formula 3 race will be given in Autocourse 1995/96.

Sports Cars

62nd GRAND PRIX D'ENDURANCE, LES 24 HEURES DU MANS, Circuit de la Sarthe, Le Mans, France, 18-19 June. 344 laps of the 8.451mile/13.600-km circuit, 2907.023 miles/4678.400 km.
1 Yannick Dalmas/Hurley Haywood/Mauro Baldi, F/USA/I (3.0t Dauer 962LM Porsche), 23h 57m 33.41s, 121.332 mph/195.265 km/h (1st Group A).
2 Eddie Irvine/Mauro Martini/Jeff Krosnoff, GB/I/USA (3.6t Toyota 94CV), 343 laps.
3 Hans-Joachim Stuck/Danny Sullivan/Thierry Boutsen, D/USA/B (3.0t Dauer 962LM Porsche), 343.
4 Steven Andskar/George Fouché/Bob Wollek, S/ZA/F (3.6t Toyota 94CV), 328.
5 Steve Millen/Johnny O'Connell/John Morton, NZ/USA/USA (3.0t Nissan 300ZX), 317.
6 Derek Bell/Robin Donovan/Jürgen Laessig, GB/GB/D (3.0t Kremer Porsche K8), 316.
7 Jean-Louis Ricci/Andy Evans/Philippe Olczyk, F/USA/CDN (3.0t Courage Porsche C32 LM), 310; **8** Dominique Dupuy/Jesùs Pareja/Carlos Palau Mallol, F/E/E (3.8 Porsche Carrera RSR), 307 (1st Group B); **9** Enzo Calderari/Lilian Keller-Bryner/Renato Mastropietro, CH/CH/I (3.8 Porsche Carrera RSR), 299; **10** Patrick Huisman/Cor Euser/Matjas Tomlje, NL/NL/SLO (3.8 Porsche Carrera RSR), 295; **11** Alfonso de Orléans Bourbon/Thomas Saldana/José Andres Vilarino, E/E/E (3.4 Ferrari 348GTC), 276; **12** René Arnoux/Justin Bell/Bertrand Balas, F/GB/F (8.0 Dodge Viper), 273; **13** Luc Galmard/Jean-Claude Police/Benjamin Roy, F/F/F (3.0t Alpine A610), 272; **14** Armin Hahne/Bertrand Gachot/Christophe Bouchut, D/F/F (3.0 Honda NSX), 257; **15** Yojiro Terada/Pierre de Thoisy/Franck Fréon, J/F/F (2.6r Mazda RX-7), 250; **16** Kazuo Shimizu/Hideki Okada/Philippe Favre, J/J/CH (3.0 Honda NSX), 240; **17** Jean-Louis Sirera/Javier Camp/Antonio Puig, F/E/E (3.0t Venturi 400GTR), 225; **18** François Migault/Denis Morin/Philippe Gache, F/F/F (8.0 Dodge Viper), 225; **19** Kunimitsu Takahashi/Keiichi Tsuchiya/Akira Iida, J/J/J (3.0 Honda NSX), 222; **20** Jean-Louis Maury-Laribière/Hervé Poulain/Bernard Chauvin, F/F/F (3.0t Venturi 600LM), 221; **21** Dominic Chappell/Jonathan Baker/Phil Andrews, GB/GB/GB (5.0 De Tomaso Pantera), 210; **22** Jun Harada/Tomiko Yoshikawa/Masahiko Kondo, J/J/J (3.0t Porsche 962 GTI), 189; **23** Stéphane Ratel/Edouard Chaufour/Franz Hunkeler, F/F/CH (3.0t Venturi 400GTR), 170; **24** Alain Cudini/Eric Hélary/'Jules' Boullion, F/F/F (3.5t Bugatti EB110 SS), 226 (DNF – accident); **25** Henri Pescarolo/Alain Ferté/Franck Lagorce, F/F/F (3.0t Courage Porsche C32 LM), 142 (DNF – engine); **26** Riccardo 'Rocky' Agusta/Almo Coppelli/Michel Krine, I/I/F (3.0t Venturi 600LM), 115 (DNF – fire); **27** Pierre-Henri Raphanel/Pascal Fabre/Lionel Robert, F/F/F (3.0t Courage Porsche C32 LM), 107 (DNF – engine); **28** Michel Ferté/Michel Neugarten/Olivier Grouillard, F/B/F (3.0t Venturi 600LM), 106 (DNF – engine); **29** Pierre Petit/Patrick Gonin, F/F (2.0t WR-Peugeot LM93), 104 (DNF – fire); **30** Franz Konrad/Antonio de Azevedo/Mike Sommer, A/BR/D (3.6t Porsche 911), 100 (DNF – engine); **31** Sylvain Boulay/Dominique Lacaud/Bernard Robin, F/F/F (3.5 ALD-BMW C298), 96 (DNF – engine); **32** Jean-Marie Almeras/Jacques Almeras/Jacques Laffite, F/F/F (3.8 Porsche Carrera RSR), 94 (DNF – accident); **33** Jean-François Yvon/Hervé Régout/Jean-Paul Libert, F/F/B (2.0t WR Peugeot LM93), 86 (DNF – engine); **34** John Nielsen/Thomas Bscher/Lindsay Owen-Jones, DK/D/GB (3.0t Porsche 968 RS), 84 (DNF accident); **35** Georges Tessier/Pascal Alexandre Dro/Bernard Santal, F/F/CH (3.0 Debora LMP2-94), 79 (DNF – engine); **36** Patrick Bourdais/Olivier Couvreur/Nicolas Minassian, F/F/F (3.5 Alpa LM Ford), 64 (DNF – suspension); **37** Jack Leconte/Pierre Yver/Jean-Louis Chereau, F/F/F (3.8 Porsche Carrera RSR), 62 (DNF – accident); **38** Peter Hardman/Richard Piper/Olindo Iacobelli, GB/GB/I (2.2t Lotus Esprit Sport 300), 59 (DNF – accident); **39** Robin Smith/'Stingbrace'/Tetsuya Ota, GB/I/J (3.5 Ferrari 348LM), 57 (DNF – clutch); **40** Dirk Ebling/Ulrich Richter/Karl Wlazik, D/D/D (3.8 Porsche Carrera RSR), 57 (DNF – engine); **41** Anders Olofsson/Sandro Angelastri/Luciano Della Noce, S/I/I (2.8t Ferrari F40), 51 (DNF – electrics); **42** Rob Wilson/William Hewland/David Brodie, NZ/GB/GB (2.0 Harrier LR9 Spyder LM), 45 (DNF – suspension); **43** Olivier Haberthuer/Patrick Vuillaume/Patrice Goueslard, CH/F/F (3.6t Porsche 911), 42 (DNF – turbo); **44** Ray Bellm/Harry Nuttall/Charlie Rickett, GB/GB/GB (3.8 Porsche Carrera RSR), 34 (DNF – engine); **45** Thorkild Thyrring/Andreas Fuchs/Klaas Zwart, DK/D/NL (2.2t Lotus Esprit Sport 300), 28 (DNF – stub axle); **46** Eric van de Poele/Paul Gentilozzi/Shunji Kasuya, B/USA/J (3.0t Nissan 300ZX), 25 (DNF – ignition); **47** Fabio Mancini/Oscar Larrauri/Joël Gouhier, I/RA/F (3.4 Ferrari 348GTC), 23 (DNF – fuel pump); **48** Boris Said III/Michel Maisonneuve/Frank Jelinski, USA/F/D (6.2 Callaway Corvette), 148 (DNF – disqualified).
Fastest race lap: Boutsen, 3m 52.54s, 130.826 mph/210.544 km/h.
Pole position: Ferté (Alain), 3m 51.05s, 131.670 mph/211.902 km/h.
Did not start: Ferdinand de Lesseps/Jacques Tropenat/Paul Belmondo, F/F/F (3.0t Venturi 600LM), did not qualify; Christian Heinkele/Guy Kuster/Hans J.B. 'Jon' Hugenholtz, F/USA/NL (2.0t Lotus Esprit S3), did not qualify.

PPG Indy Car World Series

AUSTRALIAN FAI INDY CAR GRAND PRIX, Surfers Paradise Street Circuit, Queensland, Australia, 20 March. Round 1. 55 laps of the 2.795-mile/4.498-km circuit, 153.725 miles/247.396 km.
1 Michael Andretti, USA (Reynard 94I-Ford Cosworth XB), 1h 53m 52.770s, 80.994 mph/130.346 km/h.
2 Emerson Fittipaldi, BR (Penske PC23-Ilmor D), 1h 53m 54.096s.
3 Mario Andretti, USA (Lola T94/00-Ford Cosworth XB), 1h 54m 00.650s.
4 Jimmy Vasser, USA (Reynard 94I-Ford Cosworth XB), 1h 54m 34.577s.
5 Stefan Johansson, S (Penske PC22-Ilmor D), 1h 55m 01.217s.
6 Mauricio Gugelmin, BR (Reynard 94I-Ford Cosworth XB), 1h 54m 22.328s.
7 Teo Fabi, I (Reynard 94I-Ilmor D), 54 laps; **8** Mike Groff, USA (Lola T93/00-Honda), 54; **9** Nigel Mansell, GB (Lola T94/00-Ford Cosworth XB), 54; **10** Scott Goodyear, CDN (Lola T94/00-Ford Cosworth XB), 53.
Most laps led: Andretti (Michael), 55.
Fastest qualifying lap: Mansell, 1m 34.877s, 106.053 mph/170.676 km/h (record).
Championship points: **1** Andretti (Michael), 21; **2** Fittipaldi, 16; **3** Andretti (Mario), 14; **4** Vasser, 12; **5** Johansson, 10; **6=** Groff, 8; **6=** Gugelmin, 8.

SLICK-50 200, Phoenix International Raceway, Arizona, USA, 10 April. Round 2. 200 laps of the 1.000-mile/1.609-km circuit, 200.000 miles/321.869 km.
1 Emerson Fittipaldi, BR (Penske PC23-Ilmor D), 1h 51m 41.615s, 107.437 mph/172.903 km/h.
2 Al Unser Jr, USA (Penske PC23-Ilmor D), 1h 51m 55.097s.
3 Nigel Mansell, GB (Lola T94/00-Ford Cosworth XB), 199 laps.
4 Stefan Johansson, S (Penske PC22-Ilmor D), 197.
5 Jimmy Vasser, USA (Reynard 94I-Ford Cosworth XB), 197.
6 Mike Groff, USA (Lola T94/00-Honda), 196.
7 Robby Gordon, USA (Lola T94/00-Ford Cosworth XB), 195; **8** Baul Boesel, BR (Lola T94/00-Ford Cosworth XB), 195; **9** Scott Sharp, USA (Lola T94/00-Ford Cosworth XB), 194; **10** Adrian Fernandez, MEX (Reynard 94I-Ilmor D), 194.
Most laps led: Fittipaldi, 124.
Fastest qualifying lap: Paul Tracy, CDN (Penske PC23-Ilmor D), 20.424s, 176.263 mph/283.668 km/h (record).
Championship points: **1** Fittipaldi, 37; **2=** Vasser, 22; **2=** Johansson, 22; **4** Andretti (Michael), 21; **5** Mansell, 19; **6** Unser Jr, 16.

TOYOTA GRAND PRIX OF LONG BEACH, Long Beach Street Circuit, California, USA, 17 April. Round 3. 105 laps of the 1.590-mile/2.559-km circuit, 166.950 miles/268.680 km.
1 Al Unser Jr, USA (Penske PC23-Ilmor D), 1h 40m 53.582s, 99.283 mph/159.781 km/h.
2 Nigel Mansell, GB (Lola T94/00-Ford Cosworth XB), 1h 41m 32.689s.
3 Robby Gordon, USA (Lola T94/00-Ford Cosworth XB), 1h 41m 39.854s.
4 Raul Boesel, BR (Lola T94/00-Ford Cosworth XB), 104 laps.
5 Mario Andretti, USA (Lola T94/00-Ford Cosworth XB), 104.
6 Michael Andretti, USA (Reynard 94I-Ford Cosworth XB), 104.
7 Mauricio Gugelmin, BR (Reynard 94I-Ford Cosworth XB), 104; **8** Adrian Fernandez, MEX (Reynard 94I-Ilmor D), 104; **9** Teo Fabi, I (Reynard 94I-Ilmor D), 104; **10** Stefan Johansson, S (Penske PC22-Ilmor D), 102 (DNF – fuel).
Most laps led: Unser Jr, 61.
Fastest qualifying lap: Paul Tracy, CDN (Penske PC23-Ilmor D), 52.780s, 108.450 mph/174.534 km/h (record).
Championship points: **1=** Fittipaldi, 37; **2=** Unser Jr, 37; **3** Mansell, 35; **4** Andretti (Michael), 29; **5** Johansson, 25; **6** Andretti (Mario), 24.

78th INDIANAPOLIS 500, Indianapolis Motor Speedway, Speedway, Indiana, USA, 29 May. Round 4. 200 laps of the 2.500-mile/4.023-km circuit, 500.000 miles/804.672 km.
1 Al Unser Jr, USA (Penske PC23-Mercedes Benz), 3h 06m 29.006s, 160.872 mph/258.899 km/h.
2 Jacques Villeneuve, CDN (Reynard 94I-Ford Cosworth XB), 3h 06m 37.606s.
3 Bobby Rahal, USA (Penske PC22-Ilmor D), 199 laps.
4 Jimmy Vasser, USA (Reynard 94I-Ford Cosworth XB), 199.
5 Robby Gordon, USA (Lola T94/00-Ford Cosworth XB), 199.
6 Michael Andretti, USA (Reynard 94I-Ford Cosworth XB), 198*.
7 Teo Fabi, I (Reynard 94I-Ilmor D), 198; **8** Eddie Cheever, USA (Lola T93/00-Menard), 197; **9** Bryan Herta, USA (Lola T94/00-Ford Cosworth XB), 197; **10** John Andretti, USA (Lola T94/00-Ford Cosworth XB), 196; **11** Mauricio Gugelmin, BR (Reynard 94I-Ford Cosworth XB), 196; **12** Brian Till, USA (Lola T93/00-Ford Cosworth XB), 194; **13** Stan Fox, USA (Reynard 94I-Ford Cosworth XB), 193 (DNF – accident); **14** Hiro Matsushita, J (Lola T94/00-Ford Cosworth XB), 193; **15** Stefan Johansson, S (Penske PC22-Ilmor D), 192; **16** Scott Sharp, USA (Lola T94/00-Ford Cosworth XB), 186; **17** Emerson Fittipaldi, BR (Penske PC23-Mercedes Benz), 184 (DNF accident); **18** Arie Luyendyk, NL (Lola T94/00-Ilmor D), 179 (DNF – engine); **19** Lyn St James, USA (Lola T94/00-Ford Cosworth XB), 170; **20** Scott Brayton, USA (Lola T93/00-Menard), 116 (DNF – engine); **21** Raul Boesel, BR (Lola T94/00-Ford Cosworth XB), 100 (DNF – water pump); **22** Nigel Mansell, GB (Lola T94/00-Ford Cosworth XB), 92 (DNF – accident); **23** Paul Tracy, CDN (Penske PC23-Mercedes Benz), 92 (DNF – turbo); **24** Hideshi Matsuda, J (Lola T93/00-Ford Cosworth XB), 90 (DNF – accident); **25** John Paul Jr, USA (Lola T93/00-Ilmor D), 89 (DNF – accident); **26** Dennis Vitolo, USA (Lola T93/00-Ford Cosworth XB), 89 (DNF – accident); **27** Marco Greco, BR (Lola T94/00-Ford Cosworth XB), 53 (DNF – electrics); **28** Adrian Fernandez, MEX (Reynard 94I-Ilmor D), 30 (DNF suspension); **29** Dominic Dobson, USA (Lola T94/00-Ford Cosworth XB), 29 (DNF – accident); **30** Scott Goodyear, CDN (Lola T94/00-Ford Cosworth XB), 29 (DNF – mechanical); **31** Mike Groff, USA (Penske PC22-Ilmor C), 28 (DNF – accident); **32** Mario Andretti, USA (Lola T94/00-Ford Cosworth XB), 23 (DNF – fuel system); **33** Roberto Guerrero, USA (Lola T92/00-Buick), 20 (DNF – accident).
** includes 1-lap penalty for passing under a yellow flag.*
Most laps led: Fittipaldi, 145.
Fastest qualifying lap: Unser Jr, 2m 37.887s, 228.011 mph/366.948 km/h (over four laps).
Did not qualify: Jeff Andretti, USA (Lola T93/00-Ilmor); Ross Bentley, USA (Lola T93/00-Ford Cosworth XB); Gary Bettenhausen, USA (Penske PC22-Ilmor D); Pancho Carter, USA (Lola T93/00-Ilmor C); Stéphan Grégoire, F (Lola T92/00-Buick); Buddy Lazier, USA (Lola T93/00-Ilmor C); Roberto Moreno, BR (Lola T94/00-Ford Cosworth XB); Tero Palmroth, SF (Lola T93/00-Ford Cosworth XB); Johnny Parsons, USA (Lola T93/00-Ford Cosworth XB); Willy T. Ribbs, USA (Lola T94/00-Ford Cosworth XB); Mark Smith, USA (Lola T94/00-Ford Cosworth XB); Al Unser, USA (Lola T94/00-Ford Cosworth XB); Alessandro Zampedri, I.
Championship points: **1** Unser Jr, 58; **2** Fittipaldi, 38; **3** Andretti (Michael), 37; **4** Mansell, 35; **5** Vasser, 34; **6** Gordon, 30.

MILLER GENUINE DRAFT 200, Wisconsin State Fair Park Speedway, West Allis, Milwaukee, Wisconsin, USA, 5 June. Round 5. 192 laps of the 1.000-mile/1.609-km circuit, 192.000 miles/308.994 km.
Scheduled for 200 laps, but stopped early, due to rain.
1 Al Unser Jr, USA (Penske PC23-Ilmor D), 1h 36m 57.964s, 118.804 mph/119.197 km/h.
2 Emerson Fittipaldi, BR (Penske PC23-Ilmor D), 1h 36m 59.458s.
3 Paul Tracy, CDN (Penske PC23-Ilmor D), 190 laps.
4 Michael Andretti, USA (Reynard 94I-Ford Cosworth XB), 189.
5 Nigel Mansell, GB (Lola T94/00-Ford Cosworth XB), 189.
6 Robby Gordon, USA (Lola T94/00-Ford Cosworth XB), 189.
7 Bobby Rahal, USA (Lola T94/00-Honda), 189; **8** Raul Boesel, BR (Lola T94/00-Ford Cosworth XB), 188; **9** Jacques Villeneuve, CDN (Reynard 94I-Ford Cosworth XB), 187; **10** Bryan Herta, USA (Lola T94/00-Ford Cosworth XB), 187.
Most laps led: Unser Jr, 155.
Fastest qualifying lap: Boesel, 22.310s, 161.363 mph/259.688 km/h.
Championship points: **1** Unser Jr, 79; **2** Fittipaldi, 54; **3** Andretti (Michael), 49; **4** Mansell, 45; **5** Gordon, 38; **6** Vasser, 36.

ITT AUTOMOTIVE DETROIT GRAND PRIX, Belle Isle Park Circuit, Detroit, Michigan, USA, 12 June. Round 6. 77 laps of the 2.100-mile/3.380-km circuit, 161.700 miles/260.231 km.
1 Paul Tracy, CDN (Penske PC23-Ilmor D), 1h 52m 29.642s, 86.245 mph/138.797 km/h.
2 Emerson Fittipaldi, BR (Penske PC23-Ilmor D), 1h 52m 38.856s.
3 Robby Gordon, USA (Lola T94/00-Ford Cosworth XB), 1h 52m 39.955s.
4 Teo Fabi, I (Reynard 94I-Ilmor D), 1h 52m 54.194s.
5 Michael Andretti, USA (Reynard 94I-Ford Cosworth XB), 1h 52m 56.007s.
6 Bobby Rahal, USA (Lola T94/00-Honda), 1h 52m 56.796s.
7 Jacques Villeneuve, CDN (Reynard 94I-Ford Cosworth XB), 1h 53m 07.463s; **8** Mauricio Gugelmin, BR (Reynard 94I-Ford Cosworth XB), 1h 53m 20.706s; **9** Bryan Herta, USA (Lola T94/00-Ford Cosworth XB), 1h 53m 21.739s; **10** Al Unser Jr, USA (Penske PC23-Ilmor D), 1h 53m 22.136s.
Most laps led: Unser Jr, 52.
Fastest qualifying lap: Nigel Mansell, GB (Lola T94/00-Ford Cosworth XB), 1m 09.582s, 108.649 mph/174.853 km/h (record).
Championship points: **1** Unser Jr, 83; **2** Fittipaldi, 70; **3** Andretti (Michael), 59; **4** Gordon, 52; **5** Mansell, 46; **6=** Vasser, 36; **6=** Tracy, 36.

BUDWEISER/G.I.JOE'S 200, Portland International Raceway, Oregon, USA, 26 June. Round 7. 102 laps of the 1.950-mile/3.138-km circuit, 198.900 miles/320.099 km.
1 Al Unser Jr, USA (Penske PC23-Ilmor D), 1h 50m 43.706s, 107.777 mph/173.451 km/h.
2 Emerson Fittipaldi, BR (Penske PC23-Ilmor D), 1h 50m 45.536s.
3 Paul Tracy, CDN (Penske PC23-Ilmor D), 1h 51m 16.177s.
4 Robby Gordon, USA (Lola T94/00-Ford Cosworth XB), 1h 51m 40.040s.
5 Nigel Mansell, GB (Lola T94/00-Ford Cosworth XB), 1h 51m 40.040s.
6 Jacques Villeneuve, CDN (Reynard 94I-Ford Cosworth XB), 101 laps.
7 Alessandro Zampedri, I (Lola T93/00-Ford Cosworth XB), 101; **8** Stefan Johansson, S (Penske PC22-Ilmor D), 101; **9** Mario Andretti, USA (Lola T94/00-Ford Cosworth XB), 100; **10** Adrian Fernandez, MEX (Reynard 94I-Ilmor D), 100.
Most laps led: Unser Jr, 96.
Fastest qualifying lap: Unser Jr, 1m 00.071s, 116.862 mph/188.071 km/h (record).
Championship points: **1** Unser Jr, 105; **2** Fittipaldi, 86; **3** Gordon, 64; **4** Andretti (Michael), 59; **5** Mansell, 56; **6** Tracy, 50.

BUDWEISER GRAND PRIX OF CLEVELAND, Burke Lakefront Airport Circuit, Cleveland, Ohio, USA, 10 July. Round 8. 85 laps of the 2.369-mile/3.813-km circuit, 201.365 miles/324.066 km.
1 Al Unser Jr, USA (Penske PC23-Ilmor D), 1h 27m 32.000s, 138.026 mph/222.132 km/h.
2 Nigel Mansell, GB (Lola T94/00-Ford Cosworth XB), 1h 27m 54.941s.
3 Paul Tracy, CDN (Penske PC23-Ilmor D), 85 laps.
4 Jacques Villeneuve, CDN (Reynard 94I-Ford Cosworth XB), 85.
5 Stefan Johansson, S (Penske PC22-Ilmor D), 84.
6 Raul Boesel, BR (Lola T94/00-Ford Cosworth XB), 84.
7 Adrian Fernandez, MEX (Reynard 94I-Ilmor D), 84; **8** Mauricio Gugelmin, BR (Reynard 94I-Ford Cosworth XB), 84; **9** Teo Fabi, I (Reynard 94I-Ilmor D), 83; **10** Alessandro Zampedri, I (Lola T93/00-Ford Cosworth XB), 83.
Most laps led: Unser Jr, 82.
Fastest qualifying lap: Unser Jr, 59.232s, 143.983 mph/231.718 km/h.
Championship points: **1** Unser Jr, 127; **2** Fittipaldi, 86; **3** Mansell, 72; **4** Gordon, 66; **5** Tracy, 64; **6** Andretti (Michael), 59.

MOLSON INDY TORONTO, Exhibition Place Circuit, Toronto, Ontario, Canada, 17 July. Round 9. 98 laps of the 1.780-mile/2.865-km circuit, 174.440 miles/280.734 km.
1 Michael Andretti, USA (Reynard 94I-Ford Cosworth XB), 1h 48m 15.978s, 96.673 mph/155.580 km/h.
2 Bobby Rahal, USA (Lola T94/00-Honda), 1h 48m 22.779s.
3 Emerson Fittipaldi, BR (Penske PC23-Ilmor D), 1h 48m 23.495s.
4 Mario Andretti, USA (Lola T94/00-Ford Cosworth XB), 1h 49m 18.374s.
5 Paul Tracy, CDN (Penske PC23-Ilmor D), 97 laps.
6 Robby Gordon, USA (Lola T94/00-Ford Cosworth XB), 97.
7 Andrea Montermini, I (Lola T93/00-Ford Cosworth XB), 97; **8** Teo Fabi, I (Reynard 94I-Ilmor D), 97; **9** Jacques Villeneuve, CDN (Reynard 94I-Ford Cosworth XB), 97; **10** Scott Goodyear, CDN (Lola T94/00-Ford Cosworth XB), 97.
Most laps led: Andretti (Michael), 71.
Fastest qualifying lap: Gordon, 58.154s, 110.190 mph/177.334 km/h (record).
Championship points: **1** Unser Jr, 127; **2** Fittipaldi, 100; **3** Andretti (Michael), 80; **4** Gordon, 75; **5** Tracy, 74; **6** Mansell, 72.

MARLBORO 500, Michigan International Speedway, Brooklyn, Michigan, USA, 31 July. Round 10. 250 laps of the 2.000-mile/3.219-km circuit, 500.000 miles/804.672 km.
1 Scott Goodyear, CDN (Lola T94/00-Ford Cosworth XB), 3h 07m 44.099s, 159.800 mph/257.173 km/h.
2 Arie Luyendyk, NL (Lola T94/00-Ilmor D), 249 laps.
3 Dominic Dobson, USA (Lola T94/00-Ford Cosworth XB), 248.
4 Teo Fabi, I (Reynard 94I-Ilmor D), 246.
5 Mark Smith, USA (Lola T94/00-Ford Cosworth XB), 240.
6 Hiro Matsushita, J (Lola T94/00-Ford Cosworth XB), 239.
7 Willy T. Ribbs, USA (Lola T94/00-Ford Cosworth XB), 236; **8** Al Unser Jr, USA (Penske PC23-Ilmor D), 231 (DNF – engine); **9** Raul Boesel, BR (Lola T94/00-Ford Cosworth XB), 225 (DNF – engine); **10** Emerson Fittipaldi, BR (Penske PC23-Ilmor D), 209 (DNF engine).
Most laps led: Boesel, 120.
Fastest qualifying lap: Nigel Mansell, GB (Lola T94/00-Ford Cosworth XB), 30.804s, 233.736 mph/376.161 km/h.
Championship points: **1** Unser Jr, 132; **2** Fittipaldi, 103; **3** Andretti (Michael), 80; **4** Gordon, 75; **5** Tracy, 74; **6** Mansell, 73.

MILLER GENUINE DRAFT 200, Mid-Ohio Sports Car Course, Lexington, Ohio, USA, 14 August. Round 11. 83 laps of the 2.250-mile/3.621-km circuit, 185.800 miles/299.016 km.
1 Al Unser Jr, USA (Penske PC23-Ilmor D), 1h 40m 59.436s, 110.387 mph/177.650 km/h.
2 Paul Tracy, CDN (Penske PC23-Ilmor D), 1h 41m 01.056s.
3 Emerson Fittipaldi, BR (Penske PC23-Ilmor D), 83 laps.
4 Robby Gordon, USA (Lola T94/00-Ford Cosworth XB), 82.
5 Michael Andretti, USA (Reynard 94I-Ford Cosworth XB), 82.
6 Adrian Fernandez, MEX (Reynard 94I-Ilmor D), 82.
7 Nigel Mansell, GB (Lola T94/00-Ford Cosworth XB), 82; **8** Raul Boesel, BR (Lola T94/00-Ford Cosworth XB), 82; **9** Jacques Villeneuve, CDN (Reynard 94I-Ford Cosworth XB), 82; **10** Mario Andretti, USA (Lola T94/00-Ford Cosworth XB), 82.
Most laps led: Tracy, 56.
Fastest qualifying lap: Unser Jr, 1m 07.773s, 119.517 mph/192.343 km/h (record).
Championship points: **1** Unser Jr, 153; **2** Fittipaldi, 117; **3** Tracy, 91; **4** Andretti (Michael), 90; **5** Gordon, 87; **6** Mansell, 79.

NEW ENGLAND SLICK 50 200, New Hampshire International Speedway, Loudon, New Hampshire, USA, 21 August. Round 12. 200 laps of the 1.058-mile/1.703-km circuit, 211.600 miles/340.537 km.
1 Al Unser Jr, USA (Penske PC23-Ilmor D), 1h 43m 31.594s, 122.635 mph/197.362 km/h.
2 Paul Tracy, CDN (Penske PC23-Ilmor D), 1h 43m 42.484s.
3 Emerson Fittipaldi, BR (Penske PC23-Ilmor D), 1h 43m 33.326s.
4 Raul Boesel, BR (Lola T94/00-Ford Cosworth XB), 198 laps.
5 Michael Andretti, USA (Reynard 94I-Ford Cosworth XB), 198.
6 Dominic Dobson, USA (Lola T94/00-Ford Cosworth XB), 197.
7 Jimmy Vasser, USA (Reynard 94I-Ford Cosworth XB), 195; **8** Adrian Fernandez, MEX (Reynard 94I-Ilmor D), 195; **9** Bobby Rahal, USA (Lola T94/00-Honda), 193; **10** Willy T. Ribbs, USA (Lola T94/00-Ford Cosworth XB), 192.
Most laps led: Fittipaldi, 90.
Fastest qualifying lap: Fittipaldi, 21.753s, 175.093 mph/281.785 km/h (record).
Championship points: **1** Unser Jr, 173; **2** Fittipaldi, 133; **3** Tracy, 107; **4** Andretti (Michael), 100; **5** Gordon, 90; **6** Mansell, 79.

MOLSON INDY VANCOUVER, Vancouver Street Circuit, Pacific Place, Vancouver, British Columbia, Canada, 4 September. Round 13. 102 laps of the 1.653-mile/2.660-km circuit, 168.606 miles/271.345 km.

1 Al Unser Jr, USA (Penske PC23-Ilmor D), 1h 53m 27.321s, 89.166 mph/143.499 km/h.
2 Robby Gordon, USA (Lola T94/00-Ford Cosworth XB), 1h 53m 29.612s.
3 Michael Andretti, USA (Reynard 94I-Ford Cosworth XB), 1h 53m 34.429s.
4 Scott Goodyear, CDN (Lola T94/00-Ford Cosworth XB), 1h 53m 39.788s.
5 Mauricio Gugelmin, BR (Reynard 94I-Ford Cosworth XB), 1h 53m 40.171s.
6 Arie Luyendyk, NL (Lola T94/00-Ilmor D), 1h 53m 42.164s.
7 Bobby Rahal, USA (Lola T94/00-Honda), 1h 53m 45.003s; **8** Mark Smith, USA (Lola T94/00-Ford Cosworth XB), 1h 53m 59.692s; **9** Emerson Fittipaldi, BR (Penske PC23-Ilmor D), 101 laps (DNF – accident); **10** Nigel Mansell, GB (Lola T94/00-Ford Cosworth XB), 101 (DNF – accident).
Most laps led: Mansell, 39.
Fastest qualifying lap: Gordon, 54.570s, 109.049 mph/175.497 km/h.
Championship points: 1 Unser Jr, 193; **2** Fittipaldi, 137; **3** Andretti (Michael), 114; **4** Tracy, 107; **5** Gordon, 104; **6** Mansell, 83.

TEXACO/HAVOLINE 200, Road America Circuit, Elkhart Lake, Wisconsin, USA, 11 September. Round 14. 50 laps of the 4.000-mile/6.437-km circuit, 200.000 miles/321.869 km.
1 Jacques Villeneuve, CDN (Reynard 94I-Ford Cosworth XB), 1h 42m 37.930s, 116.922 mph/188.168 km/h.
2 Al Unser Jr, USA (Penske PC23-Ilmor D), 1h 42m 38.539s.
3 Emerson Fittipaldi, BR (Penske PC23-Ilmor D), 1h 42m 40.533s.
4 Teo Fabi, I (Reynard 94I-Ilmor D), 1h 43m 01.796s.
5 Adrian Fernandez, MEX (Reynard 94I-Ilmor D), 1h 43m 05.567s.
6 Raul Boesel, BR (Lola T94/00-Ford Cosworth XB), 1h 43m 09.981s.
7 Scott Goodyear, CDN (Lola T94/00-Ford Cosworth XB), 1h 43m 11.950s; **8** Stefan Johansson, S (Penske PC22-Ilmor D), 1h 43m 14.134s; **9** Bobby Rahal, USA (Lola T94/00-Honda), 1h 43m 14.934s; **10** Scott Sharp, USA (Lola T94/00-Ford Cosworth XB), 1h 43m 15.360s.
Most laps led: Paul Tracy, CDN (Penske PC23-Ilmor D), 35.
Fastest qualifying lap: Tracy, 1m 45.416s, 136.602 mph/219.839 km/h.
Championship points: 1 Unser Jr, 209; **2** Fittipaldi, 151; **3** Andretti (Michael), 114; **4** Tracy, 109; **5** Gordon, 104; **6** Mansell, 83.

BOSCH SPARK PLUG GRAND PRIX, Pennsylvania International Raceway, Nazareth, Pennsylvania, USA, 18 September. Round 15. 200 laps of the 1.000-mile/1.609-km circuit, 200.000 miles/321.869 km.
1 Paul Tracy, CDN (Penske PC23-Ilmor D), 1h 31m 30.292s, 131.141 mph/211.050 km/h.
2 Al Unser Jr, USA (Penske PC23-Ilmor D), 1h 31m 38.751s.
3 Emerson Fittipaldi, BR (Penske PC23-Ilmor D), 1h 31m 44.46s.
4 Raul Boesel, BR (Lola T94/00-Ford Cosworth XB), 196 laps.
5 Stefan Johansson, S (Penske PC22-Ilmor D), 195.
6 Teo Fabi, I (Reynard 94I-Ilmor D), 194.
7 Jacques Villeneuve, CDN (Reynard 94I-Ford Cosworth XB), 193; **8** Scott Goodyear, CDN (Lola T94/00-Ford Cosworth XB), 191; **9** Michael Andretti, USA (Reynard 94I-Ford Cosworth XB), 191; **10** Mauricio Gugelmin, BR (Reynard 94I-Ford Cosworth XB), 190.
Most laps led: Tracy, 192.
Fastest qualifying lap: Fittipaldi, 19.397s, 185.596 mph/298.687 km/h.
Championship points: 1 Unser Jr, 225; **2** Fittipaldi, 166; **3** Tracy, 130; **4** Andretti (Michael), 118; **5** Gordon, 104; **6** Mansell, 83.

TOYOTA GRAND PRIX OF MONTEREY FEATURING THE BANK OF AMERICA 300, Laguna Seca Raceway, Monterey, California, USA, 9 October. Round 16. 84 laps of the 2.214-mile/3.563-km circuit, 185.976 miles/299.299 km.
1 Paul Tracy, CDN (Penske PC23-Ilmor D), 2h 00m 00.763s, 92.978 mph/149.634 km/h.
2 Raul Boesel, BR (Lola T94/00-Ford Cosworth XB), 2h 00m 22.180s.
3 Jacques Villeneuve, CDN (Reynard 94I-Ford Cosworth XB), 84 laps.
4 Emerson Fittipaldi, BR (Penske PC23-Ilmor D), 84.
5 Teo Fabi, I (Reynard 94I-Ilmor D), 84.
6 Arie Luyendyk, NL (Lola T94/00-Ilmor D), 84.
7 Adrian Fernandez, MEX (Reynard 94I-Ilmor D), 84; **8** Nigel Mansell, GB (Lola T94/00-Ford Cosworth XB), 83; **9** Andrea Montermini, I (Lola T93/00-Ford Cosworth XB), 83; **10** Dominic Dobson, USA (Lola T94/00-Ford Cosworth XB), 83.
Most laps led: Tracy, 84.
Fastest qualifying lap: Tracy, 1m 10.059s, 113.768 mph/183.093 km/h.

Final championship points

1	Al Unser Jr, USA	225
2	Emerson Fittipaldi, BR	178
3	Paul Tracy, CDN	152
4	Michael Andretti, USA	118
5	Robby Gordon, USA	104
6	Jacques Villeneuve, CDN	94

7 Raul Boesel, BR, 90; **8** Nigel Mansell, GB, 88; **9** Teo Fabi, I, 79; **10** Bobby Rahal, USA, 59; **11** Stefan Johansson, S, 57; **12** Scott Goodyear, CDN, 55; **13** Adrian Fernandez, MEX, 46; **14** Mario Andretti, USA, 45; **15** Jimmy Vasser, USA, 42; **16** Mauricio Gugelmin, BR, 39; **17** Arie Luyendyk, NL, 34; **18** Dominic Dobson, USA, 30; **19=** Mark Smith, USA, 17; **19=** Mike Groff, USA, 17; **21** Scott Sharp, USA, 14; **22** Willy T. Ribbs, USA, 12; **23** Bryan Herta, USA, 11; **24** Andrea Montermini, I, 10; **25** Alessandro Zampedri, I, 9; **26** Hiro Matsushita, J, 8; **27** Eddie Cheever, USA, 5; **28** John Andretti, USA, 3; **29=** Marco Greco, BR, 2; **29=** Christian Danner, D, 2; **31=** Davy Jones, USA, 1; **31=** Franck Fréon, F, 1; **31=** Brian Till, USA, 1.

IMSA Camel GT Championship

ROLEX 24 HOURS AT DAYTONA, Daytona International Speedway, Daytona Beach, Florida, USA, 5/6 February. Exxon World Sports Car Championship, Round 1. Exxon Supreme GT Series for IMSA GTS/GTO/GTU, Round 1. 707 laps of the 3.560-mile/5.729-km circuit, 2516.920 miles/4050.590 km.
1 Scott Pruett/Paul Gentilozzi/Butch Leitzinger/Steve Millen, USA/USA/USA/NZ (Nissan 300ZX), 24h 00m 54.016s, 104.806 mph/168.669 km/h (1st GTS class).
2 Bob Wollek/Jürgen Barth/Dominique Dupy/Jesús Pareja/Jack Leconte, F/D/F/E/D (Porsche 911 turbo), 683 laps.
3 Dirk Ebeling/Karl Wlazik/Ulrich Richter/Gunter Doebler, D/D/D/D (Porsche 911 RSR), 671 (1st GTU class).
4 Harald Grohs/Mark Sandridge/Bernd Maylaender/Frank Katthoefer, D/USA/D/D (Porsche 911 RSR), 670.
5 Irv Hoerr/Tommy Riggins/R.K. Smith/Price Cobb, USA/USA/USA/USA (Oldsmobile Cutlass), 665.
6 Cor Euser/Maurizio Sala/Franz Konrad/Antonio Hermann, NL/BR/D/BR (Porsche 911 RSR), 664.
7 John Heinricy/Boris Said/Andy Pilgrim/Stuart Hayner, USA/USA/USA/USA (Chevrolet Corvette), 658; **8** Edgar Doeren/Luigiano Pagotto/Sandro Angelastri/Gualtiero Giribaldi, D/CH/CH/I (Porsche 911 RSR), 656; **9** Bob Schader/Jeremy Dale/Ruggero Melgrati/Price Cobb, USA/CDN/I/USA (Olsmobile Spice AK93), 651 (1st WSC class); **10** Wayne Taylor/Jim Downing/Hugh Fuller/Charles Morgan, ZA/USA/USA/USA (Mazda Kudzu DG3), 650.
Fastest race lap: John Morton, USA (Nissan 300ZX), 1m 51.829s, 114.604 mph/184.437 km/h.
Fastest qualifying lap: Fermin Velez, E (Chevrolet Spice WSC94), 1h 45.934s, 120.981 mph/194.700 km/h (record).

CONTAC 12-HOURS OF SEBRING INTERNATIONAL CAMEL GRAND PRIX OF ENDURANCE, Sebring International Raceway, Florida, USA, 19 March. Exxon World Sports Car Championship, Round 2. Exxon Supreme GT Series for IMSA GTS/GTO/GTU, Round 2. 327 laps of the 3.700mile/5.955-km circuit, 1209.900 miles/1947.145 km.
1 Steve Millen/Johnny O'Connell/John Morton, NZ/USA/USA (Nissan 300ZX), 12h 01m 22.068s, 100.634 mph/161.954 km/h (1st GTS class).
2 Derek Bell/Andy Wallace/James Weaver, GB/GB/GB (Chevrolet ATS Spice), 322 laps (1st WSC class).
3 Jim Downing/Wayne Taylor/Tim McAdam, USA/ZA/USA (Mazda Kudzu DG3), 314.
4 Andy Evans/Ross Bentley/Butch Leitzinger, USA/CDN/USA (Chevrolet Spice WSC94), 309.
5 Mark Sandridge/Joe Varde/Nick Ham, USA/USA/USA (Porsche 911 RSR), 305 (1st GTU class).
6 Jim Pace/Butch Hamlet/Barry Waddell, USA/USA/USA (Nissan 240SX), 305.
7 Ornulf Wirdheim/Franz Konrad/Ferdinand de Lesseps/Charles Mendez, S/D/B/USA (Porsche 911 turbo), 299; **8** Jochen Rohr/Jeff Purner/John O'Steen, USA/USA/USA (Porsche 911 RSR), 298; **9** Enzo Calderari/Lilian Keller-Bryner/Renato Mastropietro, CH/CH/I (Porsche 911 RSR), 293; **10** Scott Lagasse/Ken Schrader, USA/USA (Chevrolet Consulier), 289.
Fastest race lap: Bentley, 2m 03.342s, 107.992 mph/173.797 km/h (record).
Fastest qualifying lap: Jeremy Dale, CDN (Oldsmobile Spice AK93), 2m 01.376s, 109.742 mph/176.612 km/h (record).

GRAND PRIX OF ATLANTA, Atlanta Motor Speedway Circuit, Braselton, Georgia, USA, 17 April. Exxon World Sports Car Championship, Round 3. 93 laps of the 2.520-mile/4.056-km circuit, 234.360 miles/377.166 km.
1 Jay Cochran, USA (Ferrari 333SP), 2h 01m 10.723s, 116.040 mph/186.749 km/h.
2 Gianpiero Moretti/Eliseo Salazar, I/RCH (Ferrari 333SP), 92 laps.
3 Andy Wallace, GB (Chevrolet ATS Spice), 92.
4 Jim Downing/Wayne Taylor, USA/ZA (Mazda Kudzu DG3), 91.
5 Ross Bentley/Andy Evans, CDN/USA (Ferrari 333SP), 91.
6 Fermin Velez/Hugh Fuller, E/USA (Chevrolet Spice WSC94), 90.
7 John Macaluso, USA (Buick Tiga DBIV), 80; **8** Jeremy Dale/Bob Schader, CDN/USA (Oldsmobile Spice AK93), 77; **9** Joseph Hamilton/Stan Cleva, USA/USA (Mazda Tiga), 77; **10** Scott Lagasse, USA (Chevrolet Consulier), 72.
Fastest race lap: Cochran, 1m 14.855s, 121.194 mph/195.043 km/h (record).
Fastest qualifying lap: Mauro Baldi, I (Ferrari 333SP), 1m 13.030s, 124.223 mph/199.917 km/h (record).
Other race/class winners (Exxon Supreme GT Series for IMSA GTS/GTO/GTU, Round 3. 17 April. 42 laps, 105.840 miles/170.333 km).
GTS: Steve Millen, NZ (Nissan 300ZX), 55m 57.096s, 113.498 mph/182.657 km/h.
GTO: Joe Pezza, USA (Ford Mustang), 40 laps.
GTU: Jim Pace, USA (Nissan 240SX), 39.

TOYOTA TRUCKS LIME ROCK GRAND PRIX, Lime Rock Park Circuit, Lakeville, Connecticut, USA, 30 May. Exxon World Sports Car Championship, Round 4. 132 laps of the 1.540-mile/2.478-km circuit, 203.280 miles/327.147 km.
1 Gianpiero Moretti/Eliseo Salazar, I/RCH (Ferrari 333SP), 2h 00m 28.019s, 101.246 mph/162.940 km/h.
2 Jay Cochran, USA (Ferrari 333SP), 2h 00m 44.721s.
3 Andy Evans/Charles Morgan, USA/USA (Ferrari 333SP), 131 laps.
4 Wayne Taylor/Jim Downing, ZA/USA (Mazda Kudzu DG3), 130.
5 Price Cobb/Rick Sutherland, USA/USA (Oldsmobile Spice AK93), 129.
6 Jeremy Dale/Bob Schader, CDN/USA (Oldsmobile Spice HC94), 129.
7 John Macaluso, USA (Buick Tiga DBIV), 121; **8** Paul Debban/Leigh Miller, USA/USA (Buick Kudzu DG2), 121; **9** Scott Lagasse, USA (Chevrolet Consulier), 119; **10** John Jones/Jeffrey Lapcevich, CDN/CDN (Buick Tiga FJ94), 100.
Fastest race lap: Cochran, 50.208s, 110.421 mph/177.705 km/h (record).
Fastest qualifying lap: Salazar, 50.508s, 109.765 mph/176.649 km/h (record).
Other race/class winners (Exxon Supreme GT Series for IMSA GTS/GTO/GTU, Round 4, 60 laps, 92.400 miles/148.703 km).
GTS: Irv Hoerr, USA (Oldsmobile Cutlass Supreme), 55m 08.940s, 100.528 mph/161.784 km/h.
GTO: Joe Pezza, USA (Ford Mustang), 58 laps.
GTU: Bill Auberlen, USA (Mazda RX-7), 56.

GLEN CONTINENTAL XI, Watkins Glen International 'Long Course', New York, USA, Exxon World Sports Car Championship, Round 5, 26 June. Exxon Supreme GT Series for IMSA GTS/GTO/GTU, Round 5. 80 laps of the 3.400-mile/5.472-km circuit, 272.000 miles/437.742 km.
1 Gianpiero Moretti/Eliseo Salazar, I/RCH (Ferrari 333SP), 2h 59m 56.349s, 90.697 mph/145.963 km/h (1st WSC class).
2 Irv Hoerr, USA (Oldsmobile Cutlass Supreme), 3h 00m 55.894s (1st GTS class).
3 Steve Millen/Johnny O'Connell, NZ/USA (Nissan 300ZX), 78 laps.
4 Darin Brassfield, USA (Oldsmobile Cutlass Supreme), 77.
5 Hans-Joachim Stuck/Hurley Haywood, D/USA (Porsche 911 turbo), 77.
6 Brian DeVries, USA (Oldsmobile Cutlass), 76 (1st GTO class).
7 Bob Schader/Jeremy Dale, USA/CDN (Oldsmobile Spice HC94), 75; **8** Charles Morgan, USA (Chevrolet Camaro), 75; **9** Rob Dyson/James Weaver, USA/GB (Ferrari Dyson 348), 75; **10** Eduardo Dibos, PE (Mazda RX-7), 75 (1st GTU class).
Fastest race lap: Salazar, 1m 46.560s, 114.865 mph/184.857 km/h (record).
Fastest qualifying lap: Salazar, 1m 43.486s, 118.277 mph/190.348 km/h (record).

1994 INDY GRAND PRIX, Indianapolis Raceway Park, Indianapolis, Indiana, USA, Exxon World Sports Car Championship, Round 6. 10 July, 82 laps of the 2.500-mile/4.023-km circuit, 205.000 miles/329.916 km/h.
1 Eliseo Salazar/Gianpiero Moretti, RCH/I (Ferrari 333SP), 2h 00m 16.573s, 102.265 mph/164.579 km/h.
2 Andy Evans/Fermin Velez, USA/E (Ferrari 333SP), 2h 00m 25.137s.
3 James Weaver/John Paul Jr, GB/USA (Ferrari Dyson 348), 82 laps.
4 Jeremy Dale/Bob Schader, CDN/USA (Oldsmobile Spice HC94), 81.
5 Jim Downing/Wayne Taylor, USA/ZA (Mazda Kudzu DG3), 79.
6 Tony Kester, USA (Mazda Tiga), 78.
7 Charles Morgan/Hugh Fuller, USA/USA (Chevrolet Spice), 76; **8** Henry Camferdam/Roger Mandeville, USA/USA (Mazda Hawk MD3R), 75; **9** Oliver Kuttner, USA (BMW Pegasus), 75; **10** Leigh Miller/Paul Debban, USA (Buick Kudzu), 73.
Fastest race lap: Salazar, 1m 23.622s, 107.627 mph/173.209 km/h (record).
Fastest qualifying lap: Salazar, 1m 22.533s, 109.047 mph/175.495 km/h (record).
Other race/class winners (Exxon Supreme GT Series for IMSA GTS/GTO/GTU, Round 6, 35 laps, 87.500 miles/140.818 km/h).
GTS: Irv Hoerr, USA (Oldsmobile Cutlass Supreme), 56m 12.084s, 93.414 mph/150.335 km/h.
GTO: Joe Pezza, USA (Ford Mustang), 34 laps.
GTU: Jim Pace, USA (Nissan 240SX), 33.

MONTEREY SPORTS CAR GRAND PRIX, Laguna Seca Raceway, Monterey, California, USA, 24 July. Exxon World Sports Car Championship, Round 7. 82 laps of the 2.214-mile/3.563-km circuit, 181.548 miles/292.173 km.
1 Andy Evans/Fermin Velez, USA/E (Ferrari 333SP), 2h 00m 48.609s, 90.165 mph/145.107 km/h.
2 Eliseo Salazar, RCH (Ferrari 333SP), 2h 00m 56.115s.
3 Jeremy Dale, CDN (Oldsmobile Spice HC94), 82 laps.
4 Jay Cochran/Russell Spence, USA/GB (Ferrari 333SP), 82.
5 James Weaver, GB (Ferrari Dyson 348), 81.
6 Paul Debban/Leigh Miller, USA/USA (Buick Kudzu), 78.
7 Henry Camferdam/Roger Mandeville, USA/USA (Mazda Hawk MD3R), 78; **8** Wayne Taylor/Jim Downing, ZA/USA (Mazda Kudzu DG3), 77; **9** Craig Nelson/Dan Clark, USA/USA (Lexus Spice), 76; **10** Oliver Kuttner, USA (BMW Pegasus), 74.
Fastest race lap: Velez, 1m 23.017s, 96.009 mph/154.512 km/h (record).
Fastest qualifying lap: Andy Wallace, GB (Oldsmobile Spice), 1m 21.378s, 97.942 mph/157.624 km/h (record).
Other race/class winners (Exxon Supreme GT Series for IMSA GTS/GTO/GTU, Round 7. 24 July. 38 laps, 84.132 miles/135.397 km).
GTS: Johnny O'Connell, USA (Nissan 300ZX), 56m 31.122s, 89.314 mph/143.737 km/h.
GTO: Joe Pezza, USA (Ford Mustang), 37 laps.
GTU: Jim Pace, USA (Nissan 240SX), 36.

1994 IMSA GRAND PRIX OF PORTLAND, Portland International Raceway, Oregon, USA, 7 August. Exxon World Sports Car Championship, Round 8. 75 laps of the 1.950-mile/3.138-km circuit, 146.250 miles/235.367 km.
1 Jeremy Dale, CDN (Oldsmobile Spice HC94), 1h 41m 37.757s, 86.343 mph/138.956 km/h.
2 Gianpiero Moretti/Eliseo Salazar, I/RCH (Ferrari 333SP), 1h 41m 48.997s.
3 Jim Downing/Ferdinand de Lesseps, USA/F (Buick Kudzu DG2), 71 laps.
4 Roger Mandeville/Harry Camferdam, USA/USA (Mazda Hawk MD3R), 70.
5 Andy Wallace/Hugh Fuller, GB/USA (Oldsmobile Spice), 67.
6 Bob Schader/Rick Sutherland, USA/USA (Oldsmobile Spice), 66.
7 Paul Debban/John Macaluso, USA/USA (Chevrolet Kudzu DL4), 60; **8** Wayne Taylor, ZA (Mazda Kudzu DG3), 59; **9** Bobby Brown/Brian DeVries, USA/USA (Buick Tiga DBIV), 59; **10** Andy Evans/Fermin Velez, USA/E (Ferrari 333SP), 54.
Fastest race lap: Velez, 1m 09.595s, 100.869 mph/162.333 km/h (record).
Fastest qualifying lap: Wallace, GB, 1m 08.403s, 102.627 mph/165.162 km/h (record).
Other race/class winners (Exxon Supreme GT Series for IMSA GTS/GTO/GTU, Round 8. 41 laps, 79.950 miles/128.667 km).
GTS: Steve Millen, NZ (Nissan 300ZX), 55m 11.431s, 86.917 mph/139.880 km/h.
GTO: Tommy Riggins, USA (Oldsmobile Cutlass), 40 laps.
GTU: Butch Hamlet, USA (Nissan 240SX), 39.

'THE CHECKER' IMSA CAMEL GRAND PRIX, Phoenix International Raceway, Arizona, USA, 1 October. Exxon World Sports Car Championship, Round 9. 117 laps of the 1.500-mile/2.414-km circuit, 175.500 miles/282.440 km.
1 Jeremy Dale, CDN (Oldsmobile Spice HC94), 2h 00m 09.282s, 87.637 mph/141.038 km/h.
2 Gianpiero Moretti/Eliseo Salazar, I/RCH (Ferrari 333SP), 116 laps.
3 Jim Pace/Wayne Taylor, USA/ZA (Mazda Kudzu DG3), 115.
4 Andy Wallace/Hugh Fuller, GB/USA (Chevrolet Spice), 114.
5 James Weaver, GB (Ferrari Dyson 348), 114.
6 Andy Evans/Fermin Velez, USA/E (Ferrari 333SP), 110.
7 Stanley Dickens/Jim Downing, S/USA (Buick Kudzu DG2), 109; **8** Jay Cochran, USA (Ferrari 333SP), 107; **9** Roger Mandeville/Henry Camferdam, USA/USA (Mazda Hawk MD3R), 106; **10** Leigh Miller/Paul Debban/Bob Schader, USA/USA/USA (Buick Kudzu DL4), 106.
Fastest race lap: Wallace, 56.902s, 94.900 mph/152.727 km/h (record).
Fastest qualifying lap: Dale, 55.725s, 96.904 mph/155.953 km/h (record).
Other race/class winners (Exxon Supreme GT Series for IMSA GTS/GTO/GTU, Round 9. 52 laps, 78.000 miles/125.529 km).
GTS: Johnny O'Connell, USA (Nissan 300ZX), 55m 53.073s, 83.744 mph/134.773 km/h.
GTO: Paul Gentilozzi, USA (Chevrolet Camaro), 52 laps.
GTU: Bill Auberlen, USA (Mazda RX-7), 50.

Final championship points
WSC drivers

1	Wayne Taylor, ZA	190
2	Jeremy Dale, CDN	187
3	Jim Downing, USA	178
4	Andy Evans, USA	169
5	Bob Schader, USA	160
6	Eliseo Salazar, RCH	158

7 James Weaver, GB, 127; **8** Fermin Velez, E, 108; **9** Paul Debban, USA, 100; **10** Hugh Fuller, USA, 96.

WSC manufacturers

1	Oldsmobile	163
2	Ferrari	159
3	Mazda	158
4	Buick	137
5	Chevrolet	136
6	BMW	72

GTS drivers

1	Steve Millen, NZ	137
2	Johnny O'Connell, USA	129
3	Irv Hoerr, USA	117
4	Darin Brassfield, USA	85
5	Eric van de Poele, B	34
6=	Paul Gentilozzi, USA	28
6=	Scott Pruett, USA	28
6=	Jeffrey Pattinson, USA	28
6=	Bruce Trenery, USA	28

GTS manufacturers

1	Nissan	175
2	Oldsmobile	140
3	Porsche	70
4	Chevrolet	49

GTU drivers

1	Jim Pace, USA	105
2	Eduardo Dibos, PE	101
3	John O'Steen, USA	88
4	Bill Auberlen, USA	76
5	Mark Sandridge, USA	71
6	Butch Hamlet, USA	63

GTU manufacturers

1	Nissan	139
2	Porsche	129
3	Mazda	124
4	Lotus	12
5	Ferrari	11
6	Dodge	2

GTO drivers

1	Joe Pezza, USA	113
2	Brian DeVries, USA	87
3	Charles Morgan, USA	57
4	Tommy Riggins, USA	43
5	Flip Groggins, USA	31
6	Rob Morgan, USA	24

NASCAR Winston Cup

DAYTONA 500, Daytona International Speedway, Daytona Beach, Florida, USA, 20 February. Round 1. 200 laps of the 2.500-mile/4.023-km circuit, 500.000 miles/804.672 km.
1 Sterling Marlin, USA (Chevrolet Lumina), 3h 11m 10s, 156.931 mph/252.556 km/h.
2 Ernie Irvan, USA (Ford Thunderbird), 3h 11m 10.19s.
3 Terry Labonte, USA (Chevrolet Lumina), 200 laps.
4 Jeff Gordon, USA (Chevrolet Lumina), 200.
5 Morgan Shepherd, USA (Ford Thunderbird), 200.
6 Greg Sacks, USA (Ford Thunderbird), 200.
7 Dale Earnhardt, USA (Chevrolet Lumina), 200; **8** Ricky Rudd, USA (Ford Thunderbird), 200; **9** Bill Elliott, USA (Ford Thunderbird), 200; **10** Ken Schrader, USA (Chevrolet Lumina), 200.
Fastest qualifying lap: Loy Allen, USA (Ford Thunderbird), 47.329s, 190.158 mph/306.030 km/h.
Drivers' championship points: 1= Marlin, 180; **1=** Irvan, 180; **3** Labonte (Terry), 170; **4** Gordon, 165; **5** Shepherd, 160; **6** Earnhardt, 151.

GOODWRENCH 500, North Carolina Motor Speedway, Rockingham, North Carolina, USA, 27 February. Round 2. 492 laps of the 1.017-mile/1.637-km circuit, 500.364 miles/805.258 km.
1 Rusty Wallace, USA (Ford Thunderbird), 3h 59m 43.00s, 125.239 mph/201.552 km/h.
2 Sterling Marlin, USA (Chevrolet Lumina), 3h 59m 48.15s.
3 Rick Mast, USA (Ford Thunderbird), 492 laps.
4 Mark Martin, USA (Ford Thunderbird), 491.
5 Ernie Irvan, USA (Ford Thunderbird), 491.
6 Brett Bodine, USA (Ford Thunderbird), 491.
7 Dale Earnhardt, USA (Chevrolet Lumina), 491; **8** Kyle Petty, USA (Pontiac Grand Prix), 490; **9** Ken Schrader, USA (Chevrolet Lumina), 489; **10** Michael Waltrip, USA (Pontiac Grand Prix), 489.
Fastest qualifying lap: Geoff Bodine, USA (Ford Thunderbird), 24.132s, 151.716 mph/244.163 km/h (record).
Drivers' championship points: 1 Marlin, 355; **2** Irvan, 335; **3** Earnhardt, 302; **4** Martin, 294; **5** Labonte (Terry), 282; **6** Shepherd, 280.

PONTIAC EXCITEMENT 400, Richmond International Raceway, Virginia, USA, 6 March. Round 3. 400 laps of the 0.750-mile/1.207-km circuit, 300.000 miles/482.803 km.
1 Ernie Irvan, USA (Ford Thunderbird), 3h 03m 03s, 98.334 mph/158.253 km/h.
2 Rusty Wallace, USA (Ford Thunderbird), 3h 03m 04.70s.
3 Jeff Gordon, USA (Chevrolet Lumina), 400 laps.
4 Dale Earnhardt, USA (Chevrolet Lumina), 400.
5 Kyle Petty, USA (Pontiac Grand Prix), 400.
6 Mark Martin, USA (Ford Thunderbird), 400.
7 Rick Mast, USA (Ford Thunderbird), 400; **8** Brett Bodine, USA (Ford Thunderbird), 400; **9** Terry Labonte, USA (Chevrolet Lumina), 400; **10** Dale Jarrett, USA (Chevrolet Lumina), 399.
Fastest qualifying lap: Ted Musgrave, USA (Ford Thunderbird), 21.867s, 123.474 mph/198.712 km/h (record).
Drivers' championship points: 1 Irvan, 520; **2** Earnhardt, 467; **3** Marlin, 461; **4** Martin, 449; **5** Labonte (Terry), 425; **6=** Gordon, 402; **6=** Schrader, 402.

PUROLATOR 500, Atlanta Motor Speedway, Hampton, Georgia, USA, 13 March. Round 4. 328 laps of the 1.522-mile/2.449-km circuit, 499.216 miles/803.410 km.
1 Ernie Irvan, USA (Ford Thunderbird), 3h 24m 58.00s, 146.136 mph/235.183 km/h
2 Morgan Shepherd, USA (Ford Thunderbird), 3h 24m 58.35s.
3 Darrell Waltrip, USA (Chevrolet Lumina), 328 laps.
4 Jeff Burton, USA (Ford Thunderbird), 328.
5 Mark Martin, USA (Ford Thunderbird), 327.
6 Lake Speed, USA (Ford Thunderbird), 327.
7 Greg Sacks, USA (Ford Thunderbird), 327; **8** Jeff Gordon, USA (Chevrolet Lumina), 326; **9** Ricky Rudd, USA (Ford Thunderbird), 326; **10** Jimmy Spencer, USA (Ford Thunderbird), 326.
Fastest qualifying lap: Loy Allen, USA (Ford Thunderbird), 30.405s, 180.207 mph/290.015 km/h (record).
Drivers' championship points: 1 Irvan, 705; **2** Martin, 604; **3** Earnhardt, 594; **4** Shepherd, 573; **5** Labonte (Terry), 551; **6** Marlin, 549.

TRANSOUTH FINANCIAL 500, Darlington Raceway, South Carolina, USA, 27 March. Round 5. 293 laps of the 1.366-mile/2.198-km circuit, 400.238 miles/644.121 km.
1 Dale Earnhardt, USA (Chevrolet Lumina), 3h 1m 20.00s, 132.432 mph/213.128 km/h.
2 Mark Martin, USA (Ford Thunderbird), 3h 1m 27.40s.
3 Bill Elliott, USA (Ford Thunderbird), 293 laps.
4 Dale Jarrett, USA (Chevrolet Lumina), 293.
5 Lake Speed, USA (Ford Thunderbird), 293.
6 Ernie Irvan, USA (Ford Thunderbird), 293.
7 Ken Schrader, USA (Chevrolet Lumina), 293; **8** Harry Gant, USA (Chevrolet Lumina), 292; **9** Ricky Rudd, USA (Ford Thunderbird), 292; **10** Ted Musgrave, USA (Ford Thunderbird), 292.
Fastest qualifying lap: Elliott, 29.704s, 165.553 mph/266.432 km/h (record).
Drivers' championship points: 1 Irvan, 860; **2=** Earnhardt, 779; **2=** Martin, 779; **4** Schrader, 668; **5** Rudd, 657; **6** Speed, 647.

FOOD CITY 500, Bristol International Raceway, Tennessee, USA, 10 April. Round 6. 500 laps of the 0.533-mile/0.858-km circuit, 266.500 miles/428.890 km.
1 Dale Earnhardt, USA (Chevrolet Lumina), 2h 58m 22.00s, 89.647 mph/144.273 km/h.
2 Ken Schrader, USA (Chevrolet Lumina), 2h 58m 29.63s.
3 Lake Speed, USA (Ford Thunderbird), 500 laps.
4 Geoff Bodine, USA (Ford Thunderbird), 499.
5 Michael Waltrip, USA (Pontiac Grand Prix), 497.
6 Bobby Labonte, USA (Pontiac Grand Prix), 496.
7 Rusty Wallace, USA (Ford Thunderbird), 494; **8** Sterling Marlin, USA (Chevrolet Lumina), 491; **9** Bobby Hamilton, USA (Pontiac Grand Prix), 488; **10** Dave Marcis, USA (Chevrolet Lumina), 486.
Fastest qualifying lap: Chuck Brown, USA (Ford Thunderbird), 15.357s, 124.946 mph/201.082 km/h (record).
Drivers' championship points: 1 Earnhardt, 964; **2** Irvan, 924; **3** Martin, 884; **4** Schrader, 838; **5** Rudd, 812; **6** Marlin, 757.

FIRST UNION 400, North Wilkesboro Speedway, North Carolina, USA, 17 April. Round 7. 400 laps of the 0.625-mile/1.006-km circuit, 250.000 miles/402.336 km.
1 Terry Labonte, USA (Chevrolet Lumina), 2h 36m 33.00s, 95.816 mph/154.201 km/h.
2 Rusty Wallace, USA (Ford Thunderbird), 2h 36m 37.00s.
3 Ernie Irvan, USA (Ford Thunderbird), 400 laps.
4 Kyle Petty, USA (Pontiac Grand Prix), 400.
5 Dale Earnhardt, USA (Chevrolet Lumina), 400.
6 Ricky Rudd, USA (Ford Thunderbird), 400.
7 Geoff Bodine, USA (Ford Thunderbird), 399; **8** Harry Gant, USA (Chevrolet Lumina), 399; **9** Ken Schrader, USA (Chevrolet Lumina), 398; **10** Rick Mast, USA (Ford Thunderbird), 397.
Fastest qualifying lap: Irvan, 18.905s, 119.016 mph/191.538 km/h (record).
Drivers' championship points: 1 Earnhardt, 1119; **2** Irvan, 1099; **3** Martin, 1008; **4** Schrader, 981; **5** Speed, 939; **6** Wallace, 886.

HANES 500, Martinsville Speedway, Virginia, USA, 24 April. Round 8. 500 laps of the 0.526-mile/0.847-km circuit, 263.000 miles/423.257 km.
1 Rusty Wallace, USA (Ford Thunderbird), 3h 25m 43.00s, 76.707 mph/123.449 km/h.
2 Ernie Irvan, USA (Ford Thunderbird), 3h 25m 43.46s.
3 Mark Martin, USA (Ford Thunderbird), 500 laps.
4 Darrell Waltrip, USA (Chevrolet Lumina), 500.
5 Morgan Shepherd, USA (Ford Thunderbird), 500.
6 Todd Bodine, USA (Ford Thunderbird), 500.
7 Chuck Brown, USA (Ford Thunderbird), 500; **8** Rick Mast, USA (Ford Thunderbird), 499; **9** Bill Elliott, USA (Ford Thunderbird), 499; **10** Ted Musgrave, USA (Ford Thunderbird), 499.
Fastest qualifying lap: Wallace, 20.374s, 92.942 mph/149.576 km/h.
Drivers' championship points: 1 Irvan, 1274; **2** Earnhardt, 1249; **3** Martin, 1178; **4** Wallace, 1071; **5** Schrader, 1051; **6** Speed, 1012.

WINSTON SELECT 500, Talladega Superspeedway, Alabama, USA, 1 May. Round 9. 188 laps of the 2.660-mile/4.281-km circuit, 500.080 miles/804.801 km.
1 Dale Earnhardt, USA (Chevrolet Lumina), 3h 10m 32.00s, 157.478 mph/253.436 km/h.
2 Ernie Irvan, USA (Ford Thunderbird), 3h 10m 32.06s.
3 Michael Waltrip, USA (Pontiac Grand Prix), 188 laps.
4 Jimmy Spencer, USA (Ford Thunderbird), 188.
5 Ken Schrader, USA (Chevrolet Lumina), 188.
6 Greg Sacks, USA (Ford Thunderbird), 188.
7 Lake Speed, USA (Ford Thunderbird), 188; **8** Sterling Marlin, USA (Chevrolet Lumina), 188; **9** Morgan Shepherd, USA (Ford Thunderbird), 188; **10** Steve Grissom, USA (Chevrolet Lumina), 188.
Fastest qualifying lap: Irvan, 49.540s, 193.298 mph/311.084 km/h.
Drivers' championship points: 1 Irvan, 1454; **2** Earnhardt, 1429; **3** Martin, 1227; **4** Schrader, 1211; **5** Speed, 1158; **6** Shepherd, 1144.

SAVE MART SUPERMARKETS 300, Sears Point International Raceway, Sonoma, California, USA, 15 May. Round 10. 74 laps of the 2.520-mile/4.056-km circuit, 186.480 miles/300.110 km.
1 Ernie Irvan, USA (Ford Thunderbird), 2h 24m 27.00s, 77.458 mph/124.656 km/h.
2 Geoff Bodine, USA (Ford Thunderbird), 2h 24m 36.56s.
3 Dale Earnhardt, USA (Chevrolet Lumina), 74 laps.
4 Wally Dallenbach Jr, USA (Pontiac Grand Prix), 74.
5 Rusty Wallace, USA (Ford Thunderbird), 74.
6 Ted Musgrave, USA (Ford Thunderbird), 74.
7 Morgan Shepherd, USA (Ford Thunderbird), 74; **8** Mark Martin, USA (Ford Thunderbird), 74; **9** Ken Schrader, USA (Chevrolet Lumina), 74; **10** Harry Gant, USA (Chevrolet Lumina), 74.
Fastest qualifying lap: Irvan, 1m 39.132s, 91.514 mph/147.278 km/h.
Drivers' championship points: 1 Irvan, 1639; **2** Earnhardt, 1599; **3** Martin, 1369; **4** Schrader, 1349; **5** Shepherd, 1295; **6** Wallace, 1290.

COCA-COLA 600, Charlotte Motor Speedway, North Carolina, USA, 29 May. Round 11. 400 laps of the 1.500-mile/2.414-km circuit, 600.000 miles/965.606 km.
1 Jeff Gordon, USA (Chevrolet Lumina), 4h 18m 10.00s, 139.445 mph/224.415 km/h.
2 Rusty Wallace, USA (Ford Thunderbird), 4h 18m 13.91s.
3 Geoff Bodine, USA (Ford Thunderbird), 400 laps.
4 Dale Jarrett, USA (Chevrolet Lumina), 400.
5 Ernie Irvan, USA (Ford Thunderbird), 400.
6 Ricky Rudd, USA (Ford Thunderbird), 400.
7 Harry Gant, USA (Chevrolet Lumina), 399; **8** Todd Bodine, USA (Ford Thunderbird), 398; **9** Dale Earnhardt, USA (Chevrolet Lumina), 397; **10** Michael Waltrip, USA (Pontiac Grand Prix), 397.
Fastest qualifying lap: Gordon, 29.762s, 181.439 mph/291.998 km/h (record).
Drivers' championship points: 1 Irvan, 1799; **2** Earnhardt, 1737; **3** Martin, 1470; **4** Schrader, 1440; **5** Martin, 1436; **6** Shepherd, 1374.

BUDWEISER 500, Dover Downs International Speedway, Dover, Delaware, USA, 5 June. Round 12. 500 laps of the 1.000-mile/1.609-km circuit, 500.000 miles/804.672 km.
1 Rusty Wallace, USA (Ford Thunderbird), 4h 52m 36.00s, 102.529 mph/165.005 km/h.
2 Ernie Irvan, USA (Ford Thunderbird), 4h 52m 36.34s.
3 Ken Schrader, USA (Chevrolet Lumina), 500 laps.
4 Mark Martin, USA (Ford Thunderbird), 500.
5 Jeff Gordon, USA (Chevrolet Lumina), 500.
6 Darrell Waltrip, USA (Chevrolet Lumina), 499.
7 Michael Waltrip, USA (Pontiac Grand Prix), 499; **8** Sterling Marlin, USA (Chevrolet Lumina), 498; **9** 'Hut' Stricklin, USA (Ford Thunderbird), 498; **10** Wally Dallenbach Jr, USA (Pontiac Grand Prix), 497.
Fastest qualifying lap: Irvan, 23.691s, 151.956 mph/244.550 km/h (record).
Drivers' championship points: 1 Irvan, 1979; **2** Earnhardt, 1816; **3** Wallace, 1650; **4** Schrader, 1605; **5** Martin, 1601; **6** Rudd, 1476.

UAW-GM TEAMWORK 500, Pocono International Raceway, Pennsylvania, USA, 12 June. Round 13. 200 laps of the 2.500-mile/4.023-km circuit, 500.000 miles/804.672 km.
1 Rusty Wallace, USA (Ford Thunderbird), 3h 52m 55.00s, 128.801 mph/207.286 km/h.
2 Dale Earnhardt, USA (Chevrolet Lumina), 3h 52m 55.28s.
3 Ken Schrader, USA (Chevrolet Lumina), 200 laps.
4 Morgan Shepherd, USA (Ford Thunderbird), 200.
5 Mark Martin, USA (Ford Thunderbird), 200.
6 Jeff Gordon, USA (Chevrolet Lumina), 200.
7 Ernie Irvan, USA (Ford Thunderbird), 200; **8** Brett Bodine, USA (Ford Thunderbird), 200; **9** Rick Mast, USA (Ford Thunderbird), 200; **10** Bill Elliott, USA (Ford Thunderbird), 200.
Fastest qualifying lap: Wallace, 54.692s, 164.558 mph/264.830 km/h (record).
Drivers' championship points: 1 Irvan, 2130; **2** Earnhardt, 1991; **3** Wallace, 1835; **4** Schrader, 1775; **5** Martin, 1761; **6** Shepherd, 1622.

MILLER GENUINE DRAFT 400, Michigan International Speedway, Brooklyn, Michigan, USA, 19 June. Round 14. 200 laps of the 2.000-mile/3.219-km circuit, 400.000 miles/643.738 km.
1 Rusty Wallace, USA (Ford Thunderbird), 3h 11m 58.00s, 125.022 mph/201.203 km/h.
2 Dale Earnhardt, USA (Chevrolet Lumina), 3h 11m 58.72s.
3 Mark Martin, USA (Ford Thunderbird), 200 laps.
4 Ricky Rudd, USA (Ford Thunderbird), 200.
5 Morgan Shepherd, USA (Ford Thunderbird), 200.
6 Ken Schrader, USA (Chevrolet Lumina), 200.
7 Joe Nemechek, USA (Chevrolet Lumina), 200; **8** Michael Waltrip, USA (Pontiac Grand Prix), 200; **9** Ted Musgrave, USA (Ford Thunderbird), 200; **10** Darrell Waltrip, USA (Chevrolet Lumina), 200.
Fastest qualifying lap: Loy Allen, USA (Ford Thunderbird), 39.858s, 180.641 mph/290.714 km/h.
Drivers' championship points: 1 Irvan, 2244; **2** Earnhardt, 2166; **3** Wallace, 2020; **4** Martin, 1931; **5** Schrader, 1925; **6** Shepherd, 1782.

PEPSI 400, Daytona International Speedway, Florida, USA, 2 July. Round 15. 160 laps of the 2.500-mile/4.023-km circuit, 400.000 miles/643.738 km.
1 Jimmy Spencer, USA (Ford Thunderbird), 2h 34m 17.00s, 155.558 mph/250.346 km/h.
2 Ernie Irvan, USA (Ford Thunderbird), 2h 34m 17.008s.
3 Dale Earnhardt, USA (Chevrolet Lumina), 160 laps.
4 Mark Martin, USA (Ford Thunderbird), 160.
5 Ken Schrader, USA (Chevrolet Lumina), 160.
6 Geoff Bodine, USA (Ford Thunderbird), 160.
7 Todd Bodine, USA (Ford Thunderbird), 160; **8** Jeff Gordon, USA (Chevrolet Lumina), 160; **9** Morgan Shepherd, USA (Ford Thunderbird), 160; **10** Lake Speed, USA (Ford Thunderbird), 160.
Fastest qualifying lap: Earnhardt, 47.037s, 191.339 mph/307.930 km/h.
Drivers' championship points: 1 Irvan, 2424; **2** Earnhardt, 2336; **3** Wallace, 2105; **4** Martin, 2096; **5** Schrader, 2080; **6** Shepherd, 1920.

SLICK-50 300, New Hampshire International Speedway, Loudon, New Hampshire, USA, 10 July. Round 16. 300 laps of the 1.058-mile/1.703-km circuit, 317.400 miles/510.806 km.
1 Ricky Rudd, USA (Ford Thunderbird), 3h 37m 24.00s, 87.599 mph/140.977 km/h.
2 Dale Earnhardt, USA (Chevrolet Lumina), 3h 37m 24.69s.
3 Rusty Wallace, USA (Ford Thunderbird), 300 laps.
4 Mark Martin, USA (Ford Thunderbird), 300.
5 Todd Bodine, USA (Ford Thunderbird), 300.
6 Morgan Shepherd, USA (Ford Thunderbird), 300.
7 Ted Musgrave, USA (Ford Thunderbird), 300; **8** Kyle Petty, USA (Pontiac Grand Prix), 300; **9** Rick Mast, USA (Ford Thunderbird), 300; **10** Sterling Marlin, USA (Chevrolet Lumina), 300.
Fastest qualifying lap: Ernie Irvan, USA (Ford Thunderbird), 29.944s, 127.197 mph/204.704 km/h.
Drivers' championship points: 1 Earnhardt, 2511; **2** Irvan, 2507; **3** Wallace, 2270; **4** Martin, 2256; **5** Schrader, 2171; **6** Shepherd, 2070.

MILLER GENUINE DRAFT 500, Pocono International Raceway, Pennsylvania, USA, 17 July. Round 17. 200 laps of the 2.500-mile/4.023-km circuit, 500 miles/804.672 km.
1 Geoff Bodine, USA (Ford Thunderbird), 3h 40m 28.00s, 136.075 mph/218.991 km/h.
2 Ward Burton, USA (Chevrolet Lumina), 3h 40m 29.26s.
3 Joe Nemechek, USA (Chevrolet Lumina), 200 laps.
4 Jeff Burton, USA (Ford Thunderbird), 200.
5 Morgan Shepherd, USA (Ford Thunderbird), 200.
6 Ricky Rudd, USA (Ford Thunderbird), 200.
7 Dale Earnhardt, USA (Chevrolet Lumina), 200; **8** Jeff Gordon, USA (Chevrolet Lumina), 199; **9** Rusty Wallace, USA (Ford Thunderbird), 199; **10** Dale Jarrett, USA (Chevrolet Lumina), 199.
Fastest qualifying lap: Bodine, 54.922s, 163.869 mph/263.721 km/h.
Drivers' championship points: 1 Earnhardt, 2657; **2** Irvan, 2564; **3** Wallace, 2413; **4** Martin, 2331; **5** Shepherd, 2225; **6** Schrader, 2217.

DIEHARD 500, Talladega Superspeedway, Alabama, USA, 24 July. Round 18. 188 laps of the 2.660-mile/4.281-km circuit, 500.080 miles/804.801 km.
1 Jimmy Spencer, USA (Ford Thunderbird), 3h 03m 50.00s, 163.217 mph/262.673 km/h.
2 Bill Elliott, USA (Ford Thunderbird), 3h 03m 50.025s.
3 Ernie Irvan, USA (Ford Thunderbird), 188 laps.
4 Ken Schrader, USA (Chevrolet Lumina), 188.
5 Sterling Marlin, USA (Chevrolet Lumina), 188.
6 Mark Martin, USA (Ford Thunderbird), 188.
7 Ricky Rudd, USA (Ford Thunderbird), 188; **8** Wally Dallenbach Jr, USA (Pontiac Grand Prix), 188; **9** Kenny Wallace, USA (Ford Thunderbird), 188; **10** Terry Labonte, USA (Chevrolet Lumina), 188.
Fastest qualifying lap: Dale Earnhardt, USA (Chevrolet Lumina), 49.496s, 193.470 mph/311.360 km/h.
Drivers' championship points: 1 Irvan, 2739; **2** Earnhardt, 2723; **3** Martin, 2481; **4** Wallace, 2450; **5** Schrader, 2382; **6** Shepherd, 2348.

BRICKYARD 400, Indianapolis Motor Speedway, Speedway, Indiana, USA, 6 August. Round 19. 160 laps of the 2.500-mile/4.023-km circuit, 400.000 miles/643.738 km.
1 Jeff Gordon, USA (Chevrolet Lumina), 3h 01m 51.00s, 131.977 mph/212.396 km/h.
2 Brett Bodine, USA (Ford Thunderbird), 3h 01m 51.53s.
3 Bill Elliott, USA (Ford Thunderbird), 160 laps.
4 Rusty Wallace, USA (Ford Thunderbird), 160.
5 Dale Earnhardt, USA (Chevrolet Lumina), 160.
6 Darrell Waltrip, USA (Chevrolet Lumina), 160.
7 Ken Schrader, USA (Chevrolet Lumina), 160; **8** Michael Waltrip, USA (Pontiac Grand Prix), 160; **9** Todd Bodine, USA (Ford Thunderbird), 160; **10** Morgan Shepherd, USA (Ford Thunderbird), 160.
Fastest qualifying lap: Rick Mast, USA (Ford Thunderbird), 52.200s, 172.414 mph/277.473 km/h (record).
Drivers' championship points: 1 Earnhardt, 2883; **2** Irvan, 2856; **3** Wallace, 2615; **4** Martin, 2539; **5** Schrader, 2528; **6** Shepherd, 2482.

THE BUD AT THE GLEN, Watkins Glen International 'Short' Course, New York, USA, 14 August. Round 20. 90 laps of the 2.450-mile/3.943-km circuit, 220.500 miles/354.860 km.
1 Mark Martin, USA (Ford Thunderbird), 2h 21m 07.00s, 93.752 mph/150.880 km/h.
2 Ernie Irvan, USA (Ford Thunderbird), 2h 21m 07.88s.
3 Dale Earnhardt, USA (Chevrolet Lumina), 90 laps.
4 Ken Schrader, USA (Chevrolet Lumina), 90.
5 Ricky Rudd, USA (Ford Thunderbird), 90.
6 Terry Labonte, USA (Chevrolet Lumina), 90.
7 Darrell Waltrip, USA (Chevrolet Lumina), 90; **8** Joe Nemechek, USA (Chevrolet Lumina), 90; **9** Jeff Gordon, USA (Chevrolet Lumina), 90; **10** Harry Gant, USA (Chevrolet Lumina), 90.
Fastest qualifying lap: Martin, 1m 14.540s, 118.326 mph/190.427 km/h.
Drivers' championship points: 1 Earnhardt, 3053; **2** Irvan, 3026; **3** Wallace, 2727; **4** Martin, 2724; **5** Schrader, 2688; **6** Rudd, 2629.

GM GOODWRENCH DEALER 400, Michigan International Speedway, Brooklyn, Michigan, USA, 21 August. Round 21. 200 laps of the 2.000-mile/3.219-km circuit, 400.000 miles/643.738 km.
1 Geoff Bodine, USA (Ford Thunderbird), 2h 51m 32.00s, 139.914 mph/225.171 km/h.
2 Mark Martin, USA (Ford Thunderbird), 2h 51m 32.91s.
3 Rick Mast, USA (Ford Thunderbird), 200 laps.
4 Rusty Wallace, USA (Ford Thunderbird), 200.
5 Bobby Labonte, USA (Pontiac Grand Prix), 200.
6 Kyle Petty, USA (Pontiac Grand Prix), 200.
7 Bill Elliott, USA (Ford Thunderbird), 199; **8** Terry Labonte, USA (Chevrolet Lumina), 199; **9** Darrell Waltrip, USA (Chevrolet Lumina), 199; **10** Ricky Rudd, USA (Ford Thunderbird), 199.
Fastest qualifying lap: Bodine, 39.761s, 181.082 mph/291.423 km/h.
Drivers' championship points: 1 Earnhardt, 3105; **2** Irvan, 3026; **3** Martin, 2899; **4** Wallace, 2892; **5** Schrader, 2818; **6** Rudd, 2763.

GOODY'S 500, Bristol International Raceway, Tennessee, USA, 27 August. Round 22. 500 laps of the 0.533-mile/0.858-km circuit, 266.500 miles/428.890 km.
1 Rusty Wallace, USA (Ford Thunderbird), 2h 55m 01.00s, 91.363 mph/147.034 km/h.
2 Mark Martin, USA (Ford Thunderbird), 2h 55m 01.16s.
3 Dale Earnhardt, USA (Chevrolet Lumina), 500 laps.
4 Darrell Waltrip, USA (Chevrolet Lumina), 500.
5 Bill Elliott, USA (Ford Thunderbird), 500.
6 Sterling Marlin, USA (Chevrolet Lumina), 500.
7 Michael Waltrip, USA (Pontiac Grand Prix), 500; **8** Todd Bodine, USA (Ford Thunderbird), 500; **9** Harry Gant, USA (Chevrolet Lumina), 499; **10** Rick Mast, USA (Ford Thunderbird), 499.
Fastest qualifying lap: Gant, 15.451s, 124.186 mph/199.858 km/h.
Drivers' championship points: 1 Earnhardt, 3275; **2** Martin, 3074; **3** Wallace, 3072; **4** Irvan, 3026; **5** Schrader, 2924; **6** Rudd, 2890.

MOUNTAIN DEW SOUTHERN 500, Darlington Raceway, South Carolina, USA, 4 September. Round 23. 367 laps of the 1.366-mile/2.198-km circuit, 501.322 miles/806.800 km.
1 Bill Elliott, USA (Ford Thunderbird), 3h 55m 05.00s, 127.952 mph/205.918 km/h.
2 Dale Earnhardt, USA (Chevrolet Lumina), 3h 55m 11.39s.
3 Morgan Shepherd, USA (Ford Thunderbird), 367 laps.
4 Ricky Rudd, USA (Ford Thunderbird), 367.
5 Sterling Marlin, USA (Chevrolet Lumina), 367.
6 Jeff Gordon, USA (Chevrolet Lumina), 366.
7 Rusty Wallace, USA (Ford Thunderbird), 366; **8** Jeff Burton, USA (Ford Thunderbird), 366; **9** Dale

Jarrett, USA (Chevrolet Lumina), 365; **10** Terry Labonte, USA (Chevrolet Lumina), 365.
Fastest qualifying lap: Geoff Bodine, USA (Ford Thunderbird), 29.447s, 166.998 mph/268.758 km/h.
Drivers' championship points: 1 Earnhardt, 3450; **2** Wallace, 3223; **3** Martin, 3167; **4** Rudd, 3055; **5** Irvan, 3026; **6** Schrader, 3001.

MILLER GENUINE DRAFT 400, Richmond International Raceway, Virginia, USA, 10 September. Round 24. 400 laps of the 0.750-mile/1.207-km circuit, 300.000 miles/482.803 km.
1 Terry Labonte, USA (Chevrolet Lumina), 2h 52m 59.00s, 104.056 mph/167.462 km/h.
2 Jeff Gordon, USA (Chevrolet Lumina), 2h 53m 00.790s.
3 Dale Earnhardt, USA (Chevrolet Lumina), 400 laps.
4 Rusty Wallace, USA (Ford Thunderbird), 400.
5 Ricky Rudd, USA (Ford Thunderbird), 400.
6 Mark Martin, USA (Ford Thunderbird), 400.
7 Steve Grissom, USA (Chevrolet Lumina), 400; **8** Brett Bodine, USA (Ford Thunderbird), 399; **9** Ken Schrader, USA (Chevrolet Lumina), 399; **10** Darrell Waltrip, USA (Chevrolet Lumina), 399.
Fastest qualifying lap: Ted Musgrave, USA (Ford Thunderbird), 21.765s, 124.052 mph/199.643 km/h.
Drivers' championship points: 1 Earnhardt, 3620; **2** Wallace, 3388; **3** Martin, 3317; **4** Rudd, 3210; **5** Schrader, 3139; **6** Shepherd, 3077.

SPLITFIRE SPARK PLUG 500, Dover Downs International Speedway, Dover, Delaware, USA, 18 September. Round 25. 500 laps of the 1.000-mile/1.609-km circuit, 500.000 miles/804.672 km.
1 Rusty Wallace, USA (Ford Thunderbird), 4h 26m 32.00s, 112.556 mph/181.142 km/h.
2 Dale Earnhardt, USA (Chevrolet Lumina), finished under caution.
3 Darrell Waltrip, USA (Chevrolet Lumina), 500 laps.
4 Ken Schrader, USA (Chevrolet Lumina), 500.
5 Geoff Bodine, USA (Ford Thunderbird), 500.
6 Kyle Petty, USA (Pontiac Grand Prix), 500.
7 Terry Labonte, USA (Chevrolet Lumina), 500; **8** Steve Grissom, USA (Chevrolet Lumina), 499; **9** Lake Speed, USA (Ford Thunderbird), 499; **10** Morgan Shepherd, USA (Ford Thunderbird), 499.
Fastest qualifying lap: Bodine, 23.554s, 152.840 mph/245.973 km/h (record).
Drivers' championship points: 1 Earnhardt, 3795; **2** Wallace, 3568; **3** Martin, 3428; **4** Rudd, 3319; **5** Schrader, 3304; **6** Shepherd, 3211.

GOODY'S 500, Martinsville Speedway, Virginia, USA, 25 September. Round 26. 500 laps of the 0.526-mile/0.847-km circuit, 263.000 miles/423.257 km.
1 Rusty Wallace, USA (Ford Thunderbird), 3h 24m 34.00s, 77.139 mph/124.143 km/h.
2 Dale Earnhardt, USA (Chevrolet Lumina), 3h 24m 34.66s.
3 Bill Elliott, USA (Ford Thunderbird), 500 laps.
4 Kenny Wallace, USA (Ford Thunderbird), 500.
5 Dale Jarrett, USA (Chevrolet Lumina), 500.
6 Ken Schrader, USA (Chevrolet Lumina), 500.
7 Sterling Marlin, USA (Chevrolet Lumina), 499; **8** Harry Gant, USA (Chevrolet Lumina), 499; **9** Ted Musgrave, USA (Ford Thunderbird), 499; **10** Darrell Waltrip, USA (Chevrolet Lumina), 499.
Fastest qualifying lap: Musgrave, 20.117s, 94.129 mph/151.486 km/h.
Drivers' championship points: 1 Earnhardt, 3970; **2** Wallace, 3753; **3** Martin, 3543; **4** Schrader, 3454; **5** Rudd, 3407; **6** Shepherd, 3334.

TYSON HOLLY FARMS 400, North Wilkesboro Speedway, North Carolina, USA, 2 October. Round 27. 400 laps of the 0.625-mile/1.006-km circuit, 250.000 miles/402.336 km.
1 Geoff Bodine, USA (Ford Thunderbird), 2h 32m 15.00s, 98.522 mph/158.556 km/h.
2 Terry Labonte, USA (Chevrolet Lumina), 399 laps.
3 Rick Mast, USA (Ford Thunderbird), 399.
4 Rusty Wallace, USA (Ford Thunderbird), 399.
5 Mark Martin, USA (Ford Thunderbird), 398.
6 Bill Elliott, USA (Ford Thunderbird), 398.
7 Dale Earnhardt, USA (Chevrolet Lumina), 398; **8** Jeff Gordon, USA (Chevrolet Lumina), 398; **9** Ted Musgrave, USA (Ford Thunderbird), 397; **10** Kenny Wallace, USA (Ford Thunderbird), 397.
Fastest qualifying lap: Jimmy Spencer, USA (Ford Thunderbird), 18.978s, 118.558 mph/190.801 km/h.
Drivers' championship points: 1 Earnhardt, 4121; **2** Wallace, 3913; **3** Martin, 3698; **4** Schrader, 3575; **5** Rudd, 3537; **6** Shepherd, 3407.

MELLO YELLO 500, Charlotte Motor Speedway, North Carolina, USA, 9 October. Round 28. 334 laps of the 1.500-mile/2.414-km circuit, 501.000 miles/806.281 km.
1 Dale Jarrett, USA (Chevrolet Lumina), 3h 26m 00.0s, 145.922 mph/234.839 km/h.
2 Morgan Shepherd, USA (Ford Thunderbird), finished under caution.
3 Dale Earnhardt, USA (Chevrolet Lumina), 334 laps.
4 Ken Schrader, USA (Chevrolet Lumina), 334.
5 Lake Speed, USA (Ford Thunderbird), 334.
6 Brett Bodine, USA (Ford Thunderbird), 334.
7 Terry Labonte, USA (Chevrolet Lumina), 334; **8** Derrike Cope, USA (Ford Thunderbird), 334; **9** Darrell Waltrip, USA (Chevrolet Lumina), 334; **10** Michael Waltrip, USA (Pontiac Grand Prix), 333.
Fastest qualifying lap: Ward Burton, USA (Chevrolet Lumina), 29.070s, 185.759 mph/298.949 km/h (record).
Drivers' championship points: 1 Earnhardt, 4291; **2** Wallace, 3970; **3** Martin, 3744; **4** Schrader, 3740; **5** Rudd, 3613; **6** Shepherd, 3582.

AC-DELCO 500, North Carolina Motor Speedway, Rockingham, North Carolina, USA, 23 October. Round 29. 492 laps of the 1.017-mile/1.637-km circuit, 500.364 miles/805.258 km.
1 Dale Earnhardt, USA (Chevrolet Lumina), 3h 58m 30.00s, 125.878 mph/202.581 km/h.
2 Rick Mast, USA (Ford Thunderbird), 3h 58m 30.06s.
3 Morgan Shepherd, USA (Ford Thunderbird), 492 laps.
4 Ricky Rudd, USA (Ford Thunderbird), 492.
5 Terry Labonte, USA (Chevrolet Lumina), 492.
6 Bill Elliott, USA (Ford Thunderbird), 492.
7 Mark Martin, USA (Ford Thunderbird), 492; **8** Dick Trickle, USA (Chevrolet Lumina), 492; **9** Ward Burton, USA (Chevrolet Lumina), 491; **10** Lake Speed, USA (Ford Thunderbird), 491.
Fastest qualifying lap: Rudd, 23.305s, 157.099 mph/252.827 km/h (record).
Drivers' championship points: 1 Earnhardt, 4476; **2** Wallace, 4028; **3** Martin, 3890; **4** Schrader, 3812; **5** Rudd, 3778; **6** Shepherd, 3752.

SLICK-50 500, Phoenix International Raceway, Arizona, USA, 30 October. Round 30. 312 laps of the 1.000-mile/1.609-km circuit, 312.000 miles/502.115 km.
1 Terry Labonte, USA (Chevrolet Lumina), 2h 54m 12.00s, 107.463 mph/172.944 km/h.
2 Mark Martin, USA (Ford Thunderbird), 2h 54m 15.09s.
3 Sterling Marlin, USA (Chevrolet Lumina), 312 laps.
4 Jeff Gordon, USA (Chevrolet Lumina), 311.
5 Ted Musgrave, USA (Ford Thunderbird), 311.
6 Kyle Petty, USA (Pontiac Grand Prix), 311.
7 Ricky Rudd, USA (Ford Thunderbird), 311; **8** Geoff Bodine, USA (Ford Thunderbird), 311; **9** Dale Jarrett, USA (Chevrolet Lumina), 310; **10** Darrell Waltrip, USA (Chevrolet Lumina), 310.
Fastest qualifying lap: Marlin, 27.728s, 129.833 mph/208.946 km/h (record).
Drivers' championship points: 1 Earnhardt, 4519; **2** Wallace, 4140; **3** Martin, 4065; **4** Rudd, 3927; **5** Schrader, 3920; **6** Shepherd, 3879.

HOOTER'S 500, Atlanta Motor Speedway, Hampton, Georgia, USA, 13 November. Round 31. 328 laps of the 1.522-mile/2.449-km circuit, 499.216 miles/803.410 km.
1 Mark Martin, USA (Ford Thunderbird), 3h 21m 03s, 148.982 mph/239.764 km/h.
2 Dale Earnhardt, USA (Chevrolet Lumina), 3h 21m 06.44s.
3 Todd Bodine, USA (Ford Thunderbird), 328 laps.
4 Lake Speed, USA (Ford Thunderbird), 328.
5 Mike Wallace, USA (Ford Thunderbird), 328.
6 Morgan Shepherd, USA (Ford Thunderbird), 328.
7 Derrike Cope, USA (Ford Thunderbird), 327; **8** Terry Labonte, USA (Chevrolet Lumina), 326; **9** Dale Jarrett, USA (Chevrolet Lumina), 326; **10** Michael Waltrip, USA (Pontiac Grand Prix), 326.
Fastest qualifying lap: Greg Sacks, USA (Ford Thunderbird), 29.485s, 185.830 mph/299.065 km/h (record).

Final championship points
Drivers

1	Dale Earnhardt, USA	4694
2	Mark Martin, USA	4250
3	Rusty Wallace, USA	4207
4	Ken Schrader, USA	4060
5	Ricky Rudd, USA	4050
6	Morgan Shepherd, USA	4029

7 Terry Labonte, USA, 3876; **8** Jeff Gordon, USA, 3776; **9** Darrell Waltrip, USA, 3688; **10** Bill Elliott, USA, 3617; **11** Lake Speed, USA, 3565; **12** Michael Waltrip, USA, 3512; **13** Ted Musgrave, USA, 3477; **14** Sterling Marlin, USA, 3443; **15** Kyle Petty, USA, 3339; **16** Dale Jarrett, USA, 3298; **17** Geoff Bodine, USA, 3297; **18** Rick Mast, USA, 3238; **19** Brett Bodine, USA, 3159; **20** Todd Bodine, USA, 3048

Manufacturers

1	Ford	246
2	Chevrolet	217
3	Pontiac	126

Other NASCAR Results

BUSCH CLASH OF '94, Daytona International Speedway, Daytona Beach, Florida, USA, 13 February, 2 x 10 laps of the 2.500-mile/4.023-km circuit, 50.000 miles/80.467 km.
1 Jeff Gordon, USA (Chevrolet Lumina), 15m 53.0s, 188.877 mph/303.968 km/h.
2 Brett Bodine, USA (Ford Thunderbird), 15m 53.3s.
3 Dale Earnhardt, USA (Chevrolet Lumina), 20 laps.
4 Ernie Irvan, USA (Ford Thunderbird), 20.
5 Mark Martin, USA (Ford Thunderbird), 20.
6 Kyle Petty, USA (Pontiac Grand Prix), 20.
7 Bill Elliott, USA (Ford Thunderbird), 20; **8** Ken Schrader, USA (Chevrolet Lumina), 20; **9** Rusty Wallace, USA (Ford Thunderbird), 20; **10** Harry Gant, USA (Chevrolet Lumina), 20.

THE WINSTON SELECT, Charlotte Motor Speedway, North Carolina, USA, 22 May. 70 laps of the 1.500-mile/2.414-km circuit, 105.000 miles/168.981 km.
1 Geoff Bodine, USA (Ford Thunderbird), 54m 31.0s, 115.561 mph/185.977 km/h.
2 Sterling Marlin, USA (Chevrolet Lumina), 54m 31.1s.
3 Ken Schrader, USA (Chevrolet Lumina), 70 laps.
4 Darrell Waltrip, USA (Chevrolet Lumina), 70.
5 Ricky Rudd, USA (Ford Thunderbird), 70.
6 Jeff Burton, USA (Ford Thunderbird), 70.
7 Dale Jarrett, USA (Chevrolet Lumina), 70; **8** Morgan Shepherd, USA (Ford Thunderbird), 70; **9** Ward Burton, USA (Chevrolet Lumina), 70; **10** Joe Nemechek, USA (Chevrolet Lumina), 70.

PPG Firestone Indy Lights Championship

All cars are Lola T93/20-Buick GS

PHOENIX FIRESTONE INDY LIGHTS RACE, Phoenix International Raceway, Arizona, USA, 10 April. Round 1. 75 laps of the 1.000-mile/1.609-km circuit, 75.000 miles/120.701 km.
1 Greg Moore, CDN, 30m 45.929s, 146.268 mph/235.395 km/h.
2 Steve Robertson, GB, 30m 52.617s.
3 Eddie Lawson, USA, 75 laps.
4 Andre Ribeiro, BR, 74.
5 Markus Liesner, USA, 73.
6 Dave DeSilva, USA, 72.
7 Pedro Chaves, P, 72; **8** Buzz Calkins, USA, 72; **9** Chris Smith, USA, 72; **10** Rob Wilson, NZ, 71.
Most laps led: Moore, 75.
Fastest qualifying lap: Moore, 23.895s, 150.659 mph/242.462 km/h.
Championship points: 1 Moore, 22; **2** Robertson, 16; **3** Lawson, 14; **4** Ribeiro, 12; **5** Liesner, 10; **6** DeSilva, 8.

TEXACO CLEAN SYSTEM 3 CHALLENGE, Long Beach Street Circuit, California, USA, 17 April. Round 2. 47 laps of the 1.590-mile/2.559-km circuit, 74.730 miles/120.266 km.
1 Steve Robertson, GB, 58m 37.529s, 76.482 mph/123.086 km/h.
2 Greg Moore, CDN, 58m 39.380s.
3 Pedro Chaves, P, 47 laps.
4 Nick Firestone, USA, 47.
5 Dave DeSilva, USA, 47.
6 Rick Hill, USA, 47.
7 Doug Boyer, USA, 47; **8** Scott Schubot, USA, 47; **9** Jack Miller, USA, 47; **10** Bob Dorricott Jr, USA, 47.
Most laps led: Robertson, 24.
Fastest qualifying lap: Eddie Lawson, 57.780s, 99.065 mph/159.430 km/h.
Championship points: 1 Moore, 38; **2** Robertson, 37; **3** Chaves, 20; **4** DeSilva, 18; **5** Lawson, 15; **6=** Firestone, 12; **6=** Ribeiro, 12.

FIRESTONE MILWAUKEE INDY LIGHTS RACE, Wisconsin State Fair Park Speedway, West Allis, Milwaukee, Wisconsin, USA, 5 June. Round 3. 75 laps of the 1.000-mile/1.609-km circuit, 75.000 miles/120.701 km.
1 Steve Robertson, GB, 45m 59.752s, 97.835 mph/157.450 km/h.
2 Eddie Lawson, USA, 45m 59.859s.
3 Greg Moore, CDN, 75 laps.
4 David Pook, USA, 74.
5 Rob Wilson, NZ, 74.
6 Dave DeSilva, USA, 74.
7 Pedro Chaves, P, 73; **8** Buzz Calkins, USA, 73; **9** Jack Miller, USA, 73; **10** Scott Schubot, USA, 73.
Most laps led: Robertson, 68.
Fastest qualifying lap: Andre Ribeiro, BR, 26.156s, 137.636 mph/221.503 km/h.
Championship points: 1 Robertson, 58; **2** Moore, 52; **3** Lawson, 31; **4=** Chaves, 26; **4=** DeSilva, 26; **6** Pook, 14.

FIRESTONE DETROIT INDY LIGHTS RACE, Belle Isle Park Circuit, Detroit, Michigan, USA, 12 June. Round 4. 36 laps of the 2.100-mile/3.380-km circuit, 75.600 miles/121.666 km.
1 Steve Robertson, GB, 54m 14.920s, 83.615 mph/134.565 km/h.
2 Eddie Lawson, USA, 54m 16.229s.
3 Pedro Chaves, P, 36 laps.
4 Andre Ribeiro, BR, 36.
5 Nick Firestone, USA, 36.
6 Alex Padilla, USA, 36.
7 Greg Moore, CDN, 36; **8** Chris Smith, USA, 36; **9** Rob Wilson, NZ, 36; **10** Scott Schubot, USA, 36.
Most laps led: Robertson, 36.
Fastest qualifying lap: Robertson, 1m 18.727s, 96.028 mph/154.542 km/h.
Championship points: 1 Robertson, 80; **2** Moore, 58; **3** Lawson, 47; **4** Chaves, 40; **5** DeSilva, 26; **6** Ribeiro, 25.

PORTLAND FIRESTONE INDY LIGHTS RACE, Portland International Raceway, Oregon, USA, 26 June. Round 5. 39 laps of the 1.950-mile/3.138-km circuit, 76.050 miles/122.391 km.
1 Andre Ribeiro, BR, 49m 39.853s, 91.877 mph/147.862 km/h.
2 Pedro Chaves, P, 49m 40.602s.
3 Eddie Lawson, USA, 39 laps.
4 Steve Robertson, GB, 39.
5 Greg Moore, CDN, 39.
6 Doug Boyer, USA, 38.
7 Buzz Calkins, USA, 38; **8** Roberto Quintanilla, MEX, 38; **9** Rob Wilson, NZ, 38; **10** David Pook, USA, 38.
Most laps led: Ribeiro, 39.
Fastest qualifying lap: Ribeiro, 1m 06.228s, 105.997 mph/170.586 km/h.
Championship points: 1 Robertson, 92; **2** Moore, 68; **3** Lawson, 61; **4** Chaves, 56; **5** Ribeiro, 47; **6** DeSilva, 28.

BETTER BUICK CHALLENGE GP OF CLEVELAND, Burke Lakefront Airport Circuit, Cleveland, Ohio, USA, 10 July. Round 6. 32 laps of the 2.369-mile/3.813-km circuit, 75.808 miles/122.001 km.
1 Eddie Lawson, USA, 36m 14.162s, 125.524 mph/202.011 km/h.
2 Greg Moore, CDN, 36m 16.692s.
3 Pedro Chaves, P, 32 laps.
4 Nick Firestone, USA, 32.
5 Andre Ribeiro, BR, 32.
6 Doug Boyer, USA, 32.
7 Steve Robertson, GB, 32; **8** Alex Padilla, USA, 32; **9** Frédéric Gosparini, F, 31; **10** Buzz Calkins, USA, 31.
Most laps led: Chaves, 25.
Fastest qualifying lap: Chaves, 1m 06.616s, 128.023 mph/206.034 km/h.
Championship points: 1 Robertson, 98; **2** Moore, 84; **3** Lawson, 81; **4** Chaves, 72; **5** Ribeiro, 57; **6** Firestone, 35.

TORONTO FIRESTONE INDY LIGHTS RACE, Exhibition Place Circuit, Toronto, Ontario, Canada, 17 July. Round 7. 42 laps of the 1.780-mile/2.865-km circuit, 74.760 miles/120.315 km.
1 Steve Robertson, GB, 48m 22.297s, 92.732 mph/149.238 km/h.
2 Andre Ribeiro, BR, 48m 30.269s.
3 Nick Firestone, USA, 42 laps.
4 Alex Padilla, USA, 42.
5 Eddie Lawson, USA, 42.
6 Doug Boyer, USA, 42.
7 Buzz Calkins, USA, 42; **8** Bob Reid, USA, 42; **9** Enrique Contreras, MEX, 42; **10** Bob Dorricott Jr, USA, 41.
Most laps led: Greg Moore, CDN, 32.
Fastest qualifying lap: Moore, 1m 03.777s, 100.475 mph/161.699 km/h.
Championship points: 1 Robertson, 118; **2** Lawson, 91; **3** Moore, 87; **4** Ribeiro, 73; **5** Chaves, 72; **6** Firestone, 49.

FIRESTONE INDY LIGHTS MID-OHIO, Mid-Ohio Sports Car Course, Lexington, Ohio, USA, 14 August. Round 8. 34 laps of the 2.250-mile/3.621-km circuit, 75.550 miles/121.586 km.
1 Andre Ribeiro, BR, 43m 08.543s, 105.071 mph/169.095 km/h.
2 Eddie Lawson, USA, 43m 17.549s.
3 Pedro Chaves, P, 34 laps.
4 Steve Robertson, GB, 34.
5 Nick Firestone, USA, 34.
6 Patrick Carpentier, CDN, 34.
7 Greg Moore, CDN, 34; **8** Alex Padilla, USA, 34; **9** Dave DeSilva, USA, 34; **10** Buzz Calkins, USA, 34.
Most laps led: Ribeiro, 34.
Fastest qualifying lap: Ribeiro, 1m 15.735s, 106.952 mph/172.122 km/h.
Championship points: 1 Robertson, 130; **2** Lawson, 107; **3** Ribeiro, 95; **4** Moore, 93; **5** Chaves, 86; **6** Firestone, 59.

LOUDON FIRESTONE INDY LIGHTS RACE, New Hampshire International Speedway, Loudon, New Hampshire, USA, 21 August. Round 9. 71 laps of the 1.058-mile/1.703-km circuit, 75.118 miles/120.891 km.
1 Greg Moore, CDN, 37m 04.349s, 121.575 mph/195.656 km/h.
2 Andre Ribeiro, BR, 37m 22.559s.
3 Steve Robertson, GB, 71 laps.
4 Alex Padilla, USA, 71.
5 Pedro Chaves, P, 70.
6 Buzz Calkins, USA, 70.
7 Bob Dorricott Jr, USA, 70; **8** Doug Boyer, USA, 69; **9** Nick Firestone, USA, 69; **10** Jack Miller, USA, 69.
Most laps led: Robertson, 43.
Fastest qualifying lap: Robertson, 26.153s, 145.635 mph/234.377 km/h.
Championship points: 1 Robertson, 146; **2** Moore, 113; **3** Ribeiro, 111; **4** Lawson, 109; **5** Chaves, 96; **6** Firestone, 63.

CONCORD PACIFIC CHALLENGE, Vancouver Street Circuit, Pacific Place, Vancouver, British Columbia, Canada, 4 September. Round 10. 37 laps of the 1.653-mile/2.660-km circuit, 61.161 miles/98.429 km.
1 Andre Ribeiro, BR, 39m 51.696s, 92.060 mph/148.156 km/h.
2 Steve Robertson, GB, 39m 52.089s.
3 Alex Padilla, USA, 37 laps.
4 Pedro Chaves, P, 37.
5 Greg Moore, CDN, 37.
6 Scott Schubot, USA, 37.
7 Eddie Lawson, USA, 37; **8** Bob Dorricott Jr, USA, 36; **9** Bob Reid, USA, 36; **10** Buzz Calkins, USA, 35.
Most laps led: Ribeiro, 31.
Fastest qualifying lap: Padilla, 59.967s, 99.235 mph/159.703 km/h.
Championship points: 1 Robertson, 162; **2** Ribeiro, 132; **3** Moore, 123; **4** Lawson, 115; **5** Chaves, 108; **6** Firestone, 63.

NAZARETH FIRESTONE INDY LIGHTS RACE, Pennsylvania International Raceway, Nazareth, Pennsylvania, USA, 18 September. Round 11. 75 laps of the 1.000-mile/1.609-km circuit, 75.000 miles/120.701 km.
1 Greg Moore, CDN, 40m 47.866s, 110.300 mph/177.511 km/h.
2 Andre Ribeiro, BR, 40m 48.991s.
3 Jeff Ward, USA, 75 laps.
4 Steve Robertson, GB, 75.
5 Eddie Lawson, USA, 75.
6 Pedro Chaves, P, 74.
7 Alex Padilla, USA, 74; **8** Trevor Seibert, USA, 74; **9** Dave DeSilva, USA, 74; **10** Nick Firestone, USA, 72.
Most laps led: Moore, 51.
Fastest qualifying lap: Bob Dorricott Jr, USA, 23.351s, 154.169 mph/248.111 km/h.
Championship points: 1 Robertson, 174; **2** Ribeiro, 148; **3** Moore, 144; **4** Lawson, 125; **5** Chaves, 116; **6** Firestone, 66.

MONTEREY FIRESTONE INDY LIGHTS RACE, Laguna Seca Raceway, Monterey, California, USA, 9 October. Round 12. 34 laps of the 2.214-mile/3.563-km circuit, 75.276 miles/121.145 km.
1 Andre Ribeiro, BR, 51m 39.520s, 87.431 mph/140.706 km/h.
2 Pedro Chaves, P, 51m 44.504s.
3 Eddie Lawson, USA, 51m 49.66s.
4 Doug Boyer, USA, 51m 51.07s.
5 Greg Moore, CDN, 51m 54.55s.
6 Dave DeSilva, USA, 51m 58.47s.
7 Nick Firestone, USA, 52m 03.07s; **8** Steve Robertson, GB, 52m 04.38s; **9** Niclas Jonsson, S, 52m 04.92s; **10** Juan Carbonell, RCH, 52m 17.83s.
Most laps led: Ribeiro, 34.
Fastest qualifying lap: Ribeiro, 1m 18.302s, 101.791 mph/163.816 km/h.

Final championship points

1	Steve Robertson, GB	179
2	Andre Ribeiro, BR	170
3	Greg Moore, CDN	154
4	Eddie Lawson, USA	139
5	Pedro Chaves, P	132
6	Nick Firestone, USA	72

7 Alex Padilla, USA, 63; **8** Doug Boyer, USA, 47; **9** Dave DeSilva, USA, 46; **10** Buzz Calkins, USA, 41; **11** Scott Schubot, USA, 26; **12** Rob Wilson, NZ, 22; **13=** David Pook, USA, 18; **13=** Bob Dorricott Jr, USA, 18; **15** Jeff Ward, USA, 16; **16** Jack Miller, USA, 14; **17** Bob Reid, USA, 12; **18** Markus Liesner, USA, 10; **19** Chris Smith, USA, 9; **20=** Rick Hill, USA, 8; **20=** Patrick Carpentier, CDN, 8; **20=** Roberto Quintanilla, MEX, 8.